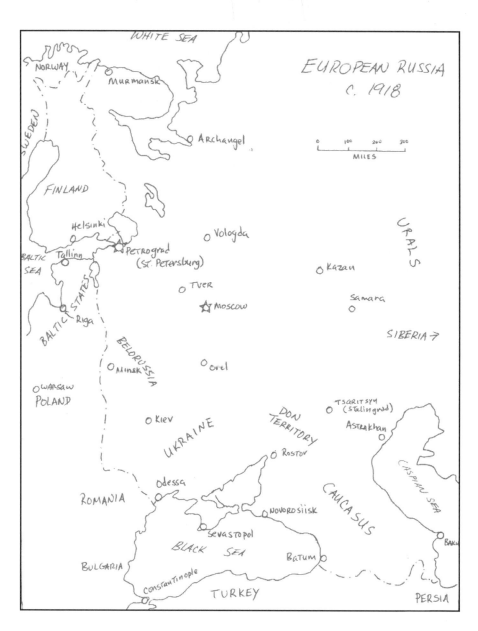

European Russia, 1918

Trust No One

Trust No One

The Secret World of Sidney Reilly

Richard Spence

FERAL HOUSE

ISBN: 0-922915-79-2

Feral House
P.O. Box 13067
Los Angeles, CA 90013

www.feralhouse.com
info@feralhouse.com

Design by Linda Hayashi

The Publisher wishes to thank
Laura Smith-Guerrero for her
protean proofing.

10 9 8 7 6 5 4 3 2 1

Dedicated to the memory of

John Potter

who, I hope, would enjoy and approve

ACKNOWLEDGMENTS

I owe a great debt of gratitude to a wide array of people who, individually and collectively, have provided invaluable assistance and information. Of these, five merit special thanks for their time, advice, insight and inspiration: G.L. Owen, Julian Putkowski, Serge Savinkov, Phil Tomaselli and, last but by no means least, my wife Ingrid who had to share her home and husband with the ghost of Sidney Reilly.

My deepest thanks are due also to: Bruce Abrams, Roy Bainton, Vladimir Bet, Nicola Best, Lev Bezymenskii, Logan Brewer, Brady Brower, Ronald Bulatoff, Aleksandr Bykov, Rachel Chrastil, Anita Citron, Nancy Dafoe, Hans Fredrik Dahl, Elena Danielson, Richard Davies, David Foglesong, Richard Freeman-Toole, Natalie Grant, John Gray, Mark Grekin, Bob Henderson, Nicholas Hiley, Mark Hull, Denis Jdanoff, Michael Kettle, Mark Kulikowski, Carol Leadenham, Eric Lee, Robin Lockhart, Andrea Lynn, Donald McCormick, Shay McNeal, Harry and Marjorie Mahoney, Galina Malinova, Sean Malloy, Molly Molloy, Eero Medijainen, Jeff Olson, Marina Pereira, Jane Plotke, Pat Polanski, Igor Prelin, Alexander Rabinovich, Judy Remmick-Hubert, Charles Rice, Dmitry Stein, Anthony Sutton, Kurt Tolksdorff, Alan Torrey, David Turner, Tatiana Wolff, Wilma Woods-Davis, Sergey Yelizarov, Aleksandr Zaitsev, and those who wish to remain anonymous.

To any I may have neglected to mention, my apologies. For all errors in fact and interpretation, I alone am responsible.

Contents:

SEARCHING FOR SIDNEY REILLY

"James Bond is just a piece of nonsense I dreamed up.
He's not a Sidney Reilly, you know."
—Ian Fleming

To some he is the "Ace-of-Spies,"
Britain's greatest secret agent and the real-life model for James Bond.
Others have hailed him as an unsung hero of Soviet espionage, the so-
called "First Man" who pioneered the Kremlin's infiltration of Western
intelligence. Still others have dubbed him "The Man Who Knew
Everything" and "The Man Who Never Made a Mistake." Less flattering
appraisals characterized him as an "astute criminal," a "double-edged
tool" and a dangerous man who would do anything for money. Could one
man really be all these things?

To one degree or another, he was all of them and more. Through his
own determined manipulation, and the willing and unwilling help of others,
the man best known as Sidney George Reilly parlayed his career as intelligence agent, businessman and arch-conspirator into the stuff of legend—
and enduring mystery. His career is proof of the old adage that truth is
stranger than fiction. Furthermore, as the following will show, Reilly was a
figure of greater depth and significance than suggested heretofore.

Perhaps the single most important fact about Sidney Reilly is that he
never truly existed at all. He was, in essence, the most visible and significant persona used by a man whose many other aliases included Salomon
and Sigmund Rosenblum, George Rose, Leon Rosenblatt, Pavel Relinsky,
Constantine Massino and Sidney Roberts. To call Reilly a simple spy

hardly does him justice. Neither does the view that holds him a Baron Münchausen-like fantasist, a colorful and dubious character of no particular significance. Neither was he an anachronism—an amateur spy and picaresque spy-adventurer more typical of the 19th century than the 20th. Perhaps Reilly is easiest to understand as a mercenary of a rather specialized sort, though it might be just as accurate to describe him as a freelance entrepreneur in the business of information and influence, a man who always maintained freedom of action and put his own interests above any national or ideological considerations.

The term that Reilly used again and again to describe himself was "a practical man." In his view, such an individual was governed by logic, necessity and self-interest. The key to understanding his often contradictory behavior is determining just what his interests were. Central among these was his belief in the immense economic potential of Russia and the need to integrate it and its riches into a global marketplace. In his appreciation of the interlocking nature of the "world economy" and the important role played by multinational corporations, Reilly was amazingly modern, even prescient, in his thinking. His fundamental approach was a version of Lenin's dictum of "flexibility in means, inflexibility in goals." It was this that allowed him to consort and connive with Communists in the interests of capitalism and, as a Jew, to abet and conspire with the most virulent anti-Semites in the pursuit of common goals.

Probably as many reading this, I first became aware of Sidney George Reilly through the 1980s television miniseries, *Reilly: Ace of Spies*. At the time, I was a newly-minted historian with what I thought to be a fairly solid grasp of modern history, particularly the Russian Revolution. While I recognized many of the persons and events portrayed in the program, Reilly was a completely new twist, and I was curious to learn how much of this man and his doings were real and how much fictional. To one degree or another, I have been on that quest ever since. For some time, I did my best to ignore Reilly while writing a biography of his partner in anti-Bolshevik intrigue, the Russian political adventurer Boris Savinkov. But Reilly haunted that story as he did my imagination. I decided to investigate an aspect of his activities barely addressed in other accounts, his role as Russian military contractor in New York during WWI. From that little acorn, the present oak has grown.

I have not set out to prove or disprove anything about Reilly. Rather, I determined early on to follow the evidence wherever it went, draw the conclusions that seemed reasonable and not be blinded by preconceived opinion—mine or otherwise.

It soon was apparent that collecting the many threads of Reilly's life and weaving them into a complete and coherent picture would be no easy task. The simplest details about his life were shrouded in myth and misinformation. Nothing could be taken for granted, and it became necessary to question and investigate every assumption and "fact." More than once I thought I had Reilly's persona and machinations figured out, only to have some fresh bit of evidence demolish my theory or send me off in a new direction. At times I felt as if I were peeling an onion from the inside or peering into the boundless complexities of a Mandelbrot set. Little by little, however, the gigantic jigsaw puzzle took form, and the picture that emerged was in many respects not the one I had anticipated.

It also became clear that tackling a subject like Reilly required some modifications in normal historical methodology. Digging into his doings often bore more resemblance to a criminal investigation than ordinary research, and I freely admit to assuming the role of historian-as-detective. Whom to believe, what to trust, motives and opportunities, were all key elements of consideration and intuition and deduction indispensable tools. As in a criminal case, there are many facets of Reilly's life that cannot be reduced to a matter of absolute certainty, but only to what the weight of evidence suggests. The most important of these, perhaps, is the question of Reilly's fate after 1925. Did he die as suggested in a variety of strangely contradictory Soviet accounts, or did he perform another personal transfiguration to live and scheme for many years to come?

In the end, Reilly's saga is a remarkable story of one man's quest to attain wealth, power and influence and to do so on a grand scale and against great odds. The audacity of his schemes, the Napoleonic scope of his ambition, were driven by a keen intellect and a character both fearless and ruthless. He did not hesitate to pit his desires and cunning against even the most powerful statesmen and captains of industry. He seldom came out the loser. Always a double-edged sword, few of Reilly's friends and collaborators, and the latter were far more common that the first, could say they trusted him. Even his most bitter enemies regarded him as an opponent of exceptional guile and determination.

There was a distinctly dark side to the man. Among many other dubious activities, he engaged in or abetted forgery, drug smuggling, gun running, blackmail, sabotage and murder. Although capable of great charm, wit and kindness, his intellect was coldly calculating, and he was equally capable of callous indifference and studied vindictiveness. In his relationships with women, he was equal parts romantic and cad. For the most part, he inflicted great suffering on those women brave or foolish enough to try and share his life.

If Reilly was sometimes not all that he claimed, he often was more than he seemed. His "myth" survives not just in the glamorized and heroic image of James Bond, but also, and perhaps more accurately, in the sinister incarnations of Eric Ambler's Dimitrios Makropoulos, Norbert Jacques' Dr. Mabuse, and Orson Welles' Mr. Arkadin.

As I pursued Reilly's twisting trail and collected the relics of his career, I was led deeper and deeper down a rabbit hole that led not to Wonderland but to a secret world of intrigue and conspiracy where strange deals and stranger bedfellows abounded. Although Reilly operated first and foremost as a freelance, he almost never worked alone. His schemes and gambits were assisted by a vast and often surprising array of backers, cronies, collaborators, and dupes. There were many enemies as well, and telling friend from foe often was no easy matter. Sometimes they were one and the same. In entering his world it is wise to recall the old Assassin maxim: "Nothing is true. Everything is permitted."

What is certain is that the secret world inhabited by Reilly and his kin was every bit as important in shaping the modern world as its more visible and accessible counterpart.

The story told in the following pages will challenge established views on several aspects of modern Russian history and broader history as well. It will reveal a startling continuity between the Tsarist and Communist security services in both methodology and personnel. It also will show that if Soviet agents managed to penetrate Western agencies and institutions, Moscow's were equally the target of infiltration and subversion, perhaps more so.

The "System" Reilly used and mastered was never so simple as left versus right, Red versus White or even British versus American versus German capital. It was indifferent to such distinctions except as tools of exploitation and manipulation. Behind its often byzantine workings there are suggestions of something eerily like Fleming's fictional S.P.E.C.T.R.E., an international criminal cartel of immense scope and resources dedicated to the acquisition of wealth and power.

Reilly's career centers on an extraordinarily rich, turbulent and critical era in recent history. The world as we know it today emerged in a chaotic and bloody birth through war, revolution and ever-accelerating social and technological change. Reilly lived through that transformation and, to some degree, abetted it. He bore witness to the opulence, intrigue and decadence of pre-revolutionary St. Petersburg, and he saw the same city, as Petrograd, devastated by war and revolution and finally, as Leningrad, experience another transformation under the Soviet yoke. He roamed the cool, dark woods of eastern Poland, strolled the streets of Victorian London, prowled the bustling canyons of Manhattan, and lurked in conspirators' dens from Moscow to Shanghai. He partook of intrigue and skullduggery in all its forms, plus war, revolution—and even a little romance. Come follow down the rabbit hole and into Reilly's world . . .

PART I
LEARNING THE CRAFT

Pleased to meet you
Hope you guess my name
But what's puzzlin' you
Is the nature of my game

—The Rolling Stones
"Sympathy for the Devil"

The crest and Latin motto used by Sidney Reilly on his letterhead. *Mundo Nulla Fides* translates as "Put No Faith in the World," or "Trust No One."

Chapter One
BEGINNINGS

It was on a cold, wet day late in 1895 that the man who would become Sidney Reilly first set foot in England. He arrived among a boatload of more or less routine travelers from France. If any of Her Majesty's functionaries gave him more than a cursory glance, they would have noticed a young man, a university student, perhaps, with the last traces of adolescent softness about his features. He was medium height with a slim build and head that seemed just a shade too large for his body. A long, large nose separated full lips from somewhat protruding eyes; above that were dark, heavy eyebrows. The face was long, almost hatchet-like, the skin sallow and topped with a thick mass of black, slightly wavy hair. Though few would have found his looks handsome, most would have thought them striking. In his smooth visage a discerning eye might have read intelligence, shrewdness and a hint of the unscrupulous.

Most of all, if anyone paid attention, they would have noticed the eyes. They were large, piercing and a shade of rich, deep brown that some would describe as beautiful and others as hypnotic. Women would fall in love with him because of those eyes and men would learn to fear the coldness and menace they could convey. But most likely, no one gave much attention to him at all, which was exactly as he wanted it. Had a curious customs agent pressed the issue, he might have discovered two very interesting things. First, that the young man was traveling with papers not his own, and second, that he was carrying a rather large sum of money.

The young traveler was no ordinary tourist, nor, of course, was he British. He had been born some twenty-one years earlier in Russian-ruled Poland and, as his features suggested, he was a Jew. As such, he might have been one of the thousands of Jewish emigrants from the Tsar's domain who were crowding into the slums of London's East End and other British cities.[1] Physical appearance aside, however, the young man had nothing in common with such refugees. He was headed for a pleasant flat in London's western suburbs, not the grimy streets of the East End. The future Ace-of-Spies was well-dressed and spoke English, albeit as yet imperfectly and with a strong accent. His mastery of the tongue swiftly improved, but the accent would remain along with one or two other idiosyncrasies. Decades later, fellow British agent Stephen Alley would recall that Reilly never quite mastered the intricacies of English slang, his favorite epithet being "Oh buggeries!"

This description of Reilly's—then Salomon Sigmund Georgievich Rosenblum—arrival in Britain, pieced together from the few surviving records and his and others' statements, bears little resemblance to the version he later offered. In that, he arrived on British shores via the jungles of Brazil and with the helping hand of a wealthy British patron, one Major Fothergill (or Frasergill). As we will see in the following chapter, this story may contain a kernel of truth, but only at a future date. For the time being, young Rosenblum had never been anywhere near a jungle, Brazilian or otherwise.[2] This fabrication, as with most of the lies that the future Reilly told about himself and his past, was designed to divert and disguise. The real question, therefore, is what Reilly sought to conceal with this tale. To do that, we must leave him for the time being on the Portsmouth docks and pick up the story at its real beginning.

Assembling an accurate picture of Reilly's origins is a surprisingly difficult task. The passage of time, loss of vital records, above all relentless obfuscation, his own and others, makes a complete resolution of this puzzle impossible. For example, in 1925, the Soviet secret police compiled a rough biography that pegged his birth on 24 March 1874 in the Ukrainian port city of Odessa.[3] According to this, his father was one Mark[us] Rosenblum, a Jewish doctor turned broker and shipping agent, while his mother stemmed from the Massino family of impoverished gentry. Beyond the fact that a marriage between a Jew and a member of the gentry, however reduced in circumstances, was highly unlikely, with the possible exception of date of birth the whole story smacks of disinformation. While there certainly are clues pointing to some early connection between Reilly and Odessa, there is no record of a Mark Rosenblum there nor, as we will see, of most of the other details in the Soviet report. Beyond this, Reilly himself never claimed Odessa as his birthplace, instead citing such diverse locales as Clonmel, Ireland and St. Petersburg, Russia. Just the same, there is no documentary evidence to support either. Obviously, he had, or felt he had, something to hide in this matter.

However, fragmentary records recollections of kin in Russia, Israel, Britain and the United States do seem to confirm that his original surname was Rosenblum (*Rosenblyum*) and a birthplace somewhere in what was then Russian Poland.[4] The Rosenblum clan from which he sprang originated in Lithuania and had a distinguished religious pedigree. Through his paternal grandfather, Jankel-Leiba (Jakov) Salomonovich Rosenblum, the future Ace-of-Spies could trace descent from Ezekiel Landau, the 18th century Grand Rabbi of Prague and rabbinical scholar Elijah ben Solomon, the esteemed Gaon of Vilna.[5]

It was not easy being a Jewish subject of the Tsar. An already adverse situation worsened following the assassination of Tsar Alexander II, the so-called "Tsar Liberator," in 1881. Jews suffered a wave of violent attacks, the so-called *pogroms*, in its aftermath. Fresh outbreaks would reoccur at regular intervals in the decades following and the dreaded cry of *Bei zhidov, spasai Rossii!* ("Kill the Yids and save Russia!") would echo down generations. While Jews were, generally speaking, a despised and mistrusted minority in the eyes of the Romanov regime, material success and upward mobility were not impossible. In the last decades of the century a class of prosperous Jewish entrepreneurs emerged in the Russian Empire's western provinces, the old Polish and Lithuanian lands of the historic Pale of Settlement[6], and spread out into the urban commercial centers of Odessa, Kiev, Moscow and even the Imperial capital, St. Petersburg. There was, after all, no distinction made about Jewish rubles, and if endemic corruption was the curse of the Tsarist Empire, it also was in some respect its saving grace. Where there was money, there usually was a way, a lesson the future Ace-of-Spies must have absorbed very early.

One such entrepreneur, born in 1845, was Gersh (also Gersz, in Hebrew, *Tsvi*) Yakovlevich Rosenblum, a contractor and middleman who worked mostly in the timber trade. Later he branched into ship provisioning and oil field construction. In so doing, he became wealthy, though not rich. Gersh was obliged, as most in his position, to abandon or bend the rigid rules that had governed orthodox Jewish life for centuries. In doing so, he doubtless regarded himself as both a "modern" and a practical man, one who embraced assimilation in appearance and manners as a necessary and even desirable condition of emancipation.[7] In commercial dealings he used the Russianized equivalent Grigorii while his German and Polish contacts called him Georg or George, or even Grzegorz. One man with slightly different identities to different people, another interesting example for his son to observe and later put to his own uses.

Gersh's father, the above Jankel-Leiba, born around 1818, hailed from the region of Lomza in what was then the Russian *Guberniia* (province) of

Grodno, now in northeast Poland.[8] Starting as a small local tradesman, he gradually built a successful career as a timber merchant, tobacco importer and, later in life, a dealer in Jewish religious works and rare books. His wife, Chana (Henrietta) Bramson, also came from a respected rabbinical family. In addition to Gersh, Jankel and Chana had at least one other son.[9] That was Vulf (Ze'ev), who later called himself Vladimir. He may at one point have studied medicine, but like his brother went into the timber business. The Rosenblum brothers leased parts of the old Sayn-Wittgenstein estates in Grodno Province. By the early 1890s, they seem to have operated a sawmill near the town of Pruzhany that lay adjacent to the primeval Bialowieza Forest.[10]

There was a definite hint of sibling rivalry in their relationship. Gersh pursued other interests and traveled widely throughout the western reaches of the Russian Empire, including the bustling port city of Odessa. It was thereabouts, around 1870, that he met and married an eligible young woman from another well-to-do Jewish family. Her original name seems to have been Beila, but she much preferred the secularized Paulina. Her family name, however, is uncertain; it may have been Altmann, or, perhaps, Berenstein or Bronstein (Braunstein). The latter possibility is interesting because it is the same surname as that of future revolutionary luminary Leon Trotsky who also came from near Odessa. That Trotsky and the Ace-of-Spies may have shared some family connection is a tantalizing possibility, but no more. In any case, at least one of Paulina's parents was said to have come from Breslau, Germany, and that, combined with the generally more cosmopolitan atmosphere of Odessa, gave her a sense of cultural superiority over her more provincial husband. Several years her husband's junior, Paulina was no great beauty but attractive, intelligent, vivacious and well educated for a Jewish woman of her time and place. She took and avid interest in art and music and seems to have possessed some talent at the piano. One of the high points of her life, supposedly, was a brief encounter with the great Polish pianist, Ignace Paderewski.

The marriage was from the start, it seems, a troubled one. She may have felt forced into the marriage and resented the overbearing influence of her mother- and father-in-law. Life with Gersh involved long separations and a dreary existence in dull, provincial towns. Right away she found her energies consumed by the responsibilities of motherhood. First came Mariam, or Maria, followed soon after by a son, Shlomo (or Shloima), later secularized to the Russo-Polish Salomon. As noted, the more or less consistent date of birth Reilly gave for himself was 24 March 1874. While we may accept this as probably correct, it is, like so many things about our subject, by no means definite. First, it is not clear whether this date was according to the Gregorian (Western) or Russian (Julian) calendar, the latter then being twelve days behind the other. On later occasions he sometimes indicated an age that would put his birth in 1873.

The question remains, however, just *where* he entered the world. One later, seemingly reliable, source named the birthplace as Bendzin, a town in southwest Russian Poland next to the German border and not far from the then-Austrian town of Auschwitz.[11] In many ways this makes sense: the town was an early center of the oil industry and timber a commodity much in demand for the construction of derricks and like facilities. Thus, Gersh, very likely could have done business there. Bendzin, perhaps, provided the first whiff of petroleum that would hover about the rest of Reilly's life. However, once again, local records record no Shlomo Rosenblum or any Rosenblum born there in 1874, nor is there any tangible evidence of the family's presence. It remains a possibility that Salomon lived for a time in Bendzin as a child, even that he was born there but the birth registered in another, more permanent locale. The best bet remains in the area of Pruzhany or the adjoining districts of Bielsk and Bialystok, though this, too, defies confirmation.

Like his father, the boy was known by a number of names. In the prevailing Yiddish vernacular, Salomon became Zalman or Zelman from which derived the childhood diminutive Ziama/Zema. Following modern practice, his mother insisted on a more cosmopolitan "equivalent name," the more Germanic Sigmund that in Polish became Zygmunt.[12] The latter doubtless helped distinguish him from two cousins also named Zalman/Salomon Rosenblum. To add to his budding multiple identities, within the immediate family Shlomo-Salomon-Zalman-Ziama-Sigmund-Zygmunt sometimes was referred to as "kleiner Georgy"—Little Georgie.

For a time the families of Gersh and Vladimir shared a large home near Bialystok. Before long Paulina found herself with another daughter, Gendla (Helena). There were, of course, servants to handle more mundane aspects of domesticity, but this only left more time on her hands. She turned her energies to her children's education, especially Salomon's, whom she was determined to raise a proper and cultured gentleman. She supposedly forbade the speaking of Yiddish in the household, insisting on proper German and Polish. She engaged tutors so that her children learned French and English and studied the classics in Greek and Latin. Conflict arose with her husband and in-laws when Paulina balked at her son's enrollment in a traditional Jewish school, or *heder*. She wanted him in a secular secondary school (*gymnaziia*) where the instruction was in Russian. The young

Rosenblums were exposed to a broad spectrum of political and social opinions. One close cousin, Lev (Leontii) Moiseevich Bramson, rose to be a leading figure in the assimilationist Society for the Promotion of Enlightenment among the Jews of Russia, and a leader of the moderate leftist Popular Socialist Party.[13] Other relatives studied to become rabbis, or gravitated to the emerging Zionist movement, or to one of the more revolutionary socialist groups, including the Bolsheviks.

Paulina's doting on her son was not simply because he was the only boy. He was sickly when small and suffered from debilitating headaches (probably migraines). He may even have had a mild form of epilepsy. If Salomon developed a strong bond with his mother, his relationship with Gersh was quite the opposite. The father's sporadic efforts to exert a controlling and conservative influence led to bitter arguments between the parents and father and son. Paulina conjured images of a big and exciting world for Salomon and with them expectations that could not be satisfied by the measured, proper example set by Gersh. To Salomon, tradition, rules, Jewishness itself, were obstacles to his aspirations. This fits with a later observation that Reilly "was extremely bothered by being a Jew" and, thus, sought to conceal his origins.[14]

However much the future Reilly was a creature of time, place and ethos, he also was something of an anomaly. There are some interesting and, perhaps, instructive parallels, between his case and that of another young man born to a well-to-do Jewish family in far-off New York a few years later. This was Arnold Rothstein, the son of a pious, law-abiding, highly respected businessman. In defiance of family and society at large, Rothstein became one of the greatest criminal masterminds in American history. An early disdain for authority and a penchant for gambling were only two of the traits the men would share. One can only wonder if some like criminal pathology was at work in Rothstein and our subject, one that each recognized when they finally met many years hence.

One of the things gnawing at Gersh was a suspicion that Salomon and his sister Elena were his children at all. Interestingly, dubious paternity was a recurrent theme in the various stories Reilly later spun about his origins. One of his more fanciful versions had it that his mother had been the brief paramour of Count Walewski, himself an illegitimate descendent of the great Napoleon, and that *Salomon* was the fruit of that illicit union.[15] It is interesting to speculate whether this tale was the result of Reilly's fascination with all things Bonaparte or the source of it. Other stories, none of which can be substantiated, peg Paulina's lover as a Polish, gentile landowner, an employee on the estate, or a mysterious stranger.

The version later digested in Robin Lockhart's *Ace of Spies* holds that Salomon was the ostensible son of a gentile Russo-Polish landowner in Ukraine and his aristocratic wife. But in truth he really was the offspring of an illicit romance between the nobleman's wife and the family's Jewish physician, Dr. Rosenblum.[16] The tale may have a basis in real life, if not Reilly's. Living in Kamenka at this time, not far from Odessa, was a prosperous Russo-German family named Hahn (Gan). Family lore records an almost identical saga of confused paternity and denunciation affecting the only son, Georgii (Jarig) Hahn.[17] Did our man somehow hear of this and appropriate it for his own use?

In pre-WWI Petersburg, Reilly claimed his mother was a Polish or Russian Jewess and his father an English or Irish ship's captain who later abandoned her. The truth that these stories disguised is very likely that Salomon's biological father was really his uncle, Vladimir. Frequent and prolonged proximity would have allowed him and Paulina to carry on an affair for years. Such a liaison would help explain a familial crisis that erupted about 1890.

Vladimir had two daughters, Sofia (Sora), who later married the influential lawyer Mikhail Vol'ff (Wolff), and the younger Felicia (Glika) who was about Salomon's age. As their parents, perhaps, living in proximity had forged a close bond between the cousins, but the family was stunned to hear Salomon proclaim his undying love for Felicia and his desire to marry her. The apparently horrified reaction to this youthful declaration makes sense if at least two of the respective parents knew that Salomon and Felicia were really half-brother and sister. Perhaps this compelled Vladimir or Paulina to confess their relationship or, perhaps, it ignited Gersh's long-simmering doubts. In any case, two things seem to have followed: the Rosenblum brothers became estranged and Paulina left her husband and moved back to her family in Odessa with Salomon and Elena.

Author Michael Kettle has speculated that it was this early disappointment in love that prompted young Rosenblum to run away from home and repudiate his family.[18] While it doubtless contributed to his growing alienation, it almost certainly was not the decisive factor in his subsequent self-imposed exile. After all, his bonds to Felicia were never entirely severed. They maintained contact, and their passion subsided into a close, lasting friendship, one of the few that Reilly would share with anyone.

In the 1890s Odessa was a bustling port city with the reputation as the "New York of Russia" because of the vitality of its commercial life and the diversity of its population. From less than 10,000 inhabitants in 1830, by the last decade of the century it had mushroomed to almost

350,000, a third of them Jews.[19] Like its American counterpart, Odessa had a rough side that included an element dedicated to crime and vice; in its criminal underworld some trace the origins of what later would be known as the Jewish Mafia. Like any boomtown, it was teeming with recent immigrants and persons going to or coming from somewhere else. For someone seeking to obscure his origins and identity, it was a perfect place to be *from*.

Even if it was not his birthplace, Odessa was to have an important influence on Salomon. According to information later gleaned by the Soviets, he and his mother lived at 15 Aleksandrovskii Prospect.[20] However, once again no clear trace of them can be found there. At this time, #15 housed a nondescript collection of Jewish-owned haberdashery and dress shops, with living quarters above. No Rosenblums lived there, but there was property leased by one Berenstein, just possibly Paulina's kin. Presumably, she received some help from them. Is it possible that she deliberately disguised or changed her childrens' names to conceal them from Gersh?

According to the same Soviet sources, Salomon, or *Zema*, completed the local *Gymnaziia* #3 in 1892 and soon thereafter enrolled in the faculty of physics and mathematics at Odessa's *Novorossiia* University where he studied for two semesters. However, here again we find the same vacuum: Odessa University records contain absolutely no trace of a Salomon, Sigmund or any other remotely similar Rosenblum in the physics-math or other departments during this period.[21] Nor is there any evidence he ever applied for admission. The records of *Gymnaziia* #3 have not been preserved, so even that defies conformation. There remains the possibility that he audited classes without formally enrolling, but he may have had other sorts of education on his youthful mind.

As mentioned above, Odessa had a thriving criminal subculture mostly centered in the Moldovanka district on the western edge of town. One of Salomon's later acquaintances who had definite roots in that quarter was a scrawny, pockmarked youth from a poor Jewish family, Boris (Borukh) Nadel.[22] He and Rosenblum certainly met in Russia prior to 1895. Nadel may have provided Rosenblum with an entrée into the Odessa underworld, but he almost certainly put him in contact with the local political underground. There was, in any case, a good deal of inter-pollination between the criminal and revolutionary spheres.[23] By early 1893, Nadel, and probably Rosenblum, were affiliated with a local revolutionary cell. Most of its members were university students. Also connected to this group was another Reilly associate, a woman, Natta (Nota) Azef. Destined to be a sort of distaff version of the Ace-of-Spies, her most notable characteristics were raven hair, striking, violet eyes, and a preference for all-black attire.[24]

Salomon's gravitation to radicalism was perfectly predictable. His temperament and upbringing had given him a healthy disdain for authority and the status quo. He and his young comrades viewed the ignorance and passivity of Russian society with contempt, and the same held true for traditional-minded Jews who clung to the irrational hope that the Messiah or a "good Tsar" would miraculously deliver them from oppression. A recent history of the Tsarist secret police notes that "most young [Russian] Jews in the late nineteenth century held radical views."[25] While this statement might be a bit broad, it certainly was the rule for those of progressive, assimilated backgrounds such as our subject's. The greater one's expectations of success, the more Russia was bound to disappoint, and the more its endemic anti-Semitism rankled. Only Revolution, many believed, could change the situation.

Salomon made other friends in Odessa. It was here the future Sidney Reilly first met a man who would have a profound impact on the rest of his life, Moisei (Moses) Akimovich Ginsburg.[26] The fortyish Ginsburg was a "commercial middleman" and commission agent with an eye to grain, shipping and Oriental commerce.[27] This suggests a possible business connection to Gersh, but it is just as possible that Ginsburg's connection ran through Paulina. There even is the remote possibility that *he* was the boy's father. In any case, he took an affectionate interest in her son.

The well-traveled Ginsburg further fired the youngster's imagination with tales of the larger world that lay as close as the next ship out of Odessa harbor. In a more practical sense, Ginsburg had connections that sooner or later would prove of great value to his young friend. A sterling example of the self-made man, he had lived in London and San Francisco and worked his way around the world as a stoker, railroad laborer and trader.[28] In Odessa Ginsburg was a prominent figure in the Jewish community and a valued intermediary in the relations of local Jews with Russian officialdom.[29] Befitting a man of the world, he was a freemason and the likely candidate to have introduced Reilly to that fraternity.[30] In contrast to his conservative public persona, Ginsburg privately held more radical opinions, something he may have shared with his young friend.

Ginsburg's involvement in Eastern commerce gave him contacts in China, Japan and India. Many of these, in turn, were British concerns. The latter included an Anglo-Greek trader named Basileos Zaharoff, also known as Zaharias Gortzakoff, Z.Z. Willamson, Z.Z., "the Greek" or, most famously, Basil Zaharoff. The Tsarist police were later convinced that

the mysterious Zaharoff was really a Russian Jew from Odessa's
Moldovanka which may well have been the case.[31] What is certain is that
the Greek had early, important connections in Odessa and that he visited
the city during 1891–93. Thus, it is possible, if no more, that he and
Rosenblum first met at this time. We will have much more to say about the
mysterious Mr. Zaharoff.

Given that freemasonry is a frequent common denominator in Reilly's
associations, it is worth pausing to provide some elaboration. From their
widespread appearance in the 18th century, masonic lodges came under
attack as secretive fonts of evil and subversion, and such charges are still
made today.[32] These fears led Catherine the Great and her successors to ban
masonry with the result that lodges would not operate openly and legally
until 1906. Sinister conspiracies aside, Tsarist officials had reason to be suspicious of these societies. While most masons were not flaming radicals, liberal sentiments were the norm and the lodges brought into contact a
volatile mixture of the visionary, the free-thinking and the discontented.
Bonds of secrecy and loyalty among members provided ideal starting points
for more purely political movements. The presence of many Jews among the
masons only increased official suspicions.

There is one other aspect of old Odessa that may have had a bearing
on the evolution of Sidney Reilly. Among its commercial buildings were
several owned by one Ralli, probably a merchant of Greek extraction.
Salomon had to have taken notice of them. Coincidentally, "Reilly" was
on various occasions rendered in Russian as "Ralli." Perhaps the name
stuck in his mind to surface years later in a very different context and for
a very different purpose.

Here again, it is useful to refer to Reilly's later version of his early years.
According to this, he left Russia to attend university in Vienna. There he
became involved with a radical, but apparently pacific, Russian student
group called the League of Enlightenment. Sometime in 1893, a fellow
member persuaded him to carry a letter back home to Odessa. No sooner
did he arrive there, however, than he was seized by the Tsar's political
police, the dread Okhrana.[33] The letter proved no innocent communication,
and young Rosenblum was in big trouble.

At best, this story is a very twisted version of the truth. Just as Odessa,
Viennese universities have no record of his attendance under any recognizable variant of his name. Furthermore, while student political cells came
and went in this period, there is none known called the League of
Enlightenment.[34] The name smacks a bit of the Jewish ORPE, the "Society
for Enlightenment . . . ." Perhaps Reilly simply appropriated this for later

use as he would other stray facts from his own and others' pasts. The reference to Vienna, however, brings to mind Felicia who had been sent there to study. That might have been reason enough for him to visit there. Such a seemingly innocent sojourn would have provided an ideal opportunity to carry communications between the Odessa cell and like-minded groups in the Austrian capital. From Vienna, he could smuggle back letters, propaganda, even money.

Later comments by Reilly to his wife Margaret tell a somewhat different story and one probably closer to the truth.[35] He confided to her that he was forced to leave a *Russian* university because he became "mixed up in a political plot which on discovery forced him to [flee] the country."[36] Whether he actually fell into police clutches or avoided that by flight is left open. Okhrana records do note a "revolutionary Jewish study group" active in Odessa that maintained contact with kindred cells through roving couriers. One of its couriers was a small-time, itinerant Jewish broker, Evno Fishelovich Azef.[37] He also was destined to become one of the most infamous police spies to plague the revolutionary movement. In fact, by 1892 he already was on friendly terms with police officials and had commenced his career as an informer.[38] And one more thing: Evno Azef was the brother of Salomon's friend Natta. Could he have been the spy who betrayed Rosenblum and his comrades?

Assuming his offenses were routine—agitation, trafficking in forbidden literature and the like—risk of serious punishment was slight. The standard response would have been expulsion from school and restriction from university towns for a few years. In addition, he would have been forbidden to leave the country.[39] Salomon, of course, was a Jew, and that raised other complications. Going on twenty, he was the ideal age for forced conscription. A recruit's life in the Russian Army was not a pleasant one, all the more so if one was a Jew from a privileged background. However, if Salomon fell into police hands, standard procedure also would have subjected him to pressure to turn informer himself, a task made all the easier if there were family and friends, like Elena and Felicia, to use as leverage. The possibility certainly exists that he did turn collaborator, something that might help explain his subsequent disappearance from Odessa and his later Okhrana connections in the West.

However, as Reilly's version continues, he had more difficulties to confront. Paulina, in poor health for some time, supposedly died soon after her son's arrest. In Reilly's later, colored version of events, this is the point when the enraged aristocratic father blurts out the truth of his paternity and damns him as "a dirty little Jewish bastard."[40]

There is one other very serious problem with this whole scenario. The Okhrana kept rather meticulous tabs on students' activities, especially comings and goings. Contemporary Odessa police records, including criminal/political investigation files and lists of students kept under police supervision, once again reveal no trace of Salomon or Sigmund Rosenblum.[41] We are thus confronted by the first real mystery in Reilly's career. While there is no doubt that Gersh and Paulina Rosenblum were real people and actually had a son named Salomon Sigmund, it is virtually impossible to document anything about the young man's life. Wherever we look, it seems, he is the Man Who Isn't There. This leaves the possibility, a rather disquieting one, that the Salomon Rosenblum who arrived in England in 1895 was not the authentic article. While the weight of available evidence argues strongly that the young man described above would evolve into Sidney Reilly, there remains the remote possibility that Rosenblum was but the first of his long line of aliases. Was the Ace-of-Spies the son of a family of prosperous Jewish businessmen or a child of the Moldovanka who somehow assumed that identity from its true owner, living or dead?

Returning to Reilly's later story, he next claimed that he left a suicide note for his family telling them to look for his corpse under the ice of Odessa harbor, after which he hopped a British steamer bound for South America.[42] There he met the aforementioned Major Fothergill, saved his life from treacherous natives, and as a reward was brought back to England and given a generous cash stipend. If this sounds like something out of a romantic novel, it was, as will be detailed later. The tale is a complete crock, though perhaps not all Reilly's handiwork. The suicide note could have been a genuine gesture, though there is no suggestion that any relations Salomon later encountered were astounded to see him among the living. The reference to the icy harbor may offer a clue as to when his exit occurred. Odessa harbor normally experiences some freezing in the winter, but almost never before December and seldom after February. That suggests a disappearance in the early weeks of the year.

This much seems certain: during the forepart of 1893, some sort of complication with the authorities compelled Salomon, the original or not, to leave Odessa in a hurry and make a serious effort to cover his tracks. Leaving the Tsar's domain without official sanction was a serious offense, though not especially difficult with the right help. The person best suited to provide that assistance was friend Ginsburg. Through his connections, Rosenblum probably received a set of false papers, or a fresh set, and passage on a ship headed at least as far as Constantinople. Ginsburg doubtless also supplied names of other persons who could be of assistance. Finally, he offered his young friend an important bit of advice: once he completed his education he should go to England. London was the center of the world and the right spot for a man with brains and ambition.

According to Margaret, Rosenblum spent the next two-plus years completing a chemistry degree at a "German" university.[43] As noted, Vienna has no record of him, nor does Heidelberg, where he later claimed to have studied Philosophy. Likewise, no trace of his can be found at Darmstadt, Bonn, Karlsruhe, Leipzig, Munich, Stuttgart and many others. The same is true for German-speaking Swiss universities in Basel, Berne and Zurich. Later informants, albeit ones hostile to Reilly, insisted he studied in Berlin.[44] Unfortunately, the most likely candidate, the Berlin Technische Hochschule, (today TU-Berlin) lost almost all of its student records during WWII. Thus, it remains a possibility. The fact that he later was able to demonstrate a convincing knowledge of chemistry and, apparently, documentation to attest this argues that he probably received formal training somewhere. But not, it would seem as Salomon Sigmund Rosenblum. Of course, as with languages, Reilly was a quick study. As a true con man he knew it was never hard to convince a person of what they wanted to believe. Fake university credentials, like false identities, were not difficult to acquire with a little money and resourcefulness. But if he was not in school or running around the Brazilian jungle, then what was he up to?

The available evidence, such as it is, puts Rosenblum in western continental Europe through the latter part of 1895, variously in Germany, France and Switzerland. In this same period, Boris Nadel took up residence in Paris and Evno Azef was an engineering student at Karlsruhe University. While both maintained active contact with the Russian revolutionary movement abroad, they also operated as Okhrana informers. Through its Foreign Agency (*Zagranichnaia Agentura*) in Paris, the Tsar's secret police spied on Russian students throughout Europe through an array of field agents and cooperative local officials and. Since 1884, the man at the helm of the Paris Agency was Petr Ivanovich Rachkovskii. Despite his corpulence, he exuded an air of energy and efficiency and was capable of great charm, albeit of a certain reptilian character. Most of all Rachkovskii possessed a quick and devious mind which made him "probably the ablest head of the Okhrana's Foreign [Agency]."[45] He also was the guiding hand behind one of the most insidious forgeries of modern times, the anti-Semitic *Protocols of the Learned Elders of Zion,* a document with which Reilly was to have a very curious relationship.[46]

It is testament to Rachkovskii's guile and resourcefulness that he would at once exploit Jews as scapegoats and as his own agents. In 1895,

Rachkovskii received a new field agent sent out by Fontanka[16], the Okhrana's central office in St. Petersburg. This was Ivan Fedorovich Manasevich-Manuilov.[47] He would prove a rather problematic operative. Born to poor Jewish parents, Manasevich was adopted and christianized by a philanthropic Russian merchant. As a youth he caught the eye of an aristocrat, Prince Vladimir Meshcherskii, who held a special fondness for pretty young boys. Among other things, Meshcherskii was the publisher of the right-wing paper *Grazhdanin*, and through his influence Manasevich took up journalism. The Prince also had connections to the Tsarist police, and doubtless it was through these that Manasevich entered the service of the Okhrana around 1890. By the time he arrived in Paris, Manasevich's looks had faded, but he dressed his paunchy figure in tailored clothes and painted the nails of his long, delicate fingers with henna-colored polish. His cover was that of a local correspondent for the Russian paper *Novosti*. He affected a particular interest in things spiritual and metaphysical through which he gained access to some of the French capitals more secretive corners.

Behind the façade of a dilapidated fop, Manasevich was cunning, greedy and utterly corrupt. This later earned him the title "the Russian Rocambole" after the picaresque, almost diabolic anti-hero of French popular fiction.[48] He refused to subordinate himself to Rachkovskii and set out to create his own network with the ostensible purpose of tracking the finances of the revolutionary groups in Western Europe. His interests also included blackmail, and through contacts in the French police, he even sought to collect dirt on Rachkovskii.[49] One of Manasevich's prime agents was a young Russian Jew working at the Grand Hotel, none other than Salomon's old Odessa chum, Boris Nadel.[50] Among other things, Nadel was a "spotter" or talent scout, and it was through him that our man gained his introduction to Manasevich in 1895. It was the beginning of a long and curious association.

It should by now come as no surprise that the surviving Foreign Agency records from this period contain no mention whatsoever of Salomon or Sigmund Rosenblum, or any name even close. Nor does his name, as either Rosenblum or Reilly, obviously show up in the massive and elaborately cross-referenced card index compiled by the Paris office right up to 1917. This omission is inexplicable given his many, many contacts with police agents and their radical quarry in the years to come. Once more, he is not where he should be.

However, among extant Okhrana records are lists of Russian subjects enrolled in German, Swiss, Belgian and other schools who were suspected of contact with revolutionary elements. Among them there appears one Leon (Lev) Rosenbaum or Rosenblat (which indicates some confusion about his precise identity) from Odessa, born in 1874.[51] He studied chemistry at an otherwise unidentified university with a school of medicine. Leon's father may have been Yakov-Mark, or Markus, Rosenblat, an Odessan whose profession was that of a "broker in ship goods." This sounds very close to the description of young Rosenblum's supposed father in the Soviet report.[52] Coincidentally or not, the name Rosenbaum later turned up in connection with Reilly, though in ways no one could ever quite pin down.[53] If nothing else, Leon Rosenbaum/blat's connection to Odessa and radicalism might explain how Salomon or Ginsburg knew him or about him and how his identity might have been appropriated. Or, was it Rosenbaum who appropriated Rosenblum? It is a dilemma that will crop up again and again as our story progresses: are we talking about one person, or two; two people, or one?

Although the similarities are less pronounced, there is another possibility. In July 1895, one Salomon Braunstein matriculated from the University of Zurich. His degree was in philosophy, not chemistry, but the former was the subject Reilly claimed at Heidelberg. Braunstein was some two years younger than Rosenblum and from Jassy, Romania, not Odessa, but both were conveniently close to the mark. There were thousands of Russian students and assorted exiles for Salomon to move among and hide among. Picking him out would be no simple task, which is exactly as he wanted.

According to information later gathered by Russian journalist Nikolai Alekseev, among the émigrés Reilly met in Western Europe in this period was still another Odessan. He was an energetic, bull-like man, Israel Leizarovich Gel'fand, better known as Alexander Helphand and later still, Parvus.[54] As a youthful radical, Helphand left Russia in the late 1880s and earned a degree in economics from the University of Basel. Afterward he became involved in the German socialist movement, though he never severed his ties to the Russian. Helphand probably knew Ginsburg; for among the latter's business associates in Odessa was his father, Leizer Gel'fand. Much as Rosenblum's, Helphand's activities in 1893–95 are frustratingly vague. About the same time Rosenblum arrived on the scene, German authorities expelled Helphand from Berlin. In the role of a socialist journalist, he thereafter shuttled between Germany and Switzerland. However, his most important job was helping set up a Swiss-based clandestine funding network for Russian and other revolutionaries. According to Alekseev's information, Rosenblum somehow got wind of this network or actually played a part in it.[55]

If Salomon did have a connection, it was an ideal vantage for an Okhrana spy. Ideology aside, he had a practical need to support himself and a healthy interest in anything that involved money. Reilly's later reflections on Russian revolutionaries displayed a grudging respect for their ideals coupled with utter contempt and cynicism regarding their ethics and methods, particularly those of the self-anointed leadership. He surely noticed that despite the supposed equality of the comrades, it was clear that some were more equal than others.

In the latter part of 1895, something definitely changed in the status and ambitions of our man. He probably completed his studies, as much as he needed anyway, and was ready to look for something bigger and more suited to his budding talents in duplicity and intrigue. Or, perhaps, he was just disillusioned with revolution and broke. He could not return to Russia without risk of arrest and worse. As so many of his displaced countrymen, he headed for Paris where, if he was not already one, he signed on as one of Manasevich's agents. The latter was very interested in the secret financial sources of the revolutionaries and eagerly enlisted Rosenblum's help. In turn, Manasevich could provide money and a certain degree of protection. However, the Tsar's police could not provide Rosenblum with the amount of cash he wanted. They divided their informants into various categories. At the top were the "collaborators" (*sotrudniki*) like Azef who functioned as deep penetration agents within the revolutionary parties. Lower down the ladder were the "piece workers" (*stuchniki* or *gastroleny*) and finally the simple informers (*zaiaviteli*), the category where Rosenblum probably belonged.[56]

At the close of 1895, he suddenly left Paris and headed to England. He would make reference to a "dark page" in his early life and intimate that he had left France because of some real or potential brush with the authorities.[57] However, almost forty years later, one Alexander Matzebovich claimed he knew what happened next.[58] A goodly share of the money flowing into revolutionary accounts came from sympathizers in Britain. Towards the end of 1895, two men, both Russian activists, left London with a cache of pounds sterling intended for one of the Swiss accounts. On a train in France, late at night, they were attacked. One of the couriers was thrown from the train, but survived, at least for a while. The other, the man actually carrying the money, was killed outright. The cash vanished. The common assumption was that the assailants were police agents who appropriated the money. Matzebovich claimed that it was Rosenblum/Reilly who engineered the robbery in league with Manasevich and that the two split the loot between themselves. To avoid the attentions of the French authorities, Salomon slipped away to England where Manasevich had new tasks in mind for him. A roughly similar story emerged through a private investigation about 1919. According to this, young Rosenblum arrived in Britain from France in 1895 in the wake of some brush with the law. While these stories constitute absolute proof of nothing, they certainly come closer to the truth than the tale of a grateful British major from the Amazon jungles.

NOTES

1. Between 1880 and 1905, some 100,000 Jewish immigrants entered Britain, the great majority of them from the lands of the Russian Empire. Another 50,000 came before the outbreak of the First World War despite Parliament's efforts to restrict immigration. This impoverished, Eastern European influx was greeted with some consternation by Britain's largely assimilated and prosperous "native" Jewish population of 60,000. See Lloyd P. Gartner, *The Jewish Immigrant in England, 1870–1914* (London, 1973).
2. A search of all relevant official lists, directories, biographical references and available public records turned up numerous Fothergills, but none fitting Reilly's description. Special thanks for Julian Putkowski for his assistance in this effort.
3. Tsentral'nyi Gosudarstvennyi Istoricheskii Arkhiv-Moskva (TsGIAM), fond 23–751, "Poiasitel'naia zapiska po delu zakliuchennogo #73," 1 (hereafter PZZ #73), 10 Nov. 1925. The TsGIAM archive was dissolved in 1961 and its collections absorbed by the current Gosudarstvennyi Arkhiv Rossiiskoi Federatsii (GARF). When and why this item was separated from the rest of Reilly's OGPU file is uncertain: see Chapter XVIII.
4. Special thanks to Vladimir Bet and Tatiana Wolff for their information and assistance.
5. *Encyclopaedia Judaica*, Vol. 6, 651–658, and Leeds Russian Archive, MS 1080, #859, Family Tree of the Wolff (Vol'ff), Rosenblum Neufeldt, et al. Families, and #322, Correspondence of Vera Bramson. Thanks also to Tatiana Wolff.
6. Generally speaking, the Pale was established in 1791 by Catherine the Great and roughly comprise the former territories of Poland and Lithuania and adjoining regions of the western Russian Empire. This imposed special laws and restrictions on Jewish inhabitants of the Pale and sharply limited Jewish residence outside its limits. For an excellent overview of Tsarist Jewish policy see Benjamin Pinkus, *The Jews of the Soviet Union* (New York, 1988), 1–48. A much more detailed treatment may be found in S. Dubnow's multi-volume *History of the Jews in Russia and Poland* (Philadelphia, 1916–20).
7. *Encyclopaedia Judaica*, Vol. 7, 1433–1451, and Masha Greenbaum, *The Jews of Lithuania: A History of a Remarkable Community*, 1316–1945 (Tel Aviv, 1995), 123–125.
8. Marriage record of Jankel [Jakov]-Leiba Rozenblium and Hana [Henrietta] Bramsohn, Lomza (Stawiski),1840, *Polish Records Indexing*, www.jewishgen.org/databases/#Poland.
9. Another brother, Moshek or Moisei, possibly died in childhood or as a young adult.
10. *Vsia Rossia*, 1895, 298.
11. Great Britain, Cabinet Office, material from briefing on Secret Intelligence Service personal file CX2616, "Reilly, Sidney G." (hereafter, SIS), Report of 13 Feb. 1922, and U.S. National Archives (USNA), RG 165, Military Intelligence Division (MID), file 9140-6073, Memorandum #5, 6 Sept. 1918, 3, statement of N.M. Rodkinson.
12. The adaptation and alteration of Jewish names usually followed a basic pattern, although there were no absolutes and many individual variations. The original Hebrew name, the *Shem HaKodesh*, i.e. Shlomo, seldom was used outside religious matters. The vernacular *kinnui*, such as Zalman, would be the name by which a person generally was known. Official records would further modify that name into more "gentile" forms. An additional/alternative "secularized equivalent" name was largely a matter of

individual taste, but often started with the same letter or bore some resemblance in sound of meaning to the original, e.g., Salomon=Sigmund, Gendla=Helena, Israel=Alexander, etc. Special thanks to Anita Citron, Mark Grekin and other members of Jewishgen and the Odessa Study Group for their help and advice in this matter.

13. *New York Times* [hereafter *NYT*], obituary (4 March 1941).

14. PZZ #73, 1.

15. Presumably this would have been either Charles Colonna-Walewski (1848–1916) or Alexandre-Antoine Colonna-Walewski (1840–1898), both sons of Count Alexandre Walewski (d. 1868), the illegitimate offspring of Napoleon and Countess Marie Walewska. Both spent most of their lives in France and Italy.

16. Robin Bruce Lockhart, *Reilly: Ace of Spies*, paper edition (London, 1967), 21–24.

17. Thanks to Judy Remmick-Hubert for this information.

18. Michael Kettle, *Sidney Reilly: The True Story of the World's Greatest Spy* (London 1983), 14.

19. Mark Grekin, "Odessa and Its Jews as Seen through Dates and Numbers," www.jewish gen.org/databases/VsiaRossiiaOdessa.htm.

20. PZZ #73, 1.

21. Ukraine, Odessa State Archive, fonds 45/2, /4 (admissions) and /5. Special thanks to Sergey Elizarov and Galina Malinova for assistance with this information.

22. Hoover Institution Archives (HIA), Stanford, Paris Okhrana Collection, Boris Nadel personal file, box 23, IIIf, folder 25. Richard Deacon [Donald McCormick], *Peddler of Death: The Life and Times of Sir Basil Zaharoff* (New York, 1965), 103, 195.

23. A case in point is that of "Misha Yaponchik" (Moishe Vinnitskii), "king of the Odessa bandits," who assumed a vivid and violent political role after 1917: see Viktor Savchenko, *Avantiuristy grazhdanskoi voiny* (Moscow, 2000), 129–159.

24. Viktor K. Kaledin, *K.14-OM.66: Adventures of a Double Spy* (London, 1934), 228. Azef had several siblings.

25. Charles Ruud and Sergei Stepanov, *Fontanka 16: The Tsar's Secret Police* (Toronto, 1999), 338, n.1.

26. Ginsburg's original surname was Mess or Mass, and he hailed from the southeast part of Russian Poland. He was not, as has sometimes been supposed, related to the more illustrious line of Baron Goratsii (Horace) Ginzburg.

27. *Vsia Rossiia*, 1895, 1598, 1600.

28. Ginsburg's true surname was Mess and he originated in the southern part Russian Poland. A basic biography is found in G. B. Sliozberg, *Dela minuvshikh dnei*, Vol. III (Paris, 1934), 293–297.

29. His name appears on an 1886 petition of prominent Odessa Jews to the Russian authorities regarding the appointment of Rabbi Simon Shvabacher: Shprinzak Central Archive for Jewish History, Hebrew University, Jerusalem.

30. N. Svitkov, *Masonstvo v' russkoi emigratsii: Sostavlennoe na osnovanii mas.* Dokumentov (Paris, 1932), 23. On the subject of Russian freemasonry, see also Nina Berberova, *Les Francs-Maçons russes du XX siècle: Des hommes et des loges* (Paris, 1988).

31. Deacon, *Peddler*, 68–71 sums up most of the evidence for Zaharoff's Jewish origins. The French investigator journalist Roger Mennevee, who carried out perhaps the most determined inquiry into Sir Basil's career, was convinced of an early link to Odessa and Russia. Mennevee's original materials may be found in the University of California, Los Angeles, Main Library, Special Collections, Mennevee Papers, dossier "Zaharoff."

32. For a broader look at freemasonry, the British variant in particular, see Stephen Knight, *The Brotherhood: The Secret World of the Freemasons* (New York, 1984). For an example of the grand conspiratorial viewpoint, see John Daniel, *Scarlet and the Beast: A History of the War between English and French Freemasonry*, Vol. I (Tyler, TX, 1994), particularly Chapter 19 concerning Russia and the Russian Revolution.

33. The so-called Okhrana (or Okhranka) was the popular name for two separate but closely related organizations, the Imperial Department of Police (*Departament Politsii*) and the Special Corps of Gendarmes (*Osobyi Korpus Zhandarmov*) which were charged with combating subversion and maintaining internal security under the supervision of the Imperial Interior Ministry (MVD). As will be seen, the Okhrana was in more than one respect the model and predecessor of the Soviet secret police. On the history and character of the organization, the above cited *Fontanka 16* is the most recent work based on Russian archival sources. Also very useful, particularly on the Foreign Agency, is Frederic S. Zuckerman, *The Tsarist Police in Russian Society, 1880–1917* (New York, 1996). A post-Revolution exposé of the Foreign Agency can be found in V.K. Agafonov, *Zagranichnaia Okhrana* (Moscow, 1918). Memoirs of former Okhrana officers include Gen. P. Zavarzin, *Souvenirs d'un chef de l'Okhrana, 1900–1917* (Paris, 1930). As noted, the surviving files of the Agency are held by the Hoover Institution Archives in Stanford, California.
34. Presumably, in Russian *Liga* or *Soiuz Proveshchenii*.
35. SIS, "Extract from typescript left with Captain Isaacs . . . ," c. Nov. 1931. This document was a synopsis or statement compiled by Margaret to prove her marriage to Reilly, and provided various details about his and her own activities. See Chapter XVIII for more details. Unfortunately, Isaacs saw fit to digest only a small portion of it. Copies of this or a similar document existed until the 1960s, and I am grateful to Dmitry Stein for his insights concerning same.
36. Ibid.
37. The classic study of Azef's career is B.I. Nicolaevsky, *Aseff the Spy: Russian Terrorist and Police Stool* (New York, 1934). Anna Geifman's *Entangled in Terror: The Azef Affair and Russian Revolution* (Wilmington, DE, 2000), adds new information and insight. See also Ruud and Stepanov, 125–151.
38. Ruud and Stepanov, 126–127, and Agafonov, 229.
39. As examples, see the cases of Aleksandr Grammatikov in E.C. Elwood, "Lenin and Grammatikov: An Unpublished and Undeserved Testimonial," *Canadian Slavonic Papers*, Vol. 28, #3 (Sept. 1986), 308 and Boris Savinkov in Richard Spence, *Boris Savinkov: Renegade on the Left* (Boulder, CO, 1991), 14–15.
40. Lockhart, *Ace of Spies*, 24.
41. Odessa archive, Fond 2/2, Investigations and 314, Supervision.
42. The PZZ #73 synopsis places the Fothergill-South American episode c. 1897-1900, which may, as we will see, have basis in fact. It also renders the officer's name as *Frazerdzhill*.
43. SIS, Isaacs.
44. USNA, MID, 9140-6073, Memorandum #2 for Lt. Irving, 23 Aug. 1918, quoting Mr. Cordley of Flint Arms.
45. Ben B. Fisher, "Okhrana: The Paris Operations of the Russian Imperial Police," Center for the Study of Intelligence, Central Intelligence Agency (1997), www.odci.gov/csi/monograph/okhrana/5474-1.html#rotc8.
46. Norman Cohn, *Warrant for Genocide: The Myth of the Jewish World Conspiracy and the Protocols of the Elders of Zion* (New York, 1967), 80–82 and *passim*.
47. HIA, Okhrana, box 23, IIIf, folder 27. This mostly covers his 1904–06 period of service. See also P. E. Shchegolev, *Okhranniki, agenty, palachi* (Moscow, 1992), 160–217.
48. Ibid., 160. See also Shchegolev's earlier *Russkii Rokambol'* (Leningrad, 1925). Rocambole was the creation of French writer Victor-Alexis Ponson du Terrail. The adventures of this early amalgam of superhero and archvillain appeared in the popular press between 1857–70 and later appeared as several published volumes. One wonders if young Salomon read them.
49. Ibid., 163–165.
50. Ibid., 165–166.

51. HIA, Okhrana, box 182, XIIIh, files 7 (index cards) and 10, "Repertoire des Étudiants, hommes et femmes, en relations plus ou moins suivres avec les principaux refugies Russes," 1891–1895.
52. *Vsia Rossiia*, 1895 and 1903, Odessa business listings.
53. SIS, C/5982, Sinclair to Norton, FO, 18 June 1931.
54. Z.A.B. Zeman and W.B. Scharlau, *The Merchant of Revolution: The Life of Alexander Israel Helphand* (Parvus) (London, 1965).
55. Alekseev's informant was Alexander Matzebovich, see note #59 below.
56. HIA, V.N. Russiian Collection, folio 317, "The Work of Okhrana Departments in Russia," 22. Russiian was an ex-Okhrana officer.
57. SIS, "Most Secret," 27 July 1939.
58. Reilly, SIS, Memo from British Consul General, Paris, 8616/148, 24 Sept. 1932; Extracts from notes and drafts of N.N. Alekseev, 1930–32. Thanks to the late Viktor Bortnevskii for assistance with Alekseev and his writings.

Chapter Two

A SPY'S PROGRESS

So we come back to the blustery, rain-soaked dockside in Portsmouth. If Reilly's later account was in any way accurate, he had some £1,500 in his bags, in current value roughly $75,000. This was no great fortune, but as a stake for a young man on the make it was a good start indeed. The next step was to discard Leon Rosenblat, or whoever he was on arrival, and revert—or assume—Salomon Sigmund Rosenblum. He thus severed any easily traceable links between his immediate past and his new life in Britain. He headed straight for London and took lodgings at 50 Albert Mansions, South Lambeth. At the time this lay on the southwest fringes of London, and if by no means an exclusive area, it was suitable enough for a man of his apparent means. He spent a good deal of money on clothes and other appurtenances the befitted his new incarnation, that of a young Polish aristocrat who had come to Britain to perfect his English and, of course, escape the Tsar's unbearable oppression of his homeland. In this one can see the blending of truth and fiction that would be the hallmark of Sidney Reilly. This guise was sufficient to satisfy nosy neighbors and landladies as to his lack of any obvious means of support, and it undoubtedly helped in his approach to his first important contact in London.

This was Wilfrid Michael Voynich (Habdank-Wojnicz), a figure perhaps best known today for his association with the mysterious "Voynich Manuscript." The latter, a weirdly illustrated antique tome written in an indecipherable alphabet was indicative of Voynich's public persona, that of a bibliophile and antiquarian book dealer who specialized in obscure works. In the 1890s, Voynich was a tall, thirtyish man with a broad face that seemed in a state of perpetual amusement. His other idiosyncrasies included one shoulder lower than the other and a habit of speaking English with Polish syntax.[1] Rosenblum's interest stemmed from Voynich's other role as Polish nationalist and supporter of anti-Tsarist revolutionaries. Born near Grodno, not far from Salomon's boyhood haunts, in 1865, Voynich endured his first arrest in 1885 as a result of his participation in an illegal Polish student organization at Warsaw University (where he studied, interestingly enough, chemistry). He escaped from prison, was again arrested, and exiled to Siberia, and yet again evaded custody. After a long trek he reached England in 1890 with the aid of a false passport and money provided by British sympathizers. Clearly, he was someone who had much in common with young Mr. Rosenblum.

Among Voynich's closest friends was another revolutionary exile, the anarchist Sergei Stepniak (Kravchinskii) who had assassinated a Tsarist police chief in 1878. More importantly, he helped establish the Society of Friends of Russian Freedom (SFRF) in London in 1890 and an American branch the following year. The Friends aided political prisoners in escaping Russia and settling abroad and in smuggling revolutionary literature into the Tsar's domain.[2] Stepniak and Voynich also had founding roles in the allied Russian Free Press Fund which aimed to become a vehicle for disseminating anti-Tsarist propaganda inside Russia.[3] Stepniak died suddenly in London in 1895 when he fell—or was pushed—under the wheels of a train. If it was murder, there can be little doubt who was behind it. Soon after, Voynich started his book business in Chelsea, but he maintained his association with the SFRF and related groups.[4]

Rachkovskii regarded the London émigrés and the SFRF as nothing less than "the most formidable revolutionary threat in Europe" and was determined to keep them under close surveillance and do everything possible to disrupt their activities.[5] As early as 1891, Rachkovskii reported to St. Petersburg that he had covert agents operating among the London émigrés and was on the lookout for more. In late 1895, the same time as Rosenblum's arrival on British shores, Rachkovskii brought over from New York an operative who recently had done excellent work in disrupting the activities of the American Friends of Russian Freedom. This was Aleksandr Evalenko, a man who later claimed to know much about Sidney Reilly and his past.[6] Evalenko may have helped engineer the death of Kravchinskii, but his most obvious role over the next few months, was to win the confidence of the Free Press Fund. In any case, it was here that he probably first encountered the future Ace-of-Spies.[7]

With the demise of Kravchinskii, Voynich became a special focus of Rachkovskii's attention. Personal conflicts with other exiles led Voynich to break with the Free Press Fund and set up a rival propaganda front.[8] Always quick to take advantage of rifts among his enemies, Rachkovskii sought an agent to penetrate and exploit this new opening. Rachkovskii's main man in London was a Frenchman with the interesting name of Emile Farce.[9] He supervised a network of operatives which included British detectives, some of them moonlighting from Scotland Yard, and a bevy of informers. It is not hard to guess Rosenblum's role in this apparatus. He was to worm his way into Voynich's confidence and use that vantage to gather information. The gambit was successful. Voynich took a shine to the dark-eyed young man and offered advice on the collecting of books and *objets d'art*, an activity in which the future Ace-of-Spies would invest a real fortune in the years to come. Financial matters, no doubt, were very much on Rosenblum's mind. The £1,500 was dwindling fast and the Okhrana's pay could not support him in the style to which he wished to become accustomed. Voynich did him two more favors: he offered him a job scouting estate sales and rival shops, and he introduced him to his wife.

Ethel Lillian Boole Voynich's relationship with Reilly has long obscured her husband's role in the picture.[10] The daughter of the noted mathematician George Boole, she was intelligent and opinionated. Her most outstanding physical characteristic was a "glorious head of golden hair." [11] While undoubtedly attractive, it seems doubtful that Rosenblum established a romantic relationship with her. In addition to being ten years his senior she reputedly was "stern and humorless" and seemingly disinclined to romantic fancies.[12] Her interest in Rosenblum likely stemmed from their presumed devotion to the common cause and his evident interest in her advice and associations. Like her husband, Ethel had been a close friend of Stepniak, had traveled in Russia, and was a devoted partisan of the revolutionary cause. Most interesting to Rosenblum, perhaps, she sat on the executive committee of the Friends of Russian Freedom.[13]

Ethel Voynich usually is linked to Reilly though her 1899 novel, *The Gadfly*, a saga of romance, intrigue and betrayal set during the Italian Risorgimento. Exactly where or when the rumor started is unclear, but it goes that the hero of the book's hero, "Arthur Burton," was modeled on Rosenblum. There are many parallels: Arthur's confused paternity, a betrayal that forced him to fake his suicide and flee to South America, and his subsequent career as a mysterious revolutionary figure. But Salomon surely later borrowed these from Voynich's story, not the other way round. For her part, Ethel could not recall who the character was based on, but the most probable inspiration was Stepniak.[14] Ethel conceived the story in 1886, began writing it three years later and completed it in early December 1895.[15] *The Gadfly* attained astounding popularity in Russia where over decades it went through more than a hundred printings. That may have

inspired Reilly to take credit for its inspiration. Salomon Rosenblum was in
the process of concocting a new identity, and what could work better than
a fictional character.

On 18 June 1896, some six months after he had entered Britain,
Sigmund Salomon Georgjevitch Rosenblum became a fellow of the
Chemical Society.[16] This is the last recorded instance of his use of the name
Salomon for many years. He thereafter used Sigmund exclusively, and for
the time being, so shall we. The following March, Sigmund G. Rosenblum
also joined the membership of the somewhat more prestigious Institute of
Chemistry.[17] To gain admittance to these bodies, he needed to demonstrate
completion of a suitable university course or an equivalent level of practical knowledge and experience. Equally important, to gain membership in
the societies he also needed sponsors. Unfortunately the names of these
have not been preserved, but it is evident that within a few months of his
arrival in Britain, Rosenblum had made important contacts and taken the
first steps in penetrating the precincts of the British Establishment. In the
case of the IC, one of his sponsors almost certainly was Lucy Everest Boole,
Ethel's sister and a noted chemist in her own right. Yet another member was
Sir Thomas Boverton Redwood, one of Britain's foremost petroleum
experts and "the *éminence grise* of British oil policy before the First World
War."[18] Furthermore, among the foreign Fellows was Russian chemist
Dmitrii Ivanovich Mendeleev. Although best noted for his compilation of
the Periodic Table of Elements, Mendeleev was an extremely important
figure in the evolution of the Russian oil industry.[19] Indeed, around the
Chemical Society and the allied Institute hung the strong odor of petroleum
and that, surely, was one of the things that attracted our hero.

Through his association with the above societies and their influential
members, Sigmund landed a job as a consulting chemist with the Electric
Ozone Company.[20] This concern manufactured raw chemicals and also
ozone generators for the production of such compounds and purification of
air and water.[21] Ozone had potential application to filtration systems
aboard surface vessels and submarines, which may have piqued
Rosenblum's interest, among others.

One person with a healthy interest in such new technology and its uses
was the aforementioned Basil Zaharoff. He was now to play, if he had not
already, an important, if largely hidden, role in Rosenblum's progress.[22] In
the years to follow, he earned the nicknames of "Mystery Man of Europe"
and "The Merchant of Death." During his long life (1849–1936), Zaharoff
most famously, or infamously, pursued the calling of international arms
dealer, but his multifaceted interests included oil, shipbuilding and high

finance. By the 1920s he was one of the richest men on Earth and one of
the most feared, though most people had never heard of him. His wealth
and contacts earned tremendous political influence in London, Paris and
other capitals and made him a Commander of the French Legion of Honor,
a Knight of the Bath and a Spanish Duke. On the other hand, he is said to
have cheated and robbed his friends, bribed and blackmailed government
officials, assassinated opponents, provoked and financed wars and to have
been nothing less than the Devil incarnate. He would be Sidney Reilly's
most significant role model. In 1897, Zaharoff already was connected with
Britain's giant Vickers Corporation, a firm in which the Greek became a
major shareholder. He also had many Russian connections, including the
Okhrana.[23] In London, Zaharoff consorted with a fellow (?) Greek, John
Mitzakis, another expert on Russian oil *and* another agent of
Rachkovskii.[24]

Zaharoff attributed his success to what he called *le système*—The
System. A early, simple case of the System in action was his sale of a costly
submarine to the impoverished Greek Navy, just the thing, he convinced
them, to offset the advantage of the larger Turkish fleet. As soon as the contract was signed, he set off for Constantinople where he showed it to the
Turks and thereby convinced them to buy two.[25] In a nutshell, the System
meant betting on all sides while manipulating the odds to best maximize
your own profit.

By the time Reilly met him, Zaharoff was nearing fifty, making him,
perhaps, a sort of ersatz father or uncle. He possessed aristocratic good
looks, intimidating steel blue eyes, combined with an immaculately
groomed mustache and goatee. Overall, he rather looked like the common
picture of the Devil. In addition to the System, Zaharoff offered other bits
of wisdom. The first was that in politics it was best to "Begin on the left . . .
and then . . . work over to the right. Remember it is sometimes necessary
to kick off the ladder those who have helped you climb it."[26] Another was
that often the easiest means to gain influence over a man was through a
woman.[27] Finally, while betting on all sides in a contest, always keep the
biggest wager on the strongest man. The future Ace-of-Spies would scrupu-
lously observe these rules in the years ahead. What would Zaharoff have
seen in Rosenblum? A younger version of himself, perhaps; in any case a
young man with intelligence, ambition and a large conscience, qualities he
could appreciate and use.

It may have been through Zaharoff that Reilly met another luminary of
the Vickers empire, Sir Francis Barker. He was a man of broad interests and
connections, but most importantly was fascinated by all things Russian.[28]

He was, for instance, president of the British-Russian Club and Chairman of the Executive Council of the Russian-British Chamber of Commerce. Such interests inevitably brought him into contact with the likes of Redwood and with others to be discussed below.

In the meantime, Sigmund kept his eyes open for the Okhrana. Under the code name "*Khimik*" ("The Chemist"), he helped keep Manasevich abreast of the radical intrigues brewing in London. One development that certainly merited his attention in 1896 was the gathering in London of the Second Socialist International. Among its attendees were radical delegates from all over Europe and beyond, among them a Russian delegation that included Alexander Helphand. A contact, unwitting or not, inside the conclave would have been extremely useful in gleaning information on surreptitious dealings between the Russians and their support network in London.

Sigmund's direct with the Okhrana in London was probably Scotland Yard detective Michael Thorpe.[29] Late that year, Thorpe was involved in the arrest of Russian revolutionist Vladimir Burtsev in the sanctuary of the British Library. Burtsev avoided extradition to Russia but ended up serving almost two years in English prisons. Rallying to his defense were Voynich and the SFRF that established a special Burtsev Defense Fund. Thorpe's primary function for both his British and Russian employers was that of "spotter" and case officer for street-level agents. Surviving Okhrana records document his recruitment of a Russo-Lithuanian immigrant, Casimir Pilenas, first as an informant for Scotland Yard and later for the Paris *Agentura*. Interestingly, Pilenas' enlistment occurred in 1898, and it may be that Thorpe picked him up as a replacement for Rosenblum. In any case, the two spies' careers were to have some startling parallels, most notably because both would become agents of London's future Secret Intelligence Service.

However, more important to our man's future was Thorpe's Scotland Yard boss, Police Superintendent William Melville, the man who personally handled the arrest of Burtsev. The model for the "ever-watching Chief Inspector" of the Victorian penny dreadful, Melville was a major, if unsung figure in pre-WWI British intelligence and a man obsessed with the struggle against anarchism and all kindred forms of radicalism.[30] He kept watchful eyes on London's Russian émigrés and in so doing had developed a collaborative relationship with the Paris Okhrana and its agents.[31] In this way, he made the acquaintance of young Mr. Rosenblum. He was, in all probability, the future Reilly's first chief in the realm of British "secret service" and an important influence on the rest of Reilly's career. A native of County Kerry in the far west of Ireland and a devout Roman Catholic, the forty-four-year-old Melville was a seemingly odd man to be heading what was, in effect, Britain's political police. Nevertheless, joining Scotland Yard in 1872, he proved one of the Crown's most steadfast and resourceful servants.

Did Rosenblum have a hand in Burtsev's undoing? Possibly, though more likely given his proximity to Voynich and comrades, he passed along information about their subsequent schemes to gain Burtsev's release. He definitely was in a position to know about the arrest and its orchestration, something he could share with Burtsev when their paths next crossed. About this same time, Sigmund commissioned some personal stationery. The upper left corner bore the image of a stylized two-headed eagle reminiscent of both masonic symbolism and the Romanov crest. At the eagle's feet was a Latin motto: *Mundo Nulla Fides*, "Put no faith in the world," or, more simply, "Trust No One."

During the autumn of 1896, Voynich sent Ethel and his young friend to Italy on a buying trip. Along with business, they seem to have taken the opportunity to enjoy themselves. From Venice they headed south to Tuscany and Florence and from there further south to Rome and Capri, the last a favorite watering hole for Russian expatriates. During the trip, Sigmund spent some of the last of his cash on a set of original drawings of the Arc de Triomphe by the French architect Chalgrin complete with notations on Napoleon's hand. This would be the foundation of a huge collection of Napoleonic books and artworks, most of which, including the Chalgrin drawings, he would sell in New York a quarter century later.[32]

Budgetary concerns probably moved Sigmund to abandon the flat in Lambeth in 1897 and move himself and his belongings into the less spacious Imperial Chambers, a bachelors' residence on Cursitor Street, just off Chancery Lane. But at the same time he was making contacts that would prove very important for his future prospects. Probably the most influential of these was Sir Henry Montague Hozier, the imperious Managing Secretary of Lloyd's of London.[33] It seems likely that he made Rosenblum's acquaintance through Melville, though it could have been the other way around. In any case, Hozier was the one man Reilly acknowledged as his early "mentor" in Britain, and probably the model for "Fothergill."[34] Hozier's tempestuous personal life included two divorces, rampant infidelity and even an abortive attempt to kidnap one of his daughters.[35] Via the same daughter, he became Winston Churchill's father-in-law. In 1873, he was one of a select group of Army officer's chosen for the War Office's new Intelligence Branch.[36] His intelligence work did not end when a year later he joined Lloyd's. It was certainly no coincidence that when he moved his family from 18 Queen Anne's Gate in 1884, the premises promptly became the new headquarters of the Intelligence Branch.[37] Hozier's role as secretary of Lloyd's had nothing to do with insurance, *per se*. Rather, he personally oversaw the activities of Lloyd's Maritime Intelligence Service, a worldwide network of agents and signal stations that fed a constant stream of naval data to the London office.[38] By formal agreement, Lloyd's "worked in harmony with the Admiralty" and supplied a constant stream of information to its Naval Intelligence Division.[39]

One of Hozier's associates in the above work was Albert Kaye Rollit, a wealthy solicitor who variously served as MP, director of the London and British Chambers of Commerce and President of the Law Society. He was very interested in oil and shipping, and among his many friends was the Chemical Society's Boverton Redwood. Most notably, however, he sat on the British Board of Trade's Commercial Intelligence Committee, a body that worked hand-in-glove with Lloyd's. Beyond this, Rollit, Hozier and even Melville were freemasons.[40] And so, of course, was Sigmund Rosenblum.

An interest shared by Hozier, Rollit and Rosenblum was horses, particularly the sporting kind. That may have provided the means of Reilly's introduction to another equine-fancier, the Reverend Hugh Thomas, age 65, a Welsh Cambridge graduate who came from a long line of Anglican divines. The Reverend was a collector of books and artworks that also offers possible contact via Voynich. Through patience, luck, contacts and inheritance, Thomas had accumulated a town house in London's Paddington district, a country house and horse farm in nearby Kingsbury Manor, an estate in Wales, plus the hoard of antiques and artworks that furnished them. In addition, he held stocks and cash assets in the amount of several thousand pounds. These were of intense interest to Rosenblum. The pressing question was how to get his hands on them.

The answer was provided by the Reverend's 23-year-old wife, Margaret Callahan Thomas, whom he wed in 1893. Another native of Ireland, Margaret was the offspring of a ship's captain named Edward Reilly Callahan.[41] The latter may or may not have provided the inspiration for our subject's future surname as well as the model for Reilly's fiction about an Irish sea captain father of his very own. Trained as a nurse, it was that calling that probably brought her into the Reverend's employ. Although raised a Catholic, Margaret adopted her spouse's faith and, despite her Irish roots, a fervently English identity. This desperate desire to be English may have given her something in common with Sigmund. In addition to the

Reverend's wealth, she also benefited from his social connections. To her dying day, one of Margaret's most prized possessions, one of the few Reilly left her, was a full-length photograph of herself dressed for presentation at court.[42]

Margaret's looks, if later descriptions are any indication, were rather plain, but beneath the auburn hair and behind the blue eyes lurked a passionate, devious, and violently jealous nature. Like Sigmund, who was her own age, she wanted more out of life than what birth had provided her. As her marriage to a man almost three times her age suggests, she was willing to make the necessary sacrifices to achieve that end. The aging Reverend had a bad heart. With the end of his mortal span likely to be sooner than later, he desperately wanted an heir to carry on his name. That was the hoped-for result of his May-December union, but after almost five years of valiant effort, Margaret had not conceived.

Margaret later recounted to Captain William Isaacs (Military Intelligence) that she first met Rosenblum at her husband's Kingsbury Manor estate in the summer of 1898.[43] That was impossible because she and Rosenblum were *married* at that time. The original almost certainly read summer of 1896 or 1897. As opposed to the edifice that today bears the name, the Manor then comprised a large tract of rural land to the northwest of London. Margaret, probably, was neither emotionally nor physically satisfied by her aged spouse. Rosenblum was young, exotic and attentive, and became a frequent visitor at the Manor and the house on Upper Westbourne Terrace. He gave her a pet name, "Daisy," from the Russian name for the flower, *Margaritka*, which she would keep longer than him. What happened next takes little imagination and who, exactly, seduced whom is unimportant. By the spring of 1898 she was madly in love with the dark-eyed Rosenblum, and she was pregnant.

One suspects that the Reverend Thomas was no doddering cuckold. He wanted an heir, and if he could not accomplish that himself, he might not have been too proud to let a more able man do it for him. Whatever anyone suspected, the child legally would be his. In early 1898, Margaret announced she was pregnant. The Reverend thought a sunnier climate would be ideal, and made plans for a trip to the Mediterranean. Whether Rosenblum was part of the plans or invited himself along is unclear, but he planned to tag along. Departure was delayed when Thomas suffered a mild heart attack. Recuperating at Kingsbury, on 4 March he made out a fresh will that left everything to his wife. However, the document pointedly provided for the possibility of a child who would have proprietary rights to his estate.

The timing of the will is curious, but then so are many other things about what followed. Maybe Thomas sensed his time was at hand and that he needed to have his affairs in order, or perhaps he was encouraged to tidy up his affairs by his wife and helpful young friend. Margaret offers no clues on this point; indeed, she pointedly avoids it. Nine days later, Thomas died in a railway hotel room in Newhaven with Margaret and his personal nurse at his side. They supposedly were waiting for Rosenblum to join them. As in so many instances to come, he was conveniently out of sight when something unpleasant occurred. The death was ruled heart failure, and perhaps it was just that, the exertions of preparing for the trip simply being too much for his failing system. On the other hand the nurse, the only other witness to the Reverend's passing, seems to vanish off the face of the Earth. The same for the doctor who signed the death certificate, variously an S.W. or T.W. Andrews, a man who by all extant professional records never existed in the first place.[44] Then there is Sigmund's handy acquaintance with chemistry and medicine. Did Margaret and her lover conspire to murder her aged husband? We may reasonably suspect so, but the evidence as it stands would hardly be sufficient to convict. Under the circumstances, however, doubts arose about the exact cause of Thomas' departure from the world, and these were not allayed when a scant five months later the widow Thomas became Mrs. Rosenblum.

The Reverend was out of the way, but there was still the matter of the unborn child. He or she would have claims to the estate and a meddling solicitor to look out for their interests. Sigmund wanted the estate free and clear. Arrangements were made and the situation rectified. One must wonder if the same Dr. Andrews lent a hand. Whatever else she may have done in the years to follow, this haunted her for the rest of her life. Her inner Catholic told her she was damned to hell, and from that moment forward, she came to believe, her relationship with Reilly was cursed.

On 22 August 1898, Sigmund Georgjevich Rosenblum and Margaret Callahan Thomas were joined in a quick civil ceremony in the Holborn Registry Office. The only other attendees were the two witnesses, both friends of the groom. One was Joseph Harold Bell, an assistant in the offices of the Admiralty's Nautical Almanac lodged in the Verulam Building off central London's Gray's Inn Road.[45] Could that have disguised some intelligence function? In any case, his duties brought him into contact with Lloyd's and Hozier. The other, Charles James Cross, was a solicitor with ties to Leslie Sanderson, to be noted above.

A close examination of the marriage certificate reveals a number of interesting details. Rosenblum gave his age as twenty-five, a year older than indicated in most other references. This may have been in deference to Margaret who was, in fact, some three months older than he. Or it may simply have been another effort to fudge and obscure his origins. This might also explain a peculiar inconsistency, one that passed muster in Holborn, but would never have done so in Russia. The groom entered his name as Sigmund Georgjevich Rosenblum, the middle item being the patronymic that identified his father. But on the same form he gave his father's name as Grigory Jakovlevich Rosenblum. The two names are quite distinct in Russian, but, as we know, both derived from his father's true name of Gersh. Still, the inconsistency is odd and certainly deliberate. Was Sigmund having some sort of private joke, a subtle admission that his father was not really his father?

Margaret vacated the Kingsbury estate and at her new spouse's urging began to liquidate the Reverend's assets. Perhaps due to haste, the air of scandal, or perhaps because the Reverend was not as good a collector as he thought, a sale at Christie's netted only a fraction of the estimated value. Sigmund wanted much more money and had plans to get it. At age twenty-four, he was fluent in at least five languages (Russian, Polish, German, French and English), a solid background in chemistry (with potential application to munitions and oil), a strong interest in basic physical and other sciences. He was cunning and unburdened by moral inhibitions. In short, he had all the makings of an excellent spy. He was now in a position to trade information gleaned from the Okhrana and radical circles to his British friends and, of course, vice versa—the basic recipe for the System.

There were further lessons to be learned. He had frequented horse races as a means of meeting the right people and placing bets seemed an easy way to expand his assets. Luck, however, did not attend his wagers. Barely a week after their wedding, as Margaret later recalled it, her new husband suddenly announced he was going to Spain; she was not invited to accompany him. He suddenly was "well-supplied with money." [46]

To put Reilly's coming ventures in context, we need to pause and consider the broader meaning of "British intelligence" and the nature of its interest in Russia.

At the close of the 19th century, Queen Victoria's empire possessed a variety of intelligence-gathering agencies which tended to operate independently as opposed to collectively.[47] The War Office Intelligence Branch/Division (WOID), the Admiralty's NID, the Commercial Intelligence Committee and Scotland Yard's counterintelligence section were the main elements. Then, of course, there were the quasi-official entities such as Lloyd's. To this could be added the intelligence-gathering activities of the Indian Government and Colonial Office. Where overseas espionage was concerned, the Foreign Office also exercised a strong pro-prietary interest if no particular direction.

While Sigmund was back in London by mid-December, his exact loca-tion and activities for some three months remain vague. There certainly was some intelligence dimension to this new mission. But what was there in Spain to interest him or others? One possibility is that he went there on Melville's behest to collect information on anarchists, Spain being a partic-ular hotbed of that movement. Melville believed in a vast anarchist con-spiracy reaching across borders and around the world. That November, he went to Rome to attend an International Anti-Anarchist Conference that aimed to create a system of "strategic international surveillance" over anar-chist and kindred groups.[48] Information collected by Rosenblum may have been of some use.

A more likely stimulus for his journey was Spain's recent defeat at the hands of the United States and the latter's acquisition of most of the Spanish Empire, including Cuba and Puerto Rico. The war catapulted America into the league of a major colonial and naval power and extended its interests and influence, particularly in the Caribbean and Latin America. Such shift in the balance of power was bound to arouse the attention of interests in London. As it happened, Britain was locked in thorny boundary disputes with Brazil and Venezuela over the frontier with its Guiana colony. In 1895, Washington and London had clashed over this very issue, and it was rea-sonable to expect the Americans to become more assertive under the new circumstances.

All this draws our attention back to the jungles of South America where Sigmund was supposed to have adventured before coming to England. Interestingly, the 1925 Soviet synopsis places the Fothergill expedition story between 1897 and 1900, a time frame that fits the "Spanish" sojourn.[49] In the summer of 1898, Her Britannic Majesty's Government also dispatched a Mr. J.H. Reddan to Spain to search archives for materials supporting the British case in Guiana. His researches were paid for out of the Secret Service budget, a general fund for intelligence and other sensitive work, but that is not the most interesting thing about his venture. Reddan had done the same sort of work before, but in late 1895 he had raised a fuss about his pay and threat-ened to go over to the other side—the Venezuelans and Americans—if not sat-isfied. Nabobs at the Foreign Office and elsewhere were concerned enough to suggest that Reddan should be shadowed and, if necessary, his property and papers searched.[50] Scotland Yard's attention was solicited which brought the matter before Melville. In the end, Reddan received some sort of satisfaction, for he returned to the work in 1898, but not without some mistrust in high circles.[51] The best bet, therefore, is that Melville or someone tapped Rosenblum to keep tabs on Reddan in Spain, a simple enough task for a tyro operative.

This mission may have led to a trip to South America itself. Rosenblum had the advantage of not being obviously British, particularly handy where discretion or secrecy was desired. At this time there was much concern about the Brazilian national debt, most of it owed to British creditors, and plans in London to refinance the obligation. Part of this arrangement assigned Brazilian port duties as security for the loan, and having an unobtrusive agent on hand to collect information would have been most useful. For good measure, in late 1898 plans were underway for an international naval exposition in Rio de Janeiro, something that would draw warships from around the world, including some of the latest models, another certain target of intelligence interest. Finally, also in 1898, the British Board of Trade dispatched businessman Thomas Worthington on a "special mission to South America" that included Brazil, Uruguay and neighboring states. Worthington's mission was closely linked to Commercial Intelligence that was, of course, Rollit's domain.[52] Did Rosenblum also shadow Worthington as a confidential observer? Interestingly, among the British businessmen on Worthington's itinerary was one Frederick Fothergill of Montevideo.[53] If nothing else, it may explain where Sigmund picked up the name. What we may be reasonably sure of is that somewhere here lay the budding Ace-of-Spies' trial mission for "British intelligence."

In his absence, Margaret continued the sale of the Reverend's valuables. Upon his return, Sigmund ventured some of the proceeds in a renewed assault on the race tracks and gambling tables. The result was a "disaster."[54] Even harder for Margaret to bear was the time and money her new husband lavished on prostitutes and chorus girls. All but ignored by her spendthrift spouse, she whiled away her time in the empty house on Westbourne Terrace. As she later confessed to a sympathetic ear she had loved her husband "with complete abandon," but out of his flagrant betrayals gradually arose hatred.[55] The latter did not replace the love, but existed alongside it, an emotional paradox that seems to have tortured Margaret even more.

Sigmund's patronage of brothels and the seamier side of the theater world may not have been wholly for recreational purposes. Such venues were wonderful places to pick up confidential and often incriminating information, dirt that could be put to profitable use by someone with a little daring and few scruples. Even Melville, a man of strict propriety in his personal life, exploited madames and courtesans for information on a regular basis, and it is quite possible that Rosenblum abetted such work.

It is about this same period, late 1898–early 1899, that Reilly may have had his first brush with Aleister Crowley, the British occultist who subsequently proclaimed himself the Great Beast incarnate. Crowley had recently visited Russia on a "scouting" mission for the Foreign Office, or so he claimed.[56] Upon returning to London, he took rooms on Chancery Lane, right in Rosenblum's neighborhood, and embarked on a string of "magickal" rituals. He also affected the persona of Count Svarov, a Russian nobleman. It seems unlikely that Rosenblum could have ignored this performance. It was no more than passing curiosity, perhaps, but it was the beginning of a strange series of encounters between these two men of mystery.

Meantime, there were schemes to pursue. Back in London, on 16 December 1898, Rosenblum wrote the chief of the reading room at the British Museum requesting a reader's card. He described himself as "a chemist and physicist and a member of various scientific societies."[57] As for his purpose, he expressed a desire to study tapestry and medieval art, "in both of which I am greatly interested." Accompanying his own was a letter of recommendation from Leslie Gordon Sandford. He was another solicitor with offices on Arundel Street, just a short distance away from Rosenblum's Cursitor digs. Sandford claimed personal acquaintance with Mr. Rosenblum whom he described as "a fit and proper person" and a "man of high scientific achievements." Rosenblum, he added, "is engaged in scientific work of great importance to the community." The Museum duly granted admission on 19th December.

The practical purpose of Sigmund's study was the chemical composition of inks, paints and dyes, a field of inquiry unlikely to have been for his own amusement. One application for the investigation of such pigments was their attempted recreation, and the most likely application of that was forgery. This brings us back to Wilfrid Voynich whose specialty was the unearthing of medieval and Renaissance manuscripts either thought long lost or completely unknown. When he opened a new shop in 1902, Voynich exhibited an astounding collection of no less than 160 "unknown or lost books."[58] While the great majority of these were certainly authentic, there is a chance that some were fakes, or, as Voynich might have it, "reproductions."[59]

There were, of course, other applications for such knowledge and skill, notably the counterfeiting of currency. It may be no coincidence, therefore, that in the spring of 1899, word reached St. Petersburg of a ruble-counter-feiting operation in London. It was no small operation, and the Tsar's officials had no doubt that the aim was to use the fake funds to bankroll revolutionary plots. Okhrana central ordered Rachkovskii to investigate the matter, but that was not all. In April, a high-level team set out from Petersburg headed by criminal prosecutor Fedor Iosifovich Gredinger. Gredinger and Rachkovskii turned to Melville for help. Among those involved in the plot was an Indian Army officer, Capt. Brant, a German engraver and a "merchant," Rosenblum.[60] The latter's help was critical in moving the funny money out of Britain. Almost certainly, this was our man. The scheme lay within the familiar realm of illicit revolutionary finances and, of course, the technical aspects of counterfeiting corresponded nicely to Sigmund's recent investigations at the British Museum.

The Russian response, especially the arrival of Gredinger, placed Melville in an awkward position. Young Rosenblum was a valuable inform-ant, but the involvement of his name in the counterfeiting plot was bound to lead to embarrassing questions, especially if they discerned his link to Scotland Yard. Certainly, the Russians could not be allowed to get their hands on him. Sigmund needed to get out of Britain, and he needed a new identity to go under.

NOTES

1. The most thorough description of Wilfrid Voynich and his background is in E. Millicent Sowerby, *Rare People and Rare Books* (London, 1967), 3–33. See also Herbert Garland, "Notes on the Firm of W.M. Voynich," *Library World* (April 1934), 225–228, and the obituaries in the *London Times* [hereafter *LT*] (22 March 1930), 17, and *NYT* (20 March 1930), 27.
2. Barry Hollingsworth, "The Society of Friends of Russian Freedom: English Liberals and Russian Revolutionaries, 1890–1917," *Oxford Slavonic Papers*, vol. #3 (1970), 54–57.
3. Donald Senese, *S.M. Stepniak-Kravchinskii: The London Years* (Newtonville, MA, 1987), 72.
4. Ibid., 81 and *passim*.
5. HIA, Okhrana, box 215, XXVa, #2, agent report from New York, 12 June 1907, and XXVb/2, report on revolutionary finances compiled c. 1908.
6. MID, 9140-6073, Memorandum #9, 27 Sept. 1918.
7. HIA, Okhrana, box 22, IIIf, folder 14; Senese, 101.
8. Senese, 81.
9. HIA, Okhrana, box 16, IIIf, folder 40.
10. E.A. Taratuta, "Na Ovoda nadavaiut masku," *Literaturnaia gazeta* (12 June 1968), 9.
11. Sowerby, 10.
12. Senese, 59.
13. SFRF, "Second Annual Report of the Executive Committee," British Library. Again thanks to Bob Henderson for help with this information.

14. Taratuta, 9, and Tibor Szamuely, "The Gadfly and the Spy," *Spectator* (17 May 1968), 665.

15. Boris Polevoi and Evgeniia Taratuta, "Komu zhe podrazhal Pavka Korchagin," *Izvestiia*, (12 June 1968), 3.

16. Royal Chemical Society Library, *Fellows of the Chemical Society, 1896, May–June*. As S.G. Rosenblum he remained listed as a member through March 1900. Thanks to Nicola Best for her assistance in locating this information.

17. *Fellows of the Chemical Society, Jan.–May 1897.*

18. Daniel Yergin, *The Prize: The Epic Quest for Oil, Money and Power* (New York, 1991), 139.

19. V.E. Parkhomenko, *D.I. Mendeleev I russkoe neftianoe delo* (Moscow, 1957).

20. SIS, Isaacs.

21. Also known as the Electric Ozone Syndicate. In 1898 the firm published a booklet entitled "Ozone: Its Commercial and Sanitary Applications, etc." that described the varied uses of the technology. There also may have been a link between EOC and the nearby Ozone Generator Co. PRO, BT 10921/82889. Thanks also to Bob Henderson of the British Library for help with this information.

22. In addition to Deacon's *Peddler of Death* cited above, there are numerous biographies of Zaharoff, of varying reliability. The most recent, with valuable archival data on his relationship with Vickers, is Anthony Allfrey, *Man of Arms: The Life and Legend of Sir Basil Zaharoff* (London, 1989). The best overall examination of his business and political connections probably remains Roger Mennevee's *L'Homme Mysterieux de l'Europe: Sir Bazil Zaharoff* (Paris, 1928). The rare Rochat-Cenise, *Roi des Armes: La vie mysterieuse de Basile Zaharoff* (Bienne, 1943) contains unique information.

23. Richard Deacon, *History of the Russian Secret Service* (New York, 1972), 117–119.

24. John Mitzakis, *The Russian Oil Fields and Petroleum Industry* (London, 1911), 16; PRO, HV 1/8 , William Melville Memoirs, 13–14.

25. Deacon, *Peddler*, 50–51.

26. Robert (Lord) Boothby, *I Fight to Live* (London, 1947).

27. Rochat-Cenise, 84–85, Deacon, *Peddler*, 62, quoting Zaharoff's 1930s interview with Rosita Forbes.

28. *LT*, obit. (30 Jan. 1922), 14c, and (9 Feb. 1922), 13b, for a list of persons attending his funeral.

29. HIA, Okhrana, box 19, IIIe. In a 13 Aug. 1904 letter to L.A. Rataev (Rachkovskii's successor), Thorpe noted that he began to assist Farce in 1894. Thorpe became a full-time employee of the Okhrana in 1901. He and other Scotland Yard officers served the Foreign Agency with the knowledge and approval of their superiors.

30. Michael Smith, *New Cloak, Old Dagger* (London, 1996).

31. PRO, HV 1/8, Melville Memoir, 7–8, 15–17.

32. The American Art Galleries, *The Notable Collection of Mr. Sidney G. Reilly of New York and London: Literary, Artistic and Historical Properties Illustrative of the Life of Napoleon* (New York, 1921), item 53.

33. Almost all Soviet documentation concerning Reilly originally was contained in a KRO-OGPU (counterintelligence) investigative file #249856 (see Chapter XVIII). For simplicity's sake, all items clearly originating with this file will henceforth be designated "KRO." Numerous selected documents from this file and others currently reside in the *Tsentral'nyi Arkhiv Federal'noi Sluzhby Bezpasnosti Rossiiskoi Federatsii* (TsAFSB, Central Archive of the Federal Security Service of the Russian Federation), AN 302330, *Razrabotka Trest'*, Chast' II, Vol. 37. For other references based on this information, see Iurii Miliutin [Igor Prelin], "Konets shpiona Reilly," *Sovershenno Sekretno*, #12 (1990), 21–23, and an earlier version of the preceding article, "Zhizn i smrt' Sidneia Reilli," 19.

34. TsAFSB, Protokol, 9 Oct. 1925.

35. Mary Soames, *Clementine Churchill: The Biography of a Marriage* (Boston, 1979), 5–10, 27.

36. Thomas Fergusson, *British Military Intelligence, 1870–1914* (Frederick, MD, 1984), 54.

37. Soames, 7.

38. *LT* obit., and "The Lloyd's Agency System." Thanks to Norman Hooke of Lloyd's Maritime Information Services for the last item.

39. In 1901 the arrangement became a formal 50-year agreement to supply the Admiralty with information in times of war and peace, and continued through and after WWI. See PRO, ADM 116/4, Cockerell, 130, Gibb, 157.

40. *Who Was Who, 1916–1928*, 905, *LT* obituary (16 Aug. 1922), 9, and Francis Vane, *Agin' the Governments* (London, 1929), 81–83, and Melville, *Who Was Who, 1916–1928*, 727.

41. Leon C. Messenger, "The Nanny with the Glass Eye," Central Intelligence Agency, *Studies in Intelligence* (Winter 1985), 28.

42. Messenger, 27–28. Margaret later claimed that the pearl earrings she wore in the picture, and still possessed, had been a gift from Reilly. Nor was she explicit as to whether she meant the British or Russian court. Given that the picture had to have been taken sometime between 1893 and 1901, it seems extremely unlikely that Reilly would have had the clout to gain an audience in either. Almost certainly it was the British court and her entrée was Rev. Thomas. In that case, the earrings still might have been a present from Reilly, though probably she just preferred to think of them so.

43. SIS, from Isaacs.

44. Among other things, Andrews (or Andrew) listed himself a member of the Royal College of Surgeons. That body has no record of any such member under any of the variant names.

45. *Imperial Calendar*, 1898, London.

46. SIS, from Isaacs.

47. The best single source on the origins and evolution of British intelligence is Christopher Andrew, *Secret Service: The Making of the British Intelligence Community* (London, 1985), esp. 1–33. See also the aforementioned Fergusson, *British Military Intelligence, 1870–1914*. Both works, however, focus largely on the War Office aspect of early intelligence. On the naval angle, see Hector Bywater and H.C. Ferraby, *Strange Intelligence: Memoir of Naval Secret Service* (London, 1999; reprint of 1931 edition). The surviving records of these early years, again almost exclusively WO-related, may be found in the Public Record Office files HD 1–4, particularly HD 3.

48. The conference convened on 24 November 1898 and included fifty-four delegates representing twenty-one representatives, including the chiefs of several police/security agencies. See Candace Falk, et al. (eds), *The Emma Goldman Papers*, "Chronology 1869-1900," UC Berkeley Digital Library, sunsite.berkeley.edu/Goldman/Guide/chronology6900/html.

49. PZZ #73, 2.

50. FO 80/452, "Employment of Mr. J.H. Reddan on British Guiana Boundary Arbitration, HD 3/102, "Activities of Mr. Reddan," 1896, and references in HD 3/130, c. 1906.

51. HD 3/106, "Correspondence and Papers about Mr. Reddan's Mission to Spain," 1898.

52. *Who Was Who, 1929–1940*. Upon his return, Worthington became the director of the BOT's Commercial Intelligence Branch.

53. Great Britain, Somerset House, Probate record for F.W. Fothergill, 1915.

54. SIS, from Isaacs.

55. Messenger, 31.

56. Aleister Crowley, *The Confessions of Aleister Crowley: An Autohagiography* (New York, 1969), 151.

57. British Library Archives. Special thanks to Bob Henderson of the BL for his help in locating these documents.
58. "The Voynich Collection of Unknown Books," *LT* (23 July 1906), 4.
59. So far as can be told, no public suggestion of fraud ever attached itself to Voynich's discoveries. However, forgery, though not necessarily Voynich's, has been proposed in the matter of the strange "Voynich Manuscript." See J.B.M. Guy, "Voynich Revisited," *Cryptologia*, #15 (1991), 161–166.
60. HIA, Okhrana, Vc, "Relations with Scotland Yard," esp. Racgkonskii to Melville, 17 April 1899 and XXVb.

Chapter Three
EASTERN HORIZONS

In April 1899, Margaret's husband suddenly announced that he was going abroad. He supposedly commanded her to sell the Paddingdon house and move to a flat in St. Ermin's Chambers in fashionable St. James. However, among the listed residents at St. Ermin's address in 1900 no Mrs. Reilly is evident, but there was a Reverend *David* Thomas.[1] Not quite the same name as her late spouse, of course, but perhaps good enough as a convenient blind. Whatever the case, Rosenblum further commanded that she was to communicate with him under a new name.

At the beginning of June 1899, Sigmund Georgjevich Rosenblum picked up a British passport bearing the name Sidney George Reilly. From that moment, like Salomon before him, Sigmund vanished from the face of the Earth. He later explained to associates in British intelligence that he had changed his name "for his own convenience."[2] So far as Margaret knew, he would never legally adopt the name, not even by the simple expedient of declaration by deed poll.[3] As we will see, he did in fact, but not for another nine years later. That certainly was no mere oversight as he later claimed. The new Mr. Reilly wanted no paper trail to connect him to the compromised and discarded Rosenblum.

The real questions are how he received the passport and why. Under prevailing regulations, passports were surprisingly easy to obtain.[4] For the native born, which Reilly purported to be, all that was required was a supporting document signed by a magistrate, mayor, minister of religion, or simply a solicitor or notary. Sidney would have had no trouble getting that. Was the Irish angle a subtle hint of Melville's own Hibernian hand in the matter? Whatever the case, in the years following, Reilly kept the birth date of 23 March 1874 but routinely gave his place of birth as Clonmel, Ireland. Years later, a cursory investigation by MI5 revealed no such person born in

Clonmel or anywhere else on the Emerald Isle, a fact confirmed by a more recent search of Irish records.[5]

Few traveling Britons bothered to acquire passports at this time, and most countries did not require them. The three exceptions were the Ottoman Empire, Rumania and, most notably, Russia, which gives us a clue to Reilly's ultimate destination. Of course, the document also came in handy as personal identification, something very useful to our otherwise none-too-British subject.

Reilly's whereabouts for the better part of the next two years is difficult to pin down in any detail. About the only thing he, or someone, later offered was that he went to Holland to spy on Dutch aid to the South African Boers.[6] During the summer of 1899, long-simmering tensions between the fiercely independent Boer Republics and British imperial ambitions reached the boiling point. Open war broke out in October, but in the months preceding, the Boers sought to stock up on arms and ammunition in anticipation of hostilities. That sort of activity, of course, was of vital interest to the War Office and others and attracted the attention of Melville as well. The Netherlands would have been an excellent nearby locale for the newly-minted Reilly to perform useful work while keeping a low profile.

Dutch aid to their Boer cousins was not what concerned London, however. The South African Republics had other supporters in Europe, most notably in Germany and Russia, and aid from those quarters passed through the Netherlands. This may explain why Sidney is supposed to have carried out his assignment in Holland disguised as a German. If so, this may be where he first employed another identity, Sigmund Stern, a German or German-American. As Stern or Reilly, he likely made forays into the Reich and, perhaps, France as well, though Rachkovskii's presence probably made Paris a place best avoided.

Sometime in 1900, he entered Russia. As noted, a British passport was indispensable for this mission. The Tsar's Gendarmes kept an eye out for Russian subjects who had left the Empire illegally. If caught, they faced fines and imprisonment.[7] Moreover, as a draft-dodger, Sidney faced forced induction. Risks to be sure, but Russia was about the last place Rachkovskii would be looking for him. Part of Reilly's mission was continuation of his Boer work. Boer sympathizers in Petersburg and Moscow, with the tacit approval of their government, not only solicited guns and money for South Africa, but volunteers as well. A central figure in this effort was an up-and-coming Russian tycoon and politico, Aleksandr Ivanovich Guchkov.[8] He recalled first meeting the Ace-of-Spies at this time.[9] Reilly presented himself as the son of an Irish father and a Russian mother who was in Russia as representative for a group of London capitalists. His father, he claimed, had imbued him with Irish nationalist sympathies that made him a secret partisan of the plucky Boers. Guchkov was not altogether convinced, but found the curious "Irishman" an interesting character. Years later, knowing much more of Reilly and his methods, Guchkov concluded that the former must have been acting as a British agent even in 1900.

But he had more to do in Russia than sniff out Boer connections. The smell of oil drew him to the Caucasus. In 1897 the Oleum Syndicate, a powerful group of British investors, had plunged into the burgeoning Russian petroleum industry.[10] More British investors followed, among them many associates of Hozier and Rollit, and perhaps those worthies themselves. Lloyd's Bank contemplated financing drilling ventures in neighboring Persia. Gauging Russia's mood and how a move into Persia might impact British investment in the Tsar's domain were questions of immediate and serious concern. Having a man on the spot would have been very useful. In the summer of 1900, War Office Intelligence acknowledged the presence of a special agent traveling between Baku and other points in the Caucasus and reporting to the British Consul in Batum. While it is by no means certain this was Reilly, the time, place and circumstances certainly fit.[11]

It probably was in Baku at this time that Reilly had his first brush with Leslie Urquhart. The latter was a Scottish engineer engaged in the petro business and later the British vice consul in Baku. He was destined to become Reilly's partner in many intrigues and enterprises, as we shall see. Whether or not Sidney took the opportunity to actually visit Persia, is uncertain, but not impossible. The Shah's frontier lay only 150 miles from Baku, and the Persian capital of Tehran twice that distance via the Caspian route.

Also very interested in matters of oil was the Admiralty. Since the 1880s it had seen debate between the advocates of coal and oil as the preferred fuel of the Royal Navy. A key point in this argument was Britain's lack of significant petroleum resources of her own. Reliance on foreign sources entailed obvious risks, especially in Russia's case. Simply put, many in London also viewed Russia as Great Britain's most dangerous rival. The two empires had long vied to control a huge swath of territory stretching from the Middle East to the Far East.[12]

Of all Britain's intelligence bodies, the NID was then probably the largest and, arguably, the most effective. Lt. Col. William P. Drury, who entered its service in 1900, recalls: "Secret information from a hundred sources all over the globe poured into the Department day and night." "In

all the naval and military (and indeed many of the political) movements of
the world, projected or accomplished," he adds, "we were behind the
scenes and knew what was going to happen sometimes long before the
Press."[13] NID and WOID maintained small permanent staffs of officers like
Drury who rarely engaged in field operations.[14] Her Majesty's Government,
like most, preferred to maintain an image that it never engaged in anything
as unseemly as espionage at all. Most hands-on espionage was performed
by agents without visible ties to British officialdom. Reilly was perfect for
the part; if he was caught, he was easily dismissed as a radical Jewish fugitive traveling on a stolen passport.

Then there was his old stomping ground of Odessa. Much Russian aid
to the Boers passed though it, and Odessa also was a transit center for
Caucasian oil.[15] Most of that trade was in the hands of Jewish middlemen,
among them associates of Ginsburg, who could provide many useful
details. Odessa assumed a special importance to military planners in
London. In the event of war, they feared the port would be used to mount
a Russian attack against the Turkish Straits or even Egypt and Malta. Thus,
data on naval and military facilities there were of great significance. As it
happened, in 1900 a new British consul in Odessa, ex-Royal Navy officer
Charles S. Smith, began forwarding such reports to London, reports provided by an adept local source.[16]

In the latter part of 1900, Reilly popped up in Paris. The main attraction there was the grand International Exhibition that commenced in the
spring and continued through November. The huge gathering of people,
art and innovations from around the world was bound to exert a powerful appeal. Of course, he found time to divert himself in other ways. It
was at this juncture that he began an affair with Eve Lavalliere, a leading
light of Montmartre's *Theatre des Varietes* and former common-law wife
of its director, Fernand Samuel (Adolphe Louveau). She was a sterling
example of his irresistible attraction to actresses and the like. Though
brief, the affair had lasting impact. Thirty years hence, Margaret still
voiced special bitterness about this betrayal, perhaps because Reilly consorted openly with the woman, something that only added to her humili-
ation. As for Lavalliere, she later attempted suicide and ended her days in
a religious order, though whether Sidney had anything to do with that is
impossible to say. More interesting, perhaps, is that during WWI she
would face accusations of being a spy because of her love affair with a
German diplomat, Baron Hellmuth von Lucius.[17] As we will see, both
Lavalliere and Lucius were to cross Reilly's path in curious ways during
the years to come.

Through the same crowd that brought him into contact with Lavalliere and Fernand, Reilly encountered a man with whom he would have occasional dealings for many years to come. This was the Duc de Morny, the second to be exact. The Duke was the grandson of Empress Josephine Bonaparte and the half-nephew of late Emperor Napoleon III. Morny capitalized on his famous lineage and on the reputation of his father, the first Duke, who was a master of speculative finance and a political force during the Second Empire. The son, by comparison, gained an unsavory reputation by squandering money on unsuccessful schemes and the high cost of cutting a proper figure in Paris society.[18] Morny also was connected to the Zaharoff crowd in Paris. What most attracted Reilly's attention was the familial link to the Bonapartist pretender to the French throne, Prince Victor Bonaparte.[19] The latter, interestingly enough, lived in Holland and in early 1901 was involved in secret meetings with British agents who wished to "sound out his views.[20] Sidney had no part in those talks, but he might have had a hand in bringing them about.

Reilly came to rest in London in early 1901, no richer, it seemed, for his travels. At best, his work on Britain's behalf would have paid no more than a few hundred pounds.[21] To Margaret's dismay, his restlessness had not abated. He expressed a sudden homesickness for Russia and wanted to return there as soon as possible. Through the liquidation of remaining assets, Margaret, by her later estimation, had accumulated a tidy nest egg of some £12,000, over $500,000 in modern equivalent. Reilly wanted part of the money to stake himself in a new business in Russia; the remainder would remain safely in the bank, or so Margaret believed. To assuage her loneliness, humiliation and, no doubt, guilt, she had started to drink, an activity that tended to loosen her tongue and excite her temper. Perhaps for this reason, and despite the tension between them, Reilly decided that she would accompany him on his new journey.

On 26 March 1901, with the help of a cooperative solicitor (likely Sandford), Margaret received a passport in the name of Mrs. Sidney G. Reilly. Soon after, she and her husband headed to St. Petersburg. There Reilly met with Danish Capt. Hans Nils Andersen, head of the Copenhagen-based East Asiatic Co.[22] The line specialized in commerce between the Far East and the Baltic, and Andersen had recently formed a Russian subsidiary, the Russian East Asiatic Steamship Co. (*Rossiiskoe Vostochno-Aziatskoe Parokhodstvo Obshchestvo*) or RVAPO. The Dane was well acquainted with Ginsburg, and it seems a good bet that the latter provided the necessary introductions. In other respects, RVAPO was a very well connected firm. Among its directors were Robert Robertovich San Galli and E.K. Grube, businessmen with direct ties to the Imperial Ministry

of Finance. Another was Admiral K.K. De Livron who represented the
Russian Admiralty.[23] Lurking in the background was the huge Sino-Russ
syndicate that eventually would give rise to the Russo-Asiatic Bank, a con-
cern destined to have a very important role in Reilly's career. Beyond this,
Hans Andersen himself was closely connected to German interests in
Russia. That generated suspicion, not without justification as we shall see,
that he was Berlin's agent in business and other matters.[24] Andersen, in fact,
probably was the man who introduced Reilly to Berlin's secret service. The
Dane offered Sidney a managerial post with RVAPO, but not in Petersburg.
Instead, it was some 6,000 miles away in the oddly named Manchurian
town of Port Arthur. This came as a shock to Margaret who had expected
to remain in the capital or at least European Russia. She and her husband
embarked on the newly-constructed (and still incomplete) Trans-Siberian
Railway headed for the Far East.

The ice-free harbor of Port Arthur lay at the southern tip of
Manchuria's Liaotung Peninsula. In the mid-1890s, Japan emerged from
more than two centuries of self-imposed isolation and made its debut on the
world stage by trouncing decrepit Manchu China in a brief war. Under the
peace terms, Japan was to have control of Port Arthur. Mobilizing the
opposition of other powers, the Tsar forced the Mikado to abandon this
prize and, in short order, grabbed it for himself. Thus, the stage was set for
a later Japanese-Russian showdown. In 1897 Russia squeezed a 25-year
lease on the port from the Manchus and proceeded to pour in millions of
rubles to transform it into the Romanov Empire's most important bastion
in East Asia. A new Russian town, complete with bristling fortifications and
state-of-the-art naval facilities, rose up beside the old Chinese one.
Ambitious Russians envisioned Port Arthur as another Hong Kong, an
entrepôt for all of northern Asia. By the time Reilly set foot there in the
latter part of 1901 it was a bustling commercial center with a distinctly cosmopolitan flavor. In addition to Russians and, of course, Chinese, the city
drew British, American, German and Japanese merchants all eager to do
business in one thing or another.

It was no accident that the local office of East Asiatic shared the
same address as Ginsburg & Co.; he was RVAPO's chief agent on hand.
Also housed in the building was the Russo-Chinese (*Russko-Kitaiskii*)
Timber Co. and the Russian Volunteer Fleet. The latter operated private
vessels leased by the Tsarist Government for commercial and military
purposes. By 1899, Ginsburg had established himself as a significant
player in Far Eastern commerce and soon earned the nickname of "Port
Arthur Ginsburg" (*Ginsburg Port-Arturskii*). He again took Reilly under

his wing, and before long Sidney took on duties for Ginsburg's local operation.

Ginsburg played an important, somewhat controversial, part in local affairs and had connections that reached back to the highest quarters in St. Petersburg. By 1902, Ginsburg had become entangled in a web of schemes and quarrels within the Sino-Russ combine. In addition to banks, mining and timber concerns, the syndicate also controlled the Chinese Eastern Railway, the vital branch line that cut across Manchuria. The present intrigues centered on the Russo-Chinese Timber Co. which aimed at extending Russian economic influence into northern Korea, an area Japan considered to be exclusively within its sphere of domination. The driving force behind this venture was a wily speculator and ex-cavalry officer, Aleksandr M. Bezobrazov who persuaded Tsar Nicholas himself to advance two million rubles as capital.[25]

Opposing such provocative ventures was Russia's astute Minister of Finance, Sergei Witte. Somewhere in the middle was Grand Duke Aleksandr Mikhailovich, cousin and brother-in-law to Tsar Nicholas and a man destined to become one of Reilly's most important Russian associates.[26] Despite other differences, Witte and the Grand Duke feared that Bezobrazov's adventure was bound to provoke a confrontation with the Japanese, a view that proved prophetic. Reilly, thus, was in an excellent position to channel information on Bezobrazov's moves to Witte. Of course, there was nothing to stop him from sending information in the opposite direction as well.

Even Basil Zaharoff had a finger in the Manchurian pie. In Petersburg he cultivated the acquaintance of Bezobrazov and friends and encouraged their expansionist dreams.[27] Zaharoff was indifferent to the success or failure of the economic schemes, but like Witte, he could see that that this would increase the likelihood of a confrontation between Russia and Japan. Unlike Witte, that is precisely the end he hoped to achieve. The Greek, after all, was an arms salesman and helping to foster wars was a prime means of drumming up business. What Zaharoff could get from Reilly, therefore, were timely updates on the rise in tensions and prospects for hostilities.

Through his association with the Russo-Chinese Bank, Ginsburg worked closely with its local *comprador*, the Chinese merchant Tso Li (Dzau Lee).[28] Reilly developed a friendship with Li, who became the Ace-of-Spies' mentor in matters of Oriental manners and business practices. Li may be the inspiration for Reilly's later story of "Tso Lim," an Eastern sage who became his guru. However, Sidney's supposed claim to have spent time in a lamasery studying Buddhism certainly was an entirely fictitious elaboration.[29]

Ginsburg's single most important commission was chief provisioner of the Russian Pacific Fleet. What troubled some was his very close relationship with Japanese firms and even the Mikado's Navy. Well before hostilities broke out, rumors circulated that he was a Japanese or British spy. Such doubts, coupled with his Jewishness, would later earn him a new nickname—the "Russian Dreyfus."[30] Similar doubts were bound to attach themselves to his assistant, Reilly. In the years to follow, various Russian and *British* officials would mince no words in labeling Reilly a Japanese spy at Port Arthur. There, is, however, no objective proof of that. Surviving Japanese intelligence records are scant and identify agents only by code name or number. Thus, it is impossible to verify or refute that Sidney was among them. However, if he was not in Tokyo's service, he certainly did something to give that very strong impression. In later years, Sidney made no bones about his presence in Port Arthur before and after the outbreak of the Russo-Japanese War, but usually suggested, in Russian circles at least, that his service had been on St. Petersburg's behalf. However, as a later report noted, when pressed on just what he did in Port Arthur, his answers were "evasive." [31]

The Ace-of-Spies had ample opportunity to visit Paris in advance of his departure for the Far East. What makes that significant is that in early 1901 a new Japanese military attaché arrived there, Colonel Motojiro Akashi. Akashi had the special responsibility of organizing a Japanese intelligence network in Europe, one aimed, as might be expected, against Russia.[32] Moreover, the Colonel was a member of the "Black Dragon Society" *(Koku Ryukai)*, a secretive, ultra-patriotic association that aimed to extend Nippon's domination over Manchuria and much of the adjoining territories of Siberia and China.[33] From this standpoint, Russia was the #1 obstacle to the achievement of this manifest destiny. If Akashi did not approach Reilly he missed a great opportunity. Reilly's position in Port Arthur and his proximity to Ginsburg gave him access to vital details of the Russian Pacific Fleet's dispositions and readiness. It allowed him to monitor the supply of timber and concrete for the construction of docks and fortifications as well as opportunity to inspect their layout. Ginsburg also happened to be a local agent for the Tokyo-based Takata & Company, a trading firm that had an office in London.[34] Most importantly, Takata was the company that Akashi subsequently used to funnel guns and money to Russian dissidents.[35] And Reilly's vantage steadily improved. By the beginning of 1904, Ginsburg had selected him as managing director of the entire Port Arthur operation.[36]

Some Russians later insisted that Sidney's sojourn to the Far East was from the outset instigated by "British intelligence."[37] There almost certainly was some truth to that. In 1902, Great Britain and Japan concluded an alliance clearly directed against Russia. Beyond that, British planners had strong incentive to stay abreast of Russian plans and capabilities in the Far East and regional developments in general. It is worthy of note that Rollit and several of his brother freemasons were ardent Japanophiles and staunch supporters of the alliance.[38] One of the few documents to emerge from this period is a report sent by Reilly to London from Tokyo in early December 1902. Although its exact provenance is uncertain, it seems authentic.[39] The report offers a survey of conditions in China. The Manchu Dynasty, Reilly offered, "was finished" and the Celestial Empire would soon become, if it was not already, the "playground of the Great Powers." China possessed no intelligence capability to speak of, nor any cogent military power. But this vacuum, he warned, was bound to be filled by someone, just as China itself was destined to regain its equilibrium and strength. The Manchus would indeed fall in 1911, and the basic thrust of Reilly's other predictions would prove valid as well. The report was headed "E.C.F.," or more likely given Reilly's peculiar hand, "E.C.I."—Eastern Commercial Intelligence or East China Intelligence. The timing of the report followed the recent (July–September) negotiation of a commercial treaty between China and the Powers in Shanghai, negotiations in which the British delegation played the dominant role.[40]

It was during Reilly's time in the Far East that William Melville's career took an interesting turn of its own. In late 1903, age fifty-one, Melville suddenly retired from Scotland Yard. He at once set up a private investigation bureau in London under the name of "W. Morgan, General Agent," with offices on Victoria Street only a few blocks from his old one. In fact, he was not in private business at all. He now worked for the War Office Intelligence Division. As its operative, he handled particularly sensitive intelligence gathering as a screen or "cut-out" to mask the hand of His Majesty's Government. Code-named "M," one of his tasks was to keep watch on "suspicious foreigners" in Britain and to find "suitable men to go abroad to obtain information."[41] His new responsibilities did nothing to lessen his interest in radical conspiracies and Russian involvement therein. If anything, it increased, and he continued his collaboration with the Okhrana and its local agents. Reilly, thus, would have been of more value to him than ever.

The System was nothing if not flexible. Working for Japan and Britain in no way ruled out spying for Russia at the same time. In Port Arthur,

Reilly definitely established contacts with the Russian military, something that would form a critical component of his future Russian networking. After the outbreak of hostilities, he passed information to the Russian Army's counterintelligence (*Kontrrazvedka*) office in Harbin and closer to home gained the confidence of the naval commander of Port Arthur, Admiral Ivan Konstantinovich Grigorovich.[42] The Harbin counterintelligence office, interestingly enough, was run by a former Paris Okhrana man, Arkadii Harting (Garting), about whom we will have more to say in the next chapter. As one of Rachkovskii's key lieutenants since the 1880s, Harting likely knew Reilly to be a useful asset, if not necessarily an absolutely trustworthy one. Moreover, Harting's other sources of information were mostly poorly paid and thoroughly unreliable Chinese agents, so he had little to lose, and potentially much to gain, by tapping Reilly for information.[43] However much opposing employers knew of or suspected such double-dealing, so long as the information one supplied was accurate and useful, none could afford to do without it.[44] That was the way the System worked.

While in the Far East, the Ace-of-Spies also found time to pursue other business and personal alliances. In partnership with Ginsburg, he speculated in land along the right-of-ways of the Chinese Eastern and Southern Manchurian Railways, especially timber and mining properties.[45] This activity brought him into contact with a Polish mining engineer, Anton Ferdinand Ossendowski. Ossendowski was also a secret anti-Tsarist and very likely a Japanese agent himself, and/or another agent provocateur for the Okhrana.[46] A like dubious character was the jeweler and gambler Aron Simanovich Simanovich, destined to become the personal secretary of the infamous Rasputin.[47] Yet another of Rasputin's future associates, and rival, was the Mongolian herb doctor and Russian political agent, Petr Aleksandrovich Badmaev. Reilly is purported to have supplied confidential reports to Badmaev on Far Eastern affairs, but for whose ultimate enlightenment it is unclear.[48] Also on hand was a rising entrepreneur, Abram Zhivotovskii, later to become one of Reilly's closest business associates. Involved in the timber trade in and around Port Arthur was a young Scotsman, William Barclay Calder. He, too, would work very closely with Sidney in years to come in, among other things, the service of British intelligence.

On the distaff side was the shadowy Natta Azef who, like Reilly, was honing her skills as a mercenary spy. At this time she had become a member of a "powerful freelance organization" of international spies that obtained Port Arthur's defense plan for Japan.[49] Was Sidney a member of the same organization? According to a later Soviet report, the man who originally "purloined a map of the defenses of Port Arthur . . . which he promptly sold to the Japanese for a good price," was Sidney Reilly.[50] Remaining Japanese records note receiving the Port Arthur plans before the outbreak of hostilities, but suggest the immediate sources were Chinese. But whether these Chinese operatives (Tso Li perhaps?) obtained the plans themselves or merely conveyed them from another source is uncertain. Reilly, in any case, certainly would have taken the precaution of having buffers between himself and the Japanese.

Sidney also formed his own timber-importing firm, *Grinberg & Raille*, which mostly supplied wood for railway and harbor construction. The partner may have been A. L. Grinberg, later a representative for Belgian firms in Russia, or possibly an American entrepreneur, Nathan Greenberg.[51] The latter possibility is strengthened by the fact that the timber they imported was American. Shipping logs all the way across the Pacific when ample were available much closer at hand may not seem a smart business. The fact was that the booming lumber industry in the U.S. Northwest supplied a great deal of wood to the Far East at competitive prices and generally better quality that local stocks. But there may have been another dimension to Reilly and Grinberg's enterprise. Ships bringing back timber carried something outbound, and one of those commodities may have been human; specifically, Japanese contract laborers. This was the heyday of Japanese emigration to the U.S. West Coast, and one of the pioneers in the trade was Tadao Kamiya, a man later counted among Reilly's most important Tokyo business associates.[52] Thus, Sidney was laying the basis for future business in Japan and in America.

Amidst all this activity, Reilly had more personal matters to attend to. In Port Arthur he encountered the woman who became, perhaps, the nearest thing to a true love of his life. That she was a figure of mystery no less than he should not be surprising. To appreciate this, we must go back a few years to Japan where the British colony was rocked by a sensational murder. In October 1896, Walter Hallowell Carew, prominent businessman and manager and secretary of the Yokohama United Club, died from a lethal dose of arsenic.[53] Evident guilt fell on his wife, Edith, who was tried, convicted and sentenced to hang by a consular court. In her defense, Mrs. Carew tried to cast blame on an Anne or Annie Luke, a young woman whom her late husband had loved and abandoned in England some years before. According to materials submitted to the court, Luke had come to Japan a few months earlier intent on attaining reconciliation or revenge.[54] The very existence of this woman was in some doubt, but at least one witness verified that a strange "Woman in Black" matching the description

given by Edith had lurked about Walter's funeral. There also were a series
of notes found among the dead Carew's effects or later sent mysteriously to
the coroner all signed "A.L." "Annie," or "Anne Luke." In one of these
notes, "Annie" pleaded with Walter: "I must see you. Why have you done
nothing since you got my cards?. . . . I am living wherever I can find shel-
ter, but you can find me and help me if you will."[56] During the inquest,
another note appeared in which "A.L." confessed to the crime in order to
spare an "innocent fool" the noose and intimated that she would take her
own life in a way to assure she would never be found.[57] Pure Victorian
melodrama, perhaps, but it also bears an eerie similarity to the note
Salomon Rosenblum supposedly left before he vanished from Odessa. Years
later, journalist Richard Hughes speculated that there may have been more
to the Luke-Carew relationship than tragic romance, that she may have had
a connection to Japanese intelligence. That might explain her amazing ability to avoid detection by the Mikado's authorities.[58]

The new love whom Reilly acquired in Port Arthur was Anne Luke,
presumably identical with the "Woman in Black" of the Carew case. It is
just possible that he had met her before. Recall that involved in the death
of Reverend Thomas was a nurse who later vanished. The nurse's name
seems to have been Anne, and while the chance that she was one and the
same with Anne Luke seems a slight one, it remains a tantalizing possibility. It is also worthy of note that among the firms with which Walter Carew
had business was Ginsburg's. Perhaps she, like Reilly, was somehow in
Ginsburg's employ. Beyond that, in Japan Carew had been close to a
British consular official, Maurice de Bunsen who, in turn, was a good
friend of Sir Francis Barker.[59] Pure coincidence, perhaps, but another
example that the Secret World was a small one. Whoever she was, Reilly
would maintain a longer and more intimate bond with her than any other
woman, albeit one that included serial abandonment and marriage to at
least three other women. She would become the special secret of an obses-
sively secretive man. When Sidney visited Japan in 1902, Luke accompanied him. Margaret's hopes of reestablishing, or simply establishing, a semblance of normal life with her husband were dashed. She had endured past
infidelities, but this time her rival was no passing prostitute or good-time
chorine.

With the money he earned from his various jobs and ventures, Reilly
purchased a large house overlooking Port Arthur's New Town. He filled it
with a burgeoning collection of oriental artworks and staffed it with a brace
of Chinese servants. Margaret spent most of her time there, isolated and
ignored by her husband. She turned more and more to drink and, possibly,

to the stronger remedy of opium. Soon enough, Reilly found her presence tiresome and awkward. As for her, whatever he had done to her, she still loved him, and it was her damnation that she always would. Deciding he had had enough, Sidney shipped her back to Europe, to a private hospital in Belgium, where she could recover and stay far away from him and his affairs. He would find, however, that it was not so easy to be rid of Daisy.

On the frigid morning of 8 February 1904, the inhabitants of Port Arthur awoke to the sound of explosions and clouds of acrid smoke billowing up from the anchorages of the Russian Fleet. In a prototype of the Pearl Harbor attack some thirty-seven years later, Japanese torpedo boats were attacking the stationary Russian warships with devastating result. The war some wanted and others dreaded had begun. While Russia possessed far greater military resources than her Asian opponent, applying them effectively at the end of a 6,000-mile, still uncompleted rail line would prove an impossible task. Japan's modern army and navy took the initiative and an immediate advantage that they held throughout the conflict.[59]

In some later versions of events, Reilly claimed he quit Port Arthur *before* the outbreak of war, though in other cases he mentioned being there *during* the campaign.[60] The recollections of others place him in the beleaguered bastion well into the following siege. According to Ginsburg, Reilly remained there until after the Japanese invested the fortress, at least through June, when he suddenly and inexplicably vanished. The full siege did not commence until the end of July. Royal Navy Commander Sir Guy Gaunt, who monitored the war from aboard the HMS *Vengeance*, later charged that Reilly escaped Port Arthur barely "a half-hour ahead" of the Japanese who finally took possession on 2 January 1905.[61] Allowing for some exaggeration in Gaunt's account, that suggests the Ace-of-Spies was still in Port Arthur well into the autumn. Adding strength to that possibility is the fact that upon occupying the city, the Japanese military authorities immediately issued an order for Reilly's arrest and put a 10,000-yen reward on his head.[62]

Reilly's abrupt disappearance excited much talk that he had been a spy, though opinion was divided as to whose. His flight and the subsequent Japanese reward seemed to discount the notion that he had been Tokyo's agent. But that probably was just what it was intended to do. Reilly's escape almost certainly required some Japanese assistance. Their sea blockade allowed Chinese boats to move between Port Arthur and the nearby ports, but subject to search.[63] One of the closest ports, interestingly enough, was Weihaiwei, a British concession where our man could expect to find a safe haven. Ginsburg later averred that Reilly briefly resurfaced in Shanghai and then vanished again.

His utility in the Far East was for the time being ended, and it was not a wise idea to return to Russia just yet. Unrest was brewing there, stimulated by the losing war in Manchuria. In January 1905, soon after the fall of Port Arthur, troops and police fired on a peaceful demonstration in Petersburg precipitating the infamous "Bloody Sunday" massacre. Abetted by the helping hand of Akashi, unrest grew into revolution and by the following autumn, Nicholas' very throne was in jeopardy. Over the past three-plus years, Reilly had played the System with skill, ruthlessness and general success. Now thirty, he had matured into an experienced secret agent with an ever-widening nexus of contacts and connections. He would make his way back to Europe, but first he would take a detour through America, the Land of Opportunity.

NOTES

1. *London Post Office Directory*, 1900.
2. R.B. Lockhart to author, 29 May 1995.
3. PRO, FO 372/2756, #7096, British Consul, Brussels to FO, 29 May 1931.
4. Great Britain Passport Regulations, 1898.
5. MI5, PF 864103, "Reilly, Sidney George," note dated 22 March 1918. This file is slated to become part of the KV2 record group in the PRO in 2002. Thanks to Mark Hull for assistance in the search of vital records in Dublin.
6. Lockhart, *Ace*, 35.
7. Thanks to Phil Tomaselli for assistance with this information.
8. For a bio, see A.S. Senin, *Aleksandr Ivanovich Guchkov* (Moscow, 1996).
9. D.S. Stein Papers, Guchkov to Alekseev, 16 Nov. 1931.
10. A. Beeby Thompson, *Oil Fields of Russia and the Russian Petroleum Industry* (London, 1904), 123 and *passim*. Thompson himself was affiliated with Lloyd's.
11. PRO, HD 3/117, re Mr. White in Petrovsk, 16 July 1900.
12. For an excellent overview, see Peter Hopkirk, *The Great Game: On Secret Service in High Asia*, also subtitled *The Struggle for Empire in Central Asia* (London, 1990).
13. W.P. Drury, *In Many Parts: Memoirs of a Marine* (London, 1926), 185.
14. Ibid., 185–187.
15. James Henry, *Baku, An Eventful History* (London, 1905), 113.
16. PRO, HD 3/111 and 3/132.
17. On Eve Lavalliere (1868–1929) and see Omer Englebert, *Du moins je sais disait Eve Lavalliere*, (Paris, 1983) and Lucie Delarue-Mardus, *Eve Lavalliere* (Paris, 1935). On Margaret's reaction, see Messenger, 31. Special thanks to Brady Brower for information regarding Lavalliere and Samuel.
18. *NYT*, 16 July 1920, 11:3, and 15 April 1935, 19:3. The original Duc de Morny (d. 1865) was the illegitimate half-brother of Napoleon III.
19. Full name Napoleon Victor Jerome Frederic Bonaparte (1862–1926).
20. PRO, HD 3/111, Court to Sanderson, 12 May 1901.
21. A 15 Feb. 1906 report in HD 3/133 indicates a expenditure of some £200 for agents in Baku, Orenburg and two other Russian towns.
22. *Ostasiatiske Kompagni Aktieselskabet*, formed 1897.
23. A.N. Bokhanov, *Delovaia elita Rossii* (Moscow, 1994), 125, 220; *Ves' Peterburg*, 1902.

24. Michel de Enden, *Raspoutine et le crepuscule de la monarchie en Russie* (Paris, 1976), 239-240.
25. B.A. Romanov, "Kontsessiia na Yalu," *Russkoe Proshloe*, #1 (1923), 87–108. On these schemes see also Andrew Malozemoff, "The Rise to Power of the Bezobrazov Group and the Decline of Witte," in his *Russian Far Eastern Policy, 1881–1904* (Berkeley, CA, 1958), 177–207.
26. David Chavchavadze, *The Grand Dukes* (New York, 1990), 193; see also Grand Duke Alexander's memoir, *Once a Grand Duke* (New York, 1932). From 1902–05, Aleksandr oversaw the operation of the Ministry of Merchant Marine.
27. Rochat-Cenise, 104–105.
28. USDS, 894.515/7, Russo-Asiatic Bank, 9 Dec. 1918.
29. R. Lockhart, *Ace*, 39–40.
30. F.A. L'vov, *Likhodei biurokraticheskago samovlast'ia kak neposredstvennye vinovniki pervoi Russko-Iaponskoi voiny* (St. Petersburg, 1906), 7. This work is an attack on the Bezobrazov scheme by an embittered investor who later brought suit against Ginsburg and others.
31. Rossiiskii Gosudarstvennyi Arkhiv Voenno-Morskogo Flota (RGAVMF), fond 1358, opis 1, delo 97, Raport #515, 14 June 1918.
32. Michael Futrell, "Colonel Akashi and Japanese Contacts with Russian Revolutionaries in 1904–05," *St Antony's Papers #20, Far Eastern Affairs 4* (London, 1967).
33. Richard Deacon, *Kempei Tai: A History of the Japanese Secret Service* (New York, 1983), 42–48. Motojiro Akashi, *Rakka ryusui: Colonel Akashi's report on His Secret Cooperation with the Russian Revolutionary Parties during the Russo-Japanese War*, trans by I. Chiharu, ed. By O.K. Falt and A Kujala (Helsinki, 1988), esp. 17–18. See also *Iznanka Revoliutsii: Vooruzhennoe Vozstanie v Rossii na Iaponskiia sredstva* (St. Petersburg, 1906), an Okhrana-sponsored expose of the Japanese–Revolutionary link.
34. The firm was formed by Shinzo Takata/Takada in 1880 on the basis of an earlier British-owned company.
35. Akashi, 49.
36. Vladimir Krymov, *Portrety neobychnykh liudei* (Paris, 1971), 78. Krymov interviewed Ginsburg in Japan in 1917.
37. PZZ #73, 2.
38. Rollit was a recipient of the Order of the Rising Sun.
39. Deacon, *Kempei Tai*, 49–50. Shortly before Deacon's [McCormick's] passing, the author discussed the document with him. He was able to provide additional details and suggestions, but could not further identify its original source, although he thought a naval intelligence connection likely.
40. The chief British representatives were Lord Inchcape (James Mackey), an associate of Hozier, and William Clark. The Treaty was signed on 5 Sept. 1902.
41. PRO, KV 1/8, Melville, 3–4.
42. N. Alekseev, "OGPU I pokhishchenie gen. A.P. Kutepova," *Vozrozhdenie* (30 Jan. 1933).
43. E.K. Nojine (Nozhin), *The Truth about Port Arthur* (London, 1908), 90.
44. USNA, Records of the Department of State (DS), Counselor's Office, CSA file 215, Agent Sharpe to Bannerman, 13 Dec. 1924, Exhibit "A," Memorandum re S.G. Reilly, 4 Sept. 1918. This quotes Gen. M.I. Kazakov, Chief of the Petrograd Okhrana. The identical item appears in Reilly's SIS file.
45. HIA, Vrangel Collection, box 110, file 22, White Russian Secret Service Report, Nov. 1920, 7, and SIS, Russian Secret Service Report, 1 Nov. 1920. The latter appears to be a translated and somewhat edited version of the former.
46. For a basic bio see George F. Kennan, "The Sisson Documents," *Journal of Modern History*, Vol. 28, #2 (1956), 146–52.
47. Aron Simanovich, *Vospominaniia lichnogo sekretaria Grigoriia Rasputina* (Tashkent, 1990).

48. Boris Gusev, *Doktor Badmaev: tibetskaia meditsina, tsarskii dvor, sovetskaia vlast'* (Moscow, 1995); see also Deacon, *Russian Secret Service*, 115–117.
49. Kaledin, 228. Kaledin (probably a pseudonym) claimed to have been an officer of the former Russian Imperial Court Okhrana, a body quite separate from the regular political police and charged with the protection of the Imperial family and the handling of highly sensitive political cases.
50. PZZ #73, 2.
51. Bokhanov, 124.
52. Japanese immigration flourished from 1898 to 1907 when it was limited by the so-called "Gentlemen's Agreement."
53. FO 46/510, "Murder of W.R.H. Carew, 1896–98," contains the inquest and other records of the case. Edith's trial proceedings are in TS 36/104. "R v. Edith Hallowell Carew . . ." and other details may be found in HO 144/937/A58585.
54. *NYT* (2 Feb. 1897), 7:3, (5 Feb. 1897), 7:1. There also seems to have been some prior relationship between Luke and the Carews' governess, Mary Jacobs, including the possibility that Luke and Jacobs were one and the same.
55. FO 46/510.
56. Ibid.
57. Robin Lockhart, *Reilly: The First Man* (London, 1987), 3–4, citing Hughes. The latter had a long interest in Japan and espionage; see his *Foreign Devil: Thirty Years of Reporting from the Far East* (London, 1960). Curiously, this makes no mention of Reilly.
58. De Bunsen served in Japan c. 1891–93 and later was active as a British agent in Latin America.
59. For a general treatment of the war, see David and Peggy Warner, *The Tide at Sunrise: A History of the Russo-Japanese War, 1904–1905* (New York, 1974).
60. RGAVMF, Ibid.
61. USNA, MID, 9140-6073, Memorandum #2 to Lt. Irving, 1. On his presence in the Far East, see Gaunt's memoir, *The Yield of the Years: A Story of Adventure Afloat and Ashore* (London, 1940). Reilly's spying for Japan also is noted in his SIS file: CX 021 744, N.G. to London, 3 March 1918.
62. Krymov, 79.
63. Nojine, 91.

Chapter Four
THE COUNTERFEIT ENGLISHMAN

The long voyage from Shanghai to the America gave Reilly time to collect his thoughts and consider options. He was almost thirty-one, and a knowledgeable eye might have detected a slight thinning and receding of his lustrous black hair and deepening hollows under the eyes. The years in the Far East had left their mark in other ways. In addition to European languages, he had picked up at least a smattering of "several oriental ones."[1] Japanese correspondence and documents later found in his New York office argue some knowledge of that tongue. In any event, Reilly developed a permanent taste for the oriental, both in art and personal style. From Chinese silk shirts to Japanese print waistcoats and exotic colognes, even, perhaps, in his "inscrutable" persona, he later always smacked of the East. One New York acquaintance described him as a man of "Semitic origin and Oriental in appearance."[2] A sketch in his SIS file called him a "Jewish-Jap type."[3]

What had become of Anne Luke? She may have been traveling with him, as his wife, perhaps, and his wife she would become at some point in the near future. It also was about this time or soon after that she became pregnant, and delivered a son, presumably Reilly's. Anne would discover, as Margaret already knew and others would learn, that an involvement with Reilly most often meant life without him.

During the Russo-Japanese War, both belligerents had submarines building in American shipyards as the Tsar's and Mikado's navies raced to augment their forces. Submarines, relatively cheap and quick to construct, were a logical choice. Early in 1904, the Russian naval agent in the U.S., A.G. Butakov, opened negotiations with the Simon Lake Company. In September of the same year, the American engineer and promoter, Hart O. Berg, traveled to Petersburg to finalize the deal, and in November work began on five boats in the company's Bridgeport, Massachusetts yard. Also involved in the deal was the Charles R. Flint Arms Company of New York, later one of Reilly's bitterest opponents on the American scene. Their feud with him dated back to this period and almost certainly involved the sub contract.

The fabrication of the sub sections, which would have final assembly in Russia, should have taken four to five months. However, due to vague "delays," not one arrived in Russia until after the termination of the war. Subsequent investigation by the Russian Navy determined that a Japanese agent had bribed Lake officials to drag out construction.[4] Reilly was the ideal man to handle that job. He arrived on the East Coast at the close of 1904 or early 1905 which put him there at just the right time to monkey-wrench the Russian deal. The method of obstruction evidenced the same aggressive simplicity that he would employ on a much grander scale ten years later. The Japanese Navy had contracted four Holland subs from Electric Boat that, under high security, were ready for shipment to Yokohama also at about the time of Reilly's arrival. That was information St. Petersburg would have been very anxious to know.

Taking advantage of the contacts he had made via Grinberg & Reilly, Sidney probably slipped into the U.S. via Seattle or Vancouver but not as Sidney Reilly. In at least one case, as we will see, he reverted to his Rosenblum identity. He headed for New York where he looked up Vladimir Mikhailovich Rogovin, a former Tsarist diplomat who had taken up the familiar trade of broker and commercial agent in Gotham.[5] Rogovin was a special representative of the Russian Admiralty for war contracts, including the above subs. Above all, he was out for his own gain. Sidney would have little trouble enlisting his assistance that established a basis for further collaboration some years down the road.

Reilly's second bit of business on American shores centered on a petroleum concession in far-off Persia. In early 1901 an enterprising Australian capitalist named William Knox D'Arcy secured an exclusive sixty-year concession to exploit the oil resources of three-quarters of the Persian Empire, modern Iran. D'Arcy's initial financial backer was Lloyd's Bank behind which loomed Henry Hozier. Where Lloyd's was concerned the Admiralty was never far removed, and so it was in this case. The Royal Navy's Fuel Oil Committee and its leading "oil maniac," Admiral John "Jackie" Fisher, were determined to secure a dependable source of oil for Britain. Sharing this dream was another Committee member, the eager young Winston Spencer Churchill. Yet another man with an interest in the Persian find was William Melville. As chief "special op" for the War Office and, by extension, the Admiralty, Melville had contact with John Mitzakis, an expert on all matters concerning oil in the region. For good measure, Mitzakis also had connection to Zaharoff and the Okhrana.[6] Moreover, Melville seems to have had a personal acquaintance with D'Arcy. Through his agents, including Reilly, "M" kept an eye on negotiations and applied selective pressure without tipping the hand of His Majesty's Government.

The critical question was whether D'Arcy's concession would really produce the oil. Much would depend on the amount of money invested, but all that cash could end up being dumped down a dry hole. Few wanted to take the risk. Exploratory wells in the isolated hill country near the modern Iran-Iraq frontier gave promising indications but no more. It was the fall of 1903 before black gold gushed in commercial quantity, but not enough to offset expenses that were some £200,000 and rising fast. Lloyd's directors were unwilling to venture further capital, and a strapped D'Arcy either had to find new backers or sell out. Fisher and friends wanted to make sure the concession did not fall into non-British hands, but conservative heads at the Treasury refused to step in.

It is at this point that Reilly is said to come into the story, though in two rather different ways. According to the version presented by Lockhart, in early 1905 Sidney was again enlisted by British spy-chief "C" to scuttle a deal between the desperate D'Arcy and the French Rothschilds.[7] Reilly is supposed to have infiltrated a meeting aboard the Rothschilds' private yacht at Cannes disguised as a Catholic priest. Under the pretext of soliciting a charitable donation from the unsuspecting French financiers, Sidney found the opportunity to approach the Australian and convince him through promises of money and appeals to patriotism that the Persian concession must remain with London. In short order, so goes the tale, Fisher arranged a deal through the British-owned Burmah Oil Company and everyone lived happily ever after.

Indeed, such an arrangement was finalized in May 1905, and the Admiralty became the major shareholder in the so-called Anglo-Persian Oil Company, the basis of today's British Petroleum. D'Arcy's shipboard dallying with the Rothschilds also took place and broke off abruptly, but the negotiations actually transpired in the first two months of 1904.[8] At that time, of course, Reilly was still in Port Arthur. Moreover, it would be another year, a long and worrisome year for D'Arcy, before he received a firm commitment of British backing. Sidney could not possibly have played the role described above.

The smell of oil and money inevitably attracted John D. Rockefeller's American colossus, Standard Oil. Standard disposed of immense resources and influence and was always on the lookout for more. In early 1904, D'Arcy opened negotiations with New York that dragged on for several months. The Australian welcomed Standard as a partner, but Standard's chairman John D. Archbold wanted to buy the concession outright.[9] Another interested party was Zaharoff, who had his own stake in Anglo-Persian. Yet another was the pugnacious Dutchman Henri Deterding, head of Royal Dutch Petroleum (later Royal Dutch-Shell).

The second version of Reilly's involvement centers on D'Arcy's dallying with Standard. As presented by French writer Anton Zischka and others in the 1930s, Reilly once more appeared in a priest's robes, but this time as a means to get close to D'Arcy aboard a New York-bound liner.[10] In reality he was acting as "special agent for the English Secret Service." His goal was not to stop the desperate entrepreneur from selling his concession to the Rothschilds, but to Standard. The Ace-of-Spies appealed to the intensely religious D'Arcy's faith and philanthropic zeal. Believing he was entrusting the valuable concession to a man of God, D'Arcy delivered the priceless patent to Reilly, who dutifully handed it to his masters in London. This tale has even less to recommend it than the previous. D'Arcy was not a religious fanatic, a Canadian or a petroleum engineer who had spent years wandering the Persian wastes in search of oleaginous riches. He was a lawyer and investor of conventional piety who never set foot in the country.

However, D'Arcy's flirtation with Standard was real, and there is evidence to support one very interesting aspect of Zischka's story. That is a tale of two ambitious offices boys, Charles Stump and William Winkfield. They worked in Standard's 26 Broadway offices with access to Archbold's private office. Desiring more money than their humble positions paid, the pair hit on the idea of removing letters from their boss' confidential files and selling their contents to William Randolph Hearst's muckraking *New York Journal*. Hearst was on the lookout for evidence that Standard was buying the votes of various U.S. senators, and he found it aplenty. The result was major political scandal complete with congressional investigation.[11] But how does that concern Reilly? Among the items pilfered from Archbold was a letter, written by someone in late 1904/early 1905 from one Rosenblum. It offered to sell Standard the details of D'Arcy's concession and operations and, for additional compensation, help in obstructing it. Archbold later confirmed the existence of the letter, but it was of no real interest to him or Hearst.[12] The thieves supposedly encountered similar indifference when they attempted to sell the Rosenblum Letter to parties in London.

If Reilly had no direct part in the D'Arcy negotiations, how could he have known enough to make such an offer to Standard? The answer brings us back to two men, Russian Finance Minister Sergei Witte and British spy master Melville. London feared D'Arcy's dealing with the Rothschilds not because of the latter's ties to Paris, but to *St. Petersburg*. As Jews, the Barons Rothschild had no love for the Tsarist regime, but as financiers they had a large stake in that Empire's oil industry and they wanted to expand their interests.[13] Their partner in this effort was none other than Witte who also had a long personal interest in petroleum. In return for his help in the Russian sphere, the House of Rothschild helped him raise much-needed capital in France. Such negotiations were handled by the personal aide of Baron Eduard Alphonse de Rothschild, Jules Aron, later the Rothschilds' man in Russia.[14] In Paris, Aron worked hand-in-glove with Witte's agents, Artur Rafalovich and Adolf Rothstein, the latter dubbed "Witte's alter ego."[15] Rafalovich, in turn, was the "energetic collaborator" of Zaharoff, and, for good measure, worked closely with Rachkovskii's Okhrana operation.[16] Jules Aron was the very man who approached D'Arcy about a possible Rothschild deal in late 1903. From London's vantage, it was not far-fetched to see the Rothschilds as the cat's paw of the Russians, all the more so since Witte was known to be violently opposed to D'Arcy's concession as a threat to Russia's interests in the region and to the Russian oil industry itself.[17]

The Rothschild-Witte link explains how Reilly could have learned all the salient details of the Persian concession. The information was passed to the Russian Consul General in New York, M. Olarovskii, whose offices housed the local branch of Witte's Imperial Russian Financial Agency. If Archbold took the bait and brought the immense power of Standard to bear against a British-D'Arcy pact, Witte would have scuttled the objectionable deal at no cost or obligation to Russia.

Witte, of course, was not the only party interested in Standard's potential action. Melville may have played a critical part in bringing the Australian to the Admiralty's table. For our purposes, it is sufficient that Melville was privy to the Persian negotiations and was equally capable of giving Reilly all the information he needed. Why would he? The same as Witte; to determine just how interested the Rockefeller boys really were. Archbold's indifference was proof that the American giant had no intention of making a big play in Persia. That came as great reassurance to wary London financial circles, and it may have been a critical element in making the Admiralty's deal possible.

Reilly probably concocted the subsequent "sea-going priest" fables to inflate his importance, but also to conceal his real role and the System at work. Thus, Stump's and Winkfield's effort to hawk the Rosenblum Letter in British circles produced no interest nor apparent repercussions for our hero. As an SIS memo later put it, no one ever employed Reilly because of his trustworthiness but because he was "of a certain use to us." He was an "intriguer of no mean class," devoid of principle or patriotism in any conventional sense, but he had "means of finding out information all over the world," information that often was otherwise unobtainable.[18] In short, he might be a crook, but he gave good value for the money. In the Secret World, utility was of much greater importance than loyalty. That explains why the Russians, despite ample evidence of his connivance with the Japanese, English, and even the Germans tolerated him and continued to employ his services.

In New York, Reilly encountered the Okhrana's resident agent, Aleksandr Evalenko, whom we last met as Rachkovskii's troubleshooter in London. One more Jewish radical turned police informer, Evalenko had become "one of the wealthiest and most active Russian revolutionists" in the local émigré colony and a man who was "in [on] all the secrets of the movements to overthrow the Czar's Government."[19] From this vantage he continued to inform on and undermine the Friends of Russian Freedom and like groups. He concentrated on ferreting out the sources of money and weapons sent from America to the growing revolutionary movement. He had firm evidence of the SFRF's involvement in this traffic and, much more importantly, he had pinpointed the Friends' principal financial backer. That was American-Jewish banker Jacob Schiff.[20]

Born in Germany in 1847, Schiff emigrated to the U.S. shortly after the Civil War and found a position in the New York banking house of Kuhn & Loeb, a company closely linked to the Rothschilds. Rising to the top, he built the firm into the chief rival of the powerful J.P. Morgan combine. An immaculately trimmed white beard and twinkling blue eyes gave Schiff a rather grandfatherly air. However, in addition to being an astute businessman, he was a fellow of strict principles and intense idealism. The latter included his support of the SFRF. Schiff loathed the Tsarist regime for its oppression of his co-religionists and was more than willing to help its enemies. At the outset of the war in Manchuria, for instance, Kuhn & Loeb floated a $200,000,000 Japanese loan in the U.S. Such efforts, in fact, largely financed the Mikado's war effort.[21] Schiff even paid for the printing of thousands of pieces of anti-Tsarist propaganda that the SFRF distributed to 50,000 Russian prisoners of war.[22] He also used his influence to discourage other firms from making loans to Russia, and a few years later he would almost single-handedly scuttle the renewal of the Russian-American trade treaty by the U.S. Congress.

Little wonder, therefore, that the Romanov regime came to view the New York banker as "one of the most dangerous men . . . against us."[23]

Thus, while in New York Reilly collected all the information he could on Schiff and his activities. This provided a means to double-check the validity of Evalenko's reports. As a friend of the Voynich's, the Ace-of-Spies had easy admittance to American SFRF circles where he presented himself as a revolutionary sympathizer. Evalenko suspected that the newcomer was there as much to spy on him as the Tsar's enemies. At the same time he sensed that this counterfeit Englishman was dangerous to deal with but even more hazardous to ignore.[24] When Reilly at last sailed for Europe in early 1905, he must have breathed a sigh of relief. But they would meet again.

Reilly's American interlude was a valuable experience. Always a quick study, he used the opportunity to size up both the strengths and weaknesses of American business and how they might be exploited to his advantage. He appreciated the real and potential power of Yankee capital and industry. Just as it had assisted Japan's military efforts, it was bound to play a crucial role in any future and larger war. If he admired Americans' energy and inventiveness, he developed an active contempt for their combination of naïveté and arrogant overconfidence. These traits, he concluded, led them to overestimate their capabilities and underestimate their opponents', sometimes with disastrous result. They were no less greedy than their foreign counterparts and so were equally susceptible to the simple lure of profit and the well-placed bribe. Ten years later, these insights would give Reilly an important edge in the scramble for American war contracts.[25]

Reilly surfaced in Paris around February 1905. Precise dates become difficult to establish at this juncture, one of the murkiest in his career. There may be a clue in an intercepted wire from the Japanese mission in Paris. Dated 5–6 February, this noted the departure of a special agent to America to replace one who had just departed.[26] At the same, a Captain Yamamoto, one of Akashi's men, arrived in Paris on an important "secret mission."[27] In the City of Light, Sidney certainly reconnected with the Okhrana Foreign Agency, now under new management. Rachkovskii had returned to Russia where he took over as vice director of the Department of Police, though he by no means abandoned interest in foreign operations.

Rachkovskii's replacement in Paris was Arkadii Markovich Harting, whom we last met in Manchuria directing counterintelligence operations against Japan. Harting and Reilly had much more in common. His true name was Avraam Hekkel'man. Following the now-familiar pattern, he was a Jew and one-time radical student turned Okhrana informer. First recruited in the 1880s, under the name Landezen he operated as a deep-cover agent among émigrés in Switzerland and France where he became involved in a plot to assassinate Tsar Aleksandr III. The episode earned him a criminal record in France but an "honorary citizenship" from the Russians, albeit with the proviso that he formally convert from Judaism.[28] In 1893 Harting worked in the Okhrana's Berlin office which raises the distinct possibility that his connection to or knowledge of Reilly dated back that far.

In early 1905 the Russo-Japanese War was still raging, and not going at all well for the Tsar. Inside the Empire unrest was mounting helped along by the efforts of Akashi. Harting's primary aim was to counter the Japanese intrigues. His right hand in this effort was none other than Manasevich-Manuilov, Reilly's partner in crime from a decade earlier. Manasevich headed a special operation devoted to penetrating Japanese and other diplomatic missions. His initial efforts achieved little, but simultaneously with Reilly's arrival on the scene, things improved dramatically. In short order, Manasevich got his hands on Chinese and American codes, both of which Reilly could have helped supply. Most significantly, however, he managed to secure Japanese diplomatic ciphers. Through bribery, he first penetrated the Mikado's embassy in The Hague and soon after those in Brussels and Paris.[29] But this success was short-lived. In June, a frustrated Rachkovskii ordered Manasevich to take immediate action against Akashi's operation being directed from Stockholm.[30]

Then disaster struck. Due to what Rachkovskii called Manasevich's "carelessness," an Okhrana agent inside the Brussels telegraph office was exposed. Not only did this alert the Japanese that their codes had been broken (they promptly changed them), but it also shed unwelcome light on the whole Russian operation. This fiasco, coupled with questions about Manasevich's dubious handling of Okhrana accounts, allowed Rachkovskii to demand his return to Russia.

What was Reilly's part in all this? There is no way to be sure, but there is a pattern that will become routine where he is involved. He first won Manasevich's confidence by offering a helping hand, quite unofficially of course; Manasevich got to keep all the credit. It was a bit like the Trojan Horse. Having penetrated the Okhrana operation, Reilly awaited his opportunity. That came in June with Rachkovskii's order to go after Akashi, something that might have posed a risk to Sidney himself. Obeying the rule of always keeping the biggest bet on the strongest man, he brought Manasevich's operation crashing down. If the latter sensed he had been used, it does not seem to have left any hard feelings. Perhaps he even found a way to profit from it. Over the next several years, he and the Ace-of-Spies would be intimate partners and co-conspirators in a variety of schemes.[31] When Manasevich returned to Petersburg in September, Sidney Reilly was by his side.

Reilly's return to Western Europe also reunited him briefly with Margaret. He would later claim that he came back to find that she had emptied their bank account and squandered the money, leaving him all but penniless.[32] Needless to say, Margaret remembered the situation quite differently, and probably more accurately. Reilly himself pilfered the London account while in Port Arthur, and when "Daisy" arrived in Brussels, it was she who faced destitution. It must have been with a mixture of relief and rage that she greeted his return. Reilly suggested that their union was a thing of the past, but he saw no reason to complicate matters with a divorce. Margaret wanted her husband but more that that, she wanted her money. That, of course, had been lost in the Far Eastern or tied up in new ventures, or so he claimed. He had prospects of restoring his—and their—fortunes in Russia. She should stay put, and he would send for her when the time was right. He sweetened the deal by paying her extra for certain favors. From time to time, he would letters that she was to mail to another address in Brussels. Other times she would receive letters to be forwarded to Russia.

Sidney's overture to Margaret was not motivated by residual affection or any glimmer of guilt. If he wanted to rid himself of her there were more permanent means to that end, means he was perfectly willing to employ. She remained among the living because she was useful. Despite her lapses, in the main she had proved herself a reliable co-conspirator, particularly when sufficient motivation was applied. Reilly now exploited her as a letter-drop for secret communication with someone. The most likely answer is Melville or his agents. Brussels had the dubious distinction of being Europe's espionage capital. It also was a city with which Melville had great familiarity.[33] In 1910, the Belgian capital became the base of the "permanent foreign agent" of the new British Secret Service Bureau, probably on Melville's suggestion.[34] Furthermore, under the circumstances "M" was acutely interested in Russian matters. The Russo-Japanese War and Britain's alliance with Tokyo significantly raised the possibility of Anglo-Russian conflict. On the advice of unnamed superiors, Melville initiated contact with "Poles, Nihilists and other discontented Russian elements."[35] The same ilk he had spied on and arrested a short time before were now sounded out as potential allies. In the event of war, Melville was to play the same role as Akashi. While London's interest cooled after 1905, some of the doors thus opened, noted Melville, remained open. In any case, there always was need of reliable information from darkest St. Petersburg where Reilly was about to establish himself. Daisy, knowingly or not, was now part of Reilly's link to British intelligence.

In Paris, Reilly supposedly had an encounter with another figure from his Rosenblum past, his "half-sister, Anna."[36] As recounted by Lockhart, the apparent shock of seeing her long-presumed dead brother, coupled with her own tormented personal life, caused her to jump out a Parisian hotel window. This tale seems another amalgam of fact and fiction, mostly the latter. Sigmund Rosenblum had no sister Anna. His younger sibling Elena did commit suicide, presumably over a failed romance, but not in Paris. Parisian press and police records indicate no death matching the above during the period. The most interesting thing about this story, though, is the invocation of the name "Anna." The best bet is that this was a reference of Anne Luke who had either come with him from the Orient or now rendezvoused with him in Paris. With child, like Margaret she needed money. To keep her, the child and himself safe, Reilly had to keep them out of sight.

A further question about Reilly's whereabouts and activities during 1904–05 is raised by Michael Kettle's assertion that he spent much of the period attending first London's City and Guilds Technical College and later Trinity College, Cambridge.[37] He did so, says Kettle, under the identity of *Stanislaus* George Reilly, an Indian-born Irish engineer. A Stanislaus Reilly did attend both schools from the fall of 1904 through the autumn of the following year. Beyond that, he spent most of his career in India employed in public works and railroads. This Indian career, Kettle insists, was a phony alibi, "carefully kept up to date all his life, which Reilly [gave] whenever the situation required it."[38] At first glance, this seems plausible enough. Kettle notes that some details of Stanislaus Reilly's resume defy confirmation, though others, notably his 1877 birth record in Calcutta, and his 1952 death certificate in England are on file. Kettle's case gets another boost from Sidney Reilly's later assertion that he attended the Royal School of Mines.[39] The RSM was an outgrowth of the Technical College, though it did not exist as such until *after* Stanislaus' attendance. Moreover, Stanislaus' records show he studied electrical engineering, while Sidney gave his field as chemistry.

Kettle seemingly makes a strong case with an analysis of the handwriting of Sidney and Stanislaus Reilly which shows them from the same hand, or at least probably so. However, this claim does not hold up to closer examination, especially against a larger set of examples. In fact, there are *no* significant similarities and the two signatures are not from the same hand.[40] Other evidence clearly shows Sidney and Stanislaus Reilly were two different men. Contemporary editions of *Thacker's Indian Directory* and similar reference works show Stanislaus to have been more or less continuously employed in the Raj's domain from the late 1890s through at least

1930. He also has a record of service in the Indian Army during WWI, and public records attest to a lone wife and a spinster daughter who inherited his small estate. Finally, such fastidiousness in a "phony" identity was completely contrary to the Ace-of-Spies method. Our subject elsewhere avoided giving his identities any elaborate (and traceable) paper trail, not even Sidney Reilly. No record was preferable to a record that could be traced and disproved. Still, there just may have been some connection between the two men, if unknown to Stanislaus. Remember, it was Reilly's habit not to invent identities but to borrow them. It is possible, if no more, that he used Stanislaus' name—or simply his surname and initials—on some handy occasion. That raises the possibility of some early link between Reilly and India. And as it happened, there was one.

It was during 1905, in London or Petersburg, that Reilly first made the acquaintance of (later Sir) George Owens Thurston.[41] The latter was a naval engineer and chief of construction for Vickers. Among his clients worldwide were the Japanese and Russian navies. However, perhaps the most significant thing about him for our purposes is that he was now and for many years to come a close personal friend and advisor to Basil Zaharoff. Thurston certainly forms an important link in the chain linking Reilly and the Greek. Doubtless Thurston, and probably Sir Basil, encouraged Sidney to return to Russia at least partly on their behalf.

Manasevich and Reilly arrived in St. Petersburg around October, just as the revolutionary wave crested and Nicholas' days on the throne seemed numbered. In September, the disastrous Japanese war was brought to end by a treaty negotiated in Portsmouth, New Hampshire. Representing Russia was Sergei Witte who returned the man of the hour. In September a general strike shut down the Imperial capital and other cities. Under pressure from Witte and members of his own family, Nicholas caved in and issued the October Manifesto that promised a constitution and elected parliament, or Duma. Liberals rallied to support the Tsar, while the radical Soviets were crushed. By year's end, Nicholas was again in control.

In the aftermath of war and revolution, Russia stabilized and for the better part of a decade experienced an unprecedented burst of rearmament and economic expansion. It was a wonderful place to play the System. However, there were hazards as well, notably a sharp rise in violent anti-Semitism. The Tsarist regime fanned the flames by condemning the revolutionary disturbances as an insidious Jewish conspiracy. *The Protocols of Zion*, already noted, was an integral part of this counter-propaganda campaign. Bloody pogroms sprang up across the Empire. In 1906, one struck Bialystok, very near Reilly's boyhood home and still the abode of many of his kin. Under the circumstances, it was more important than ever to conceal or compensate for his Jewish antecedents. Thus, in Petersburg he styled himself an English expatriate "who had become for all intents and purposes Russian."[42] As such, he set out to assemble and exploited an ever-widening network of contacts in Russia's commercial, political and underground spheres. Before long the name and influence of the mysterious Briton would even penetrate the precincts of the Imperial Court.

In 1906, the directory *Ves' Peterburg* ("All St. Petersburg"), listed a new name among its array of businessmen, professionals and public servants—*Sidnei Georg'evich Raille* doing business as a *komisioner* (commission agent) at #1/2 Kazanskaia Ploshchad (Square).[43] On hand to assist his climb up the social and Secret World ladders were a bevy of old friends and fellow intriguers. In the immediate aftermath of the war, Zaharoff arrived in St. Petersburg to cash in on Russia's rearmament bonanza. Friend Ginsburg was on the scene as well. Having brushed off accusations of treason in Port Arthur, he was ensconced as a "first guild" tradesman with interests in banking and insurance, both spheres of acute interest to Reilly.[44] Zaharoff and Ginsburg each had links to the Brothers Zhivotovskii, Abram (recently encountered in Port Arthur) and David, ambitious *affairistes* with an eye on high finance and Russia's burgeoning armaments industry.[45] The Zhivotovskiis had their roots in the Grodno-Bialystok region which means they may have known something of Reilly's true origins. However, Abram Zhivotovskii's most interestingly connection was his supposed kinship with one Lev Davidovich Bronshtein, better known as the above-mentioned revolutionary firebrand, Leon Trotsky. Sources cannot agree on just what relationship joined the two, Abram being described variously as Trotsky's brother-in-law, cousin and uncle, but it seems most likely that they were related by marriage.[46]

Besides business, another thing that Reilly, Ginsburg, Abram Zhivotovskii, and Zaharoff (reputedly even Trotsky) had in common was freemasonry. We noted this earlier as a frequent common denominator in Sidney's London associations.[47] In Petersburg it was almost universal among his contacts and cronies. To simplify matters, when first noted, an (M) after the name will indicate known masonic affiliation. The real question, of course, is what difference does that make? In the semi-liberalized atmosphere after 1905, Russian freemasonry emerged from the shadows. By 1914, some forty lodges flourished, including ones in the Duma and the military. While the total number of masons was probably less than 2,000 out of a total population of some 150,000,000, the brethren counted among their number a sizable share of the Empire's, commercial, political and intellectual elite. In the Romanov family itself, no less than five Grand Dukes were reputed brethren of one variety or another.[48] In Moscow, Reilly affiliated with the *Vozrozhdenie* ("Renaissance") lodge whose members included Aleksandr Guchkov, now leader of the center-right Octobrist Party and one of the brightest stars in the Russian political firmament. In Petersburg, Sidney linked himself to the prestigious *Astrea* lodge.

While masonic ideology was not monolithic and factionalism abounded, it would be fair to say that the overwhelming current was liberal and anti-autocratic. On the other hand, frankly revolutionary sentiments could be found as well; both Lenin and Trotsky were alleged to be brethren.[49] There was no "masonic conspiracy" in Russia, which is not to say that there were no conspiracies among masons. The main lodges were caught up in "purely political" agendas.[50] In 1912, for instance, representatives of many lodges constituted the so-called Supreme Council of the Peoples of Russia.[51] Later rumors held that the body spawned a "shadow government" that plotted to undermine and replace the regime of Nicholas II. What is certain is that among its adherents were many of the men who five years later would constitute the post-Tsarist Provisional Government, among them Guchkov and a young socialist attorney, Aleksandr Kerenskii.[52]

Salomon Rosenblum ran into some old acquaintances as well. The first was cousin Leontii Bramson (M), now a Popular Socialist Duma deputy and prominent figure in Jewish cultural and political affairs. Bramson once greeted his cousin on the avenue, only to be completely ignored. Another relation was Felicia's sister, Sofia Rosenblum, now the wife of Mikhail Mavrik'evich Vol'ff, a well-connected attorney. Among other things, Vol'ff was legal counsel for the St. Petersburg Private Bank, a firm with which Reilly had dealings.[53] Sofia was Reilly's link to Felicia with whom he had never entirely lost touch. She was in Warsaw and was, or soon would be, a widow with two young sons to care for. In March 1913, possibly on the occasion of her birthday, or possibly of his own, he sent her a rare edition of the *Rubaiyat* of Omar Khayyam. Inside it he inscribed, in German, a quote from the 29th stanza:

"Into this universe, and why not knowing,
Nor whence, like water, willy-nilly flowing,
And out of it, as wind along the waste,
I know not whither, willy-nilly blowing"

What, precisely, this passage was meant to convey we can only guess, but it suggests a pensive side and, perhaps, just a hint of regret and self-doubt.

Reilly's nominal employer in Petersburg was the firm of Mendrokhovich & Lubenskii. Its business was the brokering of military and naval contracts for the Russian Government. Mostly it acted as a local agent or intermediary for foreign companies seeking business.[54] The lead pair were an unlikely combination. Iosif L'vovich Mendrokhovich, was another Jewish entrepreneur who had overcome obstacles to attain of position of some wealth and influence. His partner, the Polish Count Tadeusz Lubenskii, was a Catholic landowner and engineer. Among the foreign companies Mendrokhovich and his partner dealt with was Vickers, and that, of course, involved them with Zaharoff, Vickers' primary foreign representative.[55]

The relationship of Zaharoff, Reilly and Vickers in Russia has been a matter of some confusion and, perhaps, a little deliberate disinformation. The picture has been that they were rivals and that Reilly competed with Vickers. In reality, Reilly was a St. Petersburg agent of Metropolitan (Metro) Vickers, a subsidiary specializing in electrical power and engineering work.[56] Thus, he and Zaharoff worked for the same people or, more to the point, he worked with and for the Greek. In certain cases, perhaps, it was to their common advantage to make it appear otherwise. Sidney's Metro-Vickers connection linked him to a Russian filial, *Elektricheskaia sila* ("Electrical Power"), a firm involved in important engineering works throughout the Empire and with a diverse array of foreign and domestic interests. For instance, a big stake in ES was held by German concerns, among them Siemens & Schukert (Krasin's outfit), Blohm & Voss and the Deutsche Bank. Reilly's position thus gave him the ability to further Berlin's interests and to keep interested Britons and Russians well-informed about same.

The Russo-Japanese War cost Russia most of her naval strength. The vaunted Baltic Fleet had sailed more than halfway around the world only to be outfought and annihilated by the Japanese in the Straits of Tsushima.[57] During 1906, most of what remained of the Imperial Russian Navy was rendered obsolete by Britain's launching of the *HMS Dreadnought*, an advanced battleship design that set a new standard for the world's navies. In response, the Duma voted hundreds of million of rubles for the construction of new ships. Additional millions poured into the modernization of Russia's humiliated Army. The result was intense competition among Russian and foreign firms to secure a piece of the action. Bribery, fraud, blackmail and every form of commercial skullduggery was employed by these contending interests. At Mendrokhovich & Lubenskii the firm and its agents profited from commissions on these deals, but far more money changed hands under the table. Through M & L, Reilly had a finger in one of the first naval contracts, the construction of the armored cruiser *Riurik*. The contract, as might be expected, went to a Vickers-owned yard in Scotland.[58]

A company with which M & L did steady business was the German Blohm & Voss. Again according to legend, Reilly conspired with Mendrokhovich to snag the Blohm & Voss deal, then used his position to copy ship blueprints sent from Hamburg and deliver the duplicates to the waiting hands of the British Admiralty.[59] Again, there may be a kernel of truth to the tale. Blohm & Voss did acquire Russian contracts, but for the construction of wharves and dry-docks, not vessels. The most important of these was the construction of a big new shipyard for the Putilov Works, but that did not commence until 1911. We will have much more to say about the latter firm and its guiding light, Aleksandr Ivanovich Putilov (M) in the next chapter.

Back in London, the War Office, Admiralty and Commercial Intelligence would have been eager recipients of the sort of information Reilly could supply. An indication of what they were after survives in pre-1909 British intelligence records. In November 1906, not long after Reilly's establishment in Petersburg, Maj. Cockerill of the WOID sought Foreign Office approval to use secret service funds to purchase two pieces of information: the current peace strength organization plan of the Russian Army and the 1907 railway construction estimate of the Tsar's Ministry of Ways and Communications.[60]

Sidney was situated to acquire information quickly and discreetly. He also had a secure way to transmit it via Margaret and Melville, but Reilly may have had a contact of sorts closer to home. This was Royal Marine Captain Cyrus Hunter "Roy" Regnart who arrived in Petersburg in late 1905 to study Russian. To do so, he took temporary leave from the Admiralty's NID, but his aim was to return to its service as a qualified Russian interpreter, which he did in July of the following year.[61] It is doubtful that he and Reilly had significant contact while Regnart was in Russia. That would have been risky for both, but then the Captain, like Reilly, had a reputation for independent behavior.[62] After returning to NID, Regnart served as its "point of contact with the world of secret agents," and its liaison with War Office intelligence.[63] The latter included Melville, and Regnart's recently acquired language skills indicated a special interest in things Russian. After 1909, Regnart would come under Cumming's new SIS command. Regnart may have had Reilly in mind when he later observed that many of the agents he dealt with "were queer, and their motives more than doubtful."[64]

Perhaps the best evidence of Reilly's past and ongoing work for Britain is the fact that in 1912 he received the status of Honorary British Subject.[65] The honor was relatively rare and generally the reward of foreign nationals for "prior service" to the British Crown. Mostly these were employees of embassies and consulates, but since Reilly had no such affiliation, his service was of some other nature. According to Nikolai Alekseev, a confidential prewar investigation by Russian authorities revealed that Reilly had become a British subject in recognition of a "secret assignment" he carried out during the Russo-Japanese conflict. That may be part of the story, if not the whole one.[66]

A number of questions might be answered if we knew *who* recommended and approved the award. Unfortunately, that little detail is missing. Such matters were was handled on a "case by case" basis and based on precedents that bypassed normal bureaucratic channels that avoided a messy paper trail.[67] Another riddle is why Reilly received only honorary status as opposed to outright naturalization. The probable answer is that the latter might have entailed sticky questions about how a Russian national named Salomon Rosenblum became Sidney Reilly in the first place. From Sidney's standpoint, the award was a long-overdue and token recognition of his service. The status may also have been of some value in his business activities and, should there be a sudden negative turn in his relationship with Russian officialdom, it might have offered some protection; in any case more than he would have as a Russian Jew and political fugitive.

To be sure, Reilly's later Secret Intelligence Service file indicates no concrete connection between him and that organization until early 1918. In fact, it reveals almost no information about his earlier career. But SIS, as noted, did not exist until 1909 and, most importantly, aside from a few operational reports, the new agency inherited almost no institutional memory from Melville's bureau. Nor did it have ready access to Naval Intelligence files. Most of Melville's documentation, to the extent it was preserved at all, fell to Vernon Kell's counterintelligence MI5. That agency, as we shall see, claimed abundant information on Reilly's past, most of it bad. What eventually became of that is yet another mystery.

The few scraps SIS later dug up regarding Reilly's past derived almost solely from sources connected to its wartime station in New York. One background report clearly stated that "Sydney [sic] Reilly is a British subject," a marked contrast to the usual denial or equivocation of that point in other British sources. Another clue is buried in a 1918 American Military

Intelligence report. This mentions that a favorable report emanated from a British official who "had known Reilly for some time."[68]

That official was Robert (later Sir Robert) Nathan. The son of a prominent Anglo-Jewish family, from 1888 through 1914 Nathan served in the Indian Civil Service, a seemingly odd place to have made Reilly's acquaintance.[69] In 1904, while Reilly was active in Port Arthur, Nathan took on "special duties" for the Indian Home Department that entailed intelligence and counter-sedition work.[70] The Far East, including China, fell within Nathan's broad purview. By 1905–06, as Commissioner of the Dacca Division, he took a direct hand in the smashing of Indian nationalist plots.[71] Just as the Okhrana smelled British collusion with Russian revolutionaries, so Nathan fretted over Russian meddling in India. Reilly's access to official and unofficial channels of information in St. Petersburg made him a valuable asset to Nathan, as others.

Honorary subject or not, Reilly's standing among the British community in Petersburg was questionable. The American Norbert Rodkinson initially worked next door to him on Kazanskaia Square and their paths continued to cross in the ensuing years. "Few reputable Englishmen . . ." claimed Rodkinson, "would have anything to do with him."[72] Cecil Mackie, a secretary in the British Embassy and leading member of the local New English Club, later recalled that there always was some doubt about the legitimacy of Reilly's status.[73] The common opinion was that he was a Jew from somewhere in Poland or the south of Russia and certainly not British in any true sense.

There were exceptions to Rodkinson's rule. Among the "respectable" local British or Anglo-Russians with whom Sidney had commercial and, presumably, mutually satisfactory contact was Alfred "Fred" Hill, a prosperous building contractor and another member of the influential English Club. Two others were John Merrett of the Petersburg engineering firm of Merrett and Jones, and Ernest Mitchelson, another engineer and managing director of the Neva Cable Works. All were connected to Reilly through naval contracting, but there may have been more than mere business involved. In the not-too-distant future, each would share with him a connection to British intelligence.

To keep the System in balance, if Reilly traded Russian secrets to Britain in one sphere, he was obliged to reverse the situation in another. In February 1906, immediately after his arrival in Petersburg, the British Embassy began to experience a string of baffling thefts of sensitive documents, a predicament almost identical to that recently suffered by the Japanese in The Hague and Paris. His Majesty's Ambassador, Sir Cecil

Spring-Rice, reported to London that the aim of these thefts seemed to be to uncover British funding of the illegal activities of "Jews and revolutionaries."[74] Spring-Rice knew nothing about this, but we know from Melville that such contacts did exist, something Reilly knew as well. The Gendarme officer orchestrating the Embassy attacks, Maj. Gen. Mikhail Stepanovich Kommisarov, had taken over the operation previously run by Manasevich. Reilly visited the Embassy often and had ample opportunity to familiarize himself with the premises and personnel. As with Manasevich, he could have steered Kommisarov in the right—or wrong—direction. In mid-April, a exasperated Spring-Rice informed the Foreign Secretary that he had found a local spy "to get to the bottom of the Russian business." However, the man found the proposed reward, 500 rubles (about $250 or £50), beneath his dignity.[75] Was Spring-Rice trying to hire Reilly to chase his own tail? Only a guess, but given Sidney and the System, not an implausible one.

Reilly may have lent the Okhrana a hand in the compilation of a brief tome titled *Iznanka Revoliutsii* ("The Under-Side of the Revolution") that appeared in Petersburg during 1906. The anonymous work was an exposé of Akashi's dealings with assorted revolutionaries and it caused no little discomfiture in those circles. The appearance of a German edition in 1907 caused such stir that Tokyo recalled Akashi from Berlin where he had assumed the post of military attaché. As we know, as late as June 1905, the Russian police were not well-informed on Akashi's activities, so where did these new details come from? Cashing in what he knew about Akashi would have been a smart move to re-ingratiate himself with the Okhrana masters of his new home.

Of course, that did not rule out his supplying information to Tokyo. In the aftermath of the war, the Japanese continued to receive a steady stream of information from Russia. One of these informants, based in Petersburg, was code-named "Tacticion" (Tactitian, Russian *Taktik*, Japanese *Senjutsuka*). The name had first cropped up in Japanese codes pilfered by Manuilov in the West, which suggests that "Tactition" had worked for Japan during the war. The informant may have been Reilly, but there is no way to be certain.

According to Prince Sergei Konstantinovich Belosel'skii-Belozerskii, who encountered Reilly in various venues before WWI, one service the Ace-of-Spies provided the Tsar's police was spying on Zaharoff.[76] Among Reilly's alleged revelations was that Zaharoff was a Russian Jew named Manuil Sakhar, an army deserter with a revolutionary past. Or was Reilly using on his own background to fill in the blanks? The System had no place for sentimental loyalty.

Reilly, after all, only would been following Zaharoff's dictum of "kicking off the ladder those who helped you to climb it." Lockhart suggests that his motivation was rivalry in business, and that Zaharoff unsuccessfully tried to buy him off.[77] But Reilly was already in the Greek's employ. The truth may be that he was simply Zaharoff's double agent, feeding the Okhrana satisfying but ultimately misleading information.

Belosel'skii also claimed that Reilly supplied the Okhrana with information on two dubious revolutionaries-*cum*-police agents.[78] He supposedly reported that along with betraying revolutionary secrets to the police, these agents were selling out Okhrana confidences to the other side. One of these men was Evno Azef, and whether or not Reilly provided the information, the gist of the charge was quite true. The second was a Georgian Bolshevik, one Iosif Dzhugashvili, later known as Stalin. Assertions that Stalin was an Okhrana spy in his early years have been the subject of debate for decades. However, available evidence makes a convincing case that Stalin collaborated to one degree with the Tsar's policemen between 1906 and 1912.[79] Belosel'skii supposedly derived his information from a friend and senior Okhrana officer, Col. Evstratii Pavlovich Mednikov.[80] Mednikov was the Department of Police's outstanding detective, a Russian Melville. He also had interest in the Azef case, but there is nothing concrete to connect him to either Stalin or Reilly.[81] Whatever the reliability of Belosel'skii's recollections, as filtered through McCormick, this much *is* certain: Stalin was active in Petersburg during 1910–1913, and the Okhrana arrested him no less than three times in this period, only in the last case sending him to Siberia. Reilly made it his business to monitor Okhrana gossip; if there was any talk about Stalin's police connection, he was bound to have picked up on it. That knowledge may have proved very handy in years to come.

Besides the British, Russians and, possibly, Japanese, Reilly developed his links to Berlin's intelligence apparatus. One connection ran through his ex-employer and continuing associate Hans Andersen and the Danish East Asiatic Co. However, perhaps the most important was Kurt Orbanowski, director of the big Putilov shipyard project handled by Germany's Blohm & Voss. The project got underway in 1911, and through his connections, Reilly secured himself a role as a broker of shipping, machinery and materials (including timber). Orbanowski was a naval architect by profession, but Russian counterintelligence pegged him as an important agent for the Kaiser's naval intelligence department, the *Marine Nachrichtenstelle*.[82] As such, he reported to Captain (later Admiral) Paul von Hintze, the Kaiser's naval attaché and later military plenipotentiary in Russia and a man very interested in naval affairs, both public and secret.[83] Through Orbanowski,

Hintze made Reilly's acquaintance, and their relationship was destined to assume new dimensions in wartime America.

Yet another Reilly crony with German connections was Antony Jechalski, AKA Tony Farroway. Of Russian-Polish-Jewish origin, Jechalski was an engineer trained and employed in Germany before returning to Russia in 1912.[84] Long before he and Reilly joined forces in America, Jechalski had a solid reputation as a "German spy."[85] In Moscow he worked for Simon Landau, owner of various factories and banks in Poland and a close associate of Ginsburg and the Zhivotovskiis. Landau also had strong ties to Berlin and Vienna and during the coming war Russian counterintelligence considered him an important German agent of influence.[86]

If a man is known by the company he keeps, Reilly had no shortage of dubious associates, and it seemed a logical conclusion that he was a bird of the same feather. But just what sort of bird, exactly? According to Norbert Rodkinson, it was "well-known in Petrograd [Petersburg] that Reilly was a spy" who "served at will any side that paid him the most."[87] In the same period, Russian journalist Vladimir Krymov heard straight from an Okhrana officer, Nikolai Gerard, that Reilly was an "English spy."[88] In an effort to get to the bottom of these stories, around 1913 Reilly's friend Boris Suvorin, went straight to the then-chief of the Okhrana, Stepan Beletskii.[89] Beletskii dismissed the accusations against Reilly as nothing but "absurd rumors."[90] He knew the Englishman well and had nothing negative to say about him. But Beletskii was not an objective source. He maintained a close, unofficial relationship with Manasevich who acted as his "personal informant" in confidential affairs. It is reasonable to suspect that Reilly played a similar role.[91] Thus, in defending Sidney's secrets, he was defending his own.

Shortly after the outbreak of the World War, Suvorin put like questions to officials of Russian military counterintelligence, such as Col. Aleksandr Semenovich Rezanov, the Petersburg military prosecutor and longtime Kontrrazvedka officer, and the chief of the critical Northern Front counterintelligence department, Gen. Nikolai Stepanovich Batiushin.[92] Both assured Suvorin that they knew all about Reilly but had "nothing suspicious" against his name.[93] Once again, they and/or Suvorin may have been less than honest. Like Beletskii, Batiushin relied on Manasevich as an informant, and Rezanov was a personal friend of Suvorin and, moreover, of Reilly as well.[94] As we will see later, persons vouching for the Ace-of-Spies were almost always his collaborators.

The positive views were contradicted by Col. Matvei Kazakov, head of the Petersburg Gendarme Division. He expressly warned a fellow officer that Reilly was a "very suspicious man" with a long history of intrigue with the Germans and Japanese.[95] Years later, inquisitive journalist Nikolai Alekseev discovered the same when he quizzed former police and military officers about Reilly. As note above, this revealed a secret report that identified him as a British operative before the war. Even so, that seemed to have little impact on Reilly's access to Russian military circles and his many friends in high places. Through these he secured Russian citizenship and passport, in addition to his British status.[96] Clearly, some people in Petersburg found him very handy to have around.

NOTES

1. PZZ #73, 1. He certainly spoke Russian, Polish, German, French and English, and perhaps Yiddish could be counted here as well. He knew at least some Italian and had studied Latin and Greek. In addition to Japanese, we may assume he picked up some Chinese as well.
2. MID, file 9140-3074, Memorandum #2, 23 Aug. 1918, 1.
3. SIS, CXM 159, #5 to Vologda, 29 March 1918.
4. "Podvodnye lodki v rossiiskom Imperatorskom Flote," www.navy.ru/users/lapin/Imperial/index.htm.
5. NYT (12 Jan. 1924), 13:2.
6. PRO, HV 1/8, Melville Memoir, 13–14.
7. Lockhart, Ace, 46–48.
8. R.W. Ferrier, The History of the British Petroleum Company, vol. I (London, 1982), 61.
9. Ibid., 62.
10. Anton Zischka, La Guerre secret pour la pétrole (Paris, 1933), 15–26. See also Jesco von Puttkamer, Erdoel, Geld und Blut: Von Rockefeller bis Rickett (Augsburg, 1935).
11. Perhaps the best digest of the scandal and its ramifications can be found in R. Swanberg's Citizen Hearst (New York, 1961).
12. Zischka, Ibid., and Frank C. Hanighen, The Secret War (Westport, CT, 1934), 19–32, and 289. Zischka claimed to have the Rosenblum Letter story straight from Archbold. This was independently confirmed by Hanighen who found the story was supported by French data. This specific reference is to a French military intelligence (Deuxième bureau) file #28779/1925. Such a dossier did exist but ended up among those French records first appropriated by the Germans in WWII and subsequently by the Soviets. Held for decades in Moscow's secret Special Archive (the same repository that held Reilly's KRO file), many of the French files returned to Paris in the early 1990s. Sidney's, however, was not among them.
13. The Rothschild's firm was the "Société Comerciale et Industrielle de Napthe Caspienne et de la Mer Noire," also known by its Russian acronym, BNITO, second only to the Nobel's in production. For an overview of the competing interests in Russian and Middle Eastern oil see Daniel Yergin, The Prize: The Epic Quest for Oil, Money and Power (New York, 1991), 114–206. Older, but still useful is Dr. Wilhelm Mautner, Der Kampf un und gegen das russische Erdoel (Vienna, 1929).
14. Bokhanov, 74.
15. A.A. Fursenko, "The Oil Industry," in Rondo Cameron and Victor Bovylin (eds.), International Banking, 1870–1914 (New York, 1991), 451–452.

16. McCormick, *Peddler*, 108. Rothstein enjoyed an added advantage of being an in-law of the French Rothschilds; he was married to one of the Baron's cousins.

17. Ferrier, 44–45, and Boris Ananich, "Rossiia i kontsessiia d'Arsi," *Istoricheskie zapiski*, #66 (1960), 281–290.

18. SIS, Memo to Maw from Morton, 31 Jan. 1922.

19. Agafonov, 341; HIA, Okhrana, IIIf, folder 14. For American coverage of the case, see *NYT*, "Says Czar Has Part in Police Crimes," (4 Sept. 1909), 7 and "Find That Evalenko Was a Russian Spy," (13 Oct. 1910), 1, etc.

20. Naomi Cohen, Jacob A. Schiff (Hanover, NH, 1999), 124–152, *passim*., and Priscilla Roberts, "Jewish Bankers, Russia, and the Soviet Union, 1900–1940: The Case of Kuhn, Loeb and Company," *American Jewish Archives Journal*, www.huc.edu/aja/97-1.htm, 4–8.

21. *NYT*, Schiff obit. (26 Sept. 1920), 2.

22. *NYT*, Statements of Kennan (24 March 1917), 1–2.

23. Ibid., 130.

24. MID, 9140-6073, Memorandum #9; Alekseev, *Zapiski*.

25. GARF, fond 6173, opis 1, delo 41, [Reilly to Hermonius], "Doklad o sostoianii ruzheinago i patronnago dela v SShSA," 8/21 Dec. 1915.

26. HIA, Okhrana, XIIIa, folder 2.

27. Ibid.

28. HIA, Okhrana, IIIb, folder 4.

29. HIA, Okhrana, XIIIa, folder 2.

30. Ibid.

31. HIA, Baron P.N. Vrangel Collection, box 110, file 22, White Russian Intelligence Report [1920] (hereafter Report), and SIS, Summary of Russian Secret Service Report, 1 November 1920.

32. Lockhart, *Ace*, 40.

33. Alan Judd, *The Quest for C: Mansfield Cumming and the Founding of the Secret Service* (London, 1999), 203.

34. Bradley F. Smith, "The Birth of the SIS: A Newly Released Document," *Intelligence and National Security*, vol. 13, #2 (summer 1998), 183–189. The 1909 document in question (from PRO CAB 16/232) describes not so much the creation of a new organization than a reorganization of the old.

35. PRO, HV 1/8, Melville, 9–10.

36. Lockhart, *Ace*, 43.

37. Kettle, 15–17.

38. Ibid., 17.

39. "Angliiskaia kontrrazvedka za rabota (Pokaznaniia Sidneia Reili)," *Izvestiia*, (17 June 1927), 2.

40. Kettle, 16–17.

41. MI5, Reilly, Thurston to WO, 19 Jan. 1918.

42. Pepita Reilly, x.

43. *Ves' Peterburg*, 1906, 551.

44. Ibid., 161.

45. There were at least four Zhivotovskii (also Zhivatovskii) brothers: Abram, David, Isidor and Tevel; *Vsia Rossiia*, 1900, 29, 460, 461, 515.

46. See, for example, USNA, Department of State (DS), 000-909, citing MID "Who's Who" of suspects, 28 Dec. 1918, in which "Abraham Jivotoffsky" is identified as Trotsky's uncle and a "Bolshevist," and DS 861.00/4878, Memo, 21 July 1919, and DS, CSA [Chief Special Agent] file 215, Sharpe to Bannerman, 18 Dec. 1924, 1–2.

47. On Russian masons, in addition to the lists in the cited works of Berberova and Svitkov, see also Oleg Platonov, *Istoricheskii Slovar' rossiiskii Masonov XVII-XX vekov* (Moscow, 1996).

48. Aleksandr Mikhailovich, his brothers Georgii Mikhailovich and Nikolai Mikhailovich, and the siblings Nikolai Nikolaevich and Petr Nikolaevich; Platonov, 93.

49. Platonov, 81–82, 99, and Svitkov, 22, 30.

50. Richard L. Rhoda, "Russian Freemasonry: An Overview from 1731 to 1996," http//:members.aol.com/houltonme/rus.htm.

51. Boris Bashilov, *Istoriia russkago masonstva*, http//:lib.alk.ar.net/POLITOLOG/OV/intellectuals.htm.

52. Kerenskii at one time served as the general secretary of the SCPR.

53. *St. Peterburg Chastnyi Kommercheskii* Bank; Bokhanov, 107.

54. Nina Berberova, *Zheleznaia Zhenshchina* (New York, 1981), 71.

55. J.D. Scott, *Vickers: A History* (London, 1962). According to Scott, "Zaharoff had a leading voice in the company's foreign affairs between 1900 and 1914."

56. Anthony Summers Collection (ASC), A. Winch to Summers, 1 Dec. 1971.

57. The main components of Admiral Z.P. Rozhdestvenskii's Baltic Fleet were eight battleships, eight cruisers and nine destroyers. They left the Baltic in October 1904 and reached the waters between Korea and Japan in late May 1905. After a running fight on the 27th against the larger and better-led Japanese force, only five destroyers escaped. All the other vessels were sunk or captured and some 10,000 Russian seamen dead or wounded.

58. Allfrey, 268; Rochat-Cenise, 106–107.

59. Lockhart, *Ace of Spies*, 64–65; Pepita Reilly, x.

60. PRO, HD3/133, Cockerill to Hardinge, 30 Nov. 1906.

61. PRO, Service Record of RMLI Capt. C.H. Regnart. Thanks to Phil Tomaselli for information from this file.

62. Judd, 163–164, 261.

63. Ibid., 202.

64. Ibid., 163.

65. PRO, FO 610/136.

66. N. Alekseev, "OGPU . . . ," 3.

67. Val Traylen, PRO client manager for Home Office Records, PRO, 27 Sept. 2000, re: Honourary Subject status. Thanks also to Mark Hull.

68. MID 9140-6073, Memorandum #2, 23 Aug. 1918, 3.

69. He was one of several Nathan brothers, most notably Sir Matthew and Walter, in His Majesty's service.

70. *LT*, Nathan obit., "Secret Service in the War" (28 June 1921), 10.

71. Richard J. Popplewell, *Intelligence and Imperial Defence: British Intelligence and the Defence of the Indian Empire*, 1904–1924 (London, 1995), 104, 107–108.

72. DS, 811.11 21911, appended Office of Naval Intelligence (ONI) report re: Reilly, Lt. Sidney G., 15 April 1919, 2.

73. PRO, FO 369/1025, 201915, Mackie to Consular Department, 10 Dec. 1918.

74. PRO, HD3/132, Spring-Rice to Hardinge, 1, 10, 15 March 1906.

75. PRO, HD3/133, Spring-Rice to Hardinge, 12 Apr. 1906.

76. Deacon, RSS, 143–145, and McCormick to author, 23 February 1994.

77. Lockhart, *Ace*, 64–65.

78. Deacon, RSS, 146–147. In a conversation with the author in March 1994, McCormick [Deacon] confirmed that Prince Belosel'skii was the source of this information and that the latter conveyed it to McCormick about 1948 or 1949 not long before the Prince's death in London.

79. The most complete survey of this period and Stalin's police connections is Roman Brackman, *The Secret File of Joseph Stalin: A Hidden Life* (London, 2000). See also: Edward Ellis Smith, *Young Stalin: The Early Years of an Elusive Revolutionary* (London, 1967), and Eric Lee, "The Eremin Letter: Documentary Proof that Stalin Was an Okhrana Spy?," *Revolutionary Russia*, vol. 6, #1 (June 1993), 55–96. Also,

HIA, Edward Ellis Smith Collection, "The Department of Police 1911–1913: From the Recollections of Nikolai Vladimirovich Veselago."

80. McCormick to author, 14 March 1994. For background on Mednikov see Ruud and Stepanov, 59–62 and *passim*.
81. Ruud and Stepanov, 131, 143–144.
82. A.S. Rezanov, *Nemetskoe shpionstvo; Kniga sostavlena po dannym' sydebnoi praktiki I drugim' istochnikam* (Petrograd, 1915), 205–206; SIS, YN3 to London, "Report: Sidney G. Reilly," 28 Nov. 1924 and USNA, USDS, CSA file 215, Sharpe to Bannerman, 13 Dec. 1924, 14.
83. Wilhelm Kosch (ed.), *Biographisches Staatshandbuch*, I (Bern/Munich, 1963), 533.
84. MID, 9140-1496, (Bureau of Investigation file on Farroway-Jechalski), Jechalski deposition, 4 Aug. 1917.
85. MID, 9140-1496., War Dept., Chief-of-Staff to A. Bruce Bielaski, Bureau of Investigation, 2 April 1918.
86. Bokhanov, 175, and "Germanskaia razvedka glazami russkoi kontrrazvedki," in V.G. Orlov [A. Zdanovich, ed.], *Dvoinoi agent: Zapiski russkogo kontrrazvedka* (Moscow, 1998), 210.
87. MID, 9140-6073, Memorandum #5, 6 Sept. 1918, 3.
88. Vladimir Krymov, *Portrety neobychnylh liudei* (Paris, 1971), 71.
89. Stepan Petrovich Beletskii became vice director of the *Departament Politsii* in 1909 and director in 1912; PTsR, VII, 307.
90. Krymov, 71–72.
91. P.E. Shchgolev (ed.), *Padenie tsarkogo rezhima* (hereafter PTsR), vol. VII, "Imennoi ukazatel' k I–VII t.t., 375.
92. Batiushin served on the staff of the Russian Army in Manchuria during the Russo-Japanese conflict and was in contact with (probably working under) the local intelligence boss Harting. Thus, he may well have known Reilly from this time. He later ran the military counterintelligence section in Warsaw where he worked alongside Rezanov.
93. Krymov, 72.
94. Ernst Henri [Semen Rostovskii], *Professional'nyi antikommunizm: Kistorii vozniknoveniia* (Moscow, 1981), 46; PTsR, IV, 393, 514.
95. SIS, Confidential Memorandum re: S.G. Reilly, 4 Sept. 1918.
96. Ibid. With the aid of the right official, it was a fairly simple matter to purchase Russian citizenship. For a contemporary description of the process, see Jonas Lied, *Prospector in Siberia: The Autobiography of Jonas Lied* (New York, 1945), 129.

Chapter Five
THE MAN WHO KNEW EVERYTHING

To grasp the full implications of Reilly the Spy in prewar Russia, we need to take a closer look at Reilly the Man of Affairs. He did not stay put at Mendrokhovich and Lubenskii. Although he maintained ties to the firm, by 1908, he moved from Kazan Square to #9 Pushkinskaia, just off the Nevskii Prospect, Petersburg's Wall Street. He also acquired a partner of sorts, Erast Petrovich Shuberskii, engineer, speculator and a man with many "important connections."[1] Shuberskii also went into partnership with Mendrokhovich. Erast was the younger brother of Vladimir Shuberskii, a powerful figure in the Russian business world and an associate of Zaharoff. Vladimir was an officer of the Russo-French Commercial Bank alongside Zaharoff's intimate Artur Rafalovich, and held seats on the boards of various railways, machine works, and insurance companies. Through the Russo-French Bank, the elder Shuberskii was linked to Rasputin's banker friend Mitka Rubinstein. His connections also included the above intelligence/Okhrana officer, Aleksandr Rezanov.[2]

Some years later, a White Russian report emphasized Reilly's intimacy with Petersburg banking circles, but his contacts went much further.[3] For instance, Vladimir Shuberskii also was a member of a supervisory committee for maritime and riverine insurance.[4] This was an especially valuable connection for Reilly whose primary business was that of "naval agent and ship broker."[5] By 1908–09, he also had further connection to the realm of insurance via the "Russian Company for the Insurance of Capital and Profits" (ROZKD in Russian), which was, roughly, a Russian equivalent of Lloyd's.[6] Association with ROZKD allowed him to collect two commissions on the same deal: one for brokering the construction or chartering of a vessel and another for insuring it. The same firm brought him into renewed contact with Robert Robertovich San Galli (M), earlier with

RVAPO. San Galli sat on the board of the *Pomoshch'* insurance firm and ran the San Galli Iron Works (involved in arms contracts) and San Galli Trading Company.[7] Reilly did business with all of them. The same realm brought him into contact with Emile Bajeau, a French subject and local manager of the Parisian *Urbaine* insurance company. In much the same way Reilly served British (and German?) interests, Bagot acted as agent for French intelligence.[8]

The above were only a small part of the Ace-of-Spies' growing commercial nexus. Old friend Ginsburg boasted an office on the Nevskii Prospect and executive positions in both the St. Petersburg International Bank and the Salamandra Insurance Co.[9] In partnership with Reilly, the Zhivotovskii brothers expanded their lumber operations to provide timber for the Blohm & Voss docks. By 1912, Abram found himself director of the Tula Copper-Rolling and Munitions Factory. The Tula complex was a product of collaboration between Adolf Rothstein's St. Petersburg International Bank and the French Paribas[10] bank in which Zaharoff held interest, along with the Rothschilds and several German banks.[11] In turn, Tula was part of a larger armaments complex to which Zaharoff, in 1906, sold the license to manufacture the Maxim machine gun.[12] Armaments, banking and Zaharoff were three common denominators in most of Reilly's Russian business affairs.

The years from 1904 to 1907 were a watershed in Russia's political development, and to appreciate the circumstances in which Reilly now found himself, we must pause and consider briefly some of these changes. Nicholas' promised constitution, the so-called Fundamental Laws, proved a bitter disappointment to Russia's liberals and further incitement to the revolutionaries. In effect, the Tsar's autocratic power was unchecked. Nicholas soon dissolved the factious Duma and dismissed Prime Minister Witte (M). When the second Duma (1907) proved equally difficult, Nicholas' new Prime Minister, Petr Stolypin, amended electoral rules to guarantee a majority of compliant deputies. The opposition bided their time.

One important change was the emergence of clear-cut political parties, both legal and illegal. After 1907, one of the most significant was the rightist-liberal "Octobrists" led by ex-Boer partisan and Reilly's lodge brother, Aleksandr Guchkov.[13] On the revolutionary left were the Socialist Revolutionaries, or SRs, and the Marxist Social Democratic Labor Party, or SDs. The SRs styled themselves the champions of the peasant masses and embraced a strong current of anarchism, including a penchant for terrorism. They formed a semi-autonomous Fighting Organization that conducted a campaign of assassination against Tsarist officials. The SDs, on the other hand, saw themselves as the vanguard of the industrial proletariat. In 1903, they split into two main factions: the moderate Mensheviks and the smaller, more radical Bolshevik. The last was the ideological fiefdom of its leader, Vladimir Il'ich Ul'ianov, better known as Lenin.

As also made clear in the White Russian report, Reilly maintained his close ties to Manasevich-Manuilov. In 1906, the latter went to work for Witte as a kind of "one-man secret service" and returned to Paris on clandestine assignments for the Prime Minister; matters, we may suspect, in which Reilly took due interest.[14] After the Tsar dismissed Witte from the premiership, Manasevich returned to journalism. Under the pseudonym "The Mask," he was a reporter and gossip columnist for the Petersburg daily, *Vechernee Vremia* and its sibling paper *Novoe Vremia*.[15] Both papers were run by the Suvorin family. This job was ideal for the collection of all sorts of information that he turned into a lucrative blackmail racket. Whoever encountered Manasevich was bound to run into the mysterious Englishman.[16] Clustered around the newspaper was a dubious crowd that included journalist-*cum*-police spy, Boris Rzhevskii, the veteran Court intriguer Dr. Badmaev (M), and aforementioned banker-speculator Mitka Rubinstein. Still another was the vice director and subsequent chief of the Okhrana, Stepan Beletskii, the same who later pronounced Reilly "OK." For good measure, Col. Rezanov worked at *Novoe Vremia*.[17]

Boris Suvorin was another important contact. He was the younger son of Aleksei Sergeevich Suvorin, Russia's equivalent to William Randolph Hearst. The Suvorin empire included newspapers, publishing houses, and even its own forest to keep the enterprises supplied with paper. As junior member of the dynasty, Boris had a reputation as a playboy and a spendthrift. Editorship of *Vechernee Vremia* was intended to settle him down, and perhaps it did to some degree. He and Reilly became fast friends, bound by common interests and, perhaps, a certain love of intrigue. The "Englishman" was a regular fixture around the VV offices and even got himself on the payroll. Vladimir Krymov, the Suvorins' business manager, found the situation puzzling. Reilly never wrote a word, but Boris held him in awe and sought his counsel on almost any matter. "Sidney knows things that no one else knows," he assured Krymov.[18] While he remained skeptical, Krymov admitted that the strange Englishman possessed an astonishingly wide range of information and could speak on almost any subject with apparent authority. He was especially well versed in matters touching on Napoleon, a topic on which he was inclined to expound in great detail. Krymov also vouched for the fact that Reilly had superb command of several languages. At a gathering of foreign journalists and diplomats at the fashionable Café de Paris ("Kiuba's"), the Ace-of-Spies chatted up the attendees in their native tongues with ease and fluency. Krymov noted his lean visage almost always presented a cool, sardonic detachment; a mask behind which his inner thoughts and feelings were well hidden.[19] He found this "man who knew everything" a genuine sphinx—fascinating, enigmatic and certainly dangerous.

Through Suvorin and Manasevich Reilly gained admittance to the real power centers of the Russian capital. These were not government ministries nor even the Imperial Court, but the salons and private clubs where the diverse currents of late Tsarist society met and mixed in unexpected ways. Among the most influential of these "circles of adventurers, half-social, half-political," was one hosted by Baroness Evgeniia Rozen, known to her intimates as "Baroness R."[20] Separated from her noble husband and without visible means of support, she somehow managed to maintain herself and a resident bevy of female "friends" in luxury and to provide food, drink and other diversions to a more or less constant parade of guests. Behind her stood a shadowy benefactor known only as "the engineer." Rumors hinted that he was a foreigner, perhaps Zaharoff. Or was it Reilly?

According to one Tsarist minister and habitué, the Baroness' salon was the sort of place where grand dukes and princesses rubbed shoulders with courtesans, actresses, and spies. It was a place where deals were made, plots hatched and secrets traded as easily as sexual favors.[21] Rachkovskii was a regular, as was the dissolute Rasputin who found the wine and women much to his liking. Always on hand was the Baroness's own "special friend," the Princess Stephania Dolgorukaia. The latter was a Spanish adventuress who through a marriage of convenience secured the name of one of the oldest families in Russia. This she used to "carry through profitable transactions" of vague and presumably dubious nature.[22] She was close to the Spanish Embassy in Petersburg, a quarter with which Reilly also cultivated acquaintance, possibly with her help.

Baroness R herself reputedly introduced Reilly to Rasputin.[23] If not, the two certainly ran into each other elsewhere. Other common haunts were the *Kupecheskii* ("Merchants") Club, an exclusive gambling establishment, and the Villa Rode cabaret where the Mad Monk regularly caroused. Reilly developed a close acquaintance with Aron Simanovich (M), the gambler who finagled his way into becoming Rasputin's personal secretary. Simanovich served as the Holy One's link to a circle of Jewish bankers that included both Ginsburg and Rubinstein. The former lobbied the holy man to use his influence with the Imperial Family to effect better treatment for Russia's Jews, as well as more mundane favors.[24] When Sidney moved out of the Pushkinskaia address, Simanovich moved in. Like Reilly, Simanovich also had a collaborative relationship with the Okhrana, keeping it abreast of Rasputin's private affairs. It seems more than coincidence that Simanovich's private gaming club on the Fontanka was adjacent to the Okhrana's main office.

Reilly's salon-trawling also brought him into contact with a figure of a rather different stripe, a man who was destined to become one of his most important collaborators in years to come. Making the rounds of the Imperial Capital's soirees in late 1905 and early 1906 was Boris Viktorovich Savinkov (M), the so-called "Horseguard of the Revolution." In theory, he was one of the most wanted men in Russia. The son of a Tsarist magistrate and a hereditary nobleman, the sloe-eyed, balding Savinkov was one of the leaders of the SR terrorist wing. Among its recent successes was the murder of the Tsar's uncle, Grand Duke Sergei. At more than one late-night gathering, Savinkov proudly brandished his Browning pistol to the perverse delight of the assembled guests. With a trademark gardenia on the lapel of his English suit and decked out in his favorite yellow spats, he was seemingly a hard man for the police to miss. Like his comrade and immediate superior Azef, Savinkov was not the chosen of the gods, but of the Okhrana.[25] Savinkov and Azef were a classic example of police "double penetration." Under the rules they knew nothing about the other's role. Savinkov's services to the revolution and to the Tsar were equally devoid of genuine conviction. Vain and misanthropic, he was driven by love of adventure and an ego of Napoleonic proportions. He saw himself a Nietzschean Superman who transcended ideological and moral limitations. In betraying comrades to the police, he reasoned he actually was doing the Revolution a service. In Reilly Savinkov found a man who shared many of his feelings and for whom he seems to have felt genuine respect and admiration, at least to the extent he was capable of these. To Sidney's *simpatico* ear, Savinkov would confide things he would not reveal even to the Okhrana.

Reilly played middleman in secret dealings between Savinkov and Guchkov. In 1910, through Sidney, Guchkov funneled money to the exiled Savinkov in order to abet the latter's effort to revive terrorism.[26] As an avowed supporter of the monarchy, Guchkov would seem to be an unlikely candidate to bankroll such activity. However, just as Savinkov was a rather odd revolutionary, Guchkov was not your typical liberal. He may have been loyal to the monarchy, but not to Nicholas. If Savinkov's assassins could eliminate the latter, so much the better for Guchkov.

Another figure making the rounds of St. Petersburg's and Moscow's salon society was writer Andrei Belyi. In his novel *Petersburg*, Belyi offered up thinly disguised and unflattering portraits of Savinkov and Azef; most of his characters had real-life models. Some years later, in his *Moscow* novellas, he conjured up the dark presence of Eduard Eduardovich von Mandro. A cad, arch-cynic and probable spy, Mandro was a man whose origins, associations and wealth were mysterious. Rumors made him out a Greek or a Jew with ties to Odessa and Britain, though no one could be sure. It all has a distinctly familiar ring, and the resemblance between Mandro and Reilly cannot be entirely accidental.[27]

Savinkov was not Reilly's only link to the revolutionary camp and its murky realm of police spies and provocateurs. Another was Leonid Borisovich Krasin (M). An electrical and mechanical engineer and astute businessman, Krasin outwardly seemed a perfect specimen of the successful bourgeois, though his neatly trimmed Van Dyke beard and pointed nose and ears gave him a slightly foxy appearance. In fact, Krasin had been affiliated with the Social Democrats since the late 1880s.[28] When the SDs split into Mensheviks and Bolsheviks in 1903, Krasin adhered to the latter. His first encounter with Reilly may date back to 1900. Krasin was in Baku about the time of Reilly's visit there. In any event, by 1906, Krasin operated a technical office at Petersburg's 55 Fontanka. His work brought him into regular contact with Karl Orbanowski, the German contractor and intelligence operative who collaborated with Reilly.[29]

At the same time, engineer Krasin had the more secret job of the Bolsheviks' "minister of finance." As such he was intimately involved with the campaign of robbery and other illicit means used to finance the organization.[30] Reilly certainly had his share of experience in that realm. In the Caucasus, along with Stalin, Krasin met and compared notes on terrorism with Savinkov. Arrested by the Okhrana in 1907, Krasin fled to Germany. There he seemingly withdrew from active revolutionary activity, and in 1910 the Bolsheviks dropped him from their ranks. The reason was his supposed mishandling of party funds, but behind this lurked darker suspicions that he was an Okhrana informer.[31] In fact, he had been one from 1894 to at least 1902, interestingly the same time Reilly was active in the same sphere.[32] In any case, Sidney certainly knew about it and was bound to find a way to use the knowledge to his advantage.

Krasin raised further eyebrows when he later returned to Russia as representative of the German Siemens-Schukert firm. By 1913 he was back doing business in Petersburg once again in the same sphere as Reilly. His intimacy with German concerns stirred allegations that he was Berlin's agent as well. Later charges identified Krasin as a channel for German funding to the Bolsheviks as far back as 1906–07.[33] At the very least, as we will see, Leonid Krasin was a man of very uncertain allegiances.

Another Bolshevik of sorts, with whom the Ace-of-Spies rubbed elbows in prewar Petersburg, was Veniamin ("Benny") Sverdlov. A minor arms broker linked to the Zhivotovskii-Ginsburg clique, he was the younger brother of Yakov Sverdlov, one of Lenin's closest lieutenants and destined to be a key figure in the early Soviet hierarchy. The whole family had a radical political upbringing. Sverdlov may have provided the early link between Reilly and another character bound to play an important role, Genrykh (Henryk) Grigor'evich Yagoda. Close to the Sverdlovs, in 1913 Yagoda served as a humble clerk in the Putilov Work's insurance office, another place he might have crossed Reilly's path.

From an immediate standpoint, perhaps the most important member of Sidney's "revolutionary" nexus was Aleksandr Ivanovich (or Nikolaevich) Grammatikov (M). His story is now routine. Born to an aristocratic family of Greek extraction, he gravitated to radicalism at Moscow University and endured the usual arrests and expulsions. By 1905 he was affiliated with the Bolsheviks and gained the confidence of Lenin. However, Grammatikov's subsequent lenient treatment at the hands of the Okhrana raised accusations that he, too, was a police spy. Lenin personally came to his defense.[34] But Grammatikov *was* an Okhrana informer and had been for some time. By 1907–08, according to police records, code-named "Chernyi", (Black) or "Ivan Petrovich," he was living in Brussels and connected to groups involved in the study and manufacture of explosives.[35]

Here several interesting threads converge. Reilly met with Grammatikov in 1908 in the Belgian capital. In the meantime, in far-off Bengal, an anti-British Hindu society, the *Anusilam Samiti*, based in Dacca, dispatched one of its members to Paris "to learn bomb-making under the instruction of Russian revolutionary exiles."[36] The Russian radical communities in Brussels and Paris were closely connected, so it is quite possible that Grammatikov had ties to the above bomb-makers or knowledge of their activities.

In India, the *Anusilam Samiti* and its allies were the object of intense interest to Robert Nathan, the Raj's Commissioner in Dacca, and special agent of the Indian Home Office. Grammatikov, therefore, had access to information of considerable worth to British authorities. Reilly, once more, was available to play middleman. Soon after, Nathan presided over the destruction of *Anusilam*.[37] A decade later, Nathan would lend his crucial endorsement to Reilly's undertaking of a British mission inside Russia.

During 1912, Grammatikov turned up in Petersburg as a lawyer in the employ of Boris Suvorin. At the same time, he acted as Reilly's personal attorney and became one of his closest associates in both business and personal affairs. Grammatikov maintained a low-key affiliation with the political left, but shifted his allegiance from the Bolsheviks to the SRs. All the while, he worked for the Okhrana.

In 1906 Okhrana chief Harting dispatched a new deep cover agent to Paris. Under the name Georges Patrick, he posed as a Frenchman and rented an apartment on the rue de la Glaciere. There he befriended a cavalcade of revolutionary exiles, among them Azef, and Savinkov.[38] Patrick dutifully reported on them and was in turn kept under observation by other agents. Georges Patrick, AKA Georgii Zus, was in reality Vladimir Avgustovich Brandes, a relation of yet another of Reilly's business associates, Avgust Avgustovich Brandes, councilor of the Imperial Court and official of various banks and insurance companies.[39] In 1910 new orders sent Patrick to New York, where he eventually took over as resident agent from Reilly's old antagonist, Aleksandr Evalenko.

Evalenko had been exposed as a police agent and forced him to flee to Russia. Back in Petersburg, he was convinced that Reilly had something to do with his downfall, and he most likely was right. To understand why, we must return to a character last encountered in Chapter One, Vladimir Burtsev, the Russian émigré arrested by Melville in 1897. Following his release from British prison, he dedicated himself to exposing police spies in revolutionary ranks and earned the nickname of "Sherlock Holmes of the Revolution." The key to Burtsev's success was information acquired from Okhrana turncoats and other "inside" sources. In the Evalenko case, he relied mostly on Leontii Petrovich Men'shchikov, a former deputy to Harting and officer of the Okhrana's "Special Department."[40] Indeed, among the persons Men'shchkov helped expose was Harting himself. It was in early 1906, immediately after the arrival of Reilly and Manasevich in Petersburg, that Men'shchikov secretly broke with the police and began supplying Burtsev with information. Another coincidence, perhaps.

Some thought otherwise. Among them was the new Deputy Minister of Internal Affairs, P.G. Kurlov, who in the wake of the Evalenko revelations ordered a search of Manasevich's residence. In January 1910, while Reilly was in Paris, the search turned up a veritable private archive of Okhrana reports and internal communications, including ones to and from Col. Mednikov, Reilly's alleged contact in the Moscow Okhrana.[41] If nothing else, it further demonstrates that through Manasevich, Reilly had access to the most sensitive of police secrets. Among Manasevich's files investigators also inexplicably found a manuscript dealing with conditions in India and a detailed outline of the Indian civil and military administration. Was that a contribution from Sidney, gleaned through his dealings with Nathan? Fortunately for Manasevich, in 1911 Kurlov lost his post and the inquiry ended. Reilly probably breathed a little easier as well.

Reilly also found time to manage a personal life, though even that was not wholly detached from the System. He played the part of a wealthy, single man-about-town and indulged, with moderation, in all the delights and vices Petersburg had to offer. Sexual diversions were provided by a cavalcade of actresses, singers and the occasional bored wife. He maintained a more regular liaison with a French *artiste*, Myrtil Paul. Among others with whom he dallied was the tempestuous opera diva, Ganna Walska. Born Chana Paucz in Poland in 1887, Walska shared with the Ace-of-Spies ruthless ambition, a fascination with Napoleon and disguised Jewish ancestry.[42] Walska made up for the limitations of her voice by exploiting her dark, voluptuous beauty to snare a succession of rich husbands. In 1907 she was the wife of the Baron Arkadii von Ettingen (sometimes d'Ettingen). Her tryst with Reilly was brief. Perhaps it meant his material success had not yet reached the critical mass to justify the prolonged interest of Madame W.

But in Reilly's world, old friends, old enemies and old loves were never quite forgotten, especially if they were useful. An example was Eve Lavalliere, who appeared in Petersburg in 1911 in the company of her German paramour, Baron von Lucius. The Baron held a post in the Kaiser's Embassy and worked closely with Hintze for the better part of two years. In 1913, the Baron came under a cloud when rumors, probably emanating from the Okhrana, accused him of contact with revolutionaries. Soon after, Berlin shifted him to the wilds of Albania.[43] Did Reilly exploit Lavalliere to compromise the Baron as a favor to his friends at Fontanka 16?

Yet another female from Reilly's past to pop up was the redoubtable Natta Azef. According to Kaledin, in prewar Petersburg she "adopted the strange career of unmasking poor dabblers in espionage" and marketed her findings to foreign embassies or any other entities willing to pay her price. "She was . . ." adds Kaledin, "one of the most ruthless counterspies . . . and a woman of mystery known only to a select few."[44] Among her confidantes were Suvorin's friend, General Nikolai Stepanovich Batiushin of the General Staff, Imperial Prosecutor S.V. Zavadskii and the police chief of St. Petersburg, Gen. V.F. Galle.[45] Batiushin, of course, was one of Reilly's fans as well. Natta even married one of the Ace-of-Spies' aeronautics pals, Nikolai Mikhailovich Raevskii, and so transformed herself into the respectable Madame Natalia Raevskaia.[46]

What about the other women in his life? Margaret was restless in Brussels and had not seen a penny of her money. By some means, she kept track of his progress, and learning he had become a "prosperous shipping broker" determined to share in his good fortune.[47] She arrived in Petersburg quite unexpected sometime in 1908. He was not at all pleased to see her, but taken off-guard, humored her, even putting her up in an apartment on Pochtamtskaia Street. There was to be no reconciliation or restitution for Daisy. She eventually discovered that he had "committed bigamy" and was now married to another woman.[48] As his legal spouse, she threatened to go to the British Embassy and to the Russian authorities and lay claim to his assets. He may have reminded her that she was the wife of Sigmund Rosenblum, a man who no longer existed. She, however, knew that he had never bothered to legally change his name and the British passport he carried was, in fact, fraudulently obtained. But her errant husband had many friends in Russia and there was little she could do to harm him. So, instead she decided to harm herself; a dead woman would at least force him to do some explaining. She found a pistol, put the gun to her head, and fired. But even in self-destruction she was thwarted. At the last instant her hand wavered and the bullet deflected through her right eye socket.[49] She came to in a private hospital run by a physician who was an intimate of her husband.

Reilly later spun a suitably recast version of this episode. Annoyed by her demands and drinking, he offered her £10,000 for a divorce but she stubbornly refused. In the end, he had to use threats of violence to chase her out of the country. Later, taking advantage of her service with a Red Cross unit in the war-torn Balkans, he planted a story that she had been killed in a road accident.[50] On the whole, Margaret's version is more convincing and she certainly bore the scars to prove it. What probably happened was that he prevailed upon the helpful doctor to declare his wounded spouse deceased on the spot rendering her position in Russia very tenuous indeed; it was no crime to murder a woman already dead.

But who was this other wife? Reilly would not take his next known plunge into matrimony until 1915, in New York, and he would not even meet that woman until 1911. Again, the likely candidate is Anne Luke. Was she with him in Petersburg? If so, he kept her very well hidden. Or did he keep her stashed elsewhere, back in Port Arthur, perhaps? They must have had contact, for according to later reports she bore him a second child, a daughter, sometime before the outbreak of WWI.

Partly as a result of Margaret's antics, Reilly spent much of the next year outside the Tsar's domain. Another impetus behind his travels was a new passion, aviation. As many others, the Ace-of-Spies was as fascinated by the thrill and danger of flying as by its technical and commercial aspects.[51] In the rickety and perilous machines that took to the skies in the early years of the century, he saw great military and commercial promise.

Again, it probably is no coincidence that Zaharoff was another air enthusiast; in 1909 he endowed a Chair of Aviation at the University of Paris. However, the friend who was Reilly's entrée into Russia's flying society was Boris Suvorin. In 1908 Suvorin was a founding member of the Imperial All-Russian Aero Club, known by its Russian initials as IVAK.[52] With Suvorin's sponsorship, Reilly joined the club and became a full member two years later. IVAK was another gathering place for Russia's high and mighty. Among the members were such personages as General F.F. Palitsyn, chief of the Imperial General Staff, Minister of Trade and Industry, I.P. Shipov, high-raking nobleman and banker A.V. Ratkov-Rozhnov (M) and the "Russian Rockefeller," oil magnate Emanuel Nobel (M).[53] Guchkov was another, and so was Natta's husband Nikolai Raevskii who edited IVAK's official organ, *Vozdukhoplavitel'* ("Flight").

The imperial patron of the Club was Grand Duke Aleksandr Mikhailovich (M), the Tsar's cousin and brother-in-law. As noted, he had links to Reilly going back to the Manchurian interlude. Known as "Sandro," the tall, genial Duke was a man of many parts and one of somewhat controversial opinions. Outwardly he was loyal to his Imperial cousin, but he had serious differences with the manner in which Nicholas governed the Empire. Aleksandr was a modernizer who foresaw the "Americanization" of Russia.[54] Aleksandr's most important connection, though, was with the Russian Navy in which he was a Rear Admiral. Most significantly, Aleksandr was linked to Russian Naval Intelligence, an agency that enjoyed a reputation for great energy and efficiency in the realms of military and technical espionage.[55] In 1906 he went to France in a self-imposed exile, but returned to Russia in two years. In addition to supporting IVAK, the Duke arranged for Russian pilots to be trained in France and set up the Empire's first military airfield near his estate in the Crimea.[56]

It was through Aleksandr Mikhailovich that Prince Belosel'skii-Belozerskii made Reilly's acquaintance. About 1909, the Prince became Sandro's *aide de camp* and he was able to observe much of the Duke's personal and official business.[57] "In ordinary conversation," Belosel'skii noted, "Reilly never entered into political controversy."[58] This was not a matter of shyness or political indifference. He restricted his comments on such matters to one-on-one conversations or intimate gatherings of like-minded persons. This allowed him to tailor his opinions to those of his listeners. Thus, to

some he presented himself as a loyal monarchist, to other a pragmatic liberal, and to still others a revolutionary sympathizer. Which was the real
Reilly? To one degree or another, all and none.

Sidney and Suvorin were not content to observe aviation from ground
level. Both undertook the hazardous course to become pilots. In 1909 they
hit upon the idea of forming a company that would import and build planes
as well as operate a flight school. Dubbed *Kryl'ia* ("Wings"), by July 1910,
thanks to Reilly, the firm held exclusive Russian rights for the French
Farman, Tellier, and Avia aircraft and boasted the imminent opening of its
private airdrome at Komendantskoe Field on the northern outskirts of the
Capital.[59]

The airdrome site was part of an old leasehold held by an elderly
Englishwoman, possibly a relation or acquaintance of Fred Hill (M).
Wooing her with his "pleasing and excellent" English, Reilly secured rights
to the land.[60] It happened to be the only tract near the city suitable for a
large airfield, so the deal neatly preempted any competition. Sidney pocketed a commission and Suvorin awarded him a generous director's salary in
the company. According to Krymov, however, it was the elder Suvorin who
ended up paying most of the bills for this enterprise that, including Reilly's
commission, totaled more than 100,000 rubles.[61]

Among the competitors faced by Reilly and Suvorin was Hart Berg, the
American promoter previously encountered in Russian submarine contracts. From 1904 to 1907, Berg was a more or less a constant presence in
Petersburg where he represented, among other things, the Wright Aircraft
Company. During 1908, Hart sought to sell rights to the Wright airplane
design to the Russian Government. He secured verbal approval of the deal,
but soon difficulties arose over the fine points of the contract and an endless series of technical quibbles.[62] Berg later complained that "Russian competitors," undoubtedly including Reilly and Suvorin, had done everything
in their power to obstruct the contract.[63]

Reilly departed Petersburg around September 1908. After returning
Margaret to Brussels, he headed for London. At the beginning of October,
he came to rest at the Hotel Cecil on the Strand. First, he had some important personal business to handle. Margaret's threats brought home the
inconvenient fact that he was, in a strictly legal sense, still Sigmund
Rosenblum. To forestall future difficulties on that front, he looked up solicitor Sandford and had him to draw up a formal petition for a name change
by Deed Poll. In this, Reilly, a self-described "gentleman," noted that he
had been known as Sidney George Reilly since June 1899 and had fully
intended to enroll a name change at that time. However, for some reason,

the original document was "never enrolled and is now lost or destroyed." His caution is evident in the fact that he paid extra to have the change formally enrolled, a step with which most petitioners never bothered.

A legal detail, of course, was not the only thing that brought the Ace-of-Spies back to London. That October the Russian Socialist Revolutionary Party convened its 4th Congress there. Melville, naturally, would have had an interest in the gathering, and that may have had something to do with drawing Reilly into the picture. Among the attendees was Boris Savinkov. In addition to his overt role as a member of the SR Central Committee, Savinkov also was on hand to keep tabs for the Okhrana. He arrived fresh from yet another failed assassination attempt, this one aimed at the Tsar himself. The plot involved an effort to plant an assassin aboard the new Russian cruiser *Riurik*, a vessel that had just completed construction in Scotland. Reilly, recall, was connected to that contract. Indeed, it could have been Sidney's helping hand that allowed Savinkov and an accomplice to visit the building ship in pursuit of their plot.[64]

Overseeing the failed operation, as usual, was Evno Azef. At the same time, Azef was the subject of fresh charges of treachery by tireless mole-hunter Burtsev. He needed one final bit of information to make his accusation stick, and Savinkov provided it. The basic story is thus: in London Savinkov made contact with A.A. Lopukhin, a Russian police official and imparted to Lopukhin the details of the recent *Riurik* conspiracy.[65] Soon thereafter, Lopukhin passed the same information to Burtsev. Next, quite coincidentally it seemed, Savinkov let slip to Burtsev that Azef was one of the few having full knowledge of the plot. Burtsev and others immediately jumped to the conclusion that Lopukhin's informant was Azef himself and the Fat Man's fate was sealed. By early 1909 he was on the run with Savinkov leading the pack baying for his blood.

What part did Reilly play in this? His most likely role was to arrange the critical meeting between Savinkov and Lopukhin and, perhaps, to direct Burtsev to the latter. Why would he bother? Years later, the inquisitive Nikolai Alekseev was told by a former female associate of the Ace-of-Spies—quite possibly Natta Azef—that Reilly assisted Azef's downfall to pay back an old debt. Had the former Salomon Rosenblum realized that Azef had been his betrayer in 1893, or had he always known it? Then again, Reilly's motives could have been entirely practical. The elimination of Azef, just as Evalenko, advanced a man of greater utility.

Sidney probably remained in or around London through December when an international naval conference opened. The big item on the agenda was battleships. Given that a major part of his business involved warship contracts, these proceedings were of more than abstract interest. There might need to be some bribes paid and a little blackmail worked to ensure that the life's blood of contracts continued to flow.

It was about this time or soon after that Reilly engaged the services of Frank Dougherty. The latter was an Irishman or Irish-American who was Sidney's valet for the next several years.[66] In reality his most important role was that of bodyguard and probably, when occasion demanded, personal gunman. Dougherty had the handy knack of blending into the background, but he seldom was far from his employer's side—or back. Reilly may not have trusted anyone fully, by Dougherty's longevity in his job argues that he may have trusted him more than most.

Reilly next appeared near Calais on 25 July 1909. There he witnessed French aviator Louis Bleriot's historic flight across the English Channel. It was a very interesting gathering. Boris Suvorin, was there, along with Russian aviator Prince Sergei Bolotov who talked of making his own channel attempt, though nothing came of the notion.[67] Also among the observers were Zaharoff, GD Aleksandr Mikhailovich, and even Savinkov who was yet another flying buff.

There may have been a interesting convergence of Savinkov's and Reilly's interest in aeronautics and the former's terrorist ambitions. During 1907–08, Reilly and Savinkov took interest in the work of Sergei Bukhalo, a Russian inventor living in Munich. Bukhalo was a partisan of the revolutionary cause and claimed to have developed a superior engine that could propel a plane at close to 100 miles per hour. Savinkov envisioned using a speeding aircraft to drop bombs on the Winter Palace while Reilly's plans were to sell the patent to the Russian military. In the end, Bukhalo proved something of a mad scientist, but not before a good deal of money was squandered on his scheme.[68]

In the wake of the Bleriot flight, international aero exhibitions opened in Frankfurt and Reims. Sidney and Suvorin took them in. It is in regard to the Frankfurt meet that another tale crops up in the "Reilly Legend." According to this, following the fatal crash of a German aviator, Reilly assisted a British pilot in surreptitiously removing a new magneto from the wreck. The British flyer introduced himself as Jones and revealed that he actually was a Royal Navy officer sent by "C" to solicit Reilly's return to the fold.[69] The story, as such, is a crock. No such accident happened at the meet, nor did any British pilot named Jones take part. Was it a veiled reference to Regnart, perhaps? Curiously, about this time, if not necessarily in Frankfurt, Reilly did meet a British, or Russo-British, aviator named Waldemar or Vladimir *Smith*. Smith soon went to work for Reilly and

Suvorin's company.[70] An interesting coincidence, though probably no more, is that the summer of 1909 corresponds exactly with the reorganization of British intelligence into what would become MI5 and the Secret Intelligence Service, also known as MI1c and later as MI6. However, as mentioned, there is no indication that Reilly had any direct contact with the SIS or its chief, Commander Mansfield Cumming—the original "C"—for several years to come.[71]

At Reims, the Ace-of-Spies also introduced himself to the American pilot and aircraft designer Glenn Curtiss.[72] Curtiss was developing seaplane designs that Reilly felt perfect for the needs of the Russian Navy. In 1911 our man helped broker the purchase of twenty Curtiss hydroplanes by the Russian Naval and Military Aero Club (also under GD Aleksandr's guidance), and two years later he and Sandro backed Curtiss in a bid to build a seaplane factory in Russia.[73]

Reilly came to rest in Petersburg in the autumn of 1909. He also acquired a new address, or rather two. He changed his main location to an apartment and office at #2 Pochtamtskaia which was conveniently close to the Russian Admiralty. He also maintained a separate office at #10 Torgovaia that was strategically adjacent to the *Kryl'ia* offices at #12 and to those of the attorney Aleksandr Grigor'evich Weinstein (Vainshtein). A one-time brothel tout with a conviction for bribery, Sidney found Weinstein a useful and convivial ally and formed a mutually profitable alliance.[74]

By 1910, Reilly was the picture of a "calm, elegant, immaculate" gentleman who tooled about town in a smart carriage with his French mistress, and whose well-appointed flat displayed his growing collection of artwork and a personal library of over 3,000 volumes.[75] All this suggests an expanding and prosperous business, yet he often presented his financial situation as precarious. According to Krymov, Reilly's finances seemed in bad shape. If so, perhaps his continued penchant for gambling was to blame. But where money was concerned, as we will see, Sidney was always most deceptive. Nor did wealth dispel his dubious reputation. An incident that illustrates both points is his involvement in the questionable death of Yulii Gof'man (Julius Hofman), an officer of the Petersburg branch of the Credit Lyonais. As it happened, this was the same bank that Manasevich used for secret accounts in Paris. Whether that had any connection to Gof'man's fate is uncertain, but it is an interesting coincidence.

According to Krymov, who got the story from the Imperial Capital's Chief of Detectives, V.G. Filipov, Gof'man shot himself and left behind a note in which he confessed to embezzling money to pay gambling debts. There was some doubt, however, about just how Gof'man died and why.

Strangely, Gof'man's associates, including Reilly, claimed to know nothing of the deceased's gaming habits. Nevertheless, a large sum of money was missing. Reilly was of particular interest to investigators because he had shared living quarters with Gof'man (apparently prior to settling at Pochtamtskaia). He pointed out his own financial difficulty as evidence that *he* could not possibly have the money. Of course, such distress would have provided a powerful incentive to obtain it. Filipov considered it a "very mysterious affair" and hinted to Krymov that powerful, unseen forces were at work.[76]

Another notably unsavory connection in Reilly's Petersburg affairs involved Eduard Scheffer, another banker. It is an excellent example of how Sidney's connections to espionage, high finance and political circles combined in curious ways. He met Scheffer in Paris sometime before the war. A Swiss citizen, Scheffer was connected to the Russo-Asiatic Bank and at one point managed the London branch of the Russian Commercial and Industrial Bank.[77] In Petersburg he was suspected of being an agent for both the German and Russian intelligence services. While in Paris, he acquired a mistress named Paulette Pax, an artiste from one of Montemarte's reviews. La Pax was the intimate friend of two like women, Henriette Roggers and Myrtil Paul. The former was the mistress of General Aleksandr Aleksandrovich Mosolov (M), no less than the Tsar's chief of the Imperial Court.[78] Myrtil was Reilly's French diversion. In Petersburg, Madame Roggers presided over very private *messes rouges*, sadomasochistic orgies in which Mosolov and other notables were regular participants. Whether Sidney and Myrtil partook in this scene is unknown but, again, he most certainly knew who did.

In early 1910, Tsar Nicholas sanctioned the formation of the Imperial Russian Air Service under the GD Aleksandr Mikhailovich's personal direction. Soon after Aleksandr led a not-so-secret mission to Paris to "study the various types of airplanes made in France and their suitability for military purposes and to purchase a large number of them for the Russian Army."[79] Reilly strategically placed himself in Paris at the same time. Given that he already had the Russian licenses for Farman and other French firms, he was well-placed to assist the Grand Duke's effort and, of course, to profit from the inevitable commissions.

June of that year saw IVAK host a Flying Week in St. Petersburg, the first such exhibition in Russia. Inspired by its success, in the fall Reilly took a direct hand in organizing a spectacular All-Russian Air Festival at the Komandantskoe Airdrome, a role that secured his full membership in IVAK.[80] Aleksandr Mikhailovich opened the meet on 21 September which offered almost 50,000 rubles in prizes to the participating pilots, all of them Russian.[81] In May of the following year, Reilly himself was one of the flyers participating in the 2nd Petersburg Flying Week. The 22 May/5 June 1911 issue of the Petersburg weekly *Iskry* features the only known photograph of Reilly in this period. He is pictured among a "groups of aviators participating in aviation week," including Nikolai Raevskii, Vladimir Smith and Mikhail Vasil'ev, one of Russia's outstanding early pilots. Reilly stands out in the photo by virtue of his dark, lean features and for two other curious anomalies: he is the only one bare-headed and he sports a polka-dot bow tie, the latter regarded as a particularly British or American affectation. The same page carries a photo of the crash that took Smith's life soon after. Just a few weeks later, Reilly was in Moscow where, on 24 July, he helped fête Vasil'ev after his victory in the first Petersburg-to-Moscow air race. *Kryl'ia* helped sponsor the race and put up part of the prize money (Suvorin's money, we may assume), and Vasil'ev himself was part of *Kryl'ia's* stable of flyers.

In the spring of 1911, a new face took over at the Russian Naval Ministry, Admiral I.K. Grigorovich, another whom Reilly had met in Port Arthur. Grigorovich was willing to deal with Reilly but seems to have been reluctant to do so directly. The discreet link, therefore, ran through Grigorovich's personal adjutant, Lt. Petr Ivanovich Zalesskii. The latter possessed a beautiful, restless wife, Nadezhda (Nadia) Petrovna, or as she preferred it, Nadine, née Massino. A petite, blue-eyed brunette, Nadine was the daughter of an engineer, Petr (Pierre) Massino, who claimed Swiss ancestry but was of Jewish background. Her mother was from the Jewish Brodskii-Dreyfus family. To disguise or offset her origins, Nadine had outwardly embraced Russian orthodoxy. As she later told it, the first time she saw Sidney she "immediately decided to have him."[82] Reilly was more than willing to he had. Beyond the practical advantages to be gained by sleeping with the Naval Minister's adjutant's wife, he was smitten himself. In private communications, he referred to Nadine as *Kiska* or *Kissenka*—"Kitten"— and his jealousy in her regard gave every appearance of being the real thing. The fly in the ointment was Nadine's husband, Lt. Zalesskii. He was willing to part with his wife, but for a price, one that Reilly found too steep. That probably was not the only reason. Nadine wanted a divorce so she could marry Reilly, not merely be his mistress. As we know and Nadine did not, Reilly already had two wives, and he was not in the market for another.

It was in connection to naval contracts that Reilly continued to enjoy his greatest success. In 1911, the same year Blohm & Voss landed the Putilov project, Vickers won a contract to construct a new shipyard at

Nikolaev on the Black Sea, not far from Odessa. The following year Zaharoff became exclusive European agent for the American Electric Boat Co. With Reilly's help, EB soon secured a contract to build six new subs for the Russian Navy in Petersburg.[83] In 1913, Zaharoff initiated another grandiose scheme for a huge arsenal complex at the Volga town of Tsaritsyn, the future Stalingrad.

Trouble, however, was brewing. The Russian arms bazaar was a swamp of graft and corruption that could not forever evade public scrutiny. As Bruce Lockhart would later confess to the Foreign Office, "Vickers was especially implicated" in bribery and similar practices.[84] In the latter part of 1913, questions arose in the Duma over the Naval Ministry's decision to grant contracts for construction of battleships in Russia as opposed to purchasing ships already nearing completion in (Vickers-controlled) British yards, a move that would save some 50 million rubles.[85] The basic reason was that certain Admiralty officials and a bevy of brokers, Reilly among them, stood to make a killing in kickbacks and commissions. In the end, protests to the Tsar achieved a compromise: two ships would be bought in England and the others built at home. To Zaharoff and his minions the whole issue was moot; Vickers interests profited either way and by the time the Russians actually purchased the English vessels their price had risen to erase the hoped-for savings.

In the first weeks of 1914, new scandal erupted over the Putilov Works. During January, a French newspaper, *l'Echo de Paris*, claimed that Putilov was about to be bought up by the German Krupp syndicate. This duly alarmed French investors who offered Putilov a flood of fresh capital to save it from the Germans. The French stories proved to be false and the paper a tool of Zaharoff. What was afoot was a stock-manipulation scheme designed to first depress Putilov shares and then reap huge gains for those insiders who scooped up the rebounding Putilov stock.[86]

Putilov was one of the largest enterprises in Russia and a vital component in the Empire's armaments industry. It was the personal domain of its founder, Aleksandr Putilov, known as the "Russian Carnegie" and the "Horseman of the Apocalypse" of the last years of Imperial Russia. He also was known as a man with a "total absence of moral scruples" and strong pro-German sympathies.[87] Along with his arms and shipbuilding enterprises, he had his fingers firmly planted in the railway (including the Chinese Eastern), oil and electrical power industries.[88] He also was the dominant force in the powerful Russo-Asiatic Bank which, in turn, was a major stockholder and creditor of the Putilov industries.[89] Finally, Reilly knew Putilov through their common membership in IVAK and, of course, freemasonry.

Public outrage over the Putilov skullduggery stimulated calls for a thorough investigation of the whole rotten business of military contracts. For Reilly it was a good time to lie low. In 1911, he had taken fashionable new digs at #22 Novo-Isaakievskaia, but these he suddenly abandoned and took to sleeping on Grammatikov's couch.[90] At the same time, "Sidnei G. Raille" vanished from Ves' Peterburg. Curiously, a "Solomon Gerasimovich Rozenblium" appeared. This "engineer" did business out of an address linked to Reilly's past and future partner Robert San Galli. All just one more coincidence, perhaps.

In spring of 1914, with Nadine in tow, he set out for the French Riviera where Zaharoff also happened to be encamped. Taking a pension near Cannes, Nadine indulged herself in the sun and sea while Sidney kept his ear to the ground. Nadine, anticipating her divorce, was determined that she and Reilly marry as soon as it came through. He still hoped to dodge that bullet and still complained of poor finances. But he sensed better times coming. War clouds were gathering in Europe, a war bound to engulf Russia. From Reilly's perspective the looming conflict meant riches and as yet unimagined opportunities.

Sidney was forty years old. At an age when most men begin to reflect on their lives and accomplishments, he looked steadily ahead. Almost twenty years' experience as a spy had honed him into an efficient and formidable broker in information and a schemer and businessman of no mean class. On 28 June, a teenage assassin shot to death Archduke Franz Ferdinand, heir apparent to the Habsburg throne, in the Bosnian town of Sarajevo. Barely a month and several ultimatums later, Europe was at war. In early July, just as the crisis started to heat up, Reilly received the cable from Abram Zhivotovskii summoning him back to Petersburg. There were big plans in the works.

NOTES

1. Berberova, Zheleznaia, 68; Ves' Peterburg, 1914, 754. According to Berberova, in 1911 E.P. Shuberskii replaced Count Lubenskii as Mendrokhovich's partner.
2. Russko-Frantsuzskii Kommercherskii Bank; Ves' Peterburg, 1917, 352, 360, 778; Henri, 56.
3. HIA, Vrangel, Report, 7.
4. Bukhanov, 260, Ves' Peterburg, 1913, 722.
5. PRO, FO 371/11793, Margaret Reilly to FO, 26 Feb. 1926.
6. Rossiiskoe Obshchestvo Zastrakhovaniia Kapitala i Dokhodov.
7. Bokhanov, 220.
8. Vladislav Minaev, Podryvnaia deiatel'nost' inostrannykh razvedok v SSSR, I, (Moscow, 1940), 44.
9. Ves' Peterburg, 1908, 140, 181.

10. *Paribas = Banque de Paris et de Pays Bas.*

11. V.I. Bovykin and B. Anan'ich, "The Role of International Factors in the Banking System in Russia," in Cameron and Bovykin, 153.

12. Allfrey, 268–269.

13. The Octobrists were, in effect, the right wing of the Kadets that split off in 1906 over the matter of the Fundamental Laws. While mainstream Kadets under P.N. Miliukov (M) repudiated the semi-constitution as inadequate, Guchkov and his followers embraced it, publicly at least.

14. PTsR, VII, 375, and Deacon, RSS, 123. One of these missions involved contact with the exiled revolutionary icon (and police agent), Father Gapon, the architect of Bloody Sunday. Manasevich's presumed task was to offer Gapon financial incentive and perhaps safe return to Russia in exchange for the latter's repudiation of radicalism. Gapon was murdered in Finland in 1906 by vengeful revolutionaries—or perhaps by other police operatives.

15. The Suvorin's flagship paper, *Novoe Vremia* ("New Times") was edited by Aleksei and later by Boris's older brother, Mikhail.

16. SIS, "Russian Secret Service Report," and HIA, Ibid.

17. PTsR, VII, 404.

18. Krymov, 69.

19. Ibid.

20. Rene Fulopp-Miller, *Rasputin, The Holy Devil* (Garden City, NY, 1928), 108.

21. Ibid, and Salisbury, *Black Night, White Snow: Russia's Revolutions, 1905–1917* (New York, 1977), 279–280.

22. Fulopp-Miller, 108.

23. Winfried Ludecke, *The Secrets of Espionage: Tales of the Secret Service* (Philadelphia, 1929), 106.

24. Aron Simanovich, *Vospominaniia lichnogo sekretariia Grigoriia Rasputina* (Tashkent, 1990), 19, 37.

25. HIA, Smith, "Veselago," 34.

26. HIA, B.N. Nicolaevsky Coll., #300-6, "Konets Sidneia Dzh. Reilli," 1.

27. Andrei Belyi [Nikolai Bugaev], *Moskva* (Moscow, 1989), 65–67, *passim*, and *Berberova, Zheleznaia*, 68. Berberova argues that Belyi almost certainly adopted the name "von Mandro" from Mendrokhovich/Mandrokhovich, Reilly's erstwhile partner.

28. For further information on Krasin see: Tim O'Connor, *The Engineer of Revolution: L.B. Krasin and the Bolsheviks, 1870–1926* (Boulder, CO, 1994), and the rather uncritical but useful work by his widow, Liubov Krasin, *Leonid Krassin: His Life and Work* (London, 1930.

29. *Ves' Peterburg*, 1906, 341.

30. O'Connor, 86 and Spence, *Savinkov*, 58.

31. Michael Futtrell, *Northern Underground*, 56–65, 166–170; Misha Glenny, "Krasin," 217–21.

32. V. Orlov, *Morder, Falscher, Provokateure: Lebens kampfe im unterirdschen Russland* [English title: *Underworld and Soviet*] (Berlin, 1929), 170 and PRO, KV 2/673, "Krassin."

33. International Instituut voor Sociale Geschiedenis (IISG), Amsterdam, Savinkov Archive (SA), box 37, file *Raznoe* #2, "Donees sur le Commissaire bolcheviste Krassine."

34. R.C. Elwood, "Lenin and Grammatikov: An Unpublished and Undeserved Testimonial," Canadian Slavonic Papers, vol. XXVII, #3 (Sept. 1986), 3–4, 309.

35. HIA, Paris Okhrana, XIIIc/1, folder 1B, #219 from Vissarionov, 12 March 1908; Elwood, 309.

36. Popplewell, 104. *Anusilam Samiti* = "Improvement Society."

37. Popplewell, 107–108.

38. HIA, Okhrana, IIIf, folder 28.
39. Bokhanov, 90. Brandes was connected to the Volga-Kama Bank (*Volzhsko-Kamskii Kommercheskii Bank*).
40. PTsR, VII, 379, Agafonov, 341–342.
41. Shchegolev, 203–205: PTsR, VII, 375.
42. Ted Gardner, *Lotusland* (Santa Barbara, CA, 1996), 108–109.
43. Brady Brower to author, 12 Feb. 2001, based on information from Delarue-Mardus.
44. Kaledin, 228.
45. Ibid., note #1.
46. Kaledin gives her the married name of "Rogerski" and the title of countess. The former is certainly a corruption, accidental or intentional, of Raevskii, and Natta did style herself a countess, though not, apparently, until the 1920s in New York and Paris.
47. PRO, FO 371/11793, Margaret to FO, 25 Feb. 1926.
48. PRO, FO 372/2756, 7096, 4 June 1931.
49. Ibid. and Messenger, 31
50. Lockhart, *Ace*, 66.
51. And dangerous it was. Between 1908 and mid-1911 no less than 47 pilots died in recorded accidents out of only a few hundred active aviators.
52. *Imperialcheskii Vserossiiskii Aero-Klub*.
53. E.g., *Vozdukhoplavitel'*, #5 (May 1907), #11 (Nov. 1907), #5 (May 1908), etc.
54. Chavchavadze, 194–195.
55. Fred T. Jane, *The Russian Imperial Navy* (London, 1904), 450.
56. Ibid., 195.
57. *NYT*, "Aide to Last Czar Dies" (22 April 1951), 88.
58. Deacon, RSS, 177.
59. *Vozdukhoplavitel'*, #7 (July 1910).
60. Krymov, 70.
61. Ibid.
62. *NYT*, "Hitch in Airship Deal" (11 Dec. 1908), 5.
63. Berg to J.E. Stevens, 10 April 1917. Thanks to T.W. Warner for help with this piece of information.
64. Boris Savinkov, *Memoirs of a Terrorist*, trans., Joseph Shaplen (New York, 1931), 299; Nicolaevsky, 264–266.
65. Spence, *Savinkov*, 70–71.
66. MID, 9140-6073, Memorandum #5, 6 Sept. 1918, 3.
67. *LT* (29 July 1909), 8b.
68. Savinkov, MOT, 286.
69. Lockhart, *Ace of Spies*, 55–57.
70. *LT*, "Aeroplane Accident in Russia" (29 May 1911), 9.
71. On Cumming and the SIS, see Judd and Andrew. Also useful is Nicholas Hiley, "The Failure of British Counter-Espionage against Germany, 1907–1914," *Historical Journal*, vol. 28, #4 (1985), 835–862.
72. DS, CSA 215, Sharpe to Bannerman, 13 Dec. 1924, 2–3, also quoting Bannerman to Sharpe, 9 Dec. 1922.
73. *NYT*, "Curtiss Factory in Russia" (30 Sept. 1913), 5.
74. *Ves' Peterburg*, 1910.
75. Pepita Reilly, "Britain's Master Spy Speaks," *Evening Standard* (11 May 1931).
76. Krymov, 70. In *Ace of Spies*, 60, Lockhart repeats a muddled version of this tale: Hofman is turned into a cashier for RVAPO who poisons himself after gambling away the firm's money.
77. France, Archives Nationales (AN), Collection des dossiers d'affaires politiques constituee à la Sûreté Nationale, F7/13981, Statement of former Princess Zizianov, 23 Jan. 1933; Bukhanov, 255.

78. AN, F7/13981, Ibid.; PTsR, VII, 383.
79. *NYT*, "Russia to Buy Aeroplanes" (27 Feb. 1910), III, 4; Thomas Darcey, Alan Durkota, and Victor Kulikov, *The Imperial Russian Air Service: Famous Pilots & Aircraft of World War One* (Mountain View, CA, 1995), 2, where the Grand Duke is misidentified as "Mikhail Aleksandrovich."
80. The air show ran through early Oct. 1910.
81. *NYT*, "Russian Aviation Meet" (22 Sept. 1910), 7.
82. MID, 9140-6073, Operative #101 to Hunnewell, 6 Sept. 1918.
83. U.S. Submarine Force Library, Groton, CT, Rare Book Case, Notebook of Stephen A. Gardner, Jr., Electric Boat Co. representative, Nevskii Shipbuilding and Mechanical Works, 23 Nov. 1913. Thanks to G.L. Owen for this item. See also Allfrey, 238–239.
84. PRO, FO 371/3326, 57062, Lockhart to FO, 28 March 1918.
85. M.V. Rodzianko, *The Reign of Rasputin: An Empire's Collapse* (New York, c .1930), 98–101.
86. The Union of Democratic Control, *The Secret International: Armament Firms at Work* (London, 1932), 41. Most of the cited biographies of Zaharoff contain some mention of the Putilov affair, e.g., Allfrey, McCormick. See also: Mennevee, *Documents Politiques, Diplomatiques et Financiers* (Feb. 1928), 46–48 and Philip Noel-Baker, *The Private Manufacture of Arms* (London, 1936).
87. Michael J. Carley, "From Revolution to Dissolution: The Quai d'Orsay, the Banque Russo-Asiatique, and the Chinese Eastern Railway, 1917–1926," *International Historical Review*, vol. XII, #4 (Nov, 1990), 726.
88. Bokhanov, 208–209.
89. Bokhanov, 208–209, PTsR, VII, 401.
90. Krymov, 71.

Artur Artuzov

Crowther Smith cartoon from the
SIS collection

Basil Zaharoff

Leonid Krasin

Xenophon Kalamatiano, courtesy
of Harry Thayer Mahoney

Kurt Jahnke

Yakov Peters

Eduard Berzin

Eduard Opperput

Feliks Dzerzhinskii

Salomon Rosenblum, age 13

Genryk Yagoda

George Hill courtesy of the L.H.
Manderstam estate

Ivan Manasevi

Vladimir Styrne

Pepita Bobadilla Reilly. Curatorial Services

Newly minted Reilly c. 1900

Passport photo from 1918,
likely as Grigorii Berman

Reilly with Pepita

Reilly c. 1911

Sketch of Reilly c. 1935,
courtesy of G.L. Owen

Reilly about 1916

Reilly c. 1924

Reilly c. 1918

Reilly c. 1925

Reilly with Russian pilot pals, 1911

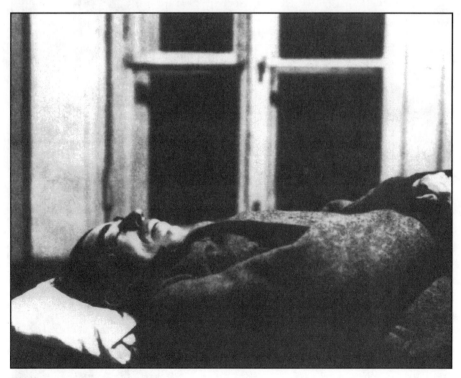

Reilly corpse

PART TWO

MASTER SPY

"The desire to rule is the mother of all heresies."
—St. John Chrysostom

Chapter Six

WAR ON THE MANHATTAN FRONT

Before leaving on the St. Petersburg-bound express, Reilly reassured Nadine that their separation would be brief. She awaited the finalizing of her Russian divorce, and fully expected Reilly to marry her when it came through. For the time being, he urged her to stay put in St. Raphael and promised to send for her the moment his course was clear. If she had not heard this line before, others certainly had. However, Nadine was not inclined to be as patient and malleable as Margaret.

Reilly's subsequent correspondence with Nadine and Margaret provides useful clues about his travels and intentions in the latter months of 1914. Nadine's first letter to her "fiancé" in Petrograd was dated 12 July. As American investigators later discovered, this and following missives made frequent mention of "an undertaking of Reilly's which she called 'The System'," and expressed her firm hope that said "System" would prove successful.[1] The Ace-of-Spies was back at his Torgovaia office by mid-July, well in advance of the actual outbreak of war. The apparent haste of Reilly and his colleagues probably stemmed from their knowledge that in the event of hostilities, the Russian Government planned to send special commissions abroad to purchase was materials. They intended to have their own agents in place to secure contracts before any official missions set up shop.

On 20 July Reilly addressed a letter to Margaret in Brussels, a city that in a matter of days would be in the direct path of the advancing German Army.[2] Perhaps he offered a heads-up to get out of Belgium before the Germans marched in. In any case, 1915 found her in Paris working as a nurse for the Red Cross. Oddly, by 1917 she was back in German-occupied Brussels, probably through her Red Cross connection. Still, one must wonder if there also was some intelligence dimension involved. For instance, Margaret later evidenced an odd familiarity with SIS officer Maj.

Claude E.M. Dansey.[3] During 1914–17, Dansey was connected with London's counterintelligence operations in France and Holland.[4] Dansey also just happened to be good friends with Reilly's American collaborator, Samuel MacRoberts. Moreover, during the early part of the war he worked with Robert Nathan who soon would meet Reilly in America.[5] Was Daisy herself a spy, and, if so, how much did her husband know about and set up that work?

In Petersburg (soon to acquire the more Russian-sounding name Petrograd), Sidney met Abram Zhivotovskii who was front man for a group of financiers and speculators connected to the Russo-Asiatic Bank. They were counting on war and intended to make a killing on it. Zhivotovskii enlisted Reilly as an agent and instructed him to proceed at once to Tokyo and place orders for munitions, weapons and other supplies that Russia would require in the impending conflict. To secure these deals, Zhivotovskii arranged that 20 million rubles (more than $100 million today) would be deposited in the RAB's Shanghai branch. As personal incentive, he guaranteed Reilly a lucrative commission on every contract obtained. Nor were Zhivotovskii and friends the only ones interested in Reilly's mission. On 26 July, Gen. Erdeli, acting on behalf of the Imperial Chief-of-Staff, issued a certificate commanding all Tsarist officials to facilitate the "expeditious and unhindered passage of the frontiers" by Mr. Sidney Reilly and his secretary, I.T. Giratovsky (Zhivotovskii).[6] The latter was one of Abram's nephews, perhaps along to look out for uncle's interests. They were going abroad, Erdeli noted, at the personal request of the chief of the Artillery Department to purchase arms and materiel "for the needs of the Army."

Reilly was not the only agent Zhivotovskii engaged. Another was Sidney's lawyer friend Aleksandr Weinstein who would handle purchasing in London. Initially another agent, the aforementioned Polish engineer, Antony Jechalski, was to take up the New York end. The financiers behind this effort deserve a closer look. At the head of the consortium was industrial kingpin Aleksei Putilov, owner of the huge armaments works bearing his name, and managing director of the Russo-Asiatic. The RAB was one of Russia's largest banks but arguably its most speculative.[7] By 1914, a wave of acquisitions and investments, most notably the Chinese Eastern Railway in Manchuria, left the Bank overextended and short of cash. Putilov, furthermore, had to answer to the RAB's other directors, several of whom were French, representatives of the Paris banks that controlled roughly half of the RAB's shares. In effect, this made direct use of RAB funds subject to all sorts of cumbersome approval and unwelcome scrutiny. The most likely scenario is that Putilov put up his own money, including whatever he could conveniently divert from RAB coffers, and channeled it through Zhivotovskii's office. He then recruited other speculative businessmen to participate in the venture. Among these were Aleksandr Guchkov and, very likely, Basil Zaharoff, who held a substantial share in Putilov and most of the other Russian firms involved.[8] Indeed, it is entirely possible that the Greek, not Putilov, was the mastermind of the entire operation.

If the gamble on war proved correct, the efforts of the above syndicate could be of great benefit to Russia's military effort. Of course, its participants also stood to make a great deal of money. Putilov and his ilk's willingness to engage in financial games at the expense of national interest, or at least the Tsar's treasury, is attested to by the former president of the Imperial Duma, Mikhail Rodzianko. He recollected that during the war Putilov, as manager of the RAB, refused to grant further credits to his own munitions and armaments works. He then demanded that the state come up with the needed "subsidy" of 36 million rubles and warned that the works might shut down if it did not.[9] To many such as Rodzianko this seemed nothing less than a naked shakedown, but their efforts to persuade Nicholas to retaliate by commandeering the factories proved futile. Rodzianko blamed the baleful influence of Rasputin, but there may have been other factors at work.

What the likes of Putilov, Zaharoff and Reilly were in the position to know better than most was that while Russian industry had made immense strides in recent years, its productive capacity remained very limited when compared to Britain and France, or most critically, Germany. Simply put, Russia's under-powered industrial plant was inadequate to supply the necessities of a huge army in an extended war of materiel. For example, just prior to the war, Russia produced roughly 60,000 tons of munitions and small arms per annum, compared to half that amount by Britain, 70,000 for France and 100,000 for Germany. The United States, by comparison, manufactured a mere 20,000 tons. These peacetime figures, however, were a poor guide to wartime potential. Two years into the fighting, Russia's output increased to some 400,000 tons, yet in the same period Britain's and France's output each climbed to around 800,000 and Germany's to over 1,000,000.[10] What this meant was that while Russia had by far the largest army in the field, as many soldiers as Britain and France combined, it could supply its troops with barely a quarter of the munitions and basic weaponry. During 1915 this resulted in a critical shortage of artillery shells and hundreds of thousands of troops being sent to the front—and into combat—without rifles. That, in turn, contributed to a string of staggering defeats and huge losses. In the same year, for instance, the outgunned

Russian Army lost nearly 3,000,000 men and retreated 300 miles, abandoning all of Poland, including Reilly's home turf, to the Germanic invaders.

Foreign purchasing, therefore, was an absolute necessity, and the American market proved by far the most important source of arms and munitions as well as motor vehicles, locomotives and even ships. By 1916, neutral America's production of basic warstuffs had mushroomed to an astounding 2,700,000 tons, almost all of it going to feed the guns of the Anglo-French armies on the Western Front, and Russia's. From 1914 through early 1917, U.S. sources supplied over a third of Russia's war materiel. The amount of money expended in these transactions was enormous, as were the profits, along with incentives and opportunities for corruption. In real terms, Russian officers and officials assigned to the American missions earned ten times as much money as they would have drawn at home, a factor that only served to further fuel greed and graft.[11] The tangible benefits of this effort, however, were far out of proportion to the costs. On average, American-made war supplies cost Russia more than three times as much per ton as those manufactured domestically. Much of the added expense, of course, was due to the great distances the goods had to travel, but a significant share stemmed from price-gouging, corruption and outright fraud.

This was the feeding frenzy into which our experienced shark Reilly was poised to plunge. In every deal he made or in which he could insinuate himself, he would extract at least one commission and, in some cases, several. For example, in addition to the up-front commission from Zhivotovskii for obtaining a contract, Reilly would extract a separate commission or consulting fee, anywhere from 1–10% of the purchase price, from the American firm making the deal. Similar arrangements were made with any subcontractors, and there usually were several. An examination of some of Reilly's contracts showed his commissions on artillery shells and rifles averaged $.25–.50 per piece while items like trucks and railway cars brought anywhere from $10 to $20, and the likes of airplanes and locomotives fetched $100–500.[12] For brokering the Russian Government's acquisition of the steamship SS *Nevada*, he collected a cool $20,000.[13] These sums must be multiplied by the sheer volume of Russia's war buying—some 2,500,000 rifles, over 11,000,000 artillery shells, 60,000 motor vehicles, at least 500 aircraft and nearly 800 locomotives, plus ships, submarines and hundreds of millions of bullets, tons of explosives and sundry material—to appreciate the bounty at hand. While Reilly was able to get his hands on only a fraction of this loot, it was enough to make him a very wealthy man. To these would be added special consulting fees, bribes, kickbacks, and under-the-table payments for all manner of services. It was the System in Paradise.

In the meantime, the European powers accelerated their rush to war. Emboldened by Berlin's guarantee of support in the event of Russian intervention, Austria-Hungary pressed a draconian list of demands on Serbia. When the latter demurred on one of the demands, on 28 July Vienna declared a state of war to exist between the two states. A wave of pro-Serbian sentiment in Russia compelled Nicholas to take action. On 30 July, the Russian Army commenced mobilization on both the Austrian and German frontiers, an action that set alarm bells ringing in Berlin. Kaiser Wilhelm was forced to yield to the insistence of his own general staff that if the Russians did not at once cease mobilization, it would be treated as an act of war. St. Petersburg could not—or would not—comply with this ultimatum and so, on 1 August, Russia was at war with Germany and Austria-Hungary. Within days, France and Britain joined the fray. It has been said that had the men who led Europe to war in 1914 understood the costs the coming struggle would exact and the forces it would unleash, they would have at once accepted peace on the enemy's terms. In any case, the world would never be the same again.

Reilly wasted no time once the course of events was clear. In early August, he and young Zhivotovskii set out for Vladivostok via Moscow and the Trans-Siberian. By luck or, more probably, careful planning, he ended up on the same train as Captain Dmitrii S. Vasil'ev, the Tsar's naval attaché to Washington who was rushing back to his American post by way of Tokyo. Sidney's connections in Russia's naval hierarchy provided a ready-made common denominator. Whatever his arrangement with Zhivotovskii, he seems to have had his sights already set on America, where Vasil'ev would prove a useful man to know, especially as he would play an influential role in approving naval wear contracts.

The two travelers reached Port Arthur at the end of August and pressed on to Tokyo. In the meantime, Japan had become Russia's ally in the war against Germany. Playing the part of a Russianized Briton, Reilly took a room at Tokyo's English Club and set about arranging contracts. He negotiated munitions orders with the Obashi Powder Co. and Nippon Celluloid and Artificial Silk Co. Most importantly, as an American report later put it, he "made valuable connections . . . that made him a great deal of money later on."[14] Among these was another British subject, W.H. Gill, who operated a brokerage office in Tokyo. Gill worked with Uchida & Co., a firm with which Reilly would have connection in New York. Uchida also may have had links to Japanese intelligence. Reilly renewed or cultivated the acquaintance of two local figures, speculator and labor contractor Tadao Kamiya and an associated Japanese engineer-businessman, Taka Kawada, both of whom later would visit Sidney in Manhattan.[15]

Vasil'ev soon continued to America, but Reilly stayed on in Tokyo as his assignment dictated. Later rumors in New York suggested that Sidney had made a brief visit there in the fall of 1914. That was not impossible, but the available evidence argues that he remained in the Far East through the end of the year. In the interim, he had kept in regular contact with "Kiska" (Nadine) whose letters followed him from Tokyo. She was anxious to join him in America, and he may have delayed his arrival there as a means of discouraging those intentions.

Over the next few months, Reilly played temporary host to General Aleksei Vasil'evich Sapozhnikov (M) and Capt. Artur Yakovlevich Zadde, Russian artillery officers also on their way to America. Thanks to his past dealings with the Tsar's military, he was "very close" to Zadde and at least acquainted with Sapozhnikov. The latter, most importantly, was headed to New York to supervise Russian munitions buying. Soon he would head Petrograd's official purchasing commission.[16] Through such men, Sidney would be able to exercise a powerful influence in that agency.

Reilly paid a brief visit to Vladivostok where he touched bases with A. Zhivotovskii who had arrived there to manage the local Russo-Asiatic branch. Against some resistance, Sidney persuaded Zhivotovskii to sanction his transfer to New York where the lifeblood of the System flowed in much greater quantity. He also jettisoned the nephew as unneeded baggage. Sidney also may have made a side trip to Shanghai. There he would have conferred with another RAB agent, Count Ladislas Jezierski. But the real reason probably was a meeting of a more clandestine sort. During November, Admiral Paul von Hintze arrived there as representative of the Imperial German Government. The Admiral, recall, had a history of diplomatic and intelligence work in Russia. He had come to China from a rent post in Mexico. Hintze was still very much involved in intelligence, or at least in the more secretive aspects of diplomacy. In Mexico, he had spearheaded German efforts to restore the recently deposed dictator, General Victoriano Huerta.[17] That involved the secret purchase and smuggling of arms from the U.S., a ticklish business given the Wilson Administration's animus towards Huerta. On the other hand, it gave Hintze intimate knowledge of German agents and organization inside the United States.

As a naval man, Hintze appreciated that geography and superior British sea power would deny Germany the means to share in America's

productive bounty. The only recourse was to divert Yankee war goods elsewhere and obstruct Allied purchases through any and all means. From
Shanghai, he hoped to lure Japan, despite its adherence to the Allied camp,
into an anti-American bloc with a Berlin-friendly Mexican regime. That,
hopefully, would force the Americans to look to their own needs first.
Thus, he was on the lookout for agents to carry on his Mexican and
American work. Reilly, a known quantity with no visible ties to German
interests, was an ideal candidate. Through his service in Russia, Hintze
appreciated the prevalence of corruption among the Tsar's servants.
Reilly's involvement in Russian war purchasing and his influence in official
circles put him in an ideal position to recruit collaborators and collect vital
information once in New York. For instance, using Russian channels,
Reilly could disguise transactions in Mexico-bound arms or even surreptitious trade with Germany. By the time he reached American shores, he had
signed on as the Kaiser's agent. What Hintze did not appreciate is that
while Reilly was offering to betray Russian confidences to Germany, he
was at the same moment planning how to trade German ones back to the
Russians—and to the British.

After finalizing the deal with Nippon Celluloid on 26 December, Reilly
set sail on the SS *Persia* bound for San Francisco, where he landed on 13
January 1915. In the information he gave to U.S. immigration, he described
himself as a merchant, Irish, a British subject and resident of Petrograd,
Russia. As for nearest friend of family there, he listed A.L. Zhivotovskii.
His birthplace he gave as Clonmel, Ireland, as he would on every other
entry into the U.S. as Sidney George Reilly. He declared this to be his first
visit to America that, as Reilly, it was.

It probably was in San Francisco that he first encountered the German
agent Kurt Albert Jahnke. A tall, dark, pockmarked Prussian, Jahnke had a
vague past that included service in the International Customs Service in
China, the German Navy or Merchant Marine, the U.S. Marine Corps and
the U.S. Border Patrol.[18] Like Reilly, Jahnke had a penchant for aliases and
playing all sides. Years later he would proclaim "the full value of a secret
service always depended on the number and standard of double agents."[19]
There is a possibility that he and Sidney crossed paths before in the Far
East. Most recently, Jahnke had followed the profession of a private detective for the Pinkerton and like agencies. On the side, he operated a private
smuggling business that handled the transport of Chinese corpses, opium
and guns. He had played an important part in Hintze's Mexican gun-run-
ning. With the outbreak of the war, Jahnke returned to the fold as an agent
of the Kaiser's "Central Office for secret military operations" based in San

Francisco.[20] Specifically, he was the resident point man for the German Admiralty's special section for intelligence and sabotage (*fur N. und S. Angelegenheiten*) and as such came under Hintze's orders. From China, the latter doubtless instructed Jahnke to cooperate with Reilly. In short order, the duo collaborated in the ostensible service of Germany, but Reilly also wasted no time in recruiting Jahnke as a double agent in Britain's service or, perhaps more accurately, in his own.

Sidney reached New York in late January. There he at once set up shop in the 115 Broadway office of Zhivotovskii's resident representative, B.M. Koppelman whom he promptly shunted aside. Reilly also made immediate connection with his old Petersburg collaborator, and longtime German agent, Karl Orbanowski. Orbanowski managed of the American Steel Export Corp. at 140 Broadway and soon became one of Reilly's Stateside business partners. More importantly, he gave Reilly entrée into the German secret apparatus in New York, opening doorways that led straight to the German Embassy in Washington. For instance, Orbanowski was a "particular friend" of another German, Adolf Pavenstedt who managed a firm called Amsinck & Co. Most importantly, he was a personal friend of German ambassador Count Johann von Bernstorff and the Kaiser's military attaché, Franz von Papen.[21] Of more immediate interest to Reilly, Pavenstedt had a hand in "Mexican revolutionary matters."[22] Yet another member of the Orbanowski-Pavenstedt crowd was August Cronemeyer, a local official of the Hamburg-Amerika Line and a key figure in handling clandestine German-American commerce in defiance of the British blockade. Reilly's Russian connections and trading fronts would come in very handy in that regard.

Through Orbanowski Reilly renewed acquaintance with Vladimir Rogovin, a "special agent" for the Russian Navy in 1904. Now he ran American Steel Foundries Co. (closely linked to American Steel Exports) and was an intimate of Orbanowski and various Germanophile Russians.[23] Moreover, Rogovin had commercial links to both the Berlin-controlled Hamburg-Amerika Line and the Japanese Uchida & Co. He sponsored Reilly for membership in the New York Club, a notorious meeting place for German agents and sympathizers.[24] A contact of similar ilk was Markus Friede, former Russian agent for Ford Motor Co. and International Taxi. In New York, he exported motor vehicles and rolling stock to Russia and was U.S. freight and purchasing agent for the RAB-owned Chinese Eastern Railway, destined to be a vital link in Russia's overseas supply network.

Several of the threads linking Reilly to the German nexus also led to the Russian official bodies in New York. The acting Tsarist Consul, Mikhail

Mikhailovich Ustinov, was a close friend of Rogovin and a fellow member of the New York Club.[25] Reilly was to enjoy an especially chummy relationship with Ustinov's secretary, Petr Rutskii. The local vice consul, Baron O.A. Korf, also had numerous German friends. So, too, did Dmitrii Florinskii, the Consulate's military attaché. At the Washington Embassy, Reilly not only counted naval attaché Vasil'ev as a useful collaborator, but also his military counterpart, Col. Nikolai Lavrentievich Goleevskii (M). From the standpoint of later American investigators, is seemed impossible to tell where German interests left off and Russian ones began, and Reilly's obvious link to this dubious crowd was to be one of the chief marks against him. However, the situation was not as simple as it seemed. The Consul's brother, for instance, Col. A.M. Ustinov, was a counterintelligence officer engaged in a dogged struggle against German agents on the home front. That Reilly maintained relations with both brothers is a hint that the System was at work in this realm as well.

During the fall of 1914 two other men arrived in New York, both of whom had connection to British intelligence and, one way or another, to Reilly. The first was Britain's naval attaché to Washington, Capt. (later Admiral) Sir Guy Gaunt. In October, he established an office at lower Manhattan's 44 Whitehall St. to monitor German war-purchasing and, more importantly, to sniff out schemes by the Kaiser's agents to obstruct Allied efforts. The garrulous, Australian-born Gaunt enjoyed playing secret agent almost as much as he loved basking in the social limelight. This was not an ideal combination, and his tendency to talk freely about his intelligence duties soon made them a very open secret among friends and foes alike. Gaunt reported to the Admiralty's Director of Naval Intelligence (DNI), Admiral Reginald "Blinker" Hall, and also communicated on a fairly regular basis with Sir Vernon Kell's MI5. He did not, however, have any connection to Cumming's Secret Intelligence Service.

Gaunt was a bit of a snob, and his prejudices included contempt for Russians and Jews. Most of the former he regarded as grafters or worse.[26] Perhaps that helped him forge a close bond with the men at 23 Wall Street; in any case, he followed the Morganites' lead on every question of mutual interest. All this made him naturally suspicious of Reilly; indeed, where he was concerned Gaunt evidenced nothing but suspicion and hostility. The Captain probably knew something of Sidney's past from his stint as an observer with the North China station during the Russo-Japanese War. Specifically, he seemed very well informed about the Ace-of-Spies' activities during that conflict, particularly his role as a Japanese spy. Gaunt's subsequent memoir, though it avoids any mention of Reilly by name, does include a very unflattering portrait of "a man in New York who professed to know all about German intrigues."[27] Sir Guy did his best to ignore this "nuisance" until, so he claimed, no less than Foreign Secretary Earl Grey ordered a meeting. Gaunt described the man as an avid "collector of bric-a-brac, genuine or otherwise," with an apartment in a fashionable Manhattan hotel full of "china, furniture, pictures and antiques." It was a reasonable if unflattering portrait of Reilly and his artwork-filled suite at the Gotham. Gaunt recorded that the intriguer even claimed to be an illegitimate son of the Kaiser, which if not Gaunt's own embellishment certainly has the ring of a Reillyesque fiction. Perhaps the tale was designed to test Gaunt's basic gullibility. Gaunt claimed he had nothing more to do with the fellow, but he was not the only British operative in town.

Another "British agent" to appear on the scene was the wandering occultist and self-proclaimed "Great Beast 666," Aleister Crowley (M). As noted, he and Reilly had their first strange brush in 1890s London. Crowley had visited Russia in 1911 and again in mid-1913, on the last occasion as impresario for a roving troupe of British showgirls, something certain to have caught Sidney's notice. Appropriately, on Halloween 1914, Crowley arrived in New York aboard the ill-fated liner *Lusitania* with what he later claimed was a vague mission to infiltrate German and Irish circles.[28] Before long Crowley, a writer of no small talent, inveigled his way onto the staff of *The Fatherland*, a stridently pro-German magazine run by George Viereck. For this and other publications, he soon produced a steady stream of anti-British vitriol which included a rather over-heated defense of German submarine warfare.[29] In retrospect, these effusions seem a mockery of pro-German propaganda, which is precisely what Crowley later insisted they were. Similarly, his bizarre antics as a *faux* Irish patriot could only have been designed to bring discredit on that quarter. Gaunt regarded Crowley as a "small-time traitor" and rejected his overtures of cooperation, much as he did Reilly's.[30] However, the Beast's activities *did* have the blessing of certain British officials in London and New York, the same ones that would embrace another apparent blackguard and German operative— Sidney Reilly.

In 1918, the British Consulate in New York, Sir Charles Clive Bayley, quietly assured American authorities that Crowley was on the "official business" of His Majesty and his activities had their "full cognizance."[31] Interestingly, Bayley had previously been London's representative in Moscow. That Reilly used the British Consulate as a point of contact is suggested by an early 1915 note from Bayley's predecessor, Courtney Bennett. In April, he informed the Foreign Office that he was receiving important details concerning German activities, including sabotage plans, from an agent with sources inside the German ring.[32] As early as January, Bennett relayed intelligence on "German-Mexican" arms plots that included a plan to sabotage the Remington-Union ammunition plant in Bridgeport, Connecticut, a firm with which Reilly was dealing at the time.[33] Bennett did not name the agent and cautioned against any public mention of the data provided lest the agent be compromised. Another clue that points at Reilly, is that said agent was somehow connected to the Russian mission in New York.

As noted, Sidney knew many officers assigned to the growing Russian military mission in the U.S, but his acquaintance ranged into other quarters. This included the manager of the Russian Volunteer Fleet office in New York operation in New York, Ivan Shestakovskii, like Reilly a former employee of the Russian East Asiatic Steamship Co. Shestakovskii, however, was hostile towards Reilly's new ally Friede and denied him use of VF ships to move his goods. This created difficulties when Fride and Reilly were soon involved in a $10,000,000 contract with the Seattle Car and Foundry Co. to supply rolling stock to the Chinese Eastern Railway. Friede, in fact, was the CER's agent in New York.[34] Fortunately, the man overseeing the Volunteer Fleet's Pacific operations was the newly-appointed Russian consul to the northwest U.S., Nikolai Bogoslavenskii. He was a friend of Zhivotovskii's and had passed through Vladivostok just about the time Reilly visited there. Shestakovskii soon found himself overruled and Friede's shipments flowed freely.

The CER contract may not have been the only thing to interest Reilly in Seattle. On 3 February, a huge explosion devastated a Du Pont powder factory near Tacoma. [35] Completely destroyed in the blast was a consignment of black powder awaiting transport to Vladivostok, part of a deal recently negotiated through the Russian Embassy. More recently, Du Pont had declined an almost identical contract from Reilly so, at he least, he would not have been disappointed to hear of the loss. Another who would have greeted the news approvingly was Hintze. Indeed, the architect of the explosion was none other than Kurt Jahnke.[36]

Back in Manhattan front, Reilly quit Koppelman's office and took one on the 27th floor of the nearby Equitable Building at 120 Broadway. He also welcomed the arrival of a useful ally from Russia. This was Isidor Martinovich (or Markovich) Kon, a friend of Ginsburg's connected to the Petrograd Commercial and Industrial Bank and the Anatol Berlin banking house, both closely affiliated with the RAB.[37] Kon had a reputation as a mathematical genius and was an expert in matters of foreign exchange. He and Reilly would become very close professionally and socially.

The 120 Broadway address is destined to loom large in our story. Situated in the heart of Manhattan's financial district, the Equitable housed a broad array of engineering, technical and import-export firms along with the posh Bankers Club, to which Sidney gained admittance, and the New York Federal Reserve Bank. Among the many foreign companies located there was the above Uchida & Co. Behind a door simply labeled "Sidney G. Reilly," our man embarked on an aggressive campaign to utilize the funds put at his disposal by Zhivotovskii. He established personal accounts at the Morgan-dominated Guaranty Trust Co. and at Empire Trust, a concern closely linked to Schiff's Kuhn & Loeb. However, the bulk he deposited in the vaults of the National City Bank and made the valuable friendship of the bank's vice president, Samuel MacRoberts (M). The latter also was a trustee of the *Rossiia* (Russian) Insurance Co., a firm in which Reilly's pal Guchkov was the leading director.[38] It was MacRoberts who helped the Ace-of-Spies bag his first big contract with the Remington Arms-Union Metallic Cartridge Co. (Remington-Union) for $1 million worth of small arms ammunition and related items. MacRoberts personally introduced Reilly to Remington-Union's head man, Samuel Pryor.[39]

Also connected to the above deal was the Charles R. Flint Arms Co. likewise headquartered at 120 Broadway. Flint had a long history of dealing with the Tsarist Government and during the Russo-Japanese War had handled Russian purchasing through credits provided by the Rothschilds. The firm's directors hoped to play a similar role in the present conflict, a hope Reilly exploited to his full advantage. Flint also had strong connections to the Mexican market that came in handy for Hintze's purposes. However, Flint dealt with at least two other Russian brokers, Michel (Mikhail) Gaurland and A.V. Perelstrauss. Both knew Reilly from Russia and neither had anything good to say about him. Gaurland later expounded on Reilly's German connections to American investigators while Perelstrauss, who had been in Port Arthur during 1904, was another decrying his past spying for Japan.[40] As Reilly's relations with Flint inevitably deteriorated, the firm's manager, Winfield Proskey, became one of his most vociferous critics on the American scene, condemning him and his cronies as "dangerous" sorts who would "do anything" for money.[41] Another Flint executive simply described Sidney as "every inch a crook."[42]

Initially, though, Flint, Gaurland and Perelstrauss showed no hesitation in doing business with Reilly. The main reason, perhaps, is that it was hard to avoid him. In April, Remington-Union handed him a bigger plum; a contract for 1,200,000 rifles that promised our dealmaker a hefty $300,000 payoff.[43] The contract engaged him "to assist in the performance of said contract and in particular in reaching an understanding with the Russian Government as the assurances required" and to "smooth over any disputes or questions that may arise."[44] Reilly even received a spot on the inspection board that would approve the finished product. The first obstacle he cleared up was the company's difficulty in obtaining the surety bond demanded by Petrograd. He handled this by marshaling the aid of Moisei Ginsburg, help for which the latter no doubt received his own special considerations. The most interesting and telling part of his contract with Remington was the stipulation that Sidney was to receive $.25 per rifle or $.25 per thousand rounds of ammunition on each and every contract the company made for the Russian market, "*whether Mr. Reilly has been instrumental in obtaining them or not.*"[45] As Pryor later described it, however much he and his partners were suspicious of Reilly and avoided taking him into their confidence, it was obvious that he exercised "tremendous influence" with Russian officials in the U.S. and Petrograd, and had connections that led "right into the Russian Court."[46] It was practically impossible to do business with the Russians without going through him. What Pryor and other Americans soon realized was that if Reilly had the power to facilitate a contract, he also had the means to obstruct it, something Pryor said resulted in "practically a hold-up" of his and other firms.[47] Despite such hard feelings, Pryor, as others, admitted that if the dubious Anglo-Russian was an unprincipled grafter, he also was "one of the most astute and clever businessmen" with whom he ever had dealings.[48]

Befitting the System, at the same time Reilly was arranging the purchase of guns from Remington and others, he was initiating a bold scheme to undercut them by setting up an American-style rifle manufacturing plant in Russia. Acting as Zhivotovskii's agent, he purchased the necessary machine tools and on 9 April signed a contract with Dickerson G. Becker, an American engineer, for the latter to act as consultant in the construction and operation of said plant.[49]

Not everything went Sidney's way. In late 1914, while he was occupied in Tokyo, Samuel Vauclain, vice president of the Philadelphia-based Baldwin Locomotive Co. ventured to Petrograd in quest of munitions and other contracts. Vauclain, a tough-as-nails businessman, was agent for Baldwin's newly-formed armaments subsidiary, the Eddystone Ammunition Co. In Petrograd, the canny Vauclain grasped at once that Reilly enjoyed "tremendous political backing" and that his connections ran directly to the office of Grand Duke Aleksandr Mikhailovich, a man with powerful influence on military purchases.[50] The Grand Duke showed the American a personal telegram from his old friend Reilly, interestingly sent via a "representative" in London, that announced a drastic price cut in a proposed deal. Vauclain responded by reducing his price even further and so walked away with the contract. He would soon discover that Reilly was anything but a gracious loser.

Potentially more serious than the setback administered by Vauclain were the efforts of the powerful J.P. Morgan & Co. to bring Allied war purchasing under its exclusive control. Morgan and his partners, shrewd and determined financiers such as Thomas Lamont and Edward Stettinius, were staunch Anglophiles who wanted to marshal America's resources for the exclusive benefit of the Entente. Naturally, they also hoped to reap ample profits. The Morganites at 23 Wall Street envisioned a "munitions trust" that would dispense with pesky independent contractors such as Reilly. They had sound reason to object to him and his ilk. Because of the contract with Remington noted above, Morgan found his firm obliged to pay Reilly at least $200,000 on subsequent deals. On 15 January 1915, Morgan partner Henry P. Davison negotiated a agreement in London by which his outfit became exclusive agent for British military purchasing; soon after the French made an identical pact. Most significantly for Reilly, Morgan's arrangement with the King's Treasury included a $12 million purchasing credit for Russia with the express proviso that Morgan approve all contractors and transactions.[51] J.P. and partners were already suspicious of the Russians, having dealt with them in some abortive loan negotiations in 1905. The fact that Reilly and most of the other Russian independents were Jews was another strike against them. If not a full-blown anti-Semite, Morgan definitely harbored prejudices in that regard.[52] As actual or suspected opponents of the Tsar, he saw Jews as inherent enemies of the Allies. He mistrusted Catholics, especially Irish Catholics, for the same reasons. Thus Reilly, a Russian Jew with an Irish name, was a type to be avoided at all costs.

The positive aspect of earning a place on Morgan's enemies list was that it automatically earned him allies or, at least, co-belligerents. Morgan's heavy-handed dominance of the American financial scene had generated resentment and resistance. Samuel MacRoberts and National City Bank had a long rivalry with 23 Wall Street and were intent on preserving their own links with Russia and, for that matter, with Germany.[53] MacRoberts was Reilly's conduit to a wide array of American contacts. They included the attorney Hoyt A. Moore, an expert on tax law and, most significantly, import-export regulations. Moore introduced Reilly to the firm of Hayes, Hirschfield & Wolf, who became his legal representatives in the U.S. for many years to come. Moore also recommended a former employee, Upton

Dale Thomas, to be Reilly's secretary/office manager at 120 Broadway. Another staunch anti-Morganite with whom Reilly came in contact was the so-called "Wolf of Wall Street," David Lamar, who, as we will see, had strong German connections of his own.

One more vital contact was John McGregor Grant (M), also situated at 120. Grant was connected to the W.R. Grace and American Express Cos. and was U.S. manager of the Swedish-Russo-Asiatic and 2nd Russian Insurance Cos. Both firms later earned a place on the British "Black List" as German fronts, but perhaps Grant's most interesting link was to the Swedish socialist-banker, Olaf Aschberg (M) and his Stockholm-based *Nya Banken*. The latter would play a pivotal role in any number of dubious transactions, most notably the clandestine transfer of German funds to Lenin's Bolsheviks.[54]

Two more dubious associates were Franklin Helm and James Slevin, "financial adventurers" with their fingers in all manner of shady affairs. Through, Helm, for instance, Reilly had access to Leon Canova, who handily headed the U.S. State Department's Mexican Division.[55] Helm also had links to the Secretary of the Treasury, William G. McAdoo, yet another figure whose name and affairs were to become entangled with Reilly's.[56] Slevin acted as Reilly's liaison to the Curtiss-Wright Aircraft Co., and through him Sidney secured exclusive rights to handle all of Curtiss Russian business, deals amounting to several million dollars.[57]

Meantime, what about Nadine? On 28 January she wired Sidney from Cannes that her divorce had come through. Naturally, she wanted to be reunited with her lover at once so they could be married. She also was very excited to see New York. There was a problem, however; in addition to all the disruptions caused by the war, she was short of cash to pay her passage and begged her intended to forward money. Reilly, as usual, had other priorities. In the familiar refrain, he explained that until his affairs and resources were in more definite shape, it was best for her to remain in France. In all likelihood, he had no intention of bringing her to America, perhaps because he was plotting to install Anne and children stateside. Yet another reason may have been the recent arrival in New York of Ganna Walska. Though no better singer, she was at the peak of her beauty and detached from her Russian husband. She would land her first American millionaire in short order, but Sidney may have seen a chance to renew their old liaison. But Kiska was not going to be put off easily.

On Valentine's Day, he received a wire from a Gotham-bound liner. It was from Nadine, who had somehow secured passage and was due to land the next day. She anticipated formalizing their bond through holy matrimony right away. Perhaps doubting her intended's commitment, she also tipped off New York police that a British subject, Mr. Sidney Reilly, was importing a woman not his wife into the U.S.A. for "immoral purposes." When Sidney met Nadine at the pier, he was confronted by plainclothes detectives who offered him a simple choice: marry the woman immediately or go to jail.[58]

One wonders if the predicament evoked memories of arrest by the Okhrana. In any event, there was no choice at all. On 16 February, he and Nadine were wed in a civil ceremony in the Manhattan registry office. Once again, it is interesting to note how he described his particulars on the requisite form. His parents had transmuted into the very British George Reilly and Pauline Alton. With continued disregard for the truth, he gave his birthplace as Ireland and the marriage as his first.[59] He also was obliged to divulge his personal residence, 260 Riverside Drive, a fashionable Westside apartment probably engaged at Nadine's insistence.

She however, was not yet satisfied and insisted on a formal Church wedding. Although of Jewish background, she took her conversion to Russian Orthodoxy seriously, or wished others to. This presented a serious difficulty in that Orthodox Lent had begun during which Church custom proscribed weddings. Never one to be thwarted by rules and regulations, Reilly immediately appealed to higher authority. As a result, the newly-arrived Orthodox Metropolitan in America, Platon, found himself ordered to grant a special dispensation for the nuptials to proceed.[60] If nothing else, it was another vivid example of the clout Reilly wielded in Russian circles. The ceremony took place at the St. Nicholas Russian Orthodox cathedral in Manhattan. Bearing witness were the consulate's secretary, Petr Rutskii, and S.S. Murkovskii, a special agent of the Russian War Ministry. Strangely, the official Church record of the union has disappeared, or, perhaps given the irregular circumstances, it was never kept at all.

In backing Sidney Reilly into a corner, Nadine could boast a coup few others, men or women, could equal. But it was something he was bound to resent and, in time, take revenge against. He later confided that once married, their relationship deteriorated quickly and he wasted no time in looking for a way out. As was his long-established custom, he diverted himself with a string of casual affairs, mostly showgirls and actresses picked up from the Broadway theaters. Among the women whose names became connected with his were two notable film actresses, Olive Thomas, the future "All American Girl," and Clara Kimball Young. She attracted Reilly's attention because of her role as a Russian revolutionary in the film *My Official Wife* that opened just about the time of his arrival in New

York.[61] Young subsequently became a regular member of the Reilly-Weinstein "rat pack."

Reilly may even have tried his hand at the movie game. By 1917, the Prudential Pictures Corporation included among its backers the Russian diplomat Florinskii and two women later earmarked as German operatives, Baroness Leonie von Seidlitz and ballet dancer Tamara Svirskaia. Another was the shadowy "Sol Blum" who may have served as representative of the firm's alleged ultimate backer, none other than Jacob Schiff.[62]

Nadine seems to have taken her husband's dalliances in stride, but towards the end of 1915, he initiated a relationship of more serious dimensions. Reilly indulged his spouse with his new wealth and accompanied her on her rounds of posh dress salons. At one such establishment, *Lucille's*, the 41-year-old Ace-of-Spies took an immediate and obvious shine to one of the models, a pretty 22-year-old, Beatrice Madeleine Tremaine. According to Tremaine's co-workers, his "infatuation" with her was obvious to all and left Nadine "very much humiliated," and frequently, they claimed, reduced to tears.[63] This ultimately cost the firm Mrs. Reilly's patronage and left a distinct bitterness towards young Beatrice; one of her ex-employers describing her as "a cold, calculating, clever woman with a baby stare and a diabolical mind."[64] Beatrice wanted to be a movie star, and Reilly was eager to help. He enrolled her in an expensive finishing school and provided a $200 a month "stipend." But the Ace-of-Spies aspired to be more than her sugar daddy. Two weeks after their meeting he proposed, declaring that Nadine already had accepted his offer of divorce. His current marriage, he explained, had been forced upon him, and that ever since Nadine had come to America (against his wishes), they "disagreed and were quarreling all the time."[65] Sidney even showed his new love a grand house on Riverside Drive that he said he would buy for her as soon as they were wed. The Tremaine affair raises an interesting question in regards to Reilly's womanizing. Was it all part of some calculated plan on his part, as in almost every other facet of his life, or is it evidence that in matters of sex, Sidney was inclined to be impulsive and even foolish?

In the forepart of 1915, three more men arrived in New York, each of whom was to have subsequent connection, one way or another, with the Ace-of-Spies. The first, who steamed in on 8 February, was another with who he shared several characteristics. This was Ignace Timothy Trebitsch-Lincoln, AKA I.T.T. Lincoln, a short, bespectacled man whose somewhat comical appearance belied a thoroughly devious, if not especially brilliant, mind. Like Reilly, Lincoln was the son of a Jewish (Hungarian) family who had transformed himself into a pseudo-Englishman.[66] He also styled himself an international spy and self-proclaimed genius. Lincoln's outstanding achievement was his improbable 1910 election to the British Parliament. Soon after he came under criminal indictment for defrauding a previous employer. With the outbreak of the war, Lincoln fled England for New York and, just as Crowley, engaged in writing anti-British propaganda for the American press. Whereas Crowley was unmolested in his apparently treasonous pursuits, Lincoln quickly faced the full force of His Majesty's justice. Britain's diplomatic representatives demanded his arrest and extradition. After arrest, escape and recapture in February 1916 he was hauled back to the Old Bailey by Scotland Yard and duly sentenced to three years penal servitude.

Lincoln's case is of interest because it shows that where real treason was involved, British power could react forcefully. Despite evidence of equal or greater perfidy on the part of Crowley and Reilly, no move was made against them and, quite the opposite, they received the active protection of British authorities. There is at least the possibility that Reilly himself had some part in bringing Lincoln to justice. The latter's initial capture stemmed from his dalliance with May Dougherty, a woman working at 120 Broadway. May was connected (perhaps by marriage) to the Dougherty Detective Bureau, a firm charged with the protection of Russian munitions ships and stores and, thus, one with which Reilly had some familiarity. Did Sidney's man Frank Dougherty also figure in somewhere? There is not enough to be sure of anything, but Reilly and Lincoln had enough points in common for the former to learn about the latter's activities. The tip that finally led to Lincoln's capture originated with a confidential source and was passed to the NYPD by Consul Bennett.

The second notable arrival was the Russian-born American businessman, Xenophon Kalamatiano. A slight, dark, serious fellow, he appeared on the scene in late March from Russia where for several years he had acted as an agent for various American firms, most importantly the J.I. Case farm implement company and the Ford Motor Co. The latter inevitably connected him to Reilly's crony Markus Friede. It seems no mere coincidence that Kalamatiano's main business contact in New York was Claude Nankivel, a motor vehicle broker ensconced at 120 Broadway and a partner of Friede. Finally, Kalamatiano came to the U.S. as representative of the Moscow Association of Trade and Industry, a body, it may be recalled, in which Reilly's longtime associate Putilov was involved.[67] The essential point is that Kalamatiano and Reilly worked with and for some of the same people well before their fateful collaboration in Russia in 1918.

The third man arrived aboard the Norwegian liner *Kristianiafjord* on 3 April. He initially identified himself as Emile Victor Gasche, a Swiss businessman in search of American war contracts. In truth, he was Captain Franz Rintelen von Kleist, an officer of the German Imperial Navy whose mission in the U.S. was to help stop the flow of American munitions to Germany's foes. Operating on the orders of the German General Staff's espionage section, *Abteilung IIIB*, Rintelen aimed to accomplish his goal through a two-pronged campaign of "buy up or blow up."[68] The first entailed placing and even paying for phony munitions orders to tie up American production. The latter was straightforward sabotage. To do this effectively, he needed a cover, and he found it under the new identity of E.V. Gibbons, a broker specializing in *Russian* war contracts. Thus, he plunged right into Reilly's sphere and cultivated many of the same contacts, most notably David Lamar.[69] In far-off Shanghai, Hintze was aware of Rintelen's mission and, we may guess, welcomed the idea of his collaboration with the Ace-of-Spies.

Reilly was obliged to render Rintelen a helping hand, but he viewed the German as an unwelcome and potentially dangerous interloper. "Gibbon's" contracts competed with his own and tapped into funds that Reilly wished to preserve for his own purposes. Beyond this, Rintelen's sabotage efforts, particularly the planting in incendiary devices aboard Russian munitions ships, threatened to bring uncomfortable scrutiny to bear on connections Sidney preferred to keep incognito. So, while pretending to help Rintelen, he simultaneously plotted his downfall.

The first step was to entice the German into the so-called "Krag-Jorgenson Scheme." In early 1915, the U.S. Army decided to sell off some 300,000 outdated but still serviceable K-J rifles. This provoked a bidding war that Reilly sought to take advantage of.[70] Probably through Orbanowski, he proposed to Rintelen that the weapons could be purchased via a fake Russian contract that would keep them out of enemy hands. Once that was accomplished, they might be moved to Mexico. Rintelen took the bait, and Reilly assumed the role of intermediary with American authorities. The plan backfired, probably just as Reilly intended, when word leaked back to Rintelen's superiors that his partner was in fact a secret agent of a hostile government. This not only undermined Rintelen's credibility with his own people, but also brought American attention to bear on his activities.

Rintelen's final undoing came in early July when Erich Muenter, a man loosely connected to the German sabotage operation, attempted to assassinate J.P. Morgan. Whether Reilly had any hand in instigating this affair is impossible to say, though he certainly would have been pleased to see Morgan dead. Muenter talked, and with Rintelen's operation threatened with exposure, Berlin abruptly ordered him home. Traveling under yet another, presumably secure, false identity, he was arrested by British authorities during the routine blockade inspection. How the British were tipped off has never been explained, but Reilly may have known a thing or two.

Meanwhile, after finalizing the Remington deal on 19 April, Reilly and Nadine sailed from New York bound for Petrograd. Upton Thomas later explained this trip as a delayed honeymoon, but as much of what Thomas had to say about his boss, this was not the whole story. Our man had other matters on his mind, the most important of which was how to evade the tightening Morgan noose. He was formulating a bold plan to bring Russian purchasing in America, indeed, the whole of its foreign purchasing, under his domination. To do this he needed to shore up his existing financial and political support and to tap new sources in Russia. The key to this plan was his old collaborator, Aleksandr Guchkov. The ambitious politician now sat at the head of the Russian Red Cross, an entity with huge sums at its disposal. Guchkov was closely connected to the so-called *Zemgor*, an agency of local and municipal governments that had still more money to spend.[71] Most importantly, he led a private effort to reorganize Russia's economy for the war effort, the War Industries Committees.[72]

First, Reilly and bride made a short stop in London. As in Rintelen's case, British naval authorities took it upon themselves to inspect the persons and cargo aboard virtually all vessels headed towards the Continent. Reilly passed smoothly through the gauntlet. In London, he went to the branch office of the Russo-Asiatic Bank as 64 Old Bond Street and from there to the Savoy Hotel. The latter housed the office of his counterpart in Britain and "old acquaintance," Aleksandr Weinstein, Reilly's former neighbor on the Torgovaia.[73] Weinstein came to London in August 1914 as purchasing agent for Zhivotovskii's band of contractors. Working with a large account at the RAB, like Reilly, he made lucrative deals for munitions and other commodities. Also like Reilly, he enjoyed flaunting his new wealth and drew some unwelcome attention amid wartime austerity. Although by all accounts fat, gap-toothed and unattractive, Weinstein was "infatuated by women," especially actresses and showgirls. He compensated for his lack of physical appeal by lavishing his many lady friends with expensive gifts. In one notorious act of extravagance, he gave every girl in the chorus of the Palace Theatre a handbag with her initials in diamonds on the side.[74]

Perhaps the most interesting thing Reilly and Weinstein had in common was the latter's current secretary, William Calder. Calder, it may be recalled, was active in the Far East around the time of the Russo-Japanese War where he probably first encountered Sidney. Later, in Russia, he had been in

Reilly's employ. After Weinstein left for New York in the summer of 1916, Calder returned to Petrograd as an agent for Bessler, Waechter & Co., a firm that, to no surprise, handled business for the same Russian concerns as his former employers. Most importantly, Calder later joined the Royal Navy Volunteer Reserve (RNVR) in Russia. Through that he became an agent of MI1c—the operative cover of the Secret Intelligence Service.[75] The question is, did Calder's connection to British intelligence predate this? And did Reilly already have a link to MI1c?

Suggestive of such a link, though of somewhat dubious provenance, is an anonymous memoir compiled in the 1960s by someone familiar with the wartime activities of SIS and MI5. As noted by Alan Judd in his biography of SIS chief Mansfield Cumming, the manuscript can neither be accepted as authentic nor dismissed as a fraud.[76] From our perspective, the most interesting allegation is that during 1915 Reilly sat in on sessions of a special "spy school" run by Cumming at Whitehall Court. Particularly notable is that among the persons conducting these seminars was William Melville, now retired. Could Reilly have attended on Melville's invitation?

Another bit of apocrypha that suggests a direct connection between Reilly and British intelligence early in the war is the so-called "Szek Affair." Alexander Szek was a half-British Austrian subject and radio expert tapped by the Germans in 1914 to help operate their wireless transmitter in Brussels. Szek had access to German codes, and soon after, British agents convinced him to hand them over, a deal that eventually cost him his life.[77] According to Richard Deacon, "it was Sidney Reilly who first gave the tip to one of Cumming's agents" about the unfortunate Szek.[78] Given that he was fully occupied in New York during this time, it is hard to see that he could have had any such involvement. Like later stories of Sidney's wartime adventuring behind the lines in Belgium and Germany, this tale is almost certainly his or someone else's embellishment, possibly Margaret's.[79] Could this also relate to Daisy's connection to Dansey?

Sidney's talks with Weinstein focused on bringing the London operation more closely in line with his own. The Ace-of-Spies argued that this was the only way to compete with the obstructionism of Morgan. In addition to Weinstein, he enlisted Moisei Skidal'skii, a former Petrograd gold dealer turned munitions tout. Also on board was Weinstein's assistant, Tony Jechalski, the Polish engineer displaced by Reilly's New York coup. While he and Reilly would cooperate closely in contracting and more secretive matters, there would be an undercurrent of rivalry and resentment, at least on the Pole's part. Over the following year, Jechalski, Weinstein, Skidelskii, and a bevy of other "blackguards" would join Reilly at 120 Broadway.

There, as an American military intelligence report later described it, they "in some extraordinary way obtained direct contracts from the Russian Government and made fat profits."[80]

Another critical contact in London was the head of the resident Russian Government Committee (RGK), General Eduard Karlovich Hermonius (Germonius) (M). This Committee not only supervised Russian war buying in Britain, but also exercised general authority over the Purchasing Committee taking shape in New York. Thus, Hermonius was a dominating figure on both sides of the Atlantic and a man Reilly needed on his side. In this, our hero enjoyed a ready-made advantage: Gen. Hermonius happened to be the uncle of Nadine, and a rather doting one at that. Through her, and doubtless through other means, Sidney secured Hermonius' confidence and support. He also gained a new means to milk bribes from anxious American contract-seekers. During the General's visits to New York, he formally eschewed meeting with local businessmen to avoid any appearance of favoritism. On the other hand, he never declined an offer to dine with his niece and her husband at the Coq d'Or or some other posh eatery, and if some of Sidney's "friends" turned up at the next table, he would never be so rude as to refuse to speak to them.[81]

Finally, Weinstein provided a conduit to a very different set of Russians—the revolutionary émigrés. Outwardly he was a Tsarist loyalist who professed "strong pro-British and pro-Ally sentiments." Early on, however, there were those in MI5 and Scotland Yard's Special Branch who saw him as "a very bad man . . . capable of anything" and a closet radical sympathizer.[82] His brother, Gregory (Grigorii) Weinstein, was a veteran Marxist activist who currently worked on the staff of *Novyi Mir*, a Russian radical paper published in New York's Greenwich Village. Also, among A. Weinstein's London cronies was Benny Sverdlov, mentioned earlier as a Reilly associate in Petrograd and a brother of Lenin's loyal sidekick, Yakov Sverdlov. Reilly initially enlisted Benny as confidential courier between himself and Gen. Hermonius, and by January 1916, Sverdlov was doing business beside the Ace-of-Spies at 120 Broadway.

These were only part of Weinstein's revolutionary connections. In London, he had at least passing acquaintance with three other exiles: Maksim Litvinov, Ludwig Martens and Jacob (Yakov) Peters. In a few years the first two would become, respectively, the Soviet regime's quasi-diplomatic representatives in Britain and the U.S. Martens, another engineer, would also find himself working near Reilly in the Equitable Building.

By far the most interesting was Peters. A lowly rag-sorter in 1915, he was destined to become one of the leading figures of the Soviet secret police, the so-called Cheka. We will have much more to say about him in coming chapters. For now it is worth noting that in 1901–11 he had been a central figure in the infamous Houndsditch Murders and the resulting Siege of Sidney Street.[83] The first was a botched robbery that involved the cold-blooded killing of London policemen and the latter a shootout in which most of the culprits, all Latvian or Russian émigrés, perished. Peters stood trial for the killing, a crime for which he undoubtedly bore some guilt but for which he was inexplicably acquitted. The key to his salvation was his status as a secret informer of the Okhrana *and* Scotland Yard.

Having tied down things in London, Reilly's negotiations with Guchkov, the Grand Duke Aleksandr and others in Petrograd over the next two months went well. The Duke's help was especially useful in keeping American competitors at bay and in influencing the appointment of officers and officials to man the New York Purchasing Committee. Reilly took keen interest in the Navy's plan to contract twelve, later eighteen, submarines from Electric Boat, and signed on as the Russian Ministry of Marine's special representative in the deal, a contract that promised millions in commissions. Guchkov, as Russia's de facto economic Tsar, assured a steady stream of orders for big-ticket items such as ambulances, trucks and locomotives.

Reilly doubtless took the opportunity to touch base with his old ally in intrigue, Manasevich-Manuilov. While continuing his work for Suvorin's papers, Manasevich had returned to state service as a special agent for the new chief of intelligence for the Northern Front, the previously noted Gen. Nikolai Batiushin. Gathering a roster of agents that included the veteran counterintelligence officer Aleksandr Rezanov, Natta Azef and the Pole Ossendowski, all prior acquaintances of Reilly's, Batiushin focused his attention on combating German espionage and subversion, particularly behind the lines.[84] The General knew that Berlin's money and agents were finding their way into Russia from abroad, particularly from Scandinavia and America. Reilly, with his many connections and sources of information, was another ideal recruit to the effort. It is important to recall that it was at or about this time that Boris Suvorin queried Batiushin about Reilly and received his assurance that our man, whatever others might think, was "OK."

Another man worth seeing was the "ex-Bolshevik" engineer, Leonid Krasin. He had continued his rise in the Russian business scene through the patronage of Aleksei Putilov. During 1915, he put Krasin in charge of one of his subsidiaries, the Baranovskii Powder Co.[85] Reilly would soon negotiate a large American contract with the same firm. Krasin also maintained his position at the head of the Russian branch of Siemens-Schukert, a German firm that curiously avoided outright expropriation by the Tsar's Government. Siemens was one of the firms that Batiushin suspected as a font of German influence.[86] Strand by strand, Reilly carefully collected the strings to manipulate the System.

With Nadine's younger sister Barbara (Varvara) in tow, the Reillys sailed from Archangel aboard the SS *Tsar*, reaching New York on 10 July. At the beginning of August he returned to the docks to greet the arrival of Uncle Hermonius. Debarking the same ship was Prince Andrei Sergeevich Gagarin (M). A friend of Grand Duke Aleksandr Mikhailovich, the Prince came as a special representative of the Russian Government to arrange the purchase of heavy artillery tractors and similar vehicles. Reilly stood ready to assist him, for a fee, of course.

Also landing in Manhattan in August was Tony Jechalski. He established himself at 120 Broadway and assumed the role of Reilly's right-hand man in business and more clandestine dealings. However, he evidenced an unfortunate knack for attracting the attention of American authorities, something that did not sit well with the Ace-of-Spies. In late November, Jechalski's name made the front page of the *New York Times*, the result of late-night carousing with Russian playboy Count Pavel Trubetskoi.[87] Like his cronies Reilly and Weinstein, Tony also took a very active interest in women, very often the same ones as Sidney.

In early October, the Russian Supply Committee (RSC)—*Russkii Zagotovitel'nyi Komitet*—officially opened its doors at the Flatiron Building in midtown Manhattan. At its head sat Reilly's chum, Gen. Sapozhnikov. Another of Sidney's "intimates" was Col. A.V. Nekrasov who ran the Committee's Artillery Department and its all-important inspectorate. And who was Nekrasov's personal secretary? None other than Tony Jechalski. Even Georges Patrick, still resident Okhrana man in New York, found a berth on the RPC's ever-expanding payroll. Reilly's influence was further enhanced by the arrival of representatives of Guchkov's WIC, Red Cross and *Zemgor*: future ambassador Boris Bakhmetev (M), and Mssrs. P.A. Morozov and R.V. Poliakov. Russian war buying was never under any central control. By 1917 no less than *thirteen* separate agencies and ministries were placing orders in America to the unending frustration of Morgan and many others.[88] One of the few persons, perhaps the only one, with a finger in all of these was Sidney Reilly.

One of the most doubtful of these buying ventures was initiated in November 1915 by Nikolai Pavlovich Riabushinskii (M), part of a family of prominent Moscow industrialists connected to Guchkov's WIC.[89]

Riabushinskii presented himself as a special representative of the Moscow WIC looking to place orders for machinery and munitions. He also was a noted art expert and brought with him to New York a collection of artworks including thirty paintings by old masters said to be worth $1 million. The paintings supposedly came from the collection of Count Gal'michev-Kutuzov, and through the auspices of the Dowager Empress they were to be auctioned off to purchase war supplies.[90] Numerous questions swirled about the effort, including Riabushinskii's precise ties to the WIC and the ownership and authenticity of the paintings. In Manhattan, Riabushinskii attached himself to the Reilly-Jechalski crowd, and with the former's help a sale was arranged at the American Art Galleries. Riabushinskii, however, proved a rather unsuccessful emissary. A penchant for high-stakes gambling led him into debt and an embarrassing suit by one of his creditors.[91] The final disposition of many of the artworks in his charge remained a mystery, and rumors circulated that he had been led astray and defrauded by certain companions. Was Reilly the art collector one of them?

Another boon to Sidney's fortunes took shape in November, the formation of the American International Corporation (AIC). Largely the creation of MacRoberts and other NCB directors, the consortium included Percy Rockefeller and Jacob Schiff's right-hand man at Kuhn & Loeb, Otto Kahn. Thus, the firm had a distinctly non-Morgan, even anti-Morgan, bent. The purpose of the Corporation was foreign trade, and its sights were set on Russia. A man such as Reilly was ideal to abet this venture. In February 1916, AIC assumed control of the Allied Machinery Co. (AMC) at 120 Broadway, and through MacRobert's intervention, Reilly became one of its directors. As an all-purpose import-export front, AMC was a perfect vehicle for his purposes. AMC later earned a spot on the Suspect List of U.S. Military and Naval Intelligence as well as American and British War Trade Intelligence.[92] In one case, American authorities discovered a large consignment of AMC-purchased machinery on the Hamburg-Amerika Line docks waiting for shipment to Sweden, "presumably for re-export to Germany."[93] The firm also did a great deal of business with neutral Spanish firms, primarily war-related goods such as copper, explosives, motor vehicles and even aircraft engines.

Curiously, among these Spanish concerns were several with links to Zaharoff's enterprises. Though that worthy openly associated himself with the Allies from the outset of the war, his wide-ranging interests extended to both sides in the conflict, and as master of the System he certainly would have had no inhibitions about facilitating and profiting from Reilly's activities. The Greek supposedly visited New York on more than one occasion in the early years of the conflict, but the great secrecy involved prevents establishing any link to Reilly, though it seems likely that Basil would have taken some interest in his protégé's doings.

One Greek with definite connections to Reilly in New York and, possibly, Zaharoff was Georges Veronius. He was affiliated with German-run Amsinck & Co. and the French Compagnie Générale de Transatlantique, a firm in which Sir Basil had a substantial interest. Despite his association with Reilly, Weinstein and others of similar ilk, the Americans had assurance from some high quarter that Veronius was "absolutely reliable" and a very useful source of information.[94]

Reinforced with financial and political support, the Ace-of-Spies launched a new contracting offensive. In late August, he signed a deal with the Mackenzie Manufacturing Co. of Toronto for 5,000,000 shells, a contract that entailed a potential commission of $2,500,000. Actual production was to be handled by the Canadian Car and Foundry Co. (CCFC) for which the ubiquitous Samuel MacRoberts handily happened to be New York representative. In the following months, Reilly secured orders for ammunition, ambulances, locomotives and ships. Three of his deals deserve special attention as each reveals details of his *modus operandi*. The first was another big shell order with Poole Engineering Co. of Baltimore. The deal was a prime example of overlapping commissions. Subcontracting firms included Reilly's Allied Machinery, Driggs-Seabury Ordnance Co. and Goodchild & McNabb of London. Reilly acted as agent for all three. More interesting, however, was that the contract lay completely outside the Zhivotovskii network. Financial backing came from a collection of American investors headed by Thomas Cochran and Harvey Gibson of the Liberty National Bank. Others involved read like a who's who of Wall Street: the investment houses of Luke, Banks & Weeks, William Saloman and Hallgarten & Co., as well as William Boyce Thompson of the Federal Reserve Bank and, most interesting of all, Charles Sabin, director of Guaranty Trust Co. Sidney was now playing in the big leagues.

The second deal involved a contract for 700 tons of nickel ore ostensibly purchased on behalf of the Russian War Ministry for the Putilov works. Its twisting channels brought together a fascinating array of persons and motives. Reilly secured the order for the Pittsburgh-based Vanadium Co., represented by Joseph de Wykoff who knew Reilly and Weinstein from Russia and currently worked closely with Rogovin and Orbanowski.[95] Also involved in the deal was the president of the Vanadium Co., J. Leonard Replogle, who had long connection to Kuhn & Loeb. Schiff's firm, in fact, was the moving force behind the contract, and the nickel's true final destination was Germany, not Russia. Equally intriguing, the source of the ore was the *Le Nickel* firm controlled by Basil Zaharoff. Using Grant's Swedish-Russo-Asiatic export front, the ore moved to Stockholm, but by the time it reached Petrograd there was not 700 tons, but only 200. Assisting the movement of the nickel to Berlin's hands was a Danish intermediary company run by none other than Alexander Helphand, Salomon Rosenblum's old comrade now turned businessman and German agent. He also was still a revolutionary, of sorts. Wykoff later tried to blame the whole thing on a simple clerical error.[96]

The final deal once more pitted Reilly against the formidable Samuel Vauclain. The latter had declined all offers from our hero, but in October 1915 he found himself confronted with an outright ultimatum. Vauclain's Eddystone Corp. had been the beneficiary of several Morgan-financed contracts including one for 2,500,000 Russian shells.[97] Reilly made it clear that Eddystone would never complete this contract unless it got its finished product past the Russian inspectors whom the Ace-of-Spies had in his pocket. Perhaps to reinforce his point, as the talks were going on, a mysterious fire broke out at the Eddystone works that were still under construction.[98] It may have been no more than another convenient coincidence, but Vauclain surely took it into consideration. Not one to bestow praise lightly on an adversary, Vauclain later offered that Reilly was "a smooth, slick article," who "when in a tight spot, proved himself an ingenious diplomat."[99] Thus, despite the risk of antagonizing Morgan, at the beginning of January 1916, Vauclain granted Reilly a "consulting engineer" contract on the Eddystone contract and even agreed to fund it out of his own pocket. Under its terms, he received a regular salary for his work in keeping "the obstreperous Russian in hand" and smoothing over any difficulties as they arose. It also guaranteed him $.25 per shell, a commission potentially worth over $600,000.[100] Finally, Reilly used his leverage to get Morozov and Poliakov added to the Eddystone board.

By the close of 1915, Sidney Reilly was the uncrowned Tsar of Russian war purchasing in America. Further testament of his influence can be seen in his 21 December report to Gen. Hermonius that addressed the state of Russian contracts and the prospects for the future.[101] He pronounced judgment on the various firms involved and warned that, overall, U.S. manufacturers had a marked tendency to overestimate their capabilities, with the result that delays and related difficulties were bound to occur. And so they did, though in many cases because of Reilly's machinations as much as anything else. The report reveals a detailed knowledge not only of

Russian contracts, but those of Britain, France and Belgium as well. Reilly had his finger on the pulse of the entire Allied arms market in the U.S.

All this business, intrigue and attendant pressures took their toll. Upton Thomas later reported that his employer suffered from "headaches" and sought help from a Dr. Bassler in Manhattan.[102] The good doctor specialized in treating nervous ailments with physical therapy and drugs, and Sidney apparently availed himself of their remedies.

The System was working well. Reilly could play Russian, German, American and British interests against each other and to his advantage. He had acquired wealth and power, though hardly enough to satisfy his grand ambitions. He had overcome great obstacles, but larger ones lay ahead, along with immense opportunities.

NOTES

1. MID, 9140-6073, Bond to Hunnewell and Smith, 9 Oct. 1918, 1.
2. SIS, Margaret to War Office, 16 Nov. 1918.
3. SIS, Minute sheet re Pepita Reilly's letter to S. Menzies, 17 Nov. 1940.
4. Anthony Reed and David Fischer, *Colonel Z: The Secret Life of a Master of Spies* (New York, 1985), 90–96.
5. Ibid., 91, 109.
6. MI5, Reilly, translated certificate dated 26 July 1914.
7. PRO, 371/4019, Bagge to Steel-Maitland, 15 May 1919, 14.
8. Deacon, Peddler, 116–117. Vickers held about 10% of Putilov's shares and Zaharoff held a smaller amount in his own name.
9. M.V. Rodzianko, *The Reign of Rasputin: An Empire's Collapse* (New York, c. 1927), 159–160.
10. The primary sources for Russian economic statistics and Russo-American economic relations are P.I. Lyashchenko, *History of the National Economy of Russia to 1917* (New York, 1949), esp. 710–784, V.V. Lebedev, Russko-amerikanskie ekonomicheskie otnosheniia, 1900–1917 gg. (Moscow, 1964), esp. pp. 146–361, and Boris E. Nolde, Russia in the Economic War (New Haven, CT, 1928).
11. M.I. Gaiduk, *Utiug: Materialy I fakty o zagotovitel'noi deiatel'nosti russkikh vooennykh komisii v Amerike* (New York, 1918), 143–144.
12. MID, 9140-6073, Bond to Hunnewell and Smith, 10 Sept. 1918.
13. Ibid., Memorandum #4, 31 Aug. 1918, 2.
14. Ibid., Memorandum #2, 23 Aug. 1918, 2.
15. Ibid., Navy Suspects List, "Reilly, Sidney," 3.
16. NA, RG 45, Office of Naval Intelligence (ONI), Summary appended to file 21010-3241. The latter file includes most of the items contained in MID 9140-1496 and -6073 plus some additional material.
17. On this effort, see Friedrich Katz, *The Secret War in Mexico: Europe, the United States and the Mexican Revolution* (Chicago, 1981), 203–249.
18. On Jahnke's background and early career, see Richard Spence, "K.A. Jahnke and the German Sabotage Campaign in the United States and Mexico, 1914–1918," The Historian, vol. 50, #1 (Fall 1996), 89–112, and Reinhard R. Doerries, "Tracing Kurt Jahnke: Aspects of the Study of German Intelligence," in George O. Kent, (ed.), *Historians and Archivists* (Fairfax, VA, 1991), 27–44.

19. USNA, U.S. Army General Staff, IRR file #XE001752," Final Report in the Case of Walter Schellenberg, 30 Sept. 1946, Appendix XV, "Jahnke and the Jahnkeburo," 2.
20. Germany, Politisches Archiv des Auswartigen Amt (PAAA), Rechtswesen 6, Saborage Claims, vol. 3, Jahnke to Reichswehrministerium Marineleitung, 29 Jan. 1925.
21. DS, CSA 215, Sharpe to Bannerman, 13 Dec. 1924, 14.
22. John Jones and Paul Hollister, *The German Secret Service in America, 1914–1918* (Boston, 1918), 230.
23. MID, 9140-6073, Some Names in the Weinstein-Reilly Investigation, 3, and Navy List, 4, 8,15.
24. Ibid., -6073, 2 and Navy List, 14–15.
25. Ibid., Navy List, 15.
26. Sir Guy Gaunt, *The Yield of the Years: A Story of Adventure Afloat and Ashore* (London, 1940), 199.
27. Ibid., 194.
28. Crowley, *The Confessions of Aleister Crowley: An Autohagiography* (London, 1929), 744, 753–754. On Crowley's intelligence-related activities in New York, see Richard Spence, "Secret Agent 666: Aleister Crowley and British Intelligence in America, 1914–1918," *International Journal of Intelligence and CounterIntelligence*, vol. 13, #3 (Fall 2000), 359–371.
29. Crowley, 752–753.
30. John Symonds, *The Great Beast* (London, 1971), 199.
31. MID, 10012-112-1, Intelligence officer, West Point to DMI, Washington, 23 Sept. 1918, 4.
32. PRO, FO 371/2584, 43179, 13 April 1915.
33. Ibid., 10004, 27 Jan. 1915.
34. MID, 9140-6073, Navy List, 3, 4, 9. The deal was for 15,000 wagons to increase the carrying capacity of the CER. At going rates, it would have netted a commission of at least $250,000—almost $3,000,000 today.
35. *Tacoma Daily News* (3 Feb. 1915), 1.
36. DS 862.20212/1101, Harrison to U.S. Embassy, Mexico City, 11 April 1918, citing intercepted German messages.
37. *Ves' Peterburg, 1912* and *Ves' Petrograd, 1914*, and *1915*.
38. Bokhanov, 129.
39. MID, 9140-6073, Memorandum #7, 12 Sept. 1918, 2.
40. PRO, FO 371/3326, #58187, "Proposal to Initiate Propaganda in Russia," 7 March 1918. Perelstrauss was a naval engineer who had helped construct the dry dock in Port Arthur.
41. MID, 9140-6073, Memorandum #2, 2.
42. Ibid., 1.
43. Ibid, Memorandum #4, 2–3, and Upton D. Thomas v. Remington Arms, New York Supreme Court, New York County, # 15332, 1919, Exhibit A.
44. Thomas v. Remington, Exhibit A.
45. Ibid.
46. MID, Memorandum #7, 2.
47. Ibid.
48. Ibid.
49. Ibid., Bond to Hunnewell and Smith, 10 Sept. 1918, 2.
50. Ibid., Bond to Hunnewell and Smith, 11 Oct. 1918, 1.
51. HIA, Russia, Posol'stvo, U.S.A., file 334/1, Anglo-Russian Sub-Committee, Agreement on Contrasts, 28 July 1916, and John D. Forbes, *J.P. Morgan, Jr., 1867–1943* (Charlottesville, VA, 1981), 89–90.
52. Forbes, 116–117.

53. On this competition, see G.L. Owen, "Dollar Diplomacy in Default: The Economics of Russian-American relations, 1910–1917," *Historical Journal*, vol. 13, #2 (June 1970), 251–272.

54. Michael Futrell, *Northern Underground: Episodes of Russian Revolutionary Transport and Communications throgh Scandinavia and Finland, 1863–1917* (London, 1963), 167–70, *passim*. See also George Katkov, "German Foreign Office Documents on Financial Support to the Bolsheviks in 1917," *International Affairs*, vol. 32, #2 (April 1956).

55. CSA 215, Sharpe to Bannerman, 13 Dec. 1924, 8.

56. Ibid.

57. Ibid., 2–3.

58. Krymov, 72.

59. City of New York, Office of the City Clerk, Marriage Register #4404-15.

60. Krymov, 72. Metropolitan Platon personally related this story to Krymov a few years later.

61. MID, Memorandum #4, 6–7. Contrary to later claims, Trotsky did not play a bit part in this film. It was made well before his arrival in the U.S.

62. Ralph Isham Papers, "Information Gathered in America and Sources of Such Information."

63. MID, Memorandum #4, 5.

64. Ibid., 6.

65. Ibid., 3.

66. On Lincoln, see Bernard Wasserstein, *The Secret Lives of Trebitsch Lincoln* (New York, 1988) and David Lampe and Laszlo Szenasi, *The Self-Made Villain: A Biography of I. T. Trebitsch Lincoln* (London, 1961).

67. *NYT* (23 March 1915), 4:5.

68. On Rintelen, see his *The Dark Invader: Wartime Reminiscences of a German Naval Intelligence Officer* (New York, 1933).

69. Rintelen, 93–94, and Henry Landau, *The Enemy Within: The Inside Story of German Sabotage in America* (New York, 1937), 47–48.

70. U.S. Justice Dept., Bureau of Investigation (BI), file OG 39368, "Sidney Reilly: Neutrality Matter," 3 April 1917.

71. *Zemskii i Gorodskii Soiuz*.

72. *Voenno-Promyshlennyikh Komiteti*.

73. MID, 9140-6073, Dillingham to Biddle, 13 April 1918.

74. MID Weinstein, 13 Nov. 1918, 1.

75. Ibid, 2.

76. Judd, 383–384.

77. Probably the most complete and accurate accounting of this affair is in Judd, 371–375.

78. Deacon, RSS, 212.

79. Lockhart, *Ace*, 71–72.

80. MID, 9140-6073, Memorandum #2, 3.

81. Krymov, 72-73.

82. MID, 9140-6073, Memorandum #2, 3.

83. See the conclusions of Donald Rumbelow, *The Houndsditch Murders and the Siege of Sidney Street* (London, 1973), and F.G. Clarke, *Will-o'-the-wisp: Peter the Painter and the anti-Tsarist terrorists in Britain and Australia* (Melbourne, 1983). For a biography of Peters, see Valentin Shteinberg, *Ekab Peters* (Moscow, 1989).

84. M. Tsekhanovskii, "General Batiushin i ego Komissiia," *Rul'*, (25–26 July 1923), and Vladimir Orlov, *Dvoinoi agent; Zapiski russkogo konterrazvedchikai* (Moscow, 1998), 179–199.

85. *Ves' Peterburg*, 1917.

86. Orlov, Dvoinoi, 209–210.

87. *NYT* (21 Nov. 1925), 1:5.

88. Gaiduk, 120.

89. Bokhanov, 219. The "Brothers Riabushinskii" had a hand in automobile and armaments manufacture as well as banking (*the Moskovskii Bank*) and insurance. Nikolai's brother, P.P. Riabushinskii, was president of the Moscow Chamber of Commerce.

90. *NYT*, (21 Nov. 1915), II, 14:3.

91. *NYT*, (31 May 1916), 12:6.

92. MID, 9140-6073, Navy List, 5.

93. Ibid., 4.

94. MID, 9140-6073, Memorandum #1, 21 Aug. 1918, 2 and Names, 3.

95. Ibid., appended French report on "de Wykoff," Jan. 1917.

96. Ibid.

97. HIA, Posol'stvo, 345-4, Vauclain to Morgan, 3 June 1915.

98. *History of the Eddystone Ammunition Corporation, 1915–1917* (privately pub., c. 1920), 7.

99. MID 9140-6073, 11 Oct. 1918, 2.

100. Supreme Court of New York, New York County, #4768-1920, "Sidney G. Reilly v. the Baldwin Locomotive Works, Eddystone Ammunition Corporation and Samuel Vauclain," original complaint and answer.

101. GARF, fond 6173, op. 1, delo 41, S. G. Reilli, "Doklad o sostoianii ruzhneinago I patronnago dela v Soedinennykh Shtatakh Severnoi Amerikki," 8/21 Dec. 1915.

102. MID, 9140-6073, #6, 5.

Chapter Seven

AN INTERNATIONAL CROOK OF THE HIGHEST ORDER

At the end of February 1916, soon after signing a new consulting contract with Max Goldsmith & Co., Reilly suddenly announced to Nadine that he was returning to Russia on business. Shortly before his departure, another man arrived at 120 Broadway from Petrograd via Liverpool. This was Ernest Michelson, an Anglo-Russian and manager of the Neva Cable Works, a firm closely linked to the Putilov outfit. There was nothing especially notable in this coincidence, but for one thing: in little more than two years, Michelson and Reilly would both be in the employ of SIS and mutually engaged in a "special mission" in Russia. Did that clandestine collaboration actually begin earlier?

Sidney traveled across the Pacific to Port Arthur and on via the Trans-Siberian. The war had not improved Petrograd. A pall of decay and creeping desperation hung over the city. Wartime inflation had driven up wages, but it had driven prices even higher, and a thriving black market coupled with endemic corruption meant that basic commodities, particularly food, were in increasingly short supply for much of the populace. The Tsar's growing fixation on military affairs left the reins of government in the hands of the Empress and her nefarious "spiritual advisor," Grigorii Rasputin. Sidney still had contacts in Rasputin's circle. Col. Nekrasov in New York was the bosom friend of Aron Simanovich, Reilly's old acquaintance and the *Starets'* personal secretary.[1] Manasevich-Manuilov kept a close eye on Rasputin on behalf of Gen. Batiushin. Darker suspicions about Rasputin held that he was conniving with German agents to push the Tsar into a separate peace.

Reilly, of course, was himself suspect in some Russian quarters. It was in the wake of his latest Petrograd visit, that local Gendarme General Kazakov offered words of advice to a fellow officer, Gen. N.Kh. Kozlov.

Kazakov described "Railley" or "Rally" as a doubtful character and likely German spy who exerted a strong influence over the Supply Committee. He urged Kozlov, part of a new crop of officers designated to clean up corruption in the RSC, that Reilly "by no means should be admitted to any [further] dealings" with that body."[2]

Sidney, as ever, had personal matters to take care of. In Port Arthur he met his "wife" (presumably Anne) and two small children and they accompanied him back to Petrograd. Any idea of bringing them to America apparently was off. Was that because Reilly was already planning to relocate his base of operations to Russia? Perhaps he felt they would be safer in the Capital. If so, this would prove a major miscalculation. In Petrograd he made arrangements for his family to be taken under the wing of a local British charitable organization. The broker Norbert Rodkinson, who knew a good deal about Reilly's activities in this period, later told American authorities that Sidney had "abandoned" his wife and children in Petrograd, entrusting their welfare to the hands of one Fred Hill who was obliged to appeal to the English community to assist in their support. As mentioned earlier in our story, Frederick William Hill, known as Frederik Alfredovich Hill to the Russians, was a leading figure in Petrograd's English Club and a prominent businessman. Among other things, he was involved in importing machine tools into Russia, something that may have given him a direct link to Reilly and Allied Machinery.[3] Fred Hill had two sons, Alfred F. "Freddie" Hill, who would end up as an intelligence officer in Russia in 1918, and George E., who worked for the British Embassy. The latter was often confused with his cousin, George Alexander Hill, yet another British officer destined to become one of Reilly's closest allies in the Secret World.

According to Rodkinson, Fred Hill personally handled the affairs of Mrs. Reilly, and rallied other members of the English Club to the cause. In October 1914, the Club agreed it would render assistance the dependents of British men on active war service. Assuming this was the basis of Reilly's appeal, it means that he already was presenting himself as being in "British service" although he would not join the Royal Flying Corps until 1917. Mackie recollected that there was some question about Reilly's status as a British subject, but that the matter was never wholly "thrashed out."[4] During 1916 an Anna Yanovna Reile appeared in Petrograd's directory living at 71 Ligovskaia. Whether she was another incarnation of Anne Luke is uncertain, but it may be another tantalizing trace of this will-o'-the-wisp of a woman.

Back on the business front, Sidney established a Petrograd branch office for Allied Machinery at 13 Torgovaia, conveniently near his old office at #10. To man this he recruited Abram Mass/Mess, a kinsman of Moisei

Ginsburg.[5] In the months to follow, AMC sent huge shipments of machine tools to Russia, though not all reached that destination. In 1917, American investigation found that some of this equipment shipped through Sweden had been diverted to Germany, just like the vanishing nickel ore.[6] Another mission for Reilly was to act as advance man for Samuel MacRoberts' plans to expand NCB's operations and influence in Russia. MacRoberts was anxious to open National City branches in Petrograd and elsewhere and to maneuver his firm into a privileged position to market a new Russian loan in the U.S. Immediately after Reilly's visit to the Russian capital, MacRoberts himself journeyed there to finalize these very aims.[7]

Another man Reilly recruited was Carl Schultzenberg Lowie (also Lowe or Levy). He was a Dane of German-Jewish origin who had recently worked in the Russian Arctic port of Archangel as local representative for Reilly's old employer, Andersen's Russian East-Asiatic Steamship Co. Shortly before Sidney's arrival, Lowie abruptly quit his Archangel post and came to Petrograd. He subsequently came to the U.S., probably with Reilly, but by June 1916, however, Lowie was back in Archangel as agent for various American insurance and shipping companies, among them AIC, W.R. Grace, Grant's 2nd Russian Insurance and Allied Machinery. Most importantly, he became the local U.S. consular agent.[8]

How he obtained this job was later a mystery, but it may have stemmed from his association with yet another pair of dubious Reilly associates, Ludwig and Mathilda Kramm. Kramm, a German-born chemist, lived with his wife in Petrograd at the outbreak of the war. Ostensibly an American citizen, he worked as representative for German and Austrian insurance companies. Sometime in late 1915–early 1916, he and Mathilda came to New York where he entered into an unofficial "consulting" relationship with the Russian Supply Committee. There he met Reilly, assuming they did not know one another already. Through his wife, a thread ran to the RSC's chief technical inspector, and Jechalski's "boss," Col. Nekrasov. Madame Kramm was an intimate of the Russian ballerina Aleksandra Miroliubskaia, Nekrasov's mistress.[9] Mathilda Kramm's most interesting contact was the newly appointed American ambassador to Russia, David R. Francis. She encountered Francis in New York during in the spring of 1916 and quickly wormed her way into his confidence, and perhaps his heart. When later reunited in Russia, rumors flew that she was the Ambassador's mistress, though he insisted she was a mere friend.[10] Her influence with Francis may have had some part in securing Lowe his post in Archangel.

Sidney was back in New York by 12 May where he signed a new contract with Goldsmith & Co. Nadine, in the meantime, had escorted her sister back to Russia and would not return Stateside until the later part of June. Perhaps these separate travel arrangements were a sign of the growing rift between them. The chief source of that rift, no doubt, was Beatrice Tremaine. His wife's absence gave Reilly ample opportunity to indulge his young paramour, and they were a very public couple at Broadway theaters and uptown clubs.

Reilly immediately plunged into blatantly crooked schemes like the so-called "Mauser" Affair. This commenced soon after Reilly arrived back at his Equitable office. From Hintze or other German agents, he knew about stocks of arms and ammunition secreted in the U.S. for potential use in Mexico. That Sidney got his hands on some of these caches is indicated by his June 1916 sale of sixty-seven Maxim machine guns, supposedly belonging to the "Mexican Government," to the RSC for a tidy profit.[11] About the same time, a story began to circulate among the Russians that a huge store of Mauser rifles, perhaps up to a million, plus hundreds of millions of rounds of ammo, were stashed in warehouses in New Jersey. As the tale spread, a number of Americans expressed interest, including representatives of Flint Arms. Prospective purchasers usually got a glimpse of what was claimed to be a much larger hoard and put down earnest money to secure their interest. In the end, they got neither the rifles nor their money back; a simple, classic con.

Reilly kept in the background, but among those promoting the scheme were a Col. Kolontaev of the RSC and William Ford, an attorney at 2 Rector Street who did legal work for the Russians—and Germans. Another player was Anthony Knapp (or Knaap), the local publisher of a pro-German Polish paper and a close friend of Tony Jechalski.[12] Another very interested party was Nicholas Biddle, Anglophile socialite and special investigator for the NYPD who later became chief of U.S. Military Intelligence in New York. Biddle, as we will soon see, also had a very close relationship to the resident SIS station. Reilly's involvement in the Mauser and like swindles explains why Director of U.S. Naval Intelligence, Adm. Roger Welles, concluded that he and his cronies were at the least "international confidence men of the highest class."[13]

Around the same time that the Mauser business was taking off, Reilly orchestrated yet another rifle-related scheme involving Flint Arms. His front men in this endeavor were Benny Sverdlov, now conveniently situated as a Russian expert inside the Flint offices, and Laurence Lyon, a Canadian who presented himself as a British officer. Through them, Reilly enticed Flint with a potential contract for 2,000,000 Russian rifles.[14] First, of course, Flint would have to pony up consulting fees to the middlemen to exert the necessary influence. Flint paid the money but did not, it seems, ever secure the contract. This episode, no doubt, did much to embitter Flint's officers against Reilly. It also is notable in that it attracted the attention of the recently established British SIS station in New York (of which more directly), in part because of the involvement of Lyon.[15]

Despite the apparent success of his many gambits, including new contracts with Goldsmith & Co. and the British-American Chemical Co. (to which the above Lyon was attached), Reilly was about to encounter some serious challenges. The first blow to fall was the 14 July agreement between the Russian and British Governments that provided that all new contracts placed by the RSC and allied agencies were to be paid for out of credits granted to London by J.P. Morgan. Morgan received complete power to select all firms and contractors involved and to set all terms, including commissions.[16] While it would take some time to implement this arrangement, Morgan and the RSC would not sign a formal agreement until November, it nonetheless was a virtual death-knell to independents like Sidney. To provide further control over the obstreperous Russians, the deal provided for the creation of a special Anglo-Russian Subcommittee (or ARSC), composed of members of the local British and Russian missions, to directly oversee the placing and completion of Russian contracts.[17] This Subcommittee reported to a Committee on Russian Supplies based in London, a body supervised by the powerful Lord Milner. These arrangements inevitably subjected Reilly and his activities to greater scrutiny by His Britannic Majesty's officials. In New York, his "interference" in contract matters provoked clashes with the ARSC's Lt. Cols. Frederick Abbot and Jack Giffard and Captain William Burton, each of whom added his voice to the chorus decrying Reilly's nefarious influence. On the other hand, as one might expect, Reilly had a friend of sorts attached to the ARSC, Lt. Arthur W. McPherson. A member of a long-established British mercantile family in Petrograd, McPherson was another prewar acquaintance and, like Sidney, was destined to assume a close relationship with British intelligence.

Another danger lay in impending changes within the Russian supply apparatus. Incessant complaints of mismanagement, graft and even treason finally forced the relief of Gen. Sapozhnikov in July and the outright recall of Col. Goleevskii who headed the critical artillery subcommittee. Sapozhnikov's replacement was Gen. A.P. Zaliubovskii who had a mandate to clean up the RSC and investigate past malfeasance. Among the matters to be probed were how Sapozhnikov's—and Reilly's—crony Col. Nekrasov had accumulated $500,000 to his name, the suspicious delays and other problems with many of the contracts and even accusations that defective goods and scrap had been shipped to Russia in place of the items ordered and paid for.[18] Zaliubovskii was to be accompanied by a special section led by Gen. Kozlov, the very officer recently warned against Reilly in Petrograd. Kozlov's chief aide was a former state prosecutor, Lt. Boris L'vovich Brasol (Brazol), who had a reputation as one of the shrewdest and most ruthless investigative minds in Russia. He also was a ferocious anti-Semite, not exactly the sort to take a charitable view of Sidney and his activities.

Kozlov's mission was a manifestation of a broader campaign against corruption and related ills inside Russia. In the early part of 1916, the Imperial General Staff sanctioned the creation of a special office to ferret out and combat speculation and espionage in the rear. In July, Petrograd was stunned to learn of the arrest of prominent financier and Rasputin crony Dmitrii Rubinstein on charges of "unscrupulous speculation" and suspicion of acting as a German agent.[19] The arrest of other businessmen soon followed, including two of the Zhivotovskii brothers. This trend would seem to have posed a major threat to Reilly and his operation, but in this regard the "political influence" noted by Vauclain and others came to his rescue. For instance, Sidney was still on excellent terms with the Grand Duke Aleksandr Mikhailovich; that fall he negotiated a private demonstration to the Duke of a new American automatic camera and ground speed indicator.[20]

About this time, Vladimir Krymov, Suvorin's former business manager, arrived in New York on a journalistic assignment. He ran into the Ace-of-Spies and took the opportunity to ask if he was not afraid his blatant profiteering would result in difficulty back in Petrograd. Reilly, according to Krymov, scoffed at the notion and opined that anyone attacking him was doing no more than "spitting from an airplane."[21] More to the point, Sidney knew he had nothing to fear from Batiushin because he was one the General's most valuable sources of information. Perhaps he even helped set up Rubinstein and Zhivotovskii.

His confidence was not misplaced, but Reilly did not ignore protective measures. Scuttlebutt around the Russian missions held that one of Kozlov's first efforts would be to investigate charges that mislabeled or fraudulent war goods had been shipped to Russia. To whatever extent Reilly himself was involved in such skullduggery, he had a vested interest in not seeing it, and doubtless some of his associates, exposed. The logical starting point for any such investigation was the veritable mountain of munitions and other Russian-purchased supplies clogging the Black Tom Island terminal in New Jersey. The sprawling railway-shipping terminal, connected to the mainland by a wide causeway, lay barely two miles from the southern tip of Manhattan. Spread among barges, warehouses and railway cars were more than 13,000 tons of explosive materials, including 4 million pounds of TNT.[22] On the night of 29–30 July, the volatile stores ignited in one of the largest non-nuclear explosions to ever rock American shores. Shrapnel and broken glass from millions of shattered windows rained over lower Manhattan and New York Harbor.

Whatever evidence Black Tom may have held had quite literally gone up in smoke, and Reilly and others could rest easier. Perhaps it was all just another happy coincidence, but the Black Tom disaster was definitely no accident. The agents of the blast were a band of German saboteurs led by Kurt Jahnke who had made a special trip from San Francisco for the job. What could never be determined, despite years of subsequent investigation and litigation, was that Jahnke and his crew had carried out the operation with the express knowledge and approval of Berlin.[23] Rather, the action seemed to have been conducted purely on local initiative, though just whose remains an interesting question. While the matter defies absolute certainty, there is excellent reason to believe that Reilly had a hand in instigating and/or abetting the disaster beyond the fact that it admirably suited his desires. Setting the explosion to achieve near total destruction required careful planning and reconnaissance. The terminal was well guarded and off limits to persons without legitimate purpose and property on the island. One of the few firms to have an onsite office was Reilly's own Allied Machinery that gave him the important ability to arrange access for designated "employees." To this must be added his connections to the German clandestine nexus, particularly lead man Jahnke. The System was working again; by setting up the destruction of Black Tom, Reilly further cemented his credibility and influence in that sphere while at the same time ridding himself and others of a nagging problem on the Russian end. As for the lost goods, well, the commissions on those had already been paid, and new orders would have to be made to replace the loss.

Gen. Zaliubovskii and his team arrived on the scene in mid-August. Reilly at once determined that Brasol was the most capable and dangerous of the lot. Fortunately, he also was the most corruptible. Brasol, age 35, bore a certain resemblance to Sidney; his dark eyes, olive complexion, and glossy, black slicked-back hair gave him a more Latin or Levantine appearance than Slavic. In other respects, the men could not have been more different. Reilly's biggest problem was getting around Brasol's virulent hatred of Jews. As usual, he found a way to exploit it to his advantage. As a Tsarist junior prosecutor, Brasol had cut his teeth on the infamous Beilis Case that erupted during 1911–13. In this, the Jewish manager of a Kiev brickyard,

Mendel Beilis, stood accused of the ancient and volatile charge of ritual murder of a Christian child. In the absence of any credible evidence, Beilis was acquitted of a crime that he certainly did not commit. Brasol remained a true believer and a tireless proponent of a much larger and more insidious Jewish Conspiracy. He was convinced that the revolutionary ferment inside Russia and all manifestations of hostility towards the Tsarist regime were part of this immense scheme, and Reilly exploited this *idée fixe* to divert the Lieutenant's attention from more mundane treason and corruption. Like many of his ilk, Brasol was willing to make exceptions when it suited his larger purpose, particularly when the Jew in question offered himself as an ally—or double agent—in exposing the plots of his co-religionists.

Reilly, of course, could also boast a long history of assistance to the Tsar's secret police and the present confidence of men such as Batiushin and Rezanov. The latter, in fact, had worked beside Brasol as a prosecutor in Petrograd. Sidney offered to pass along all he could learn regarding secret German-Jewish funding, particularly the part played by Jacob Schiff whom Brasol regarded as a most dangerous enemy of the Russian State. In furtherance of this end, Reilly put the Russian in contact with Maurice Leon, also of Jewish origin, an employee of the local French Military Mission who was obsessed with unveiling the evil practices of Schiff and the entire cabal of German-Jewish financiers.

The same information was of interest to the British. During 1916 Reilly began a close, if as yet entirely unofficial, relationship with the office of the Secret Intelligence Service recently installed at Manhattan's 44 Whitehall Street. As noted in earlier chapters, the SIS, originally the foreign branch of the so-called Secret Service Bureau, came into being in late 1909 under the leadership of Commander Mansfield Smith Cumming, a short, monocled, one-legged naval officer who almost seemed a caricature of an eccentric British spy-chief. Eccentric he certainly was, with a penchant for disguises and gadgets and the trademark flourish of signing papers with a bright green-ink "C." [24] But Cumming was no fool nor did he suffer them in his service. With the outbreak of the war it was necessary to expand his organization, and Cumming mostly did so through the selective recruitment of officers, many of them invalids or otherwise unsuitable for regular field service. One such man was Lt. Col. Sir William George Eden Wiseman. Gassed in the early months of the war (which caused permanent damage to his eyesight), in late 1915 Cumming tapped the 32-year-old Wiseman to form half of a two-man "recon" team to go to New York and size up the need and requirements to establish an SIS station on the other side of the

Atlantic. A Cambridge graduate and former collegiate boxing champ, Sir William was round-faced and slightly cherubic with the ever-present hint of a Cheshire cat smile. Before the war he had led a somewhat feckless existence as an unsuccessful playwright and representative of British banking and investment houses in the U.S. and Mexico.[25] This American experience undoubtedly recommended him to Cumming, but Wiseman's real value lay in his aristocratic pedigree coupled with an open, even charming manner and a quick and devious mind. The first two attributes worked wonders in opening doors to him in America, while the last was an essential component in the highly confidential work he was about to undertake.

Wiseman came to New York in 28 October 1915 in the company of another officer. The duo immediately presented themselves to Gaunt as "Mr. Mansfield" and "Mr. Smith," an interesting and almost certainly not accidental allusion to Cumming's name.[26] Gaunt later recalled that Wiseman masqueraded as Mansfield, but he may have been mistaken. Accompanying Wiseman on the ship over was one Sydney Mansfield, British, and he may have been the second man. In any case, Sir Guy, sensing that these interlopers intended to butt into his operation, gave them short shrift. He regarded the meddling of the "secret service" to be a mistake and even roused the opposition of Morgan & Co. to Cumming's "gumshoe merchants." [27] When they soon after sailed back to England, he must have thought it was the last he would see of them.

We can only guess what Wiseman reported to Cumming, but it is unlikely to have been complimentary to Sir Guy. The latter, it may be recalled, served the Admiralty's NID and, to some extent, MI5, though certainly in much too open a fashion to suit "C." Cumming's operation at this juncture functioned under the nominal authority of the War Office using the cover of MI (Military Intelligence) 1C, or simply, Section V ("Vee"). In practice SIS/MI1C was largely autonomous. Its designated mission was active intelligence operations abroad, including what now would be termed "covert operation," matters that called for utmost secrecy and, when necessary, outright subterfuge. In December Wiseman returned to New York. Soon after, he was joined by another officer of his choosing, Captain Norman Graham Thwaites.[28] Compared to Wiseman's feline qualities, the rugged Thwaites' were those of an energetic, friendly hound, though he was his bosses' equal in guile. He had worked for years as a journalist on the Manhattan beat, at one time acting as secretary to George Pulitzer, and had a raft of friends and acquaintances in various corners of Gotham life, including the German ones.[29] Thwaites had the added advantage of having been educated in Germany and being fluent in the language; indeed, he was able to pass for German if the situation required. These attributes gave him the particular responsibility of keeping tabs on German circles in New York and other parts of the U.S.

Cumming's men set themselves up at 44 Whitehall with Wiseman operating under the general cover of the British purchasing agency while Thwaites, who took control of the local Military Control Office (MCO), functioned as his #2 and handled the more obvious aspects of intelligence work. Behind this façade, Section V was to coordinate information and propaganda activities for all British entities in the U.S. and to conduct "the regular routine work of C.E. [contre-espionage] and activities in connection with Indian and Irish sedition." [30] Beyond this, Sir William had an even more secretive and important personal mission: to cultivate the friendship and confidence of influential Americans, men such as presidential friend and adviser Edward M. House, and thereby influence American policy towards Britain and the war.[31]

Gaunt was discomfited by Section V's presence but there was little he could do about it. He maintained an outward attitude of polite cooperation with Wiseman, but beneath the surface resentment simmered. He sniped at his rival in memos to London and kept his eyes open for anything he might use against him. In his later memoirs, Gaunt quite erroneously described Thwaites as *his* assistant, while Wiseman, he boasted, "played a very small part under me." [32] This was, simply put, an utter lie.

Whether it was Wiseman who approached Reilly or the other way around is uncertain. His subsequent reports to London, those that survive anyway, discuss intelligence activities in only the most general terms. Informants remain anonymous. Sir William had to compartmentalize counter-espionage from his propaganda and diplomatic work, so Thwaites handled most direct liaisons with agents and informants. He did tell London that his office had "dependable German agents who are trusted acquaintances in enemy circles" and retained at least two up to March 1918.[33] As noted, Reilly probably had been supplying information to the British Consulate from the time of his arrival, and Consul Bailey worked hand-in-glove with Wiseman and his organization. Sir William and the Ace-of-Spies had other things in common. Both were interested in circumventing Gaunt. Wiseman and Thwaites cultivated a close relationship with Jacob Schiff and Kuhn & Loeb, despite the firm's reputation for pre-German sympathies—or, perhaps, because of them. Reilly, of course, had links to the same sphere.

In his memoirs, Thwaites describes his confidential dealings with Reilly, Weinstein and Jechalski as early as 1916. He unreservedly praised Reilly as a man who performed "excellent intelligence work" and provided "valu-

able services" for the British cause.[34] He suggests that his first contact with
Sidney came about as a result of accusations of graft and treason against
certain Russian officials in New York, something that demonstrates
Wiseman & Co.'s active interest in local Russian affairs.

Wiseman and his associates knew that Indian and Irish nationalists in
the U.S. were receiving financial and other encouragement from the
Germans. They also were cognizant of German sabotage plans on American
shores. While Wiseman had a practical interest in limiting these activities,
he had greater desire to exploit them for propaganda purposes. In this
regard, something like the Black Tom explosion was ideal. It demonstrated
to the U.S. leadership and public that German agents constituted a genuine
threat to the lives and property of American citizens on their own soil. This
does not mean that Wiseman or SIS actively encouraged the Black Tom
scheme or its ilk, but it does mean he would have had no reason to *discourage* such outrages.

The man leading the battle against Hindu sedition on the American
front was Robert Nathan, the Indian political officer who, as previously
described, may have had a connection with Sidney as early as 1906. During
the early months of the war, Nathan spearheaded SIS infiltration and disruption of Indian and other anti-Allied plots on the Continent. According
to his *Times* obituary, in 1915 he "discovered the anarchist plot, hatched in
Switzerland and financed from Germany, for the assassination of . . . the
heads of the Allied nations." [35] That many of those involved were Russians
showed his continued interest in that sphere and provided a common
denominator for his renewed work with Reilly. Sir Robert came to New
York in March 1916 to act as Wiseman's point man in combating Indian
intrigues. He also was "instrumental in running to earth the German agents
blowing up munitions ships and munitions factories," a task in which he
worked hand-in-glove with Thwaites and, less directly, with Reilly.[36] Fellow
British agent Paul Dukes, who would meet both men soon after, recorded
that they were "great friends" who "shared much in common." [37] This,
again, suggests a relationship that long predated 1916.

Wiseman's bureau colluded with Reilly in stifling investigation of corruption and treason in the Russian Mission. The main charges centered
around Sidney's friend Col. Nekrasov of the RSC's Technical Bureau. The
so-called Nekrasov Affair, draws together several threads. With the aid of
sympathetic staffers in the RSC, Ivan Okuntsev, the publisher of a local
anti-Tsarist paper, *Russkii Golos*, gathered a dossier of incriminating evidence against Nekrasov and several other officials. His case received a
major breakthrough when a fellow named Vladimir Zybyshko (AKA

Ziganovich) came forward to reveal that he had acted as a go-between in successful efforts by the Germans and Austrians to obtain information on Russian rifle and shell contracts along with specifics on the factories producing them and the dates and routes of their shipment. He further charged that this information had been used to organize the sabotage and disruption of Russian war supplies. As Zybyshko related the tale to his friend George Lurich, another intimate of Okuntsev, he received documents from Aleksandra Miroliubskaia to convey to the German and Austrian consulates. Miroliubskaia, the aforementioned friend of Mathilda Kramm, received the material directly from her lover. Poor Zybyshko, it seems, was himself in love with Miroliubskaia and had been duped into believing that she was Nekrasov's sister, not his paramour. It was on learning the bitter truth that he decided to tell all he knew to Lurich and Okuntsev and soon after, to Guy Gaunt.

Gaunt pushed for a full investigation, and Thwaites thrust forward to handle the affair. Thwaites turned immediately to Reilly who, as Thwaites later described it, knew all of the officers involved and "gave them a clean bill of health."[38] On the basis of this, he concluded that there was "no evidence either of graft or of enemy contacts" and dropped the inquiry flat. His approach was paralleled by Boris Brasol, who not only rejected the Lurich-Okuntsev charges as "completely untrue," but countered by accusing those worthies of being German agents seeking to bring discredit on the Russian Government and its representatives.[39] When the accusations later found their way into the American press, Brasol threatened the papers with libel suits.[40]

The Affair ultimately involved, in one way or another, most of the leading Russian officials in New York. Gen. Sapozhnikov appeared at least astoundingly remiss, particularly when he admitted that Jechalski was certainly a German spy, but only a "commercial" one.[41] Indicted as accessories after the fact were consular officials Ustinov and Rutskii, men close to the Ace-of-Spies. Sidney, as usual, managed to keep his name out of the mess, publicly anyway. The only apparent reference crops up in a letter from Russian attorney Isidore Chiurig (Khurig) to Gen. Khrabrov, the successor to Zaliubovskii. Chiurig, who was himself somehow involved in the investigation, vouched for Lurich's German connections, citing as his source one Lucini, "a former employee of S.R."[42]

Chiurig, to no surprise, was another source of Thwaites'.[43] In a report on the affair later compiled by anti-Tsarist sleuth Vladimir Burtsev, Thwaites admitted having documents in his possession that incriminated Nekrasov and several others.[44] It also is noteworthy to compare Thwaites' laudatory statements about Reilly in his memoirs to what he told American investigators in 1918. Pressed by the Americans to provide information on Reilly and his associates, Thwaites then swore that he knew very little about them personally. He did admit to having approached Reilly and Weinstein regarding the Nekrasov charges and to have become "suspicious" by their conspicuous effort to get the Russian out of trouble.[45]

What Thwaites was at pains to conceal was his and the SIS's connection to Reilly and the network of German agents and double-agents that supplied them with information, information they were not always inclined to share with their new American allies. Though he avoids naming names, in his memoir Thwaites recounts the involvement of Jechalski with a would-be femme fatale, the actress Myrtis Cooney, in this skullduggery. Her name also cropped up in the Nekrasov affair. According to Thwaites, Cooney's reckless amateur spying was to blame for all sorts of the trouble. Through her meddling, Jechalski, who "had so involved himself in by prying into German affairs that he had become suspect" was arrested by the U.S. military.[46]

Despite his clandestine alliance with Thwaites and Wiseman, Reilly did not enjoy the good will of other members of the British mission. Gaunt, as noted, evidenced a special animus and denounced him as an "enemy of the Allies."[47] Two others who had nothing good to say were Cols. Abbot and Giffard of the Anglo-Russian Subcommittee. The former complained to the Americans that Reilly had created "a great deal of trouble" by holding up Russian contracts and reiterated that "it was impossible to do anything [with the Russians] unless it was done through Reilly."[48] He noted that this was well known to Thwaites who, Abbot believed, had made a thorough investigation of the "clever schemer."[49] Giffard echoed Abbot's complaints but confessed that Reilly was a "shrewd businessman" who had "great influence with the Russians" as well as many American business figures, notably Samuel MacRoberts. Giffard likewise insisted that Thwaites knew all this and more about the man.

Reilly's antics attracted the attention of French military agents in New York. This interest noticeably increased in August 1916 with the arrival of Lt. Zinovii Peshkov. The latter, as mentioned, was the brother of both Benny and Yakov Sverdlov. Enlisting in the French Army at the beginning of the war, Peshkov had lost an arm and thereafter took up a series of intelligence-related staff assignments.[50] In New York, he assisted in keeping tabs on the local Russians, Tsarist and radical, and their involvement with German agents. Reilly and friends certainly came under his scrutiny. Capt. Henri Merchel of the French Mission confided to American officers that

Reilly was a "very mysterious person" who frequently was discussed in French circles as a German agent.[51] Merchel noted that he had it straight from a member of the Russian Mission, none other than Guchkov's man Morozov, that Reilly was without doubt a German spy and was long known to be such in Russia. The French took interest in Reilly because of his dealings with one of their own countrymen, the Duc de Morny. He may be recalled as an old acquaintance of Sidney's. Now fallen on hard times, he frequented the Russian and French missions where he peddled information and tried to snag the occasional small commission. Merchel, on the other hand, was known to socialize with Reilly and his companions and, as with Thwaites, raises questions as to just how honest and thorough his comments were.

During the latter half of 1916, Reilly concluded a new set of contracts for motor vehicles, rolling stock, powder and sundry equipment, but his business ventures were facing mounting difficulties from Morgan's ascendancy on the supply front. Another problem, as Sidney himself had warned Gen. Hermonius, was the inability of certain American firms to complete the work they had undertaken. A case in point was the shell contract taken on by Poole Engineering. Behind this deal, recall, was a syndicate of Wall Street financiers led by Thomas Cochran of the Liberty National Bank. By mid-1916, it was obvious that the contract was about to collapse under the weight of mounting production delays and the burden of multiple subcontractors and commissions. Cochran and friends stood to lose their investment unless some fresh source of financial backing could be found. The advent of Morgan offered a way out. Cochran a few months later would leave LNB to become a Morgan partner. However, Morgan was unlikely to support a bailout so long as Reilly and others stood to claim costly commissions. Precisely what happened next is uncertain, but Cochran et al. undoubtedly informed Reilly they could not or would not pay him his money.

Reilly's response was one he would use quite frequently in the years to come—the American legal system. He promptly filed suit and, as Vauclain described it, the matter was "quickly and silently adjusted out of court."[52] Sidney walked away with at least a part of the money owed him, but he extracted another concession from Cochran and his codefendants. He demanded a letter from them attesting that they had found him to be "absolutely honest and upright" in his dealings. It suggests that Reilly was concerned about his reputation and intent on restraining open attacks on his person and practices. However, Vauclain and others agreed that an "honest man" never would have demanded such a letter.[53]

Reilly's fortunes suffered another setback in connection with a Russian loan floated in the closing months of 1916. Following MacRoberts' return from Russia in April, he set about organizing support for a new $50 million Russian loan to be backed by his NCB and other investors. The campaign drew in some rather strange bedfellows. Olaf Aschberg, the Swedish banker with ties to Germans and Bolsheviks, came to Wall Street to lobby for the cause, one in whose bounty he certainly hoped to share. In the boardrooms of Europe and New York, however, there were grave concerns about Russia's financial and political stability, something unlikely to make Russian bonds an attractive investment. After much negotiation, on 17 November MacRoberts announced that a syndicate had come together to back the sale of $50 million in Russian bonds. For Reilly this was welcome news because the money raised would back most of the deals he had recently concluded. The bad news was that NCB's major partner in the new offering was J.P. Morgan. Through the Morganites' cautious influence, only $25 million in bonds were offered for sale, and not all of those found ready buyers.[54]

Robbed of financing, many of Sidney's contracts collapsed. In early October, Reilly had signed a $1 million railway car deal with Newman Erb, but it fell through in November when the anticipated credits failed to materialize. Another notable, and very odd, case was a munitions contact for the Baranovskii Powder Co. This firm, it may be recalled, was controlled by Putilov and managed by the Bolshevik businessman Leonid Krasin. In this deal Reilly followed the common practice of having an innocuous frontman as prime contractor, in this case the respectable-sounding Judge Jacob Erb, a relative of the above. When the deal fell through, agents for the Judge filed suit claiming $465,000 in unpaid commissions, a huge amount on a contract that seems to have totaled no more that $3,000,000, and we can bet that only a fraction of it was destined for Erb's pocket. But this was not the only thing odd about the deal.[55] Some $1,700,000 supposedly deposited in the Empire Trust Co. simply vanished. The powder also seems to have disappeared into thin air with neither Aetna nor Baranovskii claiming to know its whereabouts. Once again, we must suspect, Reilly had his finger in a multileveled fraud.

In addition to business, during 1916, Reilly took a marked interest in Polish affairs. This seems to have been stimulated by the 15 November arrival in New York of Ignace Paderewski, the renowned pianist, currently acting as a leading representative of the Polish national movement. The Maestro had come to America to lobby support for Polish independence. While Paderewski espoused a pro-Allied orientation, the Tsarist

Government was highly dubious of his activities. For this very reason, other Polish factions had taken a pro-German or pro-Austrian stance, among them the group led by Jechalski's friend, Antony Knaap. Paderewski wished to create a unified Polish movement and was anxious to reach out to such groups. That, of course, made him all the more suspect to the Russians. In New York, Paderewski found lodging at the Gotham Hotel. Reilly himself had recently relocated to this locale (apparently sans Nadine), and it is possible that he offered these very rooms to the Maestro. There may have been, after all, some personal history between the two men. Reilly had intimated that Paderewski had known both his mother and younger sister. A few years later, Paderewski would acknowledge Reilly as an old acquaintance and possibly return the favor by offering him sanctuary on a crowded cross-channel ferry. Moreover, who else showed up in Manhattan about this time but Reilly's—and Paderewski's—old comrade, Wilfrid Voynich, still the avid Polish patriot.

Upon his arrival in New York, Paderewski also commenced an unusual interaction with Jechalski. Although the Maestro later claimed never to have liked or trusted him, Jechalski was his liaison with German-oriented Polish groups as well as "certain Jewish leaders," among them Jacob Schiff.[56] Subsequent American investigation revealed that Jechalski channeled a good deal of money into Paderewski's coffers as well as the Germanophile Polish Peoples Council.[57]

The true sources of much of this money, we may guess, were Reilly and Wiseman. What would be their interest in Paderewski and the Poles? First, the Germans and Austrians had recently granted "independence" to the Polish territories under their control that threatened to undermine pro-Allied sentiment among the Poles at home and abroad. Bolstering Paderewski and securing influence in the pro-German camp was one means to mitigate adverse effects. The perceptible decay of Russia's military and political structure already had started some thinking about alternatives in the event of a Russian collapse or, as some feared, a Russian separate peace. In such a scenario, the Poles would become important, perhaps invaluable, allies.

In the summer of 1916, Russian military fortunes evidenced a brief improvement; in June a Russian assault against the faltering Austro-Hungarian Army, the so-called Brusilov Offensive, scored Russia's biggest success of the war. The attack soon bogged down with ruinous losses. The hope of victory, now dashed, sent the Empire into a tailspin of despair and defeatism. In the Duma, Guchkov pointed the finger of blame straight at Nicholas and dared to ask if the country's predicament was the result of stupidity or treason. In the growing mood of crisis, the sinister figure of

Rasputin loomed ever larger as the apparent center of the "dark forces" destroying Russia.

Interestingly, Rasputin and the issue of a separate peace came together in New York in the autumn of 1916. Among those who had fallen afoul of the Mad Monk and his influence and been forced to flee Russia was another churchman, the monk Iliodor (Sergei Trufanov).[58] In September Iliodor had drafted a long article provocatively titled "Rasputin: The Holy Devil of Russia" and sold it to the popular *Metropolitan Magazine*. The story, so he claimed, was based on a purloined cache of Rasputin's letters to the Empress. These revealed the *Starets'* secret work on behalf of Berlin in pushing Alexandra to support a separate peace. Iliodor alleged that the Holy One even dared blackmail the British by threatening to push the Tsar into a peace unless London agreed to provide a three million ruble (about $1,500,000) "loan" to him and his associates.[59] These charges were unsubstantiated, but they seem to have hit a nerve in Petrograd and New York. Wiseman knew all about Iliodor and later considered sending him back to Russia on a propaganda mission.[60] In the meantime, however, he was embarrassing. On 3 October, *Metropolitan* abruptly announced the cancellation of the article, even though it already had gone to press and had to be physically excised from the issues. The cause of this change of heart was a strong protest from the Russian Consulate. Personally representing the Russian Government in the matter was Reilly's good friend, Petr Rutskii. Iliodor further charged that Rutskii had tried to bribe him into silence.

Sidney knew Iliodor from prewar Petersburg through Manasevich and perhaps brought him to Wiseman's attention. Sir William would have forwarded his tale to other quarters. By year's end Rasputin was dead, murdered by a band of right-wing patriots led by Prince Feliks Yusupov. From the outset, there were rumors of a British hand in the *Starets'* demise. Recently, Russian historian Oleg Shishkin has alleged that Rasputin's real killer was a "cool, professional" British officer.[61] Shishkin points the finger at the chief of London's military intelligence mission in Petrograd, Samuel Hoare, but he hardly fit the bill of an assassin. There were, however, two other men on hand who would have been right for the job, Majors John Dymoke Scale and Stephen Alley. Also involved in the Rasputin flap in Petrograd was another British intelligence man, Oswald Rayner, a friend of Yusupov. What is of interest to us is that all three of these men soon would have connection to Sidney Reilly in the common service of British intelligence.

But Sidney already had a personal connection to the British secret service apparatus in Petrograd—his old acquaintance and recent employee,

William Calder. In February 1917, immediately following Reilly's return to America, Calder left his job with Bessler & Waechter and enlisted in the Royal Volunteer Naval Reserve. He immediately joined the staff of the Petrograd Military Control Office, but his true affiliation was indicated by his forwarding address in London: 2 Whitehall Court, c/o Captain Spencer, the operational address and cover name of Cumming's SIS/MI1c.[62] This seems clear evidence that, beyond Wiseman and Thwaites, Reilly had at least unofficial links to that organization well before 1918.

In early December, Sidney suddenly arranged for his young mistress, Beatrice Tremaine, and her mother to take an extended vacation in far-off Santa Barbara, California, all at his expense. The decision to get Beatrice out of New York was connected to his own plans for departure. His concern stemmed from the fact that the lovely Beatrice not only had won the Ace-of-Spies' affections, but also the amorous attentions of Tony Jechalski. Tremaine later admitted that the Pole had fallen in love with her and that, despite Reilly's objections, she had maintained a "friendship."[63] However cruel or neglectful Reilly could be towards his women, he also was possessive of them, much as he would be in the case of a valuable painting or beautiful work of art. The same was true of much-abused Nadine who, although Reilly may not yet have realized it, was also squarely in Jechalski's sights.

Nadine had taken to frequenting nightspots such as Maxim's and the dancing studio of Maurice Mouvet, with and without her husband. Mouvet's establishment had a notorious reputation as a place where wealthy married women learned to tango and contracted liaisons with the resident gigolos.[64] One such struggling "dancer" was a young Italian immigrant, Rudolfo Guglielmi, AKA Valentino. Whether Nadine had any personal contact with him is unknown, but it is worth noting that he resembled a younger, if rather prettier, version of Sidney, something she might well have noticed. In any event, Valentino's connection to Mouvet may explain Reilly's later claim to have known the movie idol before he became famous. The picture is further clouded by the fact that Reilly knew Mouvet socially and, apparently, in some business sense as well. Beyond his wife's "dance lessons," Mouvet received payments from Reilly, perhaps for details on the indiscretions of well-heeled clients, or even for Maurice to keep a special eye on Nadine.[65]

In the meantime, Reilly once again traveled the trans-Pacific route. He stopped in Seattle to negotiate a contract for a Japanese cargo ship to undertake three trips between the U.S. West Coast and Port Arthur/Vladivostok.[66] Obviously, he was planning to transport a good deal of something, but what? If one thing had become certain in our story so far, it is that Sidney Reilly almost never traveled with a single purpose in mind. Whatever intelligence duties his journey entailed, its purpose, as usual, was business.

In light of recent setbacks, he was on the lookout for new partners and schemes. In the summer of 1916, for instance, he joined forces with Vil'gelm Karl Ottonovich Lukas, AKA William O. Lucas. A Russian subject of German-Finnish extraction, Lucas had arrived in the U.S. in late 1915 as a representative of the *Zemgor* organization to the RSC, and it is likely that his cooperation with Reilly commenced soon after. He held a lieutenant's commission in the Tsar's army and claimed to have been a flying officer. In any case, by the fall of 1916, Lucas resigned his official duties to form W.O. Lucas & Co. with offices in Chicago and New York as well as Moscow, Petrograd and Vladivostok. In full-page ads in *Ves' Petrograd* and other Russian publications, the company billed itself as a general purveyor of American machinery, vehicles, weapons and munitions. Moreover, Lucas claimed to operate an automobile factory in Seneca, New York where he produced his own line of "Lucas" vehicles.

Given his association with Reilly, it should come as no surprise that neither Lucas nor his outfit were quite what they seemed. First, the firm had no factory in Seneca Falls or anywhere else, but it did lease large warehouses in America and Russia that it filled to the rafters with auto parts, machinery and assorted weaponry. Where most of these goods came from is uncertain, but it is possible that some were diverted from official Russian contracts. The 1916 Petrograd directory shows a Vil'gelm Ottonovich Lukas residing at 13-15 Torgovaia, essentially the same address as the office of Lucas & Co., #13.[67] And 13 Torgovaia, recall, also was the address of Reilly's Allied Machinery office. Curiously, the same directory identifies this Lucas not as a businessman but as an artist at the Imperial Theater. He was, in fact, an actor and in this case his role was to play stand-in for the real boss, Reilly. The plan was to create a new vehicle for obtaining goods and contracts without the increasing burden of having the Ace-of Spies' name attached. The ship chartered in Seattle, we may guess, was to handle the transport of Lucas-purchased goods.

Nor was Lucas the only Reilly ally to appear on the American scene. In late September, Moisei Ginsburg arrived from Petrograd to set up his own office on Broadway. Ginsburg's Far Eastern connections, naturally, would be most useful to Sidney's new gambits. A like role may have been played by Reilly's Japanese associate, Tadao Kamiya. He stopped in New York in late September on his way back from Brazil. Kamiya was involved in shipping thousands of Japanese laborers to South America. In doing so, he chartered vessels that had room for non-human cargo on their return voyage. Sidney had any number of ways to take advantage of that available space.

About this time, Reilly had a hand in the formation of yet another import front, the Grace Russian Co. that operated from Russia's arctic ports. It was a joint venture of W.R. Grace and the San Galli Trading Co., another of Reilly's past Russian associates. American International controlled the firm and its Archangel agent was none other than Karl Lowe, still the American diplomatic agent in the town.[68]

Reilly's ability to finance the Lucas venture shows that, despite recent setbacks, he had accumulated a fair sum of capital. A later SIS report estimated that by 1917 he had been paid at least $2 million in commissions, and the true figure probably was higher.[69] An equal amount was still owed him, and while much of that would never be paid, he had extracted more than enough in bribes, lawsuits and under-the-table payments to make up the difference. He had, of course, considerable overhead, including the upkeep on Nadine and Beatrice and who knows how many others, plus the inevitable bribes and pay-offs in the other direction. His outlay was substantial, perhaps as much as $10,000 a month, but still only a small fraction of what he was raking in. America had made Reilly a very wealthy man.

Sidney was not shy about displaying his wealth even if he was much more guarded about its sources and extent. Chauffeured cars whisked him, Nadine and, of course, Beatrice around town, and there was no end of fine clothes, food and other expensive gifts for the chosen few. As ever, he assiduously added to his collection of rare books and art. As men of means, Reilly and Weinstein played the stock market, though reportedly not always with great success.[70] Sidney took an avid interest in more routine gambling, and he and his cronies were regular players in the high-stakes games held in Manhattan's big hotels.[71] It is in those surroundings, no doubt, that he made contacts in the New York underworld, including the "brain" of Gotham's gambling and other rackets, Arnold Rothstein.

He was back in New York by early February for on the 15th he hosted a big party at the Knickerbocker Hotel to celebrate his and Nadine's second anniversary. Weinstein, Jechalski, Ginsburg, and rest of his gang were on hand. Among the Russian attendees there was much excited conversation about events back home. There events were moving swiftly towards revolution. It was about this time, that Gen. Kozlov of the RSC recollected a phone call from Reilly. The latter, it seems, had avoided any direct contact with Kozlov up to this time but now insisted on a face-to-face meeting. The General declined the offer and stated that so far as he knew, Reilly had no formal connection to the affairs of the Supply Committee. At this, the caller "became very angry and hung up." [72]

Reilly, as always, was a bad enemy to make. Zaliubovskii's superior in London was Reilly's confidant Gen. Hermonius. He oversaw Zaliubovskii's every move with the result that he could not do anything without Hermonius' approval.[73] In Petrograd, British military attaché Sir Alfred Knox, another man who was or would become a friend of Reilly, blasted Zaliubovskii as "ignorant and difficult" and lobbied for Sapozhnikov's reappointment.[74]

Ironically, one of the biggest complaints about Zaliubovskii was his inability to come to grips with a number of "problem contracts." Pre-eminent among these were two in which Sidney played a major role. The first was the Remington rifle contract concluded by Morgan on which Reilly was owed his pre-negotiated commissions. When the firm, in acute financial distress, proclaimed that it could not pay him his due, his response amazed Vauclain and other observers. Instead of filing suit, as he had done successfully in other cases, "in the most suave and genial manner" Reilly expressed his understanding of the company's predicament and waived his rights to further commissions. Vauclain could only suspect, that this oddly philanthropic gesture was motivated by "some subtle motive of which he had no knowledge." [75] The likely explanation is that by helping to save Remington from outright collapse, he protected larger investments.

His role in another contract gone bad, the shell deal of Canadian Car & Foundry, was a very different story. The contract was far behind schedule and Morgan was balking at making further payments to suppliers and subcontractors. This meant a cessation of commission payments to Reilly and others. On 11 January 1917, CC&FC's shell assembly plant at Kingsland, New Jersey caught fire and went up in another huge explosion. The blast cost CC&FC Russia 300,000 shrapnel rounds, plus components for a million more including two million pounds of TNT. The plant itself was a total loss, but by some miracle no one was killed. A disaster for Russia to be sure, but for CC&FC and its creditors it was manna from heaven. The resulting insurance settlement saved the company from bankruptcy and provided sufficient funds to pay Sidney at least a part of what he was owed.

As with Black Tom, official blame fell on German saboteurs, and as in that case some of those definitely were involved, most notably the ubiquitous Kurt Jahnke. The key question in Kingsland is how Jahnke and his comrades gained access to the plant as employees. The vetting of Kingsland's nearly 1,400 employees was under the direction of Boris Brasol.

He engaged private detective firms and placed operatives among the work-force to ferret out German, and especially radical, subversion. One such man working at Kingsland was an Austrian-born Ukrainian, Fiodore Wozniak, also a German double-agent. In the weeks preceding the explo-sion, he warned Brasol's office of security problems at the plant and pre-dicted a catastrophe. Brasol made not the slightest effort to investigate the charges. At the same time, the British had their own agent keeping an eye on Kingsland, one Casimir Palmer. In fact, Palmer was the ex-Okhrana/Scotland Yard informer Casimir Pilenas who, like Reilly, had been recruited by Michael Thorpe. Once again, he and Sidney were working for the same outfit(s). On 9 January, just two days before the plant's destruc-tion, Palmer/Pilenas warned his current superior, Norman Thwaites, of pos-sible sabotage and pointed out *Wozniak* as the likely culprit.[76] Like Brasol, Thwaites did absolutely nothing. The subsequent fire that ignited the con-flagration started at Wozniak's workstation, but whether he set it or was set up remains in doubt. Certainly, what happened was supposed to happen, to the complete satisfaction of Sidney Reilly and others.

In the early days of March (late February in Russia), a rising tide of demonstrations and food riots gripped Petrograd. Tsar Nicholas, effectively isolated at general headquarters far from the Capital, committed a final act of political stupidity by decreeing the dissolution of the Duma. On the 12th, Guchkov and other members of that body's masonic leadership seized the initiative by proclaiming themselves a Provisional Government. Guchkov took the key post of war minister. The Kadets Miliukov and Prince Georgii L'vov, respectively, became foreign minister and prime minister. A token socialist, the laborite lawyer Aleksandr Kerenskii, held the justice portfolio. Abandoned by the military, Nicholas bowed to the inevitable, and on 15 March he abdicated for himself and his son. At the same time another, much larger, body convened as the Petrograd Soviet of Workers and Soldiers Deputies, a reincarnation of the radical assembly forcibly sup-pressed in 1905. It was dominated by Mensheviks and SRs, and contained only a handful of Bolsheviks. Russia now had a curious situation of "dual power," a predicament that would grow steadily more fractious and com-plex in the months to follow.

A local version of this situation played itself out in New York, but with a much quicker and different resolution. Most of the officials of the Russian diplomatic missions and the RSC recognized the Provisional Government, with varying degrees of enthusiasm, but another group popped up calling themselves the Russian Executive Committee. Heading this were Ivan Okuntsev, the radical editor who exposed the Nekrasov scandal, and Ivan

Narodny and Joseph Dalinda, two Russians of revolutionary sympathies and suspected German connections. Another member was Dr. Nikolai G. Kuznetsov, an automotive expert attached to the RSC. He had come to America in February where his ostensible task was to study the U.S. auto industry with an eye to adapting its products and techniques for Russia's needs. This made him ideal to assist the Ace-of-Spies' Lucas company.

On 17 March, Kuznetsov made the front page of the *New York Times* as spokesman for the above Committee, declaring that it was ready to assume control of all Russian assets and agencies on American soil.[77] The next day, the *Times* ran another statement in which Kuznetzov disavowed any association with the Committee. The reason for his change of heart, he declared, was that "a certain Russian with large business and official connections in Russia," undoubtedly Reilly, had threatened to "knock his head off" and make trouble for him in Petrograd if he did not at once quit his work for Okuntsev and friends. This same man, Kuznetsov explained, was "engaged in an enterprise to put American automobiles on the Russian market and command an illegitimately high price . . . by pretending they were manufactured in Russia."[78] Revolution or no Revolution, Sidney was determined to maintain business as usual.

The tumultuous changes in Petrograd generated new interest in Russia in almost everyone, but in few more so than Wiseman. Why this was the case is an interesting question, because Sir William had no prior acquaintance with the country, its people or language. Nevertheless, in the weeks following the Tsar's fall, he seized upon the notion of organizing a special "intelligence and propaganda service" in Russia to combat German intrigues and "guide the storm" of Russian politics by channeling support to "responsible elements," including those on the revolutionary left. The basic criterion was that the groups and individuals to be supported were solidly anti-German and opposed to a separate peace.[79] In this endeavor Reilly was an invaluable counsel. He pushed the aforementioned Father Iliodor as a sterling example of Russian patriotism and a superb orator with a strong following among the common folk.[80]

Reilly also helped acquaint Sir William with Petr Rutenberg, a onetime SR assassin and comrade of Savinkov, now an outspoken champion of the Allied cause. Rutenberg was returning to Russia where, among other things, he had excellent connections with Zionist circles. The latter were to figure prominently in Wiseman's scheme because of their presumed influence among Russian Jews, a group long open to German influence because of widespread anti-Tsarist sentiments among them.[81] Zionists wanted to secure British support for their aspirations in Palestine, so cooperation with Russia was logical quid pro quo. More broadly, Sir William wanted to cultivate all aspects of Russian Jewish opinion, and it that regard, Sidney's connections to the likes of Ginsburg and Simanovich may have proved useful. Beyond that, a list of "principal Jewish leaders" in Petrograd sent to Wiseman in May included the name of Leontii Bramson, cousin of Salomon Rosenblum.[82]

Wiseman also exploited the Jewish angle for money, most notably from Jacob Schiff. The latter was delighted by the fall of Tsarism and publicly avowed that he "loved deeply" the new Russian Government.[83] He agreed to help Wiseman through his influence with Russian bankers and Jewish activists, but also with direct outlays of cash.[84] The advantage of such money was that there was no way it could be traced to a British source; indeed, it might even be disguised as *German* money. With House's help, Wiseman convinced the Americans to put up $75,000 by claiming to act on secret British information and then tapped London for the same amount by assuring officials there of U.S. support.[85] Perhaps Reilly was coaching Sir William in the rudiments of the System.

Wiseman's—or was it Reilly's?—plan called for secrecy. Given a growing tide of anti-Allied sentiment in Russia, any direct ties had to be avoided. In a later, terse report on these activities, Wiseman alluded to many agents, one of them "a well-known international socialist," but gave no names.[86] One of the few persons who can be connected to the venture was another Briton, and family friend, the writer W. Somerset Maugham. While Maugham had practical experience as a secret agent, like Wiseman he no knowledge of Russia and as a rather obvious Englishman he seemed bound to attract unnecessary attention. That, likely, was his primary function—to distract attention from ground-level operatives like Reilly.[87]

Another actual potential recruit could have been Leon Trotsky. The veteran revolutionary arrived in New York in January 1917 following his expulsion from France and Spain for antiwar agitation. In Gotham he continued to speak out against the war, but he differentiated himself from outright defeatists like Lenin by also declaring his opposition to any separate peace by Russia.[88] That made him exactly the type Wiseman was looking for. In the wake of the revolution back home, Trotsky, as hundreds of other Russian exiles, sought the first ship home. One man to immediately take notice of this was Wiseman's agent Casimir Pilenas. He went to Sir William to denounce Trotsky as a dangerous radical with German connections. Wiseman later admitted receiving this information before Trotsky sailed, but, for reasons not explained, did absolutely nothing to prevent or obstruct his departure.[89] Had Wiseman received contrary advice from someone like Reilly?

However, Pilenas conveyed the same information to Guy Gaunt. On 28 March, Gaunt sent an urgent wire to British naval intelligence: on board the SS *Kristianiafjord* that had left New York the day before were a group of Russian socialists bent upon overthrowing the present Russian Government. They carried $10,000 courtesy of the Germans and were led by one Trotsky.[90] On 3 April, Trotsky and five companions (along with his wife and son), were taken into custody by British naval authorities at Halifax, Nova Scotia. But for the moment, let it be noted that also aboard the *Kristianiafjord* was a returning Russian officer, Col. Andrei Kolpashnikov. Apparently on his own initiative, he at once offered his services as a translator and general intercessor between Trotsky and the British authorities. Kolpashnikov, however, had been associated with the RSC and was a close associate of Rogovin, Rutskii, and John MacGregor Grant and thus, with Reilly.[91] It seems unlikely that his presence on the boat was entirely accidental. Was Kolpashnikov there to keep an eye on Trotsky and, if so, for whom?

At almost the same time Gaunt denounced Trotsky, he did the same to Sidney and in almost precisely the same terms. On 3 April, U.S. Bureau of Investigation agent L.S. Perkins relayed to Washington Gaunt's recent statement to Proskey that Reilly was anti-Ally and a probable German spy.[92] The report soon found its way to the desk of the chief of Captain Roger Welles, Chief of the Office of Naval Intelligence (ONI), who ordered an immediate investigation of the suspicious Englishman—or Russian—and his associates. Gaunt's attacks on Trotsky and the Ace-of-Spies may have been motivated by a desire to get back at Wiseman by instigating actions that might reveal his dealings with such undesirables. But in Reilly's case, Sir Guy's attack came on the eve of America's entry into the war which, thanks in no small part to the efforts of his rival, followed on 6 April. Though small and inexperienced, American intelligence services were poised to combat an anticipated wave of enemy subversion and sabotage. Reilly, from all indications, was a prime suspect.

The Trotsky arrest had another interesting twist. On 20 April, Claude Dansey landed in Halifax as part of a British delegation destined for Washington. He at once arranged the release of Trotsky and his comrades (21 April).[93] In an exchange with Wiseman, Dansey demanded to know why the Russians had been stopped in the first place. Sir William cited Pilenas whom Dansey insisted ought to be fired. He was not. Dansey's arrival may also have presented more problems for Sidney. Claude was initially slated to take over the whole British intelligence operation in the States, and his knowledge of Reilly's past may not have made him a welcome change.

Faced with these difficulties, Reilly decided it best to disappear. In April, he and Nadine slipped off to secluded Hot Springs, Virginia, from where he would make quick, furtive forays to New York over the next few months. At Hot Springs, later reports revealed Reilly frequented the company of one Fred Ostwald, a German-American with links to Orbanowski, Pavenstedt, but also, to the complete puzzlement of the Americans, to members of the British mission in Manhattan, most notably Thwaites.[94] Vague reports held that Reilly had recently enlisted Ostwald to intercede with British authorities to forestall his conscription into the King's forces. In fact, it was rather the other way around. On 13 March 1917, one Sidney G. Reilly enlisted in the Royal Flying Corps in Toronto, Canada.[95] This was distinct from his RFC commission that would not come for several months, and a detail later missing from his main service record. Ostwald was another double agent working for Thwaites and Wiseman, and Sidney was using him to communicate with Section V to arrange the enlistment. This step may well have been designed to forestall conscription, something made possible by New York State's recent decision to turn over names of all British subjects to the King's military authorities.

Nor was this the only problem he had to contend with. As Russia foundered in revolution and America lurched towards war, in late March Samuel Vauclain moved to extricate himself and Eddystone from the dead-end Russian contract and sell the plant, lock, stock and barrel to the U.S. Government. To do this, however, he had to free it of pesky things like commission claims. The latter, including Reilly's, were technically payable only on profits, so if the company books could be juggled to show it dissolved in the red, the problem was solved. On 17 March, after offering them a special "bonus," Vauclain received the approval of Eddystone's directors, including Mssrs. Morozov and Poliakov, to dissolve the firm forthwith.[96]

Some were to pay a heavy price for Vauclain's sleight-of-hand. On 11 April the Eddystone works suffered the same fate as Black Tom and Kingsland and at the hands of the same master saboteur, Kurt Jahnke. In this case, however, more than 130 workers, almost all women and teenage girls, were blown to bits when the shell-loading building went up in a titanic blast.[97] Was Reilly behind the disaster? Well, he certainly had the motive and the means to set things in motion, and whatever the truth, Vauclain would always have to wonder.

America was becoming too hot for the Ace-of-Spies. Tremaine recalled that around this time she and Reilly were "often followed by men" whom she assumed to be "detectives," but just whose she did not know. [98] In response, her lover hired Pinkerton men to shield her from these unwanted attentions. A serious blow fell on 7 July when Maj. Ralph van Deman, head of the U.S. Army's Military Intelligence Division (MID) wrote Wiseman to ask what the latter knew regarding "Sydney George Reilly, Englishman," whose name had come to MID's attention "in connection with German propaganda." [99] Two days later, Sir William replied that the individual in question, who might or might not be a British subject, had a generally bad reputation and had been "mixed up with various scandals" involving the Russian mission. He was without doubt an associate of "various undesirable characters" and it would not have been "in the least surprising if he was employed by enemy agents." [100] Sir William told no lies, but, of course, he could not let slip any hint of his real knowledge of Reilly. The American inquiry was beginning to probe too close to home.

Under the circumstances, the Ace-of-Spies' talents could be used more securely and profitably elsewhere, namely Russia where Wiseman's initiative was about to go into full swing. In addition to his many contacts among Russia's economic, political and military circles, Reilly could continue infiltrating and informing on German activities. In an earlier report to London, Wiseman had advocated sending selected "German" operatives from New York "who have special facilities for getting into the confidence of German agents." [101] During July Reilly quietly prepared for the trip. In early August, he popped up briefly in New York to settle some accounts and cash checks, and soon thereafter completely vanished from American eyes and shores. He would not return, openly at least, for almost two years. He was headed back to Russia and into a web of intrigue that would prove the greatest challenge and opportunity of his career—so far.

NOTES

1. HIA, Posol'stvo, f. 370-12, 9.
2. CSA 215, Exhibit A, Confidential Memorandum, 4 Sept. 1918.
3. Dame Elizabeth Hill, *In the Mind's Eye: The Memoirs of Dame Elizabeth Hill* (Lewes, 1999), 8–10.
4. PRO FO 369/1025, Mackie to Consular Dept., 10 Dec. 1918.
5. Sliosberg, III, 293.
6. ONI 21010-3421, Names List, 4; USDS, 661.116/32, 18 Apr. 1917.
7. *NYT*, (21 Apr. 1916), 15:4, (22 June), 5:4.
8. PRO, FO 371/3348, "Karl Lowe," 17 Dec. 1918.
9. HIA, Posol'stvo, f. 370-12, 2–5.
10. Aleksandr Bykov and Leonid Panov, *Diplomaticheskaia stolitsa Rossii* (Vologda, 1998), 128–132.
11. Ibid., Memorandum #3, 2.
12. *NYT* (15 May 1918) 10:1.
13. USDS, 862.2-412, Welles to Harrison, 14 Jan. 1919.
14. CSA 215, 6.

15. SIS, New York, 28 Nov. 1924.
16. HIA, Posol'stvo, 334-1, ARSC Agreement, 28 July 1916; PRO, MUN 4/5490, #20360, Text of Anglo-Russian Agreement, 14 July 1916.
17. PRO, Ibid., #20170, Stettinius to Denkstein, 5 July 1916, and #21514, Denkstein to Whigham, 23 June 1916.
18. HIA, Posol'stvo, 370-12, 4–5.
19. *NYT* (28 July 1916), 2:6.
20. MID, 9140-6073, 10 Sept. 1918, 3.
21. Krymov, 73.
22. Landau, 77–80 and *NYT* (30–31 July & 1–2 Aug. 1916). See also Jules Witcover, *Sabotage at Black Tom* (Chapel Hill, NC, 1987), 160–1.
23. The voluminous records of the U.S.-German Mixed Claims Commission (MCC) are in USNA, RG 76, specifically, "Opinions and Decisions, 1926–32."
24. On Cumming's career, see Alan Judd, *The Quest for C: Mansfield Cumming and the Founding of the Secret Service* (London, 1999).
25. On Wiseman, see W.B. Fowler, *British-American Relations 1917–1918: The Role of Sir William Wiseman* (Princeton, 1969) and his obituary, *NYT* (18 June 1962), 25:1. Regarding his intelligence work, much more information may be extracted in Wiseman's personal papers in the Yale University, Sterling Library, Group 666. Hereafter cited as WWP.
26. Mansfield Smith also happened to be the original name of Cumming so their names conveniently conveyed just whom they represented.
27. Gaunt, 172.
28. WWP, folder 175, "Memo for the New York Office," [1916] and f. 172, "American Section M.I.1.C.," [Oct. 1917].
29. Thwaites later offered his carefully edited version of events in a memoir, *Velvet and Vinegar* (London, 1932).
30. WWP, f. 175, Ibid.
31. Fowler, 14, *passim*.
32. Gaunt, 172. On the veracity of Gaunt's account, see Popplewell, 252.
33. WWP, f. 173, "Miscellaneous Functions of the New York Office . . . ," 28 March 1918.
34. Thwaites, 181.
35. *LT*, "Secret Service in the War, Sir R. Nathan's Work" (28 June 1921), 10. See also Popplewell, 248–249.
36. *LT*, Ibid.
37. Paul Dukes, *The Story of "ST25": Adventure and Romance in the Secret Intelligence Service in Red Russia* (London, 1938), 31.
38. Ibid.
39. HIA Posol'stvo, 370-12, Brazol to Coudert Bros., 11 June 1917.
40. Ibid., and *New York Herald* (7–8 Oct. 1917), *Washington Post* (7 Oct. 1917).
41. HIA Posol'stvo, 370-12, 6–7.
42. Ibid., Chiurig to Khrabrov, 26 Oct. 1917.
43. Ibid., 12.
44. Ibid.
45. MID, 9140-6073, Memorandum #2, 3–4.
46. Thwaites, 181.
47. BI, 39368, Agent Perkins to Director, 3 April 1917.
48. MID, 9140-6073, Report 17 Oct. 1918, 2.
49. Ibid., 3.
50. On Peshkov, see Mikhail Parkhomovskii, *Syn Rossii, general Frantsii* (Moscow, 1989).
51. MID, Memorandum #4, 5.
52. Ibid., Report 11 Oct., 2.
53. Ibid., and 17 Oct., 3.
54. *NYT* (5 Nov. 1916), VIII, 9:1 and (28 Dec. 1916), IX, 19:3.

55. Ibid. (28 Nov. 1916), 20:2.
56. MID, 9140-1496, Statement of L. Kraevna, 15 May 1918.
57. Ibid., Memo of New York Intelligence Office, 23 Nov. 1917.
58. PTsR, VII, 346–.347.
59. *NYT* (24 Oct. 1916), 8:1.
60. WWP, f. 260, "Russia," [1917]. 1.
61. Will Stewart, "Was Rasputin Assassinated by British Foreign Secretary?," *Express Newspapers* (30 April 2000). Shishkin's book detailing these allegations, *To Kill Rasputin*, was not available at the time of this writing.
62. MID, 9140-6073, "Weinstein," 13 Feb. 1918.
63. MID, 9140-6073, Memorandum #4, 4.
64. *NYT* (16 Apr. 1917), 13:3.
65. MID 9140-6073, Memorandum #5, 3.
66. Ibid., Memorandum #4, 3.
67. *Ves' Petrograd, 1916*, 405.
68. USDS, RG84, 12F54, Memo of Fleet Counterintelligence Bureau, 1 Dec. 1917.
69. SIS, CXM 212, 29 March 1918.
70. MID, 9140-6073, Memorandum #5, 6 Sept. 1918, 4.
71. Ibid., 3.
72. CSA 215, 13 Dec. 1924, Exhibit A.
73. PRO, MUN 4/5490, #31482, Crease to Booth, 18 Nov. 1916.
74. Ibid., #23377, WO to Knox, 30 Sept. 1916.
75. MID, 9140-6073, Report 11 Oct. 1918, 2.
76. Landau, 198.
77. *NYT* (17 March 1917), 1:7.
78. *NYT* (18 March 1917), II, 3:3.
79. WWP, 10/261, "Intelligence and Propaganda Work on Russia, July to December 1917," 19 Jan. 1918, 1.
80. WWP, 10/260, "Russia," [1917], 1, and 10/255, "Russia," 18 May 1917, 2.
81. Ibid., 10/277–282.
82. Ibid., 10/277, #61, Report Sent to New York, 5 May 1917.
83. *NYT* (13 April 1917), 8:2.
84. PRO, FO 115/2317, Wiseman to FO, 16 April 1917 and WWP, f. 112, "Russian Affairs," 26 May 1917.
85. Fowler, 111–118.
86. WWP, f. 261, "Intelligence . . . ," 1.
87. On Maugham's recollections of his Russian venture see *A Writer's Notebook*.
88. Ian D. Thatcher, "Leon Trotsky in New York," *Historical Research*, vol. 69, #169 (1996), 176.
89. PRO, KV/2,502, Wiseman to Dansey, 20 April 1917.
90. PRO, FO 871/3009, Report from NCO Halifax to DID, 3 April 1917 and National Archives of Canada (NAC), vol. 2543, file H.Q.C. 2051/1.
91. *NYT* (5 June 1919), 13:2 noting attendees at Kolpashnikov's nuptials.
92. BI, 39368, Ibid.
93. PRO, KV/2, 502.
94. MID, 9140, 817/8, Report of P. Ault, 17 June 1917, 3–4.
95. Royal Naval Air Service Museum, Yeovilton, RFC/RAF Officer's Aperture Cards, PI 21220, Reilly, Sidney George.
96. HIA, Posol'stvo, 93-2, Memorandum of EAC Board of Directors, 28 Aug. 1917.
97. *Eddystone*, 14; Landau, 113.
98. MID, 9140-6073, Memorandum #5, 5.
99. Ibid., Van Deman to Wiseman, 7 July 1917.
100. Ibid., "Memorandum for Major Van Deman," 9 July 1917.
101. WWP, 10/255, "Russia," 18 May 1917, 3.

Chapter Eight
THE RUSSIAN QUESTION

To avoid trouble from the increasingly nosy Americans, Sidney slipped into Canada. In late August, he sailed for Archangel, probably in the company of a group of officers sent from Toronto to join a British military equipment mission in Russia.[1] Bolshevik information later noted that he came to Russia in 1917 as an "expert" attached to the British Military Mission.[2] His goal was to gather information on German land and naval forces held by the Russians, presumably before access to that was lost. That may have been true, but he certainly had other things in mind. By chance or design, also just arrived in Archangel was Reilly's friend and ex-employee, Lt. William Calder, RNVR. In late June 1917, Calder had shifted from the British Military Control Office On Petrograd to MCO Murmansk where he was engaged in "special service outside the Admiralty," i.e. MI1c duties.[3] By the time of Reilly's appearance on the scene, he temporarily shifted his base of operation to Archangel. There he was involved with "propaganda materials," something that provided a link to Wiseman's enterprise and Reilly. Also in Archangel was Karl Lowie, still on duty for Grace, San Galli and the U.S. Consular Service.

From the Allied standpoint, things in Russia were bad and getting worse. The fall of Tsar Nicholas initially offered hope that a free Russia would pursue the war with new vigor and unity. Instead, antiwar and even anti-Ally sentiment was gaining momentum. The Russian Army had mobilized some 14 million men for the trenches, and by 1917 over half of these were dead, wounded or prisoners. Industrial production, despite the genuine effort of Guchkov and others, declined, the transportation system was in ruins and inflation drove the price of ever scarcer basic commodities higher and higher. The faltering Provisional Government seemed incapable of solving any of these problems.

Bolshevik leader Vladimir Lenin arrived in Petrograd in mid-April. He came from Switzerland with the direct assistance of the Germans. In fact, he and his party had been the recipients of the Kaiser's financial assistance for some time. While not a German agent *per se*, Lenin lived by the rule of "flexibility in means, inflexibility in goal," which meant that he was willing to take money from anyone and do anything to achieve control of Russia and igniting World Revolution. Lenin at once called on the popular Soviet assemblies to seize power and end the war. In April, his proposals found limited support even among his own Bolsheviks. But Lenin's persistence, the manifest incapacity of the Provisional Government and mounting public frustration saw the tide gradually turn in his favor. In July, an abortive insurrection forced Lenin to flee to Finland and landed many of his lieutenants in jail. However, by autumn, he and his growing body of followers, now including Trotsky, awaited the opportunity to seize power.

The leader of the Provisional regime, Aleksandr Kerenskii, had other things to worry about. Of particular interest to us is his acting War Minister—Reilly's past partner in intrigue, ex-terrorist and Okhrana informer, Boris Savinkov. Ever the intriguer and power-seeker, Savinkov had his own eyes on the leadership slot. To achieve this, he conspired with an ambitious general, Lavr Kornilov, who harbored his own dictatorial ambitions. In late August Kornilov, encouraged by Savinkov and Guchkov, marched on the Capital with the apparent aim of quashing the Soviet. In a sudden about-face, Kerenskii released Trotsky and other Bolsheviks from jail and asked their help. The coup fizzled, the scheming Savinkov got the sack, but Kerenskii emerged looking weak and isolated. On 13 September, Lenin's supporters took charge of the critical Petrograd Soviet, and a week later that of Moscow.

Such was the atmosphere Reilly found when he rolled into the Capital in mid-September. In Petrograd, he established contact with Maj. Scale who ran the British Military Intelligence Section attached to the Russian General Staff, the agency with which the Ace-of-Spies now cooperated, and which he would formally join in a few months' time. Reilly's many contacts within the Russian military, especially the *Kontrrazvedka*, were his greatest asset in the present effort. Though demoralized by the failure of the Kornilov "revolt" and marginalized by the radical soldiers' and sailors' committees, the officer corps presented a body in which patriotic and pro-Allied sentiments still predominated. A secret officers' organization already operated under the leadership of the new head of the high command, Gen. M.V. Alekseev. In October, a special "Aviation Conference" opened in Petrograd that provided a convenient cover for conspiratorial networking. The conference drew a wide array of officers from the Russian military's aviation, artillery and technical branches, including many whom Reilly knew personally. One attendee was his old pal Gen. Sapozhnikov, ex-chief of the RSC.

Among Allied officers in attendance was Capt. George Alexander Hill, Royal Flying Corps (RFC), on special assignment to the Director of Military Intelligence. Hill later reported that underlying the conference was "a strong political movement."[4] He will play an important part in the rest of our story. A man of some mystery in his own right, twenty-four-year-old "Jolly George" Hill was born at Kazan, in central Russia, the son of Frederick George Hill, an English merchant.[5] That George later sought to obscure his place of birth suggests some sensitivity about it, perhaps the fact that it made him a nominal Russian, and subsequently Soviet, citizen.[6] The elder Hill had many Russian acquaintances, including some with revolutionary sympathies. To one degree or another, he shared those sympathies. Also, F.G. Hill was the cousin of the aforementioned and like-named Fred Hill, protector of Anne. How this figured into George Hill's relationship with Reilly is unclear, but it is, if nothing else, another interesting coincidence.

Reilly also insinuated himself into the Conference, keeping a low profile. He may have been the author of a report reaching Wiseman dated 6/19 October detailing conditions in the Russian Army.[7] Though the Army was, relatively speaking, better armed than ever, morale was "very poor everywhere." Simply put, Bolsheviks or no, the Army was unlikely to last the winter. To give him legitimacy with Russian officers and officials and a measure of protection, on 19 October Sidney George Reilly received a temporary commission as a 2nd Lt. in the RFC, appropriately enough, as a "technical officer."[8]

His commission soon became known in New York, where it aroused curiosity and consternation. Majors Abbot and Giffard, Sidney's antagonists on the contracting front, could only voice "astonishment" that such a rotter had become an officer in the British Army.[9] Gen. Kozlov of the RSC expressed similar puzzlement. The British Recruiting Office in New York, where Reilly's commission supposedly originated, claimed to know absolutely nothing about it. Further probing led them to Thwaites. Capt. Merchel of the French Mission vouched definite knowledge that Reilly had joined the RFC with Thwaites' help.[10] Thwaites only offered that he would get to the bottom of the matter when he next visited England and that Reilly almost certainly would be recalled or asked to resign. He intimated that the dubious subject's enlistment was allowed to proceed because at the time "very little was known against him," a statement contradicted by his simultaneous contention that he regarded Reilly a highly suspicious sort because of his connection to the Nekrasov Affair.[11] Odder still was evidence showing that the direct agent of Reilly's enrollment and his nominal commanding officer was Maj. T.F.G. Strubell, head of the RFC aviation station in Toronto, who was unavailable for comment. Given Reilly's highly dubious standing, it was necessary for Wiseman and his crew to maintain a discreet distance from their secret agent.

Thwaites later told a different tale. Reilly approached him in 1917 and, motivated by patriotic desire to "do his bit" asked the Major to arrange enlistment. In a 1925 SIS report, Thwaites simply noted that the subject had obtained his commission "through the influence of certain officers in the [New York] British Mission, (M.I.[1c]).[12] He later let slip something else: in the fall of 1917, Reilly was not training in Canada but operating in Russia "when Kerensky was dropping to his doom."[13] As for Sidney, he told Beatrice, perhaps with some honesty, that he joined up "to get away from everything, particularly his wife."[14] Sidney used Tremaine to keep up his Canadian alibi; she later claimed to have received regular letters from her betrothed in Toronto throughout the fall, though she could not produce them. At the same time, Reilly continued to pay his young love $200 a month "allowance."

Keeping in mind the System, we must wonder if Sidney had entirely severed his ties to the Kaiser's agents. Interestingly, in the spring of 1917 von Hintze left his post in China to become Berlin's ambassador to Norway. On the way back to Europe, he passed through Yokohama where he again touted the virtues of a Berlin-Tokyo Axis. But he added a new twist, the addition of Russia under a future pro-German regime.[15] Russian affairs were very much on his mind. His Norwegian post put him conveniently close to Stockholm, the chief locus of German-Bolshevik intrigue. Working in the German Embassy in Stockholm where he oversaw "espionage and propaganda" was none other than Hintze's past collaborator Baron von Lucius. Moreover, the Baron "came under suspicion of having been in active touch with the Russian Bolsheviki."[16] In fact, he was a pivotal figure in Berlin's connection to that quarter.[17]

Meanwhile, in Petrograd, the aviation conference ended with some success on the clandestine level. In Petrograd, the *Orel'* (Eagle) officers' organization undertook the collection and transfer of volunteers, money and supplies to the southern city of Rostov-on-Don. There an anti-German, and implicitly anti-Bolshevik, military force was gathering under the aegis of the Don Cossack General, A.M. Kaledin. Allied support for this venture was based on the hope of preserving some semblance of an Eastern Front against Germany and its allies.

Reilly now assumed the alias of Konstantin Massino, a Russian merchant from the south, possibly Odessa. Behind the scenes, he began to assemble a team of agents to handle the clandestine end. Like him, they were all connected in one way or another to the defunct Okhrana. As one of the detested symbols of the old regime, the Tsarist police establishment had fallen on hard times since March 1917. The Provisional Government formally disbanded it and dragged its leaders, men such as Beletskii and Komissarov, before a public hearing to confess their individual and collective sins. Although decapitated, the body of the Okhrana was still very much alive. Its thousands of officers, agents and informants were cast adrift to fend for themselves. A few gravitated to the Provisional regime's feeble effort to organize a security/counterintelligence service, while others sold their services to the Germans. Many more would find their way into the revived secret police of the Soviet state.

One of Sidney's recruits was Manasevich-Manuilov. It may be recalled that the veteran intriguer had been an agent of Gen. Batiushin's special committee to combat speculation and espionage. In early 1917, Manasevich headed a section investigating banking activity but came under accusation of using his position to extract bribes and blackmail, which undoubtedly was the case. In jail at the time of the March overturn, Manasevich arranged his release by offering to tell all he knew, or enough, about past police intrigues to the new regime's investigating commission. He claimed to know something about the links among the Germans, Bolsheviks and certain Russian banks.

Reilly approached another veteran of the Batiushin committee, Lt. Vladimir Grigor'evich Orlov. A former military prosecutor and expert investigator, Orlov was a boyhood chum of Boris Savinkov and knew Brasol from their mutual work in prosecuting political cases. That job brought him into contact with a wide array of revolutionaries, including Feliks Dzerzhinskii, one of Lenin's key lieutenants and the future head of the Soviet secret police. Orlov was now one of Gen. Alekseev's main agents in Petrograd, and for good measure, he established links to German intelligence in the Capital.[18] Other members included the versatile Pole Ossendowski, Reilly's friend Grammatikov and another former police agent with journalistic roots, Evgenii Petrovich Semenov.

It is possible that Reilly also solicited the help from revolutionary muckraker Vladimir Burtsev. A dedicated radical but also a Russian patriot, the old nemesis of the Okhrana was one of the first to denounce the

Bolsheviks as a new threat to freedom. Earlier in 1917, he had amazed many comrades on the left by coming to the defense of Manasevich, widely regarded as one of the most vile examples of police agent, by arguing that Manasevich's recent work had been in the true service of the nation. By the end of the year, Burtsev would find himself sharing a prison cell with ex-Okhrana chief, and other Reilly collaborator, Beletskii. Burtsev took the opportunity to quiz Beletskii on the Tsarist police's manipulation and support of Lenin's party.[19]

Then there was Savinkov. Seething over his recent dismissal by Kerenskii, Boris had attached himself to the Union of Cossack Forces and managed to get himself elected to its executive committee. There he tirelessly agitated against Kerenskii and the rising Bolsheviks. He rightly pegged Lenin as the next Russian strongman and, thus, his new rival. Wiseman later reported that his agents worked "to form a strong Cossack combination to support any government which took a strong line on the war."[20] In late September, Boris journeyed to the Don to confer with Kaledin and Alekseev.

Sidney's attention focused on the connections between Lenin's Bolsheviks and the German General Staff, a question that had surfaced early that summer. There may have been a link here to Robert Nathan's mission in Switzerland early in the war. Then, recall, Nathan unearthed an "anarchist" plot financed by Germany. The German "bag man" in this affair was a Swiss socialist, Karl Moor (AKA "Beyer") who had a long history of infiltrating and subsidizing Russian émigrés on behalf of Berlin.[21] Through his investigation of Moor, Nathan discerned the broad outline of German intrigues with Russian radicals, a matter that now cried for more thorough examination, especially in regard to the Bolsheviks. Assisting Nathan in the operation was veteran anarchist-smasher and Reilly mentor William Melville. If Nathan did not know the Ace-of-Spies already, Melville provided the necessary introduction.

The British were not the only ones interested in a Berlin-Bolshevik axis. The French had their own suspicions. In May 1917, the previously mentioned Lt. Zinovii Peshkov left his post in New York and returned to Paris. There he contacted a Parisian police official with the odd name of Charles Faux-Pas-Bidet. Bidet, as we will call him, specialized in keeping tabs on Russian radicals and had extensive files on their activities and was the man who engineered Trotsky's expulsion from France in 1916. He was convinced that Germany subsidized the antiwar movement among the Russians. In June, Peshkov and Bidet, the latter now enrolled in the French Army, headed for Petrograd bringing with a dossier of materials culled from Bidet's archive. To this was added information recently obtained by the

French military intelligence section in Petrograd headed by Capt. Pierre Laurent. Among Laurent's agents was insurance man Emile Bagot, an excellent source on the local scene and its denizens and, of course, another Reilly contact.

Within days of Peshkov's and Bidet's arrival on the scene, the first public accusations of a Bolshevik-German alliance appeared in the press.[22] Involved in this complex network were two rent links to Reilly territory, The Russo-Asiatic Bank and Olaf Aschberg's *Nya Banken*, and an older one, veteran revolutionary gadfly Alexander Helphand-Parvus.[23] Given these threads, Sidney was an ideal man to investigate their connections which may have involved collaboration with Peshkov. At the end of August, Paul Dukes, a young Britisher connected to the Anglo-Russian Commission in Petrograd, received a confidential assignment from London to proceed to Paris and comb through French files on the Bolsheviks.[24] Dukes next headed to Petrograd where he delivered the information to Maj. Scale. From Scale, the dossier would have passed to Reilly and his gang.

While the collected information was highly suggestive, it failed to establish an unequivocal link between the Germans and Lenin's minions. With time growing short, Reilly recalled Voynich's advice, that what could not be found might be reconstructed. And he had able forgers at hand. With experience detecting and concocting fabricated evidence, Orlov probably handled the technical end. As pitchmen for the finished product, the Ace-of-Spies enlisted Ossendowski and Semenov. In the aftermath of the Bolshevik coup, the forgers added additional items to show the ongoing dependence of Lenin on German largesse.[25] While the bulk of the assembled dossier, ultimately some seventy documents, was phony, it is important to note that the conspiracy it detailed was essentially true, though this would not finally be proven until the release of German foreign ministry files in the 1950s.[26] The immediate question was how to employ the collection to maximum effect. British and French motives were so suspect among Russians than any direct connection to those quarters would discredit it at once. Moreover, at this late hour it seemed doubtful that anything could stem the rising Bolshevik tide.

The logical recipients of the dossier were the Americans. Not only did the Yanks preserve a wide measure of credibility among Russians, but involving them meshed perfectly with Wiseman's plans. On 27 October, Sir William sailed for London. On the same ship, certainly by no accident, was Edgar Sisson, an American journalist heading to Petrograd to assume control of the U.S. propaganda agency, the Committee on Public Information (CPI). On the bosom of the Atlantic, Wiseman chatted up Sisson and care-

fully primed him for what he would soon find in Petrograd. In the weeks
that followed, Sisson not only swallowed the bait, but even forked over at
least $50,000 for the dossier—a nice payoff for Reilly and his pals.[27] When
Sisson returned to Washington the following March, he carried the incriminating file with him. This admirably served Wiseman's desired end of keeping American policy in Russia in step with London's.

The Sisson gambit was not the only benefit Reilly provided Wiseman
and the nascent anti-Bolshevik resistance. Another key rests in a series of
checks and IOU's signed by Reilly in the weeks preceding his departure
from New York. American investigators later questioned these but were
assured by his man Thomas that they represented nothing more than routine commissions payments or personal transactions. Ranging from a few
to several thousand dollars each, the recipients, men such as Vladimir
Rogovin, an Armenian named Umaniants, and an American businessman
Henry Kuntz, all had one thing in common: they did business in Russian
and had bank accounts there. On closer examination, Kuntz's case seemed
very odd. Other papers indicated that Reilly recently had obtained a court
settlement against Kuntz in Russia.[28] So why was Sidney *paying* him
money?

The answer is provided by Maksim Trester, a member of the RSC's
Technical Bureau and a close associate of Reilly. Trester later confessed that
in the summer of 1917 he and Sidney sailed together back to Russia. On the
way, Reilly gave him an IOU for the contents of his Russian bank accounts,
some 15,000 gold rubles.[29] The aim was to buy up caches of "clean" rubles,
money that could not be traced directly to him or, more importantly, British
hands. Moreover, he also secured a string of accounts at various Russian
banks, under various names, through which additional funds could be laun-
dered. Simply put, it was the Allied equivalent of the secret German nexus
detailed above. It also was part of a massive "ruble-raising" scheme that
would reach its peak a year later. Management of these illicit funds, of
course, offered our hero ample opportunity to enrich himself in the process,
an opportunity he was sure not to miss.

Wiseman's idea was to funnel this covert aid not to Russians but other
groups more committed to the Allied cause. The most important were the
Poles. In the spring of 1917, the Provisional Government had recognized,
with some reluctance, the Poles' right to form their own state and military
formations. Also important was the 50,000-strong Czecho-Slovak Legion.
If given sufficient support, such groups might be enough to preserve some
semblance of an Eastern Front. Reilly, of course, had connections to Polish
nationalists via Paderewski and Jechalski and to the Czechs through the

Czech-American, Emanuel Voska.[30] In New York, the latter had run an efficient espionage ring tied to the Russian Purchasing Committee and
Wiseman that undoubtedly brought him into contact with Reilly.[31] The
tough, square-jawed Voska came to Petrograd in the summer of 1917 as
another operative of Sir William. However, at the same time he was an
American agent with a commission in the U.S. Army. That did not altogether please Wiseman who felt the Yanks were trying to undercut his operation.

In October, another American appeared in Petrograd who presented
Reilly with a more direct challenge. This was Xenophon Kalamatiano, the
Russo-American entrepreneur mentioned earlier in connection with Friede
and Nankivel. In Chicago, Kalamatiano had put together a consortium of
35 American firms dubbed the International Manufacturers Sales Company
of America (IMSC) with the specific aim of penetrating the Russian market.
Backed by $300 million in capital, this enterprise dwarfed Reilly's rival
Lucas & Co.[32] Moreover, Kalamatiano's Chicago office was only a block
away from Lucas' and their New York ones were in the same building, 17
Battery Place. Kalamatiano returned to Russia in May 1916 and established
a Moscow office at 6 Bolshaia Lubianka, an address soon destined to
become the nerve center of the Soviet secret police.

When Kalamatiano again resurfaced on the Russian scene in the fall of
1917, he came not only as a businessman, but also as an agent of U.S.
Intelligence. Similar to the Ace-of-Spies' relation to the British, he had acted
as an "informal unsupervised and unpaid volunteer agent" for the U.S.
State Department as early as 1915–16.[33] His formal role as American spy
commenced on the eve of the Bolshevik coup under the auspices of the
American Consul in Moscow, Maddin Summers. Summers put
Kalamatiano in charge of a special Publicity and Propaganda Section, soon
to be expanded into the Information Service (IS).[34] When Voska departed
the scene in November, Kalamatiano took over his network of Czech and
Russian agents, a move that further extended American independence and
influence.

This was precisely what Reilly and Wiseman wanted to contain.
Kalamatiano later admitted that his operation experienced leaks from the
start, apparently from inside the Moscow Consulate.[35] The culprits were
two ex-Okhrana informers, one a friend of Kalamatiano's wife, who
acquired copies of Kalamatiano's reports beginning in October. Espionage
writers William Corson and Robert Crowley, argue that the former Tsarist
spies forwarded the reports to the head of the Soviet Cheka, Feliks
Dzerzhinskii.[36] However, the Cheka would not come into being until

December, and, as we will see, would not assume any effective counterintelligence capabilities for some months to come.

The hand engineering the infiltration of the American IS in late 1917 was almost certainly Reilly's. His long association with the Okhrana gave him ready means to contact an exploit *in situ* sources. Sidney also may have been able to get his hands on Kalamatiano's reports via New York. The American sent copies of his reports to Nankivel's 120 Broadway office. It would have been simple for Reilly's agents to acquire those papers for Wiseman's consumption. This nexus may explain a later, cryptic remark by an American diplomat that proof of Reilly's "treachery" could be found in his communications with New York.[37]

Lenin's cohorts, directed by Trotsky, finally made their move on the night of 6–7 November. Wiseman ordered Maugham out of Petrograd just before the blow fell and most of his other agents ran for cover. Reilly, however, lingered to watch the Bolsheviks take their first unsteady steps in power. Lenin's success was not certain. In Moscow anti-Bolshevik military cadets took control of the Kremlin and threatened to seize the whole city. Petrograd teemed with officers and political opponents ready to turn on the new masters at any moment. Among them was Savinkov who lurked about the city for a few days, at one point taking refuge in the British Embassy.

While Sidney's movements during the next few weeks are vague, he seems to have remained in or near Petrograd using his Massino guise. According to one report he focused attention on cultivating and "corrupting" officials of the fledgling Soviet regime which sounds like his style.[38] Most of these, in fact, were ex-Tsarist servitors. One such was Aleksandr Aleksandrovich Yakushev, a former waterways specialist with the Ministry of Ways and Communications. The best bet is that they had met before, for in addition to shipping the two men shared an abiding interest in actresses. The Cheka later discovered that as Massino, in late 1917, Reilly chatted with Yakushev backstage at the Miniature Theatre in the company of one its performers, Milochka Yur'eva.[39] Most interesting, however, is that soon Yakushev would become a personal aide to none other than Trotsky.

Perhaps to disguise what he really was up to, this period later gave rise to tales of Reilly's hair-raising adventures behind German lines, the theft of Berlin's naval codes and even a meeting, in disguise, with the Kaiser.[40] There is not the slightest evidence to support any of it. Information later collected by the Soviets had him *arriving* at Murmansk in December aboard the British battlecruiser *Queen Mary*.[41] The latter was impossible; that ship was sunk at the Battle of Jutland in 1916. However, this probably is a muddled version of an *exit* from Russia. According to his service record, he had never left Canada. The same notes show that on 3 December, he received the grade of Equipment Officer 3.

In Murmansk, Reilly reportedly approached the leader of the local soviet, Aleksandr Mikhailovich Yur'ev. While a professed Bolshevik, Yur'ev's loyalty to Moscow was questionable. He subsequently proved quite willing to support the Allies against his government's directions.[42] Murmansk also happened to be the spot where his friend Calder now ran the British Military Control Office, so he was right on the spot to help Reilly make a smooth exit.

What, if any, measures did our spy take to safeguard wife and progeny in Petrograd? Did he arrange their transfer to a safer locale or leave them be? And what of the other Mrs. Reillys? On 22 September, Daisy, from Brussels, wrote the British Embassy in The Hague asking for information on the whereabouts of her husband. Her letter has long since been removed from the consular files of the PRO, but its purport remains.[43] The interesting thing is that she knew he had left New York and seemed convinced that someone in British officialdom would know where he was. Interestingly, Claude Dansey had been in New York from April–June 1917 where he met with Wiseman and Nathan.[44] Thus, he could have picked up information about Reilly and his plans and passed it on to Margaret. Why would he have been so helpful? Years later, a rumor surfaced that Dansey and Margaret had been "intimate."[45] While a romantic entanglement between a disfigured, middle-aged woman and the reputedly homosexual Major seems highly unlikely, it does not rule out some other sort of friendship. Then again, perhaps Dansey used Daisy as an alternative means of keeping tabs on the dubious Mr. Reilly.

As for Nadine, in June 1917, the same time her husband dropped from sight, she abruptly moved out of their Manhattan apartment and relocated to a hotel far out on Long Island and later still to the secluded Allenhurst Club in New Jersey. Aside from Weinstein, Jechalski and a few other of her husband's friends, she kept to herself and was well supplied with money. According to American investigation, Nadine, unlike Beatrice, received no letters from her husband nor did she write to him.[46] Reilly, however, was not out of her thoughts. An informant told U.S. Navy investigators that she displayed several pictures of him in her bungalow and otherwise "seems to be very fond of him."[47] There is evidence that Nadine knew something of her husband's whereabouts and anticipated his movements. In December she announced plans to go to England with the intention of reuniting with her errant husband.[48] At the last minute, however, her passport was refused by Thwaites' office.

Meanwhile, on 20 November Wiseman delivered a report to the War Cabinet based on Maugham's, and probably Reilly's, findings. It was highly negative toward the Soviet regime and its prospects for the Allied cause. The latter was in a rather precarious state. The depleted French Army had been wracked by mutiny, and the British exhausted by a string of costly, fruitless offensives. On 5 December, Lenin declared an armistice in the East. The Russian Army soon melted away and a million German troops were freed to reinforce the Western Front.

The basic debate in London was how to salvage something from the Russian debacle—by supporting the Bolsheviks' opponents or by accommodation with the "Bolos" themselves? Although supporters of the latter approach were the minority, they were not without influence. An outspoken proponent of the "pro-Bolshevik" position was a young Scot diplomat recently returned from Russia, Robert Hamilton Bruce Lockhart. "Bruce" was handsome, charming and well-educated, by birth and upbringing an almost perfect specimen of the British ruling class. He had served His Majesty in Russia since 1912, and in the summer of 1917, he was a "fair-haired boy" in line for the plum position of commercial attaché, a job that was "a road to higher things."[49] Not even a very public affair with a married woman, a Jewish one no less, did much damage to his prospects, though it did get him reassigned to London in the fall. Beneath his insouciance and boyish charm, Lockhart seethed with insecurities and resentment. Repulsed by the values of his class, he developed an infatuation with the revolutionary left.[50] While he later denied that he acted out of ideological motives in his pro-Bolshevik advocacy, he could not disguise a certain hero worship of Lenin and Trotsky.[51] In December Lockhart's efforts finally secured the support of the powerful Lord Alfred Milner who approved his return to Russia with the aim of forging a working relationship with the Bolsheviks.[52] In mid-January, he set out for Petrograd.

Those who viewed the Bolsheviks as traitors to the Allied cause and a menace to political order everywhere were not happy. Among them were Nathan, Scale and Wiseman who were on the lookout for an agent to represent their interests. Lucky for them it seemed, Sidney Reilly came to town. MI5 later pegged his arrival as 1 January, though from where they could not determine.[53] He was lodged at the Savoy hotel sharing rooms with two other officers. MI5 could not fathom how he had ended up in the RFC uniform he sported so proudly along Piccadilly. Sidney had come from Russia and was willing to go back, but this time as a formal British operative. If he was going to risk his neck for HMG, it was only reasonable that it grant him such recognition and all the protection it could offer. Wiseman soon sailed back to New York, which left the matter in Nathan's hands.

For the time being, Nathan tapped Paul Dukes to shadow Lockhart. He had proved his worth in the matter of the German-Bolshevik investigation. In his memoirs, Dukes wrote that he first met Reilly in Nathan's rooms at the Albany, though he is rather hazy about just when it was. Dukes also insisted that Reilly was present when he (Dukes) was first interviewed for a job with the SIS.[54] In his book, Dukes admits to altering or withholding information about Nathan at the request of superiors. He does not, for instance, mention him by name and refers to him as "head of the political section."[55] Dukes also was misleading about when his intelligence work really began. According to his personal diary, his interview with *Cumming* took place at 2 Whitehall in late July 1918.[56] As we will see, Sidney could not possibly have been present. However, a War Office cable dated April 1918 notes that Dukes could not undertake work for the Foreign Office because he was already "too valuable to MI1c [SIS]"[57] So, his meeting with *Nathan* and Reilly must have taken place earlier, probably just prior to his departure for Russia in January. Traveling separately via Scandinavia, he landed in Red Petrograd on the 27th—exactly the same day as Lockhart and his crew.

Meanwhile, on 10 January, Reilly moved from the Savoy to decidedly more private and elegant digs at the St. James Palace Chambers at 22 Ryder Street. The address is an interesting one. First, the same Chambers had been Zaharoff's London residence of record for several years; did he, in fact, provide the rooms for Sidney? Moreover, Ryder Street also housed offices for Cumming's Section V, the very section that Wiseman oversaw in New York. Was this, too, a mere coincidence? On the 19th, doubtless at Nathan's urging, Reilly addressed a letter to Col. Byron at the War Office as the first step in applying for a post with its Intelligence Department.[58] He attached a letter from George Owens Thurston attesting that the writer had known Mr. Reilly for thirteen years and knew him to possess "great abilities as a linguist." Thurston also noted that his friend had done a great deal of work for the Russian Government and had an "extensive and accurate knowledge of Russian affairs." Reilly had always been a "diplomatic business-man," and he had no knowledge of anything "disparaging to his character." Sidney also provided a translated copy of the certificate issued him by the Russian Chief-of-Staff and as additional references listed Gen. Hermonius and Maj. Strubell. The last, he assured, could provide "full information about my circumstances and standing in New York."

On 1 February William Melville passed away at his home in Clapham. The old warhorse kept his finger in clandestine affairs to the end. In a surprising bit of candor, his brief *Times* obituary noted his attachment to the

"Intelligence Department of the War Office" since his departure from Scotland Yard almost fifteen years earlier.[59] In his final days, therefore, Melville might have provided his own endorsement to Reilly's application. While Sidney was not a sentimental man, it would not have been unlike him to make an unobtrusive appearance at the funeral to pay last respects to another denizen and ally in the secret world.

Reilly's exact whereabouts for the next few weeks are vague. He certainly seems to have done more than wait patiently on Ryder Street. Stories later circulated in Russia that in the early part of the New Year he was operating in, of all places, Odessa.[60] A British mission thereabouts under the direction of a Canadian, Lt. Col. J.W. Boyle. While mostly concerned with transport and economic work, Boyle's staff did contain officers linked to military intelligence and MI1c, notably George Hill and one John Gillespie. The latter name was to become another of Reilly's aliases, but did he first employ it here? In his own subsequent report, Hill notes working with Gillespie in the south but definitely makes him out to be distinct from Reilly. However, the writer Savchenko insists that Sidney was operating in Odessa and cultivated a wide range of contacts including a local warlord, the "Red Napoleon" Mikhail Artem'evich Murav'ev.[61] Another, supposedly, was a young Left SR named Yakov Bliumkin whom we will encounter a bit further on. Savchenko also records that an elderly woman named Rosenblum, possibly our man's mother (!), was sheltered in a house near the British Consulate.

Savchenko almost certainly is mistaken about the above, but there is an odd, unsigned report in Wiseman's papers from someone connected to the Boyle mission at this juncture.[62] The report describes efforts to organize and assist Russian officers and other pro-Allied groups in Odessa and Kiev. One of the persons the writer worked with was the British consul in Odessa, J. Picton Bagge, a man later very well disposed towards Sidney. The writer records he departed Kiev on 22 February 1918, which would have provided just enough time for Reilly to reappear in England in early March. However, the general tone of the report does not sound like Reilly. The best bet is that later reports of his presence in Odessa were based on confusion of him with the genuine Gillespie.

However, during February Reilly very likely did make a quick trip to Stockholm in order to pick up fresh information on the Bolshevik-German nexus. Isidor Kon was there and working hand-in-hand with Aschberg. So, too, was Abram Zhivotovskii. According to American intelligence, the last was on some sort of "Bolshevik mission" to the Germans.[63] Reilly also could have touched base with Krasin who had patched up his differences

with Lenin and returned to the Bolshevik fold. Also in the Swedish capital
was Sidney's man Lowie who had been forced out of Archangel after being
denounced as a German spy. Lowie soon sailed again for New York.

Another stop may have been Paris where Reilly would have wanted to
consult the files of the old Paris Okhrana. These were now under the personal care of Ambassador V.A. Maklakov (M), a good friend of Guchkov
and a man who would cooperate with Sidney in the future. The files of the
Paris Agency were a gold mine of information on revolutionaries, including, surely, the likes of Salomon Rosenblum. One must wonder if Reilly
availed himself of the opportunity to remove any inconvenient items.

There may be veiled references to Reilly's peregrinations in a cable from
Charles Ascherson to Wiseman in early March. Ascherson was Wiseman's
"opposite number" in London and his personal liaison to Cumming.
Ascherson reported that "Jean," the agent's code name, "has not gone to
Stockholm as intended," but, for reasons unexplained, turned back to
London. He further noted that the French were "making trouble" about the
same agent and would not allow him to return to Paris because they "con-
sider him a Russian subject" and were determined to keep Russians out of
France. Ascherson admitted that "Jean" was an uncertain quantity who
merited "careful watching."[64] That certainly has a familiar ring to it.

Reilly definitely was back in London by 6 March, for on that day MI5
operatives, probably acting on Cumming's request, put him under surveillance. For the next few days, they kept tabs on his comings and goings without finding out anything of significance.[65] He seldom left his Ryder Street
rooms before noon and spent a good deal of time at the Savoy. He traveled
frequently by cab, but the shadows made little effort to follow.

On 15 March, "C"'s desk diary records what by all indications was his
first meeting with the Ace-of-Spies. The man who provided introductions
was Nathan's ex-comrade in Indian Service, Maj. John Scale. Also lurking
in the background was Claude Dansey. Cumming sized up his visitor as
"very clever—very doubtful—has been everywhere and done everything."[66]
He accepted Reilly's services and saw to it that the new agent was provided
with £1250 in traveling funds, including £750 in easy-to-conceal diamonds.
Even so, Cumming pondered the "great risk" involved, for the dubious
character was soon to have contact with most of the British network operating in the Red domain.

The inquiry on Reilly, however, had only just begun. In February 1918,
Col. Hercules Pakenham arrived in Washington to head the British Military
Intelligence Liaison Office. As such, he served as representative of Kell's
MI5. On the direct instructions of Kell and with the encouragement of

Gaunt, Pakenham ordered Thwaites to turn over control of the New York Office including all dossiers in its possession.

In this battle for control, Reilly's candidacy became an issue. Probably in response to a request from Cumming's office, on 20 February, Kell ordered Pakenham to ask American authorities for an immediate and full investigation of Aleksandr Weinstein, who was under suspicion "through his being associated with Sydney J. [sic] Reilly."[67] Pakenham's request went first to MID chief Ralph Van Deman, and from there to his man in New York, Nick Biddle, and from Biddle to his assistant, Charles Dillingham. Biddle, as mentioned, was a buddy of Thwaites, and quite possible Reilly; so was Dillingham. It was not until 22 March that Dillingham reported back to say that he had interviewed Weinstein and Thwaites. Weinstein had insisted Thwaites had a complete file on him and there was nothing more to be said. Thwaites simply admitted that if Weinstein was perhaps not the most honest businessman, he was "OK" and that there was "nothing against him either in London or in New York."[68] Reilly's name was carefully avoided. An annoyed Pakenham emphasized that what Weinstein or Thwaites had to say was "not sufficient" and demanded that the Americans undertake an independent inquiry.[69] On 6 April, Van Deman was obliged to remind Biddle that "Major Thwaites is not the ranking officer of the British Intelligence Service . . . in this country," and Pakenham was. Even so, the latter was powerless to exercise any "jurisdiction and control" over the New York office. Thwaites doggedly refused to turn over anything. Reilly, in any case, was already in Russia.

Thwaites, however, was more forthcoming with "C" and the information he provided was by no means favorable. On 3 March, someone in New York, presumably Thwaites, reported "Sydney [sic] Reilly is a British subject . . . who has made money since the beginning of the war through . . . corrupted members of the Russian Purchasing Commission."[70] His spying for the Japanese was duly noted. The subject had been "under observation" by New York Section V since 1916, and "we consider him untrustworthy and unsuitable to work suggested." On the 13th, just two days before the meeting with "C," and apparently in response to a further inquiry, the same source offered a confidential statement from an official of the National City Bank, though not MacRoberts.[71] This characterized the Ace-of-Spies as "a shrewd businessman of undoubted ability but without patriotism or principles and therefore not recommended for any position which requires loyalty as he would not hesitate to use it to further his own commercial interests." Thwaites added that this was "precisely confirmed by our own view of the man." Finally, on the 20th, New York offered more information attesting to Reilly's "unscrupulous" nature, but also noted his "connections in almost every country," including Germany, Japan and, especially, Russia.[72] Thwaites concluded by pointing out that "there must be strong motive for Reilly leaving [a] profitable business here and [a] wife of whom he is said to be very jealous, to work for you."

So what was going on? The above assessment was not unfair but hardly an endorsement. However useful Reilly may have been as an informant, perhaps Thwaites thought it another matter to bring him right into the SIS fold. The warning that Sidney would always put his own interests first and his probable ulterior motives, was something we, too, must keep in mind as the story continues. However, once Cumming had made his decision, apparently at or soon after the 15 March meeting, Thwaites was duty-bound to support it.

At the same time, the MI5 investigation plowed on. In early April, they finally heard back from the Irish Command that reported no Sidney Reilly had been born in Clonmel in 1874. On 8 April, MI5 received a report from an informant "well-acquainted with Russia" who identified Reilly as a Russian Jew, a grafter, possible German agent and overall a "most undesirable" character.[73] Perhaps more worrisome to Kell's people was a telegram intercepted on 22 March from Reilly to the Bolshevik's "ambassador" in London, Maksim Litvinov. In this, Sidney mentioned previous attempts to reach Litvinov and he now needed to meet with him urgently. What Sidney was after, certainly, was a Soviet visa to help smooth his way past Red officialdom. MI5 found it all very mysterious, but on the 29th they received a brief assurance from Cumming's MI1c that "we know all about the telegram and it is all right."[74] By this time, Reilly was already on his way to Russia.

So he got the job. Given that Cumming was no idiot, it can only be because he had some positive estimation to offset the negative. The question is, whose? A later investigation carried out by State Department agent Sharpe showed that Reilly had secured the Russian mission by being "favorably reported upon by . . . British Secret Service officials in New York, who were at that time under the control of . . . Wiseman."[75] If not Thwaites, this must point the finger at Nathan and Wiseman. After his return from London in January, Wiseman was consumed by sensitive political duties in Washington, thus leaving Thwaites to handle the inquiries to the Manhattan office. Even so, Cumming logically would have solicited Sir William's opinion and must have known something of his recent employment of our man in Russia. Ascherson could have conveyed Wiseman's opinion verbally, bypassing Thwaites. There may be some relevancy to the fact that at the beginning of April Wiseman received orders to proceed at once to London to confer with unnamed higher authorities.

The real key to Reilly's success, however, was Nathan. He enjoyed the convenience of working in Cumming's office. He also fits the profile of the British official, noted in a later MID report, "who had known Reilly for some time," "whose name is withheld in the British reports on file," and who handled the request for information (to Thwaites) in February. The same unnamed official held a very favorable opinion of Reilly.[76]

Sidney's recent presence in London had not gone unnoticed by other parties. Margaret later wrote that unnamed "friends" met him there in early 1918 "wearing the uniform of a Captain [sic] of the Royal Flying Corps."[77] Reilly mentioned to the friends that he would shortly be going abroad, but did not offer just where. How this information was communicated to Daisy in Brussels is uncertain, but again one must wonder if Claude Dansey played a role.

On 29 March, SIS central sent a coded wire to the British Consulate in the north Russian town of Vologda.[78] It noted that on the 25th, "Sydney George REILLI," Lieutenant RFC, was leaving England bound for Archangel and would report to the consulate in early April. There he was to contact the Passport Control Officer (MI1c) and deliver a coded message. In true cloak and dagger form, the PCO was to ask him what his business was, to which the newcomer would respond: "Diamond buying." To further aid in establishing bona fides, the wire described our man as "Jewish-Jap type, brown eyes, very protruding, deeply lined, sallow face, may be bearded, height 5'9"." "He will be at your disposal," the message continued, "utilize him to join up your organization if necessary as he should travel freely. Return to Stockholm if possible end of June." As a formal agent of the Secret Intelligence Service, Reilly received a personal code name, ST1, designating him the first operative under a new station established in Stockholm and later moved to Helsinki. At its head sat ST0, Maj. Scale, the very man who had introduced him to Cumming. Finally, on 1 April, even as he steamed towards Russian shores, Sidney received one more piece of official imprimatur—a permanent commission of 2nd lieutenant, technical officer, in the Royal Air Force that superseded the old Royal Flying Corps.

Before departing, Reilly made out a will that he entrusted to the safe-keeping of his friends, probably Nathan, at 2 Whitehall Court. He named as beneficiary his wife, Mrs. A. Reilly of 120 Broadway, New York.[79] This certainly was not Nadine or Margaret, so it must be a reference to Anne and proof, perhaps, that of all his spouses she was foremost in his thoughts. Does this mean he had succeeded in bringing her to America? Nothing else suggests so, but it does argue that someone at his Manhattan office, Weinstein or the faithful Thomas, knew about her and how to contact her if need be.

Sidney's new passport, hastily issued to him on 24 March, deserves some comment. The "Reilli" spelling of his surname corresponded neither to any accepted English variation nor to the forms previously used in Russia, *Raille, Ralli* or *Reile*. The simplest explanation is that he wanted to insure that the version on the passport coincided with the visa he obtained a few days earlier from the Soviet quasi-ambassador in Britain, Maksim Litvinov. The real reason, however, may be that *Reilli*, in English or Russian, was just different enough from the above to frustrate any cursory inquiries and obscure links to his past associations, including Anne.

What, exactly, was the nature and purpose of Reilly's mission? The above suggests that he was to be a sort of roving operative who would handle liaisons between other, *in situ* agents. After the 15 March meeting, Cumming noted, with some trepidation, that "[Reilly] is to visit all of our men in Vologda, Kief, Moscow, etc." [80] But his mission also had the sanction of Cumming's nominal superior, the Director of the War Office Military Intelligence Branch (DMI), Gen. George MacDonough. So far as the WO was concerned, Reilly's job was only to collect military information. He was to avoid meddling in *political* matters. However, a later memo from DMI to Gen. F.C. Poole, chief of the British Military Mission in Russia, stressed that Reilly, along with another officer, Lt. Ernest Michelson, were on "special secret assignment" and should not be mentioned in dispatches unless "absolutely necessary." [81]

This was the same Michelson who had visited 120 Broadway in 1916. Why and how he was now linked with Reilly and what their "secret mission" entailed remains a puzzle. There may be a clue in the fact that for years Michelson lived and worked in Tsarskoe Selo, the small town attached to the Romanovs' primary country estate just south of Petrograd. It is possible this gave him a certain familiarity with the Imperial Family or, more likely, persons connected to them. That may be connected to another "hire" Cumming made just a few days before his engagement of Reilly. On 3 March Cumming contracted the services of Henry Armitstead, an official of the Hudson's Bay Company, another man with long commercial experience in Russia. [82] As an SIS operative, Armitstead was to join yet another British mission on its way to Vologda, a special commercial one headed by Sir F.O. Lindley.

With Armitstead, Cumming also engaged a Norwegian businessman, Jonas Lied, owner of the Siberian Steamship Co. Armitstead and Lied were part of a very secret scheme to rescue the imprisoned Tsar Nicholas and his family.[83] Ultimately, the plan fell through, but it was only the first of several such schemes. How did Reilly fit into this picture, if at all? Beyond the synchronicity of his and Lied's engagement in the same general area, there is the fact that Sidney knew Lied through mutual association with the Russian Consulate in New York and via connection to Metro-Vickers chief Sir Francis Barker. And where Vickers was connected, we may suspect that Basil Zaharoff had an interest as well. Did Barker and/or Zaharoff have a part in bringing Reilly aboard? If so, what did they see as his intended role? As ever, the System was at work, and no matter how many masters Sidney appeared to serve, ultimately he always served himself.

Reilly disobeyed his orders at once. Instead of proceeding to Archangel, he landed instead at Murmansk on 4–5 April. The diversion may have been a matter of weather. Unlike the permanently ice-free Murmansk, getting a ship into Archangel at this time of year was a tricky business. At the least it was a handy excuse, for Murmansk had other advantages. Friend Calder still manned the Military Control station. The local soviet, recall, was run by Aleksei Yur'ev, who was proving most cooperative with the Allied occupiers. In this instance, however, Sidney's bet proved wrong. Calder, who expected Reilly's latter's arrival in Archangel, had gone there. The acting British commander at Murmansk, Rear-Admiral Thomas Kemp, was at once suspicious of this dark, accented stranger bearing a very fishy passport (what Irishman, after all, would spell his name "Reilli"?). Furthermore, despite his claim to be a British officer, he had arrived in civilian dress aboard a Norwegian steamer. Kemp promptly tossed him into the brig of the HMS *Glory*. Fortunately for Reilly, at the same time Maj. Stephen Alley (the possible assassin of Rasputin) came to town. He was headed back to England after handing over control of the Petrograd military intelligence/MI1c office to a new man, Commander Ernest Boyce, RN. Kemp asked Alley to check out the prisoner. He had not met Reilly before, but probably knew something of his name and reputation from Scale or others. Sidney immediately "produced a microscopic message in code, which he had secreted under the cork of a bottle of tablets."[84] Presumably this was the one he was supposed to present in Vologda. Alley at once recognized it as one of the codes used by MI1c and advised Kemp to release the prisoner and allow him to proceed to Moscow, Reilly's declared ultimate destination. Alley does not seem to have been overly impressed by the Ace-of-Spies, or at least his impression of a Britisher, later describing him as "a typical little Odessa Jew."[85] Once free, Reilly still did not make for Vologda as ordered. Instead, he headed straight for Petrograd.

To appreciate what he was about to plunge into, we need to take stock of the dramatically shifting turn of events. The Soviet-German talks that got underway in December reached an impasse in February. Despite Lenin's desire to secure peace at virtually any price, Trotsky, the lead Soviet nego- tiator, refused to accept the draconian terms pressed by the Germans, terms that included not only the loss of Poland and the Baltic Provinces but the whole of the rich Ukraine as well. He called their bluff by proclaiming a state of "no war, no peace" and walked out of the talks. Berlin and its allies responded by renewing hostilities. At first glance this seemed to be exactly what Lockhart and others had hoped for; Russia was back in the war. However, the old Russian Army was gone and the Bolsheviks were yet to organize a new one. The result was not really war but an almost entirely unopposed enemy advance along the entire length of the front. It was obvi- ous that unless the Germans were appeased they would occupy Petrograd and even Moscow. In the end they advanced to within eighty miles of the former. In this predicament, Lenin's argument carried the day, though still against great opposition even within his own party. On 3 March the Soviet regime bowed to the harsh terms of the Treaty of Brest-Litovsk. In the face of the inexorable German advance, most of the remaining Allied diplomatic missions decamped from Petrograd and relocated to Vologda which lay about halfway between Moscow and Archangel. The presence of these Allied missions certainly was the main reason Reilly had been ordered to go there. Skeleton crews were left to man the old embassies and consulates. The vulnerability of Petrograd prompted Lenin to move his government lock, stock and commissars to Moscow that became the Soviet Republic's new capital.

Despite these setbacks, Lockhart remained convinced that the Bolsheviks could be roused to fight, especially with Trotsky at the head of the new Peoples Commissariat of War. The determined Scotsman pleaded with London not to abandon the Soviet infant to Berlin's grasp. His job was not made any easier when on 9 March, the day following the Bolshevik cen- tral Committee's ratification of the peace treaty, a small force of British Royal Marines occupied Murmansk, ostensibly to safeguard the vast array of military stores piled there. The situation grew worse on 5 April when Japanese forces made a like move against Vladivostok. This, Lockhart recalled, put Trotsky in a very "difficult mood."[86] These were the first creeping steps of Allied intervention.

Lockhart faced his most serious opposition, however, from within his own camp. He was unpopular with many of the British military officers, above all the MI1c men. Alley had left Petrograd, in part, because he could not stand Lockhart and his successor, Boyce, openly expressed his "disgust" with the Scot's appointment.[87] The basis of this sentiment was the suspicion that Lockhart was much too sympathetic with the Bolos. If there were doubts about his loyalty, no one expressed them publicly. To the likes of Boyce and His Majesty's Naval Attaché in Petrograd, Capt. Francis Cromie, recent events seemed to prove that Lenin ran the show and that he was, *de facto* or *de jure*, Berlin's puppet. The only question was if, or rather when, the Germans would kick in the door and seize the rest of the country, including such assets as the Russian Baltic Fleet. There were those in London who worried about the same thing.

The big picture, in fact, was even more complicated. If policy-makers in London were divided as to whether to deal with or squash the Bolsheviks, so too were those in Berlin. The powerful First Quartermaster General of the Kaiser's high command, Erich Ludendorff, wanted to topple the troublesome revolutionary regime and replace it with a government of pro-German monarchists.[88] German agents were laying the groundwork for a like coup in Moscow and Petrograd. In the first week of April German troops landed in Finland where they gave armed support to local White Finns battling Red ones. In the weeks that followed, the Germans and their Finnish allies pushed ever nearer Petrograd, stopping barely twenty miles from the old capital and putting the Russian Baltic Fleet within easy grasp. However, leading the call for a more restrained policy in Berlin was Reilly's old friend, Admiral von Hintze. He advocated continued support for the Bolsheviks as the surest means to dominate Russia and limit Allied influence. Hintze also was involved with Krasin in drafting supplemental Russo-German economic treaties that, he argued, would guarantee Germany's dominance in the East whatever the war's outcome in the West.[89] Bearing in mind the System, did Reilly return to Russia a German agent, or potential German agent, as well as a British one?

The first word Cumming received from his new agent was a long cable dated 16 April from the British Embassy in Petrograd.[90] Cumming noted to Scale that this seemed "very odd," all the more so as Reilly made absolutely no effort to explain his changed itinerary.[91] Stranger yet, his report was "all politics," not the military information he was supposed to be collecting. The message began with this blunt assertion: "Every source of information leads to definite conclusions that today BOLSHEVIKS only real power in Russia." Even so, he immediately added, "opposition in country constantly growing and if suitably supported will ultimately lead to overthrow of BOLSHEVIKS." In classic System style, Reilly went on to advocate "action . . . in two parallel directions." First, collaboration with the Bolos to attain "immediate practical objects"; second, collaboration with the opposition with the goal of "gradual re-establishment of order and national defence."

The protection of Murmansk and Archangel were important, but the most pressing issue, he stressed, was the evacuation of huge stores of weapons and munitions in and around Petrograd to prevent them from falling into German hands, and the destruction or disabling of the Baltic Fleet for the same reason. Bolshevik cooperation was essential to the realization of these goals, but could only be achieved through offering the Reds tangible benefits. Among his suggestions in that area were a "substitution [or] moratorium for final repudiation of foreign loans," and the "semi-acknowledgment of their Government." The most important thing was money—lots of it. Hard cash, Reilly stressed, was the "most important factor with Bolshevik leaders and explains all German success." To gain the upper hand, Britain might have to expend as much as a million pounds, and even then, he warned, "without any real guarantee of ultimate success." Time was critical, he warned, and "you must be prepared to meet obligations at any moment and at shortest moment." The same held true for the opposition that were "ready to throw themselves into German arms" if Allied support, above all monetary support, was not forthcoming.

Reilly went to urge the purchase of prominent newspapers, notably friend Suvorin's *Novoe* and *Vechernee Vremia* which could be used as vehicles for pro-Allied propaganda and a "trumpet of national resistance." He expected this would take about £100,000, but "we are assured," he added, "that this can be done with the tacit consent of certain influential Bolsheviks." The essence of Reilly's approach was that it might be possible to overthrow the Bolsheviks as much by co-opting certain of their number as by backing their opponents. These were the same basic themes that he would repackage and reiterate for the next several years.

Given that Reilly had been in Petrograd barely a week, the report was remarkable not only for the breadth of its vision, but also for the amount of information gathered. What, exactly, had he been up to and to whom had he been talking? The first step was to establish, or re-establish a local cover and base of operations. He resumed the identity of Konstantin Massino residing at 10/10 Torgovaia, conveniently proximate to his existing commercial offices. The flat belonged to Elena Boguzhevskaia, an old mistress and the first of the many female accomplices he would employ over the next few months. As part of the current arrangement, she assumed the title of "Mrs. Massino."

The next move was to touch bases with Boyce. Interestingly, on 13 April, just days after Reilly's arrival in Petrograd, Bruce Lockhart, in Moscow, complained that two of Boyce's officers, Lts. MacAlpine and Lessing, were "intriguing" against him in an effort to get him recalled.[92] A.I.

Lessing was a man with long connection to Russian banking and commercial circles that certainly gave him prior acquaintance with Reilly.[93] Most telling, perhaps, Boyce and crew make absolutely no effort to appraise Lockhart of Reilly's presence; indeed, the Scot was to remain utterly ignorant of this for weeks. Perhaps this merely reflected the very secret nature of the Ace-of-Spies' assignment, but it also worked for him to study and undercut Lockhart from behind the scenes. While the two may seem to have been advocating the same policy—support for the Bolsheviks—that made Lockhart, in Reilly's mind, at best redundant and at worst, a troublesome competitor. Beyond this, remember, Sidney advocated his policy as a matter of cold, tactical expedience, whereas Lockhart's was tainted by personal and political affections.

In the meantime, Lockhart had started a torrid love affair with Moura (Maria) Ignatievna Benckendorf, later better known as Moura Budberg. She was the wife of a Tsarist diplomat, socialite and a volunteer translator-clerk at the British Embassy. A sloe-eyed brunette of much personal and sexual magnetism, Moura encountered Lockhart soon after his arrival and promptly seduced him, a none-too-difficult task.[94] The man who introduced them, according to Lockhart, was the aforementioned Capt. George Hill, now in Moscow on duty for DMI, and soon MI1c. This in itself is a bit interesting because Hill otherwise seemed to have no close connection to either party. A woman of highly dubious morals and genuine cunning, Madame Benckendorf made it her business to collect information and assorted gossip floating around the Embassy. She passed some of it along to Lockhart. But beloved Bruce was not the only recipient of her sexual and informational favors. Moura had already made her peace with the new order on her own special terms. Whatever she knew, the Bolos—some at least—knew as well.

The third, and perhaps most important, step was to reconnect with his Russian collaborators from the previous fall and recruit more. Manasevich was out of the picture. Despite his initial cooperation with Dzerzhinskii's fledgling Extraordinary Commission to Combat Counter-Revolution and Sabotage, the VChK or Cheka, he had been arrested and shot as he tried to slip into Finland.[95] But Grammatikov and Orlov were still around and quite safe in Soviet employ. Sasha Grammatikov, of course, had solid revolutionary credentials and had once earned the personal recommendation of Lenin. He still represented the Suvorin interests and was a frequent visitor at the British Embassy where he had the confidence of Boyce and others. Undoubtedly, he already supplied them with intelligence gleaned inside the local Red administration. Grammatikov was the obvious man to spearhead Sidney's newspaper gambit.

The most important links ran through Vladimir Orlov. In January, the ex-Tsarist prosecutor took the identity of a Polish Bolshevik who had "disappeared," Boleslaw Orlinski. As Orlinski, he obtained a modest but strategic position in the archive section of the Council of Peoples Commissars-*Sovnarkom*—the executive of the Soviet republic headed by Lenin himself. By the time of Reilly's arrival, Comrade Orlinski had risen to the post of chief of Petrograd's *6th Ugolovno-sledstvennaia komissiia*, or Criminal Investigation Commission, commonly called the *Ugrozyska*.[96] That body was in turn linked to the new Peoples Commissariat of Justice (*NKYu*) and later to the Cheka.[97] In April, Orlinski enrolled a new member in his detective force, another Pole, Sidnei Georgievich Reilinski (or Rellinskii).[98]

Orlov was still a most determined anti-Bolshevik. In February he had organized a secret White intelligence organization in Petrograd, known as the *Orga* or *Biuro* that functioned with impunity and considerable success for the next seven months. His effort had the official blessing of Gen. N.N. Yudenich, Gen. Alekseev's man in Finland, and the active cooperation of Boyce and the French intelligence section still headed by Bidet. By the time of Reilly's appearance on the scene, Orlov's net had some eighty agents serving "in all more or less important Bolshevik institutions collecting secret military and political information for the Allies."[99] Ever versatile, he also supplied much the same information to the new German Consulate in Petrograd, a link that would prove very useful to the Ace-of-Spies.[100] Orlov's contact there was Berlin's commercial attaché, Walter Bartels. Bartels, in turn, reported to a special Russian section of the German Foreign Ministry. And that section was run by none other than Admiral von Hintze, soon enough to become the Kaiser's foreign minister.

Orlov and Reilly owed much of their conspiratorial success to the assistance, conscious or not, of two brothers, Vladimir Dmitrievich and Mikhail Dmitrievich Bonch-Bruevich, both big men in the Soviet hierarchy. Vladimir, the younger, was a veteran Bolshevik and confidant of Lenin. In the wake of the October Revolution, he took charge of the *Sovnarkom* Administrative Office, of which the archival section was a part. But Vladimir wore another hat; he was boss of the Soviet regime's first security service, a body that predated and paralleled the Cheka. It began as the Committee for Combating Pogroms attached to the Petrograd Soviet and charged with maintaining order in the Capital. Bruevich, however, turned his hand to combating political enemies, and by the beginning of 1918 he changed its name to the Commission for the Struggle with Counter-revolution and Sabotage, and later still, to avoid confusion with the Cheka, the Investigation Commission.[101] Within this tangle of organizations, Bruevich also oversaw the operations of the *Ugrozyska*. Interestingly, almost all the later documents secured by Ossendowski and Semenov supposedly originated with Bruevich's organization and were "obtained and photographed" in its offices.[102] Orlov certainly had the means to do that.

It was Mikhail Bonch-Bruevich who personally recommended "Orlinski" to his brother.[103] During the war, General Bruevich had commanded the staff of the Northern Front and was a close collaborator of Gen. Batiushin and his special commission in which Orlov served. Indeed, Mikhail B. took a keen interest in counterintelligence and was known as an "indefatigable fighter" against German espionage.[104] He also was one of those senior officers who offered their services to the new order. Lenin named him chief-of-staff of the Supreme Command and in March, he assumed the even grander mantles of Chief of the Supreme Military Council and Commander-in-Chief of the All-Russian Main Staff. General Bruevich was now the functional head of the Soviet military, though the forces under his command amounted to very little. The only effective units consisted of a few remnants left over from the old Army, most notably some 15,000 troops of the Latvian Rifle Corps. The General was determined to reconstruct a new army as quickly as possible. A new army, naturally, would also mean a restored military intelligence service. Little wonder, therefore, that Reilly thought he would make an excellent member of his new team.

In his memoirs, General Bonch-Bruevich recollected that among his "frequent foreign callers, was Sydney Reilly who represented himself as a lieutenant of a Royal Engineer Battalion attached to the British Embassy."[105] A simple lapse of memory, perhaps, though it is unlike a military man to confuse an engineer with a flying officer. But this is not the most interesting ambiguity in Bruevich's account. His chronology is vague, but there is the definite suggestion that his first contact with Reilly took place in late *1917* as opposed to 1918. He does set one notable encounter at the time of the German landings in Finland, the first half of April, a time frame that fits Reilly's return to the city. Addressing the general in Russian of which "a native Muscovite might justly have been proud," Reilly laid out a detailed scheme to deploy the Baltic Fleet at its island base of Kronstadt.[106] Bruevich claimed he smelled a rat because the Englishman's plan was almost identical to one recently set before him by a group of "reactionary" naval officers. Sure enough, he deduced that both plans had the same "treacherous aim of laying out battleships and cruisers open to a German U-boat attack."[107] As a result, he ordered the ships moved to an anchorage closer to Petrograd. Nevertheless, "Reilly continued to invent excuses to come see me, until I gave orders not to receive him."[108] He even reported the pernicious foreigner to his brother.

Reilly's reports to London suggest a very different picture. Between mid-April and the beginning of June, he noted no less than eight extensive interviews with General Bruevich, first in Petrograd and later in Moscow.[109] There is not the least indication that the General was reluctant to speak, particularly about his efforts to raise a new army or his candid opinions of fellow officers and politicos like Trotsky. Bruevich seems to have gotten along very well with the latter and wished to see him become "sole military and naval commissar" in the government.[110] That, too, differs from Bruevich's later, Stalin-era, characterization of Trotsky as a meddlesome nonentity.[111] In early June, Reilly relayed to London his description of sitting in the General's office while the two and Trotsky, via telephone, drew up new anti-sabotage/espionage procedures to employ against the Germans. He was no passive observer. According to the account, Bruevich "asked me to suggest what other steps could be taken in this direction." Sidney, for his part, glowingly characterized Bruevich as the "brain centre of the whole [military] organization" and a true patriot and anti-German who begged for Allied help to "us, the officers, who alone can save the situation."[112]

As ever, Reilly's version of affairs should be taken with a grain of salt, but in this instance his portrayal rings truer than Bruevich's. In any event, the reports were taken very seriously in London and distributed to the Director of Military Intelligence, the Admiralty and Foreign Office. Of course, given that our man was only identified as ST1, it is possible that someone reading them did not realize they were the handiwork of the notorious Mr. Reilly. One anonymous, approving note reads: "ST1 is reliable, & I am designing a questionnaire for him."[113] Information from his reports was to be included in other documents, but care was to be taken to avoid "compromising the General." Thus, from some in London's standpoint, the Ace-of-Spies had the chief of the nascent Red Army as a confidential informant, perhaps an outright agent.

Reilly had so far done an excellent job of establishing himself inside the Bolshevik domain and cultivating an array of valuable contacts and collaborators. In late April he headed to Moscow to continue the process in the very shadow of the Kremlin. The *real* game was about to begin.

NOTES

1. PRO, WO 106/1145, General Report for 1917.
2. PZZ #73, 2.
3. PRO, ADM 337, RNVR Service Record for Lt. William B. Calder.
4. PRO, FO 371/3350, 203967, "Capt. G.A. Hill's Report on His Work in Russia for DMI," 11 Dec. 1918, 1/17.

5. PRO FO 395, Batum Consular records, 3 Feb. 1895. In his later Canadian Service Record, Hill gave his birthplace as Tashkent in Russian Central Asia and later still, London.
6. See, for instance, his Canadian service record, CAC, RG 150 (1992-93/166) CEF file 51224 and British, PRO, AIR 76.
7. WWP, 10/258.
8. PRO, AIR 76, Service Record of Lt. Sidney G. Reilly (PI 21220).
9. MID, 9049-6073, Report 17 Oct. 1918, 2–3.
10. Ibid., Memorandum #4, 5.
11. Ibid., Memorandum #2, 3.
12. SIS, Thwaites to C, "Capt. Sidney Reilly, MC, late RAF," 29 Oct. 1925.
13. Thwaites, 183.
14. MID, 9140-6073, Memorandum #4, 4.
15. NYT (28 Apr. 1917), 12:3, (28 June 1917, 3:7).
16. Ibid., (2 Feb. 1920), 4:5.
17. Futrell, 163.
18. Orlov, Dvoinoi, 294–295, and Morder, 7–8, passim.
19. Burtsev, "Lenine and Malinovsky," Struggling Russia, Vol. I, #9–10 (17 May 1919), 138–140. Burtsev's suspicion was that Lenin had colluded with the Okhrana via police agents in his ranks much as he later did with the Germans.
20. WWP, f. 261, 1.
21. IISG, Boris Souvarine Coll., file Nicolaevskii: Recueil Geneve, "Iz rannei istorii Kominterna . . . ," note #10.
22. The material appeared in a small right-wing paper, Zhivoe Slovo, but managed to achieve wide currency in the Capital.
23. Futrell, 161–176.
24. PRO, FO 395/109, period covering 30 Aug. to 8 Sept. Much of the material collected by Dukes also ended up in the hands of MI5.
25. FO 371/4363.
26. Le Complot German-Bolcheviste (Paris, 1920). The best analysis is George Kennan, "The Sisson Documents," Journal of Modern History, vol. 28, #2, 130–154.
27. Sisson's account is in his One Hundred Red Days (New York, 1931).
28. MID, 9140-6073, Report 10 Sept. 1918, 4.
29. Izvestiia VTsIK (29 Nov. 1918), 1, 3.
30. On the Anglo-American intrigues with the Poles and Czechs, see Rhodri Jeffreys-Jones, American Espionage: Secret Service to CIA (New York, 1977), 79–89.
31. Emanuel Voska and Will Irwin, Spy and Counter-Spy (New York, 1940), 115–173.
32. Ves' Petrograd 1917, 38.
33. William R. Corson and Robert T. Crowley, The New KGB: Engine of Power (New York, 1985), 48 and G.J.A. O'Toole, Honorable Treachery: A History of U.S. Intelligence, Espionage and Covert Operations from the American Revolution to the CIA (New York, 1991), 294.
34. USDS, 125.6313/298, Dearing to Kalamatiano, 8 Dec. 1921, and 125.6314/182, "Consulate General at Moscow," 15 Oct. 1917, 8.
35. USDS, 361.1121K121/50, 'Lockhart Trial," 9.
36. Corson and Crowley, 51–52.
37. PRO, FO 371/3319, Findlay to FO, 30 Sept. 1918.
38. V.A. Savchenko, Avantiuristy grazhdanskoi voiny (Moscow, 2000), 291.
39. Revolt Pimenov, "Kak ia iskal Shpiona Reili", Radio Samizdat Archive #1089 (Leningrad, 1968), 24, 54, and Lev Nikulin, Mertvaia zyb' (Moscow, 1965), 256.
40. Lockhart, Ace, 17–19 and Reilly, viii.
41. Savchenko, 292–293. PZZ #73 puts this in early 1918.

42. For a Soviet interpretation of Yur'ev's "treachery," see V.V. Tarasov, *Bor'ba s inter-ventami na severe Rossii* (1918–1920 gg) (Moscow, 1958), digested in W. Bruce Lincoln, *Red Victory: A History of the Russian Civil War* (New York, 1989), 179–181.
43. PRO, FO 383/379, 117983, referring to 151889 of 1917, originally in FO 383/259.
44. Reed and Fisher, 109.
45. SIS, Notes on interview with Pepita Reilly, 17 Nov. 1940.
46. MID, 9149-6073, Memorandum #1, 4.
47. Ibid., Operative #101 Report on Mrs. Reilly, 2.
48. Ibid., Memorandum #4, 4.
49. PRO, FO 368/1798, FO to Lindley, 3 May 1917.
50. See, for instance, Lockhart's comments in his *Retreat from Glory* (London, 1934), 20–22.
51. B. Lockhart, *British Agent* (London, 1961 [orig. pub. 1932]), 122–123, 132–133, *passim*.
52. Ibid., 104–110.
53. MI5, Reilly, Report from A.L.W., 9 March 1918.
54. Robin Lockhart to author, 8 April 1996, and a 1966 letter from Lady Diana Dukes to Lockhart.
55. Paul Dukes, *The Story of "ST 25"* (London, 1938), 30–31.
56. HIA, Dukes Collection, 1918 Diary.
57. FO 395/109 and Tomaselli to author, 12 Dec. 2000.
58. MI5, Reilly, Reilly to Byron, 19 Jan. 1918 and Thurston to Whom It May Concern, 19 Jan.
59. *Times* (5 Feb. 1918), 3a; (6 Feb. 1918), 9c.
60. Savchenko, 292–293.
61. Ibid.
62. WWP, 10/264, attached to "Russian Affairs," 3 July 1918.
63. USDS, 000-909, "Who's Who: A Ready Reference List of Persons in the Public Eye," 28 Dec. 1918.
64. WWP, file 4, Ascherson to Billy [Wiseman], 3 March 1918.
65. MI5, Reilly, Reports of 6–9 March 1918.
66. Judd, 437–438.
67. MID, 9140-6073/6, Van Deman to MI5 [Apr. 1918], and Van der Kley to Thwaites, 6 Sept. 1918.
68. Ibid., Dillingham to Biddle, 22 March 1918.
69. Ibid., note appended to Van Deman to MI5.
70. SIS, CX 021744, 3 March 1918.
71. Ibid., CX 023100, 13 March 1918.
72. Ibid., CX 023996, 20 March 1918.
73. MI5, Reilly, Report from Col. W.H. Courtenay, 11 April 1919.
74. Ibid., Maj. Kendall, MI1c to MI5g, 29 March 1918.
75. CSA 215, 13 Dec. 6.
76. MID, 9140-6073, Memorandum #2, 3.
77. Reilly, SIS, Margaret Reilly to Air Board, 4 Jan. 1919.
78. Reilly, SIS, CXM 159, 29 March 1918.
79. PRO, AIR 76, Reilly Service Record.
80. Judd, 437.
81. PRO, WO 33/962, DMI to Poole, 28 May 1918.
82. Hudson's Bay Company Archives, RG 22/5/103, Cumming to Sale, 21 May 1918.
83. The most recent and thorough examination of these plans is Shay McNeal, *The Plots to Rescue the Czar* (London, 2001).
84. HIA, Lockhart, box 6, Alley to Robin Lockhart, 13 May 1966.
85. Anthony Summers Coll. (ASC), A. Winch to Summers, 24 Jan. 1972.

86. House of Lords Record Office (HLRO), Beaverbrook Papers, R.H.B. Lockhart Diaries, 1918, 6 Apr.
87. Sisson, 294 and Andrew, 212, 530, n. 33.
88. MID, 9728-182/1, Contre-Espionage Report from A.D. 6, 14 March 1918.
89. E.H. Carr, *The Bolshevik Revolution* vol. III (New York, 1953), 85, 314–315.
90. SIS, CX 127753, 16 Apr. 1918.
91. Reilly, SIS, CXM236 to Stockholm, 20 Apr. 1918.
92. HLRO, Lockhart, 13 Apr. 1918.
93. Bokhanov, 170.
94. HLRO, 2 Feb. Perhaps the most complete and incisive study of the mercurial Moura, AKA Baroness Budberg, is Nina Berberova's *Zheleznaia Zhenshchina: Rasskaz o zhizni M.I. Zakrevskoi-Benkendorf-Budberg, o nei samoi i ee dryz'iakh* (New York, 1982).
95. *Vserossiiskaia Chrezvychainaia Komissiia.*
96. Orlov, *Dvoinoi*, 296–298.
97. VChK ("Vecheka") from *Vserossiiskaia chrezvychainaia Komissiia po borbe s kontr-revoliutsiei i sabotazhem.*—"All-Russian Extraordinary Commission for the Struggle with Counter-Revolution and Sabotage." A longer version of the title also noted the struggle against speculation and abuse of office.
98. PZZ, #73, 1.
99. HIA Nicolaevsky, Orlov bio; Bortnevskii to author, 12 July 1995.
100. Orlov, *Dvoinoi*, 303.
101. *Komissiia po borbe s kontrrevoliutsiei I sabotazhem* and *Issledovanaia komissia.*
102. PRO, FO 371/4363, CX 2769, Maclaren, 7 April 1918.
103. Orlov, *Dvoinoi*, 298.
104. Ibid., 298–300, 326.
105. M.D. Bonch-Bruevich, *From Tsarist General to Red Army Commander* (Moscow, 1958), 263.
106. Ibid., 264.
107. Ibid., 264.
108. Ibid., 265.
109. PRO, WO32/5669, 127830, ST [Reilly] to MI1c, 3 June 1918.
110. Ibid., 127851, ST Report #7, 29 May 1918.
111. Bonch-Bruevich, 265–166.
112. PRO, WO 32/5669, 127955 and 126833.
113. Ibid., 127851, 29 May 1918.

Chapter Nine
PLOTS AND COUNTER PLOTS

The events of late spring and summer 1918 are the only ones about which Reilly felt obliged to make a written account, at least that we know of. The basic purpose of this account, as in most such cases, was to justify his actions and to exculpate himself from the doubts and accusations that hung over the episode for years to come. Given its self-serving quality, Sidney's account was far from a complete or honest record, but then neither was anyone else's. Almost everyone involved would have something to hide. Among others, Bruce Lockhart was permitted to review and excise from Reilly's manuscript what he deemed "very inaccurate statements about me."[1]

The centerpiece of these intrigues, as we will see, was the so-called "Lockhart" or "Ambassador's Plot."[2] Various accounts generally ascribe some role to Reilly as a British operative, but often as evidence of his supposed rampant egomania.[3] On the other hand, American author Edward Van Der Rhoer and Soviet dissident writer Revolt Pimenov charge that Reilly's participation proves he was a Bolshevik agent.[4] To one degree or another, all are correct, though each misses the essence and complexity of what really was afoot.

According to his version of events, Sidney went to Moscow in the company of Grammatikov. They traveled in a special car as members of the Petrograd Cheka, Reilly using the Reilinskii identity provided by Orlov.[5] On the way to Moscow, he passed through Vologda where he once again became Reilly and made his long-overdue visit to the local British Consulate. The secretary was John Gillespie, a former British propaganda agent now working for MI1c. He almost certainly was the same Gillespie who recently worked with Hill in Ukraine, but from this point on his and Sidney's identities become inextricably mixed. Indeed, so far as the Cheka later could determine, Reilly and Gillespie were the same man.[6] They certainly bore a strong general resemblance that probably explains why Reilly chose him. Gillespie—or was it the Ace-of-Spies?—subsequently organized an "anti-Soviet conspiracy" in Vologda based on detachments of ex-officers.[7] He also buried a large case full of money on the local consulate grounds. Where that may have come from, we will see below. By adopting such alternate personas, the Ace-of-Spies was compartmentalizing his activities. Massino (AKA "Constantine"), Reilinskii, Gillespie and others each handled discreet activities usually in different locales.

He arrived in Moscow as Lt. Sidney George Reilly, RAF uniform and all. There, on 28 April, as General Bruevich's personal guest, he attended an address by Trotsky at the Bolshoi Theatre. The essence of this speech, as Reilly immediately reported to London, was Trotsky's plan for a new "proletarian" army to safeguard the revolution and wage "merciless class war" against the bourgeoisie as opposed, it seemed, to the Germans.[8] A short time later, Reilly took a train back to Petrograd with Grammatikov, or at least he appeared to. In reality, the traveler, he later explained, was "someone who bore a passable resemblance to me," doubtless the genuine Gillespie.[9] Thus he threw off unwelcome observers and gained time to establish other identities in Moscow before resurfacing as Reilly.

To understand his future moves, we need to take stock of the currents and crosscurrents swirling around him. First, there was a sizable British presence in Russia, but no one was in charge, least of all Lockhart. As agent ST1 of SIS/MI1c, Sidney reported to Scale (ST0) in Stockholm and under the vague supervision of Boyce (ST2) in Petrograd. That was simple enough. But then there was Naval Attaché Cromie, also quartered in the Embassy and close to Boyce, who cultivated his own links to anti-Bolshevik elements and reported to the Admiralty. As an ostensible branch of military intelligence, MI1c agents theoretically came under the authority of the Director of Military Intelligence (DMI) and the War Office. In Russia, the DMI was represented by the chief of the British Military Mission, General F.C. Poole. He also supervised the Petrograd-based Military Intelligence Section run by Lt. Col. C.J.M. Thornhill. A 28 May memo from DMI tried to make sense of this situation by putting Thornhill "in charge of all officers doing military intelligence in Russia except those engaged on secret service [MI1c], whose relations with him will be defined on some later date."[10] Nonetheless, MI1c men were supposed to cooperate with Thornhill "in every possible way" and to keep him and Poole appraised of "any military of political information they may obtain." Because the latter had other duties, however, DMI next named Boyce to "run all secret service" under the nominal oversight of Thornhill. However, to muddle matters even further, London identified Lts.

Reilly and Michelson as being on *special* secret service and emphasized that they were not to be mentioned unless "absolutely unavoidable." So whom, if anyone, did Reilly answer to?

Lockhart saw himself as the de facto head of the British Mission in Russia and sought to force Thornhill, *et al.,* to report to and through him.[11] They refused. During May, his situation was rendered more nebulous by the arrival in Vologda of Sir Francis Lindley as "Senior Officer of the Diplomatic Corps." In June, Foreign Secretary Sir Arthur Balfour told Lindley that while Lockhart "will work under your general supervision," he "should be allowed to retain the measure of initiative originally entrusted to him."[12] Clear enough?

Occupying a strange, but pivotal, position in this mess was Capt. George Hill. He was the informal liaison between Lockhart and the British intelligence mission in Petrograd. But as Lockhart's aide Capt. Hicks reported to Poole in May, "Hill has commenced military intelligence work on his own initiative" and was sending reports straight to London. "Hill arranges his work entirely as he pleases," Hicks added, "and we know nothing about . . . part of it."[13] Hill and Reilly were to become very close collaborators in this most secret work.

Lockhart developed his own sources of information. Through his mistress Benckendorf, he cultivated Capt. Cromie. Moura, however, also collected information for the Germans and the Bolsheviks.[14] Did Bruce know or suspect that? A letter from Moura to Lockhart in June or July seems rather suspicious.[15] Responding to Lockhart's worries that their private communications might be discovered, she wrote: ". . . getting all anxious when I spoke of letters being searched. What did you think? That I put Cromie in [my] confidence . . . ?" "[I] am more careful with him than you think," she added, ". . . he is a gramophone for all the infernal gossip in the Embassy. That's why I cultivate him." Later she noted that Cromie was "pleased as Punch" to receive a note from the Scot and swore that "Lockhart is the only one to keep me informed." "How little is needed to satisfy a little vanity," Moura concluded. While he surely was a fool for love, Lockhart probably was not a conscious traitor.

The big concern of Cromie and the Admiralty was German seizure of the Baltic Fleet. To forestall that, he had recruited Russian naval officers to sabotage the vessels as need be. As we have seen, Reilly was vitally interested in the same question, and many of the officers who cooperated with Cromie also served in Orlov's organization. But the connections did not end there. The sabotage plan required money, and to get it Cromie had become involved in the surreptitious purchase of rubles.[16] That, too, interested the Ace-of-Spies.

The ruble-buying also supported another hush-hush operation, almost certainly the "special secret mission" that Reilly was part of. At its head sat Lt. Col. Terence Keyes, who reported to Gen. Poole and the FO in London.[17] Basically, the scheme aimed to buy up control of banks and industrial assets with the aim of securing preeminence in the future Russian economy. In early 1918, the front man for Keyes was Hugh Farran Leech, known as Faran Faranovich to the Russians.[18] Ostensibly a representative of the Midland Bank, he worked out of the Petrograd Embassy.[19] Even more interesting, Moura Benckendorf was Leech's secretary, or was until he discharged her because of complaints that she was a "German agent."[20] The source of that accusation most likely was Reilly. The reason was because Sidney planned to discredit Leech and take his place. He explained to one puzzled Russian that "English Government circles were dissatisfied with Leech's activities . . . and all these activities were to be taken over by [me]."[21] And that is exactly what happened. By early August this gave the Ace-of-Spies access to a large cache of ready, untraceable cash. The takeover was not without repercussions, however; it earned him the lasting enmity of Col. Keyes. What made Reilly the right man for this job were his long-established links to Russian banking and business circles, especially the shadier aspects thereof. A big part in the scheme was played by émigré financiers in Stockholm who were in contact with Scale. We will have more to say of them in future chapters, but for now it is worth noting that among them were several of Reilly's pre-Revolutionary associates, including Isidor Kon and V.F. Davydov.[22]

A key Reilly associate in this and similar deals was Polish sugar magnate and arch-speculator, Karol Jaroszynski (Yaroshinskii).[23] In addition to his part in the "Banking Scheme," Jaroszynski had intimate ties to the ex-Tsar and his family. That, in turn, linked him to British-inspired efforts to rescue or ransom the Imperial Family, the very same ones that Lied and Armitstead were part of.[24] The question is: did Reilly play a part in this as well? Was his takeover of Leech's operation part of a plan to divert money to the rescue efforts? Within this tangled web almost anything is a possibility and very little a certainty. While there is nothing concrete to tie Sidney to the rescue plots, he definitely was in a position to know about them.

Meanwhile, in Moscow, Reilly was expanding his network of contacts and collaborators. On the British end was Hill who secured Poole's OK to stay on in Moscow to assist in military identification and propaganda work.[25] Among other things, Hill had his own line of communication to Trotsky.[26] Trotsky and Reilly both were willing to place an unusual amount of trust in Jolly George. And, of course, Hill also had Lockhart's confidence.

That came in handy, because the Scot had grown increasingly suspicious of the actions of Lessing and other MI1c agents. He was disturbed by stories that Lessing was in contact with "certain international Jews" who, while inclined to be pro-German, might be willing to assist British efforts in Russia.[27] That might have been a reference to Sidney himself. Lockhart added that Lessing "seems to be working on some policy unknown to us." The result was a cable from DMI demanding that Lessing cease and desist all "unauthorized political activities."[28]

Reilly was in Moscow for nearly two weeks before Lockhart knew of his existence. This was not, as we will see, because he was keeping a particularly low profile. It was because nobody in the British Mission bothered to tell Lockhart. He finally got wind of Reilly on 7 May when Lev Karakhan, Soviet Deputy Peoples Commissar for Foreign Affairs, let drop that a "so-called English officer" with the improbable name of "Relli" had recently interviewed Vladimir Bonch-Bruevich (and Karakhan himself) in the Kremlin. The bold interloper had even demanded to see Lenin.[29] A later Soviet report noted the same.[30] Karakhan added that the fellow insisted he had been sent from London to correct Lockhart's "defects" in dealing with the Bolshevik regime. Lockhart demanded an explanation from Boyce who sheepishly admitted that there was a new agent just arrived from England. By his own admission, Bruce "blew up in a storm of indignation" and insisted the new man come see him at once.[31] The following day he summoned Reilly and "dressed him down like a school master," or so he claimed and despite the fact that he had no authority over him whatsoever.[32] The Ace-of-Spies reputedly found the whole thing rather amusing.

Lockhart's diary does not recount anything so elaborate. The notation for 8 May merely records that during the evening he saw "Reilli," the British officer that interviewed Bonch-Bruevich: ". . . He is either mad or a crook." The "crook" part suggests something concerning the ruble and banking scheme or the use of the money for illicit purposes. "Mad" might simply be a response to Reilly's going about Moscow as a British officer barging in on Bolshevik officials. What we must bear in mind is that he never drew attention to himself in one area without the objective of diverting attention from another.

In the wake of his encounter with Reilly, Lockhart's communications with London, heretofore fairly reliable, experienced an inexplicable deterioration. The Scot's messages soon took a week or more to reach Whitehall, if they got there at all. Incoming telegrams arrived late, garbled, or were lost altogether. The Petrograd and Murmansk cable offices, through which these communications ran, were managed by Boyce and Alley. Reilly's messages experienced no such difficulties.

Sidney's interview with Karakhan was no act of rashness. The latter was a wiry, black-bearded Armenian who like Trotsky had not become a Bolshevik until mid-1917. That was not all they shared in common. Karakhan had been secretary of the Soviet delegation at the Brest-Litovsk talks, and as Trotsky he opposed the bitter pill Lenin persuaded the Party to accept. As Deputy Commissar for Foreign Affairs, he now served as Trotsky's right-hand man. From 1905 to 1910, Karakhan had worked in Harbin and Vladivostok, and it was in Manchuria that he experienced his first arrest by the Okhrana. Had he, too, turned informer? Sidney had many contacts in the Far East and had recently perused the Okhrana archives. That certainly gave him the means to concoct a charge if need be. By one means or another, he turned Karakhan into one of those "influential Bolsheviks" on whose "tacit consent" he could depend, or even demand. Karakhan, had decided to test Reilly's influence by dropping a word to Lockhart. The result must have convinced him.

Karakhan put Reilly in touch with the head of the Moscow or M-Cheka, Yakov Peters. We have met him before. He was the London-based Latvian radical who seven years earlier saved himself from the gallows by turning informer for the Okhrana, if he was not such already. One of Peters' London comrades, and a longtime agent of the Okhrana and Scotland Yard, was Casimir Pilenas, most recently an agent of Wiseman in New York. Thus, the Ace-of-Spies stood to know all about Peters' past. Is this what he meant when he later confessed that Reilly threatened to "expose him"?[33] But Reilly had more to work with. The plump-faced Latvian had left an English wife and daughter back in London, whom he hoped to see again. Interestingly, the later Soviet report on Reilly makes note of the fact that in 1918 "Peters' family were in England."[34] As carrot to stick, Sidney added to blackmail the appeal of sweet reason. Faced with the imminent threat of German and/or Allied intervention plus an ever-growing array of domestic opponents, the Bolshevik position was precarious, something Peters was in an excellent position to know. He had already demonstrated his willingness to switch sides to save his skin. Reilly did not present himself as a man hostile to the Revolution, *per se*. It might achieve great things for Russia, but not if Lenin's short-sighted policies delivered it to the grasp of the Germans and completely alienated Britain and France.

Decisive battles on the Western Front raged as they spoke. If Germany prevailed, Russia would lie completely at Berlin's mercy. The defeated Allies would be unable and unwilling to aid a nation whose defection contributed to their downfall. If the Allies triumphed without Russia's help, they still would have no reason to look kindly on a regime that had betrayed them. The only hope for the nation and the Revolution was to reverse Lenin's policy and return to the Allied fold, at least temporarily.

Peters and Karakhan were only the start. Over the following weeks, Sidney would draw in a select group of Chekists and military officers, mostly Latvians. One of these probably was twenty-seven-year-old Genrikh Yagoda, whom we met earlier as a minor employee at the Putilov Works. He, too, had a background as an Okhrana informer.[35] In early 1918 he served the Bolshevik regime as a chief of Red Guards in Petrograd, but about June 1918 he transferred to the Moscow security command. His subsequent rise had much to do with the patronage of Yakov Sverdlov, head of the Soviet's Central Executive Committee (VTsIK). Yakov, of course, was the brother of Reilly's business partner, Benny Sverdlov. Perhaps the latter provided the necessary inside information on Yagoda.

The cooperation of Peters would explain why the Cheka, especially the Moscow or M-Cheka, was unable to get a handle on Reilly in the months to come. By contrast, the modest efforts of Soviet naval counterintelligence turned up a surprising amount of information. For instance, in early May, he took an apartment in the name of Lt. Sidney Reilly, RAF at 24 Miasnitskaia Street, #75 and lived there in grand style for several weeks.[36] This residence on one of Moscow's main thoroughfares put him in the immediate vicinity of the main post office and central telegraph exchange as well as the offices of the old Finance Ministry. Interestingly, Sidney engaged these quarters *before* his departure from England.[37] He seemed a man of about fifty (actually forty-four), "lively and energetic" but inclined to keep to himself. A chauffeured car shuttled him about town. Most days his car took him to the British Mission near the Bolshoi Theater. He made absolutely no effort to disguise his connection to the Mission; he evidently enjoyed a "high position" there and generally "behaved like a boss." Other members of the mission seemed to hold him in "profound respect" but refused to talk about him.[38] He was running some secret department and was without doubt connected to the British Secret Service. Through diplomatic couriers he maintained regular contact with Petrograd, Archangel and other points north.

Some of above is echoed in the recollections of Anton Evgenievich Beloi, a Russian engineer who knew Reilly prewar and now encountered him in Moscow. Sidney sported his well-tailored British uniform at breakfast with Beloi and others at the "Hermitage," one of the restaurants still open in the Red Capital. In contrast to his usual guardedness, Beloi thought he seemed exceptionally candid about his hostility to the Bolsheviks and his conviction that their regime was not long for the world. His Majesty's Government was already "taking decisive measures" to deal with the problem and he was part of them.[39] It was here, too, that he outlined his plan to take over Leech's ruble-raising operation.

The Red naval reports took great interest in Reilly's ever-widening array of Russian contacts. They fell into three general categories. First were the military officers. He clearly had many acquaintances among naval officers, especially those connected to the pre-Revolutionary Admiralty staff.[40] His marriage to the former wife of the ex-Naval Minister's secretary, Zalesskii, seemed to have special significance. He even approached the chief of naval counterintelligence, Lt. Abramovich.[41] Sidney claimed to have been well acquainted with the past head of that service and wanted to establish fresh collaboration between naval *kontrrazvedka* and "British counterintelligence."[42] It was this overture that stirred Abramovich to put him under surveillance. However, Abramovich, a non-Bolshevik, did not report his findings to the Cheka.

A different sort of military contact was Maksim Trester, Reilly's crony from the RSC in New York. Trester now held the post of chief of the Moscow Military District's motor pool. Under the identity of Konstantin Massino, Reilly approached him soon after he arrived in Moscow and demanded that he hand over the money stipulated in their previous arrangement. Over the next few months, Trester provided him with at least 20,000 rubles.[43] He also helped Sidney secure a new identity in the person of K.P. Vasil'ev, a Soviet official handling automobile spare parts. As Vasil'ev, he secured a pass permitting him unrestricted travel on government trains running between Moscow and Petrograd.

The second sphere of contacts were mostly humble, but well-placed, functionaries in the Red administration. One was twenty-five-year-old Olga Starzhevskaia, a staffer in the Soviet's All-Russian Central Executive Committee (VTsIK), Sverdlov's bailiwick.[44] That put her inside the Kremlin. Sidney seduced her and arranged for her to move into a love nest on Malaia Bronnaia Street, thus providing himself with another alternate address/safe house. Her job gave her means to eavesdrop on the most confidential communications of Lenin's Government. In the VTsIK she worked directly under Varlaam Avanesov, an Armenian Bolshevik whose other duties included a post in the Cheka alongside Peters.[45]

Starzhevskaia later confessed that she long believed her lover to be the businessman Konstantin Pavlovich Massino.[46] He seemed to be a supporter of the Bolsheviks, she claimed, but they never really discussed politics. She absolutely denied that he ever asked her to supply him with any information from her work. The Cheka did not take this denial too seriously, and neither should we. For example, she did admit to providing him with official passes to various offices and installations, a rather odd favor for a purely romantic associate.

As Sidney Reilly, our hero found a similar accomplice in Maria Leokhnovskaia, a wireless operator attached to the special telegraph section that handled the "most secret communications of the Government."[47] Through her, Reilly received regular reports on all such traffic. The same report linked him to an official of the Commissariat of Justice, one Landsberg, another likely link with Orlov. A like accomplice was I.I. Khrizhanovskii, an official of the Soviet Central Supply Administration who provided data on the supply of food and fuel to Moscow and other cities.

Reilly probably had an at least indirect link to a White agent that sat in on *Sovnarkom* meetings where Lenin himself presided. This was Arkadii Alfredovich Borman (M), son of longtime liberal activist Ariadna Tyrkova (M) and later stepson of British journalist Harold Williams (also destined to play a role in Reilly's affairs).[48] Acting on the orders of Gen. Alekseev's organizations, Borman found his way into the Soviet Commissariat for Trade and Industry as an economic *spetsialist* (*spets*) and rose quickly in the Red hierarchy. The Alekseev link, of course, he shared in common with Orlov. Borman became especially close to Leonid Krasin, who was now lead man in the Bolshevik economic apparatus.[49] Krasin, with Borman at his side, handled sensitive economic negotiations with the Germans, negotiations in which the Ace-of-Spies was very interested.

Borman's memoirs provide an interesting glimpse into the environment in which Reilly operated. The Bolsheviks did not have the numbers to staff their commissariats and had no means to effectively screen those they engaged. The result was that every institution was "flooded with counter-revolutionaries," though most of these lacked direction or any motivation beyond simple self-preservation.[50] Still, it would not have been difficult, mused Borman, for an *organized* group to infiltrate Soviet administration and destroy it from within. The Cheka was no exception. It was full of dubious elements and flailed about blindly mostly arresting innocent persons. In the meantime, the Bolsheviks' "real enemies traveled in commissar's trains and occupied important positions in People's Commissariats and military staffs."

The third sphere of Sidney's network was what might be termed the "theatrical connection," for most of its members were actresses or others connected to the theater/entertainment scene in Moscow and Petrograd. Most of them were young women who served as couriers and were the con-

necting links between Reilly and other associates—or targets. A male operative was Vladimir Kostomarov, an impresario and theater manager who
helped Reilly meet and recruit others in the artistic world. Sidney frequented the "Aquarium" cabaret where he hobnobbed with resident
dancer-*cum*-courtesan, *Ogonek*. During rides in his car, he quizzed her
about her numerous personal relationships with Red officials and naval
officers.[51] A like confidante was the Ukrainian actress Maria Vsevolodova,
another favorite of Soviet officials. His female accomplices also included a
humble waitress and a cinema usherette. The first was a delegate to the
Soviet of Workers' Deputies, and the two women shared an apartment on
Moscow's wooded outskirts ideal for private meetings of all kinds.[52]

The inter-pollination of these connections can best be seen in Dagmara
(or Dengmar) Karosso (Karozus), an artist at the Moscow Arts Theatre,
Grammatikov's niece and the den mother for a bevy of other "Reilly girls"
living at 3 Sheremetev'skii Lane, #85.[53] Adjoining Moscow University, this
abode lay just west of the Kremlin. Dagmara was the mistress of Count
Aleksandr Dmitrievich Sheremet'ev (M), a prominent composer and former
conductor of the Imperial Court choir who owned this and other houses on
appropriately-named Sheremet'evskii Lane.[54] Reilly knew the Count via the
Grand Duke Aleksandr and was a "frequent visitor" at the address from
the moment of his arrival in Moscow.[55] Dagmara shared the abode with
three other performers, Maria Manon, Evgeniia Likhotinskaia, and
Yelizaveta Otten. Contrary to his later statements, our man frequented the
place quite openly as Lt. Sidney Reilly.[56]

All the women worked for him to some degree, but his primary relationship was with Otten with whom he was "romantically involved."[57]
After abandoning his Miasnitskaia flat in early July, he moved in with her
at the Sheremetev'skii address. George Hill called Otten Reilly's "chief
girl."[58] According to Starzhevskaia, it was Otten who introduced her to
Reilly—as Massino. Just as Starzhevskaia, Otten later insisted that she had
no knowledge that her paramour was a spy, though she knew he was an
officer attached to the English Mission and admitted to destroying certain
correspondence he had entrusted to her. Some of that involved secret letters
to the acting British Consul in Moscow, Arthur Woodhouse, an exchange
in which Otten played the intermediary role.[59] Perhaps it was the fact that
times were desperate, the girls were hungry and Reilly was a man with
money, or perhaps it really was evidence of his "sexual magnetism," but
one way or the other Reilly certainly had his way with women.

Sheremet'evskii Lane included at least one other thing of interest. Next
to Otten and friends, at #5, lived Aleksandr Borisovich Rosenblum, director

of the Moscow Prisoners' Aid Society, and his son Mikhail Aleksandrovich. While there is nothing concrete to connect them to Reilly or his nearby scheming, their proximity is another curious coincidence.[60]

A close friend of the girls at Sheremet'evskii and frequent visitor was another young *artiste*, Maria Fride. She was the sister of Col. Aleksandr Vladimirovich Fride, another Latvian Rifles officer who served the Bolsheviks as chief of military communications. That post gave him access to all communications passing to and from the various fronts. Reilly later claimed that it was Fride who introduced him to Orlov, but that makes absolutely no sense given Reilly's and Orlov's obvious prior connections. The true situation had to be the reverse because Orlov's Petrograd network included Latvian officers who knew Fride; the Colonel himself may have been part of the *Biuro* network. An interesting question is whether Fride was related to Sidney's business partner in Manhattan, Sergius Friede (originally *Fride*). In any case, Fride was a very valuable asset.

Complicating the situation, however, was that in May Fride and his sister started working for another Allied spy master, the American Kalamatiano. In March, U.S. Moscow Consul Maddin Summers picked Kalamatiano to head an intelligence-gathering operation dubbed the Information Service (IS). As Chief Observer, by May Kalamatiano recruited and managed a net of some fourteen agents covering central and southern Russia; Fride was #5.[61] The cover for this activity was his International Manufacturer's Sales Company with headquarters on the Lubianka. By summer the number of his operatives grew to more than thirty. Despite later claims by Kalamatiano and his superiors that the IS was devoted to the passive collection of political and commercial data, his recruitment of men like Fride argued otherwise.

Reilly, of course, still viewed Kalamatiano's efforts with suspicion but was determined to exploit them to his own benefit. Such suspicions were shared in London. For instance, in early May the British Consulate in Stockholm reported that J.P. Morgan was rumored to be hunting for Russian banks. A Consulate officer wondered if he should quietly inform his American counterpart that His Majesty already had "interests" in that realm; the reply from Whitehall was to strictly "avoid the subject."[62]

Reilly saw further evidence of the American threat in the connection between Kalamatiano and the incoming U.S. Consul in Moscow, DeWitt C. Poole, to American millionaire Charles R. Crane. Crane was a Russophile with personal links to the Imperial Court and Russian political circles. Among these were Guchkov, Grand Duke Aleksandr and, interestingly enough, Count Sheremet'ev. Crane also was a big backer of Kalamatiano's syndicate. Though he held no official position in the U.S. Government, he was a member of Woodrow Wilson's "Brain Trust" and an influence on Washington's Russian policies. From Sidney's perspective, Kalamatiano was the cat's paw of men like Crane who were bent on establishing American economic and political domination of Russia. That made them even more dangerous than the Reds.

The cultivation of Fride secured a valuable foothold inside the Yankee camp. As Reilly described it, he and Fride arranged a couple of "surreptitious meetings" after which the Colonel "became my most willing collaborator."[63] By contract, Reilly claimed to have avoided all contact with Kalamatiano for some time to come. The American remembered the arrangement very differently. According to him, it was Reilly who suggested using Maria F. and the Sheremet'evskii house as a common drop point for the Colonel's reports. Miss Fride delivered Sidney's copies directly to Otten. Thus, it is unlikely that Col. Fride ever set eyes on him at all, at least as Sidney Reilly.

In his later confession, Fride admitted that apart from Kalamatiano, for more than two months he also supplied reports to a second American, one "Johnston."[64] He seemed to be a commercial agent of some sort. They met near the Kuznetskii Bridge, but Fride also recalled that Johnston had two addresses, one on Sheremet'evskii Lane and another on Miasnitskaia Street—just as Reilly. Likewise, Johnston disappeared from the latter place the same time as Sidney. The best bet, therefore, is that Johnston was Reilly in yet another guise. It would not have been difficult to pass himself off as an American, and Fride was not the only one so deceived. A Soviet naval report from mid-June recorded that several persons interviewed insisted that Reilly was an officer in the *American* Army.[65] Also, the Ace-of-Spies may have used a similar ploy in Vologda by passing himself off as an American insurance agent, Edward C. Riley.[66] The latter was quite real, but the local Cheka was convinced they were one and the same. Why the subterfuge? It was another example of Reilly's compartmentalization. Impersonating Johnston permitted him to collect information from Fride that he did not have to share with Kalamatiano. Next, should Fride be caught or prove treacherous, there would be no direct link to Sidney or British interests. Only the Americans would be compromised. Such precaution was all the more necessary if Reilly himself planned to do the compromising.

Sidney doubtless had other spies inside the Information Service. One was Dmitrii Ishevskii, who first connected himself to Kalamatiano's organization in late 1917. A journalist, Ishevskii was a friend and protégé of Manasevich-Manuilov and well trained in his mentor's methods of deceit and exploitation. Claiming dissatisfaction with Ishevskii's performance, Kalamatiano fired him, whereupon he demanded hush money.[67] To no great surprise, he later ended up in the Cheka's service.

Nor were Fride and Ishevskii the only things that connected Reilly and Kalamatiano. In late 1917 the latter had several Czechs among his agents, holdovers from the Voska network. In his *British Connection*, Deacon/McCormick cites a document dated 27 April 1918, purportedly from "Czech intelligence" to Oliver T. Crosby, the U.S. Treasury's special representative to the Inter-Allied Financial Committee in London. The writer asks if "we can expect the promised funds which Kalamatiano tells us Reilli has arranged to transmit to our troops?"[68] Unfortunately, the provenance and authenticity of this communication cannot be verified, but all things suggest it is genuine or at least based on real information. Crosby was indeed involved in channeling American money to anti-Bolshevik forces, including the Czechs. Moreover, Crosby was linked closely to the aforementioned Charles Crane, himself a close friend of Czech leader Thomas Masaryk. Most significant, perhaps, was that in order to disguise the source of the funds (the U.S., after all, was supposed to be neutral in Russia's internal affairs), they were funneled through *British* hands.[69] Wiseman, in fact, was in London during April conniving with Crosby in such secret funding schemes. Reilly was the perfect man on the spot to handle the Czech money.

The Czech, Latvian, American, British and even Cheka threads all come together in the case of yet another Reilly contact, Boris Savinkov. Over the past few months the redoubtable intriguer had journeyed south to Don Cossack territory to seek alliance with Generals Alekseev and Kornilov. With the cautious blessing of Alekseev, he returned to Moscow in February and began to organize an underground force of ex-officers. Among his recruits were several Latvian officers, most notably Col. Frederik Bredis, head of Savinkov's counterintelligence section. Bredis and friends were former comrades of the Latvian commanders now guarding the Kremlin and the Red leadership. Dubbed the "Union for the Protection of the Motherland and Liberty," hereafter the Union, Boris' organization was handicapped by lack of money. In May, at the same time as Reilly's arrival on the scene, Union finances suddenly improved and it quickly expanded to a force of some 2,000 in Moscow, with more supporters in surrounding towns. This energetic expansion took place without the least hint of opposition from the local Cheka.

Reilly also may have encouraged Savinkov in a plan to assassinate Lenin. The elimination of his guiding hand would definitely simplify the co-optation and manipulation of other members of the government. On 22

May, Union gunmen narrowly missed their mark, when a confused time schedule caused Lenin to show up an hour early for a speech. The failure, however, would not dissuade Reilly from using the same "direct method" in future.

Sidney directed Savinkov to another possible donor: Lockhart. On 15 May, the Scot met with a Union representative, Capt. Aleksandr Vilenkin. Lockhart knew Vilenkin from the latter's past association with the British Embassy. There followed a face-to-face meeting with Savinkov himself. Lockhart dutifully informed superiors in London of the contact and asked permission to continue it. But they may not have been the only ones he informed. Shortly after the interview with Lockhart, Savinkov learned that the Moscow Cheka was planning a move against his organization. The warning came from Reilly who doubtless received the tip straight from Peters. Sidney urged Boris to move the operation out of the Capital. Savinkov dallied and the Cheka blow finally fell on 29 May. A hundred Union members were caught in the sweep, including Vilenkin, but Boris and most other key officers escaped.

The Cheka official history explains the move on Savinkov as the result of a lucky break: a lowly Union member being treated in a local hospital unwisely confided the details of his clandestine association to a loyal nurse.[70] The story smacks of a cover for some other informant. While the Union was no sterling example of security, it did observe the basic conspiratorial rule by which no ordinary member would know the identities and locales of key leaders. But Lockhart, via Vilenkin and Savinkov, did have such information. A former Unionist and friend of Vilenkin probably hit the nail on the head, when he offered that Lockhart "betrayed secrets through his mistress," Moura Benckendorf.[71] Moura's hand would explain the need for the Ivanov story, for she was an agent worth protecting. The probable scenario is that Lockhart blabbed the information to Moura, who gave it to Dzerzhinskii or Peters. The latter then warned Reilly, who warned Savinkov. It was not beyond the Ace-of-Spies to have set up Savinkov with Lockhart as a test of the Scot's reliability.

The affair raised serious questions for Peters' M-Cheka. Trotsky demanded to know how the "Sword and Shield of the Revolution" had overlooked a conspiracy involving thousands of persons growing under its nose for months. The main onus fell on the Cheka's top man, Feliks Edmundovich Dzerzhinskii. A Polish nobleman by birth and ex-Catholic seminarian, the gaunt, aesthetic figure of "Iron Feliks" has passed into legend as the archetype of the ruthlessly clever Soviet intelligence boss. Perhaps because one is only as good as one's opposition, this estimation has been parroted by most Western commentators. While he definitely was ruthless, an indefatigable worker and a dedicated revolutionary, it is not at all clear that he was any genius at intelligence work.[72] As an underground activist, he was arrested repeatedly with no indication that he learned from his experience. The real question is whether Feliks was ever really in control of the Cheka at all.

In June, Orlov, with Peters' help, was assigned to the M-Cheka. According to Orlov, one day Dzerzhinskii strolled through his office and recognized him. He had good reason; Orlov had prosecuted him following an arrest in Warsaw in 1912. Feliks simply welcomed the ex-Tsarist agent to the side of Revolution and offered his personal assistance as needed.[73] It also was in June that Reilly received another alias, that of Georgii Repinskii, Chekist.[74] Here, too, we must suspect the helping hand of Peters and a connection to Orlov's simultaneous transfer.

In London the "political" nature of Reilly's reports raised concerns about just what he was doing. According to a War Office memo, "in June it became apparent that [Reilly's] utility as a military agent was being impaired by the fact that he was in touch with Mr. Lockhart, who was using him for some political purpose."[75] The exploitation certainly was the other way around, but it was clear that ST1 was ignoring orders "not to get into any official position or to get mixed up with politics." As a result, new orders arrived directing him to proceed at once to Siberia to investigate German POW camps, the whole idea being to get him "away from the Political atmosphere in which he was involved." For reasons no one later could, or wanted to, explain, he never undertook the Siberian mission. Whether he was working on his own initiative or on the unwritten orders of someone else in London remains a mystery, but what is clear is that no one had any real control of his actions.

Meanwhile, thousands of miles away in New York, things were happening that would impact his affairs in Russia. Throughout the spring and summer of 1918, Sidney remained in regular contact with his Manhattan office, now under the care of Thomas and Weinstein. Through them, even while he plotted in Russia, he pursued business in New York. Soon after his arrival in Petrograd, Thomas, acting on his instructions, filed suit against the ABF-Economizer Co. This small firm produced a fuel-saving device suitable for autos, aircraft, and even submarine engines. Reilly had secured the rights to market it in Russia, but he wanted more. A year earlier, he had made a loan to the cash-strapped company and received a controlling share of the company stock as collateral.[76] The Ace-of-Spies now called in the debt. The ABF device's military applications also had attracted the interest of the U.S. Navy. Reilly's effort to grab control stimulated fresh interest about him and his associates.

This brings us back to Tony Jechalski whose relationship with Sidney was to take an even more ambiguous turn. On 23 April, Thomas handed the Pole a check for $2,000. It bore Reilly's signature, indication that it had been made out some months in advance.[77] Thomas claimed it was repayment on a "loan" Jechalski made to Reilly in 1917. Given that he had no need to borrow such a trifling amount from his underling, the more likely explanation it that it was another purchase of rubles. It also may have been an advance for services Jechalski was to perform. He soon departed on a tour of the American West supposedly on the lookout for oil and mining properties. In May, Jechalski visited San Antonio, Texas, where his activities, especially his conspicuous cultivation of American military officers, raised suspicions. His known association with Reilly did not help. In fact, in November 1917, an unidentified "British officer" had informed U.S. officials in San Antonio that one Sidney Reilly of New York was a past Japanese spy and a current tool of German interests in America and Mexico.[78] On 29 May, U.S. Military Intelligence and Bureau of Investigation agents nabbed Jechalski as an "enemy suspect" and locked him up in the stockade at Fort Sam Houston. He would remain for more than five months. The very next day, Nadine cabled London wanting to be put in touch with her husband.[79] If her purpose was to tell him about Jechalski, why was it important that Reilly know that in Russia? Did she suspect that Sidney might somehow be behind the arrest?

Tony's arrest may have been simple bad luck, but his retention in custody raises questions. He had an excellent lawyer, Arthur Garfield Hays of New York, but even he was unable to gain his client's release. An interesting bit of synchronicity is that Jechalski's time behind bars corresponds closely to Reilly's stint in Russia. His release followed by just a few days our man's reappearance in London. Was this, too, more than coincidence? In July, Reilly's factotum Thomas wired Jechalski $50, presumably to provide spending money in the stockade, but that was not the only connection. Payments to lawyer Hays also came from 120 Broadway, and Hays had been Reilly's partner in the war contracts game.[80] Was Hays being paid to get Jechalski out of jail or to keep him *in*?

There always had been an undercurrent of rivalry in the Reilly-Jechalski partnership and that extended to the sexual arena. American investigators were astonished to learn, but we should not be, that Nadine had been an all-night visitor at Jechalski's apartment after her husband "went to Europe."[81] It is a sure bet that Reilly got wind of the affair even in Moscow.

While not one to make a fuss over fidelity, as the Tremaine episode indicated he was possessive and already annoyed by Jechalski's poaching on his territory. Forcing the latter to cool his heels in a Texas lockup, and thus keeping him well away from Nadine, might have been just the comeuppance Reilly would have ordered.

Then there was Thomas' 18 June payment of $6,000 each to Weinstein and Carl Lowie, the latter recently arrived from Stockholm. Thomas explained the first as a delayed commission payment and Lowie's, "a friend of Reilly's for a great number of years," as repayment of money advanced to Nadine during her 1916 trip to Russia. Possibly, but another explanation is that it was an exchange for rubles Lowie had stashed in Archangel. Soon after the exchange, he left New York back to northern Russia. On 21 August he landed in Archangel but was at once arrested by local White Russian counterintelligence on charges of being a German spy.[82]

Lowie regained his freedom through the intercession of the acting American naval attaché in Archangel, Lt. Sergius Martin Riis. In the Reilly mold, Riis concocted a largely phony autobiography that had him born in New York state to Danish immigrant parents, and as a graduate of the U.S. Naval Academy and/or the nearby Marine Corps School.[83] In reality, Riis was a Finn or Dano-Estonian who immigrated to America soon after the Revolution of 1905. In the late '30s, Riis boasted that he had been "an active student for more than thirty years of . . . underground political and espionage affairs."[84] In 1909, he formed his own detective agency, the S.M. Riis Confidential Service. The firm specialized in factory security and suppression of labor spying. For this reason, his was one of the agencies hired by Boris Brasol to keep tabs on plants engaged in Russian war work. Thus, Riis and Reilly must have had some measure of acquaintance, so it is all the more interesting that he stepped in to rescue Lowie. In Archangel, Riis handled local intelligence and security matters, and worked closely with the American Information Service *and* MI1c via Commander Malcolm Maclaren, RN, an officer with direct links to Boyce and Reilly.[85] Riis later claimed that since WWI he had "been attached to the British Secret Service, serving under men who are leaders in their profession."[86] Was one of these men Sidney Reilly?

The ABF affair and Jechalski's arrest breathed new life into the stalled investigation of Reilly and Weinstein.[87] It is even possible that a resentful Jechalski helped guide the Americans in the new direction. The driving force this time was the Navy's Office of Naval Intelligence (ONI). An important aspect of the investigation was monitoring of cable traffic passing to and from Reilly's Broadway office. This revealed regular communication between Thomas and Weinstein and Reilly in Russia. The result was that just as Reilly's plots were coming to a climax in Russia, he was coming under close and hostile scrutiny in the U.S.A.

During June and July, a noose—several nooses, really—seemed to draw tighter and tighter around the Bolsheviks' throats. In the Western capitals, armed intervention was a foregone conclusion; the only questions were when and in what force. In early June even Lockhart seemed to accept the handwriting on the wall. He burned incriminating documents and wired London that "if you do not intervene in the next few weeks or days . . . we shall lose a golden opportunity."[88] Whether this represented his heartfelt opinion is open to question. By voicing opposition to intervention he would have insured his recall and loss of all remaining credibility. By going along with the new program he was assured of keeping at least a finger in the mix.

In Berlin the mood also turned hostile. The successive offensives on the Western Front had failed to break the British and French armies and the Americans were arriving in ever larger numbers. It seemed time to secure all possible gains in the East. Berlin's ambassador in the Red Capital, Count Wilhelm von Mirbach, urged his government to finish off the Red vermin. In early July, German agents extended an offer of general amnesty and repatriation to all Latvian troops in Red service in exchange for their neutrality in the event of a German occupation of Moscow. The shifting German policy meshed with Reilly's increasing interest in the Latvians. In keeping with the System, their subversion would serve a useful purpose whether Allied or German interests prevailed in Russia. Adding credence to this, a later Soviet report insisted that as of June, Reilly's main aim was to incite a "*coup d'etat* by the [Latvian] Riflemen," but that he played a "double game [by] performing jobs for German Intelligence."[89] What else would we expect?

Meanwhile, Savinkov's Union, encouraged by French money and promises of intervention, lay plans for a mass rising. Inside Moscow the Bolsheviks' disgruntled junior partners in the Soviet Government, the Left SRs, hatched their own scheme to seize power. In late May the Czecho-Slovak Army Corps, perhaps stimulated by the money Reilly had helped supply, rose in arms against Bolshevik authority, and under the cover of Czech guns, an anti-Bolshevik government opened for business in the Volga town of Samara.[90] In the south, Alekseev's so-called Volunteer Army joined rebellious Cossacks to overwhelm local Reds. Things did not look good for Lenin & Co.

Assuming that Bolshevik power was bound to soon fall by one means or another, Reilly turned some of his attention to the Russian Orthodox Church. In Petrograd, he contacted Archpriest K.M. Aggeev, president of the Church's financial department. On 14 June, Sidney compiled a report for Lindley extolling the Church as the "one fundamental moral factor in Russian life" and the key to the nation's return to social and political equilibrium. The Church's ability to exert moral influence, however, was handicapped by the Bolsheviks seizure of its assets. Simply put, it needed money, as much as 20–25 million rubles (roughly £500,000, or $2,500,000), to "flood the country with propaganda" to counteract the spirit of Bolshevism now and for the future.[91]

A week later, from Moscow he sent a similar memo to SIS and noted his negotiations with N.D. Kuznetsov, Patriarch Tikhon's "legal advisor and right-hand-man." [92] Kuznetsov also was the Patriarch's "intermediary" with the Bolsheviks. According to Reilly, certain Reds, faced with mounting opposition and declining confidence, were willing to relax their policies towards the Church and seek its support. The same Bolsheviks would permit Allied financial aid to religious bodies and with such money "10,000 religious agitators" could be unleashed upon the countryside. Perhaps, Reilly suggested, the Archbishop of Canterbury could put up the needed funds on behalf of the Anglican Church. Moreover, the Patriarch was ready to give Allied intervention his formal blessing. It is unclear whether Reilly ever received formal or informal sanction for this scheme, but by one means or another, he later claimed to have delivered 2 million rubles to the Patriarch's hands.[93]

Reilly spent most of June and the first part of July in Moscow, though Red naval surveillance noted at least two brief trips to Petrograd. Besides his dealings with Church officials, he also drew closer to George Hill, Cromie and others. Although Hill later insisted that he and Reilly maintained entirely separate organizations, the Captain's after-action report shows that they were thoroughly otherwise. Hill, it may be recalled, had developed his own close relationship with several Soviet officials, most significantly Trotsky and, like Sidney, the brothers Bruevich. With the sanction of Trotsky and General Bruevich, Hill had an important advisory role with the nascent Red aviation service and Soviet military intelligence. Hill makes his first, definite mention of Reilly in late June noting that "we [Hill, Boyce, Lt. Urmston, etc.] had some excellent information via Lt. Riley's [sic] channels." [94] Urmston managed cable communications for Boyce and Hill and also handled Reilly's cables for London—and New York.

Yet another British operative involved was engineer John Merrett, who also managed to get himself confused with Reilly. Merrett had ties to Cromie, the Orlov-Yudenich network and even Farran Leech. Merrett's later reports note that he worked closely with MI1c man "Gillespie." For instance, in September 1918 Merrett would receive 250,000 rubles from Gillespie, "the last of the Intelligence Officers [in Russia]." [95] Reilly was still in Russia at that time.

Meanwhile, things started to heat up. On 20 June, V. Volodarskii, People's Commissar for Propaganda and Agitation, was gunned down in Petrograd by a young SR with links to Savinkov. Sidney might have had good reason to want Volodarskii dead. The deceased had lived in New York pre-1917 and worked at the *Novyi Mir* offices alongside Weinstein's brother Gregory. Thus, there was a chance that he knew our man by sight or reputation, something Reilly may have found inconvenient, particularly if he had tried to recruit Volodarskii and been rebuffed.

The activity of Reilly and other British operatives in Petrograd did not go unobserved. In July, an opportunistic double agent named G.G. Gol'dinger reported to the head of the P-Cheka, Moisei Uritskii, identifying the conspiratorial quarters of English agents, "Gilespi," "Dzhon Merrit" and others. To add to the confusion, Gol'dinger thought Gillespie and Merrett were the same man. Was Reilly imitating the latter as well? In any case, Uritskii took no obvious action against the foreign culprits. [96] Even so, this knowledge may have played some role in his coming assassination.

All of this brings us back to Reilly's plan for a palace coup. Reilly already had collaborators among the Latvians like Peters and Fride, but in June or early July he secured another recruit, Colonel Eduard Petrovich Berzin. Reilly's chronology on this point differs radically from sources such as Lockhart and, most significantly, Berzin himself. In his memoir, Sidney puts his first meeting with Berzin prior to 6 July and suggests that the introduction came through the local chief of French intelligence, Capt., Henri de Verthimon (Vertement). [97] However, Berzin, for good reason, subsequently insisted that he never set eyes on Reilly until the middle of *August*. A later Cheka/OGPU report seems to support Reilly's timing at least, stating that during *July* Lockhart sent him to Petrograd "to start a revolt in the [Latvian] regiments." [98]

Berzin's nominal post was commander of the 1st Latvian Artillery Division, an important part of the Capital guard. But he also led the so-called "Special Battalion" that guarded the Kremlin itself. [99] As early as March, Vladimir Bonch-Bruevich put him charge of the security unit protecting the Soviet Government's move from Petrograd to Moscow. [100] He subsequently worked closely with General Bruevich's Red staff and, of course, Peters, who in addition to his Cheka duties, exercised overall supervision of the Latvian units in Moscow. [101] Both provided other means for him and Reilly to meet. He was exactly the man Reilly needed to realize his scheme.

The only sticking point was the money that Berzin needed to secure the cooperation of other Latvian officers and troops. That was where Leech's money-raising came in. It may well be that the initial idea was to start the revolt in Petrograd as a means of drawing attention and troops away from Moscow where the real blow would fall at just the right moment.

On 6 July all hell broke loose in Moscow. That afternoon, an LSR Chekist named Yakov Bliumkin and an accomplice assassinated Ambassador Mirbach. This was the opening gun of a full-scale Left SR revolt. In a bold, or simply foolish, effort to subdue the rebels, Dzerzhinskii walked into the LSR camp and fell prisoner. The same day Savinkov's Unionists launched attacks in several towns to the north and south of Moscow, actually taking control of Yaroslavl, a town lying on the vital rail line connecting Moscow to Vologda and Archangel. For twenty-four hours, things hung in the balance, but by the evening of the 7th the LSR rising was crushed, thanks mostly to the Latvian units under Berzin and others.

Where was Reilly in all this? According to Bruce Lockhart's memoir *British Agent*, Sidney suddenly appeared in his box at the Bolshoi around 6:00 p.m. to warn him of the Mirbach assassination and the pending coup.[102] However, Lockhart's diary entry for the day records the events at the Bolshoi in some detail but makes absolutely no mention of Reilly.[103] On the other hand, his presence would not have been a difficult feat; the Cheka detachment guarding the Theater was in the hands of Peters.[104] KGB author V.F. Kravchenko later claimed that Reilly had "direct contact" with rebel commander D.I. Popov, commander of the main LSR combat unit, and American writer Edward Van Der Rhoer actually puts him at Popov's headquarters when Dzerzhinskii was arrested.[105] If Reilly did so involve himself, it almost certainly was in an effort to quell the revolt which was in complete opposition to plans which it threatened to delay or ruin altogether. Indeed, he probably approved the defeat of the rising. Replacing Lenin with an equally radical and possibly even more intractable regime of Left SRs was not what he wanted at all, nor was a bloody, chaotic shootout his style. The Ace-of-Spies always preferred conspiracy to firepower.

Reilly's whereabouts and actions between the events of 6–7 July and the beginning of August are sketchy, but in the immediate aftermath he seems to have stayed close to Moscow. That was in part necessitated by a Bolshevik decree forbidding Allied officers from leaving the place of current residence. Sidney phased out his Lt. Reilly identity and stopped wearing his uniform. Around the 14th–15th, probably as Gillespie, he headed for Vologda making a brief stop in Petrograd along the way. The primary purpose was to consult with Gen. Poole, Lindley and other Allied representatives before they pulled out of Vologda, as they already planned to do, and Russia altogether.

While in Vologda, Sidney made a fresh pitch to Lindley on behalf of the Church scheme. Whether he really planned to deliver such money to Patriarch Tikhon or divert it to his Latvian plot is an open question. In any case, once more as Sidney Reilly he presented himself before the executive committee of the Vologda Soviet (which included members of the local Cheka) on 20 July and received a special pass to travel to Moscow via Petrograd. Not only was this unusual given the tight restrictions on Allied personnel, but the pass stipulated that he was to proceed without obstacles or hindrance en route.[106] The Ace-of-Spies' connections were serving him very well.

Interestingly, and likely by no accident, his departure from Vologda preceded by just a day the arrival of a special Cheka team from Moscow charged by Dzerzhinskii with "unraveling the Allied Secret Services" and their nefarious connections. By the 23rd, Reilly was at rest in Petrograd and temporarily ensconced in the "British Intelligence Section attached to HQ Russian Staff," Boyce's cover, and sent a final appeal to Lindley regarding the Church matter. The following day, Lindley et al. departed for Archangel and Reilly hopped a train back to Moscow. He had Boyce's tacit approval to push ahead with the Latvian gambit and, by one means or another, sufficient money to do so.

It is possible, if no more, that Reilly's visit to Vologda may have been connected to another matter. On the night of 16 July, in the distant Ural town of Ekaterinburg, ex-Tsar Nicholas Romanov and all or most of his family were murdered by a band of local Chekists. That, at least, is the generally accepted story, although exactly what happened that night and the days following are a source of enduring mystery and controversy. One of the rescue plans concocted by British agents called for spiriting the family out of Russia via Vologda and Archangel.[107] One possibility is that just such an abortive rescue triggered the massacre in Ekaterinburg, which may explain the uncertainty and obfuscation surrounding the event ever since. If so, it was another secret that Reilly could carry and exploit in years to come.

It was about the beginning of August, Hill later recalled, that he learned MI1c planned to leave an officer behind in the event of a general evacuation of Russia. Reilly was that man.[108] At one of their secret meetings, Sidney warned Hill that he should curtail his recruitment of Russian officers. The effort was bound to be penetrated and compromised, he cautioned, and was best left in the hands of Savinkov's or Alekseev's people. If nothing else, it shows that Reilly was not oblivious to such dangers and never too trusting of Russians, Latvians or anyone else.

In Moscow new troubles were brewing. Following his near-death experience in the Left SR uprising, on 8 July a shaken Dzerzhinskii resigned his post as head of the Cheka. This put Peters in charge of the whole operation, seemingly a great boon for Reilly. Iron Feliks, however, maintained an active interest in the efforts he had personally initiated to penetrate and reveal the intrigues of the Allied missions. He certainly understood that the Bolshevik regime's position had changed radically in the past few weeks. With the Germans preoccupied by relentless Allied counter blows in the West, the Left SRs crushed, and Savinkov on the run, the Allied missions were the only remaining immediate threat. If they could be neutralized, Bolshevik power would gain a critical and much needed breathing space.

Back in June, Dzerzhinskii had enlisted two eager Latvians, Jan Buikis and Jan Sprogis, to infiltrate the pro-Allied activities of their fellow countrymen in Petrograd. As Buikis later recalled it, this effort was slow to produce results. Using the names Shmidkhen (AKA Schmitheim) and Bredis, during July Buikis and comrade wormed their way into the group of Latvian officers cultivated by Cromie.[109] By the beginning of August, they had gained Cromie's confidence to the point that he agreed to provide them with a recommendation to persons in Moscow. Buikis later claimed the intro was to Lockhart, but a contemporary British account insists that Cromie's letter was addressed to another Latvian officer with ties to Savinkov, Col. Gopper. One may suspect the hand of Moura Benckendorf in the matter. Being privy to Cromie's and Lockhart's communications, she could have pointed the Latvians in his direction.

Perhaps most important to us, at the same club they met with Cromie, Buikis and pal also encountered Reilly.[110] Buikis even claimed that Sidney interviewed them before they left Petrograd to see Lockhart and knew they intended to see the Scot. That seems doubtful because Reilly seems to have been fully occupied in Moscow at the time. In the Red Capital, he held a series of urgent meetings with Hill, Boyce and another British officer, Lt. Laurence Webster, during 1–3 August. In addition to being MI1c and head of the Passport Control Office in Moscow, Webster also held the money raised through the ruble-buying. Lockhart was now involved in that end of the business, signing IOU's as ranking representative of His Majesty's Government. At these conclaves, Reilly received Boyce's formal "authorization" to proceed with his plan and a guarantee of money to carry it out.[111] As Hill recollected it, "[Reilly] was receiving very excellent information from all possible sources," and "Reilly knew the situation better than any other British officer in Russia, and he had the more delicate threads in his hand." As a result, Hill and Boyce as well agreed "to leave the political control and our policy in his hands."[112] In effect, the Ace-of-Spies was now in charge of British intelligence in Russia.

On 5 August, a fresh difficulty appeared. In the days preceding, the long-anticipated landing of Allied troops in the northern ports—the intervention—had taken place. The news at first threw the Bolsheviks into a panic; believing that an overwhelming Anglo-French force would descend on Moscow, some talked of abandoning the city. However, when it was apparent that the Allied forces were but a few thousand men, the Red leadership was emboldened and struck back by arresting every Allied officer they could find. Boyce and Webster were grabbed, but not before the latter managed to transfer the MI1c funds to the relative security of the American Consulate. Reilly got a timely tip-off from Hill, and after destroying papers, the two headed for one of their many safe houses. A Cheka descent on Sidney's old Miasnitskaia address struck thin air. Reilly took a new identity, possibly Vasil'ev, and became a worker in the "Technical Department" of the Red General Staff.[113] Hill also went undercover.

On the 7th, Sidney moved out of Otten's place, though things on Sheremet'evskii Lane remained quite undisturbed. These changes did nothing to curtail his conspiratorial activities. Soon after, Hill recounted that "Lt. Riley's [sic] naval connections reported, and much information was obtained in regard to the morale, movements and plans of the naval circle."[114] "Sabotage and destruction plans" for the Baltic fleet and other military assets were still very much part of the agenda.

Peters, in the meantime, was having troubles of his own. Since late July he had been under mounting pressure from Dzerzhinskii to make headway on the investigation of the Allied missions, and Feliks' anxiousness increased in the wake of the landings. Iron Feliks was especially worried about what the perfidious English were doing. In his defense, Peters argued that the recent arrests of Allied officers yielded nothing more incriminating than a few items pilfered from the Hotel Astoria!

In the meantime, Buikis and Sprogis arrived in town and went straight to Feliks with Cromie's letter. If Buikis' recollection is correct, he and his comrade had their first, brief encounter with Lockhart about 3 August followed by a second meeting a week later.[115] These meetings apparently failed to produce meaningful results, and Dzerzhinskii hauled in Peters to discuss how best to exploit the situation. Buikis remembered clearly that Peters was present at the meeting and that it was *he* who insisted that a higher-ranking officer, *Berzin*, be used to approach Lockhart.[116] His real intention, of course, was to make sure that ally Berzin handled any liaison with the British, not Dzerzhinskii's men.

Even so, the situation was fraught with uncertainty. As Peters doubtless knew, Lockhart himself was a not altogether certain quantity. Beyond this, the Soviet regime's remarkable turn of good fortune, most notably the feeble display of the Allies, must have forced an opportunist like Peters to consider his options. Perhaps Bolshevik power could survive after all. If so, was there more to gain by double-crossing Reilly than helping him? Thus, neither he nor Berzin breathed a word of Buikis and Co.

Lockhart's actions raise a number of questions. He later justified his willingness to admit these total strangers to his confidence because of his faith in Cromie's recommendation. Or was it Moura's? In any case, it was powerful faith, for only days before the Scot himself had reported to London that the British network in Petrograd was full of Bolshevik agents, and a little checking would have revealed that Shmidkhen himself was under suspicion there.

Over the next few days, Dzerzhinskii's men approached Berzin posing as anti-Bolsheviks anxious to secure British support. Pretending to take them at face value, he accepted their offer to take an appeal to Lockhart. He demonstrated his own impeccable loyalty by "reporting" their treachery back to Peters, on 10 August.[117] On the 14th he accompanied Buikis to Lockhart's flat where the Scot agreed to put Berzin in contact with "Konstantin"—Reilly—who could supply the funds necessary to buy the cooperation of other Latvians. A few days later, Lockhart met with his American and French counterparts, Consuls Poole and Fernand Grenard, and the chief of the French Military Mission, Gen. Jean Lavergne, and secured their agreement to channel funds to the dissident Latvians via Reilly.[118] As Hill later put it, Lockhart arranged that "Reilly should take charge of all questions dealing with the [Latvians]," and "from the first the Allies desired to leave to policy to him."[119]

It is not clear if all the Allied representatives knew just how far he planned to take the Latvian scheme. The later view from the lofty perspective of the Foreign Office, echoed in Lockhart's official explanation, was that Reilly was supposed to restrict himself to securing the Latvians' neutrality in the event of further Allied moves against the Bolsheviks, *not* to engineer the overthrow of the Red regime.

One man who did know exactly what Reilly was about was George Hill. He knew all about the meetings with Berzin and by mid-August Reilly had put Hill "in contact with the whole affair, so that [he] could take over if need arose." Thereafter, he carefully briefed Hill after each meeting, "and explained to me all that had been done."[120] Hill, of course, never mentioned just what that was.

In his subsequent statement cooked up with Peters, Berzin claimed he met "Konstantin" for the first time on 15 August. Over the next week, in a series of meetings, the Colonel claimed he bilked the evil English spy out of 1,200,000 rubles which, as obedient servants of Revolution, he and Peters handed over to the Cheka treasury.[121] How much they actually received and siphoned off for themselves only they and Sidney knew. Berzin's testimony sounds an obviously false note in his claim that Reilly throughout was uncharacteristically loquacious, boasting about his plans and detailing every aspect of the conspiracy. For instance, after first suggesting that Lenin, Trotsky and other key Reds be arrested and imprisoned, Sidney later, according to Berzin, thought it a better idea to shoot them on the spot. For good measure, the Colonel noted a specific threat against loyal comrade Peters.[122]

On the other hand, Berzin's description doubtless contains many authentic details, at least to the extent he and Peters understood them. For instance, he records that Reilly knew the location of several batteries of British-made heavy guns that could be brought to Moscow to overcome any unexpected opposition. He also knew, probably via Borman, the secret location of a special train loaded with gold to be sent to Germany. The train was guarded by a battalion of Latvian troops and his agents among them would divert the train to Moscow, thus providing all the money needed to pay the garrison and bankroll a new government. Once the signal was given, subverted Latvian units in the Capital would occupy the State Bank, telephone exchange, Kremlin, and all Soviet offices. After the armories were secured, special officers' detachments drawn from Savinkov's and Alekseev's followers would seal off the workers' districts and disarm the Red Guard. Yagoda might have helped there. In Petrograd, Latvians and other rebels would gather at the British Embassy while mutineers would take control of the Baltic Fleet and open fire on Red strong points throughout the city. Elsewhere in the North, two Latvian regiments, also well-penetrated with agents, would mutiny and seize Vologda, thus opening the door for an advance by Allied troops in Archangel. Finally, the Patriarch would come forward to bestow his blessing on the rebellion. Sidney expected the whole thing to be ready to go by 28 August when Lenin was scheduled to summon a meeting of the Party Central Committee.[123] This was no half-baked scheme.

Reilly's next, and presumably final, step was to secure the cooperation and coordination of his Allied opposite numbers, Verthimon and Pierre Laurent of the French mission and, of course, Kalamatiano. Soon all were well integrated into his plans. French agents handled the liaison with the

Savinkov people and would undertake the critical demolition of railway bridges linking Petrograd with Moscow and Vologda, thereby preventing any interference or reinforcement from that quarter. Kalamatiano was knee-deep in the ruble-raising scheme. Fride admitted that he and Kalamatiano, and perhaps Reilly as well, often met in the office of William Camber-Higgs, the British businessman who acted as a front for the money scheme. According to Berzin, Reilly told him that of 700,000 rubles handed over, 200,000 came from the Americans and the balance from the French.[124] So what had become of the British funds?

All these elements came together at a meeting at the U.S. Consulate on the night of 25 August. In attendance were Kalamatiano and American Consul Poole, de Verthimon, French Consul Grenard and, for some inexplicable reason, a French journalist, Rene Marchand. Reilly was there too, of course, but for the benefit of Marchand and other uninitiated he passed himself off as an American named "Ser Reis" (Marchand thought "Rice"), almost certainly a play on "Sergius Riis."[125]

Sidney later described how Marchand crept into the room where Reilly and de Verthimon were going over "details about liaison" and eavesdropped on the conversation.[126] Marchand himself later recalled how Reilly coolly expounded on the demolition of the bridges and seemed in control of the proceedings.[127] While noticing the Frenchman's decidedly suspicious behavior, amazingly neither Sidney nor Verthimon made any effort to question him and Marchand was allowed to leave the Consulate unmolested. Almost certainly, things did not happen that way at all. Marchand, for instance, did not reveal anything about the meeting for several days until word had leaked from other quarters. One of those was Reilly himself.

To understand why the Ace-of-Spies would scuttle his carefully-laid plans, we need to step back a few days. After "setting up" Berzin and Reilly, Lockhart did not sever connections with Dzerzhinskii's provocateurs Buikis and Sprogis. In another very questionable move, on 17 August Lockhart wrote out special passes for Buikis and two comrades to undertake "an important mission to British Headquarters" in Archangel and urged military authorities to render them all possible assistance.[128] A truly inexplicable aspect of this already dubious arrangement was that Buikis' pass was made out in his *real name*; did Lockhart know he was not dealing with "Shmidkhen"? Once in the north, Buikis and friends were to contact Gen. Poole to discuss the collaboration of the Latvian units with the Allies. Moreover, Lockhart records that at the same meeting he determined, for some reason, to put them in direct touch with Reilly.[129] Next, on the 22nd Dzerzhinskii decided to return to the helm of the Cheka. Commencing on the 25th, the very day of the American Consulate conclave, Iron Feliks ordered raids against the White officers' organization in Moscow, bagging more than hundred in the following twenty-four hours. Among them were several officers linked to Reilly's plot via Orlov and Savinkov.[130] These arrests, or more likely, the unexpected overture of Buikis, alerted the Ace-of-Spies to the real and present danger.

His logical first thought was that Peters had betrayed him. On the 27th he ordered Berzin, no longer trustworthy under the circumstances, to Petrograd with the ostensible purpose of contacting Latvians there. That night Sidney showed up at Karakhan's in a state of intense agitation. Karakhan phoned up Peters, who soon arrived to find Reilly in a most foul and threatening mood. Peters admitted that Dzerzhinskii's agents had wormed their way into the plot, but argued, with some reason, that he could not have moved against them without arousing suspicion. So far, however, they had not stumbled on the main conspiracy. To Sidney's mind, however, the whole plot was fatally compromised. Peters described the Ace-of-Spies' cold rage and explicit threat to expose him, and doubtless Karakhan and others, unless the situation was set right. To prevent further exposure, everything had to be shut down at once. The most important thing was that British agents and networks be affected as little as possible. To accomplish that, attention and blame would be shifted to the French, or even better, the Americans.[131]

And that is precisely what happened. On the 29th Peters issued a statement accusing Allied missions of fomenting counter-revolutionary plots and on the same day ordered a raid on the French mission and the homes of Verthimon and others. In the meantime, Reilly rushed to Petrograd. He met Berzin at his Massino flat on Torgovaia and abruptly ordered him back to Moscow to assist Peters. The next day he conferred with Cromie, probably to keep the excitable attaché from starting any mischief on his own and to gauge just how much Cromie knew about the operation.

There were other matters to attend to. On the morning of the 30th, Petrograd Cheka boss Moisei Uritskii fell to the bullets of another SR-linked assassin. Perhaps Sidney feared that Uritskii, might unravel the connection between Reilly and the Cheka and, thus, Peters. Uritskii's killing, however, had another useful function. At word of the shooting, Dzerzhinskii rushed to lead the investigation, leaving the M-Cheka completely in Peters' hands.

That evening, as he emerged from a speaking engagement at the Mikhel'son Factory, a gunman—or gunwoman—fired two shots into Lenin. Peters promptly arrested Fania Kaplan, a young woman with links to the

Left SRs. In short order she dictated a confession to Peters who then ordered her executed and her body dissolved in acid.[132] Not even her fingerprints remained. As has been determined since, Fania Kaplan most certainly did not shoot Lenin. Almost as certainly, we can finger Peters as the guiding hand, again acting in collusion with Reilly and probably on his direct order. Even in this last, desperate gamble, luck was not with them. Lenin still lived.

Back in Petrograd, Sidney supposedly sought out Boyce and Cromie, though without much success. According to Hill's report, Reilly told him he finally made contact with Boyce about noon and "explained the whole" of the Latvian Plot, possibly including the collusion with Berzin and Peters.[133] Boyce insisted that Cromie should be informed and left for the Embassy to fetch him, promising to return by 3 p.m. After hanging around Boyce's flat until about 6 p.m., Reilly finally gave up and went home. He did not hear about what had happened at the Embassy until some time later.

However, in his own version of events, Reilly tells a very different tale. According to this, he arranged to meet *Cromie* at a café at noon.[134] When the latter failed to appear by a quarter after, Sidney went straight to the Embassy, where he bore witness to the bloody aftermath of a Cheka raid on the premises in which Cromie was killed. This would seem to be no later that 1 or 1:30 p.m.

A Cheka assault indeed took place that day, but by all other accounts no earlier than 4 or 5 p.m. A brace of armed Chekists, some of them from Moscow, forced their way into the British Embassy on the grounds that Savinkov and some of his henchmen were hiding there. At their head was a commissar of the P-Cheka, Semen Leonidovich Geller, a most curious Bolshevik. A former policeman under the Kerenskii regime, until very recently he had been an SR with ties to Savinkov, just like the man who had shot Uritskii.[135] On the Embassy's second floor, Geller and his men encountered an armed Cromie and in the ensuing, confused shootout, Cromie and one Chekist were killed and two others wounded, one of them by Geller's fire.[136] Presumably, Geller's shots also felled Cromie, though afterwards no one seemed sure.

As Boyce had pointed out, Cromie knew a great deal about the Latvians and other matters, perhaps too much, and he had a notable tendency to talk. What would he have done under interrogation? Reilly may have felt some genuine regret at Cromie's fate, but he also knew that a very dangerous loose end was now neatly tied up. More to the point, did the Ace-of-Spies, who certainly had the means to know Geller, conspire to have Cromie silenced?[137] And what was Sidney really doing most of the afternoon: waiting patiently at Boyce's, or did he make a visit to Cheka head-quarters on the Gorokhovaia? Was Comrade Reilinskii or Repinskii of the Cheka also on hand at the Embassy that fateful day?

NOTES

1. HLRO, Lockhart Diary #15, 10 Feb. 1931.
2. In Russian, *Zagovor Lokarta* or *Zagovor Poslov*.
3. Lockhart, *Ace*, 79–100, and John Long, "Plot and Counter-plot in Revolutionary Russia: Chronicling the Bruce Lockhart Conspiracy, 1918," *Intelligence and National Security*, vol. 10, #1 (Jan. 1995), 122–143.
4. Pimenov, "Kak iskal . . . ," and Edward Van Der Rhoer, *Master Spy* (New York, 1981).
5. PZZ, #73, 2.
6. PZZ, #73, 1, Aleksandr Bykov, "Reili, Raili, Gillespi . . ." *Ekho Planety*, #5 (1998), 18–21 and Bykov and Panin, 82–91.
7. Ibid.
8. PRO, WO 32/5669, 126833, 30 April 1918.
9. Reilly, 16–17.
10. PRO, WO 33/962, DMI to Poole, 28 May 1918.
11. Ibid., noting that "Lockhart has been informed that in future all intelligence will be controlled by Thornhill."
12. PRO, FO 175/74, Balfour to Lindley, 7 June 1918.
13. PRO, FO 371/3328, Lockhart #118, 22 April 1918, Hicks #146, 3 May 1918.
14. Moura.
15. HIA, Lockhart, Box 12, ? July 1918.
16. PRO, ADM 137/1731, NID to Cromie, 27 May 1918.
17. Keyes was Indian Army and had arrived in Russia in 1917. On his role see Leeds University, Russian Archive, Lindley Memoir, MS 1372/2, 56, *passim*.
18. PRO, ADM, 137/1731, Cromie #147, 23 May 1918. Cromie did not entirely approve of the Yudenich officers whom he thought reactionary and pro-German.
19. Leech.
20. PRO, 371/3740, Report of R. Farina on interview with Leech, April 1919.
21. Krymov, 74.
22. PRO, 371/3326, 57379, Woodhouse #66, 30 March 1918, 63184, #91, 6 April 1918, 91807, Poole to Keyes, 29 April 1918.
23. Ibid., 109730, 19 June 1918.
24. For a full description of these convoluted plans, see McNeal, especially chapters IV and V.
25. PRO, Hill Report, 6/22.
26. Ibid.
27. PRO, 371/3316, Lockhart #136, 29 April 1918.
28. Ibid., 93675, DMI (McDonough) to FO, 25 May 1918.
29. HLRO, Diary #3, 7 May 1918.
30. PZZ #73, 2.
31. R. Lockhart, *British Agent* (London, 1961, orig. pub. 1932), 161.
32. Ibid., 162.
33. TsAFSB, "Iz Protokol pokaznanii E. Petersa," [Peters confession], 27 Dec. 1937 and 18 Jan. 1938. Thanks to G.L. Owen and Valentin Shteinberg for assistance with this item. Shteinberg found this and related documents in the KGB/FSB archives when working on his biography of Peters, *Ekabs Peters* (Moscow, 1991).
34. PZZ #73, 2.

35. Brackman, 234.
36. Russia, Rossiiskii Gosudarstvennyi Arkhiv Voenno Morskogo Flota (RGAVMF), fond 1358, opis 1, delo 97, Raport 573, 8 Aug. 1918.
37. Ibid.
38. Ibid.
39. Krymov, 74.
40. RGAVMF, Raport 515, 14 June 1918.
41. Sergei Kobiakov, "Krasnyi sud'," *Sovremennye zapiski*, #8 [c. 1920], 226.
42. RGAVMF, Raport 515.
43. TsAFSB, 114037, (Lockhart Case File), "Zakliuchenie sledstvennoi komissii VTsIK," summary of Starzhevskaia and Trester testimony, *Izvestiia*, (1 Dec. 1918), 2–3.
44. Ibid.
45. George Leggett, *The Cheka: Lenin's Political Police* (Oxford, 1981), 444–445.
46. TsAFSB, "Zakluichenie," and *Izvestiia* (1 Dec. 1918), 2.
47. RGAVMF, Raport # 595, 15 Aug. 1918.
48. A.A. Borman [ed. by Viktor Bortnevskii], "Moskva–1918 (iz zapisok sekretnogo agenta v Kremle)," *Russkoe Proshloe*, kniga 1 (1991), 115–149 and Bortnevskii, *White Intelligence and Counter-Intelligence during the Russian Civil War*, Carl Beck Papers # 1108 (Pittsburgh, 1995), 16–17.
49. Bortnevskii, 17.
50. Ibid.
51. RGAVMF, Raport 592, 14 Aug. 1918.
52. Ibid., Raport of 29 Aug. 1918.
53. Ibid., Raport 592.
54. *Vsia Moskva* 1914, 680.
55. RGAVMF, Raport 573.
56. Reilly, 6, 17–18.
57. RGAVMF, Raport 592.
58. PRO, Hill Report, 20/39.
59. RGAVMF, Raport 595.
60. Living at 4 Mal. Khariton'evskii Lane, not far from Reilly's address on Miasnitskaia, was the engineer Aleksandr *Gershkovich* Rosenblum. Was this Reilly's half-brother?
61. USDS, 811.20261/33, Kalamatiano report #1, 26 Oct. 1918, 2 and TsAFSB, 114037, *Pokaznanii* A.V. Frid', 2, 14, 19 Sept.
62. PRO, FO 371/3328, 79675, Howard #1219, 4 May 1918.
63. Reilly, 19.
64. TsAFSB, Frid, 2 Sept.
65. RGAVMF, Raport 515.
66. Bykov, "Reili . . . ," 19–21.
67. USDS, 361.1121K121/50, "Lockhart Trial," 9.
68. Deacon, *British Connection*, 28, 263.
69. These covert arrangements are described in Oleh Pidhainy, et al., "Silver and Billions: American Finances and the Bolshevik Revolution," *New Review of East European History*, vol. 14 (Dec. 1974), 1–47, especially 20–23, 33–34, and USDS, 861.00/8101.
70. *Krasnaia kniga VChK*, I (Moscow, 1989, orig. 1920), 51–54.
71. Private communication to author, May 1993.
72. Dzerzhinskii was arrested by the Okhrana at least five times, something that suggests no inherent aptitude in clandestine matters.
73. Orlov, *Dvoinoi* 299, *Morder*, 108–109.
74. PZZ #73, 2.
75. PRO, FO 371/3319, French to Campbell, 10 Oct. 1918.
76. Supreme Court, New York County, #17299-18, Sidney G. Reilly against Walter S. Josephson.

77. MID, 9140-6073, 10 Sept. 1918, 4.
78. BI, OG 39368, Agent Farland, 23 Nov. 1917. The identity of this officer is a mystery, but he may have been Capt. A.E.W. Mason (the writer) who was on assignment in the region at the time and was connected to Gaunt. That would explain his knowledge and opinion of Reilly.
79. MI5, Reilly, Extract from Air Ministry Papers on Reilly.
80. MID, 9140-6073, 10 Sept. 1918, 2.
81. Ibid., Memorandum #8, 16 Sept. 1918, 2.
82. PRO, FO 371/3348, 189631, 13 Nov. 1918 and 208058, 17 Dec. 1918.
83. Neither institution has any record of him.
84. MID, PF 60340, Riis to ONI, 11 Sept. 1939, 3.
85. Guy Richards, *The Rescue of the Romanovs* (Greenwich, CT, 1975), 161. In his later *Yankee Komisar* (New York 1935), Riis refers to Maclaren as "MacGloin."
86. MID, PF 60340, Ibid.
87. MID, 9140-6073, #1, 21 Aug. 1918, and Van der Kley to Thwaites, 6 Sept. 1918, 1.
88. PRO, FO 371/3332, Lockhart #251, 4 June 1918.
89. PZZ #73, 2.
90. Formed on 8 June, this was the so-called *Komuch* (*Komitet chlenov Uchreditel'nogo sobraniia*) regime, a left-leaning body based on the elected Constituent Assembly dismissed by Lenin in January.
91. PRO, FO 175/5, Report by S.T., 14 June 1918.
92. FO, 371/3515, Affairs in Russia, 6 June 1918.
93. Ts AFSB, 302330, vol. 37, Styrne to Pilyar, 2 Oct. 1925.
94. PRO, Hill Report, 11/28.
95. Tomaselli to author, 16, 21 April and 5 May 2000.
96. Vasilii Berezhkov, *Vnutri i vne bol'shogo doma* (St. Petersburg, 1995), 57.
97. Reilly, 26–27.
98. PZZ #73, 2.
99. *Osobie Zadanie*, 101.
100. E.P. Berzin's name appears as the 1918 chief of what would become the KGB's 9th Main Directorate, the special guard section for the protection of the Soviet leadership and key installations.
101. PZZ #73, 2.
102. B. Lockhart, *British Agent*, 180–181.
103. HLRO, Diary #3, 6 July 1918.
104. Yakov Peters, "Vospominaniia o rabote v VChK v pervyi god revoliutsii," *Proletarskaia Revoliutsiia* (24 Oct. 1924), 17.
105. V.F. Kravchenko, "Pervyi shagi VChK (Novoe o Zagovore Lokkarta)," *Sovetskoe gosudarstvo I pravo*, 1967, #3, 113; Van Der Rhoer, 53.
106. Bykov, *Diplomaticheskaia . . .* , 90.
107. McNeal, Chapter Eight.
108. PRO, Hill Report, 12/29.
109. *Osoboe zadanie*, 96–97.
110. Ibid., 83; Pimenov, 18.
111. PRO, Hill Report, 13/30.
112. Ibid.
113. Ibid., 14/31.
114. Ibid., 15/32.
115. Kravchenko, 100. The initial meeting supposedly took place at the British Mission. Given that these offices were closed on 5 August, it had to have occurred prior.
116. *Osoboe zadanie*, 101.
117. TsAFSB, 114037, Berzin *Protokol*, 303.
118. PRO, FO 371/3348, 190442, Lockhart to Balfour, 5 Nov. 1918.

119. PRO, Hill Report, 17/36.
120. Ibid.
121. TsAFSB, Berzin, 305; Peters, 24.
122. Ibid, Berzin, 303–305.
123. Ibid.
124. Ibid. On 8 August, General Lavergne wired Paris that he had turned over a million rubles to Laurent and Verthimon. "Their schemes are developing," he added, "and are producing excellent results": France, Archives Nationales (AN), Fonds Clemenceau, 6N/221, #676, Lavergne, 8 Aug. 1918.
125. M. Ya. Latsis, *Dva goda bor'by na vnutrennem fronte* (Moscow, 1920), 19–20.
126. Reilly, 31–32. Marchand offered his version of events in *Allied Agents in Soviet Russia* (London, 1918).
127. Rene Marchand, *Why I Support Bolshevism* (London, 1919), 46.
128. Kravchenko, 101.
129. R. Lockhart, *British Agent*, 194.
130. "Grandioznyi zagovor v Moskve," *Izvestiia VTsIK* (31 Aug. 1918), 4. Latsis (p. 22–23) calls this a "White-SR" plot and says the arrests began on the 24th.
131. TsAFSB, E. Peters, 27 Dec. 1937.
132. On the Kaplan case see Evgenii Danilov, "Taina `vstrelov' Fanii Kaplan, *Zvesda Vostok*, #1 (1991), 113–130, and Boris Orlov, "Tak kto zhe strelial v Lenina?," *Istochnik*, #2 (1993), 63–88.
133. PRO, Hill, 22/41.
134. Reilly, 45–46.
135. Vasilii Berezhkov, *Vnutri I vne "Bol'shogo Doma"* (St. Petersburg, 1995), 38–39.
136. Ibid., 40, and "K obysku v' zdanii Angliiskago posol'stvo," *Krasnaia gazeta* (2 Sept. 1918), 1.
137. Far from making him a revolutionary hero, Geller's actions at the Embassy placed him under a cloud. Expelled from the Cheka, he teamed up with Gol'dinger and others in smuggling and speculation, activities that led to both men's execution in January 1920.

Chapter Ten

FEAST OF ASHES

The Grand Conspiracy had failed, but not because it was inherently impossible nor because of any exceptionally clever counter-measures by Dzerzhinskii. It came very close to success. In the end, the plot collapsed from the sheer weight of its complexity. It was a juggling act, and even the Ace-of-Spies could only manage to keep so many balls in the air, particularly when others were tossed in from outside. Plus, there was betrayal from inside that Reilly may or may not have realized. He certainly detected the intrigues of Buikis and Sprogis, but those amateurs never penetrated the core of the plot. Then there was Moura Benckendorf but she, too, was only privy to what she could coax out of Lockhart and Cromie. In fact, there was a Bolshevik agent much closer to Reilly and at the very heart of the conspiracy.

It was the threat of exposure as opposed to its reality that provoked Sidney to call off the game. He handled the dissolution like the controlled demolition of a derelict building, the structure collapsing so as to minimize collateral damage. First, he, Peters and Berzin had a mutual interest in protecting themselves and each other. The immediate battle might be lost, but not the war. Next, as he instructed Peters, things had to be fixed so as to minimize harm to British interests and leave a British intelligence network intact for future operation. That meant bringing most of the debris down on the heads of the French and, above all, the Americans.

In the first days of September, Boyce, Lockhart and most of the other remaining members of the British mission were swept up by the Cheka though none were to suffer any harm. Hill, by some odd stroke of luck, remained free and, like Reilly, in hiding. Lockhart remained at large until the 4th when, on the advice of Karakhan, he went to see Peters about Moura. For the next month, those two Bolsheviks, along with Madame Benckendorf, guarded Lockhart first in the Lubianka and later in a private cell in the Kremlin. Dzerzhinskii, oddly, made no effort to visit or interrogate the putative head of the vast counter-revolutionary conspiracy. In fact, Iron Feliks was a sick, exhausted man, and would soon depart on a much-needed "vacation" to Switzerland leaving, as usual, everything in the hands of trusty Peters. Reilly, no doubt, picked Lockhart to be the scapegoat for British involvement in the plot simply because he was the least involved in it. The Scot suffered his share of anxiety, but at no point was he in any real danger. In early October, Peters released him to join the exodus of British officials from Red Russia.

Meantime, in the aftermath of the Cheka's raid on the British Embassy, Sidney returned to Moscow. He touched bases with Grammatikov and Orlov and caught the night train for Moscow on 1 September traveling as Comrade Repinskii. The next morning, as he neared the Capital, Sidney claimed to have seen a newspaper announcing the discovering of a "great anti-Bolshevist plot" instigated by the Allied missions and involving Lockhart and the Latvian.[1] Marchand's treachery was to blame. According to this, Fride and Berzin and many others already were in custody. The tale is complete fabrication; not a word of the "Latvian/Lockhart Plot" would reach the Soviet press until the 3rd, and Marchand did not write his letter telling what he knew of the conspiracy until the day after. However, a later Soviet report notes that the conspiracy was "unmasked" on the 2nd, so Sidney seems to have been oddly prescient of the Cheka's progress.[2]

Back on 1 September, Maria Fride visited #3 Shetermet'evskii carrying a set of reports from her brother. She had come specifically to meet Reilly, but instead she found Peters' men lying in wait. A quick search discovered Maria's stash and her arrest was immediately followed by the Colonel's. In short order, the whole American network was rolled up. Reilly, we may guess, deliberately set her up with just that in mind. Thus, it was with no fear that he went straight to Otten at Sheremetev'skii as soon as he hit town. Otten later testified that he stayed the night, retrieved some papers, but at no point betrayed any particular haste or concern.[3]

On the night of the 3rd, the Ace-of-Spies appeared at the door of another girlfriend, Olga Starzhevskaia, at her place on Malaia Bronnaia. He seemed tired and agitated, she claimed, and revealed that he was not the merchant Massino but an English officer wanted by the Reds. When she asked why, Reilly replied that she could read all about it in the papers. Olga wanted to talk more, especially about how this was going to affect her and her job, but her paramour claimed illness and refused to discuss the matter. He left early the next morning bearing Massino's identity papers and she never saw him again.[4] The Cheka did not get around to visiting Starzhevskaia until 12 September, the day *after* Sidney left Moscow.

Reilly's reversion to the Massino alias shows that he had no immediate concern of being detected under that name. But Berzin, recall, had visited the Massino flat in Petrograd, knew him to be identical with Reilly and, so he confessed, had already "revealed" that to Peters.[5] So why was the Cheka not looking for Mssr. Massino?

A man soon asking the same question was Kalamatiano. On 30 August, just before the storm broke, he left Moscow for Samara, the Volga town held by the anti-Bolshevik *Komuch* Government. There he met with Czech representatives and collected reports and messages to take back to Moscow. While there he heard about the shootings of Uritskii, Lenin and Cromie and the arrests following the exposure of the "Allied Conspiracy." Despite such warning, on 18 August Kalamatiano returned to Moscow confident that his own alias was secure. After all, the only persons who knew it were Consul Poole, now safely out of Moscow, Col. Fride, who Kalamatiano was sure would not betray him, and Reilly. The Chekists nabbed Kalamatiano at the gates of the American Consulate. Handling his interrogation, once again, were Peters and Karakhan. They revealed detailed information about the recent meeting at the Consulate, but it was evident to Kalamatiano that Marchand could not have been the source of all their information. "The Bolsheviks . . . had definite data of everything that had been talked of . . . on 25th August," he reported, "They knew all who had been present . . ."[6] Marchand, of course, had overheard only part of the plot and could not, in his report, identify either Reilly or Kalamatiano by name. Beyond that, there was no way the Frenchman could have given away Kalamatiano's alias or the names and addresses of his agents, all arrested. The damning information, he soon learned, came from Berzin. In the latter's statement to Peters, he claimed that when visiting Reilly's flat in Petrograd he discovered lying out in plain view a list of all the American and French agents in Moscow, complete with code names and addresses. While Kalamatiano may have had his suspicions about Reilly's character, he knew him to be a "professional" and such "criminal carelessness" was inexplicable in someone of his experience.[7] Another thing the American could not fathom, and something the Chekists made no effort to explain, was why Reilly had not been arrested since it was obvious they "knew just where he was to be found."[8] Kalamatiano also could not fail to notice that whereas most of Reilly's agents and the British as a whole either avoided arrest or were soon set free, he and his people were held for trial.

When the trial finally got underway in late November, Peters stage-managed the whole production. Handily, he and Berzin were the only prosecution witnesses. Soviet prosecutor Nikolai Krylenko painted Kalamatiano as the mastermind of the wicked affair. It was small compensation to the American that Reilly and de Verthimon were along with him sentenced to death, for their verdict was in absentia. He took bitter note that none of "Reilly's people" suffered serious punishment. Otten, Trester, and Camber-Higgs received acquittals. Dagmara, Likhnovskaia and most of his known accomplices were not even charged. Starzhevskaia alone took a fall, but only for three months detention and a ban from state employment. In contrast, no less than seven Information Service agents got sentences of five years and the unfortunate Col. Fride, the firing squad.[9] This led Kalamatiano to the conclusion that Reilly had betrayed him. He was absolutely right even if he did not fully appreciate why. From prison, Kalamatiano managed to communicate this to Consul Poole who was on his way out of Red territory.

On the morning of the 4th, George Hill received a visit from one of "Reilly's girls" who reported that her boss was safe and in Moscow having just arrived in "a first-class compartment" from Petrograd.[10] He was at an apartment she had found for him "in the back end of town" and Hill met him there a few hours later. For some reason, Jolly George was not on the Cheka's arrest list and while he stayed in disguise just in case, he was able to move around freely. Reilly told Hill a rather different version of his recent escapades. He claimed not to have hit Moscow until the 3rd and have known nothing of the arrests and collapse of the plot until then, certainly a less than truthful account. Sidney insisted that he was willing to come forward and face arrest, "if it would help," but neither seems to take that notion too seriously.[11] The immediate problem was how to get out of Moscow and Bolshevik territory. George suggested he head for Siberia or the Ukraine where anti-Bolshevik forces were operating, but Reilly decided to exit via Petrograd and Finland if he could, but he made no move to quit Moscow just yet. On the 5th, Hill recorded that he "moved Lt. Reilly into new quarters at a Soviet office," which certainly seems a case of hiding in plain sight.[12]

Hill reappeared on the 6th and handed Reilly a German passport under the name of Georg Bergmann, a Baltic-German from Riga. Hill had intended to use this himself, but had decided that he was safe enough without it. As an honorary Reich subject, Herr Bergmann could ride in a special compartment on the train to Petrograd. On the evening of the 8th, Hill saw Sidney off at the Petrograd station. The Cheka was nowhere to be seen. However, in a later Soviet deposition, Sidney stated that he "liquidated my affairs in Moscow" only on the 11th.[13] A minor discrepancy, perhaps, but it may mean that after departing under Hill's eyes, he slipped back to Moscow to take care of some unfinished business, business he wanted to make sure Hill knew nothing about. Could it have been a secret meeting with Peters or Karakhan? As usual, no one but Reilly knew exactly what he was up to.

Among the many other things on his mind, there must have been some room for thoughts of Anne. Fred Hill had left Russia in late 1917, so she would have had to depend on her own devices and whatever help her husband could provide through intermediaries. One of these may have been Fred Hill's son, Capt. Alfred "Freddie" Hill who happened to work for Lockhart and had at least some dealings with the Reilly-Boyce-George Hill nexus. Sidney certainly was subject to surveillance of one sort or another and that called for immense caution. A possible clue to Anne's presence is mentioned in one of the naval reports that noted he had a *sister* in Petrograd with whom he was keeping in contact.[14] Was this a replay of the charade used in 1905? Sidney's only surviving sister, Maria, was nowhere near Petrograd. In any case, Reilly could not risk trying to slip out of Russia with a wife and children in tow. What he could have done was to arrange her evacuation to some safer locale, perhaps in the White-held south. Orlov certainly could have helped. Another may have been Chaim Meyer Kogan, an Odessa merchant with whom Reilly had frequent, if vague, contact during July and August. He had the means to move goods and people between Bolshevik and anti-Bolshevik zones.

If the Cheka could not, or would not, locate Reilly, the Americans had no problem doing so. Kalamatiano's suspicions had reached DeWitt Poole who landed in Norway at the close of September. Poole immediately went to the British representative in Oslo, Sir Mansfeldt Findlay, and argued that Reilly "has either compromised Lockhart . . . or has even betrayed him." [15] Poole echoed Kalamatiano's concern that neither Reilly nor Berzin had been arrested and that the former was still in Russia. Poole noted that American officials in New York had intercepted a cable from Reilly that indicated he was still at the Torgovaia address, the very one visited by Berzin and definitely known to the Cheka, as of "some days ago." He insisted that Reilly be arrested and questioned the moment Allied officials could put their hands on him.

Findlay promptly forwarded Poole's charges to Sir Francis Lindley in Archangel and straight to the Foreign Office in London. The first response came from Rex (later Sir Reginald) Leeper, head of the FO's Political Intelligence Division and its liaison with MI1c. Leeper, destined to become one of Sidney's staunchest supporters, vouched that he had seen several reports from Reilly and had "always found them quite satisfactory." [16] Leeper offered that whether ST1 had "acted falsely or merely unwisely," Poole's account at least cleared Lockhart of any of the Bolshevik charges or other suspicions. Stronger support came from Col. Charles French of the War Office. Having discussed the matter with Cumming, French admitted that the subject had a habit of ignoring and exceeding his instructions, but advised Findlay and Poole "not to raise a hue and cry about Reilly until we know more about the circumstances." [17] For his part, George Hill considered that Reilly was being "most unjustifiably libeled and that for his own sake and as a British officer he should . . . be completely cleared [of] . . . all rumours and libels." [18] Alley and Boyce chimed in with their support, and even Lockhart vouched that the accusations were baseless. Of course, each had their own interests at stake; if Reilly was a traitor, what did that make them?

Sidney at last surfaced in Stockholm about 20 October. On the 23rd, SIS station chief Scale informed Cumming that Reilly and Boyce were in town and both would be leaving for London "by the next boat." [19] Not a word was said—or asked—about where ST1 had been and what he had been doing for almost two months. The subsequent story was thus: in Petrograd he had assumed, as circumstances dictated, a string of new identities. One was Edward C. Riley, the American working for New York Life Insurance Co., whose name and description conveniently matched Reilly's. The other was a Baltic antiquarian, Grigorii Berman, who may or may not have been a mutated version of Hill's Georg Bergmann. At the same time, Sidney continued use of the Massino identity or at least the Torgovaia address. Typically, Reilly muddied the episode with a variety of conflicting details. For instance, he later estimated his stay in Petrograd at ten days to a fortnight at most, which would put his departure around 22–26 September. That timing fits his last known communication from the city, according to Poole, and the curious fact that only on the 23rd did the Cheka get around to tossing the Torgovaia flat. As in Moscow, did they conveniently wait until he was gone?

The only documentary evidence to attest to Reilly's whereabouts in this period puts his exit around 8–10 October, some two weeks later. This "evidence," however, is far from conclusive. It is a 10 October letter written and given by Sidney to Arie (Harry)Van den Bosch, the Dutch captain who supposedly carried him out of Red Petrograd to the German-occupied Estonian port of Tallinn (Revel). The letter contains a mini-biography replete with trademark Reilly falsehoods. Van den Bosch would not have needed such credentials from his passenger. A Dutch diplomat and businessman, he knew Reilly from their mutual interest in ship and dock building in prewar days, including the Putilov project.[20] The purpose of the letter was to prove, if anyone should demand it, that Reilly was aboard the Dutchman's boat in the Gulf of Finland on that date.[21] Why would that have been necessary? One factor may have been to downplay the amount of time he spent in German-occupied locales, something that could have raised more eyebrows in London.

In his fairly detailed, if not necessarily more accurate, story later given to the Soviets, Reilly claimed he had been taken from Kronshtadt, near Petrograd, by a *Finnish* captain. The Finn delivered him to Tallinn where he lingered for another ten days as Grigorii Berman. He then set out for Helsinki in early October, and from there, eventually, Stockholm. Why he did not proceed directly to Stockholm from the nearer Tallinn is another unanswered—and unasked—question. The Soviets, however, discovered an alternative story. In this version, he escaped via Riga "disguised as priest" and from there sailing for Scandinavia aboard a Dutch steamer.[22] So what was the truth?

Perhaps the closest thing to an accurate version of Reilly's escape from Russia comes from his engineer friend Evgenii Beloi. As later related to Krymov, the tale is far from complete, but Beloi had no discernible ax to grind. As noted, he had last seen Reilly in Moscow. Beloi provides no exact dates, but sometime in the fall, in Petrograd, he received a phone call from a mysterious woman. She (Boguzhevskaia?) stated that an "old friend" of his was in town and wanted to see him on urgent business.[23] The friend could not leave his abode, so Beloi would have to come to him. After some hesitation, the engineer agreed and soon paid a visit. Answering the door was a heavily-bearded man he at first did not recognize, but the voice and eyes revealed him to be Reilly. Sidney admitted that he was the true architect of the plan Soviet papers were calling the "Lockhart Plot." He added that he had been given the authority and means to overthrow of the Bolsheviks, and the plan might have succeeded if some of the Latvians he was dealing with had not lost their nerve and decided to betray the plot. Reilly was, as usual, being less than honest. He explained his amazing ability to evade arrest as a case of sheer luck. He further claimed to have headed straight back to Petrograd when the Cheka wave broke and to have laid low there ever since waiting for his beard to grow out. The passport he held in the name of a Latvian [Baltic] merchant (Bergmann? Berman?) featured a bearded face and he needed to match it. A false beard, apparently, just would not do.

Reilly was ready to get out of Russia, and he sought Beloi's help in arranging a safe exit. He first directed the engineer to Fernando Contreras, secretary of the Spanish Embassy. Sidney knew Contreras through a mutual friendship with Princess Dolgorukaia, the confidante of Baroness Rozen. He gave Beloi a coded message for Contreras. Sidney knew that Madrid's Embassy was organizing a group of its own subjects to leave the country and was allowing selected other foreigners to accompany it. The Spaniard, however, smelled trouble and had no desire to get mixed up in a spy's affairs.

Some days later, Beloi learned that it was possible to arrange private passage from the small port of Oranienbaum, about twenty miles west of Petrograd. On the pretext of going to the countryside to buy food and carefully avoiding Red checkpoints, he and Reilly reached the town and found someone with the information they wanted. Passage to Finland was possible, not from Oranienbaum, but from a smaller place down the coast used by smugglers. The necessary arrangements were made, and that night Reilly slipped aboard a small boat and set out upon the dark waters. Four years later, Beloi bumped into him in Berlin and asked what finally happened. "You know, that was a long time ago," Sidney replied, "and I have forgotten all about it."

In the waning days of October, Stockholm was the rallying spot for many British operatives coming out of Russia. In addition to Reilly and Boyce, Michelson and Paul Dukes landed there hot on the heels of our man. Dukes was about to take a much bigger role in the spy game, one in which Reilly would take a keen interest. While Sidney was fifteen years his senior, he and Dukes shared a number of things in common: an interest in Oriental art and philosophy, freemasonry, and a certain love of intrigue for intrigue's sake. But there may have been more connecting them. Dukes, as noted, had a special audience with Cumming in July 1918 that began his formal enlistment in SIS. Stage-managing the appointment was Robert Nathan, the same gray figure looming behind Reilly's recruitment. In this case, it may have Sidney who recommended Dukes. The latter had spent much of June in Moscow and carried a copy of Reilly's "Church report" to Vologda on his way to Archangel. Returning to the same port in early September, Dukes marked time in North Russia until 13 October when he abruptly set out for Sweden. Had he been waiting for a summons from Reilly? In any event, it was the beginning of a long and interesting friendship.

Boyce and the Ace-of-Spies were back in London by 6 November. On the Western Front, the Germans were in full retreat and the Armistice was only a few days away. Victory was in the air, but for Reilly there were no trumpets and drums. But neither was there a waiting inquisition. Despite the ruin of his grand scheme and the insinuations of Kalamatiano and

Poole, Cumming seemed pleased with his work. In short order the name of Lt. Sidney G. Reilly appeared on the list of officers recommended for the Military Cross (MC). On the other hand, this was a very modest recognition and not what Sidney wanted and expected. He hoped for a promotion to a more prestigious rank, captain or even major, and a full-time posting to the SIS. Neither were forthcoming. Beyond this, while Reilly had his fans in Cumming's organization, there were others, mostly in the Foreign Office, who wanted nothing to do with him. The degree to which their antagonism was based on recent events or on longer institutional memory is uncertain. His being a foreigner and a Jew did not help. Over the next few years these "swells" would make repeated efforts to give the unwelcome Reilly "the boot." [24] So long as he had the backing of "C," he took such harassment in stride, but beneath the surface the hostility stung him and the lack of recognition was a burr that would irritate more and more.

Given the attitude in the Foreign Office, the Ace-of-Spies initiated a campaign to win friends and influence people there. On the afternoon of the 6th, he and Boyce lunched with Lockhart at the Savoy Hotel, Reilly's base of operations for the next few weeks. It was a private meal in Sidney's rooms where he freely expounded his "very interesting" views on Bolshevism and regaled them with the tale of his recent escape.[25] Over the next few weeks, Reilly aggressively courted Lockhart's favor. It is unlikely that our man held any genuine affection for the Scot and vice versa. What they did have in common were the recent and mutually incriminating events in Russia which earned them some of the same enemies. However, one of the common friends Lockhart and Reilly shared was Rex Leeper, Political Intelligence chief and one of the FO's "Russian experts."

On 8 November, Sidney had a general debriefing with Cumming. On hand for the occasion was Wiseman who arrived in London from New York a few days before. The Ace-of-Spies pleaded to both that he needed to get back to Russia right away. "C" was interested in the proposition but non-committal. He admired Reilly's effort and resourcefulness, but still did not trust him. Perhaps he suspected that there was more to his agent's urgency than an overactive sense of patriotic duty.

Later in November, Reilly sent Lockhart a letter from the Savoy laying out his predicament and begging the Scot's help. Sidney had just heard that his proposed return to Russia was off, for the moment at least. "I have told "C" (and I am anxious that you should know it too)," he wrote, "that although I am naturally keen on going back to my wife and my business, I consider that there is a very earnest obligation upon me to continue to serve—if my services can be made use of in the question of Russia or

Bolshevism." [26] He felt that the "the State should not lose my services," and confessed that he felt a need to do something that would erase "those unfortunate libels" [Kalamatiano's and Poole's accusations]. If a "half-way decent job would be offered me," he added, "I would chuck business altogether and devote the rest of my wicked life to this kind of work . . . [and] I should like nothing better than to serve under you." Cumming, he noted, had promised to take this up with the FO, but nothing had come of the effort if had been made at all.

Attached to the above missive was a report that outlined his views on Bolshevism and his notion of an "International Declaration" to oppose it. [27] Bolshevism, he stressed was a "a world problem which must be faced immediately and resolutely," but he feared that Britain's leadership and most Allied diplomats failed to grasp the menace at hand. In Germany, where the Kaiser's regime had fallen to a socialist-dominated coalition, in the defunct Habsburg Empire, and even in Sweden and Switzerland, "Bolshevik forces are straining at the leash." Sidney professed to "see the great cataclysm relentlessly approaching," and if this insidious influence went unchecked, he offered, "next year we will have civil war all over the world." He was quick to add that by "Bolshevism" he did not mean Marxism or Socialism per se or even theoretical Bolshevism. The latter, he argued, had real value "as a system for the social reconstruction of the world." Indeed, he went so far as to opine that "this system contains practical and constructive ideas for the establishment of a higher social justice," and in that respect it was bound to "conquer the world, as Christianity and the ideas of the French Revolution have done before it." He even praised the Soviets, the popular, radical councils that the Bolsheviks had co-opted, as "the nearest approach, that I know of, to a real democracy." In the next breath, however, the Ace-of-Spies blasted Bolshevism *in practice* as a perverted force "run amuck" and bent on the "destruction of all attainments of culture, economical and political chaos, the extinction of all liberties and all principles of justice."

To combat this menace, Reilly placed little faith in the Russian "Whites" or Allied military intervention. He advocated that the forthcoming Peace Conference issue a unified Declaration from the Allied Powers demanding that Lenin—and his rivals—accept an armistice on all fronts, abolish revolutionary tribunals, grant general political amnesty and agree to the prompt, free election of a national assembly. Sidney did not "for one moment expect that Lenin will meekly submit to the ultimatum," but given the latter was a "practical statesman" and his previous acquiescence to German demands at Brest-Litovsk, he was confident that the declaration backed up with overwhelming military force would back the Bolos into a cage. Should Lenin & Co. remain defiant then armed intervention should proceed in a "speedy and decisive manner." If it came to that, Reilly did not see the establishment of an immediate democratic order in Russia. Instead, there would be a "police order" and a dictatorship for an indefinite time. Finally, he noted that the success of either approach, intimidation or military conquest, depended on the cooperation of the United States, the only nation "in a position to undertake and carry through such a gigantic task."

Whether the above represented Reilly's true convictions is, as always, a question. Keeping in mind his habit of matching comments to the prejudices of the recipient, the condemnation of "Bolshevism" coupled with high praise of Marxist principles neatly meshed with Lockhart's own leftist sentiments. On the other hand, we will see echoes and elaboration of these basic arguments in Reilly's future proposals on the Russian Situation.

On 12 November, ostensibly to celebrate the conclusion of the Armistice, Reilly hosted Lockhart and Leeper at another lavish dinner at the Savoy. Sidney was his most charming self. Decked out in RAF uniform, he toasted the end of the war against Germany, but offered that the war against Bolshevism was just beginning. Later, in the relaxed atmosphere of his upstairs suite, he got down to the real business of the evening: he wanted Leeper's and Lockhart's support for a new mission to Russia, to the South this time, the Black Sea region and Odessa. From that vantage Reilly offered to scope out the Ukraine and oil-rich Caucasus and, if possible, to venture back into central Russia all the way to Archangel. That would entail immense risk (or would it?), but he was willing if he was assured "some form of recognition for the risks taken."[28] Leeper thought his host "one of the most useful agents we could have in Russia" and agreed to push the idea. The next evening, Sidney met Lockhart, J.D. Gregory, head of the FO's "Northern Division" (that included Russia) and Hugh Walpole, formerly of His Majesty's Propaganda Office in Petrograd at a performance of the *Ballet Russe*. Sidney pressed his new plan and persuaded them all to accompany him back to the Savoy. They were joined there by George Hill who had rolled in on the 11th. Reilly hit on the idea that he and Hill should go back as a team. Jolly George immediately accepted.

On 27 November, Leeper received a disappointing memo from his superior, Reginald Hoare. "The proposal to send Major Reilly to South Russia for intelligence purposes has fallen through," he wrote.[29] There was no explanation as to why, but Reilly doubtless suspected the FO "swells" at work. However, Hoare offered that it might be possible to send out a couple of agents under cover of the British Trade Corporation. J. Picton Bagge, the former British Consul in Odessa, proposed to lead a mission to the Black Sea region on behalf of the Board of Trade. Leeper concurred that "Major Reilly" (anticipating his imminent promotion) and "an assistant of his own choosing" should tag along. Three days later, Bagge's mission got the green light. Sidney accepted the job but was far from satisfied. He knew he was being entrusted with an intelligence mission but was not being given formal credit for it. Officially, he and Hill were on a "special mission" for the Foreign Office, not Cumming, and were to "travel as civilians as . . . assistants to Mr. Bagge.[30] It was not at all the sort of thing he had in mind. Nor was the above the only reason for Reilly to feel slighted. Hill, who so far as Sidney was concerned had served under him in Russia, received a Distinguished Service Order, a rather more prestigious honor than his paltry MC. Then there was the irksome fact that Cumming had tapped tyro Paul Dukes to take over the British network in Petrograd, a task for which Reilly certainly thought himself better suited.

Cumming may have considered him too hot a property to send back into the thick of things. The so-called "Lockhart Trial" opened in Moscow on 25 November and was covered by most of the European press. As noted, the "evidence" presented shifted most of the attention onto the unlucky Kalamatiano, but Reilly's and Lockhart's names featured prominently. This provoked some sharp and potentially embarrassing questions from Labour members in Parliament and added to the conviction in certain quarters that it would be best to get Mr. Reilly out of town and well away from such disquieting inquiries.

In the aftermath of the "Lockhart" trial, Peters and his Cheka henchmen discovered another conspiracy inside the Red Navy staff. They arrested most of its officers on charges of being counter-revolutionaries in league with imperialist agents. Prominent among the accused was Lt. Abramovich, the man who had initiated Reilly's surveillance in Moscow. Despite all appeals, Abramovich went before the firing squad. His attorney Kobiakov thought it had to do with certain things he knew about Trotsky, but might it also have been a result of what he knew about Reilly?[31]

Like a bad penny, Margaret decided to pop up now. Having seen his name in accounts of the "Lockhart Affair," she was anxious to know where he was. She sent a letter addressed to the "Intelligence Department for Russia" in the War Office, so she had some notion as to how to find him.[32] She also knew, for instance, that Sidney had been "actively working against the Bolcheviste [sic] government on behalf of Britain." The WO ignored her. She also wrote the British Consulate in Brussels demanding information on her errant spouse. The Consul forwarded her letter to the FO thus initiating a most untimely inquiry into Reilly's status as a British subject, among other things. In response, the FO explained to Daisy that her husband had indeed been implicated in a plot, had gone into hiding for a time and subsequently made his way to Finland.[33] Beyond that, they admitted to nothing, carefully avoiding any mention of his return to Britain. Not to be put off so easily, she pursued her quest. Latching onto the RAF connection, she wrote to the Air Board on 4 January.[34] "Will you not have pity on me gentlemen," she pleaded, "and let me know . . . what has become of my dear husband?" "I desire ardently to hear from him," she added, "[and] my financial situation is also rather strained." This note produced a response from Capt. D.S. Talbot of the Air Ministry who pointed her in the direction of Cumming's office in Whitehall. She managed to get herself to London and in early February addressed a plaintive letter to "Captain Spencer," Cumming's cover name at the War Office.[35] "I appeal most earnestly," she wrote, "to let me know where [my husband] is and know if I can communicate with him." This was getting a bit too close for comfort, and "C" forwarded the message to Reilly in Odessa with the pointed suggestion that something be done to placate the woman and get her out of SIS' hair. On 19 February Sidney sent a curt wire to SIS London: "Please pay Mrs. Reilly from my account £100; please inform her I shall [make] further provision after I return."[36] With cash in hand, Margaret once again crept back into obscurity.

Then there were those pesky Americans. Back in New York the ONI-driven investigation of Reilly and his cronies rolled on. They interviewed anyone they could find concerning Reilly's character and connections, among them ex-Okhrana agent Aleksandr Evalenko whom they located in New York in July 1918. He had some old scores to settle. Evalenko had been in and out of Russia several times since 1910 and had encountered Reilly there. He was more than willing to tell all he knew or suspected concerning Sidney's past dealings with the Tsar's police and the Japanese.[37] Navy sleuths looked up opera diva Ganna Walska, now married to the second of her American husbands, and quizzed her about Reilly, Jechalski and friends.

Cable intercepts, as noted, yielded clues that seemed to support Kalamatiano's accusations of Sidney's dalliance with the Bolos. In September, agents conducted a general search of the office at 120 Broadway and seized business records along with assorted personal correspondence.[38] This gave ample proof of Reilly and Weinstein's extensive involvement in war contracting and association with a host of suspicious characters. By early 1919, the ONI concluded that if there was not sufficient evidence to indict or arrest the subjects, there was no doubt that they were "rotters" and should be kept under close observation.[39]

Navy investigators were particularly interested in Sidney's and Jechalski's relationship with a former employee of the Sperry Gyroscope Co., a Pole named Josef Pawlowski. In late September, agents hauled in Pawlowski and gave him the third degree on his dealings with the Reilly gang. He admitted to knowing Jechalski from Russia and that the fellow Pole introduced him to Reilly in New York in 1916.[40] Sidney first secured Pawlowski a job as translator with his associate Newman Erb. In March 1917, with a recommendation from another of Reilly's friends, Col. Petrovskii of the Russian Supply Committee, he landed a position in the drafting department of Sperry. Soon thereafter, blueprints of a new gyroscope and other designs went missing. In what seemed a most suspicious coincidence, the very day Pawlowski started work at Sperry, Jechalski opened a bank account for him at the Guaranty Trust Co. and deposited $500 into it. What especially aroused the Navy men was that representatives of the Japanese Navy had made past attempts to buy the gyro patent. Noting Reilly's reputation as a Japanese spy, ONI was certain that he had connived to obtain the design for them through Pawlowski. It was one more thing to convince the Americans that he was a dangerous and undesirable man to have around.

The Yanks even planted a female informer in Nadine's circle at the Allenhurst Club. The woman reported that Mrs. Reilly seemed "very fond" of her husband and had several photos of him in her bungalow. One struck the operative as especially interesting: "[a] face—intelligent, intensely shrewd and calculative [sic], smooth and unscrupulous."[41] Nadine's constant companion was Weinstein, though the relationship appeared to be platonic. Weinstein, as usual, was protecting Reilly's interests, perhaps by trying to keep her away from Jechalski who soon was back in New York and working for Paderewski's Polish Mission.

Whatever her sexual fidelity, Nadine knew well enough to keep her mouth shut about her husband's business affairs. Sidney, on the other hand, knew she could cause him a great deal of trouble if she chose. He had, it may be recalled, thwarted her effort to follow him to England in late 1918 and she still hoped to join him there. He had no intention of bringing her over, but knowing her capacity to take matters into her own hands he decided to take preemptive action. He began writing her apologetic, endearing letters soon after he left London and throughout his coming sojourn. It was the same old story; she should be a good, quiet girl until he returned.

Back in London, it was 10 December before Reilly and Hill met Bagge and received final instructions from Leeper. The pair were to pose as commercial agents interested in contracts for sugar, grain and other commodities. In reality, Reilly, with Hill as his second, was to collect data on the economic and, above all, political situation in south Russia. The next couple of days were taken up with last minute preparations and meetings with Leeper, Lockhart and Cumming. Sidney packed most of what he needed in an elaborate, custom-designed portfolio that had nooks and crannies for everything from multi-colored inks to rubber bands and a knife. He also had time to print up new visiting cards. On one side they proclaimed "Sidney G. Reilly, Member of the British Commercial Mission in Russia"; on the opposite, the same in Russian. The final, vital item was a Courier's Passport issued on the 12th that guaranteed priority transport on the journey East.[42]

Hill barely made the train at Victoria Station later that afternoon. In Southampton, Sidney recalled running into Maj. Strubell, the RAF officer he had nominally served under in Canada. Whether this encounter was purely incidental or had some other purpose he does not say. The Channel crossing was choppy and horribly crowded. It was here, recalled Hill, that they ran into Ignace Paderewski on his way to represent Poland's cause at the Paris Peace Conference.[43] The pianist turned statesman greeted Reilly like an old friend and offered the Englishmen the sanctuary of his cabin for the night, perhaps in recompense for our man's help in New York a few years before. Via Paris, Marseilles and Malta it took ten days to reach Constantinople and the gateway to the Black Sea aboard a succession of vessels, including one Reilly described as "the dirtiest ship [I] ever saw."[44] The weary travelers disembarked in the Crimean harbor of Sevastopol on Christmas Eve.

As noted in earlier chapters, the southerly regions of the European Russia had offered sanctuary to anti-Bolshevik and counter-revolutionary forces since 1917. Militarily, the most important of these were the Cossacks of the Don, Kuban and Terek regions who had, with varying degrees of success, thrown off the Red yoke and established a fragile independence. These Cossack hosts operated in loose alliance with the Volunteer (or "White") Army formed by Generals Alekseev and Kornilov. Unfortunately for the Whites, both these capable and popular commanders were now dead. The reins of command fell to General A.P. Denikin, a competent but rather unimaginative officer. The situation was complicated by the fact that Denikin was obliged to recognize the military and political overlordship of Admiral A.V. Kolchak in far-off Siberia. Kolchak, dubbed "Supreme Ruler," took power in a British-backed coup in November 1918. To further confuse the situation, a bevy of local "governments," nationalist movements and warlords were scattered across the landscape. Perhaps the most significant was the Ukrainian national movement led by S.V. Petlura, a force that battled the Reds, the Whites and anyone else that stood in its path. The icing on this bizarre cake was Allied intervention. The British dominated the scene in north Russia and the Japanese in Siberia, but in the Black Sea region the French played the major hand. London, of course, had a powerful interest in the nearby Caucasus where oil was the main attraction, and where petroleum was concerned, Reilly was seldom far away.

In Sevastopol, he compiled a general picture of this chaotic environment in a "Précis of Situation in South Russia." [45] He also took advantage of the local amenities, including a quiet Christmas dinner and a "splendid bath." [46] With lice-born typhus raging, basic hygiene was a matter of survival as well as aesthetics. Sidney interviewed a number of Russian officers on hand, notably Admiral B.A. Kanin, who commanded what was left of the Black Sea Fleet and Denikin's "War Secretary," Gen. A.S. Lukomskii. However, the man he was most pleased to see was old friend Sasha Grammatikov. Grammatikov also fled Petrograd in the autumn and made for Odessa. On Christmas Day, Sidney wired Sasha to come at once to the Crimea, and he dutifully appeared the following day. He immediately returned to Odessa to act as Sidney's eyes and ears. As we will see, Reilly may have had him on the lookout for more than military and political news.

Another Sevastopol contact was Lt. Grigorii Maslennikov, an ex-officer of the Black Sea Fleet and erstwhile Savinkov Unionist, now representative of an anti-Bolshevik intelligence service called the Azbuka ("Alphabet"). [47] Azbuka was a private, volunteer spy net run by Vasilii Vitalievich Shulgin, a rightist politician-*cum*-journalist with ties to Guchkov and Suvorin. The service operated agents in Kiev, Moscow and other cities of central Russia linked by an efficient courier system. For Reilly it was an invaluable source of information and a means to contact some of his own people still operating in Red territory. Shulgin needed money and Sidney helpfully offered to secure a stipend from London.

Catching a ride on the HMS *Acorn*, Reilly and Hill, accompanied by Maslennikov, arrived in the Caucasian port of Novorosiisk on the 29th. They were met by Col. H.B. Clayton, a comrade of Nathan and Dansey in wartime counterintelligence, who provided "interesting information." [48] Gen. Poole and Terence Keyes were also around but off at the front. Reilly was glad to miss Keyes who, thanks to their recent encounter in the ruble business, was full of ill will towards the Ace-of-Spies. After a brief, chilly meeting a short time later, he recorded that Keyes "behaved like a cad" and "just hates me." [49] Another questionable quantity to come sniffing around was sometime French agent Rudolph Ehrlich, a former actor. He had worked for Faux-pas-Bidet and Laurent and now served the French command in Odessa. Reilly recorded that "[Ehrlich] pretends to be very friendly and is placing himself at my disposal." [50] Still, he suspected that Ehrlich's real purpose was to spy on him—but for whom? The Frenchman soon came through with "some interesting information on under-surface work here." [51]

In the Kuban capital of Ekaterinodar, Sidney met a host of friendly faces. Arriving there on New Year's Eve, he was received by Maslennikov and a very cheery Gen. Poole. Soon after, Boris Suvorin loomed up like a ghost from the past, and Reilly immediately enlisted him to start a propaganda campaign on behalf of the Volunteer Army and the Allies. Accompanying Suvorin was Osip Einhorn, an Odessa businessman well versed in all things concerning petroleum.

Reilly's first task was to size up the potential of the Volunteer Army and its Cossack allies. He met with members of Denikin's "Special Council," an advisory cabinet composed of officers and politicians and businessmen "representing all shades of moderate opinion." [52] Most were affiliated with the so-called National Center, a body dominated by the same cabal of liberal freemasons that had run the defunct Provisional Government. Also on board was Reilly's erstwhile partner, Erast Shuberskii, who ran Denikin's transport department. From such men he gathered valuable data on the state of commerce and finance as well as military and political affairs. Ekaterinodar put Reilly near the Maikop oil fields, long a focus of British investment. Interests in London were anxious to see these properties protected and production resumed.

Speedy restoration of trade and industry, Reilly reasoned, would help stabilize the political atmosphere, but without money, real money, local powers were helpless to stem the decline. After consulting some of his Russian banking friends, he proposed the idea of a *valiuta* or hard currency loan to support a new ruble in the liberated territories. It would take the form of gold bullion or a solid foreign currency deposited in resurrected Russian banks. From this would evolve an elaborate and ambitious scheme to revitalize—and control—the whole of Russia's economy. Unfortunately in the postwar world very few countries had such ready cash, and certainly not Britain or France. The masters of gold and hard currency were the Americans. That presented a serious problem unless the Yankees could be persuaded to put the money in British hands, much as they had the earlier subsidies to the Czechs and Whites. A disturbing note was that the Yankees, in the form of Standard Oil of New Jersey, were already at work in the region buying up everything they could from cash-strapped local regimes and destitute owners.

On 10 January, Reilly and Hill finally secured an audience with
Denikin. Sidney sized up the General as a "higher staff officer type," digni-
fied, cultured and relatively broad-minded, but lacking any "great power of
intellect" or any marks of a true leader.[53] Whatever one could say about the
Bolsheviks, he noted, they did not lack for men with real drive and brutal
genius. Sidney was more concerned about the Cossack chiefs, especially the
Don Ataman (warlord), Gen. P.N. Krasnov, whom he characterized as a
reactionary dictator surrounded by a sordid clique of "rabid monarchists"
and anti-Semites.[54] Heading up Denikin's political department, Reilly noted
with disgust, was Gen. Kommisarov, the disgraced Okhrana officer who
once bossed and bullied Manasevich. More recently Kommisarov had been
Rasputin's bodyguard, obviously not a very good one. With men like that
in charge, "bribery and abuse of power abound everywhere," and the general atmosphere was "hostile to any concept of democracy."

Around the same time, Reilly sought out Noi Gordon, a former direc-
tor of the Russo-Asiatic Bank, to get his thoughts on financial matters. Our
man also was interested in the views of the Left. There he interviewed Isak
Israilovich Shik, who offered the "Inter[national] Socialist point of view."[55]
Shik, interestingly enough, was an in-law of Sidney's Rosenblum cousins.
Was he exploiting that connection here?

A few days later, in Rostov, Sidney and Hill took part in a Russian New
Year's celebration. Everyone got "horribly drunk," Reilly confided in his
diary, including Jolly George who ended up directing the equally intoxi-
cated band in his dressing gown. It was the "Old Regime all over," he
added, with an equal touch of nostalgia and disdain.[56] Hill also recounted
a vivid impression of his companion at this juncture. He took particular
note of Reilly's face with its "long, straight nose, dark, penetrating eyes,
large mouth and black hair brushed back from his forehead," and watched
as he "with precision smoked one Russian cigarette after another." "With
equal precision," added Hill, "he was taking in everything going on around
him, systematically recording his impressions and reactions."[57]

Whatever Reilly envisioned for Russia, it was not restoration of the old
order. In his papers from this period are notes for a report, apparently never
written, titled "Causes of Fall of Great Empire."[58] In this, he described the
fundamental flaw of the Tsarist regime as the lack of any true bond between
the government and the people. Under Nicholas II, "Government had disappeared . . . it became a shadow—only Rasputin was real." But the Mad
Monk merely represented the moral rot that, in Sidney's view, emanated
from the Church itself. Its inability to rein in Rasputin was symptomatic of
its general demoralization and that, in turn "was the principal source of the

poison which infected the entire state organism." This, of course, was the same Church that some months before he had pitched as the vehicle of Russia's moral resurrection.

While in Rostov, Sidney ran into a past acquaintance from New York, Lt. Arthur McPherson, late of the Anglo-Russian Supply Committee at 120 Broadway. Whatever the exact nature of their relationship, McPherson was happy to share with him his "pretty story about officer as commercial traveler." [59] The suggestion is that the Lieutenant was himself on some sort of intelligence assignment. In any case, in 1920 MacPherson would be working for SIS in Helsinki and Riga.

Reilly prepared to sail from Novorosiisk back to Sevastopol on 25 January. He had completed five reports for Bagge and was working on a sixth detailing all he had seen to date. If the overall impression was far from positive, neither was it altogether hopeless. His biggest problem was coding the reports for transmission, something he found tedious and rather difficult and finally paid a cipher clerk to do it for him. Thus, there was at least one aspect of the spy's craft at which he was not adept. Interestingly, he prepared a separate set of reports for Cumming. Only a list of the titles remain, including "Bolshevism," "Church," "Bessarabia," "Sovdepia" [Bolshevik Russia] and "Odessa." These were not encoded but personally entrusted to Hill who was to return to England as soon as they reached Odessa.

Reilly also found time to keep up personal correspondence. He wrote at least half a dozen letters to "Kissenka" (Nadine), plus others to Cumming, Lockhart, Leeper and, oddly, Harley Granville-Barker.[60] The latter was a well-known British dramatist who had worked as a part-time agent for Wiseman in the States. Sidney likely met him in that context. He now employed Barker as a confidential intermediary with Sir William who was at the Paris Peace Conference as a "Special Adviser" to the American delegation. Wiseman's job was much the same as it always had been: to keep a careful eye on American activities and do all possible to keep Washington's policies in line with London's, especially in Russia. Thus, what Reilly picked up about Standard's intrigues in the Caucasus and Wiseman's inside information from Paris provided a very useful mutual exchange.

Reilly and Keyes had done their best to avoid each other, but they were forced to share a boat back to the Crimea. Keyes continued to behave "like a cad and fool," and Sidney took to calling him "Kizi-Wizi."[61] He was convinced that Keyes was to blame for the subsequent delay in getting passage to Odessa, a place Reilly was increasingly anxious to reach. The week-long wait in the Crimea was not a complete waste, however. Reilly ran into an

American officer, Maj. Haig Shekerjian, who was more than willing to share views on the Russian situation and, most importantly, to listen to Reilly's. A Turkish Armenian by birth, Shekerjian was on a tour of duty with British forces in the Near East and attached to the U.S. Army's Military Intelligence Division.[62] He, too, was bound for Odessa, and Sidney assiduously courted him as a useful contact inside the local American military mission. Other interesting information came from Maslennikov's courier who had just returned from Moscow and Kiev. There was news of starvation and typhus epidemics ravaging Red territory and mounting popular unrest. Reilly still entertained hope that Bolo power would crumble from within and he still looked to Lenin's Latvian praetorian guard to bring this about. Back on 11 January, he noted encouraging news from Moscow about discontent among the Latvians who constituted "the greatest latent danger for the Bolsheviks."[63] Their disaffection might be furthered, he argued, by a "vigorous propaganda campaign in the Baltic Provinces." Reilly was nothing if not persistent.

Reilly set foot on Odessa early on the morning on 3 February. If it was not yet a city of the damned, it was headed in that direction. French troops, with some reluctant Greeks in tow, occupied the port in late 1919 under the command of General Henri Berthelot. The tenuous Allied grip was threatened not only by Red forces pressing on its environs, but also by Petlura's Ukrainian Army, the sworn enemy of all Russians, Red or White. The eventual fall of the city to either Lenin's or Petlura's hordes seemed a foregone conclusion and nervous refugees were frantically looking for ways out of the trap.

Sidney's first step was to check in with Bagge at the British Consulate. Over the next several days he kept a busy schedule of meetings with an array of Russian and Allied representatives. Perhaps the most significant of these was Karol Jaroszynski, the Russo-Polish financier who some months earlier had played front man in British plots to rescue the Imperial Family and buy up Russian banks. The latter scheme was very much alive. Together with Reilly and Bagge, Jaroszynski drew up a bold plan to expand acquisitions from banks to railways, oil fields and factories; in effect, to bring the bulk of Russia's economy into a single, giant syndicate.[64] Sidney was to become one of the scheme's most effective and persistent advocates. What the Pole needed most, of course, was money, lots of it. Whether His Majesty's Treasury would be willing to provide such funds was a major question, and behind it lay the threat that if London did not, the Americans might. In Jaroszynski's syndicate, Reilly saw the best hope of averting American domination of Russia, and he was not the only one.

Also on hand was K.M. Aggeev, the Russian Orthodox Church official with whom Sidney had hatched the idea of a British subsidy for religious propaganda. Despite Reilly's expressed reservation about the Church, he agreed to revive the idea and carry a personal appeal to the Archbishop of Canterbury.[65] What most attracted him to this scheme, we may guess, was the possibility of siphoning off some of the cash for his own purposes.

Among Reilly's Odessa contacts was another set of familiar names and faces, notably Vladimir Orlov and Natta Azef. Like Sidney, Orlov had an amazing knack for landing on his feet. Reaching Odessa via Berlin, Denikin named him chief of counterintelligence for the Southwestern District, an area embracing much of Ukraine. Since the Volunteer Army was in no position to pay much for his services, the ever-versatile Orlov continued to supply information to the Germans as well as the British and French. He gave Reilly detailed reports on the Ukrainian and Belorussian independence movements, the condition of finance, industry and trade in the Soviet zone and even a dossier on Jaroszynski that described his secret overtures to French and German quarters.[66] He also filled him in on the activities of a local gang of Jewish black-marketeers led by Mssrs. Hari (Chary) and Hepner. The group also included Kogan, the man with whom Reilly had strange dealings months earlier in Moscow. Orlov had managed to leave Petrograd with a priceless collection of files culled from the Okhrana archive, files that detailed the persons and careers of many key Bolsheviks. Those, too, were of great interest to persons in London and elsewhere.

Natta Azeff, AKA Madame Raevskaia, pursued her usual role of freelance counterspy, apparently in league with Orlov. Her raven hair and shapely, athletic figure reminded Reilly of Nadine, a woman much on his mind at the moment. He paid his old colleague in the secret world a personal kindness by ordering from London a consignment of black and dark blue cloth, Natta's preferred colors, along with matching black stockings and an invaluable store of Pears' Soap.[67]

Somewhere in this tangled web of agents and double-agents may have been Sergius Riis. When we last met him, he was Acting U.S. Naval Attaché in Archangel. According to his bizarre memoir, he and MI1c/RN man Maclaren fled Petrograd soon after Cromie's murder and embarked on a months-long trek through the heart of Soviet Russia disguised as Red commissars.[68] The tale is certainly mostly a crock since Riis's presence in Archangel can be documented as late as November 1918. However, his whereabouts in the early 1919 is a blank, and his story of surfacing in Odessa around February may hold a kernel of truth. If so, it is another case of the strange synchronicity between his movements and the Ace-of-Spies'.

Another American Reilly encountered in Odessa was a U.S. Army soldier, Edward Remick. Explaining that he "needed to practice his flying," Sidney invited Remick to come along for the ride. The latter had been raised in one of the nearby German colonies, and his knowledge of area landmarks might have come in handy. Remick recalled that his companion "spoke German as good as I" and noted that "he had lived in Odessa when he was younger." Currently, Reilly explained, he was working for the British but admitted "they didn't like him and made faces behind his back, but he didn't care." To Remick, he seemed a thorough enemy of the Bolos.[69]

In eight reports composed over the next month, Sidney damned the French and heaped scorn on Petlura's separatist ambitions. He was only slightly less negative towards the local Whites whose leadership and policies struck him as misguided if not outright idiotic. On 18 February, he reported "the French have no friends here in any classes of population."[70] Berthelot had no control over his subordinates and the absence of the British was "universally regretted." French dickering with the Petlurists, a "stillborn movement," alienated the Russians and undermined confidence in the Allies as a whole. A few days later, he described Berthelot's effort to force French officers on Volunteer units as "inimical and tactless" and provoking "complete confusion." Reilly was particularly critical of Berthelot's adjutant, Col. Henri Freydenberg, whom he held responsible for pushing negotiations with the Ukrainians.

As for Denikin, on 6 March, Sidney wrote that the General's policy of summary execution of officers found serving in Red or Ukrainian ranks was short-sighted and produced a "bad impression" on the French.[71] The same held for the Volunteer command's harassment of Jewish officers and Jews in general. On the other hand, Reilly noted that local opposition to the Volunteers was "mostly Jewish." He urged London to use Keyes or other representatives to press for a change in such policies. Many excellent officers, he noted, served the Reds out of necessity or a sense of professional duty and cited Bonch-Bruevich as a sterling example. A more sensible approach might win them over. Such men, he added, were most likely to overthrow the Bolsheviks themselves. If so, a fresh civil war would ensue in which the issue would be "doubtful" for the likes of Denikin and Kolchak. That being said, he held out hope for the White cause if it could be brought under more practical, namely British, influence. Only a revived Russian national movement, he argued, could provide an ideological tonic to Bolshevism.

What impact did Reilly's reports have in London? They certainly received a positive reception from War Secretary Winston Churchill, a gung-ho advocate of intervention and militant anti-Bolshevik. By early March, Sidney's reports were circulating to the War Cabinet and even the King. Walford Selby of the FO's Russian Department declared them full of "useful information," and Rex Leeper, already a Reilly fan, praised his work as "very interesting & reliable" and full of "the political information we require." [72]

However, almost as soon as he set foot in Odessa, Reilly was anxious to leave. This was more than a reaction to the chaotic political and military conditions. At the meeting with Bagge, the collective decision was that Hill would return to Paris at once with the current reports. Sidney saw him off late on the 4th; he enjoyed Hill's companionship and was sorry to see him go. That, however, does not explain the peculiar funk that now overtook him. In his memoirs, Hill recalls that soon after their arrival, on the 3rd or early on the 4th, they were walking along Aleksandrovskii Prospect and passed in front of #15. This, remember, supposedly was the address young Salomon Rosenblum lived at with his mother many years before. Reilly suddenly "went white and fell down in the street, obviously suffering an intense emotional crisis." [73] He quickly recovered his equilibrium, but refused to discuss the incident or its cause.

Perhaps it was some old, painful memory that provoked the attack, but there may have been more acute and stressful things on his mind, like Anne. His anxiousness about getting to Odessa could have been because he expected, or hoped, that she would be there. If so, he soon discovered she was not. Was she dead, in hiding, or did Peters have her securely under his thumb? Probably Sidney himself did not know, and that was what tormented him. With this in mind, we might better appreciate the bleak mood he recorded in his diary the following night: "Went home to cold and dark room feeling very lonely." [74]

Adding to Reilly's discomfiture may have been an article that appeared in the local paper *Prizyv* ("The Call"). This announced that a certain "Foreigner Who Knows Russia" was in town on a special mission. [75] The same man had played a leading part in the recent "Ambassadors' Plot" and who because of that faced a death sentence in Red hands. Was this a warning or a threat? In either case, Sidney could conclude that his presence had become a bit too public.

The very next morning he cabled his desire to leave and redirect his energies to the matter of "Prince's Island." [76] This referred to a proposal made by U.S. President Wilson in January for a peace conference of Russian factions, including the Bolsheviks, to be held on Prinkipo (Prince's) Island near Constantinople. Speaking for Lenin, on 4 February, Soviet Foreign

Commissar Georgii Chicherin accepted the proposal. To Reilly this was a potentially disastrous situation. He had no doubt that the instigators of Wilson's overture were Morgan and like American capitalists eager to force a deal in Russia that would leave the devastated country open to their exploitation. Nor were his suspicions far off-base. Early in 1918, the U.S. Ambassador in Stockholm, William Buckler, quietly sounded out Moscow's man Litvinov on the possibility of American recognition in exchange for the Reds' recognition of Russia's foreign debts, at least its American ones. Wheels started moving in Washington to dispatch a delegation under William Bullitt for direct talks in Moscow.

In the meantime, Lenin's main agent in New York, Ludwig Martens, had set up a "Soviet Bureau" and was actively courting Wall Street. Martens, of course, had recently done business beside Reilly at 120 Broadway. Among those already sniffing at his bait was the Ford Motor Co., and by March it concluded a tractor deal with the Ivan Stakheev Co. acting as intermediary for Martens and Moscow. Back on 10 February Reilly had recorded a conversation with Jaroszynski regarding the very same Stakheev.[77] Behind Stakheev stood Jaroszynski's archrival in the ranks of Russian capitalists, P.P. Batolin.[78]

Sidney proposed that he return to Paris and, if and when the Russian conference materialized, go to Prinkipo as a special advisor. Bagge backed the idea, noting Reilly's "great knowledge of Russian politics and his [excellent] relations with Russians of all classes."[79] Receiving no response, a week later Reilly wired again. He argued that he had completed meaningful work in Odessa and had plenty of information on "all political questions." "Unless it is desired to employ me on another mission," he added, "may I respectfully suggest that I be ordered to return home as my further stay here is a waste of time."[80]

In London, however, these entreaties found opposition. Friends like Leeper considered him "one of the most useful agents we could have in Russia" and thought it "a great pity" for him to leave.[81] Leeper wondered if Reilly might be persuaded to undertake a mission deep into Soviet territory, despite the obvious risks. A Brahmin of the Foreign Office, Lord Drogheda, opined that Reilly's attendance at Prinkipo might be useful, but that he should stay in Odessa for the present.[82]

Hill, at the same time, was taking longer than expected to reach Paris where he might enlist the help of Wiseman and others. On 15 February, he wired Sidney from Bucharest warning him "*do not* [ital. original] leave Russia until I telegraph you."[83] "Our friend has done a bit of damage," he added, "his latest on you will drive you crazy . . . you can rely on me doing

all in my power 1) to get home w/o delay, 2) do all I can." Most likely this
was a reference to Keyes, but it suggests that some may have wanted to
keep him in Odessa as a means of keeping him out of sight and trouble in
the West. Hill finally made London on the 21st and sent his stranded comrade a brief wire: "Reports sent in. Wiring fully few days. Nadine well New
York." [84] Hill also passed on another bit of information that must have
brought Reilly some satisfaction. Among those lurking around Paris, ostensibly as a member of the Polish delegation, was Tony Jechalski. Just before
Hill's arrival, Jechalski had been arrested by French authorities "in connection with some spying activities" and faced expulsion from the country. [85]

Meanwhile conditions in Odessa deteriorated. Red forces began a concerted advance on the city and the French troops approached outright
mutiny. It was only a matter of days until the French decamped and the
Bolsheviks were back in charge. In his final report from the doomed city,
Sidney railed against French "bungling and malfeasance" and criminal
duplicity of Freydenberg. [86] Rescue from Odessa finally came from Rear-
Admiral Richard Webb, His Majesty's Assistant High Commissioner in
Constantinople. Reilly's grim assessments so alarmed the Admiral that he
summoned him and Bagge to the Turkish capital to give a firsthand
account. On 10 March, Webb arranged Sidney's departure for London so
that he could give the FO "a full personal account" as well. [87] No doubt it
was more than some there would want.

Reilly rolled into Victoria Station on the 18th and presented himself to
Cumming. Despite the acknowledged value of his recent service, there was
no offer of decoration or promotion. Nothing was happening at Prinkipo,
so "C"'s problem was what to do with his independent-minded agent.
Alongside the other complaints, voices in the FO now charged that he had
abandoned his post.

Sidney had some personal business to attend to. The same day he set
foot in London, he asked Cumming's office to lend a hand in bringing
Nadine over from New York. MI1c forwarded the matter to MI5 where
one wag opined "these wives of Reilly are rather tiresome." [88] However, in
the end, powers-that-be determined that it would "not do either the
Bolsheviks or the Germans any good to let MI1c's man have a little license."
Nadine grabbed the *Baltic* on 26 March and was reunited with her husband
in early April. Had absence truly made Reilly's heart grow fonder, or was
he most interested in getting her away from the attentions of Jechalski? Or
was Nadine carrying some vital information, something that could only be
conveyed to the Ace-of-Spies in person? While Nadine continued to call
herself Mrs. Sidney Reilly, she and her husband seem to have maintained

separate residences in the months following; certainly he had very little time for her. It appears the marriage was over in everything but name, but Sidney felt no need of a divorce and Nadine was, perhaps, unwilling to part with the financial advantages he could provide.

In the meantime, Cumming dispatched Reilly and Hill to Paris where they were to "hold ourselves in readiness to give expert information should it be required, to observe what was happening in Paris, particularly in connection with Russian affairs, and possibly to act as liaison officers with the newly-formed Committee of [Russian] Ambassadors."[89] It was about this time that Reilly first made the acquaintance of Churchill. The introduction has been credited to Sir William Bull, a Tory MP and friend of Cumming.[90] In fact, it was Cumming himself who did the honors.[91] Winston had an adventurous, even reckless, side that political responsibilities forced him to subdue. Reilly would become, in some respects, an alter ego whose devious exploits provided vicarious satisfaction. From Sidney's perspective, Churchill was a genuine Englishman of rank and influence, rather what he longed to be. Even their political opinions seemed to match. It was the beginning of a long and beautiful friendship.

Boris Savinkov was in Paris trying to boss around the unofficial Russian [anti-Bolo] delegation. As "special military representative" of Admiral Kolchak, he lobbied for Allied military aid to the White armies. On 29 March, Reilly watched him address the exiled Russian Chamber of Commerce. The crowd of businessmen and journalists, some them old associates, received Savinkov's strident denunciation of Bolshevism with genuine, if impotent, enthusiasm. However, most of his former comrades on the Left saw him as a "despicable and hated renegade."[92] One exception was Vladimir Burtsev, who had also turned against the Bolsheviks. But Boris garnered no real affection from the right either; the Tsarist diplomat Sergei Sazonov, was aghast to find himself working beside "an assassin."[93] Reilly, however, claimed to see in Savinkov nothing less than a Russian Napoleon. Thus encouraged, Churchill dubbed him a "terrorist for moderate aims."[94] Sidney's admiration, as we will see, was something less than sincere. He may have liked Savinkov, but he knew him to be a man of great ambition and little or no convictions and moral scruples. That made him potentially very useful.

Reilly and Hill set up camp at the Hotel Majestic, the center of Paris' diplomatic wheeling and dealing. Although RAF officers, they tried to pass themselves off as special consultants to the British Naval Delegation, a stunt that quickly drew fire from the Admiralty.[95] As a result, they had to shift operations to the less central and less visible Hotel Mercedes. The "Russian

Front" produced new rumors and twists on an almost daily basis. The notion of an All-Russian peace conference was dead, but other feelers were in the air. To Reilly the most troubling was that the American Bullitt was bringing proposals from Moscow. Lenin was willing to dangle political—and economic—concessions in hope of coaxing the Allies, especially the U.S., into recognizing his regime. About the 25th, he and Hill got word of Bullitt's imminent arrival. Their first step was to consult with Wiseman who still acted as London's special liaison to the President and the American delegation. Sir William shared Reilly's concerns and together they plotted how to handle the situation. Bullitt was scheduled to lay the proposal before Lloyd George, whose willingness to accept an accommodation with the Bolos was distressingly apparent.

Sidney, fortunately, had a contact close to the Bullitt team, a man Hill describes as a member of the "American military delegation."[96] This was Sergius Riis who had arrived in the French capital from Russia. Riis, of course, may already have been a British agent. The next step was simple: Riis provided the essential details of the Bullitt report, and those, properly edited, found their way into the hands of Henry Wickham Steed, Paris editor of *The Times* and the *Daily Mail*. Those papers broke the story, in a most negative light, on 2 April. The Bullitt proposals drew fire all around and Lloyd George backed off his support. Another American scheme was thwarted—for the moment.

The Bullitt affair also drew unwelcome scrutiny to Reilly's presence, in Paris, and it seemed best for him to disappear for a while. Cumming summoned him back to London right after the story broke, but his presence complicated things there as well. Whether "C" decided to send him to New York or it was Sidney's own idea is uncertain, but that is what happened. Wiseman probably lent his support, as did Nathan. The latter was back in Manhattan where he had taken over the reins of Section V from Norman Thwaites. The idea was that Reilly would monitor Bolshevik influence on Wall Street and use his contacts there to persuade American businessmen that their best interests lay in cooperating with Jaroszynski's syndicate, a syndicate, of course, also backed by London.

Soon after Nadine's arrival, Reilly decided that he had to go to New York—without her. The problem was that his name was mud in American official circles, not the least in the State Department. Getting him into the country would require some finesse and a little outright deception. On 11 April the American Embassy in London received a formal request from the Foreign Office that Sidney be granted a diplomatic visa to undertake "urgent government service" in the United States.[97] He was scheduled to sail on the 14th, so speed was of the essence. Although later saying he "did not like Reilly's looks," the passport officer granted the visa but, as routine procedure, reported the matter to Washington. This made it to the State Department's L. Lanier Winslow who, finding Reilly's name on the ONI and MID suspect lists, immediately wired London for an explanation. By this time it was the 15th, and Reilly was already at sea.

Curiously, the same day Reilly submitted his application to the American Embassy, another of Cumming's operatives landed in New York. This was Capt. Humphrey Plowden, recently of the British Army in France, who was on an undisclosed mission to His Majesty's Embassy in Washington. Plowden's visit would overlap very closely with Reilly's, and given their mutual connection to SIS, this suggests some connection in their missions. But, if they did not encounter one another at this juncture, they would soon enough. Reilly soon would count Plowden as one of his closest colleagues in the brotherhood of British intelligence and anti-Bolshevism.

Meanwhile, back in London, U.S. Embassy secretary Edward Bell sought to determine who sent Reilly to the U.S. and why. It proved a difficult question to answer. Following up Winslow's request, Bell, who had never heard of Reilly, bypassed the Foreign Office and went straight to MI5, "who have a wonderful card index on all the scoundrels of the world," on the 16th.[98] He made contact with Capt. Sidney Russell Cooke who had a fat file on Reilly full of mostly negative information. Despite this, Cooke assured Bell that the subject had recently been in the employ of "the Secret Service known as M.I.1.C.," and that agency had "given him a clean bill of health some time before."[99] Cooke suspected that Reilly had gone to America on that agency's behalf and promised to check on the matter. Later that evening, he reported that Col. Stewart Menzies (Cumming's future successor) of the Secret Service told him that Reilly had gone to the U.S. "on purely private and personal business," though with the knowledge and approval of MI1c. Menzies quickly added that while his agency guaranteed the traveler "from a national point of view," they "had nothing to say in his favor from a moral or financial" one.

This hardly clarified the situation so far as Bell was concerned. He next phoned the FO's passport office to ask why they had declared Reilly to be on "official business."[100] He finally got a response from them on the 19th and was assured that Reilly had "gone to America on an official mission"— for the War Office! So he checked with the WO that confirmed the statement but suggested that the ultimate source of the order was the Secret Service. Taking the direct approach, Bell rang up Cumming, whom he knew to be "Head of the Secret Service" and relayed what he had heard from

Cooke and Menzies. Coincidentally, both those officers had suddenly gone "on holiday" and were unavailable to explain their comments. Cumming calmly suggested that Menzies had told Cooke what he did "as the easiest way out of the difficulty." [101] The mission in New York was only a "blind," he admitted; the "real facts" were that they "wanted to get Reilly out of the way for a while." Specifically, they wanted him away from Paris for a month or so, after which "he is to go again to Russia." Bell complained that the matter had put the Embassy in a "very difficult position." Cumming, agreed; he knew American authorities were suspicious of Reilly and did not blame them for "making a fuss." Bell asked that if he planned to send any more "criminals and shady characters to spend their holidays in the United States, particularly if he knew that our authorities regarded them as such, he had better let me know in advance." Bell forwarded the above to Washington on the 19th adding that, under the circumstances, it was best if Reilly was not molested.

Some additional insight into this episode, and perhaps some clarification, is provided in a note from Menzies to MI5. He noted that Reilly's American trip was a "private one" but "C" was anxious for him to have "all facilities" and guaranteed him in every respect but financial.[102] MI1c wanted him back in Paris as soon as possible "where he is doing good work."

By the time Winslow got the full report, the Ace-of-Spies had arrived in Halifax aboard the SS *Olympic*. There something else unusual happened. The *Olympic*, originally destined for New York, remained in Halifax and then turned back to Southampton, transferring its Gotham-bound passengers to the SS *Adriatic*. Sidney, however, did not re-embark on the *Adriatic*. He slipped aboard a New York-bound train and was already at his desk at 120 Broadway when the ship pulled in to the Manhattan docks. That put him one step ahead of the American agents charged with keeping an eye on him, and he would remain so the rest of his stay.

Sidney at once reconnected with Thomas and Weinstein. The former he charged with mounting a suit against Samuel Pryor and the Remington Union-Metallic Cartridge Co. for $300,000 in unpaid commissions.[103] Pryor, it may be recalled, was the man who had so vociferously denounced Reilly as a German agent almost exactly two years before. But Sidney's action was not simple revenge. He knew, possibly through Savinkov, that Remington was seeking rifle contracts from Kolchak's representatives. The suit would be a sharp reminder that no deals would be made without his participation. It was declaration that he was back in town and back to business.

At the same time Reilly represented the Russo-Asiatic Bank, or at least its exiled officials in Paris, in a suit against Morgan-dominated Guaranty

Trust. The purpose here was to stop Guaranty from disposing of Russian accounts in its hands. As described in a Department of Justice report, during WWI Guaranty Trust acquired large ruble accounts through Scandinavian deals with German banks, many of them in the name of the Russo-Asiatic.[104] Whether this had any connection to the Bolshevik finance nexus is unknown, but it was by no means out of the question. The drastic depreciation of the ruble since 1917 threatened to leave Guaranty in an "awful hole." When RAB representatives in Paris demanded payment of their New York accounts in dollars, Guaranty responded that the RAB and other pre-Revolutionary banks no longer existed as a result of the Soviet nationalization. Thus, Guaranty and its backers had a strong vested interest in seeing recognition of the Bolshevik regime and its decrees. Sidney was hardly surprised to find that Charles Sabin, a Guaranty Trust executive, was personally handling the financing of Martens' Soviet Bureau.[105] Sidney had encountered Sabin before; he was among those sued by the Ace-of-Spies back in 1916 over canceled Russian contracts.

The secret war against Bolshevism was very much on the mind of Robert Nathan. The fear that animated Nathan, Thwaites and their superiors in London was that Red Moscow had replaced Berlin as the primary nemesis of the British Empire and that a Bolshevik hand was behind her troubles from Bengal to Ireland. Nathan's aim was to uncover the clandestine links between Bolsheviks in the U.S. and their comrades in Britain, specifically how the former channeled funds to England and the Continent. Martens' bureau was assumed to play a role, and it was bound to play an even bigger part if he won American recognition and financial backing. Reilly's help could be very useful in unveiling the affairs of the Soviet Bureau and subverting its efforts.

He may have lent one helping hand to Nathan by helping him find an agent to infiltrate the transatlantic Bolshevik courier system. He was Jacob (Harry) Nosovitsky, a gangly, almost comical-looking fellow who styled himself an "international spy, conspirator and super forger." [106] A better description might be a third-rate Reilly. They did share some common background: Russian Jews with an early attraction to radicalism that gave way to a career as counter-revolutionary provocateur and spy. And for good measure, both were liars and crooks. Nosovitsky offered his services to the American Justice Department sometime in 1918. More interesting, during the war he was among those private detectives hired by the Russian Supply Committee to protect munitions plants and ships; he may even have been one of Sergius Riis' men. This explains how Reilly would know him. Also involved in Nosovitsky's recruitment was Raymond Finch, another ex-

Justice Department man and New York State investigator who now worked for Nathan.

Nosovitsky and Finch, furthermore, were connected to Boris Brasol, the Russian Supply Committee's former special investigator. Since 1917, Brasol, too, had worked in the American camp, first as a Russian expert for War Trade Intelligence and later as agent "B-1" of the MID. He remained an ardent anti-Semite. From late 1918 through early 1919, he filed no less than thirty-three reports, most aimed at detailing the link between Brasol's *bêtes noires*, Bolshevism and the International Jewish Conspiracy.[107] He even managed to dig up some legitimate dirt on Martens and friends. More importantly, he provided Reilly with useful links to like-minded Americans. Brasol's boss in the New York MID apparatus was Dr. Harris Houghton who remained a friend and confidant when their official work ended. Houghton, in turn, was the friend and personal physician of C.C. Daniels, chief of Henry Ford's private detective service in New York.[108] Brasol himself would soon become Ford's special advisor on the "Jewish Question." He also remained tight with Charkel (Charles) Wallevitch, another Jew in strange company, who remained with MID after Brasol's departure.[109]

There were more Russians. Boris Bakhmet'ev, Guchkov's friend, still oversaw the Embassy and the array of consulates for a government that no longer existed. However, as recognized emissaries, Bakhmet'ev and his financial officer, Sergei Uget, controlled the remaining accounts and credits of the former Russian regimes amounting to tens of millions of dollars. If the Soviets gain recognition, those assets would become theirs. He and Reilly shared a common goal in making sure that did not happen.

Another familiar face was Anton Ossendowski who had attached himself to the Russian Economic League, another gaggle of émigré capitalists. He linked Reilly to an American, Jerome Barker Landfield, though they may have known each other otherwise. A journalist and self-styled explorer, Landfield was prospecting for gold in Eastern Siberia and Manchuria when Reilly was thereabouts in 1901. He later showed up in Petersburg in 1906–07 and married a lady-in-waiting to the Tsarina.[110] Most recently, Landfield had served the State Department as an "adviser on Russian Affairs." After the war, he wound up in New York as secretary of the American-Russian Chamber of Commerce, hence his connection to Ossendowski and the REL. Reilly was interested in his journalistic talents and their application to anti-Bolshevik propaganda. In May, Landfield began a series of articles and letters to the editor decrying Red savagery and deceit.[111]

Reilly soon got down to his main business in the country, the recruitment of Yankee financial backing for Jaroszynski's Russian economic scheme. For this, he reverted to his role as an emissary for Bagge and the Department of Overseas Trade. In Manhattan, he turned first to Samuel MacRoberts to garner their support. Reilly reported to Bagge through the courtesy of the local SIS code clerk and routed a copy to Cumming. On 10 May, he cabled "My conversations with prominent American bankers and manufacturers have convinced me that they are fully alive to the possibilities of RUSSIA as inexhaustible market for American manufacturers and as great a field for capital." [112] "Various big, American interests," he added, were poised to plunge into the Russian market "wherever a certain measure of order is reestablished." Unfortunately, many of the "highest financial circles" had taken keen interest in a scheme proposed by Jaroszynski's rival Batolin, including Sidney's old employer the American International Corporation. Reilly took the direct approach and sounded out Batolin for a deal. The Russian was motivated by money alone and willing to work with an English and American syndicate if such was organized. He even was willing, though not enthusiastic, to combine efforts with Jaroszynski if that would prove mutually profitable.

Reilly argued to London that absorbing Batolin in an Anglo-American combine was the wisest idea. MacRoberts, he reported, felt that only the combined effort of Britain and the United States could handle the reconstruction of Russia and that in such endeavor "there could be no place for jealousy." Sidney assured Bagge that MacRoberts was a staunch Anglophile who possessed "great influence and directs the foreign policy of [various] banks." But he warned that unless some initiative was taken and soon, the Morganites would be moving on their own; perhaps they already were. With MacRoberts' help, Reilly hoped to enlist such heavy-hitters as Armour, Dupont, Ford, the Guggenheims, Standard Oil, and mining tycoon John Ryan. With that kind of power, an Anglo-American syndicate could overwhelm any rivals. There was another small detail. Jaroszynski had not been asked if he would go along with such a scheme, one that would force him into a partnership with Batolin. If he balked, Reilly casually suggested, it would be no problem to dump him and find another front man.

As Sidney was preparing to sail back to Europe, he fired off a second brief report on a meeting with Richard Martens, an ex-Russian diplomat and owner of a shipping company that once handled much of the trade between Britain and northern Russia.[113] Martens, he noted, possessed "exhaustive" information on Russia's industrial and commercial resources and would be of "great value" in the coming reconstruction of the country. He made no reference to past allegations of Martens' pro-German sympathies nor to Brasol's recent charge that he was, like Batolin, a cat's paw of the Bolos.[114] Sidney asked that Martens be permitted to come to England where he might be used to assist and influence Jaroszynski.

Before leaving, there were personal negotiations with Nadine. She and Reilly agreed that their marriage was no longer a viable proposition. However, he wanted Nadine's continued cooperation and she sought guarantees of financial and personal security. He agreed to bring her back to Europe and provide a suitable financial settlement.

Sidney sailed on the SS *Baltic* for Liverpool on 15 May. Before departing, he may have put a plot in motion than would not bear fruit until after he was safely across the Atlantic. On 2–3 June bombs exploded in eight U.S. cities. They came disguised as gift boxes from Gimbel Bros. department store in New York, and all were sent to prominent figures, including the Attorney General of the United States, A. Mitchell Palmer.[115] While there was no doubt that "radicals" were to blame, the culprits were never identified. Subsequent investigation showed that the bombs had been mailed about 25 April, during Reilly's stay, from the main post office on Cedar Street, not far from his Broadway office. Whether he had a hand in them or not, the timing and results of the Gimbel bombs could not have suited him better. They brought hostile attention to bear on Martens' Soviet Bureau; its officers were raided and ransacked by New York police on 12 June. The Red Scare was on. Palmer and his young Bureau of Investigation deputy director J. Edgar Hoover, were set to mount a holy war against Bolshevism. Reilly couldn't have been more pleased.

NOTES

1. Reilly, 55.
2. PZZ #73, 2.
3. *Izvestiia* (1 Dec. 1918), 2–3.
4. Ibid.
5. TsAFSB, Berzin, 305.
6. USDS, 361.1121K21/50, Lockhart Trial, 1.
7. Ibid., 2.
8. Ibid., 7.
9. *Izvestiia* (5 Dec. 1918), 2.
10. PRO, Hill Report, 21/40.
11. Ibid., 22/41.
12. Ibid.
13. Reilly, 78–79.
14. RGAVMF, Raport #573.
15. PRO, FO 371/3319, Findlay to FO, 30 Sept. 1918.
16. Ibid., minute, 1 Oct. 1918.
17. Ibid., French to Campbell, 10 Oct. 1918.
18. Leeds University, Historical Centre, F.C. Poole Papers, G. Hill, "2nd Lt. S.G. Reilly, R.A.F.," 56.
19. SIS, CVXM 678/110, 23 Oct. 1918.

20. Ben Knapen, *De Lange Weg naar Moskou: Nederlandse relaties tot de Sovjet-Unie 1917-1942* (Amsterdam, 1985), 78–79.
21. Reilly, 99–102.
22. PZZ #73, 2.
23. Krymov, 74–77.
24. SIS, Morton to Reilly, 4 Jan. 1919.
25. HLRO, Diary #3, 6 Nov. 1918.
26. Oxford University, Lord Milner Papers, Great War, box 365c, Reilly to Lockhart, 25 Nov. 1918.
27. Ibid., Reilly to Lockhart, 24 Nov. 1918.
28. PRO, FO 371/5414, Leeper notation to Bagge Report, 15 Feb. 1919.
29. PRO, 371/4019, Hoare to Leeper, 27 Nov. 1918.
30. SIS, Maj. Hargreaves to Capt. Shute, undated.
31. Kobiakov, 225–227.
32. SIS, Margaret to WO, 16 Nov. 1918.
33. PRO, FO, 369/1025, Villiers to FO 3 Dec, 1918 and attached note, 7 Dec.
34. SIS, Margaret to Air Board, 4 Jan. 1919.
35. Ibid., to Capt., Spencer, 4 Feb. 1919.
36. Ibid., CX 066117, 19 Feb. 1919.
37. ONI, 21010-3241, Memorandum #9, 27 Sept. 1918.
38. Ibid., Memorandum #6, 10 Sept. 1918.
39. Ibid., Memorandum #8, 16 Sept., 2.
40. Ibid., "Examination of Joseph Pawlowski," 20 Sept. 1918.
41. MID, 9140-6073, Madam Reilly, 6 Sept. 1918.
42. SIS, Attached items.
43. George Hill, *Dreaded Hour* (London, 1936), 63.
44. SIS, Reilly Diary, 10 Dec. 1918–11 Feb. 1919, 19 Dec.
45. PRO, 371/3962, 28 Dec. 1918.
46. SIS, Diary, 25 Dec. 1918.
47. Bortnevskii, 20–22, and his "Kistorii osvedomitel'noi organizatsii Azbuka," *Russkoe proshloe*, vol. 4 (1993), 160–193.
48. PRO, FO 371/3962, Report #2, 8 Jan. 1919.
49. SIS, Diary, 1 Jan. 1919.
50. Ibid., 31 Dec. 1918.
51. Ibid., 1 Jan. 1919.
52. PRO, FO 371/3962, Report #6, 21 Jan. 1919.
53. Ibid., Report #4, 11 Jan. 1919.
54. Ibid., Report #5, 21 Jan. 1919.
55. SIS, Diary, 13 Jan. 1919.
56. Ibid.
57. Hill, *Dreaded*, 62.
58. SIS, Attachments.
59. Ibid., Diary, 21 Jan. 1919.
60. Ibid., 8 Jan. 1919.
61. Ibid., 30 Jan. 1919.
62. Shekerjian took a post with MID after his return to Washington in Dec. 1919.
63. PRO, FO 371/3962, Report #4.
64. FO 371/4019, Bagge to Steel-Maitland, 14 May 1919.
65. SIS, Diary, 7 Feb. 1919.
66. Ibid., Attachments, "Spravka o Karl Iosifovich Yaroshinskom," 23 Feb. 1919.
67. Ibid., List of items for Mme. Raevskaya.
68. Riis, 24–25. He claimed to have used the name "Maxim Galinski."
69. Thanks to Judy Remmick-Hubert for this information.

70. PRO, FO 371/3963, Report #13, 18 Feb. 1919.
71. Ibid., Report #18, 6 March 1919.
72. Ibid., cover notes to Reilly reports.
73. Lockhart, *Ace*, 106.
74. SIS, Diary, 5 Feb. 1919.
75. Savchenko, 299.
76. SIS, Diary, 6 Feb. 1919.
77. Ibid., 10 Feb. 1919.
78. PRO, FO 371/4019, "Character Sketch of Carol Yaroshinski," and France, Archives Nationales (AN), AP/94/186, Noulens to Barthou, 3 Nov. 1917.
79. FO 371/3997, Bagge to FO, 6 Feb. 1919.
80. FO 371/3978, Reilly to Campbell, 22 Feb. 1919.
81. FO 371/3997, Leeper notation to #67a, 15 Feb. 1919.
82. Ibid., #356, 22 Feb. and #107, 25 Feb. 1919.
83. SIS, Hill to Reilly, 15 Feb. 1919.
84. PRO, FO 371/3962, Hill for Reilly, 21 Feb. 1919.
85. MID, 10110-920/321, Report #32, 20 Feb. 1919.
86. PRO, FO 371/3962, Report #20, 10 March 1919.
87. FO 371/3978, Webb to FO, 10 March 1919.
88. MI5, Reilly, Note by G.E. Pennington, 20 March 1919.
89. Hill, *Dreaded*, 95.
90. R. Lockhart, *Ace*, 108 and Judd, 193–195.
91. Churchill Archives Centre, Cambridge (CAC), Chartwell Papers (CHAR), 16/27, "Russian Trade," 3, 11 Sept. 1919.
92. Spence, *Savinkov*, 233.
93. Ibid., 225.
94. Churchill, *Great Contemporaries* (New York, 1937), 106.
95. Hill, *Dreaded*, 95.
96. Ibid., 102.
97. USDS, 811.111/21911, #1715, April 1919 and 862.2/412, #1222, 21 April 1919, 2.
98. 862.2/412, 5.
99. Ibid., 6.
100. 811.111/22087, #1815, 19 April 1919.
101. 862.2/412, 7.
102. MI5, Reilly, S.R.C. memo, undated.
103. New York Supreme Court, New York County, #15332, 1919, Upton Dale Thomas v. Remington Arms and Ammunition, Exhibit A.
104. MID 10110-1194/331, Synopsis of Martens Case, 10.
105. 10110-1194/64, "L.C.A.K. Martens," 14 May 1919.
106. *New York American* (NYA) (11 Oct. 1925), Sect. II, 1.
107. MID, 10110-921/128, Memorandum for Col. Dunn, 20 Dec. 1918.
108. Norman Hapgood, "The Inside Story of Henry Ford's Jew-Mania," Part I, *Hearst's International* (June 1922), 14–15.
109. Ibid., Part IV, (Sept. 1922), 134.
110. *Cyclopedia of American Biography* (CAB), vol. 40, 314–315. Landfield's wife was Princess Liubov Lobanov-Rostovskii.
111. For example, *NYT* (9 May 1919), 16:7.
112. PRO, FO 371/4019, CXC 416, Reilly for Bagge, 10 May 1919. A copy of this report also found its way into ADM 137/3038.
113. FO 371/4022, Reilly to Bagge, 15 May 1919.
114. MID 10110-920/139, Report #26, 23 Jan. 1919.
115. See *NYT* (3–4 June 1919).

Chapter Eleven
On His Majesty's Secret Service

Reilly's transatlantic passage gave him opportunity to mull over the Russian situation and his own. The iron law of the System was to always keep the biggest bet on the strongest man. So far as Russia was concerned, for the moment the Whites appeared to have a slight edge. In March, Kolchak's Siberian legions had rolled across the Urals almost to the Volga before the tide broke and the Reds advanced again. In the south, however, Denikin's Volunteers and Cossacks were making impressive gains, and to the north Gen. Yudenich was readying another White Army in Estonia for a lunge at Petrograd. Then there were wild cards like the newly-independent Poles and Finns; could they be induced to join the anti-Bolshevik crusade?

Sidney still was certain of one thing: whether under Bolsheviks or the Whites, devastated, resource-rich Russia would be inevitably opened up to foreign investment. Someone with a foot in all camps and access to the right people and information could manipulate the resulting competition for immense profit. Reilly was determined that he would be that man. Juggling the conflicting interests of the British and Americans, Batolin and Jaroszynski, plus the innumerable factions and sub-factions of White Russians—and the Bolsheviks too—would be no easy task. For the time being, it also suited his purposes to back British interests over any others. However, that, too, was subject to change.

The Ace-of-Spies walked down the gangplank at Liverpool on 25 May. His next stop was London where he further briefed Cumming on his recent travels. He probably also took time to see Sir Basil Thomson, now Director of Home Office Intelligence, a newly-created body designed to deal with "labour unrest, revolutionary matters, aliens and counter-espionage."[1] This outfit was the brainchild of Thomson and his close friend, retiring Naval Intelligence Chief Admiral "Blinker" Hall. Both were virtually obsessed with the Red Menace and were ready to combat it any way they could. Thomson and Hall also were the founding fathers of the National Propaganda Committee, a nominally private body of right-wing politicos and industrialists dedicated to the struggle against socialism in all its forms. NPC would become the Economic League, a body of which we will meet again in later chapters.

In an immediate sense, the news Reilly brought from New York, especially that gleaned from Brasol and friends, may have stimulated Thomson and his associates to dispatch a follow-up agent to American shores, Lt. Col. Ralph Isham. He was an American-born officer in charge of "Anti-Bolshevik Propaganda and General Unrest in the British Army." Nominally on leave, Isham arrived in New York in late July and subsequently returned with information on Red intrigues gathered straight from MID files in Washington. More to the point, he seems to have given special importance to reports made by Brasol and Walevitch, the latter described by Isham as a "U.S. Secret Service Agent in whom they placed greatest confidence." [2] To no surprise, the names of Jacob Schiff, the Warburgs and other Jews figured prominently as sources of Bolshevik financial support. Isham's inquiry also turned up the name of Prudential Pictures Corp. that allegedly had been turned into a vehicle for the recruitment of a "Semitic Russian Army." That firm, recall, was one that Reilly may have had some connection with during the war.

Sidney pushed on to Paris where he rendezvoused with Wiseman. Wilson had departed the Peace Conference and Sir William's useful work with the American delegation was at an end. Amid mounting inter-Allied tensions, he had been mostly successful in maintaining harmony between British and American policies, but he was none too confident about the future. The looming question was which of these great powers "is going to be greater, politically and commercially?" [3] Nor was this a purely abstract question so far as he was concerned. Wiseman was planning to return to New York to take up private life as broker for none other than Jacob Schiff's Kuhn & Loeb. Of course, that by no means meant he was abandoning London's cause or the fold of British intelligence. Like Reilly, he was a strong proponent of the Jaroszynski scheme and saw an Anglo-American joint venture as the ideal solution to many problems. With a little luck, he could get Schiff to throw his considerable weight behind the syndicate and act as counterweight to the Morganites.

By June, Sidney was back in London where he ensconced himself in a luxurious suite in the Ritz Hotel overlooking Piccadilly. He was flush with cash retrieved from his Manhattan accounts and indulged in a spending spree to expand his collection of books and *objets d'art*. Along with Hill and Boyce, he was a regular at gatherings of former intelligence agents in Russia hosted by Stephen Alley at the posh Café Royal on Regent Street. Through Alley, Sidney made friends with William Field-Robinson, an SIS man assigned to Paris who would become another of his intimate collaborators in more than the King's business. The group dubbed itself the "Bolo Liquidation Club," but the informal atmosphere disguised a more serious purpose. As the name suggests, the members were self-proclaimed die-hard opponents of Bolshevism, and the get-togethers provided a perfect opportunity to exchange views and information and, perhaps, discuss strategies not necessarily in keeping with official policy. There was obvious relevance to Thomson's concerns, and Basil was a frequent guest if not a full-fledged member. But the "Bolo Liquidation Club" was more than it seemed in other respects, for sitting around the jolly table was at least one Soviet agent.

On the romantic front, Nadine remained somewhere in the background, but Reilly had found new interests. Alongside assorted courtesans and temporary diversions, two women achieved a somewhat more lasting significance. The first was an eighteen-year-old art student, Caryll Houselander, who replaced Tremaine and an outlet for the forty-five-year-old Ace-of-Spies' Pygmalion (or Svengali) impulses. A shy, gangly redhead fresh from a convent school, the aspiring artist Houselander was in the throes of a Bohemian interlude that would end in devotion to Catholic mysticism a few years hence.[4] A vision provoked by reading of the death of the Tsar kindled her interest in things Russian. Through émigré friends she met Sidney. The result, as she later described it, was "as dry grass is swept by a flame."[5] Perhaps she saw him as one of the "unlikely souls" to which she felt drawn her life through, or, possibly, he was a substitute for the father who had abandoned her as a child. In any event, she had no inhibition about embarking on an affair with a dark, mysterious man more than twice her age. Sidney evidenced a great interest in her artwork and acquired several pieces. Some of Caryll's friends were none too keen on her paramour—one called him "brusque" and "swarthy"—and were concerned by her emotional dependence on him.[6] For Reilly, however, Houselander seems to have remained a purely occasional diversion.

The other *femme* was a very different sort, a professional dancer and married woman. She was Eleanor Toye, daughter of the famed Italian stage star, Eleanora Duse. Her estranged spouse, Francis Toye, served in Naval Intelligence during the War and probably maintained some link to that realm. Interestingly, her brother-in-law, Edward Toye, was a close friend of Lockhart's. Eleanor allegedly had her own connection to MI5.[7] All of this suggests that there may have been more to her romance with Reilly than sex. On-again, off-again over the next few years she would serve as his personal secretary and semi-regular bedmate. As with Houselander, the relationship never developed beyond that, perhaps to her chagrin. Toye later disparaged Reilly's sexual technique, describing him as "the kind of man who would make love while reading the *Financial Times* on the pillow."[8] Perhaps it only meant that the paper held his interest better than she did. Toye allegedly expressed the more intriguing opinion that Sidney was bisexual, a view with which Hill supposedly concurred.[9] While there is no visible evidence to substantiate such a charge, it would not have been out of character. Given that Reilly assumed so many roles in his career, taking or feigning an interest in homosexual activity might have been very useful in certain circumstances. The watchword of the System, remember, was flexibility.

What of Margaret? Mollified by the financial arrangements made after his return from Odessa, she had retreated to Brussels plying the trade of governess. Like the proverbial bad penny, however, she was bound to pop up. As for Nadine, she seems to have remained in New York through 1919 but, as we will see further on, joined Reilly in London and Paris early the following year.

Reilly's new status was special consultant on Russian affairs to SIS, a role that increased his access and influence in certain high quarters. One of his main tasks was the vetting of Russian émigrés in London and Paris with an eye to ferreting out Red agents.[10] Besides reporting to Cumming, such work tied in closely with Basil Thomson's efforts. In July, Sidney, along with Boyce and Rex Leeper, reviewed a proposal to set up a "Central Russian Propaganda Committee" in London that would handle the production and dissemination of anti-Bolshevik propaganda.[11] As proposed, the Committee members were to be Thomson, Leeper, Ariadna Tyrkova-Williams (mother of Arkadii Borman), and old Reilly chums Burtsev and Boris Suvorin. Also included was another journalist with ties to the Suvorin press and the Okhrana, Mikhail Rumanov. Reilly reviewed the proposal on Thomson's behalf but gave it a "lukewarm" recommendation.

The reason was that the Committee competed with a like proposal Reilly was cooking up. This took the form of a "Socialist Information Bureau" that would seek to rally leftist opinion, Russian and non-Russian, to the anti-Bolshevik cause. In addition to Savinkov, the central figures in this effort were to be Burtsev and ex-Bolshevik Grigorii Aleksinskii. During August and September, Reilly provided Thomson with favorable reports on both men, reports that also found their way into Churchill's hands.[12] Sidney argued that Burtsev had "access to most exclusive information" that derived, in part, from "the Russian Governmental Secret Service," i.e. the Okhrana. He also praised Burtsev's "political tolerance, [and] undoubted patriotism and honesty." The clear implication of the reports was that if Britain did not step in to assist these men, the French or even the Americans would seize the advantage. Even so, he cautioned, it was absolutely essential that "every trace of the source from which these pamphlets are being financed . . . would necessarily have to be disguised." [13]

Another radical émigré in whom Reilly took a personal interest was Petr Rutenberg. His acquaintance with Rutenberg went back to the prewar period and most recently they had encountered each other in New York, Petrograd and Odessa. When Rutenberg had trouble entering Britain in September, Reilly personally intervened to remedy the matter. In a long memo to Thomson and SIS, he blasted recent reports from Contantinople that, among other things, besmirched Rutenberg's reputation by linking him to a clique of Jewish speculators in Odessa. [14] Interestingly, he noted that one of these reports probably emanated from Vladimir Orlov, a man "for whom I have the highest respect," and attributed Orlov's antagonism to a personal grudge. From his own experience in Odessa, Sidney attested Rutenberg's bona fides. His effort was successful and Reilly was able to report to Churchill's secretary Arch Sinclair that Rutenberg's visa had been arranged and the "obnoxious remark on his passport" expunged.

Sidney's assistance to Thomson may have included acting as liaison to Arthur Maundy Gregory. [15] An actor and theatrical manager, Thomson tapped Gregory before the war as a general snitch and purveyor of information on suspected foreign spies. By 1919, Sir Basil had enlisted Gregory to keep an eye on radical Labour MP Victor Grayson, suspected of contact with Soviet agents and the IRA. Much as Manasevich-Manuilov, Gregory was greedy and corrupt and ran a lucrative sideline in blackmail. Such knowledge made him a very useful man to Thomson and others. That Reilly knew Gregory seems quite possible, but whether, as alleged, he actually recruited him for SIS or the like seems doubtful.

Another alleged example of Reilly's services was his approach to Trebitsch-Lincoln following that worthy's release from British custody in the summer of 1919. Lincoln, it may be recalled, had earned London's enmity through his highly publicized anti-British antics in wartime New York. He now faced imminent deportation to his native Hungary, a land wracked by defeat, Bolshevism and civil war. Years later, in Shanghai, Lincoln recollected that soon after his release, Reilly brought him an offer from unnamed persons in the British Government. [16] These persons, Reilly explained, were concerned about the attitudes and plans of right-wing forces in Germany, especially efforts to overthrow the fledgling Weimar regime and repudiate the Versailles Treaty. Or, out of spite and desperation might they seek common cause with the Soviets? The gist of the proposal was that instead of going to Hungary, Lincoln would go to the Netherlands. There, he would utilize his German contacts to infiltrate rightist circles. That, in any case, is precisely what he did.

Reilly also served as a discreet contact man for certain Russians seeking an audience in London. On 4 June, Sidney arranged a meeting between Guchkov and Churchill with the apparent aim of securing British backing for Guchkov's band of liberal exiles. Soon after, the head of Guchkov's "intelligence section," Nikolai Alekseev, met Reilly through Winston's secretary, Archibald Sinclair. The latter lauded Reilly to his chief as the "keenest and ablest of all the anti-Bolos . . . in London." [17] At the Ace-of-Spies' opulent quarters at the Ritz, Alekseev realized that he had encountered this mysterious figure before during their recent, mutual travels in the Russian south. There was a dawn of recognition in Sidney's dark eyes as well. The ice broken, he launched into one of his broad discourses on Russia and its predicament. Alekseev was impressed, but he also was curious to know where Reilly got his information, his influence and his very evident wealth. He put these questions to Guchkov who confided that Reilly was a "professional conspirator" with an excellent understanding of Russian affairs and very methodical in his undertakings. Exactly what those encompassed was always a matter of some doubt, and Guchkov offered that the subject's current "passion" for anti-Bolshevism undoubtedly masked the ulterior motives he always had. Moreover, Reilly was adventurous by nature, perhaps to a fault, and obsessed with Napoleon and money.[18]

Reilly, in turn, tapped Guchkov for information. In September, Sidney passed to Sinclair and Thomson reports of a 100,000-strong Russo-German mercenary army gathering in the Baltic for a projected march on Petrograd and Moscow.[19] The story was basically true, although both the size and strategic ambitions of the force were much exaggerated. It fit Reilly's purpose by further sowing alarm and uncertainty in the quest of mobilizing British support behind his schemes.

Another Russian to whom Sidney lent a helping hand was A.N. Krupenskii, a former Tsarist emissary to Japan. Reilly provided him with directions to the Admiralty's Naval Intelligence offices and personal introduction to Commanders Ernest Boyce and George Le Page, the latter ill-fated Cromie's assistant in Petrograd. They were keen to see the collection of materials on Russian naval assets around the globe that Krupenskii had acquired and was anxious to barter.

Sidney's most important Russian contact remained Boris Savinkov. He used Savinkov to further gain Churchill's confidence by touting him as the future strongman of Russia. Samuel Hoare (Lord Templewood), head of British intelligence operation in Russia c. 1916–17, also regarded Boris as the most versatile and capable of the Paris-based Russians. He also knew him as an inveterate schemer and there was almost "no plot of which he was not the central figure." [20] Lloyd George, however, thought Savinkov a "seductive nihilist" and could never fathom just why he objected to the Bolsheviks.[21] The main question is what Reilly saw in him. Claims by Hill and others that Sidney placed an almost religious faith in Savinkov are unfounded. While he talked up Boris to already sympathetic ears, in other circumstances he disparaged Savinkov's abilities as a political leader. In a later "assessment" prepared for SIS, Reilly noted Boris' courage and persistence (or obstinacy) but pointed out a crippling lack of organizational skills and practical knowledge coupled with political vision that seldom rose above the level of terrorist conspiracy.[22] He confided to émigré poet and diarist Zinaida Hippius that Savinkov was no *homme d'etat*. Hippius, in turn, suspected that Reilly used Savinkov as a front behind which he pulled all the strings.[23] It was an astute judgment. Savinkov's fundamental value to Reilly lay in his man-of-action persona and his lack of any political or moral scruples. Those were things our man could put to good use.

In June, the Ace-of-Spies' lobbying prompted Churchill to order his personal "political spy" in Paris, Col. Edward Louis Spears, "to get in touch with the Savinkoff group and let me know more about them." [24] Over the next few months, Boris' visits to London usually entailed a call on Winston in Reilly's watchful company. This mutual admiration society had its limits, however. Savinkov later recalled his shock and annoyance when Churchill displayed a map of south Russia showing the position of Denikin's forces laid out in colored pins and proudly declared "here is my army!" [25] It was as if Russia was another Africa or India to be carved up as Britain willed. Boris also suspected that behind British interest in Russian matters he detected the faint but unmistakable odor of petroleum. At the time, the terrorist put his affront and suspicions aside and nodded approvingly.

Sir Edward Spears' recalled that he met Reilly "through Savinkov." As he described it some forty years later, he never took a real liking to the Ace-of-Spies whom he saw as a "clever but not very pleasant individual, speaking perfect English but with an awful accent." [26] Spears claimed he "never looked upon [Reilly] as a spy," though he recalled that Sidney told him he had been "accepted as member of the German Staff during the war." [27] In light of subsequent differences, Spears preferred to forget or downplay their relationship, for there is ample evidence that the two forged a close and curious alliance for at least the next few years. An Englishman raised in France, the tall, debonair, Spears served as British liaison to the French High Command during the war.[28] However, his evident sympathy for things Gallic raised doubts in the post-war environment and this, despite Churchill's backing, denied him the posts he really wanted.

There may have been other issues at work. Spears had only recently changed his name from the original Spiers because of its distinctly German flavor. Behind this also lay the not terribly *secret* secret that the Spiers line was of Jewish origin.[29] Whether this element of common ancestry had any bearing on the relationship between Spears and Reilly is impossible to say, but we may be confident that if Sidney could find any way to exploit it to his advantage, he did. The more obvious key to their relationship was that Spears, frustrated in his diplomatic ambitions, turned to commerce. Reilly, with his wide array of contacts, seemed an ideal partner. Sidney inevitably drew Spears into the murky realm of émigré finance. Their mutual contact was Otto Ottonovich Brunstrom, a Russo-Finn with past and current ties to Putilov (the de facto chief of the exiled businessmen and financiers in Paris) and Zhivotovskii and, naturally enough, a veteran associate of Reilly.[30]

Throughout the summer and fall, Reilly shuttled between London and Paris, sometimes at the behest of Cumming, at other times on his own business, though we may guess that he drew no great distinction between the two. For instance, on 5 September, a note from SIS Maj. A.J. Hargreaves indicated that Reilly was heading to Paris on a "special mission" for "C." He ordered Sidney to Paris again on 10 October on a "special mission for WO/MI1c" with the stipulation that he return to London within the week.[31]

While SIS memos are mum on the exact purpose of all this coming and going, much of it related to the evolving Jaroszynski scheme. To succeed, the scheme needed political backing, but most of all money. Picton Bagge was still a leading advocate, as was Leeper and, as Churchill's stand-in, Arch Sinclair. As Reilly sketched it, the scheme called for two huge, parallel syndicates. The first, "K. Jaroszynski Ltd.," would control his personal assets including six banks, twenty-two sugar mills, assorted enterprises and large tracts of land. The other, "The Russo-British Trust, Ltd.," would be a wholly English concern serving as "finance vehicle" to buy up concessions and other assets for the Jaroszynski outfit.[32] The whole point, as Bagge explained to Sinclair, was to ensure Britain a "leading position" in the future Russian economy. The plan encountered much skepticism and obstruction, especially in the Foreign Office. Feeling he had not received a "sympathetic reception in England," Jaroszynski threatened to go elsewhere, and there was no doubt that "elsewhere" was New York.[33] Reilly, whom Sinclair described as Jaroszynski's "right-hand man," persuaded him to hang on.[34] Sir Archibald reported to Churchill that Sidney, at Wiseman's behest, had been at Jaroszynski's side during talks with Lord Reading and other of His Majesty's officials.[35]

Reilly also kept in close touch with Wiseman in New York. On 26 July, he wired, using SIS code, that "the Russian scheme is proceeding slowly but favorably" and that British officialdom would take "definite action" soon.[36] By mid-August, he reported that the plan had received a green light from the Government, including Curzon, and had the "strong approval" of Churchill.[37] This message passed through Thwaites' hands as well. Sidney anticipated the rapid formation of a "British Financial Group" that would include the Baring, Hambro and Midland banks along with capitalist bigwigs like Lord Northumberland. Once the syndicate was formed, he added, Wiseman would have a place on the executive board which seemed the best way to bring in the Americans such as Kuhn & Loeb. In the meantime, Sidney cautioned Sir William to keep an especially close eye on moves of American bankers and Batolin. In early September, he cabled Weinstein and instructed him to keep Wiseman supplied with all information regarding Batolin and other relevant matters.[38] He simultaneously urged Sir William to put complete trust in Weinstein. His concern was that Morgan or others would use Batolin as a go-between to make a deal with the Soviets.

The New York grapevine paid important dividends. On 8 October, Sidney reported to Bagge that Batolin had recently formed a company in America dubbed the Peoples Industrial Trading Co.[39] The firm had a million dollars behind it courtesy of the Armour Co. and National City Bank. More important to Reilly, perhaps, its legal advisor was Henry Kuntz, the man he had crossed paths and swords with a few years before. Kuntz and his associates were already preparing a shipment of machinery and autos to Russia. At the same time, the American-Russian Industrial Syndicate had appeared, backed by the Guggenheim Bros., W. Averall Harriman and Sinclair Oil, among others. These were "some of the biggest interests in the United States," Reilly warned, and "the information is so instructive that I think I can dispense with all comment." The Yankees were on the march, and the Italians and Germans, too, for that matter, and unless London got off the dead point there would be nothing left.

During September, Reilly went to Paris to hammer out a agreement with Putilov and other émigrés on the formation of a special council to manage the planned consortium of Russian banks. As Sinclair reported it to Churchill, Sidney was devoting his main energy to the project and "he might be described as the moving spirit behind these somewhat sluggish Russians."[40] Reilly's "unrivaled flair for Russian politics," Sinclair added, enabled him to rally Savinkov, Aleksinskii and Rutenberg behind the scheme, thus giving it an important political dimension. What ultimately emerged was the Russian Financial Executive Committee with offices in London and Paris. At its head, naturally enough, sat Jaroszynski, but the real achievement was to bring him together with Putilov (Russo-Asiatic Bank), Boris Kamenka (Azov-Don Bank), and the Nobel Brothers (oil and Volga-Kama Bank). Jointly, this cabal truly did control Russia's economy— on paper.[41]

At the same time, Putilov, Jaroszynski and friends joined forces in the so-called *Société Commerciale, Industrielle et Financiere pour la Russie*, better known by its Russian acronym, *Torgprom*. In early October, Reilly reported to Bagge about this development and warned that behind it was a powerful consortium of French banks and even the French Government itself.[42] The Parisians had "proved very much more receptive and enterprising than our friends in the City" and had offered the Russians a large amount of cash and credits. The clear implication was that London would lose out entirely unless it presented a better deal. That may have been true, but, as with his dire warnings about the Americans, Sidney was playing the System.

As ever, a vital consideration in all this wheeling and dealing was oil. One of Reilly's key contacts in that sphere was A. Baldwin Raper, a thirty-year-old ex-RAF officer and world traveler and new Tory MP. Raper visited Russia before the war and had an avid interest in aviation, factors that probably place him among Sidney's prewar acquaintances. During the war, Raper served on the Russian Aviation Mission and, most importantly, on a "special mission" to Finland in April 1918. Reilly praised Raper as a loyal friend and anti-Bolshevik and an indispensable link to like-minded men in Parliament.[43] But Raper also had close ties to Royal Dutch Shell. Along with that firm's #2 man Robert Cohen, Raper would take a seat on its new subsidiary, Shell-Mex Petroleum.

Though Dutch in origin, Royal Dutch and its hard-driving boss, Sir Henri Deterding, were practically British concerns by this time. In the world battle for oil, RDS was the traditional nemesis of Standard and of newcomers like Sinclair. Deterding was every inch as ambitious and ruthless as his rivals.[44] Cohen, the scion of a prominent Anglo-Jewish family, was cut from the same cloth. He was, for instance, suspected of delivering his original employer, Shell Transport and Trading Co., into Deterding's hands back in

1906. Cohen probably made Reilly's acquaintance in wartime New York where he represented RDS in oil purchases and worked with Wiseman.[45] Deterding saw the Jaroszynski scheme as means to gain a dominant or even exclusive position for RDS. In the fall of 1919, Cohen began negotiations for the export of crude oil from the north Caucasus fields then under White control. Perhaps Reilly's earlier inquiries had some influence on this. In any case, as the "moving spirit" behind Jaroszynski and the Nobels, Sidney made sure he had his finger firmly planted in the black morass.

Another man with a strong interest in oil and Russia was Basil Zaharoff. The venerable "mystery man of Europe" had sunk much of his fortune into the Greek effort to wrest control of Constantinople and Anatolia from the defeated Turks. Zaharoff's dreams of a new Greek Empire were part of larger ambitions for the whole of the Near East, plans in which petroleum played a critical role. Among his many postwar ventures and acquisitions was the *Société Générale des Huiles de Petrole* (General Petroleum Society). He also held a sizable share of Anglo-Persian stock. Thus, the eventual disposition of the huge Russian oil fields was of interest to Zaharoff too.

The fate of the Jaroszynski scheme rested on the military success of the Whites. By the beginning of October Denikin's Volunteers took Orel, barely 200 miles from Moscow. In the same period, Kolchak's Siberian forces rallied and pushed the Red Army back while Yudenich's troops battled their way to the outskirts of Petrograd. For a brief moment, the Bolsheviks again appeared to be on the edge of complete ruin, but the White advances were checked and thrown back. Retreat turned into rout, and at the dawn of 1920, the Reds advanced victoriously on every front. In the south, each day brought them nearer to the coveted oil fields.

In response to the changing situation, at the beginning of December, Reilly drafted a lengthy memo on "The Russian Problem" for SIS and the FO.[46] He began by sounding a grim, even alarmist, note. The Russian Problem, he warned, was "assuming an ever more complicated and . . . more hopeless character." It constituted nothing less that the "greatest threat to the world's political, social and economic stability" which made "restoration of normal life in Russia . . . the world's most urgent task." The measures used so far to combat the Bolshevik menace had proved inadequate, most notably the White generals. At the same time, Sidney evidenced no spirit of reconciliation with the Leninites. Bolshevism represented "the worst form of autocratic tyranny known to History, exercised by a band of unscrupulous international adventurers." There could be no deal with this ilk despite Moscow's constant, and increasing, calls for negotiations with the Allies and the Border States. Such arrangements, he cautioned, would be a repeat of the Brest-Litovsk pact, affording "the Bolsheviks a breathing spell in which to gather strength for a second propagandistic attack on Europe."

So what was to be done? No solution to Russia's distress could be found so long as the Reds retained power. Thus, a new military alliance had to be forged among the remaining anti-Bolshevik Russians and former subject peoples of the Tsarist Empire such as the Poles, Finns and Latvians. These groups opposed Bolshevism but feared "still more the uncertainty of a possibly reactionary Russia bent in conquest." The Allies had to step in forcefully. In their weakened state, the Whites could be pressured into making the needed concessions. The same held true for the nationalist regimes that would have to abandon many of their more extreme political and territorial aspirations. The ultimate result would be an Allied, or simply British, sponsored "Inter-State Conference" that would forge a general pact (independence for Poland and Finland, "broad autonomy" for everyone else) and set up a common military command.

Even this, warned Reilly, would not be sufficient without the active assistance of Germany which exerted a "powerful but almost entirely clandestine influence . . . upon all phases of this problem." Through "an army of hundreds of thousands of conscious and unconscious agents" the "hidden hand of Germany" still intrigued to prop up the Soviet regime as a means to keep Russia weak and exploitable at some future date. Abetting this effort was "that occult octopus known as 'International Capital', whose tentacles reach . . . to New York, Berlin, London or Paris." The only way to get these forces on the side of the anti-Bolshevik alliance was to make it profitable. Thus, the only solution was an "economic understanding as regards Russia" between London and Berlin or, possibly, London, Berlin and Paris. German banks, he stressed, still controlled large amounts of Russian bank stocks. If these were combined with those already held by the Jaroszynski syndicate, almost complete control of the Russian economy would be assured. To no surprise, Sidney proposed that Jaroszynski himself be placed at the head of this joint enterprise. Such a powerful combine, he continued, would undoubtedly attract the interest and support of American capital and the important "sympathies . . . of Jewish financial circles" (i.e., Kuhn & Loeb).

Despite the anti-Bolshevik tone of Reilly's memo, remember that the System kept all options open. On 7 December, just two days after completing the memo, Sidney met at his Ritz suite with James O'Grady, a trade union official and Labour MP who had just returned from Copenhagen.

There, as part of a Parliamentary delegation, he had negotiated with Soviet representatives for the repatriation of British civilians and POWs held in Red Russia. Lurking about the Soviet delegation were two of Reilly's old associates, Leonid Krasin and Yakov Peters. Krasin's primary focus remained on the economy, and with the military struggle now turning in the Reds' favor, he was giving more thought to normalized relations, including the resumption of foreign trade. Behind the scenes, Krasin let it be known that he was willing to do business, and the word was carried back to London. Peters, who narrowly avoided death in an "anarchist" bombing in September was on hand to look after the Cheka's interests. His boss Dzerzhinskii also had a strong interest in economic matters and, of course, in any opportunity to extend Soviet intelligence operations abroad. Reilly would have supposed no less.

In an unlikely coincidence, two more days after his chat with O'Grady, Sidney received fresh orders from Hargreaves to proceed to Paris on more "special duty" for the War Office and to return as soon as it was completed.[47] At almost the same time, another man departed London bound for Helsinki. This was Paul Dukes, who a year earlier had taken over the British intelligence apparatus in Petrograd. For eight months, he guided a conspiratorial effort "on a very large scale." This included the subversion of Red forces in Petrograd and at the front, counterfeiting, the murder of Lenin, Trotsky and other Bolsheviks, and even incorporated earlier plans to blow up the railway bridges linking Petrograd to the rest of the country.[48] In the end, though, his operation was betrayed. After a failed attempt to extricate Dukes by sea, he slipped across the Latvian border at the end of August. When he landed in London in mid-September, Reilly met him at the station and hustled him off to an interview with Churchill.

Over the next few weeks, Dukes, often with Sidney at hand, met with Curzon, Leeper and others. Of particular note was a meeting with the Ace-of-Spies and Nathan in the latter's rooms at the Albany on 4 November. Nathan had been in New York where as head of the SIS station he worked with Basil Thomson to detect and undermine the trans-Atlantic Bolshevik nexus. He now wanted to expand that battle in Europe. Several days later, Dukes recorded another meeting at the Albany with "C3" or "C&," possibly indicating the presence of Cumming. The upshot was that on 18 December, Dukes reached Helsinki where he remained for two days before hopping a steamer straight back to England. The implication is that he went to retrieve something—or someone—that had come out of Russia.

Reilly returned to the Ritz and on the 15th he wrote Savinkov to say that he shortly expected some information valuable to them both. By

Christmas, he was once more, on SIS orders, at the Mirabeau in Paris. On the 27th, he was in Prague, where he sent a report via the British Legation to Maj. Desmond Morton, one of Cumming's chief assistants and the head of SIS's "Production" section that handled agent control and the acquisition of raw information. Morton had become one of Sidney's strong supporters in the agency. On 4 January, he thanked him for the data and sent out "a request for information of something of the same nature," and which would be "extremely useful if we could get the full facts."[49]

What was it that Morton found so interesting? As noted above, having secured the victory in Russia, Lenin and his comrades were gearing up a new offensive to gain recognition and aid from the West. To Nathan and Reilly this presented a threat and an opportunity. Unlike Jaroszynski and his fellow émigrés, who mostly held only paper ownership, Lenin had physical possession of those riches. That gave Moscow tremendous leverage to work its own version of the System by playing Western interests against each other. As usual, the cash-rich Yankees would be the main target of Bolshevik blandishments with the renewed threat of Britain being left out in the cold. There were ominous signs that Soviet efforts in that direction were on the increase. In September, Michael Gruzenberg, AKA Mikhail Borodin, a Russian-born U.S. citizen, returned to America on a mission for Moscow. He earlier had attempted to smuggle diamonds and other valuables into the U.S. for the benefit of Martens and indigenous Communist activities.

Reilly and Nathan huddled at the Albany to come up with a new strategy. The plan they came up with was to take the initiative by making an overture to the Soviets and drawing them into a special arrangement with England. The plan involved risks and would face stiff opposition, but where better to keep an eye on the pesky Reds than in one's own backyard? In any case, the dangers of having a Bolshevik mission in town would be more than offset both by the commercial advantages and the opportunity to infiltrate and subvert it. Through his recent travels, Reilly had gotten word that Krasin and others in Moscow were amenable to the idea as well.

For the time being, it was essential to keep Western interests focused in the same direction. On 10 January, Reilly was back in Paris putting himself "*au fait*" of the latest developments in the Russian situation. In a letter to Leeper, he opined "barring a miracle, disaster is as good as complete."[50] The Whites were well and truly finished, but this did not mean the situation was hopeless, nor had he abandoned the idea of a big Russian syndicate. He again insisted that "as matters stand today," the Russian problem could not be solved without the active participation of the Germans. As further incentive for Berlin's cooperation, he advocated a five-year moratorium on reparations payments. Given that the French would object violently to such unilateral action by London, Sidney further suggested the use of a convenient, neutral go-between, his old Danish boss at the Russian East Asiatic Steamship Co., Hans Andersen. Andersen had excellent relations with the Germans and "vast interests" of his own in Russia. One must wonder, had Sidney returned to his traditional supporting role as a German agent? He was ready to make the overture to Andersen (perhaps he already had) and to personally take the case to Ronald Campbell and Philip Kerr (later Lord Lothian), the respective personal secretaries of Lord Curzon and Lloyd George. "For goodness sake," he pleaded, "let us get off the dead point."[51] At the Foreign Office, Reilly's proposal made it as far as Arthur Balfour who nixed it on the grounds that Andersen was "unacceptable," no doubt because of the Dane's long history as a German agent. Otherwise, Balfour thought the scheme, and its advocate, had possibilities.

There were other gambits to be played. Taking a different tack, Reilly told Leeper that the Poles were now the key to military containment of the Bolsheviks. Sidney had cultivated Polish representatives in Paris months earlier. The central figure was Capt. Karol Wedziagolski, an old revolutionary comrade of Savinkov's now attached to Warsaw's delegation in Paris. Most importantly, Wedziagolski was a confidant and personal emissary of Poland's military strongman, Josef Pilsudski. Wediagolski was a rarity among Poles, a Russophile who supported a united struggle against Bolshevism. A major obstacle to such an alliance had been the stubborn refusal of Kolchak, et al. to recognize Polish independence. As a result, the Polish Army had so far maintained a general neutrality in the Russian civil strife. The eclipse of the Whites, therefore, offered new opportunities. The Warsaw-raised and reciprocally Polonophile Savinkov seemed the ideal man to lead a Russo-Polish rapprochement.

Before arriving in Paris in August 1919, Wedziagolski wrote Savinkov proposing an alliance between resurgent Poland and Russian "democrats." Soon after, he found himself invited to a conclave at Savinkov's home. In addition to host Boris, Wedziagolski recalled three other men present: Spears, a British intelligence officer, "Broderick," (most likely Lt. Alan Brodrick of Spears' staff) and "that genius of the intelligence service, the mysterious Captain Sidney Reilly." The Pole had heard much of Reilly and was fascinated by him in the flesh. "He knew scads of people," Wedziagolski recounted, "all-knowing, interested in everyone, and a man with a splendid command of the Russian language."[52] Wedziagolski came away with the feeling that London, or certain influential parties there, was anxious to encourage a Russo-Polish pact. Nevertheless, while Reilly and his associates "were interested in everything related to Russia and the Bolsheviks," he could never quite pin down where they stood. "From conversations with them," he remembered, "it was impossible to conclude that they were definitely anti-Bolshevik."[53]

Many of the Russians in Paris had reservations of their own, mostly about Savinkov. He had burned many bridges, and few figures of note were willing to join the Russian Political Committee he hoped to set up in Warsaw. One who did was the venerable "patriarch of Russian populism," Nikolai Chaikovskii. To secure his cooperation, Wedziagolski accompanied Savinkov on a visit to Chaikovskii in Paris towards the end of 1919. There once again were Spears, Brodrick and Reilly.

Wedziagolski soon returned to Warsaw and put Savinkov's offer before a receptive Pilsudski. Right after New Years, he wired Boris to come to the Polish capital at once for direct talks. Savinkov was anxious to go, but waited for Sidney to return from Prague. What Reilly was bringing was information on the reception of the large community of Czech-based émigrés to a Russo-Polish pact. Reilly reported that the mood was cautious, but not actively hostile. Savinkov and Chaikovskii set out for Warsaw on 16 January. The visit convinced Boris that Pilsudski was determined to fight the Bolsheviks as soon as circumstances permitted. Boris' vision hinged on the creation of a new "democratic" Russian army to fight alongside the Poles, thus denying Lenin the mantle of defender of Russian land and honor. An army, naturally, required money, and Savinkov looked to Sidney to secure the necessary funds from London.

By the forepart of 1920, so far as SIS was concerned, Reilly had given excellent value as a British agent. Still, his palpable rewards for this service were nil, especially in the realm of outward recognition. During 1919–20, both Dukes and Nathan received knighthoods, while our man remained a lowly 2nd Lt. with an MC. In early October 1919, Desmond Morton, appealed to his WO superior Col. Menzies to "consider forwarding the name of Lieut. Reilly for an honorary commission as Major." Reilly, advised Morton, "is now engaged on important work for the Foreign Office which necessitates his conferring with soldiers and civilians of high rank, and he finds his low, temporary rank a great hindrance."[54] Morton was sure the FO would back up the nomination and offered to secure "a written statement from them to that effect." Menzies, however, demurred noting that the subject was an RAF officer, "so how can I help?" He also warned that the WO was "adamant" in their refusal to give even temporary promotions lest they be held financially liable in the event of the officer's death.[55] Reilly, perhaps, did not seem a good risk.

Morton persevered, but it was apparent that the FO presented the main opposition to Sidney's promotion and to his continued association with His Majesty's Government. Not only Reilly was in trouble; Field-Robinson in Paris also was targeted for termination at least partly because of his association with him. In an early January letter to Reilly in Prague, Morton explained that Robinson was bound to lose his post, but "there are reasons for the change." In any event, he assured, "'C' is very just to everybody who works for him and if [Robinson] is a friend of yours, you may be quite certain he will not be let down." As for Reilly himself, Morton offered "you are quite safe, or ought to be now, after the numerous efforts that have been made . . . to apply the boot." If Sidney was pushed out, he added, "you will not be alone, as all our nefarious past will by that time have come to light." In such an event, "we better club together, buy an island in the West Indies and start a republic of our own. You," he ventured, "may be president if you give me the job of chancellor of the exchequer." [56]

What Morton did not mention and, perhaps, did not know, was that same day the FO gave a final thumbs-down to Reilly's promotion. Furthermore, in April 1920 he faced mandatory demobilization from the RAF. He seems to have taken all this in stride, but it must have rankled and weighed in his subsequent calculations. If Britain would not reward him for his services, there were others who might. In any case, it did not stop him in years to follow from dubbing himself "Captain" Reilly. Perhaps this was sheer defiance, but the oddest thing is that no one seems to have questioned it, including his many adversaries.

In the meantime, fresh intrigues were afoot. In Paris, Reilly watched over urgent negotiations between Royal Dutch's Deterding and rival Standard to buy up stock in the Nobel's Russian oil fields before they fell into Red hands. Neither company really wanted the worthless paper, but neither did they wish to see their rival take it all for themselves. At the close of January, Nathan departed quietly for Riga where he was to undertake sensitive negotiations with Soviet emissaries. The plan was to initiate talks about reopening Anglo-Russian trade, a move already "tacitly decided" by certain parties in London.[57] This was to be the first step in re-establishing a British mission in Russia, a mission he hoped to head. Plagued by worsening health, however, Nathan had to turn back to England. The deal made in Riga called for further talks in Copenhagen. The Soviet delegation, Reilly doubtless anticipated, would be headed by his old friend Krasin.

While Nathan conducted the talks in Riga, on 7 February Reilly drafted a parallel memo on the "Possibilities of Trade with Russia."[58] In essence, this was another permutation of the Jaroszynski scheme. The key element was the creation of a "Russian International Bank" to be financed by British as well as German, American, French and even Italian capital. Sidney, however, emphasized that initiative and control would remain "in British hands." In sharp contrast to his prior advice, he now offered that the Soviet Government could be convinced to go along with this plan and become an active partner in it. Moscow's part would be to deposit most of its remaining gold reserve the Bank's capital. This would then be used to issue special "trade currency" inside Russia. The Bank also would take responsibility for collecting Russia's huge foreign debt, another sticky point in normalizing relations. The material benefits and "positive influence" of this scheme, he argued, "would lead to a gradual extinction of the destructive features of the Soviet regime." So the Bolsheviks could be civilized after all. Reilly had shifted his wagers on the System's betting line.

While Nathan waited in London anticipating the next round of negotiations with the Bolsheviks, Sidney was off again to Paris. On 5 March, Maj. Hargreaves reported to "C" that Reilly and "wife #2" [Nadine] had appeared at the Adam Street offices the day before and demanded passports and passage money for the cross-Channel trip. This note proves that someone in SIS knew that our man had at least two wives. However, Hargreaves' concern was that he knew "nothing about the journey nor whether it is to be at our expense." Cumming was unavailable, and he was at first reluctant to approve it, but Morton stepped in to vouch that the trip was in regard to Reilly's planned meeting with a Russian named "Baratov."[59]

In fact, the man in question was Gen. Pavel *Bazarov*, who may be recalled as one of the officers Sidney met during his travels in south Russia. Ensconced in routine splendor at the Hotel Lotti, Sidney wrote Nathan on the 13th noting that he had seen Bazarov but had not yet "settled with him," suggesting some financial arrangement was involved. Bazarov was Denikin's intelligence man in the French capital. In that role, he worked closely with Vladimir Orlov who had entrusted Bazarov with a portfolio of captured Bolshevik decrees and "character sketches" of prominent Reds. Among them were dossiers on Krasin and others involved in the current negotiations, material Nathan wanted to see.

The material on Krasin painted the picture of a venal, ideological *poseur*, an Okhrana informer, and tool of German interests.[60] Everything suggested he could be cultivated to play a like role for British ones. Also noted was Krasin's friendship with the Norwegian Jonas Lied.[61] The latter continued to play an ambiguous role in relation to the Russians and British intelligence. In addition to Reilly and Nathan, Lied was on very chummy terms with Basil Thomson.[62] In February 1920, he returned to Red Russia with the avowed aim of resurrecting trade, perhaps as a substitute for Nathan. Returning to London in early May, he sought an audience with Lloyd George where he aggressively pitched the resumption of trade with Russia and the acceptance of Krasin as head of Soviet mission Krasin.[63] That was just what Sidney and Sir Robert were counting on.

In mid-March, events erupted in Germany that offered to change the situation radically. Right-wing *Freikorps* troops under the nominal leadership of ex-Kaiserian official Wolfgang Kapp seized control of Berlin, putting the Socialist-dominated Weimar government to flight. For several days, Germany's political fate hung in the balance. It all was of intense interest to Sidney who had continuously emphasized the German influence in Russian affairs. In fact, since January, he had been supplying Field-Robinson and the Paris SIS with a steady stream of information on the intrigues between various Russian factions and German reactionaries. Some of this may have derived from Trebitsch-Lincoln who had managed to insinuate himself into the very heart of the rightist conspiracy. Also worthy of note that staying at Berlin's Adlon Hotel, the *putschists'* headquarters, was Norman Thwaites. He later recalled keeping a very close eye on Lincoln's activities. We can again rest assured that Thwaites' presence in Berlin was no simple accident.[64] Others involved in the German situation were Spears, veteran SIS Russia-hand Malcolm Maclaren, Orlov and, of course, Savinkov.[65] Boris happened to be on "very friendly" terms with one of the key figures in this circle, Aleksei Aleksandrovich Oznobishin (M) and perfectly willing to betray this confidence to Reilly.[66] What made this Russo-German plotting interesting, and potentially dangerous, was the intention of certain Russian monarchists, most notably Gen. Vasilii Biskupskii, to raise an army for a joint attack on Poland with a militarist in Berlin or the Bolsheviks, or both.[67]

In a 14 March letter to Nathan, Sidney offered "for once, it is the expected that has happened."[68] The repercussion of the German counter-revolution on the Russian situation could be "enormous." If the Berlin rightists succeeded, "it means the rapid termination of the Bolshevist regime and a goodbye to all those beautiful conclusions of [Lloyd George] & Co." On the other hand, if the desperate Socialists joined forces with the German Communists ("and I don't see how they can avoid it"), then "Lenin, Trotsky *über alles*."

Sidney informed Robinson that he had tried to "get a pigeon" into a meeting of pro-German Russians in Paris, but owing to the short time available was unable to do so "without spoiling the whole game."[69] Instead, he proposed to Nathan to dispatch Savinkov to Germany as a confidential agent, and Boris was eager to go. The only rub was that

Savinkov's "financial position was very bad" and he would need some help from SIS coffers if he was to "do useful work." [70] Sidney suggested £100, but on the 18th, Cumming's paymaster approved £300. This is proof that in this instance, at least, Savinkov was a paid agent of British intelligence. Nathan subsequently explained this largesse as stemming from SIS' desire to "leave no stone unturned . . . to find out the inwards of what is going on in Berlin." [71] By 20 March, however, the Kapp venture collapsed, smothered by a wave of popular protest and general strike. Nor did the Communists grab the initiative. While the German situation remained highly volatile, Reilly put Boris' trip on hold. There was no word from him or Sidney about returning the money.

On 27 March, Reilly finally sent Nathan the Krasin and related dossiers along with assorted data complied by Savinkov's people in Paris. Sidney passed on word from his private sources that accompanying Krasin in the future Copenhagen talks would be one Julius (Yuli) Grossjean, a Bolshevik of French origin.[72] This was the same man that a subsequent Scotland Yard report described as an important Bolshevik agent and courier and possibly a Chekist.[73] Was he Peters' man, perhaps? Be that as it may, Sidney noted that Grossjean was the "intimate friend" of Capt. Feliks Volkhovskii who also happened to be one of Boris' "most trusted assistants." [74] Reilly even arranged that Volkhovskii should come to London once the Red mission arrived to "pump" his friend. The last comment is especially interesting because it implies that he took the imminent arrival of a Soviet mission in London as a *fait accompli*. Much of Sidney's inside dope on the Krasin mission probably derived from a British agent close to it, one he probably helped recruit. Known as "D 57" in SIS reports, this informant may have been Simon Liberman, a Menshevik *spets* with a pre-revolutionary specialty in the timber trade. Reilly later praised him as "particularly honest." [75] However, it is not impossible that D 57 was Krasin himself or his secretary, Yulii Figatner.

In February, Reilly told Savinkov that personal affairs were calling him overseas. In the above letter of the 27th, he informed Sir Robert that he could not postpone his departure further and offered apologies to the Chief. "I intend to be back here [Paris] within three weeks," he insisted, and noted "Robinson knows my address." However, he also gave "Robbie" the special privilege of opening and forwarding his mail, suggesting he really expected to be away longer than a few weeks. Indeed, he would be away more than two months.

Reilly's initial destination was America, but given the complications that had arisen on his last visit, it was a journey to be undertaken with some caution. For that and other reasons, he could not travel openly as Sidney Reilly. He most likely caught the SS *Carmania* from Liverpool at the end of March. Conveniently sailing on the same ship was Wiseman on his way back on some undisclosed errand for the British Government and, probably, SIS. Among Sir William's fellow passengers was a certain Vincent O'Kane, who roughly approximated Reilly's age and dimensions.[76] Debarking in New York on 7 April, O'Kane told U.S. Immigration that he was Irish and headed to Shanghai where he had a position with Standard Oil Co. His only substantive difference from Sidney was gray hair, but that was a simple enough disguise to throw off anyone looking for a man of Reilly's standard description.

Another interesting coincidence is that just three days after O'Kane and Wiseman landed, another SIS man, Humphrey Plowden, also arrived from Liverpool. Plowden's last visit to New York a year previous, it may be recalled, also coincided with Reilly's. What is doubly curious about the present case is that almost no sooner than he had set foot in Gotham, Plowden hopped a ship back to London and after a whirlwind visit there, again landed in New York on 28 April. Given his need to stay undercover, Sidney could not have risked communicating with "C" via cable or official channels. Plowden's perambulations, therefore, may have served as a means to convey information or material to or from Reilly.

Such security would not have been excessive. Washington and New York were still full of officials who thought our hero little less than the Devil incarnate. In March 1920, Reilly's name came up during U.S. Senate hearings regarding Martens and his Soviet Bureau. Martens endeavored to divert the issue from his subversive antics by bringing up the recent activities of Allied agents in Russia, specifically the "Lockhart Plot." Answering these charges on behalf of the State Department was DeWitt Poole who had raised the alarm about Sidney some months before. Asked about Reilly's role, Poole experienced a sudden lapse of memory and denied any knowledge of the British agent.[77] In fact, Poole remembered him very well and still bore him nothing but ill will.

The personal business Reilly had to attend to in New York was legal. Among others, his case against Walter Josephson and the AB-Economizer Co. was still dragging its way through the courts and needed to be wound up. Reilly had bigger game in his sights. During his last stateside visit he instigated a suit against Remington Union for unpaid Russian commissions. That case was settled out of court in November 1919 with a chagrined Remington shelling out a sizable sum to get him off their backs. Thus encouraged, Sidney resolved to go after Samuel Vauclain and the Eddystone

Corp. The wily Vauclain, it may be remembered, had cheated Reilly out of some $650,000 in commissions by bribing the Eddystone board, including its Russian representatives, to dissolve the firm without profit in early 1917. Vauclain then sold the business to the U.S. Government without financial encumbrances. However, he never actually got around to paying Mssrs. Morozov and Poliakov the promised bonuses. At the end of January 1920, they informed the Russian Financial Agent in New York, Sergei Uget, that they would sue for the money. This was Sidney's warning shot. On 3 February 1920, Upton Thomas filed suit for his boss demanding all of the unpaid commissions plus interest, thereby initiating a legal battle that would rage for almost five years.[78]

Vauclain and his Baldwin Locomotive associates had no intention of rolling over like Remington. Realizing that they could not contest the legitimacy of the contract with Reilly, they opted to portray him as a foreign crook, something not hard to do. The last thing Sidney wanted to do was expose himself to public examination in a Manhattan courtroom, and that meant avoiding subpoenas from Vauclain's lawyers. His counter-strategy was to keep the case hanging while his attorneys asserted he was out of the country and he fished around for other means to coerce Vauclain into settlement.

Weinstein was another man to look up. He had moved uptown to offices on Madison Avenue, but kept in close touch with other members of the old Reilly gang at 120 Broadway. In his role as Reilly's general factotum, Thomas maintained a presence at the Equitable and handled his investments and other interests. Sharing the office was Tikhon Agapaev, the ex-Russian naval officer and accused embezzler who also remained very close to Weinstein and was his "right hand man in every negotiation."[79] At the same time, Agapaev was linked to Boris Brasol through local White Russian organizations.

Brasol was another denizen of 120 Broadway. He was still close to Ford's people, but his blatant Jew-baiting had brought his work for MID to an end, formally at least. He now kept himself busy as a consultant to both the U.S. Congressional and New York State (Lusk Committee) hearings on radicalism and as an expert on Russian law to Wall Street firms. Among Brasol's patrons was Coudert Bros. law firm which was still legal agent for the "Russian Government," i.e. the pre-Soviet agencies and representatives. In his spare time, Brasol was chairman of the Unity Association of Russia, vice chair of the Russian National Association (both monarchist groups) and U.S. representative of the Paris-based Supreme Monarchist Council (VMS).[80] All this made him an excellent medium of influence and information.

Another man to land in Gotham was the wandering Sergius Riis. He had just returned from duty in the Black Sea ended abruptly by a Navy superior.[81] Just what the American Navy had against Riis they would never come out and say, but from this point forward they regarded him as a most suspicious and undesirable character. He still had friends elsewhere. In mid-April, the same day he landed in New York, Riis wrote State's Russian Division asking for assignment to any duties "required in Russia or Baltic States." [82] And so he received; in May he shipped out for Riga to take up the job of "assistant in charge of intelligence" at the U.S. Legation. There, Riis would handle Washington's key intelligence-gathering and listening post on Soviet Russia. He also would develop a close relationship with the local SIS station run by Meiklejohn and Boyce. Some of his American coworkers would find the arrangement just a little *too* close.

Another useful man to see in New York was Capt. A.W. James. Under the alias "Charles Fox," he ran the much-reduced "British Secret Service" operation in Gotham.[83] James/Fox carried on Nathan's surveillance of Irish and Indian nationalists and dug into Bolshevist doings. His chief agent was an American, Raymond Finch, formerly close to Thwaites and, more interesting, a co-worker of Brasol's on the Lusk Committee.[84] James also provided a secure means to communicate with Nathan back in London. For instance, the SIS file contains a 4 May note from Nathan to an earlier query from Sidney regarding one "Levinson-Levi." [85] Reilly's note is gone from the file but it requested letters of attestation for Levinson, with the aim of getting him into Britain. Basil Thomson, Nathan wrote, was willing to write one, but the Department of Overseas Trade "did not see their way" to do likewise. The subject of this correspondence must have been L.O. Levinson-*Levin*, another member of *Torgprom* who was, or very recently had been, in New York.

Two more contacts were promoter Franklin Helm who had been one of Sidney's associates in the wartime German nexus, and the "J.P. Morgan of the underworld," Arnold Rothstein. Rothstein's attention was focused on the advent of that "Great Experiment" in American social policy, Prohibition. The "Brain" saw the ban on the legal production and sale of alcohol as a potential gold mine of illicit profits. In the spring of 1920, he initiated operations on two fronts. First, he negotiated with British distillers for a steady supply of high-quality hooch.[86] Reilly was an ideal intermediary. Next, Rothstein looked to diversify his product line by establishing a pipeline of opium and other narcotics from the Far East to the U.S. East Coast. Here, too, Sidney's influence and broad connections could prove useful, perhaps invaluable. It was at this juncture, the forepart of 1920, that

Rothstein dispatched his lieutenant Jacob "Yasha" Katzenberg to Hong Kong and Shanghai to set up the operation.[87]

Helm was, as usual, hip-deep in promotions and schemes. He lobbied on behalf of his old employer, the German Government, to sway U.S. Congressional support towards a softer reparations policy.[88] But Helm also had keen interest in Oriental affairs. Later investigation by the State Department not only established his intimate link to Reilly, but also to more respectable members of the business world, most notably Woodrow Wilson's late Secretary of the Treasury, William G. McAdoo, and American railway expert, John F. Stevens. Reilly and McAdoo, recall, had been tangentially linked through the covert funding of Czech operations in Russian during 1918. McAdoo was now back in private practice at, where else, 120 Broadway. Stevens had worked at Brown Bros., Reilly's New York stockbrokers, but now held the top slot in the Inter-Allied Technical Board (IATB) in Siberia. That body oversaw the operation of the Trans-Siberian and Chinese Eastern Railways. When Stevens left for the East, Helm took over his slot at Brown Bros., and the two remained in contact.[89] Thus, through Helm, Sidney could pick up information about developments in the Far East, especially ones concerning the CER.

Reilly had been connected to the Chinese Eastern in one way or another since the turn of the century. The line was now of acute interest to him and others. Among these was Putilov and the *Torgprom*. The CER remained the only substantial asset in the hands of the Russo-Asiatic Bank. Putilov and friends sat up and took notice when, in February 1920, Morgan partner Thomas Lamont went to China as representative of a international financial consortium (American, British, French and Japanese) interested in advancing a large loan to the Chinese Government. The latter, a shaky junta of warlords led by General Wu Peifu, was in dire need of money. As in any loan, a key question was collateral, and among the few profitable assets Wu could put on the table was the Chinese Eastern Railway.

However the knotty question was who, exactly, "owned" the line? The original 1890s agreement between the Tsarist and Manchu regimes granted physical control of the railway and related concessions to Russia, but compensated the Chinese with shares of the bonds and stock. During the Russian Civil War, which still sputtered on in the Far East, control of the line was held by Kolchak's minions. As White power crumbled, Wu Peifu began to make noises about proclaiming Chinese sovereignty over the CER. During April and May 1920, the Bolsheviks chimed in by renouncing all "unequal" Sino-Russian treaties, including the CER agreement. In return, they asked that the line be transferred to Moscow's control and, naturally, that Beijing offer the Soviets formal recognition. From Reilly's standpoint, there was good reason to suspect that Lamont intended to gain control of the Chinese Eastern in order to leverage a deal with Moscow for a favored position in the Russian market. If successful, this would secure an invaluable "doorway" through which all manner of goods and capital could flow. That might render the Russo-British plan under discussion in Copenhagen a dead issue.

Reilly did not tarry long in Manhattan. As O'Kane or some other alias, he pushed on to San Francisco where he probably met two men, the dapper American William R. McGarry and the local Russian Consul, Yurii Romanovskii. McGarry was a businessman and writer with ties to the U.S. State Department and British interests. He claimed to have worked for British intelligence during the war, and as a narrator for British war films, he definitely had a connection to Wiseman's propaganda operation.[90] There were other threads linking him to Reilly. As ex-editor of *Pan-Pacific Magazine*, he knew Helm from prewar promoting on the West Coast and also Landfield. More recently, he had become a commercial and political agent for Kolchak's regime and thus came into contact with Brasol and Bakhmet'ev.[91] Also close to McGarry and Romanovskii was Mikhail Rumanov who had figured in the abortive Russian propaganda effort reviewed by Reilly some months earlier. Various rumors actually placed McGarry in Russia during the critical spring of 1918, while others put him in London or working for U.S. MID in Paris.[92]

In March 1920, McGarry and Romanovskii had initiated the preparation and publication of a strange book originally titled *Prisoners of Tobolsk*, subsequently changed to *Rescuing the Czar*. The author of record was "James P. Smythe," McGarry's alias, but the book purported to be the edited diaries of a Russian nobleman, Aleksei Syvorotka, and an Anglo-American officer, Charles James Fox. The latter, of course, bore a strong resemblance to "Charles Fox" in New York. The book told the fantastic story of the rescue not only of Tsar Nicholas, but also his entire family. They were spirited across the heart of Asia to Shanghai under the guiding hand of the redoubtable Fox. The story is almost certainly fiction, but the question is why it was produced and by whom. The real issue was not the fate of Nicholas and his family but of the large personal fortune and state assets to which they had title. These riches were now scattered around the world. The Bolsheviks held but a fraction; most rested in foreign banks. If reasonable doubt could be generated that Nicholas or one of his heirs was still alive, it could impact the value and disposition of these resources. Among many other things, the late or ex-Tsar was a major stockholder in the RAB and the disputed CER.

A recent analysis by writer Shay McNeal demonstrates that *Rescuing the Czar* contains many legitimate and not readily accessible details about the persons and events connected to the Imperial family's final months. McGarry, or whoever put the work together, had access to some well-informed sources. McNeal's research also suggests that the money and influence behind the book was of *British* origin.[93] So where does Reilly fit into this picture? Perhaps James tapped him to look over the work performed by McGarry et al. Would that mean the effort was somehow the work of SIS, or that they merely took a passive interest? The book's publisher recalled that around May, a "mysterious person" arrived to edit proofs of the text.[94] Reilly, though not visibly involved in the actual plots to rescue the Romanov's in 1918, was close to persons who were, such as Lied. He would have had enough information to add corroborative details to the yarn and, perhaps, make sure it did not reveal too much.

Sidney's eye, naturally, was on the money. Throughout 1919 and early 1920, San Francisco was the center of numerous, often secretive, financial deals on behalf of Kolchak, mostly involving the purchase or anticipated purchase of war supplies. In June 1919, McGarry and Romanovskii were involved in a bold scheme to transfer the whole of Kolchak's gold reserve, more than $300 million, to the safekeeping of American banks.[95] Of course, originally it was the Russian states'—the Tsar's—gold. The fate of much of this bullion remains a mystery to this day. Between pilfering, train wrecks and secret transactions, tens of millions of dollars simply vanished. For instance, in the fall of 1919 Kolchak's regime deposited over $500,000 in bullion in the Vladivostok branch of the RAB to pay for machine guns ordered from the Marlin-Rockwell Corp.[96] The gold was to be credited to the account of Reilly's old friends at National City Bank which would pay the manufacturer with dollars on the American end. The actual gold in Vladivostok, however, eventually disappeared into some very large crack. A similar transaction, in which Reilly had a hand, if only an outstretched one, was the $2,500,000 in gold placed in the Vladivostok branch of the British-owned Hongkong and Shanghai (Hong-Shang) Bank to pay for the Remington-Kolchak rifle contract.[97] Again, this bullion was guarantee for Remington's future payment in dollars from Russian accounts held by NCB in New York. Those accounts were under the direct control of Ambassador Bakhmet'ev. Remington fulfilled its contract but was not paid a penny. Given Sidney's influence with both Bakhmet'ev and NCB and the fact that he was then embroiled in a suit against Remington, it is reasonable to suspect he had something to do with it. The net result was that Remington became the owner of the gold in Vladivostok, but had no means to get hands on the stuff. In the end, the firm accepted a partial cash payment from Bakhmet'ev and abandoned all claim to the troublesome gold. By early 1920, at least a half-million still sat in the Hong-Shang Bank in Shanghai, while another million arrived in San Francisco. After paying off debts to the U.S. War Department, Bakhmet'ev still had $400,000 in his coffers. Where the remaining million went, no one seemed to know, but Reilly may have had some ideas.

Churchill later made reference to another mysterious deposit of gold in San Francisco in 1920, one made by "individuals who spoke English with a strong foreign accent."[98] Was one of them Sidney? This relates to a gold cache of some $50 million that Kolchak put up to back a proposed foreign loan in early 1919. This scheme was part of the Jaroszynski syndicate so dear to Reilly's heart and intended to finance the purchase of Russian banks and other assets. At least half the bullion ended up in the Hong-Shang's Hong Kong branch. On 28 May 1920, two shipments of gold variously estimated at $20–28 million arrived in San Francisco from Hong Kong, presumably part of the Kolchak hoard. From there it was consigned to the care of Morgan & Co. "for credit to the British Government," ostensibly as payment on the above loan.[99] Soon after, Bakhmet'ev's New York accounts received a large infusion of fresh cash. What surely was going on here was the laundering of Kolchak, i.e. Russian state, gold into "British" assets. Reilly must have contemplated how to pocket some of this for Savinkov and, of course, for himself.

Sidney would have been the ideal agent to supervise the transfer of the above gold from Hong Kong. From San Francisco, he headed there, perhaps accompanied by Katzenberg. Sidney had good connections in the British colony. M.M. Ustinov, ex-Russian consul in New York, was stationed in Hong Kong before the war and close to the reigning Russian diplomat there, D. von Ettingen.[100] In May, Nikolai Yakunikov (Yakoonikoff, AKA Nick Yard), came to Hong Kong from Vladivostok. Until recently he had served Kolchak's command staff as "intelligence officer for the exchange of information with the heads of the Allied intelligence services."[101] He credited the British Military Mission with helping him get out. Thirty-one-year-old Yakunikov was the son of a "prosperous import-export merchant in Petrograd" and before the war had worked in the Russian Bank for Foreign Trade's London office. All this points to a prior acquaintance with Reilly or at least with British intelligence. In any case, Yakunikov happily encountered a man he knew at the Russian Consulate, the "American manager of the Russo-Asiatic Bank." More than one person could have claimed that title, and Reilly was one of them. He helped Yakunikov get to Shanghai and gave him an introduction to another Russian there, George Moszkowski.

Actually a Pole, during the war Moszkowski was an instructor at the Military Automobile School, a realm Sidney knew very well.[102] He later served with the British Army in Persia and now managed the RAB branch in Shanghai. He promptly hired Yakunikov for a job in Harbin, the administrative hub of the Chinese Eastern Railway.

On 2 June, Thomas Lamont was in San Francisco fresh from protracted loan talks in Beijing. The loan, however, was a dead issue along with any immediate prospects of getting control of the CER. Reilly may have shadowed Lamont all the way back to New York. Meanwhile, things were happening in Europe that required the Ace-of-Spies' special attention.

NOTES

1. Mark Hollingsworth and Charles Tremaine, *The Economic League—The Silent McCarthyism* (London, 1989), 5.
2. Yale University Library, R.H. Isham Papers, box 2/16–17, "Information Gathered in America and Sources of Such Information."
3. British Library, Balfour Papers, Wiseman, "The Attitude of the United States and President Wilson Towards the Peace Conference," undated.
4. Up to her death in 1954, the reclusive Houselander authored more than a dozen books, among them *The Reed of God*, and hundreds of other pieces of Catholic devotion and mysticism. For brief synopses of her career, see Margaret King at www.peregrina.com/caryll/caryll.html and Robin Maas, "Caryll Houselander: An Appreciation," www.catholic.net/RCC/Periodical/Crisis/Oct95/Maas.html. A fuller biography is Maisie Ward, *Caryll Houselander: That Divine Eccentric* (New York, 1962).
5. Ward, 73.
6. Ibid.
7. R. Lockhart, *First Man*, 160.
8. Ibid.
9. Ibid.
10. N. Alekseev, "OGPU . . . ," 3.
11. PRO, FO 371/4020, "Anti-Bolshevik Propaganda," 29 May 1919.
12. CAC, CHAR, 16/25, "Russian Propaganda" and attached memoranda "A" and "B."
13. Ibid., Reilly, "Memorandum to Sir Basil Thomson," 22 Aug. 1919.
14. Ibid., "Rutenberg," 11 Sept. 1919.
15. Www.spartacus.schoolnet.co.uk/SSgregory, and /SSreilly
16. Lincoln supposedly related this story to Evgenii Kozhevnikov during WWII. On Kozhevnikov, see Chapter XVIII.
17. CAC, CHAR 16/28, Sinclair to Churchill, 4 Dec. 1919.
18. Alekseev, "OGPU . . . ," 3.
19. CAC, CHAR, 16/27, Sinclair to Churchill, 15 Sept. 1919.
20. Lord Templewood, *The Fourth Seal: The End of a Russian Chapter* (London, 1930), 324–325.
21. David Lloyd George, *Memoirs of the Paris Peace Conference*, vol. II (London, 1932), 214–242.
22. PRO, FO 371/5439, 14 Nov. 1920.
23. Temira Pachmuss (ed.), *Between Paris and St. Petersburg: Selected Diaries of Zinaida Hippius* (Chicago, 1975), 245.

24. Martin Gilbert (ed.), *Winston Churchill*, Companion Vol. I (London, 1977) 697–698.
25. *Boris Savinkov pered Voennoi Kollegiei Verkhovnogo Suda SSSR* (BSVKVS) (Moscow, 1924), 90–92.
26. HIA, Lockhart, box 6, Spears to R. Lockhart, 2 Jan. 1967.
27. Ibid. Reilly's supposed comment about being a member of the "German Staff" may actually refer to some episode in his 1918 exit from Russia.
28. For a biography of Spears, see Max Egremont, *Under Two Flags: The Life of Major-General Sir Edward Spears* (London, 1997).
29. Ibid., 2–3.
30. Bukhanov, 94. Spears notes the link to Putilov in his letter to Lockhart.
31. SIS, Hargreaves, 5 Sept. and 10 Oct. 1919.
32. CAC, CHAR, 16/28, "Anglo-Russian Economic Relations," Bagge to Sinclair, 15 Oct. 1919.
33. Ibid., Sinclair to Churchill, 17 Oct. 1919.
34. Ibid., Sinclair to Churchill, 11 Nov. 1919.
35. Ibid.
36. WWP, 6/176, CXG 465, 26 July 1919.
37. Ibid., CXP 962, 19 Aug. 1919.
38. Ibid., CXG 484, 10 Sept. 1919.
39. CAC, CHAR, 16/28, Reilly to Bagge, 8 Oct. 1919.
40. Ibid., 16/27, Sinclair to Churchill, 11 Sept. 1919.
41. Ibid., 16/28, "Russian Financial Executive Committee," [Nov. 1919].
42. Ibid., Reilly to Bagge, 10 Oct. 1919.
43. GARF, fond 5831, delo 170, 14 June 1922. See also Raper's RAF service file in AIR 76.
44. For a highly critical, but basically accurate, survey of Deterding's career, see Glynn Roberts, *The Most Powerful Man in the World* (London, 1939).
45. HLRO, LG, F 41/7/31, Northcliffe to Lloyd George, 14 Nov. 1917.
46. Cambridge University Archives, Lord Templewood Papers (TP), II, #106.
47. SIS, "Lt. S.G. Reilly, R.A.F.," 9 Dec. 1919.
48. Dukes played down the "hostile" intentions of his work, but these were attested to in an early 1921 report to U.S. MID by Zinaida Kennedy, one of the caretakers of the American Embassy who was drawn into Dukes' effort; MID 9771-245.
49. SIS, Morton to Reilly, 4 Jan. 1920.
50. CAC, CHAR 16/57, Reilly to Leeper, 10 Jan. 1920.
51. Ibid.
52. Karol Wedziagolski, *Boris Savinkov: Portrait of a Terrorist* (Kingston, ON, 1987), 132.
53. Ibid., 150.
54. SIS, Morton to Menzies, 3 Oct. 1919.
55. Ibid., Menzies to Morton, 16 Oct. 1919.
56. Ibid., Production [Morton] to Reilly, 4 Jan. 1920.
57. HLRO, LG, 202/3/3/, Report by E.F. Wise, 18 April 1920.
58. CAC, CHAR, 16/28, "Memo on Possibilities of Trade with Russia," 7 Feb. 1920.
59. Reilly, SIS, Section H (Hargreaves) to CSS (Cumming), 5 March 1920.
60. IISG, Savinkov, box 37, "Donees sur le Commissaire Bolcheviste Krassine" and PRO, KV 2/673.
61. HIA, Vrangel, Report, 18–19, Lied, 230–231.
62. HLRO, LG, F/90/1/7, Kerr to Lloyd George, 4 May 1920.
63. Ibid., F/90/1/7 and /6, Kerr to Lloyd George, 3 May 1920.
64. Thwaites, 261–266.
65. Reilly, SIS, attached report of Field-Robinson, G/1367, 31 Jan. 1920.
66. Ibid., G/1428, 26 March 1920.

67. Ibid.
68. Ibid., Reilly to Nathan, 14 March 1920.
69. Reilly, SIS, attached report G/1413, 18 March 1920.
70. Ibid., Reilly to Nathan, 14 March 1920.
71. Ibid., Nathan to Reilly, 20 March 1920.
72. Ibid., Reilly to Nathan, 27 March 1920.
73. HLRO, LG, F203/1/7/h, "Gold and Precious Stones."
74. Reilly, SIS, 27 March 1920. Feliks Volkhovskii (in the original "Volkovissky") was a prewar SR activist who later worked beside Savinkov under Kerenskii.
75. TsAFSB, 302330, Reilly Lubianka "Diary," 4 Nov. 1925.
76. Information given to U.S. immigration gave O'Kane's age as forty-two whereas Reilly was forty-six.
77. U.S. 66th Congress, 2nd Session, Senate Sub-Committee of the Committee on Foreign Relations, *Russian Propaganda* (Washington, DC, 1920), 355–356.
78. NYSC, NYC, 4768-1920, Sidney Reilly v. Baldwin Locomotive, et al.
79. CSA 215, Sharpe to Bannerman, 13 Dec. 1924, 10.
80. *Vyshchii Monarcheskii Soviet.*
81. USDS, E845, McCully to Bristol, 20 Feb. 1920.
82. USDS, 121.55/714, Riis to State, 14 April 1920.
83. MID, 9944-A-178, "British Espionage in the United States," 15 Feb. 1921.
84. MID, 9771-745/45, "Memorandum on British Secret Service Activities in this Country," 2 Nov. 1920.
85. Reilly, SIS, Nathan to Reilly, 4 May 1920.
86. On Rothstein, see Leo Katcher, *The Big Bankroll: The Life and Times of Arnold Rothstein* (New York, 1994).
87. Hank Messick, *Lansky* (New York, 1971), 230–231.
88. *NYT* (27 April 1921), 2:6 and (23 Oct 1922), 19:1.
89. CSA 215, Sharpe to Bannerman, 13 Dec. 1924, 8.
90. HIA, Gretchin Haskin, "Rescuing the Tsar: A Story for Two Revolutions," 157–158.
91. Ibid., 143–144.
92. Ibid., 157–158.
93. McNeal, 240, citing McGarry to Romanovskii, 22 Nov. 1920.
94. Ibid., 231.
95. Ibid., 226, and William Clarke, *The Lost Fortune of the Tsars* (New York, 1994), 231–232.
96. USDS, 861.24/197, Bakhmet'ev to Miles, 23 Oct. 1919 and attachments.
97. Clarke, 234–235.
98. Clarke, 230, quoting Grand Duke Aleksandr Mikhailovich.
99. Ibid., 236, and Haskin, 135.
100. P.M. Ivanov, *Gonkong* (Moscow, 1990), 101.
101. American International Group (AIG) archives, "Nick Yard: A Profile," *Contact* (March 1953), 10.
102. Ibid., *Contact* (Oct.–Nov. 1932), 6.

Chapter Twelve

KNIGHT ERRANT

Events in Europe did not hold still for Reilly's return. In April, Pilsudski launched his Polish legions into Ukraine and occupied Kiev on 7 May. To the consternation of his new ally Savinkov and many other Russians, the Poles installed a resurrected nationalist regime under Petlura. The latter barely had time to unpack his bags, for a week later the Reds counterattacked and it was the Polish Army's turn to retreat. The long-expected Soviet-Polish War was on. By mid-June Bolshevik armies were on advance all along the front. Meantime, in the Crimea, Baron Petr Vrangel (Wrangel) took command of what was left of the Volunteers and Cossacks. Under his firm hand the Crimea held, and by May the Whites once more were on the attack. More politically flexible than his predecessors, the Baron still hesitated to countenance Polish or other nationalist ambitions so that an alliance between him and Pilsudski was out of the question. This left Savinkov to carry the Russian banner in Warsaw where he tried to cobble together a small force to fight at Poland's side.

Sidney was back in London by the first half of June. Interestingly, as the same time, Nadine sailed back to New York where she disembarked on the 13th. Whether she did this to avoid her husband or on his instructions is uncertain, but it is worthy of note that she still called herself Mrs. Sidney Reilly and listed herself a married woman. As ever, Reilly had other things on his mind. On 20 June, ensconced at the Albany, he announced his presence with a fresh memo on the "Possibility of Trade with Russia."[1] In this latest permutation of his favorite theme, he advised that Britain must "create a permanent trade organization working *in* and not *outside* Russia." He still believed that a special "international bank" was the means to achieve this. The result would be an entity much like the Hudson's Bay Co. Moscow would grant concessions to foreign firms to restore and operate Russia's industrial and commercial infrastructure. He also offered, with apparent certainty, that the Soviet Government would be willing to put up £25 million in gold as security for "trade warrants" and an additional £5 million as guarantee of faithful performance. Moscow would acknowledge past debts, though it might be necessary to give Lenin & Co. a moratorium on payment. It was even possible, he concluded, that the Reds might rescind nationalization in certain areas.

Arch Sinclair forwarded Reilly's memos to Churchill and others calling them "a concrete proposal for bringing about the downfall of the Soviet Government by economic means and . . . putting us in a position at the earliest possible moment to obtain food and raw materials from Soviet Russia."[2] Sinclair continued to praise Reilly as one "reputed to possess expert knowledge of finance" attested by "his personal prosperity and the authority which he enjoys among Russian financiers such as M. Jaroscynski [sic]." As a source of information and prophecy about Russia, Sinclair regarded him "without rival among my Russian and Anglo-Russian visitors."

Prophecy-wise, in his reports Sidney did anticipate the "New Economic Policy" that Lenin introduced almost a year later. Rather than psychic power, it suggests familiarity with the financial resources—and limitations—of the Soviet regime and access to someone with their finger on such information. That someone was Leonid Krasin who had arrived in London on 27 May. During Reilly's absence, a British team including Nathan and Edward Frank Wise, a veteran of the old Anglo-Russian Supply Committee, hashed out a deal with Krasin and his comrades in Copenhagen.[3] Reilly, it may be recalled, had earlier supplied Sir Robert with information that portrayed Krasin as a pragmatic, slightly corrupt, technocrat and a "resolute adversary" of Communist extremism.[4] Nathan wasted no time in presenting this material in a report to the Foreign Office and other government agencies.[5]

Described as "Mr. X," Nathan represented SIS in the negotiations, but also acted as a stand-in for émigré interests like Putilov and Jaroszynski. As the rightful owners of many of the goods to be bartered in any Anglo-Soviet accord, the exiles could raise endless difficulties unless suitably mollified. In April, Nathan consulted with a "prominent Russian banker" in London, almost certainly Jaroszynski, who wanted to know if private property and bank accounts might be restored, at least for those lending support to the venture.[6] Krasin was noncommittal, but offered that anyone who wanted to work for the common good and make money was welcome to do so if they stayed out of politics.[7]

Nathan held private talks with Krasin's chief assistant, Nikolai Kliment'evich Klyshko, a presumed non-Bolshevik who had lived in Britain for many years. He was, as Reilly, a longtime associate of Vickers and a familiar of Sir Francis Barker and Zaharoff.[8] During the war, Klyshko had worked directly under Gen. Hermonius, Sidney's collaborator and in-law.[9] After the fall of the Tsar, he joined a council of Russian political emigrants in England, among them Chicherin and Litvinov. Though on friendly terms with many of the Bolsheviks and apparently favorable toward their regime, he did not return to Russia. When the Trade Mission came to town, Klyshko became Krasin's secretary and factotum. He also may have served the interests of the Cheka.

In May 1920, Genrikh Yagoda assumed the secret police slot on the executive board (*kollegiia*) of Krasin's Commissariat of Foreign Trade.[10] In July, he gained further stature with a seat on the Cheka's own *kollegiia*, a move that put him right at Dzerzhinskii's side. Yagoda's long, serious face gave him a slightly aristocratic air. He was a Bolshevik and a Chekist, but only so far as this served his own interests. He was a man Sidney could understand and, as necessary, work with.

Krasin's arrival was most satisfying to Nathan. The free movement of goods and people would facilitate the expansion of an intelligence network within the Red domain. Reilly's appeal for the creation of a permanent trade apparatus inside Russia doubtless was part of this design. The fact that the British already had an informant close to the Mission, the aforementioned D 57, was an encouraging start. The appearance of a Bolo delegation in Britain did not sit well with everyone, however. Basil Thomson and head of the Imperial General Staff, Gen. Sir Henry Wilson, were convinced that it would be a center for subversion and sedition and were inclined to see Bolsheviks behind every corner. Their fears were not unjustified; there were those in Moscow who saw the same opportunities as Nathan.

Churchill's attitude was more difficult to pin down. While he railed against the threat posed by the presence of the Soviet mission, he also took great satisfaction in reading intercepts of the Mission's communications with Moscow and other Soviet bodies around the world, another perk from having Krasin in town.[11] Regarding Reilly's proposal, Winston's man Arch Sinclair told his boss it was a sound idea. "A man with a well thought-out policy and a set purpose," he advised, "might impose this plan on the reluctant but desperate Bolos." Sidney hoped to do just that.

In London, Reilly collaborated with Krasin in various mutually profitable ventures. The most important of these, which got underway in August, was a deal between the Soviets and International Marconi for the restoration of wireless service in Russia. At the same time, Krasin was guest of honor at a dinner at Nathan's residence, a function Sidney must have attended as well.[12] In a letter to SIS' Menzies, Churchill admitted that the Marconi business was a "scheme devised by Reilly."[13] Also involved in the Marconi deal was another man once employed on "special intelligence work" in Russia, a businessman with prewar interests in the country.[14] His name has been blanked out, but the likely candidate is Jonas Lied, the Norwegian who often crossed paths with Reilly. In the same period, Lied was denounced by Britons and Americans coming out of Russia as a "cad" and informer.[15] Someone else with a big stake in Marconi was Zaharoff, and it is possible that Reilly was acting as the Greek's stand-in in the negotiations.

Churchill, Cumming and even Basil Thomson knew about Reilly's dalliance with Krasin and raised no objections. Sidney himself gave SIS a White Russian intelligence report that described his "communication with the Bolshevik Delegation in London." How he obtained it, Nathan offered, "Heaven only knows."[16] Reilly's cultivation of the Krasin clique certainly paid dividends, or seemed to. In August someone (Nathan?) forwarded a report to SIS from Sidney who was described as an "absolutely reliable source."[17] It was a résumé of a recent conversation between Krasin and an "intimate friend," a man Reilly knew "very well." Krasin confessed that things in Russia were so bad they hardly could get any worse. The Kremlin's only hope was that things "shall be equally bad throughout the world." Through propaganda and subversion they hoped to keep the Western Powers too preoccupied with their own problems to mount any concerted threat to the Socialist Motherland. Krasin supposedly admitted that 90% of the *valiuta* supplied to the trade missions was spent on propaganda. True or not, this was exactly the type of thing that Thomson and others wanted to hear. Of course, if London knew about the Krasin-Reilly connection, persons in Moscow must have as well. Did they find the situation equally useful?

Reilly's influence with Krasin may have stemmed from more than mutual profit motive. A later confidential report delivered to MI5 concluded that Krasin, as so many others, had been an informant of the Okhrana. That, it continued, left him open to blackmail by other ex-informants, and Reilly definitely was one of those.[18] Also revealing of Krasin's character was MI5's surreptitious inspection of his private safe-deposit box sometime in 1921, something Sidney might have tipped them to. Therein they found plans for a palatial house and a large trove of Russian oil stocks.

During the summer of 1921, Reilly and Krasin were both much involved in formation of the Copenhagen-based International Clearing House Co. The avowed purpose of the outfit was import-export trade with Russia via the Baltic States. In time, it hoped to set up offices inside the Soviet Republic.[19] The Soviets were to kick in £5 million in gold to guarantee goods and contracts, just as Reilly had proposed for his scheme. To undertake this bold enterprise, the firm had a rather modest capital of $500,000, Danish and British.[20] However, there were hopes that more would flow in from German and, especially, American sources. The president was Sir Martin Abrahamson, a British merchant resident in Denmark and a longtime associate of Reilly's old friend, Hans Andersen. Andersen, remember, had been touted by Sidney just a few months earlier as the figurehead of an almost identical-sounding consortium. One of the sponsors of the ICHC was the Danish Committee for the Resumption of Trade with Russia. Behind that stood another of Reilly's past associates, Alexander Helphand. Yet another interesting character connected with the deal was Dmitrii Navashin, a former friend of Guchkov's in the Russian Red Cross. The pair remained good friends despite Navashin's work as a financial advisor to the Soviet Government.[21] It is one more example that "White" and "Red" were very simplistic and imprecise labels.

The roots of the ICHC went back to the fall of 1919, right after Reilly started his series of memos on Russian trade. Further evidence of his connection is found in involvement the so-called Transatlantic Co. Reilly and Brunstrom were involved with the outfit and so, less openly, was Zaharoff.[22] Transatlantic was a front for the Banque Transatlantique that was in turn controlled by the Greek's Banque Commerciale de la Méditerranee.[23] Also lurking in the background of the Clearing House as "close consultants" were Frank Wise and Reginald McKenna, the latter an officer of the powerful London Midland Bank so involved with the Jaroszynski scheme.[24]

The Clearing House, basically, was an attempt to bring Reilly's Russian consortium to life. In the end, it achieved little primarily because anticipated financial backing never materialized on the American end. Reilly knew just whom to blame—Morgan and its acolytes on Wall Street who still nurtured their own plans for Russian trade. During 1920, Anglo-American commercial rivalry intensified. In April, British and French representatives met at San Remo to divvy up oil concessions in the Middle East, effectively barring Americans from much of the region.[25] This exclusion especially annoyed Standard Oil. In London's City, many mandarins of high finance saw Russia as a "second India," the dominance of which would compensate Britain for the loss of other markets to the Americans.[26] At the same time, U.S. interests complained bitterly about "the American Government letting sentimental rot stand in the way of American businessmen making money or cutting out the English" in Russia.[27] The man making that argument was Guaranty Trust's representative in the Baltic States who was busy negotiating deals with the Soviet mission in Estonia. The solution advocated by his ilk was Washington's unilateral recognition of the Bolshevik regime, what Reilly had feared since 1918. Chances of that happening seemed better than ever. The discredited Wilson administration was in its final months. Few doubted that fall's election would usher in a new Republican with no commitment to non-recognition. Noting Krasin's mission in London, advocates of an "open door" for American business in Russia persuaded Washington to rescind most restrictions on U.S.-Soviet Trade, a move hailed by Martens as the first step to recognition.[28]

Krasin reported to Moscow about the increasingly ugly mood between London and Washington.[29] The British, he insisted, secretly intended to destroy the American Navy to insure their own naval supremacy. First they would seek alliance with Japan and possibly Mexico (shades of the Zimmermann Note!). A defeated U.S. would lose the Panama Canal, its Pacific islands and control of Cuba. Japan would take the Philippines and have access to the oil of California and Texas. As strange as it may seem, the American military was making plans for the same war.[30] Who fed this scenario to Krasin? Would sowing the notion of an imminent Anglo-American conflict in Moscow have furthered Reilly's interests? If it made Moscow hesitate in pursuing U.S. ties, yes. The System thrived on conflict and uncertainty.

The summer produced further ominous signs on the Manhattan Front. The men at 23 Wall Street dispatched a special agent to Europe, William "Wild Bill" Donovan, attorney, ex-MID officer and a future founding father of the American CIA. With another Morgan man, Grayson M.P. Murphy, Donovan was to make an examination of Bolshevism and its impact on Europe, particularly from an investment standpoint.[31] When Donovan returned to New York in October, among his fellow passengers was Sir William Wiseman, headed back to take up fresh work for Morgan's rival, Kuhn & Loeb.[32]

On 29 June, Reilly received a letter from Spears on behalf of the "British Corporation of Mine and Steamship Owners in Russia" (BCMSOR), a firm representing stockholders of concerns nationalized by the Reds. In addition to Spears, the firm's directors included Putilov, Brunstrom and three other men hereafter linked to Reilly's affairs, ex-

Foreign Secretary Arthur Balfour, Nathan's friend, Herbert Guedalla and
Scottish mining magnate Leslie Urquhart.[33] Balfour and Guedalla were
prewar directors of the Russo-English (*Russko-Angliiskii*) Bank that suggests their acquaintance with Reilly may have dated back to that era.[34] So,
too, Urquhart who had long association with the Baku and had owned
numerous mining properties in the Urals and Siberia.[35] He still headed the
so-called Russo-Asiatic Consolidated Mining Trust (not associated with the
Russo-Asiatic Bank) that claimed a loss of no less than £56 million to
Bolshevik nationalization.[36] Spear's letter lamented that as far as the
BCMSOR was concerned, for Russia to be opened to unbridled American
investment would be nothing less than a disaster. Brunstrom separately
sounded the same alarm, declaring a mass influx of U.S. capital as ruinous
for émigré hopes for restoration of compensation.[37] There was a sense of
desperation in the air and a plea, perhaps, for desperate measures. The
Americans had to be stopped.

The prayers of Brunstrom, et al., did not go unanswered. Just after
noon on 16 September, a massive explosion rocked the man-made canyons
of Manhattan's financial district. A wagon laden with high explosives and
iron sash-weights detonated directly across the street from the J.P. Morgan
offices at 23 Wall. Scars from the blast can still be seen today. The aftermath
was a scene of utter carnage; 39 persons were blown to bits or mortally
wounded, and some 400 injured. A gigantic manhunt, supervised by Red-
hunting Attorney General A. Mitchell Palmer, descended on New York and
spread out across the country. Nevertheless, despite years of investigation,
dozens of suspects and numerous "confessions," the outrage went unsolved
and remains so today. The one point that was never questioned by Palmer
or any other of the investigators, publicly, was that the deed was the work
of "radicals" somehow linked to Bolshevik Russia. Of course, this did not
suit Lenin's plans at all. The Wall Street Bomb excited the "Red Scare" to
a fever pitch and was the final straw in putting an end to Marten's adventure. Deported in January 1921, he and most of his comrades boarded a
ship bound for Russia. The incident also cast its pall over the upcoming
elections. As expected, Warren G. Harding took the White House, but any
further rapprochement with the Bolsheviks was politically incorrect for the
near future.

As noted, Reilly's early 1919 visit to New York had a curious synchronicity with equally unexplained bombings. Could Sidney have had a
hand in this most recent outrage? Given that he was not around New York
at any time proximate to the blast, the answer would seem a simple no, but
remember that simple answers seldom apply to the Ace-of-Spies. He never

made or planted bombs himself but had a long history of association with persons who did. One of these, recall, was the veteran German saboteur, Kurt Jahnke. Jahnke was marginally connected to the abortive Kapp Putsch in which Reilly had been so interested. During July, Paul Dukes, Sidney's stand-in and troubleshooter, made a hasty visit Berlin to exchange information with Vladimir Orlov, but he also could have met Jahnke. Dukes rushed to London where, on 27 July, he recorded a meeting with Reilly.[38]

In mid-August, Jahnke slipped out of Germany bound for Mexico on some secretive mission, but not for the German government.[39] He did not show up in Mexico until late September, so where was he in the interim? The big German was intimately familiar with New York and a master of disguise; during his many wartime sabotage forays into the U.S., he always evaded detection. At this point, he was a gun for hire and had the expertise to assemble the rather sophisticated bomb used on Wall Street. A clue is the use of the sash weights as shrapnel, a technique Jahnke pioneered back in 1915.[40] Paul "Pablo" Altendorf, an ex-MID operative-*cum*-private detective who worked on the case for the FBI, later linked Jahnke to the bombing, though he never revealed just how.[41]

Reilly had other friends to lend a helping hand. The foremost was Brasol who was, naturally, violently opposed to any normalization of American relations with the hated "Judaeo-Bolsheviks." He had personal connections within the Bureau of Investigation and the MID. For instance, his friend and employer Frederic Coudert was himself an ex-special assistant to the Attorney General and still influential in that quarter. Brasol was well placed to monitor the investigation and, if necessary, give it a nudge in the "right" direction. None of this proves that Reilly arranged the Wall Street Bomb, but it certainly shows how he might have. If nothing else, he had every reason to be pleased with the result.

Sidney was still busily at work for SIS. On 3 September, Nathan wrote Capt. Guy Liddell at Scotland Yard regarding about a collection of documents recently provided by Reilly.[42] The materials had been recently retrieved by Dukes from Orlov and delivered to our man in London. There was a set of card indexes and albums of "Bolshevik Missionaries" and assorted Red agents, including items salvaged from the Okhrana archives. Also included was a map indicating the locations of resident Soviet agents throughout Europe, a circular instructing those agents, a list of Tsarist military officers in Red service, and, for good measure, grisly photos of Bolo atrocities. Sidney already had put the trove in the eager hands of Basil Thomson and Norman Thwaites. Nathan was impressed and thought MI5, the War Office and others would also find it of "great interest."

At the end of August, "C" dispatched Reilly to Paris on a "highly important and confidential mission," one that would last for some weeks.[43] The exact nature and purpose of the venture never appears in the SIS memos, but circumstances seem to have compelled our man to don a Royal Navy uniform. This generated an angry response from the Admiralty which in September complained of his appearing in Navy dress while engaging in conduct that was "not satisfactory." "Is he still employed by 'C'?," they demanded to know.[44] On 7 September, Cumming wrote his counterpart at NID, Capt. (later Admiral) Hugh Sinclair, to affirm "Mr. Sydney [sic] Reilly is employed by me" and was still engaged on the confidential mission in question.[45] "C" asked for details of his agent's supposed misconduct. "I feel confident that the statement that he has been wearing naval uniform is not correct," he added, and thought it "at least possible that the accusation as to his conduct is also incorrect." Further reports from the Navy, these from a Russian source, insisted that Sidney had been seen in naval uniform and that he was "boasting of being in close contact with [Churchill]." Also adding to the hue and cry was Capt. J.A. Leighton, late of the Allied Armistice Shipping Commission in Rotterdam. He complained about Reilly's impersonation to MI5 and denounced the subject as a thoroughly untrustworthy person." [46] Cumming ran damage control and clung to the position that the information was not "sufficiently definite to bear out the original accusation." He stuck by Reilly, but the episode may have forced him to reconsider just how much trouble this particular agent was worth.

What was Sidney up to in Paris? His naval masquerade is probably explained by the convening in Paris of an association of Russian Navy officers, among them his crony Agapaev from New York. Its purpose was to marshal support for Vrangel's struggle, but there was good reason to suspect its infiltration by Bolshevik agents. Reilly's likely assignment was to check out the attendees. A man in naval dress was bound to gain more access and confidence.

There were other things going on the French capital that merited his attention. On 12 August, the Quai d'Orsay announced that France recognized the administration of Baron Vrangel and the government of Russia and intended to supply him with economic and military aid.[47] French emissaries in London received instructions to cease all talks and contacts with Krasin's mission. The cultivation of Russian naval officers also may have been a first step in discovering more about French plans and intentions. Opinion at Whitehall held the French move to be foolish and even counterproductive.[48] Like it or not, there was a growing consensus that the

Bolsheviks were bound to be the masters of Russia for the foreseeable future.

French policy towards Vrangel was an offshoot of their broader concern about Poland, a vital ally to which Paris dispatched arms and advisers to stem the Red advance. The turning point in the campaign came in late August when Pilsudski, bolstered by this aid, delivered a counterblow that drove Lenin's host back from the gates of Warsaw. Savinkov, in the meantime, still struggled to reach accord with one or another renegade Russian commander, to no decisive result.

There also were economic intrigues to excite Sidney's interest. One was the negotiation of a big French loan from a consortium of American banks spearheaded, naturally, by the Morganites.[49] The reasonable suspicion was that infusion of American capital into France would provide a convenient conduit for its subsequent flow into the cash-starved states of Central and Eastern Europe and Russia beyond. During these weeks Paris was the scene of byzantine deal-making between Deterding's Royal Dutch combine and Standard Oil of New Jersey (SONJ). The Rockefeller interests wanted to secure a foothold in the French/European market but needed RDS' cooperation. The arrangement made between August and October centered on the disposition of two French banks and, more importantly, the shares of Russo-Asiatic stock held by each. Deterding sought control of the aforementioned L'Union bank and SONJ took over Paribas. The final deal gave Deterding a hefty interest in the RAB and, thus, in the Chinese Eastern, the object of so much attention and rivalry. The acquisitive Dutchman was by now the paper owner of much of Russia's oil industry, and thereby interested in all questions of commercial arrangements with the Bolsheviks. By assuming a presence in the affairs of the RAB and CER, he had leverage in any deals cut with the Soviets in the Far East or elsewhere.

In the latter half of September, Reilly sent Dukes to Warsaw to keep an eye on the Savinkov situation. The Ace-of-Spies himself first headed for Brussels where a new international financial conference opened on the 20th. Krasin and Zaharoff were there, as was Deterding and even Putilov. The air was thick with tensions among the Americans, British and French, especially over oil. It was the perfect environment to work the System. Perhaps he made a brief visit on Margaret while he was there.

Reilly next embarked on quick visits to Karlsbad and Prague in Czechoslovakia, plus Vienna, Berlin, and Riga. The absence of any direct reference to these travels in his SIS file suggests that they were not undertaken at "C"'s behest. However, a 23 September message from Nathan shows that London was aware of his activities and willing to lend assistance. Nathan noted that he had received a letter from Boyce, now SIS chief in Helsinki, on the subject of one "Tchaev," a man about whom Reilly had earlier inquired. Boyce forwarded descriptions of two individuals, and Sir Robert thought "the second . . . is the person you want to know about." [50] That was S.N. Chaev, a man long connected to Jaroszynski, the RAB and, of course, the CER. He had been enmeshed in the 1918 ruble-buying scheme and was now threatening suit against His Majesty's Government for funds he claimed unpaid. What Sidney wanted with him is another mystery, but a good bet is that it revolved around Chaev's chunk of RAB shares, obviously a hot commodity at the moment.

Reilly's visit to Berlin at the beginning of October interestingly coincides with the reported appearance of Yakov Peters in that city. Accompanied by a mysterious Miss Krause, Peters was said to have brought with him a large cache of valuables for deposit in unnamed German banks.[51] Could this have been part of the gold intended for the Clearing House—or something else? According to other records, Peters had been shunted off to Tashkent in Central Asia in August where he would remain for almost two years. That, of course, does not mean that he—or someone posing as him—didn't make a quick jaunt to Berlin. The Cheka held the keys to the *Gokhran*, the Soviet State's treasure house of inherited and confiscated valuables. Perhaps the man who really showed up in Berlin was Genrikh Yagoda. In May 1920, he had assumed a slot on the executive directorate of Krasin's Commissariat of Foreign Trade. By July of that year, he also had a place on the Cheka's own *kollegiia* and was assistant chief of the secretive "Special Department" (*Osobyi Otdel*—OO). Genrikh took a particular interest in the raising of *valiuta* hard currency, the lifeblood of Soviet foreign trade, not to mention subversion and espionage.[52]

Reilly resurfaced in London in mid-October. On the 12th he informed the Board of Trade that he had finalized arrangements with Krasin regarding the Marconi deal and the linked formation of a "holding company" to handle Russian trade, a likely reference to the International Clearing House.[53] The only thing needed was the formal approval of the Soviet leadership and the arrival of the £5 million in gold and valuables to capitalize the venture. Was this what "Peter's" visit to Berlin was about?

In the meantime, Cumming, or someone, came up with a new assignment for Reilly that involved a virtual grand tour of northeastern Europe, seemingly a broad fact-finding mission. On 20 October, Morton wrote an introduction to the SIS resident in Riga, Ronald Meiklejohn, stating "the bearer of this is Mr. S.G. Reilly, who is on business for the Air Board connected to Civil Aviation." Morton asked that the traveler be given "every assistance from our point of view," and added that, "he is absolutely *au courant* with our work."[54] That the Civil Aviation bit was a cover is attested in a note to the Warsaw station in which Morton emphasized that Reilly was "employed by the Air Board and *us*."[55] Morton supplied identical notes to Berlin, Tallinn and Stockholm.

Morton told the Warsaw station that Sidney would proceed there from Paris on the 23rd and that ST25 (Dukes) should be informed so he could arrange a meeting as soon as possible. A meeting with whom is not indicated, but it surely was Savinkov and/or Polish officials assisting him. Events in that corner of the world had moved rapidly in the past few weeks. Pilsudski drove the Red Army steadily eastward. On 12 October Lenin offered an armistice and the Poles, victorious but exhausted, accepted. The terms called for both sides to disarm any forces hostile to the other operating in their domain.

This left Savinkov's small Peoples' Volunteer Army[56] (about 12,000 men) belatedly formed at the close of August, in a precarious position. Boris had joined forces with a Pancho Villa-style adventurer, Ataman Stanislav Nikodimovich Bulak-Balakhovich. The latter was a small, dark, big-eared swashbuckler with a penchant for robbery and Jew-baiting.[57] The armistice meant that Boris and his ataman would either have to invade the Soviet realm or submit to internment in Poland. Opinion in the Foreign Office was decidedly negative towards Savinkov and his adventure; he was seen as a meddling spoiler or worse. Even Rex Leeper, a former fan, now found Boris "a dangerous and embarrassing individual" and instructed London's emissary in Warsaw, Percy Loraine, to avoid him.[58] Sidney's connection to the venture could in no way improve his reputation at the FO. However, Churchill was still a Savinkov-backer and had diverted funds from Vrangel to assist the ex-terrorist's plans. The official explanation from the War office was that they desired intelligence on the situation east of the Polish demarcation line but did not want to put British officers as such in the area. Thus, the use of "Secret Service agents . . . while politically suspect, is still useful."[59]

Sidney left London on 23 October, but during a brief stop in Paris found himself recruited for another task. Spears' replacement as head of the local British Military Mission, Maj. G.J.P. Geiger, wanted Reilly's help in interrogating a recently-arrived Russian, one Vasil'ev.[60] The latter had commanded a Red Army division in Turkestan and was able to offer information on Soviet strength and intentions in that region. What really made him interesting, however, was that he now was collaborating with the French High Command and privy to their grand scheme of aiding Vrangel and a "general pacification of Russia." The problem was, Vasil'ev basically spoke only Russian and Geiger needed Reilly to put questions and translate answers. Anxious to catch his train for Warsaw, Sidney could not tarry and arranged for Geiger to send him Vasil'ev's written responses by King's Messenger that he would study and translate as time allowed. Before departing, he assured Geiger that the Russian seemed to be telling the truth. One aspect that may have been of special significance to him was that in Turkestan Vasil'ev had worked with Peters. Geiger vouched that Reilly was useful and "reliable," but in a later letter the Sinclair he cautioned that there were certain matters that should not be discussed "even with one so much in our confidence in these Russian matters as Reilly." [61] Interestingly enough, the matter at hand was Krasin who had boasted about his ability to manipulate the French with "tainted gold."

Reilly rolled into the Polish capital on the 26th to find that Savinkov had left for the front a few days before, accompanied by his mistress, a hundred Cossacks and the Committee's cash box. SIS wanted Sidney back in Berlin the following day, but he also decided on a change in plans.[62] On the 30th, a brief wire to London announced that Reilly and Dukes had departed for Savinkov's camp deep in the Polesian Marshes.[63] The wire went through the British Embassy, something soon to raise new objections in the Foreign Office.[64] In the same manner, Sidney sent along a report on Petlura's Ukrainian forces also fighting alongside the Poles. Savinkov, he argued, was prepared to "unequivocally recognize" Ukrainian independence and join Petlura in the struggle against the Bolsheviks. He was much less sanguine about the prospects of Vrangel who, Reilly noted, took an "irreconcilable attitude" towards the Ukrainians. "His Majesty's Government's good offices," he concluded, "are looked upon by all parties as the most efficient means of righting [the] situation."

Boris' brother, Viktor Savinkov, recounted Reilly's arrival at Luninets, the forward base some 250 miles east of Warsaw.[65] Viktor had heard of but never met the Ace-of-Spies and was surprised to find him a "smallish" man with a handsome, lively face and piercing, dark eyes. He presented himself as an English officer and noted his long acquaintance with Boris. He even suggested some prior knowledge of Balakhovich, which is not beyond the realm of possibility. Reilly also claimed to be the representative of commercial firms interested in buying local products, a guise perhaps intended for the benefit of curious onlookers. Boris was somewhere out in the woods. While they waited for his return, the strange Englishman addressed Viktor with a directness and attentiveness that gave him the feeling of being carefully sized up. The younger Savinkov noted the visitor's excellent

Russian and his relaxed manner. Sidney attributed this familiarity to his "Russian mother."

When Boris showed up, he and Reilly secluded themselves with Polish officers drawing up plans for the new campaign.[66] Having assumed the role of commander-in-chief of the motley PVA (a move *not* recognized by Balakhovich), Savinkov bestowed honorary commissions on his British guests. Perhaps therein lies the basis for Reilly's subsequent claim to the rank of captain. The advance finally commenced on 7 November and achieved some early success. On 10 November, Balakhovich's division stormed the important town of Mozyr, and on the 16th, Rezhitsa fell. But Red forces rallied and the anticipated peasant uprising, upon which any real success hinged, failed to materialize. Savinkov and Balakhovich soon fell out, and amid a squalid welter of massacres and pogroms, the last typhus-ridden remnants of the Peoples' Volunteer Army trickled back across the Polish frontier in early December.

Neither Reilly nor Savinkov remained for the final, dismal act, but Sidney saw enough to file detailed and candid reports with London. In the longest of these, composed in mid-November, he branded Boris' decision to leave Warsaw a "political mistake," indicative, he added, of Savinkov's "narrow perspective" and overall limitations as a leader.[67] "Like many Russians," he opined, "[Savinkov] is unpossessed of practicality." Nevertheless, he still thought that in some way Savinkov was destined to play "a leading part in the reconstruction of Russia."

In the meantime, Reilly's use of the Embassy to cable reports aroused the Foreign Office. On 2 November, Leeper warned SIS that ST1, "not, perhaps, through any fault of his own, misunderstood his position."[68] Unlike his 1919 mission, where "he went, in a way, on behalf of the F.O.," things were different now. Without arguing this point, Morton, or possibly Cumming himself, cast blame on Leeper for giving Reilly an introduction to Loraine, something that certainly implied FO sanction. SIS was willing to wire a clarification to their agent, but Leeper "thought it a pity in any way to hurt Mr. Reilly's feelings" and suggested it be handled as gently as possible.[69] Addressing the question some days later, Reginald Hoare showed no such sensitivity. "His Majesty's Government run the danger of being fatally compromised by the activities of these two gentlemen [Reilly and Dukes]," he warned.[70] He accused them of pointlessly stirring up trouble and, by their very presence, giving the appearance of British approval to actions absolutely contrary to London's wishes.

On 8 November, while he and Dukes were holed up in Luninets, a message arrived in Warsaw from Morton.[71] This advised that no more cables be sent through the Embassy because it had "fluttered the dovecotes" in the FO who could not abide that Loraine should "quote a person not on the Diplomatic List." No harm had been done, Morton assured, but added "the authorities are terrified of any person acting in conjunction with [SIS]." "As you well know," he added cryptically, "possibly they have reason to be." Morton that had something to do with the business angle Reilly mentioned to Viktor Savinkov.

The cable flap was not the only misunderstanding. In the same missive, Morton mentioned that "Mac[laren] had wired me from Berlin in a great stew as he seems to think you were going to visit him there, on what grounds I do not know." Maclaren was leaving for some unknown destination, Paris or Prague he thought, and then, maybe, back to London. Maclaren "seems very pleased with himself and hopes great results in the future." The pressing matter at hand had to do with Vladimir Orlov and his archive of anti-Bolshevik material. Finally, Morton mentioned one other item that was sure to get Sidney's attention; Dukes had just been awarded a knighthood largely on the basis of his past service in Russia.

Sidney and Dukes were back in Warsaw by the 12th where they learned of the FO's objections and Reilly wrote up his long report. He first thought he could fix the problem by simply using his and Dukes' code designations—ST1 and ST25—in place of their names, which he did in a preliminary wire to "C" and J.D. Gregory, the FO's Russian specialist. Two days later, he cabled again to say that he and ST25 were off to inspect Petlura's Ukrainian rebel army in the south. By the 18th, he was again in Warsaw and reported to Morton, with respects to Nathan and Cumming, on an interview with Pilsudski.[72] "The Poles know all about me and what I am doing here," he noted, "but that does not matter at all." "I have not done a stitch of work for the Air Ministry," he admitted, "I have not had a minute's time for anything outside Russian affairs," though he thought he might yet squeeze in a little something.

A week later Morton ordered both agents to "return to England at once." He soon amended the instructions allowing Dukes to remain in Poland, albeit no longer on SIS orders, while Reilly was to make haste home. Whether he did so is unclear. On 3 December he wrote Morton from Paris relating a recent conference with Orlov and Maclaren.[73] Orlov had fled the Crimea before the Red Army overwhelmed Vrangel's forces in November. He set up shop in Berlin where, through his old friend Walter Bartels, he became a collaborator of Weimar's Political (secret) Police. Reilly and Maclaren wanted to bring Orlov into Britain's employ as well. The "spade work" was done, our spy assured Morton, "everything now depends on how it will be utilized." Orlov was eager to help, he continued, and "we are assured of the full benefit of "O"'s work with [the Germans]." Sidney wanted to bring Orlov across the channel to meet with Basil Thomson and Cumming, and he assured Morton this could be done without "exposing ourselves." Of course, Orlov would need "support," especially of the monetary kind. The end result would be "to arrange between ourselves and [Orlov] and entirely irreproachable liaison," i.e., one undetectable to outside, meddlesome parties like the FO. Reilly went on to advise that Maclaren should go to Riga and that a man like Nathan was "urgently needed" in Warsaw. If all this could come together, he concluded, "we will . . . be better informed about Russia than ever before."

One of the things Orlov had information on was secret Bolshevik bank accounts in Switzerland. Lenin earlier ordered the accounts to be set up to keep the Party in business should it be forced from power in Russia. By 1921, some 10 million gold rubles sat safely tucked away in Geneva and Berne.[74] Reilly would have found that very, very interesting. Curiously, between October 1920 and March 1921, SIS man Plowden served as an honorary consul in Berne. Could he have been hunting for the Bolos' loot?

On 6 December, Sidney passed through Paris and dropped in on Geiger, probably to deliver the Vasil'ev report. He also offered up his latest views on the Russian situation which Geiger found a bit trite and unconvincing. Russia had entered a "Directory" state, he proclaimed, and "salvation is to come from a Savinkov-Balakavitch [sic] combine."[75] By the 9th, he was back in London where he and Dukes, who had quit Warsaw after all, dined with Churchill.[76] They also introduced Winston to Orlov. Dukes noted another meeting with Reilly on the 20th, and three days later the two skipped to Paris again with Orlov. There they conferred with Field Robinson before Dukes returned to England on the 30th, alone. Where was Reilly?

Before taking up that question, an incident occurred in London at the close of 1920 that deserves our attention. Georgii Solomon was another Russian *spets* who had taken the Bolsheviks' coin. A currency expert, in late 1920 he joined Krasin's operation, but at once found himself involved in work he found highly objectionable. At Krasin's insistence, and probably with the cooperation of the Cheka, Solomon smuggled a cache of diamonds to be sold secretly in the West. He was horrified to learn that Krasin intended to sacrifice the gems for a fraction of their true value. When Solomon balked, he was confronted by Krasin's menacing accomplice, a British officer called "Capt. Kahn" (*Kon*).[77] This man, Solomon learned, was an Anglicized Russian Jew who had some powerful influence over Krasin and connections in Paris to dispose of the diamonds without any fuss. It seems a solid bet that this was Reilly under a new alias, one borrowed, perhaps, from his banker friend Isidor Kon. The cash-hungry commissars in Moscow would be satisfied with the modest return. Afterwards the diamonds could be re-cut and resold for much more with Krasin and Sidney pocketing the difference.

Next, there is some suggestion that Reilly paid a visit to Estonia using yet another alias. At the beginning of 1921, American intelligence in the Baltic States picked up the story of one "Krommel," a Russian or Russo-German with intimate ties to the British "secret service" and the German, who claimed to have highly-placed sources of information inside Russia.[78] References to Krommel date back to the previous October when Reilly also made a brief sojourn to the Baltic. That the two were one and the same is impossible to say for certain, but there are strong indications that if Krommel was not the Ace-of-Spies, he surely had some connection. First, the subject presented himself as an "international agent" in British employ. He had in his employ one Vladimir Ivanovich Rykatkin, a Russian engineer who happened to be a friend of Krasin's and who had been active in prewar Petersburg. Rykatkin supplied Krommel's operation with 300,000 Estonian marks from some unidentified source. The matter was all the more suspicious, because other sources identified Rykatkin, who also claimed to be a British operative, as an agent of the Cheka's "Special Department"—Yagoda's realm.

Nor was that all. The January reports forwarded to the State Department put Krommel at the center of a bold plot to overthrow the Soviet Government. Krommel was close to a former Russian officer serving on the Estonian staff, Col. Aleksandr Smolen. A Latvian who had served both Reds and Whites before joining Estonian service, Smolen happened to be a former friend and comrade of Col. Eduard Berzin and Gen. Yoakim Vatzetis. The latter currently led the Latvian Division garrisoned in Moscow. Smolen allegedly maintained secret contact with Vatzetis and on behalf of Krommel had enlisted the disillusioned General in a conspiracy to subvert the *Latdiviziia*, seize the Kremlin and set up a military dictatorship. Sound familiar? The similarities with the 1918 conspiracy seem a bit much to be purely coincidental. If this plan fell through, Krommel had an alternative. He claimed that a dissident wing of the Cheka, led by Dzerzhinskii himself, was willing to seize power in the name of ridding the Soviet regime of Jews. Krommel wanted American support, especially financial backing. He was in close contact with Meiklejohn, the SIS man in Tallinn, and through him he made a specific appeal for the U.S. intelligence officer in Riga, past and future Reilly ally Sergius Riis, to come to Estonia for confidential talks. Riis readily accepted the offer, but there is no indication of what came of the affair. Obviously, no coup by Vatzetis or Dzerzhinskii materialized. The whole business probably was some sort of provocation, but whose? One explanation is that Reilly concocted the scheme as a means of conning money out of the Americans, perhaps to the ultimate benefit of Krasin and other Soviet collaborators. The alias was necessary since alarm bells would at once sound in Washington if his name came up.

In the wake of the Tallinn meeting, Riis—together with Reilly?—made a quick jaunt to the Lithuanian capital of Kaunas (Kovno). Another of Sidney's former associates in espionage had taken up residence in that city. This was Casimir Pilenas-Palmer, erstwhile employee of Scotland Yard, the Okhrana, SIS, MID and God knows who else. He had assumed a position with the Lithuanian political police as an expert on combating Bolshevism. About the same time, still another of Reilly's "friends" popped up in Finland, Otto Lucas. He now called himself Capt. William Van Narvig and claimed to be attached to the personal staff of Finnish military chief Gen. (later Marshal) Carl Mannerheim.[79] There is no real evidence of that, but as Van Narvig he probably did have connection to Finnish military intelligence. The appearance of three experienced operatives all with links to Reilly strategically placed along Russia's Baltic frontiers seems, if nothing else, an extraordinary coincidence and one very handy for Reilly.

By late January, Sidney definitely resurfaced in Prague. The Czech capital was destined to be his business and conspiratorial headquarters in Central Europe. A beautiful baroque city dominated by its brooding Castle, it had served for centuries as home and inspiration to artists, composers and writers. Among the more recent was Franz Kafka, whose paranoia-laden tales reflected the City's darker side. It was that side, no doubt, that Reilly knew best. Ensconced in the Hotel Passage, he received a letter from Nathan. Sir Robert conveyed word from "Stanley" (Morton's alias) that he had been in contact with "Z" (Orlov), now firmly on the British payroll. Part of Reilly's job in the Czech capital was to scope out the local Russian émigrés, particularly Savinkov's erstwhile SR comrades. The latter functioned under the nominal leadership of Kerenskii, though, as Sidney reported, the movement was rent with factionalism and personal feuds. There was, most notably, no chance of building a coalition between Kerenskii and Savinkov.[80] This, of course, fit Sidney's contention that Boris was the only horse worth backing.

The SIS file is silent on the Ace-of-Spies' whereabouts and activities from the end of January through late June. Still, thanks to Dukes' diary-keeping and other clues, it is possible to reconstruct a rough picture. On 12

February, Dukes saw Thwaites who had just returned from Prague, perhaps with Sidney. Reilly definitely was back in London by the close of the month, when he conferred with Dukes. Paul was going to America on a combination of anti-Bolshevik speaking tour and personal business, but Reilly coaxed him into doing a little work on his behalf.

Sidney had a large collection of books and artworks stashed in New York. He had assembled a collection of some 1,100 items relating to the person and career of his idol, Napoleon.[81] The plan was for Dukes to act as front man for an auction of this collection at Manhattan's American Art Galleries, timed to coincide with the upcoming centenary of Napoleon's death. Among the items were the drawings of the Arc de Triomphe he had purchased way back in 1897. The sale took place over 4–5 May, and netted roughly $100,000, a rather modest sum by Reilly standards. Sidney later suggested that the proceeds all went to assist Savinkov, but that was, at best, a gross exaggeration. Indeed, his claim to have sacrificed the better part of his fortune backing Savinkov's schemes was, as we shall see, a complete lie. His true contribution to Boris' cause was rather modest, totaling between $50,000 and $80,000 from 1919 through 1924.[82] Most of that he handed out in small amounts, £100 here or 1000 francs there, always keeping Savinkov on a short financial lease and, thus, always under control. Whenever possible, Reilly got others to foot the bill. Remember, when Savinkov needed £100 to go to Germany, he finagled that out of SIS rather than reaching into his own pocket.

Nor does this liquidation of Napoleoniana, representing only a fraction of his artworks, seem to have been stimulated by any acute shortage of cash on Reilly's part. What the sale probably was, at least in part, was an experiment in marketing looted valuables on the American market. Seeded among the hundreds of items in the collection were objects gleaned from the Cheka's *Gokhran* loot. The sale also would identify collectors interested in purchasing more of the same. Krasin and Yagoda would have secured much-needed *valiuta* and Reilly, of course, would have taken a cut for his role as broker.

Dukes' diary shows that he was conducting a variety of business for his friend and colleague. Soon after getting off the boat on 4 March, he had lunch at Sidney's old Bankers Club haunt at 120 Broadway. After a quick jaunt to Washington (to see whom?), he was back in Gotham by late March to hobnob with Baron Ginzburg and G.A. Izvol'skii, cronies of Bakhmet'ev and leaders of the local Society for Aid to Russia, an organization with links to Putilov's *Torgprom*. He also had meetings with former Vice Consul Petr Rutskii and ex-Okhrana colonel, Aleksandr Ivanovich Spiridovich. During

April and May, amid his many comings and goings Sir Paul recorded an encounter with Bakhmet'ev himself.

But New York also was the source of new complications. On 22 April, the familiar Henry Kuntz bore witness to the passport application of 23-year-old Armand Hammer who going abroad on business.[83] Kuntz's Peoples' Industrial Trading Co. gambit had fallen through and he now teamed up with Hammer for a new venture. Kuntz claimed to have known young Armand and his father, doctor and drug manufacturer Julius Hammer, for over fifteen years. What neither Kuntz nor the applicant mentioned was that Armand's intended destination was Russia and that his father was a dedicated Communist activist and personal acquaintance of Lenin.

Armand was on his way to take advantage of the New Economic Policy (NEP) unveiled by Lenin at the X Party Congress in March 1921. Against the fierce opposition of Marxist stalwarts, including Trotsky, Lenin rammed through sweeping changes that aimed to quell a dangerous wave of peasant insurrection and restore the country's shattered economic infrastructure. The centerpiece of the reforms was the restoration of private cultivation of land and sale of its produce, but the part that most excited the imaginations of Hammer, Reilly and others was the offering of all manner of concessions to foreign investors, the very thing Sidney had anticipated months before.

Back in London, Sidney had business with Royal Dutch/Shell kingpin Robert Waley Cohen. The topic of conversation was oil. Seeking to gain advantage on rivals Anglo-Persian and Standard, in February Cohen commenced quiet talks with Krasin about the purchase of some 175,000 tons of Russian crude, a move that some of His Majesty's officials hoped would be "the beginning of a big Anglo-Russian oil trade."[84] Cohen presumably had boss Deterding's approval even though it compelled the Dutchman to buy oil he believed to be his in the first place. Cohen explained the deal had been arranged by unnamed "brokers" who approached him on behalf of the Soviets. Was Reilly one of them? If so, one of his accomplices was Boris Said, who represented Standard of New Jersey in London. His relations with the Ace-of-Spies went back to the war when Said served Gen. Hermonius in the Russian Government Committee and visited New York. Beyond that, Said also had past connection to the Okhrana and was one of those supposed to use that as leverage with Krasin.[85] According to information in Churchill's hands, Said had been the "principal Zionist agent in London before the revolution" which gave him access to "an exceedingly large sum of money."[86] By 1920, in addition to Standard, Said reputedly worked for the Bolsheviks and lived "in style" at the Ritz. By one account

he was in personal contact with Lenin. White Russian information indicated he was close to Krasin as well as the ubiquitous Jonas Lied. However,
the same source insisted Said was on friendly terms with none other than
Basil Thomson.[87] As ever, the question is: whose side was he really on? Like
Reilly, the answer probably is whoever was paying him most. The generally
well-informed Xavier Hauteclocque later described Said as an "agent" of
Reilly whom shifting allegiances ultimately turned into a "ferocious
enemy." [88]

Come March and April, Sidney headed to the Continent, shuttling
between Paris, Berlin and Prague. The main effort seems to have been
devoted to a scheme hatched with Spears and Brunstrom to set up a tobacco
distribution business in central Europe. Also involved was Lev (Leon)
Rozen, another of Sidney's contacts from old Petersburg who now ran a
chemical and brokerage business in Poland and London. But there was
more going on here than tobacco business.

During visits to the French capital, Reilly met with Gen. Rudolf
(Radula) Gaida, a Czech officer and veteran of the Russian Civil War. He
led an army for Kolchak, but his insubordinate nature led to his expulsion
from Siberia in late 1919. The Czech government likewise found his plotting and power-seeking a nuisance and in November 1920 packed him off
to Paris to study at the *École de Guerre*.[89] Gaida retained many friends in
the Czechoslovak military, and that was where Sidney's interest came in.
Gaida provided contacts that could help in a very different sort of venture.
The recently concluded peace between Poland and the Soviets threatened to
end Savinkov's anti-Bolshevik activities in Warsaw. Prague seemed an ideal
new base of operations. He was determined to resume armed struggle
against the Bolsheviks by mounting a guerrilla campaign, and the assistance
of the Czech Army would be of immense value.

From Prague, Reilly headed to Berlin where he rendezvoused with
Franklin Helm. The latter had just come over from New York to pursue his
German connections. Holed up at the Adlon, Berlin's "Conspiracy
Central," Helm was the middleman in a recent "exchange of notes"
between Washington and Berlin seeking American support for a reduction
in Germany's reparations.[90] At the same time he was a conspicuous advocate of a scheme to secure the Germans a $3 billion credit on Wall Street.[91]
His connections with high German circles were very useful to Sidney in
sniffing out news about secret negotiations then underway in Berlin. On 17
April, Viktor Kopp, Moscow's man in Berlin reported to the Kremlin positive talks with German firms, including Blohm & Voss, concerning the construction of aircraft and submarines in Russia. On 3 May, Krasin himself

passed through Berlin on his way back to the Socialist Motherland. Behind all of these maneuverings lurked a very basic and important question: which way was Germany going to jump—East or West?

Reilly popped up in London in May and composed a long summary for SIS on Savinkov's recent escapades. Balakhovich and his ilk he dismissed as "frankly criminal elements of robbers, looters and Jew-baiters."[92] Savinkov, he claimed, was above that sort of thing, had experienced "a tremendous political evolution," and was now in touch with the "real Russia."[93] Boris placed his new hope in the peasantry whom he believed would rise en masse to throw off the Bolshevik yoke. All they needed was leadership which he was ready to provide. Sidney described a network of Savinkovite cells throughout western Russia and filial links with anti-Bolo groups as far away as the Caucasus. The weak point, Reilly argued, was Savinkov's dependence on the Poles. They had been a great help, supplying the ex-terrorist, exclusive of military supplies, with nearly 300 million Polish marks (about £100,000).[94] Such generosity could not continue much longer. Savinkov's future looked bleak unless he could find fresh sources of support. "Personal friends," among whom Reilly doubtless counted himself, had chipped in small amounts, and the French might come up with some more, but the underlying message was that London should step in to fill the gap. Reilly certainly did not believe everything that he was saying, but he was not willing to have Boris fade away just yet. Savinkov was a man who still had his uses.

After completing the Savinkov report, Reilly mostly dropped from sight and for several weeks. In early June, he appeared in Berlin where he hovered on the sidelines of a gathering of Russian monarchists. Two other men attending the meeting are of particular note. The first was Brasol, who had come over from New York bearing funds from Ford for the monarchists—and, perhaps, Savinkov.[95] The second was Aleksandr Yakushev, the former Tsarist, now a Soviet official who may be recalled as one of Sidney's contacts in 1917. Yakushev also was or had been close to Trotsky. The exact nature of his present business in Berlin will be taken up in a later chapter, where it will prove to be most significant for the Ace-of-Spies.

Whatever he was up to in Berlin almost made him miss the 13 June opening of Savinkov's All-Russian Anti-Bolshevik Congress in Warsaw that included Ukrainians, Cossacks and assorted peasant organizations. It was all Boris' show, and he harangued the delegates with fire-breathing rhetoric about "exterminating" the commissars and Chekists while offering that the Soviet system as such would be preserved as the mainstay of the New Order.[96] He pledged to deliver Russia to its peasant masses and to reconcile dissident minorities with principles of democratic federalism. The Bolsheviks were doomed, he promised, it was all just a matter of time, though it is hard to say whether he or most of his audience really believed this. The British, French, American, Italian and Belgian embassies all sent representatives, among them Sergius Riis who slipped away from his duties in Riga. Reilly, as usual, stayed to the background, the more visible representative of His Majesty being Maj. H. B. Clayton, a former friend and colleague of Nathan. The Foreign Office, where Savinkov's name was now a dirty word, was quick to raise objections. One note decried Clayton's appearance, in uniform no less, as "particularly unfortunate."[97] As for Sidney, the same hand opined "Mr. Reilly is in a position to do what he likes." In the view of some, perhaps, Sidney already was outside the realm of acceptability and accountability.

That Reilly was Cumming's man on the spot is confirmed by a telegram he dispatched to SIS on 16 June.[98] While in Warsaw, he reported, he had attended both public and secret meetings of Savinkov's organization that convinced him of an "impending insurrection" inside Russia. In Prague, he had further interviews with persons recently arrived from the Red Domain who assured him that a "great, coordinated insurrection" by the peasantry would erupt after the coming harvest and that the Red Army "will either join or remain neutral." The overall situation of the Soviet Government seemed "hopeless." However, only a few days later, Sidney took a more cautious tone in a letter to Savinkov's deputy Filosofov, warning that a peasant rebellion could not be taken for granted and should not forestall other actions.[99] Again we have one Reilly, two opinions.

Soon after he returned to London. It probably was Clayton who alerted Reilly to Nathan's dire condition. Long in poor health, Sir Robert passed away on 26 June at his rooms at the Albany. Whether Sidney arrived in time to pay his respects is uncertain, but a solid indication that he was headed in that direction is a 22 June packet from Warsaw to Morton asking than an enclosed letter be given to Reilly "immediately on his arrival in London."[100] Even the reclusive Cumming turned out for the funeral along with many other colleagues from the shadow world of espionage. With Nathan's death, Reilly lost a great friend, perhaps his *greatest* friend, in British intelligence. From this point on, the Ace-of-Spies' standing steadily began to deteriorate.

French espionage expert Hauteclocque later claimed that sometime in July Sidney appeared in Finland. Adopting a disguise, he crossed the frontier into Soviet Karelia where he engineered the escape of a prisoner from the special political "gulag" on the Solovetskii Islands.[101] Hauteclocque's tale even has Reilly disarming the guards with drugged vodka. While much of this sounds like dramatic license, the story cannot be dismissed out of hand.

However, firmer evidence puts Sidney in Vienna in relation to the surreptitious training of Ukrainian troops in Czechoslovakia. Polish information reaching London in early July described how Reilly presented himself as the representative of the British Government in negotiations with Galician (West Ukrainian) emissaries seeking help in their fight against Moscow.[102] With its large and restive Ukrainian minority, Warsaw frowned on anything that encouraged separatist ambitions. Sidney allegedly promised the Ukrainians the use of Czechoslovak Army facilities (perhaps via Gaida's influence), and intimated that London would provide the money. He declared that while England had ceased efforts to overthrow the Leninist regime outright, it still sought to detach as many regions as possible from Bolshevik control. Naturally, this report raised new questions in the Foreign Office and provoked denials from other quarters. In August the British military attaché in Prague insisted to Lord Curzon that "Mr. Reilly was not in Vienna during the period mentioned," at least not on behalf of His Majesty.[103] But how could he be so certain? The Passport Control Office in Vienna, i.e. the SIS station, blandly denied any knowledge of Ukrainian training camps in Czechoslovakia or anywhere else and made no mention of Reilly at all.[104] Chances are, the report contained more than a germ of truth, and it meshes well with his other, known movements.

During the summer months, Sidney also breezed in and out of Paris where he found time to pursue another turbulent romance. Sometime earlier, perhaps the previous summer, he had taken special note of a beautiful new face to appear on the Parisian stage, Arlette-Leonie Bathiat, later simply known as Arletty. In 1918 she had worked as a secretary at the Schneider-Creusot works, a firm, incidentally, around which Zaharoff was a frequent presence. Raven-haired and shapely, Arletty soon fell under Reilly's spell. He saw her when he was in Paris just as he still enjoyed Caryll Houselander's companionship when he was in London. Sidney may or may not have proposed marriage, but in the summer of 1921, she announced she was pregnant, something the Ace did not want to hear.[105] Like Margaret decades before, he insisted she solve the matter with an abortion. She agreed, but broke off their relationship, a move that seems to have taken him by surprise.

According to George Hill, the bitter termination of the affair plunged Reilly into a "state of acute depression" culminating in another seizure-like episode.[106] Hill claimed to have been present in Sidney's London

rooms when the attack occurred, and it was in the bleak aftermath, he further alleged, that Reilly once and only once spoke about his origins. The
tale he supposedly told that night had him the bastard offspring of a
Russo-Polish noblewoman and Dr. Rosenblum from Vienna. Perhaps the
most interesting aspect of the incident, if it occurred, is that even in the
midst of an emotional crisis, Reilly was capable of calculated lying. Or was
the breakdown a stunt to lend credibility to story he was about to feed
Hill? If so, why would he feel a need to deceive a friend like Jolly George?

Was there, possibly, something more to Reilly's depressed state of mind
than fakery or disappointment at the loss of Arletty? What, for instance, had
become of Anne since that long-missed rendezvous in Odessa? Were they still
in Russia? Were they still alive? And what did Yagoda or others know about
them? Was it some news from that hidden corner of his life that precipitated
his momentary collapse and resurrected thoughts of his early years?

Yet another story puts Reilly in Paris in July at the Hotel Lotti. His supposed mission was described in a 1930 book by German journalist
Hermann Berndorff provocatively titled *Diplomatic Underworld*.[107] While
the Reilly-related parts, like the rest of the book, are composites of fact,
rumor and imagination, Berndorff's acquaintance with Orlov,
Grammatikov and French spy-hunter Faux-Pas-Bidet meant that he had
access to some potentially well-informed sources. The gist of the tale is that
in league with two other British operatives, Sidney Roberts and George
Edwards, Reilly undertook to unveil secret negotiations between Polish and
Turkish agents in Paris, an arrangement that may also have involved the
connivance of the French Government. Berndorff connects this to recent
events in the disputed region of Upper Silesia where the Inter-Allied
Commission had brokered a cessation of hostilities (24 June) between
German and Polish partisans. The French, naturally, favored the Poles while
the British leaned to the Germans. Meanwhile in the Near East, Anglo-
French rivalry also simmered. The Greco-Turkish war raged on with
Ataturk's forces gaining the upper hand thanks, in part, to supplies of arms
and munitions from the French *and* the Bolsheviks. Thus, according to
Berndorff, a tacit French-Polish-Turkish alliance was taking shape to offset
a potential Anglo-German one. Sidney handled this situation by insinuating
an agent into the confidence of the key Polish agent, Madame Gordon, and
then arranging a surreptitious search of the rooms and papers of the local
Turkish representative, Bekir Sami Bey.

How much truth there is to this scenario is difficult to say. For instance,
Alekseev later noted "Sidney Roberts" as one of Reilly's aliases, though the
similarity in name lends itself to confusion. On the other hand, Reilly did

have some acquaintance with a George Edwards through James Slevin and Franklin Helm. He was a British businessman with interests in South America who traveled regularly between London, New York and Buenos Aires. That his business may have included some intelligence component is quite possible, but there is no obvious connection to the current Parisian intrigues. As for the Gordon woman, Berndorff declared that she had spent the war years in America, which at least suggests a prior connection to Reilly or Tony Jechalski. How interesting, therefore, that Jechalski was back in Warsaw's service and about to take up a post at the Polish Legation in Constantinople.[108]

What is certain is that SIS, and others in London, took a keen interest in the Turkish nationalists and especially the person of His Excellency Bekir Sami Bey. This was not because of his dealings with the Poles but with the Soviets. From as far afield as Shanghai, information drifted back to London linking Bekir's name to a proposed Soviet-Turkish alliance, itself part of a supposed "Pan-Asiatic Movement" aimed against British colonialism in India and elsewhere.[109] At this same juncture, several such SIS reports reached the recently-formed Inter-Departmental Committee (IDC) on Bolshevism as a Menace to the British Empire. One noted the Turks' recent receipt of a "subsidy" from Moscow, probably in gold, while another emphasized Ataturk's reluctance to accept Bolshevik help.[110] Another suggested that far from being pro-Soviet, Bekir Sami Bey was opposed to Moscow's influence.[111] If Sidney was spying on him in Paris, this must have been the sort of information he was after.

The IDC, first put together in June, would have been very receptive to Reilly's input. The chair was R.C. Lindsay, Undersecretary of State at the FO, but also on board were Rex Leeper, Basil Thomson, Arch Sinclair (representing Churchill, now Colonial Secretary) and Maj. Bray of the India Office, sitting in for the recently deceased Nathan. The SIS also had two members, names withheld in surviving documents, but Cumming surely was one and the other, perhaps, Morton. The Committee's first reports, collated in August, cited reports from agents inside Russia, including, seemingly, some with access to official and confidential documents. Most of these reports were categorized "A1," meaning "original documents actually in the possession of the S.I.S., or to which a representative of the S.I.S. has had access."[112] That Reilly was the direct or indirect source of at least some of this information seems certain. It was a role that would come back to haunt him in short order.

Meanwhile, back in New York, there were things afoot that may have had significance for him. On 1 July, both Claude Dansey and Guy

Gaunt arrived in Manhattan from England, albeit on different vessels. The first declared his intention to press on to Cuba for personal business, but Gaunt informed U.S. immigration that he would remain in the country for three months in connection with J.P. Morgan & Co. This alliance of two of Reilly's old antagonists may have had some important implications for his financial schemes in Europe, schemes generally detrimental to Morgan interests.

In mid-July, Reilly put in an indisputable appearance in Prague where he arranged a private meeting with Savinkov's old rival Kerenskii. Sidney's avowed aim was to patch up the feud between the two men and unite them in the anti-Bolshevik struggle. Whether this was Boris' or Reilly's idea is open to question, but one thing that made Kerenskii an attractive potential ally was that the former Prime Minister was receiving a generous stipend from the Czech Government. Reilly proposed that this money might better be spent abetting Savinkov's plan for sabotage and guerrilla operations. He later wrote that the two reached some agreements on "purely practical arrangements." To whatever degree Kerenskii responded, soon after the Ace-of-Spies committed an uncharacteristic error by mentioning the meeting to another local émigré, Savinkov's SR comrade Vladimir Mikhailovich Zenzinov (M).[113] The latter, perhaps a little miffed that Reilly had not come to him, reported the conversation to Kerenskii who refused to deal with Reilly further. On the 21st, at the Hotel Passage, Sidney tried to patch things up with a letter. "You accused me of indiscretion," he wrote, adding, "I should be very disturbed, if, as result of this innocent conversation [with Zenzinov], you were to refuse to find a means to accomplish the plan I suggested."[114]

Reilly told Kerenskii he was going on to Warsaw. In fact, he headed back to London, perhaps to report there about the failed mission. He had taken over Nathan's rooms at the Albany, a set of exclusive, bungalow-like flats neatly secluded from the hubbub of nearby Piccadilly. On 5 August, he completed a new memorandum on the Russian Situation.[115] It was based, he claimed, "on facts acquired from continuous personal contact with the leaders of democratic anti-Bolshevik activities in Russia." He interpreted Lenin's New Economic Policy as an admission of failure and weakness (which, to some degree, it was) but did *not* envisage a precipitate collapse of the regime. Rather, the country was likely to "plunge into a prolonged period of anarchy" but thought it pointless to speculate further about what might or might not happen. The Bolsheviks knew they were in trouble and were turning for help abroad. The Americans were "leading the way" in providing it. This was a clear reference to recent negotiations between Moscow and the American Relief Administration, headed by future U.S. President Herbert Hoover, negotiations that were to reach their conclusion in August. One of the first fruits of this Soviet-American accord, interestingly enough, was the release of Reilly's old accuser Xenophon Kalamatiano from prison. The basic aim of the Leninites, Reilly continued, was survival, and for the near future, that was to the advantage of the West as well. If Russia was to be reconstructed, the maintenance of trade was essential, and that necessitated the preservation of some modicum of stability. If the Bolsheviks should fall to some "general upheaval," chaos would reign for an "indefinite period." "The problem, therefore," he continued, "is how to bring about the downfall of the present Bolshevik Government in the least violent way, so as to preserve the administrative apparatus and the army." This sounds remarkably similar to what he first recommended to Cumming back in early 1918. He suggested the Reds' need for international help could accomplish this bloodless transformation by linking aid to certain changes in the regime. The Cheka would have to go and executive authority shifted to the hands of more "moderate types" such as Aleksei Rykov and Krasin. Lenin, Trotsky, Zinoviev, Lev Kamenev and other hardliners would be "banned from direct participation in affairs" but granted "personal immunity." Once these basic alterations were accomplished, the government would be broadened to include the Kadets, Right SRs, Mensheviks and, of course, Savinkov's Unionists. Finally, what remained of Russia's gold and portable wealth would come under the control of an "international trust fund," perhaps that last permutation of the old banking syndicate idea.

The above paper found its way into the hands of Lloyd George who, on the very same day, held a meeting with Krasin at 10 Downing Street. The main item on the agenda was whether the Soviet regime was willing to recognize past Russian debts.[116] Krasin agreed to pose the question in Moscow. To what degree the Prime Minister was reassured that he was talking with a "moderate" is unknown, but Sidney's memo must have had some influence on shaping perceptions and expectations. This was, in many respects, the high-water mark of Reilly's role in British affairs. Soon after his actions would become increasingly maverick and objectionable, and the hostility and suspicion that had always surrounded him would force all but his staunchest friends to keep a safe distance.

NOTES

1. CAC, CHAR 16/28.
2. Ibid., 16/57, Sinclair to Churchill, 24 June 1920.
3. Wise had connections to the Labour Party and most recently had served as a British delegate to the Allied Supreme Economic Council and the German reparations question.
4. PRO, FO 371/4033, 19083, 9 April 1920.
5. Ibid.
6. Ibid.
7. HLRO, LGP 202/3/4/ Secret Report #17, 5 May 1920.
8. HIA, Vrangel, Report, 20.
9. Ibid.
10. Leggett, 461.
11. David Stafford, *Churchill and the Secret State* (New York, 1998), 94.
12. PRO, KV 2/573, Report sent to Thomson, 6 Aug. 1920.
13. CAC, CHAR 16/49, "Personal and Confidential," 29 Oct. 1920.
14. Ibid.
15. UPA, Riga Records, Gade to State, 11 May 1920, Appendix B.
16. SIS, Russian Secret Service Report (summary), 1 Nov. 1920, note by Nathan. This appears to be close or identical to the report in the Vrangel file.
17. PRO, KV 2/573, CX 601, 24 Aug. 1920.
18. Ibid. 2/574, V.S.O. memo, 18 Oct. 1928.
19. University Publications of America (UPA), U.S. Diplomatic Post Records, Riga, reel 2, "International Clearing House Scheme," 21 July 1920, 1–2.
20. *NYT* (17 Oct. 1920), VIII, 4:5.
21. MID, 10058-530/65, ONI to MID, 20 Feb. 1920, and UPA, Riga Records, reel #2, Grew to State, #38, 21 July 1920, "International Clearing House Scheme."
22. GARF, f. 5801, d. 170, 19 June, 31 July, 6 Aug. 1922.
23. Xavier de Hauteclocque, "Zaharoff: Merchant of Death," *The Living Age*, vol. 342, #4388 (May 1932), 212.
24. J.T.W. Newbold, *Bondholders and Bolsheviks* (London, 1919), 14–15.
25. Yergin, 189–190, 195–196.
26. Newbold, 5–6, 12.
27. UPA, Riga Records, Gade to State, #187, 11 May 1920.
28. The new policy became effective in July, but left in place the ban on the import of export of gold from Russia. In light of the non-convertibility of the Soviet ruble, large-scale commerce still faced a major difficulty. See also the interview with Martens in *Pravda* (23 Feb. 1921).
29. HLRO, LG, 203/1/10, Krasin to Chicherin #43, 2 June 1920.
30. Thaddeus Holt, "Joint Plan Red," *Military History Quarterly*, #1 (Autumn 1988), 48–55.
31. Antony Cave Brown, *The Last Hero: Wild Bill Donovan* (New York, 1982), 75–77.
32. *NYT* (16 Oct. 1920), 15:7.
33. CAC, E.L. Spears Papers (SPRS), 1/53. Also included among the directors were former RAB man C. Chantry Inchbald, and Russian bankers V.R. Idelson and Boris and Noah Gordon.
34. *Ves' Peterburg*, 1914.
35. Urquhart's connection to Baku went back to 1896. A decade later he was British vice consul in the city; *LT* (15 March 1933), 16c.
36. Ibid.
37. CAC, SPRS, 1/53, Bruntrom to Spears, 31 May 1920.
38. HIA, Dukes 1919 Diary.

39. MID, 10541-367/149, U.S. Military Observer, Berlin to DMI, 30 July 1920, and /183, ditto to Col. Miles, Washington, 24 Feb. 1921.
40. U.S. Federal Bureau of Investigation (FBI), file 62-5394-2, Kurt A. Jahnke, "Memorandum for Mr. Hoover," 30 April 1923.
41. USDS, U-H file 812.0-683, Huddle to Gibson, Warsaw 23 March 1921, 3–5.
42. SIS, Nathan, Sec. V, to Liddell, 3 Sept. 1920.
43. Ibid., C to DNI, 7 Sept. 1920.
44. Ibid., Production, For Commander, R.N., 6 Sept. 1920.
45. Sinclair replaced Hall as DNI in early 1919.
46. MI5, Reilly, A.M.K. to Morton, 11 Jan. 1921.
47. NYT (12 Aug. 1920), 1:8.
48. NYT (14 Aug. 1920), 1:6.
49. NYT (8 Sept. 1920), 18:4.
50. SIS, Nathan to Reilly, 23 Sept. 1920.
51. NYT (22 Oct. 1920), 1:7.
52. MID, 2657-D-643, DS, 12 Jan. 1922 and 2037-1422, ID, 16 Nov. 1922.
53. CAC, CHAR 16/28, Reilly to Horne, BOT, 12 Oct. 1920.
54. SIS, Production to Meiklejohn, 20 Oct. 1920.
55. Ibid., Production to Warsaw, 20 Oct. 1920.
56. Narodnaia Dobrovolcheskaia Armiia.
57. Spence, "Useful Brigand: Ataman S.N. Bulak-Balakhovich, 1917–21," Revolutionary Russia, vol. 11, #1 (June 1998), 17–36.
58. PRO, FO 371/5423, note to #194, 8 Oct. 1920.
59. FO 371/5413, 3842, 7 Dec. 1920.
60. CAC, CHAR 16/68B, Geiger to Sinclair, 25 Oct. 1920.
61. Ibid., Geiger to Sinclair, 29 Oct. 1920.
62. SIS, Warsaw to London, 23 Oct. 1920.
63. Ibid., CXG 148, 30 Oct. 1920.
64. Ibid., Sir P. Loraine (from Reilly), 29 Oct. 1920.
65. GARF, f. 5901, d. 87 (#8), "Pokhod Generala Bulak-Balakhovicha," 45–47.
66. Ibid.
67. PRO, FO 371/5439, ST1, "Assessment of Savinkov," 14 Nov. 1920.
68. SIS, Production, Section V, 3 Nov. 1920.
69. Ibid.
70. PRO, FO 371/12602, 2649, Hoare's note to #1017, 17 Nov. 1920.
71. SIS, CX 2616, G2, 8 Nov. 1920.
72. Ibid., Reilly to Morton, 18 Nov. 1920.
73. Ibid., Reilly to Morton, 3 Dec. 1920.
74. Orlov, Morder, 228–229.
75. CAC, CHAR 16/68B, Geiger to Sinclair, 7 Dec. 1920.
76. HIA, Dukes 1920 Diary. He was in London as early as 4 Dec. when he notes dining with Churchill.
77. Georges Solomon, Parmi les maitres rouges (Paris, 1930), 248–250.
78. UPA, Riga Records, reel 1, Young to State, #270, Young to Sec. of State, 2 Nov. 1920, 6–9, and 21 July 1921.
79. R. Lockhart, First Man, 29, Deacon, Super Spy: The Man Who Infiltrated the Kremlin and the Gestapo (London, 1989). As with most of Deacon/McCormick's works, this "biography" of Lucas should be used with caution, but it does sketch his rather long and strange career in the secret world.
80. PRO, 371/6845, 1050, "Russian Social Revolutionary Party," 22 Jan. 1921.
81. American Art Galleries, Collection of Mr. Sidney G. Reilly . . .
82. TsAFSB, 302330, Styrne, "Doklad o razgovorakh s Reili 24–26 sentiabria 1925 g.," 2 Oct. 1925.

83. FBI, file 61-288, "Hammer, Armand," section I.
84. HLRO, LG, F/28/8/11, Hilton Young (Treasury) to Edward Grigg (FO), 11 Feb. 1921.
85. PRO, KV 2/574, V.S.O., 18 Oct. 1928.
86. CAC, CHAR, 16/49, "Personal and Confidential," 29 Oct. 1920.
87. HIA, Vrangel, Report, 17–18.
88. Hauteclocque, "Russian Secret Service Secrets," *The Living Age* vol. 344, #4401 (June 1933), 348.
89. Thanks to Dr. Joseph Zacek for details on Gaida's career. See also Gaida's memoir, *Moje Pameti* (Prague, 1924).
90. *NYT* (23 Oct. 1922), 19:1.
91. Ibid. One of Helm's partners in the German credit plan was William McAdoo.
92. PRO, FO 371/6910, ST/1, #187, 5 May 1921, 2.
93. Ibid., 7.
94. Ibid., 14.
95. At his trial, Savinkov denied receiving money from Ford, to his knowledge at least; see: BSPVKVS, 135–136, 249–250, n. 162. For Brasol's role as a bag man see Jerome and Suzanne Pool, *Who Financed Hitler?* (New York, 1978), 85–130.
96. Spence, *Savinkov*, 299.
97. PRO, FO 371/6830, 11555, "Notes on Meeting of Anti-Bolshevik Russians and Ukrainians," 30 Sept. 1921.
98. FO 371/6849, ST/1, 16 June 1921.
99. Amsterdam, Internationaal Instituut voor Sociale Geschiedenis (IISG), Archief Sawinkow (AS), box 34, ST to Filosofov, 22 June 1921.
100. SIS, Maclaren to Morton, 22 June 1921.
101. Hauteclocque, "L'Intelligence Service: Sidney Reilly," *La Liberte* (17 Dec. 1925), 2.
102. PRO, FO 371/6810, #218, "Galician Question and Training of Officers in Czechoslovakia," 4 July 1921.
103. PRO, FO 371/6811, 10950, 24 and 29 Aug. 1921.
104. Ibid.
105. R. Lockhart, *Ace*, 124 and interview with Dmitri Stein, Paris, 1996.
106. Michael Kettle, "Who Was Sidney Reilly?," *Sunday Times* (19 Nov. 1967), 13, and Kettle to author, 20 May 1995.
107. *Diplomatische Unterwelt* (Stuttgart, 1930), 12–31.
108. MID, 9140-1496,/348, Senior Naval officer in Constantinople to ONI, 10 Sept. 1921.
109. British Library, India Office Records (IOR), L/PJ/12/45, SIS Report #316, 8, July 1921.
110. PRO, WO 32/5728, 24270, "Bolshevik Activities against the Empire: Formation of an Inter-Departmental Committee," [Aug. 1921], 10, 17, and IOR, L/DJ/12/45, SIS report #331, "Political Problems in the Near East," 15 July 1921.
111. PRO, WO 32/5728, Ibid., 24–25.
112. Ibid., Second Report, introduction.
113. HIA, Lockhart, box.6, Reilly to Kerenskii, 21 Oct. 1921.
114. Ibid.
115. HLRO, LG, 203/3/6, 5 Aug. 1921.
116. Ibid., 203/3/7, "Notes on Interview with Russian-Soviet Representatives at 10 Downing St.," 5 Aug. 1921. Also present at the meeting was Frank Wise. Krasin was accompanied by Jan Berzin.

PART THREE
MYSTERY MAN

"The public demands certainty;
it must be told definitely . . .
that this is true and that is false.
But there is no certainty."

—H.L. Mencken

Chapter Thirteen
ODD MAN OUT

As summer 1921 drew to a close, there were no obvious signs of change in Reilly's position with SIS. On 23 August, Boyce, now running the Helsinki station, wired him that a former Russian naval officer, "Daniel Fedotoff White," had arrived from the Soviet side with an urgent message from one Redkozubov, one that had to be delivered personally to Reilly.[1] The traveler actually was *Dmitrii* Nikolaevich Fedotov-White.[2] During the early part of the war, he had been an assistant Russian naval attaché in the United States and had a fair amount to do with war contracts and the characters associated with them. Thus, he knew Sidney. Perhaps to refresh Reilly's memory, he mentioned them meeting at a dinner in New York. During early 1918, Fedotov worked with British naval intelligence in Archangel, but whether his and the Ace-of-Spies' paths crossed there as well is uncertain. He now hoped Reilly could meet him at the Hotel Astrea in Copenhagen on the 29th. Who Redkozubov was and what information he wanted to pass was not revealed. Could the information have somehow involved Anne? Whatever the case, Redkozubov elsewhere is identified as an SIS operative under Boyce's supervision. Given Fedotov's background and the fact that he had most recently worked in the Soviet Merchant Marine administration, the best bet is that Redkozubov was another former Imperial Navy officer. Sidney, however, could not be bothered; a rendezvous with Fedotov was out of the question because he had to be in Prague on the 29th.

Reilly had big business in the Czech capital. Commercially, he was riding in higher circles than ever. One rather minor angle involved the tobacco venture he and Spears, who accompanied him on the trip, had initiated some months before. Tobacco was a state monopoly in the new Republic, so they sold directly to the Czech Government. That, if nothing else, helped open doors for other deals. In this same period, Sidney was negotiator for a "French consortium" interested in modernizing Prague's gas and electric service.[3] But the biggest scheme was a plan to corner the world market on radium. This involved a pact between the Czech Government and the London-based Imperial and Foreign Co. (IFC). Sidney was the latter's special representative. The head of the IFC was Herbert Guedalla, Nathan's chum. Spears also held a directorship. Yet another was ex-Foreign Secretary Arthur Balfour. Each, recall, was linked to the British Corporation of Mine and Steamship Owners in Russia. Also taking an active interest in the deal was Churchill who in July assured Spears and Sidney of his assistance with the "matter in Prague."[4] The affair even caught the attention of Buckingham Palace that dispatched a special King's Messenger to bring some of the precious radium to Oxford University.[5] The state-owned pitchblende mines at Joachimsthal (Jachymov), near Karlsbad (Karlovy Vary), were then the world's richest source of the rare element, so rare that a single gram fetched more than $100,000.

Word of a big Anglo-Czech radium deal leaked to the European press in late July. We can suppose that Reilly had started the ball rolling during his recent visits.[6] The end result, as revealed on 16 September, was the creation of the Radium Corporation of Czechoslovakia, its stock split 50/50 between the IFC and the Czech Government.[7] The managing director of this new firm was none other than Mr. Sidney G. Reilly. A not insignificant side note was that the Radium Co. was financed by a loan from the parent IFC, and that additional funds might be channeled through it. The Radium outfit, therefore, could supply money to other enterprises or even, with a little creative bookkeeping, to someone like Boris Savinkov. Perhaps the most unusual aspect of the radium deal was the relative openness with which Reilly's name was associated with the venture. An item in the *New York Times* quoted him on the "far-reaching scientific results" anticipated. "Within fifteen years we shall have from fifty to sixty grammes of pure radium," he boasted, and expected that the Czech mines ultimately could produce as much as a hundred.[8] Given that France, Germany and America had no more than a few grams at their disposal, "henceforth Britain will be in a pre-eminent position in radiology."

Beyond its medical uses, just what did Reilly and his partners envision doing with all this radioactive material? Sidney mentioned recent experiments in Czechoslovakia indicating that "radio emanations" could stimulate the growth rates of plants and animals. Given that the discovery of nuclear fission was still some years off, there would not seem to have been any notion of a military application, but the possibility of radioactive heat as a power source might have lurked in the background.

Radium was not the only thing Reilly was after in Czechoslovakia. Reports in Paris identified him as the agent of yet another firm, the Standard Franco-American Oil Co. This was a subsidiary of Standard Oil of New Jersey and the spearhead of its all-out war with Royal Dutch/Shell for the markets and riches of Central Europe. Sidney's work on behalf of Standard was an extension of his long association with MacRoberts and the National City Bank, a close financial ally of the Rockefeller interests. It also certainly had something to do with his dealings with Boris Said. The arrangement Reilly negotiated gave Standard exclusive drilling rights in the country and a powerful advantage in marketing its own products.[9] This coup, noted the *New York Times*, was part of the "intense rivalry" between Standard and Shell. The deal, in fact, pre-empted Deterding's attempt to secure the same advantage.[10] For Reilly, of course the petroleum battle-ground was the perfect environment to employ the System.

That Cumming's office was interested in and well-informed about ST1's business activities is attested by a 26 September memo from Field-Robinson in Paris to Morton that forwarded an article from the Parisian *La Journée Industrielle*.[11] Among other things, the piece identified Reilly as a *commis-saire* of British Civil Aviation and as the special "commercial agent" of Arthur Balfour. Robinson seemed to think this would "amuse" Morton.

Amidst all this business, Reilly found time to engage in his favorite pas-time, political intrigue. On 11 September, Savinkov breezed in from Warsaw. His presence there was a growing inconvenience to the Polish Government. Moscow claimed that Warsaw's harboring of him and his restyled Peoples' Union for the Defense of the Motherland and Liberty was a flagrant viola-tion of the recent Riga Treaty and demanded his expulsion.[12] To make the point, Lenin refused to honor another treaty obligation, the payment of 30 million gold rubles to Poland, until Savinkov and his gang were sent pack-ing. Warsaw needed the money while Boris seemed adept only at making trouble. The situation was further complicated by the arrival of an official Soviet Legation, headed by Lev Karakhan. In early September, Marshal Pilsudski, summoned Savinkov to a private meeting. He asked his old ally to vacate Poland for a month or so until things cooled down. To compound matters, some weeks before the Polish Foreign Ministry had cut off its sub-sidy to Boris' group, estimated as 15 million Polish Marks per month. This sent the Union into an acute financial crisis provoking desperate messages from Maclaren and Savinkov's secretary, Dmitrii Filosofov, pleading with Reilly to come to the rescue. Again, there is no sign that Sidney invested any appreciable amount of his own money, but he did engineer a timely infusion of cash from other sources. On 6 September, Reilly, then on a quick visit to

Vienna, received a letter from Jiri Kranz, a Czech official of the Anglo-Magyar Bank. This confirmed that 3 million Polish Marks was being sent to the Union Bank in Warsaw, the firm where Savinkov had his accounts.[13] Interestingly, Kranz acknowledged a mutual friend, Stephen Alley, now with MI5, who seems to have played some role in approving or facilitating the transfer. This at least hints that Reilly had arranged a transfer of clandestine British funds to Boris's organization.

Sidney also lent a helping hand in securing a fresh base of support in Czechoslovakia. With his help, Savinkov received audiences with Czech President Thomas Masaryk, with whom he had conspired in 1918, and Prague's Foreign Minister, Eduard Benes. The latter offered sanctuary and a small stipend, but discouraged Savinkov from pursuing more "active" measures against the Soviets.[14] Reilly, however, knew they could count on stronger support from the Czech military, whose intelligence service employed a number of Savinkov's adherents as agents to keep tabs on Bolshevik and other Russian factions.

One man taking a keen interest in Reilly's doings was Bruce Lockhart, who now held the post of British commercial attaché in Prague. In a seemingly friendly gesture, he invited Reilly and Savinkov to lunch. Boris poured out his frustration over Kerenskii, who refused to see him, and railed against Russian financiers in Paris (undoubtedly Putilov and friends) who also declined to help. He solicited the Scot's help in securing a German visa to go to Paris and make his case in person. He also expressed a strong desire to visit London to confer with Churchill and Lloyd George. Lockhart immediately reported all of this to the Foreign Office. The Scot noted that Savinkov's finances had improved significantly since his arrival in the Czech capital, not through Reilly's largesse, but that of unnamed "private Czech sources."[15]

As might be expected, Savinkov and Reilly's scheming received a very negative review at the FO, especially the proposed visit to London. On 16 September, the same day as Lockhart's report, Charles Hardinge conveyed the gist of it to Foreign Secretary Curzon. Another FO hand, P.V. Evans, noted that "we are utterly opposed to Mr. Savinkoff's movement and will have nothing to do with it." Still, he thought it might create more of a fuss than it was worth to refuse him a visa, a view with which Rex Leeper concurred.[16]

Lockhart's involvement with Reilly at this juncture had a strange twist that may have had a bearing on what he reported—or did not report—to London. As Spears recalled it, Sidney prevailed upon him and Brunstrom to make a £500 personal loan to Lockhart, to help him out of a tight spot.[17]

This intervention on Reilly's part certainly did not stem from friendship. Note that, as usual, he did not put up the money himself. The ulterior motive surely was to buy Lockhart's silence or cooperation in some regard.

During September an incident occurred that brought Reilly's name into further disrepute. In the preceding months, SIS reports, forwarded by the aforementioned Inter-Departmental Committee, painted a disturbing picture of Soviet subversion. Motivated by these, on 7 September Lord Curzon composed a note to Krasin and Soviet Commissar of Foreign Affairs Chicherin alleging "flagrant breach of faith" of the Anglo-Soviet trade agreement. Signed back in March, this pledged Moscow to cease all hostile and subversive activities. Curzon attacked the "violent anti-British propaganda" conducted throughout Asia and other corners of the world.[18] The essence of Curzon's charge was true, but Moscow insisted that the British Government had fallen victim to the nefarious work of "professional forgers and swindlers" such as Orlov, a charge that also probably bore some element of truth.[19] This suggested some of the documents were forgeries or, at the least, hardly the unimpeachable information claimed by SIS.[20] In this regard, it is worthwhile to recall Sidney's hand in the earlier Sisson Documents.

Donald McCormick later claimed that reports forwarded to Curzon were altered to disguise the interception of Soviet diplomatic traffic by Britain's super-secret Government Code and Cipher School (GCCS).[21] He alleged that Reilly goaded the Foreign Office into revealing these intercepts as a means of tipping off Moscow that its codes were compromised. That seems doubtful; given his standing at the FO, it is hard to see how he could have exerted any influence there. Beyond that, the Bolsheviks continued to use the same, compromised codes. Nevertheless, the controversy did absolutely nothing to improve Reilly's repute at the FO.

On 19 September, Sidney was again in Prague and had prepared a new report for SIS on Savinkov.[22] He sent it to L.G.M. Gall, another "good friend" in Cumming's office who earlier had worked with Nathan in the Copenhagen negotiations. "I am so frightfully rushed here," Reilly noted, "[I have] written it helter-skelter." When it seemed "ship-shape," he asked Gall to show it to "people who count," among them Churchill, Leeper, Lloyd George's secretary Sir Edward Grigg and "anybody else you think useful." The note of urgency, he added, was motivated by the fact that "Savinkov is coming with me to London." He and Boris had just spent a week together going over the "financial question." "We have for [now] the daily bread," he boasted, "we are out to get the butter and we will get it too." Reilly anticipated landing in Paris on the 25th and to be in London a few days later.

In the interim, Savinkov was embroiled in a very public and bitter end to his Polish liaison. In Warsaw, an officer connected with Savinkov's Union went to the press with a convoluted story of how he fabricated documents "proving" the relationship between Savinkov's organization and the Polish Army and then sold them to Karakhan.[23] The affair may have made Karakhan look foolish, but it also made Boris and his associates an even bigger embarrassment to the Warsaw regime. Beyond this, Reilly's name cropped up in the affair that did his local reputation no good either.

On 7 October, Savinkov, then in Paris, fired off an urgent wire to London telling Reilly "I need you here absolutely."[24] Earlier that day, Filosofov, Viktor Savinkov and other key lieutenants had been summoned by the Polish Foreign Ministry and told they would have to leave the country. Against Reilly's advice, Savinkov rushed to intercede with Pilsudski. After more antics and the personal intercession of Pilsudski, Boris departed Warsaw on the 29th amidst an air of recrimination and ill will. The whole ugly denouement was duly noted by London. On 2 November, with SIS sanction, Reilly dutifully rushed to Prague to hold Savinkov's hand and keep him from making some other stupid move.[25]

He also provided London a full report on the affair, one that tried to put the best spin on a bad situation.[26] Savinkov's "activities have entered upon a new phase," he predicted. Boris remained "undaunted" and viewed the recent Polish incident as "a blessing in disguise." He was no longer bound to kowtow to Warsaw's wishes that could only enhance his popularity in Russia. All the "real work" of Savinkov's Union was now taking place inside Russia anyway, so a removal to Prague would have little practical impact. However, "a big illegal organization" remained in Poland and would continue to operate with the tacit approval of the Polish General Staff. Savinkov's plan was to set up several centers in Finland, Latvia and the other Baltic States that would supervise the activities of guerrilla bands and local cells on Soviet territory.

In Prague, Reilly also presented a copy of this report to William Howell, the U.S. charge d'affaires who forwarded it to the State Department. Howell described Reilly as "a Hebrew, born in Galicia, and now a British subject."[27] Sidney's interest in courting American opinion likely had some relation to Kalamatiano's reappearance in Washington. Three years in Red jails had not softened the American spy-master's opinion of Reilly; he still regarded Reilly as the primary agent of his downfall in 1918 and was sure to make that point upon his return home.

Back in New York, an interesting visitor showed up in mid-September. It was Mrs. Margaret Reilly who arrived aboard the SS *Lapland* from

Antwerp. To all appearances, she traveled alone. Given her continual assertion of penury, where did Daisy get money for the trip? It is worth noting that Guy Gaunt was still in New York working for Morgan. Could he have had a hand in bringing her to the States? If so, why? It seems certain that Margaret's trip had some connection to her husband. He, of course, was occupied in Europe, which might have been the whole point of her foray. With a little help from Gaunt, she would have a relatively free hand to probe around for assets. Perhaps she had gotten word of the American Art Galleries auction and hoped that by presenting herself as his spouse she could claim some of the proceeds.

Sidney, meanwhile, was finalizing the tobacco business with Spears and Rozen. Under a contract signed in London on 15 October, Rozen was entitled to a commission on each order placed by his partners on behalf of the British firm of Watson & Co. It was a simple arrangement and the sums involved rather small, but it would prove to be the source of dispute and rancor in the future. That Sidney did not give his business with Spears high priority can be seen in his neglect to pay the electric bill for their London office, an oversight that vexed Spears and excited growing doubts about dealing with the Ace-of-Spies and his multitude of shady friends.

Spears was not the only one to have such reservations. On 2 November, for no apparent reason, French military intelligence, the *Deuxième Bureau*, complied a summary report on the "*Affaire Lockhardt* [sic]" which rehashed Reilly's dealings with the Latvians and Kalamatiano. Although there was really nothing new in it, the report found its way to London and into ST1's SIS file. Who requested it and why is uncertain, but it seems to have been part of an effort by Cumming or someone on his staff to investigate Reilly's earlier career. Why had this now become an issue? Perhaps the answer lies in the recent Curzon Note flap, but there may have been other issues. Reilly's connection to Orlov, for instance, and Orlov's collaboration with the Germans took on disturbing implications if one considered Reilly's past association with Berlin's intelligence services. Then, of course, there was his familiarity with Krasin and other Soviet representatives. Someone, certainly, was curious as to just who Sidney Reilly was and who he was working for.

Things began to move with a hectic and bewildering intensity. About the time he was putting signatures to paper with Spears and Rozen, Sidney wired Dukes in New York asking that he return to Europe at once. Finding passage on a seedy steamer bound for Hamburg, Sir Paul landed there on 8 November. He was supposed to meet Reilly and proceed with him to London, but something detained Sidney in Prague. Dukes cooled his heels in the German port for a week before pushing on to England. The duo were at last reunited at the Albany on the 17th, and over the next two weeks Dukes recorded no less than five meetings with Reilly, at least one of them in the company of "C." [28] At the close of November, Paul headed to Berlin where on 2 December he met with Orlov and "K." The latter most likely was Orlov's friend and liaison to the local monarchists, Col. Aleksandr Aleksandrovich Kolberg.

Also on the 2nd, Morton sent a coded wire to the SIS resident in Berlin, Frank Foley. He informed him Reilly was to arrive in few days and "will call on you . . . please assist him." [29] The message noted that [Reilly] put us in touch with Z-51 [Orlov] and knows all concerning latter." Sidney arrived in the German capital on the 4th where he, Dukes and "K" got together. Two days after, Dukes pushed on to Riga where he conferred with resident SIS chief Meiklejohn. Also on Dukes' visiting list was another SIS man, Arthur McPherson, who had encountered Reilly in wartime New York and Odessa. Dukes also made contact with Savinkov's agents and even the head of the local Swedish Legation. Sidney, in the meantime, rushed back to Paris to pick up Boris.

What was all this about? To understand, we must return to the afore-mentioned Aleksandr Yakushev. During 1919, while in Red service, he joined a White underground organization in Petrograd with links to Dukes.[30] When that collapsed, he fled to Moscow where he resumed work for the Commissariat of Ways and Communications (*Narkomput*). During the fall of 1921, he undertook a mission to Sweden, Norway, Switzerland and Germany, something that brought him into contact with Krasin's for-eign trade apparatus. Before returning to Russia, he stopped in Estonia and looked up an old friend, Yurii Aleksandrovich Artamonov, a former officer linked to monarchist exile circles. Yakushev confided that he, too, retained monarchist sympathies and was in league with many like-minded individu-als in Moscow and Petrograd. In fact, he claimed to be their representative seeking contacts with fellow monarchists abroad. It was no use, he told Artamonov, to try and overthrow the Bolsheviks from abroad. That only could be accomplished from within Russia and was the very thing he and his comrades aspired to do. After Yakushev's departure, Artamonov reported the meeting in a letter to another friend, Prince A.A. Shirinskii-Shikhmatov, a member of the Supreme Monarchist Council (*Vysshii Monarkhicheskii Soviet*—VMS) in Berlin. Shirinskii-Shikhmatov, in turn, was intimate with Orlov's buddy Col. Kolberg. To make the story even more interesting, Artamonov happened to work for the British Passport Control Office in Tallinn, i.e., the SIS station. He was a trusted informant to Meiklejohn and even Riis in Riga. He undoubtedly passed on word of the Yakushev meeting to them.

This is what caught Reilly's notice and what Dukes was dispatched to investigate further. During December, while Dukes was on hand, another man showed up in Estonia calling himself Viktor Kolesnikov. He claimed to be a representative of the organization Yakushev had discussed, the Monarchist Association of Central Russia (*Monarkhicheskoe Ob'edinenie Tsentral'noi Rossii*-MOTsR). This group, Kolesnikov claimed, sought active collaboration with foreign intelligence services in its struggle with the Lenin regime. Artamonov, Riis, and possibly Boyce met with the visitor to hear him out. It is even possible that Dukes was in on the gathering; at the least he must have received a full report.

Naturally, things were not quite what they seemed. The Yakushev-Kolesnikov overtures had all the earmarks of provocation. Few of the experienced agents involved, least of all Reilly, would have overlooked that possibility. And provocation is exactly what it was. Dzerzhinskii decreed that Yakushev should be approached and persuaded to help organize an actual shadow government inside Russia to be dubbed the "Trust" (*Trest*). While most of its rank and file would be legitimate monarchists, thus flushing them out of the woodwork, the key positions would be held by Chekists and "reliable" operatives. They, in turn, would be used to divert and infiltrate émigré groups and the foreign intelligence services backing them. By one means or another, Yakushev agreed to cooperate and set up the meeting for Kolesnikov, in reality a Polish Chekist named Stetskovich.

There are problems with this scenario. For instance, Jonas Lied later wrote that Yakushev, whom he knew well from the old days, tried to entice him into an obvious Cheka trap in 1920, suggesting that he was an active collaborator much earlier.[31] Of course, Lied himself was accused of being a Cheka informer, so it is impossible to know whom to believe.

Yet another dubious character to pop up in relation with the Trust was Eduard Ottovich Opperput, AKA Selianinov, Staunitz, Stroilov, Levine, Kasatkin, Ring, Uppelintz and many others. His true name, as best as can be determined, was Eduard Upeninsh, a Latvian by origin.[32] The familiar Latvian link may hint as some connection to Peters and Berzin. Since 1918, Opperput, under various names, had functioned as a Red agent and provocateur from Petrograd to the Crimea, though never as a Cheka regular. Opperput has been lurking around the edges of our story for some time. In late 1917, he was a member of a Latvian military organization in Petrograd and was arrested by the Bolsheviks as a suspected counter-revolutionary. He was freed, interestingly, on the personal order of Vladimir Bonch-Bruevich and enrolled in his Investigation Commission.[33] That certainly provided an opportunity to meet Orlov and Reilly. Moreover, in 1920, as Stroilov, he served on Vrangel's staff in the Crimea where he worked in close proximity to Orlov. Early the following year, as Opperput-Selianinov, he infiltrated Savinkov's organization in Poland, even helping organize the Anti-Bolshevik Congress. Given all this, it seems all but impossible that he would have been unknown to Reilly or Orlov. After he disappeared on a mission inside Russia when a wave of arrests decimated Savinkov's cells from Kiev to Petrograd. Presumed dead, Opperput suddenly resurfaced in Warsaw in October 1921, on the very eve of Savinkov's expulsion. He claimed to have been released under a Soviet amnesty, but hinted that his freedom had been obtained through the influence of a powerful, underground anti-Bolshevik movement.[34] By December Opperput was in Berlin where he told the same story to local monarchists and Orlov. After publishing a small book highly critical of Savinkov and his organization, he again vanished into Russia.[35]

Sidney would not have been taken in by Yakushev's and Opperput's improbable stories, but he would have seen them as potentially useful to his own plans. He knew that men like these—men much like him—did not serve out of any sense of loyalty or ideological conviction, but from personal necessity and desire for reward. They were always ready to take a better deal if it was available. With the efforts of just a few people, after all, a phony anti-Bolshevik conspiracy might be transformed into a real one.

Talk of underground movements and the undermining of the Bolshevik order from within also fit perfectly with Savinkov's latest scheme-cutting a deal by which he could return to Russia and take up some role in a "broadened" Soviet Government. That, of course, meshed with the plan Reilly proposed to Lloyd George a year earlier regarding the "peaceful" transformation of the Soviet system. Sidney, in fact, was encouraging his comrade in this new gambit. According to the writer Zinaida Hippius, who worked with Savinkov's Committee in Poland during 1921, Boris' determination to reach accommodation with Moscow was evident well before he left Warsaw.[36] He fantasized that Lenin would welcome him as an ally against the Communist left wing. It was for this reason that the main person Savinkov wanted to see in Britain was not Churchill or the Prime Minister, but Krasin.

The problem was how to get him into the country. The attitude at the Foreign Office had not softened. This view was epitomized by FO Permanent Undersecretary, Eyre Crowe, who thought Savinkov "most unreliable and crooked" and refused him a visa.[37] So strong was this feeling that Cumming and Morton declined to intervene, at least directly. Reilly found a way around the problem with a little help from Field-Robinson and, perhaps, Churchill. On 2 December, Robinson wrote Spears with details about the personnel and organization of the Paris Passport Control Office, including "particulars required by your friend."[38] Robinson proposed to somehow take control of the office and "carry out a certain amount of intelligence work for 'C'." A few days later, Sidney used Robinson to convince the SIS chief in Paris, Maj. T.M. Langton, to give Savinkov a visa without asking or informing London, or at least the FO. On the 8th, Reilly and Savinkov slipped across the Channel without anyone but a select few knowing.

Two days later, they dined with Krasin at the Soviet Mission. Also in attendance was an unnamed Englishman, probably Dukes. What happened next varies from one account to another. According to Reilly, Boris approached Krasin on the idea of a coalition Soviet Government including "moderate elements of all parties," himself included. Krasin admitted the regime was on a rightward course and likely to continue on it for the foreseeable future. He did not, however, hold out any hope for the changes Savinkov envisioned and pooh-poohed the notion that there were serious divisions among the Bolshevik leadership. However, his comments did not close the door on *individual* accommodations, and for over an hour he and Savinkov spoke in private. Even so, Boris reportedly left disappointed.

However, according to Boris' later statements to Churchill and members of his own organization, it was Krasin who proposed that he come home to Moscow where an honorable and suitable position would be his.[39] Savinkov responded that he could only do so on the conditions that the Cheka was abolished, private property restored and free elections instituted for the Soviets. Krasin supposedly offered to convey the terms to Moscow. To some, Boris even claimed that he had enlisted Krasin as a secret member of the Union.

The Kremlin did grant one of Savinkov's demands, though certainly not because of him. In January 1922, the infamous Cheka—the Extraordinary Commission—ceased to exist. In its place immediately appeared the rather bland-sounding State Political Administration (*Gosudarstvennoe Politicheskoe Upravlenie*) or GPU. The change, of course, was purely cosmetic; it was still the secret police and it was still run by Dzerzhinskii and his veteran *chekisty*, a name they preserved with some pride. In little more than a year there would be a further change of title to the Unified State Political Administration, or OGPU.[40] Far from weakening its grip, Iron Feliks' organization expanded in size and scope. Something else that remained the same was that a large proportion of the personnel, in some bureaus as high as 90%, were former employers of Tsarist military intelligence, border guards, customs, foreign ministry and, above all, the Okhrana.[41] Reilly, of course, had many acquaintances in those quarters.

What Savinkov's overture to Krasin proved to Sidney and others was that the old intriguer wanted to return to Russia and was willing to make a deal with his erstwhile opponents to do so. It was all just a matter of terms and timing. As for Krasin, his outward handling of the situation polished his rather tarnished image as loyal Soviet servant, thus bolstering his stock and influence at home.

Most observers dismissed the Savinkov-Krasin meeting as the desperate act of a political has-been, but there were some who saw more sinister implications. Crowe, for instance, wondered whether the real purpose of the dog-and-pony show was to convince Churchill and other British politicians that the Soviet regime really was on a course of reason and moderation. That it occurred just before an economic conference at Cannes, where Russian questions would be high on the agenda, seemed all the more suspicious. Similar misgivings were expressed by a Polish officer, Wladyslaw Michniewicz. He took special note of a 29 December letter from Savinkov to Pilsudski describing the meeting.[42] This emphasized Boris' supposed challenge to Krasin and other "right-Bolsheviks" to break with Trotsky and Dzerzhinskii and join with him. Michniewicz interpreted this as a deliberate effort to distort the character of the Red regime and concluded Savinkov was acting as a Soviet agent of influence. If so, what did that make Reilly? Michniewicz almost certainly was wrong in his assessment, as least for the reasons he supposed.

Following the Krasin meeting, Reilly escorted Boris to a sit-down with an adoring Churchill who, in turn, set up a meeting with a much less impressed Lloyd George. Churchill was still full of fight against the Reds, but Lloyd George had concluded the Bolsheviks were the only real power in Russia, and the only faction that had to be dealt with and appeased.

Margaret later recounted a story, presumably gleaned from her husband or someone else in intelligence circles, about what happened next. According to this, someone, probably Churchill, asked Sidney to present his views on Russia to the Cabinet. There he voiced strong reservations about Russia's supposed return to normalcy and concluded by saying that he would believe the country had entered a "convalescent state" when it "turned round and massacred at least one million Jews."[43] These words "terribly shocked" the gentlemen of the Cabinet who refused to listen to any of his recommendations. In response, he "resigned as officer of intelligence." It seems very doubtful that Reilly would have addressed the

Cabinet in person, but he may have submitted another of his reports expressing these and other unpalatable views. While Margaret's rendering may be somewhat skewed, the issue of endemic Russian anti-Semitism and pogroms crops up elsewhere in Reilly's utterances. Furthermore she and others may have misinterpreted his remarks. Basically, he argued that the prominence of Jews among the Bolshevik leadership was bound to provoke a violent reaction should the regime collapse. That may partly explain his advocacy of the modification of the Soviet regime from within as opposed to its abrupt overthrow.

Sidney certainly faced the retribution of the FO for defying its edicts. Robinson mustered out of service before the storm broke and so was beyond their reach, and Spears managed to conceal his culpability. The unfortunate Langton was left holding the bag. Everyone knew, though, that Reilly was the real culprit. This was the last straw in his contentious relationship with the "swells" at Whitehall, and it was to have a serious impact on his relationship with SIS. If Cumming had found him a most useful agent, he had never thought him an altogether trustworthy one, and he had a distinct knack for exciting unease in high places. The most recent episode made him a full-fledged persona non grata. Years later, the official explanation offered by the FO was that Reilly's intrigues were "embarrassing to His Majesty's Government at a time when this country wished to establish better relations with the Russian Government." That, coupled with some of his questionable "business transactions" led to a demand that all official connection with him be severed.[44] "C" had no choice but to pull back to protect his organization from further fallout. To some extent, it was a matter of money. The FO exerted considerable influence over the "secret service budget" just recently slashed by half.[45] Cumming simply could not afford him and many others. Of course, that did not prevent him or some of his officers from continuing relations with Reilly on a purely "personal" basis. Nor were stalwarts like Churchill bound to obey the edict.

There is an interesting coincidence between Reilly's fall from grace and that of his fellow anti-Red crusader, Basil Thomson. The latter had turned the Home Office intelligence section into a de facto political police force that spent much of its time spying on the Labour Party and other working-class organizations. Accusations of "misleading and inaccurate" reports caused the dissolution of that body. Continued criticism of Thomson's activities and his refusal to be accountable to the regular police caused Lloyd George to sack him as chief of Special Branch at the close of 1921.[46] Like Sidney, Thomson did not lose his contacts in high places, especially among the British Right.

Meanwhile, on 23 December, Sidney escorted a sulky Savinkov back to Paris. On the same day, Dukes sailed for New York. Reilly promptly zipped back to the quiet of the Albany where he focused his attention on the upcoming Cannes Conference. Another very interested party was capitalist Leslie Urquhart. He hoped the Bolos could be squeezed in compensating him and other foreign property owners for their nationalized assets or, better still, offering concessions to restore and operate them. All other approaches had achieved nothing, and he was more than willing to utilize Reilly's special resources if they could help.[47] At the close of December, Urquhart and Reilly exchanged letters about the upcoming conference, an undertaking both regarded as a "great risk."[48] Urquhart was the point of contact between the Ace-of-Spies and other British business figures after the same thing and willing to invest more money to get it.

At the same time, Reilly was immersed in a flurry of meetings and communications with Dukes, Krasin, Marconi, "Claire" (Sinclair), the mysterious "Hart" and "Pinocchio," and even Thomas in New York.[49] One way or another, all shared his interest in the upcoming conference. On the 19th, he and Dukes met with Harold Williams, editor of *The Times*. Williams also was the stepfather of Arkadii Borman. The general topic of conversation was the Cannes gathering and how it should be covered. Whatever suggestions Reilly offered, in the ensuing days, Williams championed the notion that the conference should be an "economic Prinkipo," a reference to the stillborn 1919 plan for a parley of all Russian factions.[50] This, of course, followed closely Savinkov's demand that he and other non-Bolsheviks be allowed to participate in the proceedings.

Sidney himself penned an advisory memo on the subject, his last so far as can be told. On 3 January, from Paris, he sent Churchill a reworked version of his 1920 memos as a template for upcoming talks.[51] He envisioned Russia's economic renewal in the hands of two giant syndicates, one dedicated to refurbishing and running the railway system (including the Chinese Eastern), and the other in charge of iron, coal and petroleum. Each syndicate would sell concessions, splitting proceeds with the Kremlin, and settle émigré and foreign claims with shares of stock or profits. As before, the Soviet Government would put up the necessary gold to back the deal. He provided a copy to Brunstrom who forwarded it to Savinkov, now holed up in Nice where he planned to spy on the Cannes proceedings. Reilly's proposal was not out of step with plans there, and may have influenced them. On the 11th, the assembled delegates tentatively approved a bold initiative dubbed the Central Industrial Finance Corp., a huge syndicate dedicated to the economic reconstruction of Russia, provided, of course, that the Soviets accepted certain terms. It would be headquartered in London and despite the planned participation of French, German, Italian—maybe even American—capital, the predominant influence would remain British.[52] However, Anglo-Soviet relations had followed a steady downturn since the Curzon Note. In late October, for instance, chief of the Exchequer Robert Horne denounced the Anglo-Soviet trade agreement as a dismal failure and Parliament declined new export credits for Russia.[53]

What all this signaled to Reilly was that the door once more was wide open for Wall Street to step in and grab the cash-starved Russian market. And the Yanks would be represented at Genoa. Ominous signs had already appeared. Back in October, Krasin inked a deal with the U.S.-based Foundation Co. to refurbish refineries and pipelines in the Caucasus. The following month, Standard of New York representatives in Moscow reached an accord with the Kremlin over former Russian concessions in northern Persia, a deal that provoked anguished howls from Shell and Anglo-Persian. More troubling, perhaps, was the Urals asbestos concession secured by Armand Hammer in league with Reilly's old rival, Henry Kuntz. If this was not enough, a gutsy West Coast huckster named Washington B. Vanderlip had finagled a general lease on the whole, huge Kamchatka Peninsula and recruited a small army of eager capitalists, including Standard of California, to back the scheme.[54]

But reinforcements had arrived. In November, a familiar face reappeared in London, George Hill. Since 1919 he had handled SIS affairs in Constantinople and the Balkans, a job that entailed keeping tabs on Bolshevik agents. The budget crunch forced him out of intelligence in June, formally at least. In December, Hill got a chance to return to the same region on behalf of Royal Dutch to scout a possible oil concession in the Caucasus.[55] His boss was his former partner in Russia, Col. J.W. Boyle, and the mission had Krasin's formal blessing. The post not only gave Jolly George the opportunity to scope out Shell's plans for Russian oil, but rival Standard's as well. Reilly would have found such information very useful. Was it his hand that secured Hill the job? At this same time, Reilly mentioned renewed contact with Stephen Alley.[56] Officially, Alley was still with MI5, but he may have been acting as Cumming's cutout in dealing with "unofficial" agents. Alley wanted to pick Sidney's brain about Krasin, and perhaps, the Hill-Boyle mission as well.

Following the System, Reilly moved to shore up his American end. In addition to his already noted work for Standard Franco-American Oil in Czechoslovakia, he was agent Rockefeller's Standard-Nobel subsidiary in Poland, and sought business for other U.S. firms. In December, for example, he approached émigré friends in Warsaw about placing deals for the Denver-based General Engineering Co., an outfit mostly interested in mines and quarries. GEC was really after bigger concessions in Russia, and Poland would provide a base of operations nearby. In New York, Sidney stayed in communication with Franklin Helm. In November, Helm, in partnership with two other Reilly associates, James Slevin and H.C. Manger, incorporated the China & Japan Trading Co.[57] Ostensibly a general trading front, the firm's real business was the purchase and transfer of arms and munitions, including such items as aircraft and gas shells, to China. This blatantly violated U.S. neutrality laws and eventually led to criminal indictments, but not before Helm and friends had shipped a great deal of war materiel to the East. American inquiries connected Reilly with the enterprise that, as an SIS report later summarized, "seem to have some relation to the [Chinese Eastern Railway] and the Wu Peifu situation." [58]

Sidney probably bankrolled Helm's operation in the same way he had Lucas'. There was more going on here than mere profiting from China's internal strife. In late 1921, vague reports circulated in Europe and America that Krasin was on his way to Canada where he hoped to purchase military supplies from American suppliers.[59] Nothing seems to have come of that, but setting up a clandestine arms pipeline to Russia would have been possible and profitable. Helm's outfit fit the bill perfectly. This could explain the cryptic reference to the CER, the route through which arms could be transshipped from Chinese to Soviet territory.

Another Stateside associate with whom Sidney kept in close touch was Boris Brasol. In late 1921, that worthy managed to insinuate himself into the Washington Naval Conference as a Russian observer. That gathering, which ran through early 1922, sought to hash out the conflicting interests of the U.S., Britain and Japan over naval strength and, ultimately, supremacy. Anglo-American tensions were especially acute, and Brasol was on hand to pick up the scuttlebutt and pass it on to Reilly.

It probably was via Brasol that Reilly cultivated another White Russian exile, Anastasii Andreievich Vonsiatskii, the future self-proclaimed leader of the Russian Fascist Party.[60] The son of a former Tsarist gendarme chief of Warsaw, the twenty-four-year-old Vonsiatskii knew Orlov and, perhaps, Savinkov. His older brother, Nikolai, was among the Moscow officers collaborating with Orlov and Reilly in 1918, and one of those executed in August. After fighting for Denikin, the handsome but destitute Anastasii kicked around Paris in the spring of 1921 where he won the heart of an older and very rich American divorcée, Marion Reem. He also charmed Mrs. Reem's bosom friend, Constance Vauclain, none other than the daughter of Sidney's nemesis, Samuel Vauclain. Anastasii came to America with

Mrs. Reem, soon to be Mrs. Vonsiatskii. Friend Constance persuaded Daddy to give the elegant, if unskilled, Russian a job at the Baldwin Locomotive Works, at its Eddystone facility, in fact. For the next two years, Vonsiatskii had free access to the plant's offices. It is not hard to see how Reilly could have taken advantage of that. Vonsiatskii might turn up information useful to Reilly's suit, an action that, despite months of legal maneuvering, had failed to force a settlement out of the stubborn Vauclain.

The Cannes talks concluded on 23 January. Results were minimal, but it was clear that Moscow would send a full delegation to Genoa. In the meantime, back at the Lotti in Paris, the Ace-of-Spies huddled with Putilov and other members of the *Torgprom*. The exiled capitalists feared the West's complete abandonment of their claims. While seeing themselves as moderate and practical men, they were open to Reilly's suggestion that stronger and more desperate measures were in order. The pivotal meeting occurred at or soon after the 14 January refoundation of the masonic Astrea lodge in Paris, a body to which Putilov, Sidney and Savinkov had belonged in old Petersburg. Reilly convinced Putilov and former oil magnates Gustav Nobel and Stepan Lianozov to finance Savinkov's organization, something they had been reluctant to do in the past. The critical matter was what he would do with the money. Savinkov was to return to his old game of terrorism and organize the assassinations of Soviet diplomats, especially the delegates sent to carry out economic negotiations. Even Krasin's name was on the list of targets. The point was to prove to Moscow that it would have no peace until it settled with the émigrés. Boris accepted the mission, but whether his heart was in it is another question. On the *Torgprom's* end, a "secret council" was formed composed of Nobel, Lianozov, Pavel Tikston, and the Tsar's former aide-de-camp, Prince Sergei Belosel'skii-Belozerskii.[61] But the one really running the show was Reilly.

Always on the outlook for other options, Sidney pushed Savinkov in the direction of a bright new star on the European political horizon, Benito Mussolini. This ex-socialist turned founder of Fascism was yet to take power in Italy, but he already loomed as the Great White Hope of anti-Communists there and abroad. Mussolini's organization was well funded by grateful industrialists, and Reilly thought Boris might be able to coax a little money out of the future Duce. During January, Savinkov met with Fascist agents in Paris.[62] Desiring to vex the present government in Rome, Mussolini had his own reasons to disrupt the Genoa meeting. He might be persuaded to abet Boris' terrorist aims.

How much Cumming or others in London knew of Sidney's suborning of terrorism, before or after the fact, is an open question. He was back in

London on 17 January when a wire arrived at SIS headquarters from Boyce in Helsinki. This reported that Redkozubov, the same mysterious figure earlier mentioned by Fedotoff-White, was in Finland and "anxious to meet ST/1."[63] As before, this elicited little interest. Reilly replied through SIS Central's Bertie Maw that a trip to Finland was "impossible" before April. That very day (23rd) he was leaving on a trip for Vienna, Prague, Warsaw and Berlin and did not plan to return for a fortnight (6 February). He expected to be "very busy" during all of February and March. "I wanted to see how the cat will jump at Genoa," he added. Obviously, Sidney was not yet off-limits at SIS, but he recognized that things had changed. He told Maw "I am not calling at the office, as Morton may perhaps have told you, just now it is healthier for me to keep away for a while."[64] Could this have been because Morton knew or suspected what Reilly was up to?

About this time, a man left Finland bound for Paris. This was Capt. Georgii Evgenievich El'vengren, a follower of Savinkov since 1918 and veteran of innumerable anti-Soviet intrigues in Russia and the Baltic. El'vengren had been tapped by the *Torgprom's* man in Helsinki to assist Savinkov in the performance of his assignment. While there is no obvious connection to Redkozubov, the timing is suggestive, and it is possible that the two were the same.

Before leaving Paris, he summoned Savinkov, El'vengren and Filosofov (fresh from Warsaw) to the Lotti and laid out a plan. This called for striking at the Soviet delegation as it passed through Berlin. Orlov could provide the necessary intelligence and run interference with local authorities. Sidney already had information on an advance Bolshevik team under Karol Radek and suggested that he might be an excellent initial target. At this meeting, El'vengren recalled, he realized that Reilly was running the show and he and Savinkov were only there to take orders.[65]

In London, doubts about the Ace-of-Spies grew. Back in December, a certain H.F. Pougher approached the Air Board saying that Reilly had solicited him to look into any arrears in pay left over from his RAF lieutenancy.[66] The Air Board turned to SIS for an explanation. The AB could not deny that Reilly had held an RAF commission, but they could find no indication that he ever actually served under their command. Thus, it seemed to them that SIS ought to be liable for arrears. In a reply to Morton, Sidney explained that other than the nominal assignment under Strubell in Toronto, "I never had a [commanding officer] in the R.A.F., having been lent to W.O., and F.O. for special work."[67] As for Pougher, he explained that the fellow was a "small clerk at Holt's [Bank] whom I have assisted financially from time to time." Reilly promised that if Pougher could uncover any arrears, they were his to keep. Since our man was not usually given to such philanthropic gestures, we must wonder if something else was afoot here. Had Pougher been supplying the Ace-of-Spies with some sort of information or, perhaps, is there a hint of blackmail? Morton must have wondered the same.

Despite the supposed severance of ties, SIS maintained a very active interest in Reilly and his doings. On 13 February, they received a report from a "private source in the U.S.A." [68] This reiterated that during the war Reilly did a good deal of business with Germans and the attendant accusation that he was himself a German agent. Like sinister implications were drawn from his history of connections to Japanese interests. Also noted were his intimate association with the corrupt Russian missions and his "domestic difficulty." The anonymous writer concluded that there was no solid proof of German connections outside the commercial realm, but offered "the folks of the other side [Berlin] may be able to supply the missing links."

The very next day, Menzies contacted MI5 asking if they knew the whereabouts of SIS' file on Reilly that had, mysteriously, gone missing. [69] He noted that Sidney was no longer employed by his agency but he still "sometimes sends in reports." He offered that he had "always distrusted" Reilly and regarded him an "extremely clever but absolutely unscrupulous person." He now suspected that the fellow was trading on his past relationship with SIS for his own nefarious purposes. Just what the missing file had to do with this, Menzies did not say, but MI5 had no record of receiving or seeing it.

This concern must have had something to do with Reilly's most recent foray into central Europe. On 27 January, the SIS station chief in Vienna wired Maw to ask if "Sidney Reilly, who occasionally blows into this office and says he is part of our London show, is really your representative and should be talked to in all confidence?" [70] The Budapest station head had vouched that the subject was "all right," but Vienna had "the strongest intuitive mistrust of him which I only hope is unfounded!" Sidney had just wired the Vienna station from Paris and was expected in Vienna shortly. Maw forwarded the message to Morton with the note: "Personally I think Reilly knows far too much about our show . . . [but] it seems late in the day to prevent him knowing more." On the 31st, Morton instructed Maw to tell Vienna to "Give Reilly no more information than is absolutely necessary," but crossed out the added "not to arouse his suspicion." [71] Morton assured Maw that "Reilly is not a member of our office and does not serve C in that he is not receiving pay from us," a qualification that left open the possibility that Sidney *was* serving "C" in some respect. "He worked at one time during the war in Russia for C's organization and is now undoubtedly of a certain use to us," he continued. This was a wholly disingenuous statement, since Morton knew full well that Reilly had labored on Cumming's behalf long after 1918. Remember, this was the same fellow who two years prior promised Sidney that "C" always looked out for his people and that if worst came to worst, he and Reilly could go off together and start their own country. Was he hiding something?

Morton took a more straightforward path when he offered "we do not know altogether what to make of him." "There is no doubt that Reilly is a political intriguer of no mean class," he noted, "and therefore it is infinitely better for us to keep in with him." By such means, he stressed, "he tells us a great deal of what he is doing." "At the moment," Morton went on, he is "Boris Savinkov's right-hand man . . . in fact, some people might say he almost is Boris Savinkov." For that reason, Reilly "has undoubted importance." He was a "very clever man . . . with means of finding out information all over the world." "I personally would stake my reputation that he is not anti-British, at the moment at any rate, and never has been." Had that question been raised? Even so, he continued, "[Reilly] is an astute commercial man out for himself, [but] genuinely hates the Bolsheviks." That, Morton thought, "is about all one can really say of him." The clear implication was that Reilly would be a dangerous man to offend.

In reply to Vienna, Maw summed up the above with "give Reilly no more information than is absolutely necessary." The next day he wired Vienna with his own take on the matter. "To be quite frank," he began, "I quite share your view [of Reilly] and am of the opinion that he knows far too much about our organization." Because of his "un-official position with us," Maw continued, "he knows such a lot that it would hardly do to quarrel with him or, in fact, to let him see that he is receiving different treatment to that to which he has become accustomed." The man had "undoubtedly rendered us considerable service" since the end of the war, and SIS probably got more information out of him than he had received in turn. On the other hand, "we have been able in many cases to give him facilities which he otherwise would not have enjoyed." Taking Morton's tack, Maw opined that Sidney was "certainly not anti-British and was "genuinely working against the Bolsheviks as much as he is able." The bottom line was that there should be no appearance of hiding anything from him, but he should not be entrusted with "anything of real importance." Reilly might ask for help in facilitating the journey of two of Savinkov's "principal assistants" to Constantinople. If so, the request should be directed "to the competent authorities." Who were they? "The last thing in the world we should wish is to become embroiled in any way with Savinkov," Maw concluded. This pronounced sensitivity about Savinkov suggests there was some inkling of the assassination plans afoot. There could be no trail leading back to London or any SIS branch.

In Berlin, the plot thickened. Boris and El'vengren arrived there in mid-February using false passports, and were received by Orlov. The latter provided details on the persons, lodgings and habits of Radek and two other Bolshevik emissaries, Nikolai Bukharin and Khristian Rakovskii. The killing of these men might force Moscow to have second thoughts about sending more important persons into the line of fire. Orlov produced "sanitized" pistols for the assassins and even cyanide capsules in case those should be needed. It was clear that Orlov had been fully briefed by Reilly who, El'vengren deduced, considered the Englishman his "chief" and the travelers from Paris as mere functionaries.[72] El'vengren suspected that behind Reilly and Orlov lurked British intelligence.

Much time was wasted waiting for three officers from Warsaw selected by Filosofov to carry out the dirty work. It was March before the gunmen were on the streets hunting their quarry. Despite a watch on restaurants, train stations and other locales frequented by Radek and his comrades, the hunted completely eluded the hunters. Toward the end of March, with the main Red delegation on its way, an impatient Sidney suddenly arrived to "inspect" the situation. Meeting in Orlov's office, Boris blamed the former's information and voiced complete frustration. Reilly emphasized that the *Torgprom* wanted results. He ordered, and it was clear to everyone that it was an order, that the new target should be Grigorii Chicherin, the former Tsarist diplomat who headed the Commissariat of Foreign Affairs and the Genoa delegation. Reilly then vanished as abruptly as he had appeared. Subsequent efforts proved no more successful. Chicherin and friends hit Berlin on 2 April and departed, completely unscathed, on the 5th. On his own initiative, Savinkov decided to follow them to Italy where he hoped to have better luck.

Reilly, in the meantime, was back in Prague where he shifted from terrorist conspirator to international businessman. Eleanor Toye was on hand plying her trade as nightclub entertainer, but she soon returned to the role of Sidney's secretary and bedmate. Drawing him back to the Czech capital was trouble with the Standard concession. The deal had encountered opposition in certain quarters of the government and renegotiation seemed necessary to quell the objections. Reilly doubtless suspected Deterding's interference at work. At the beginning of March, false rumors reached the press that a "last minute shift" in the Czech Government had canceled the deal.

Interestingly, the original source of these stories was Amsterdam.

Oil was not the only issue in Prague. Wiseman was in town on a mission for his bosses at Kuhn & Loeb. On the table was a big bond deal for the Czech Government totaling some $50 million. Also in on the deal were K&L's London affiliate, Baring Brothers, and Standard-linked National City.[73] Wiseman took a hand in the negotiation of yet another loan package on behalf of the City of Prague worth $12 million in league with the London banking house of Helbert Wagg & Co. That firm was one with which Basil Zaharoff maintained a special relationship.[74] The involvement of Helbert Wagg put Sidney in contact with its master of arbitrage and international speculation, Isaac Albert Palache. Perhaps their paths had crossed before. Reilly and Palache shared many things in common, including a taste for fine living, women and, above all, money. Another contact at Wagg was W. Lionel Fraser, one of Admiral Hall's former NID officers who ran the foreign exchange department.

What was Reilly's part in this deal-making? The contacts he garnered in previous negotiations would have made him a very useful adviser. If a little espionage, bribery or blackmail was required, well, who was better qualified to handle that end? Another feature of the bond deal was that part of its guarantee was based on profits from the state tobacco monopoly. That would boost Reilly and Spear's venture. With all this money around, our man was bound to have pocketed some.

By mid-April Sidney was resting at the Albany. That month his name surfaced in an MI5 memo concerning Petr Rutenberg. The writer had come across Reilly's 1919 report exonerating Rutenberg of charges of corruption and crypto-Bolshevism and concluded it was a "whitewash." He consulted Menzies who offered it would be "quite wrong to place implicit reliance on anything Reilly said," especially on matters of character.[75] Menzies added unnamed "other influences" had influenced Reilly's report. This, of course, was the same man once hailed as a reliable and first-rate informant.

Reilly kept tabs on the Genoa proceedings from a distance. Remember his tendency to avoid scenes of impending catastrophe. As he anticipated, the conclave (ending 22 May) produced few results. The Soviets failed to secure recognition of credits. However, the Russian and German delegates did wander up the coast to Rapallo and concluded a bilateral agreement that normalized their diplomatic relations. The pact also provided for secret military cooperation and set the stage for German economic penetration of the Red Republic.

The biggest battle was over oil. Deterding attempted to cajole the Soviets into a monopoly deal with Shell. That gambit fizzled when details of the plan leaked to the press provoking ferocious denials from Krasin.[76] Was this just bad luck, or someone's revenge for Shell's meddling in the Czech concession?

Something else Reilly had cause to take note of was the activity of the busy young American Armand Hammer. Recall the previous winter Hammer had secured a potentially lucrative asbestos concession in Moscow, the first of several. In the interim, he set up the Allied American Corp., Alamerico, and in March Hammer showed up in London to establish an office next door to Krasin's ARCOS. Armand was fast becoming the fair-haired boy of the Kremlin. His ventures were intended not only to enhance trade, but also to provide a secure conduit for Comintern funds and other clandestine resources.[77] From Reilly's standpoint, he bore careful watching.

Also reappearing in London in April 1922 was the peripatetic Sergius Riis. His stint as American intelligence agent in Riga had ended under a cloud. The precise reason was never made clear, but his loyalty to the United States and its interests was questionable. He quickly landed on his feet by grabbing the post of military and naval attaché at the Estonian Embassy in London. He got the job through his closeness with the chief of Tallinn's intelligence service and, perhaps, the recommendation of SIS man Meiklejohn. The scuttlebutt around the Embassy was that the mysterious "Mr. R" was a spy. The question was, whose?[78]

At the Albany, Sidney found urgent messages from Warsaw. These were from Filosofov and "James" begging money to keep Savinkov's organization from ruin. Included was an odd reference to a recent £125 ($500) payment to "Harvey." "James" most likely was Capt. A.W. James (Fox) who until the preceding fall had managed the British intelligence section in New York. If so, that makes an ongoing connection with Reilly's affairs all the more curious. As for Harvey, there was a U.S military attaché/MID agent with that surname operating in the area, but nothing else to link him to Reilly. In this period, Sidney's correspondence with Savinkov and others is full of aliases and nicknames, some persons having more than one. For example, "Vins" and "Marlborough" referred to Churchill, while "Rimlianin" (the Roman) or simply "R" was code for Mussolini. "Z" was for Zaharoff. Others, like "Pinocchio," a British official, defy identification.

Savinkov's luck in Italy did not improve. On 13 April, three days after the opening of the Conference, Italian police arrested him and several followers for plotting an attack on Soviet delegates. Thanks to Mussolini's intervention, Boris was released but unceremoniously deported to France. He faced ridicule from fellow émigrés and outrage from Putilov and the

boys at *Torgprom* who accused him of incompetence or worse, not to mention wasting 80,000 precious francs. There was more at work here than
simple bad luck. The complete failure of the assassination plots, not even a
near miss, suggests obstruction or betrayal. If so, whose? To Burtsev and
others, Sidney derided Savinkov as "morally exhausted," a morphine-
addicted bankrupt with no chance of leading a serious movement.[79] But if
he truly felt this way, why did Reilly stick with him for two years, constantly feeding Boris' hopes and delusions? It surely was not out of sentimentality. Sidney knew that every old horse had its uses, and he had one in
mind for Savinkov. That was but one aspect of a larger, emerging plan.

From this period, Reilly also presented himself on the edge of financial
ruin. He sang a constant song of imminent destitution, cadged small loans
from acquaintances and ignored small debts. Most accepted his excuse that
he had squandered his fortune helping Savinkov. At the same time, his personal lifestyle, fine clothes, luxury hotels and constant travel, experienced
no obvious economy. Perhaps this was taken as more evidence that he was
just a poor manager of money. But he was far from broke or even close.
Beyond past earnings, recent commissions on deals in Czechoslovakia,
Poland and elsewhere added to the pot. The truth was that Reilly had other
plans for his money, plans that he needed to keep secret from Boris and the
world in general.

In the first week of May, Sidney rushed back to Prague to monitor the
ongoing loan negotiations. Soon after, he popped up in Berlin where different negotiations were underway. Hammer was in town brewing new deals
with the local Soviet trading front, Westorg. Of more immediate importance, however, were efforts by the British-owned Cunard Lines to open a
shipping concession in Russia. The key figure in these talks was another
émigré turned *spets*, Yulii Isaakovich Gessen. He was a former marine
insurance broker and Cunard agent in Petrograd and a man well known to
both Reilly and Aleksandr Yakushev.[80] Interestingly, back in Britain,
Cunard was one of the biggest backers of anti-Red outfits such as the
British Empire Union and the Economic League.[81]

Yakushev, in fact, was one of the Soviet negotiators, but that was not
his sole mission. He secretly billed himself as the foreign minister of the
Trust and was seeking contact with monarchist groups in Germany and
France and had enlisted Gessen as a helper.[82] If Sidney had somehow overlooked Yakushev previously, there was no way he could have missed his
antics now. Yakushev's next stop was Paris where a congress of the
Monarchist Center (*Monarkhicheskii Tsentr*) was due to open in June. And
who surfaced there on 3 June but Reilly. Whatever he knew about Yakushev

and the Trust, he breathed not a word to Savinkov.

Meantime, in Russia, Lenin had an operation to remove the bullet left in his body since the 1918 assassination attempt. Perhaps as a result of this stress, on 6 May he was felled by a stroke. To aid recuperation, he abandoned the Kremlin and convalesced at the provincial town of Gor'ka. Though he gradually returned to a semblance of his old self, it was the beginning of the end. Back in Moscow, the battle for succession had already begun.

Having apparently abandoned politics, Reilly threw himself into business or, as he put it, "*garder les affaires.*" Yet another economic conclave, this time in The Hague, was scheduled to begin in July. In league with Brunstrom, he tried to resurrect the Transatlantic Co. as the basis of a new Russian trade front. Spears, Sinclair and Churchill took an interest in the plan, as did Palache. In the end, though, nothing came of it.

While this was going on, he returned to London. On 14 June, he recorded meetings with Urquhart, Sinclair and Basil Thomson.[83] Though exiled from official power, Thomson remained an inflexible anti-Bolo and man of influence in like-minded circles. Among his "die-hard" comrades on the Right were Admiral Hall and the Duke of Northumberland (Ian Alan Percy), a filthy-rich coal and shipping magnate who was the deep pocket of right-wing causes. In the following days, Reilly noted more meetings with Baldwin Raper, his "good friend" in Parliament, and two gentlemen of the Press, Lord Northcliffe (Alfred Harmsworth), publisher of the conservative *Times* and *Daily Mail,* and H.A. Gwynne of the *Morning Post.* What all had in common was opposition to any concessions to the Reds at The Hague, the same thing that was on Reilly's mind.

The issues at The Hague were the same as Genoa—would the Bolsheviks gain recognition and/or credits, and what would they give up in turn? Oil, however, assumed a more open and important role. Ending on 20 July, the Conference failed to achieve any resolution of these questions, much as Reilly desired. At Deterding's urging, frustrated petroleum interests came out of the meeting willing to put aside their differences and form a *Front Uni* (United Front) against the pestiferous Reds. In essence, Shell, Jersey Standard and ultimately nearly a dozen other companies pledged to neither buy nor sell with Moscow until its misguided leaders agreed to a reasonable settlement on nationalized property. That, Reilly-wise, was *not* a good thing. The System thrived on rivalry, not accord.

During the height of The Hague parlays, Sidney left London for a secluded lodge at Deepdene in Surrey. In what he described to Savinkov as "absolute secrecy," he spent three days working with "friends from Holland."[84] Were these Shell people, Robert Cohen, perhaps, or were the "friends" connected to the Soviet delegation come over for a visit? Could that explain the privacy? Somehow, Reilly had been privy to confidential wires between the Red delegation and Moscow. Whatever went on at Deepdene, in the aftermath, he confidently predicted that the *svoloch* ("scum/bastards"—his epithet of choice for the Bolos) would get nothing.

At the end of July, he headed to Warsaw where trouble was brewing, more than usual anyway, between Pilsudski and his opponents. His real interest, however, was old friend Tony Jechalski who had come under hostile scrutiny and summarily dismissed from Polish service. At this same time, the Polish military attaché in Washington asked to see Jechalski's MID file, a request that soon wound up tightly wrapped in red tape. The attaché would not say why he needed the file, but in a note to the State Department, he expressed his personal doubt that Jechalski was a spy because "he is too stupid to be one."[85] Jechalski was suspected of disloyalty and someone thought a key might be found in his wartime activities, activities that centered on his relationship with Reilly. How interesting, therefore, that in early August, SIS received word from Warsaw that Polish authorities were expressing "antagonism" towards Reilly and wanted him out of the country.[86] Jechalski, soon after, showed up in Paris. Sidney may not have liked Jechalski all that much, but he was a man with uses and one, perhaps, who knew too much to be left out on a limb too long.

By 6 August, Reilly was in London working with Brunstrom on the Transatlantic scheme. Things on that front continued to go poorly. Spears, fed up with intrigue and lack of profits, called it quits and cut off relations with Sidney. Interestingly, years later, a copy of Reilly's 1908 name change petition showed up in the files of Spears' attorney. This suggests that Spears had done some digging of his own into our man's background, at least enough to learn that Reilly was really Rosenblum and originally came to England from France after some brush with the law. Had Spears, who knew his ex-partner was a dangerous character, collected this information out of curiosity or self-protection? And with whom did he share it?

Romantically Sidney continued to divert himself with the worldly Toye and the ethereal, girlish Houselander. He would break with both, however, before the year was out. He ran into Nadine in Paris where she reputedly was mistress to one of the Nobel brothers.[87] Perhaps he tapped her for scuttlebutt concerning the *Torgprom* and related affairs. The other old flame to resurface in Paris was Ganna Walska, now wed to Chicago farm-implement millionaire Harold McCormick. Sidney steered Savinkov in her direction as a prospective source of funds.[88]

If Spears abandoned him, he could still count on Churchill and others.

Among his "great friends," Reilly still noted SIS man Humphrey Plowden, whom he characterized "one of the most energetic workers in the English anti-Bolshevik movement."[89] Plowden by this time had acquired a rich American wife who supported his political views. He also held a high post on Cumming's staff, a detail Reilly did not mention to Boris. Like, Alley, Hill and Thomson, Plowden is further proof of Reilly's personal contacts with British intelligence. Was there something more at work here than just friendship?

On the business front, Sidney became interested in a big investment in Italy, one supposed to pay off by the end of October. What did take place then was Mussolini's March on Rome, through which he intimidated his way into the Italian Government. Was that what Reilly had "invested" in? If so, what was to be the payoff? Reilly also put great stock in an "oil deal" in Romania. The cash-strapped regime in Bucharest was offering concessions in its state-owned petro industry. This set off a rush that attracted Palache and Helbert Wagg, and Zaharoff who played his typical role by arranging a loan in exchange for leases.[90] Sidney jumped on the same bandwagon.

But that may not have been the only thing to interest him in Romania. It was about this time that Reilly's former mistress Myrtil Paul was found dead in a Bucharest hotel room, poisoned, it appeared, by her own hand. This seemingly simple case of suicide was complicated by a suitcase found in her room, one full of Russian documents that showed that she, or someone she knew, had been involved in espionage.[91] Whether this was for or against the Soviets is unclear, and the whole matter was vague and mysterious in the extreme. Nor was this the only strange death to which Reilly was somehow connected. According to former Russian counter-espionage officer Victor Kaledin, sometime in the early '20s, Rosa Papkevitch, a former German spy in Russia and Mexico was found dead and "horribly mutilated" in Cairo. A half-burned paper found near the body indicated that she "was at one time in touch with Captain Sidney George Reilly."[92] Was this just another bit of "Reilly apocrypha," or a glimpse of some connection otherwise completely obscured?

Luck, however, seemed to desert Reilly's business hand. On 5 September, he bemoaned to Savinkov that his bank balance had shrunk to a mere £17. Two days later, he voiced shock when the Romanian venture "collapsed," leaving him on the verge of ruin.[93] Oddly, the Romanian oil deal produced ample windfalls for Helbert Wagg and Zaharoff, so why not Reilly? He did mention that he had been forced to wire his "trustee" (Thomas?) in New York to rush him some cash. This was a tip-off to where his wealth really lay. America was going to play a fresh and major role in Reilly's emerging scheme.

NOTES

1. Reilly, SIS, CXG 175, 23 Aug. 1921.
2. D.N. Fedotoff-White, *Survival through War and Revolution in Russia* (Philadelphia, 1939), 40–53.
3. SIS, clipping from *La Journée Industrielle* (18 Sept. 1921). Also *LT* (17 Sept. 1921).
4. CAC, SPRS 1/310, Sinclair to Spears, 16 July 1921.
5. The Messenger was Professor Soddy from Oxford. *NYT* (26 Sept. 1921), 1:2.
6. *LT* (30 July 1921), 9f.
7. *LT* (30 Sept. 1921), 9f.
8. *NYT* (4 Oct. 1921), 10:3.
9. *NYT* (16 Oct. 1921), 1:2.
10. Ibid.
11. See note #3.
12. The Treaty of Riga formally ended the Russo-Polish conflict in March 1921.
13. HIA, Lockhart, box 6.
14. PRO, FO 371/6930, 10552, Lockhart to FO, 16 Sept. 1921.
15. Ibid.
16. PRO, FO 371/6930, 10683, Hardinge to Curzon, 16 Sept. 1921, and 10990, Hardinge to FO.
17. CAC, SPRS 1/299, Spears to Reilly, 5 May 1925 and 1/56, Brunstrom to Spears, 4 May 1925.
18. *LT* (21 Sept. 1921), 10a.
19. *NYT* (8 Oct. 1921), 15:3.
20. *LT* (27 Sept. 1921), 9f.
21. Deacon, *The Greatest Treason: The Bizarre Story of Hollis, Liddell and Mountbatten* (London, 1989), 54.
22. Reilly, SIS, Reilly to Gall, 19 Sept. 1921.
23. Spence, *Savinkov*, 310–312.
24. HIA, Lockhart, box 6.
25. SIS, CXG 328, 1 Nov. 1921.
26. MID, 10058-804/11 (also USDS 861.00/9159), "Boris Savinkov," 17 Nov. 1921.
27. Ibid., 804/12.
28. HIA, Dukes 1921 Diary, 17, 18, 21, 22, 28 November. The meeting with "C" was the 18th.
29. SIS, CXG 376, 2 Dec. 1921.
30. *Ocherki istorii rossiiskii vneshnei razvedki* (OIRVS), vol. II (Moscow, 1996), 112. For a somewhat different and "novelized" version of Yakushev story can be found in Lev Nikulin's *Mertvaia zyb'* (Moscow, 1965). A digest of this and other Soviet accounts is contained in Central Intelligence Agency, Historical Intelligence Collection, "The Trust," (unpublished, 1969).
31. Lied, 242–244.
32. HIA, B. Prianishnikov Coll., box 5, *Trest*, "Biografiia Opperputa."
33. Ibid.
34. Spence, *Savinkov*, 335.
35. A.E. Selianinov-Opperput, *Nardnyi soiuz zashchity rodiny I svobody* (Berlin, 1922).
36. Pachmuss, 251.

37. Gilbert, *Companion*, vol. 3, 1703–1705, Crowe to Curzon, 28 Dec. 1921 and Crowe's note to FO 317/6931, 13792.
38. CAC, SPRS 1/76, Field-Robinson to Spears, 2 Dec. 1921.
39. Gilbert, ibid., 1699–1701, Churchill to Curzon, 24 Dec. 1921. On this episode see also David Watson, "The Krasin-Savinkov Meeting of December 1921," *Cahiers du monde russe et sovietique*, #17/3-4 (1988), 465–467.
40. *Ob'edinoe Gosudarstvennoe Politicheskoe Upravlenie*.
41. Bortnevskii to author, 5 October 1995, noting comments of researcher Boris Starkov at the V World Congress on Soviet and East European Studies, Warsaw.
42. Mikhail Geller, "Pismo Borisa Savinkova marshalu Pilsudskomu," *Obozrenie*, #18 (Jan. 1986), 40–43.
43. SIS, Margaret R to "Sir," 28 Dec. 1931.
44. SIS, "Most Secret," 27 July 1939.
45. HLRO, LG, F/9/2/16, Churchill, "Reduction in Estimate for Secret Services" [March 1920].
46. Mark Hollingsworth and Charles Tremayne, *The Economic League—The Silent McCarthyism* (London, 1989), 6.
47. *NYT* (13 Oct. 1921), 32:2.
48. GARF, f. 5866, op. 1, d. 56, Urquhart to Reilly, 30 Dec. 1921. Urquhart mentions receiving letters from Reilly dated 27 and 28 December.
49. Ibid., Reilly to Savinkov, 28 and 31 Dec. 1921.
50. GARF, 5831, Reilly to Savinkov, 27 Dec. 1921.
51. CAC, SPRS, 1/301, 3 Jan. 1922.
52. *NYT* (11 Jan. 1922), 1:6. The CIFC was, in turn, to be part of an even larger International Industrial Finance Corp. aimed at the general reconstruction of Central and Eastern Europe.
53. *NYT* (14 Oct. 1921), 19:5.
54. *NYT* (11 Jan. 1922), 1:2. Among the other backers of the Vanderlip scheme were oil men Harry Sinclair and E.L. Doheny, both anxious to plunge into the Russian morass.
55. Hill, 189–191.
56. GARF, 5866, Reilly to Savinkov, 31 Dec. 1921.
57. Manger was a wartime associate of Karl Orbanowski and suspected German agent: USDS, 811.01-608, Sharpe to Kinsey, 25 Aug. 1925.
58. SIS, New York, 24 July 1925.
59. MID, 10058-530/121, DS, 30 June 1921.
60. On Vonsiatskii, see: John Stephan, *The Russian Fascists: Tragedy and Farce in Exile, 1925–1945* (New York, 1978), 92–105.
61. I. Kichkassov, *Belogvardeiskii terror protiv SSSR* (Moscow, 1928), 11.
62. BSPVKVS, 132.
63. SIS, CXG 818, 16 Jan. 1922.
64. Ibid., B.M. for Boyce, 23 Jan. 1922.
65. Kichkassov, 15.
66. SIS, Morton to Reilly, 10 Dec. 1921 and enclosure from Pougher.
67. Ibid., Reilly's reply.
68. Ibid., Report on Reilly, 13 Feb. 1922.
69. MI5, Reilly, Menzies to MI5, 14 Feb. 1922.
70. SIS, Vienna to BM, 27 Jan. 1922.
71. Ibid., Memo to Maw, 31 Jan. 1922.
72. Kichkassov, 15–16.
73. *NYT* (6 April 1922), 24:2.
74. Allfrey, 207.
75. MI5, Reilly, O.A.H to Menzies and reply, 29 April 1922.
76. *NYT* (3 May 1922), 6:3 and (4 May 1922), 2:1.

77. Probably the best source on Hammer's career is Edward J. Epstein, *Dossier: The Secret History of Armand Hammer* (New York, 1996), which incorporates material from both FBI and Soviet files. On his earlier activities see in particular 45–85.

78. Eero Medijainen, *Saadiku Saatus: Valisministeerium Ja Saatkonnad, 1918–1940* (Tallinn, 1992), 122, citing diary of Aino Kallas.

79. IISG, AS, box 17, Burtsev to Reilly, 30 Sept. 1924.

80. Hauteclocque, RSSS, 349.

81. Ron Bean, "Liverpool Shipping Employers and the Anti-Bolshevik Activities of J.M. Hughes," *Bulletin for the Study of Labour History*, #34 (1977), 22–26.

82. Hauteclocque, 350.

83. GARF, 5831, 14 June 1922.

84. Ibid., 13 July 1922.

85. MID, 9140-1496/353, DS, 15 July 1922.

86. SIS, cross ref. to Warsaw report, 2 Aug. 1922.

87. GARF, 5831, 5 Sept. 1922.

88. Ibid., 7 and 13 Sept. 1922.

89. Ibid., 12 Aug. 1922.

90. Allfrey, 207.

91. France, AN, F 7/13981, "Autour de l'assassinat de Paul Doumer: Le rôle de Madame Claude Ferrere alias Henriette Roggers," 23 Jan. 1933.

92. Kaledin, 58.

93. GARF, 5831, 7 Sept. 1922.

Chapter Fourteen
NEVER SAY NEVER

Reilly's return to Central Europe in
the autumn of 1922 had a special air of secrecy. He said nothing about it to
Savinkov, the main reason being that it concerned money, and lots of it. In
Prague, Sidney collected currency and other monetary instruments and set
out for Berlin. But he was not discreet enough, perhaps. At the Czech-
German frontier, he was searched and the funds confiscated by Reich customs.[1] In the end, the money was returned and he was permitted to go on
this way, no doubt after the payment of appropriate bribes. Was this incident just more bad luck, or deliberate obstruction? More to the point, why
was he taking the money to Berlin?

At about the same time, Putilov and the Russo-Asiatic Bank's rump
administration entered into secret negotiations with Soviet representatives
in Berlin. The latter wanted to buy control of the RAB and Putilov was willing to sell. With his grip on the bank under assault by the French and rival
Russian shareholders, Putilov and his cronies were anxious to make a deal
with the Devil himself. The real issue, however, was the Chinese Eastern
Railway. By gaining control of the RAB, the Reds aimed to secure a dominant position over the latter.[2] The "monetary instruments" Reilly brought
from Prague were almost certainly RAB shares and/or CER bonds acquired
from Russian émigrés. The question is whether Reilly was acting in concert
or competition with Putilov. It probably was a bit of both. Ultimate control
could hinge on a razor-thin majority of stock, so a modest cache in hand
might make all the difference. In any case, the negotiations would prove
long and difficult.

Nor was this the only matter of interest in the German capital. Sidney's
visit also coincided with the final phase of the Soviet-Cunard negotiations.
The resulting deal provided that Yulii Gessen would return to Russia to
manage the concession office, an arrangement that put him in close contact

with Yakushev and the Trust. As for Yakushev, he had just resurfaced in Estonia and was due in Berlin ere long, something Reilly surely picked up through the émigré grapevine. Yakushev's main task in Berlin was to wangle a meeting with Baron Vrangel's representatives.[3] He encountered plenty of skepticism, but also stimulated long-nurtured hopes. His next stop was the monarchist congress scheduled in Paris in mid-November.

At the same time, Reilly received two pieces of bad news. During the summer, he had worked with Urquhart and Krasin to put together a big concession deal that would return most of Russo-Asiatic's properties in the form of a 99-year lease. Krasin agreed to personally put the plan before the Sovnarkom. However, on 6 October, from Moscow came word that Lenin had vetoed the Urquhart Concession despite the entreaties of Krasin. Lenin justified his action by noting that so important a concession could not be granted a person whose government did not manifest a "sufficiently friendly attitude" towards the Soviet Republic.[4] There may have been other factors. One rumor held that Lenin killed the plan to placate rival French capitalists. Dzerzhinskii saw Urquhart as the stalking-horse of "British Intelligence" and the concession as a cover to flood Russia with agents and saboteurs.[5] Iron Feliks was a staunch opponent of all foreign intrusion in the Bolshevik realm, something that made him a special obstacle to Reilly's ambitions. His suspicions were not unfounded. The demise of the Urquhart Concession was a major blow to the influence of Krasin who argued, to no avail, that if Moscow rejected the deal it might as well abandon the whole idea of concessions.[6] Beyond this, Lenin ordered the breakup of Commissariat of Foreign Trade's monopoly on foreign trade. It now had to compete against a bevy of new cooperative societies and syndicates. Krasin's decline meant that Reilly had to look elsewhere for help, to the likes of Yagoda.

The second thing was the fall of Lloyd George's government in London. While Sidney had little regard for the equivocating Welshman, he took with him into the political cold many useful contacts, above all the redoubtable Churchill.

Reilly was almost fifty years old. The lines in his face had deepened into crevices and the still-lustrous eyes shone from ever deeper and darker sockets. How many more deals and plans did he have in him? How much time did he have left? If the System had served him well, it had not yet provided the truly grand opportunity, one that offered the wealth and power that would make him free of all others. Like his hero Napoleon, he was convinced that Russia held the key to his ambitions. As to how he might achieve them, he recalled the story of Troy. Much as that city, Soviet Russia was a besieged fortress whose defenses had frustrated all the brute force and strategies of its enemies. To bring down Troy, the Greeks had to get inside its walls, and they did so by offering the Trojans a gift they could not refuse, a gift that carried within it the means of their destruction. Reilly had long argued that the best or only way to bring about the downfall of the Bolshevik regime was from within, but he concluded this would not happen spontaneously or inevitably, at least not in the foreseeable future. It called for the application of very skillful hands, above all his own.

Leaving Berlin, Sidney made a quick stop in Paris where he hoped to rendezvous with Dukes, just back from New York. Sir Paul, however, was preoccupied with his new, rich American wife, a Vanderbilt no less, and the meeting did not come off. By 23 October, Reilly was back in London again where he wrote Dukes a long and interesting letter.[7] He began by apologizing for intruding on Dukes' honeymoon, but stressed the urgency of the issues and noted "our relations are such that the question of 'mind your own business' cannot arise between us." He urged Dukes to take advantage of the political sea-change in London by running for Parliament on the Tory ticket. The Conservatives, he rightly predicted, were bound to seize the majority in the next election. A certain amount of "constructive reaction" was needed to offset the "orgy of destructive radicalism" that had afflicted Britain and the rest of Europe since the war. "The title of Paul Dukes, M.P. for Russia is yours for the asking," he continued. "In the course of the next year the Russian Question will become one of the most vital ones in international politics, and you have the chance of becoming its foremost exponent." And Reilly's cat's-paw, too, of course.

Then there was Savinkov. Sidney wanted Dukes to take time to meet with Boris, with the implied agenda of helping him out monetarily. In distinct contrast to the rather negative view he voiced to others, Reilly insisted his old comrade "was and is and always will be the only man outside of Russia worth talking to and worth supporting." In the face of great difficulty, "he has kept his organization both here and in Russia alive, and he is the only man amongst the Russian anti-Bolsheviks who is actually working." "I am sticking by him through thick and thin," he added, "and . . . I shall continue to do so until I find a bigger man."

This last statement hints at Reilly's true intentions. The simple truth was that Savinkov was a political pariah surrounded by a shrinking band of hangers-on. The prime examples of these were his aide-de-camp, Aleksandr Digkof-Derental, and Derental's wife, Aimee (Liubov), who served both as Boris' personal secretary and mistress. This intimacy meant that the Derentals were in charge of keeping Savinkov supplied with morphine. An on-again, off-again user for years, he was now a full-blown addict which partly explains his constant pleas for money. Beyond this, the Derentals were not the most loyal retainers. One or both were in contact with Soviet agents by 1922. Beginning in May of that year, someone carefully preserved every letter Reilly sent to Boris, no longer destroying them as the norm, and this cache of correspondence would subsequently find its way into the GPU's hands. As secretary, Aimee Derental is the obvious suspect. Oddly, while Reilly privately despised the Derentals, he never breathed a word of criticism to Savinkov. Was this because their agenda abetted his own?

Reilly's last point to Dukes concerned a recent visit from mutual friend Norman Thwaites. Though nominally retired from in 1919, he certainly retained some link to intelligence circles. For instance, a letter addressed to him in late 1921 mentioned his connection to the "Secret Service." [8] Moreover, Norman was still hip-deep in the anti-Bolshevik movement alongside Thomson, Hall and, naturally, Reilly.[9] He recently had told Sidney that a friend of his (Hall?) was thinking of approaching Mrs. Vanderbilt (Dukes' new mother-in-law) about contributing to a fund for Russian refugees in Paris. Reilly's advice on the matter is interesting. "I hope you will agree with me," he said, "that it would be a great pity if a single cent was wasted on any of the 'has-beens'." "They may be charming people in the social sense . . . but they have never have been of any use to Russia," he added. "Inexorable historical logic has condemned them to death . . . let them die." Could any Bolshevik have put it better?

Over the next few weeks, Reilly busied himself with sundry affairs, including meetings with Brunstrom who brought him into contact with two French speculators, Andre Lebon and Michel Lessin. They represented Parisian moneymen with interests in the Russo-Asiatic Bank and Chinese Eastern Railway, interests they hoped to leverage into lucrative Russian concessions. That made them rivals of Urquhart but potentially useful allies of Reilly in the System. He reconnected with Abram Zhivotovskii who also had set up shop in Paris speculating in shares of nationalized Russian concerns and solicited investment in new concessions.[10] Rumor held that among the persons employed in his office was Trotsky's nephew. Zhivotovskii provided Reilly with an introduction, or reintroduction, to another expatriate, Yosif Abramovich Maller (Joseph Mahler), a former Petersburg merchant struggling to make ends meet in Prague. Sidney was prepared to offer him something better.

Towards the close of November, he finally connected with Dukes in London. Over dinners, they plotted new maneuvers. Dukes was to set sail again for Manhattan, and Reilly had more favors to ask of him on the American side. He probably entrusted Dukes with carrying a very important proposal, or ultimatum, to certain parties in New York.

At the same time, Sidney had renewed contact with Dmitrii Fedotov-White, the Russian officer who earlier had come bearing mysterious messages from Russia. Fedotov's recent appearance in London had sparked MI5's interests and they sent an inquiry to SIS. In December, a note from the latter quarter stated "based on private knowledge, in regard to certain journeys [Fedotov] is about to take, he is doing these on behalf of Sidney Reilly." [11] This led to a follow-up exchange between MI5's W.A. Alexander and Morton. The former wanted to know if Fedotov's mission for Reilly was "likely to be of any advantage to this country." [12] No reply or further explanation survives, but it is more indication that Reilly's affairs still raised questions and acute interest.

Despite the apparent effort, Sidney's finances showed no improvement, or so he claimed. At the end of October, he wrote Savinkov that he had been forced to liquidate more of his Napoleonic collection to make ends meet. [13] A month later, he insisted his ready cash was down to less than £3! It was in high hopes of reversing this dismal situation, he told Savinkov, that he again set out for Central Europe at the beginning of December.

There were big things brewing in Berlin. Sidney's ostensible purpose was the purchase of rights to medicinal/herbal concoctions which he hoped to market in Britain and America. However, his other aim was to check up on Yakushev and the Trust. His first stop, therefore, was Orlov who provided a report on Yakushev's antics. He reported that a second Trust operative, Opperput, was now in town. Was Opperput also checking up on Yakushev, or was he really there to meet with Reilly?

Orlov was in the process of setting up an Anti-Bolshevik Intelligence Service with the aid of the Berlin police. His operation included several operatives with expertise in forgery, a skill that came in handy for "fleshing out" information from other sources. And Orlov still provided information to SIS. For instance, it was just about December 1922 that Cumming's office began receiving regular copies of supposed Comintern and Communist Party Central Committee minutes all supposed to emanate from an agent inside the Kremlin. [14] Given the timing, it seems possible that Reilly carried these reports back to Britain.

Two others to see in Berlin were Guchkov and Kurt Jahnke. The first presided over his circle and maintained close ties to the Vrangel camp. At this very time, Guchkov was trying to convince Vrangel's adjutant, Gen. A.A. von Lampe, to create a new, super-secret White intelligence organization on the grounds that all such existing bodies were corrupted by traitors and provocateurs.[15] That this effort arose simultaneously with the Trust's overture is another curious coincidence. As for Jahnke, he had just returned from China where he had been part of a German military mission assisting Wu Peifu. That put him in a perfect position to abet Helm's and Reilly's gun and airplane running and to observe the intrigues whirling around the CER.

Jahnke also may have played a part in a different sort of smuggling. His experience, recall, included running opium to California and Mexico. He doubtless still had connections among Eastern poppy merchants that could be put to good use. Also remember that in 1920, likely with Reilly's help, Arnold Rothstein had set up a narcotics pipeline from China to the U.S. East Coast. Bankrolled by Rothstein, by 1922 an international cartel had taken shape. Its main centers were Manchuria, where dope was collected and rough-processed, the Baltic port of Riga, and Germany, where pharmaceutical labs turned this into morphine and heroin. From there it found its way to American ports and into the veins of waiting customers. The dominant figures in this pipeline were "White" Russians.[16] But the essential link that made the operation possible was Soviet Russia, through which the dope passed from the Far East to Riga. That entailed collaboration with persons *inside* the Red domain, and the most important of those was Yagoda who facilitated the product's passage from Siberia to the Baltic with a minimum of fuss and added expense. For Yagoda, it was an excellent way to accumulate *valiuta* and, no doubt, feather his own nest as well. Soviet dominance of the CER and expansion of Moscow's trading privileges would enhance this scheme. Whatever else he accomplished, Sidney Reilly probably deserves credit as one of the early architects of the international drug trade.

It was in Berlin at the close of 1922 that Reilly encountered a new love interest. Staying at the same hotel, the venerable Adlon, was a pert, brunette twenty-nine-year-old English widow. As Pepita Bobadilla, she was a London chorus girl who had attained minor notoriety on the stage. She landed her most lucrative part in 1919 when she became the wife of the successful Australian-born playwright, Charles Haddon Chambers. Barely two years later, March 1921, Chambers, age 61, died suddenly of heart failure, leaving his spouse everything, which included a sizable estate and an income of at least £2,000 a year.[17] If this tale sounds vaguely familiar, it is because it follows closely the saga of Rev. Hugh and Margaret Thomas, all the more so because Reilly was to marry both widows.

Pepita, or Pita, had at least one thing in common with Sidney; both had questionable pasts to disguise. Her true name was Nelly Louise Burton and she was born in Hamburg, the illegitimate offspring of an English mother and a German officer father.[18] Supposedly her mother previously had been married to a "South American" named Bobadilla, the source of the stage name. The mother's liaison with a Dutchman, plus the German connection, had attracted MI5's attentions during the war. In 1917, Pepita herself had tried to make contact with MI5 for some reason. She seems to have a long fascination with spies and intrigue that may explain her sudden attraction to Reilly. However, her later description of how they met is highly suspect. Having listened to dinner conversation extolling the exploits of the intrepid British secret agent "Mr. C.," (a take-off on Constantine or Cumming?) she became determined to meet this fascinating creature. A little while later their eyes met across a crowded room, sparks flew, and within a few days they were secretly engaged.

Was this their *first* meeting? The late Chambers was a friend of Thwaites and visited him in New York during the war. That suggests some acquaintance with Reilly, an acquaintance that might have extended to his wife. In 1916, Pepita was in a London review headlined by Weinstein's mistress, Gertie Millar. Reilly took a keen interest in the stage and the women who adorned it, and if Pepita caught his eye in 1922, why not earlier? All circumstantial evidence to be sure, but the fact remains that Sidney and future bride had been moving in the same circles for some time. If nothing else, it seems unlikely they would have been total strangers. As for Chambers' sudden demise, all that can be said is that Reilly was in town when it happened.

If Pepita and Sidney were carrying on an affair before late 1922, they kept it very well hidden. Sidney may have learned from the case of Rev. Thomas to put a discreet distance between Chambers' death and the couple's "discovery" of one another. On the other hand, Reilly may merely have seized the opportunity to sweep a bored, lonely and emotionally vulnerable woman off her feet. Her wealth and his apparent penury combined with the suddenness of their courtship certainly made him seem a fortune-hunter. Perhaps that is precisely the impression he wanted. Marrying Pepita helped reinforce the notion that he was a man at his financial rope's end. As for Pepita, did she set her sights on Reilly out of a taste for adventure, or because she, too, smelled money? Another possibility, if no more, is that she had some connection to German intelligence. She was, after all, by birth a German subject, and Berlin had ample reason to be interested in Reilly and his activities, as they had in the past.

From Berlin he headed again to Prague, where he found Maller and recruited him for another mission to the U.S., an interesting achievement for a man with no money. By the end of the month, Maller was set up at Manhattan's 2 Rector Street where he handled "general commerce between the U.S. and the Baltic States." [19] Strategically situated at the same address were Boris Brasol and the ABF-Economizer Co., the firm Reilly had grabbed two years earlier. Also in Prague, Sidney visited Savinkov's brother-in-law, Aleksandr Miagkov. It was more than just courtesy. He had good contacts with the local émigrés and was an excellent source of information about Savinkov's organization, things Boris might be blind to or unwilling to divulge. Miagkov's teenage daughter Lydia observed the visitor closely and was surprised that an Englishman spoke such good Russian. He was a very singular sort whose dress and appearance seemed calculated to attract attention, rather odd, she later thought, for a spy. He had "a remarkable face," the sharp features and high forehead looking as if they were "hewn with an ax." What struck her most, though, were the heavy, black eyebrows arching across the rather pallid face; "Once you saw it . . . you could never forget it." [20]

Leaving his new fiancée behind, Reilly was back to London by late January where all sorts of things awaited him. A letter from Filosofov sounded the usual frantic note about Savinkov's operation in Warsaw, but this time wondered whether Boris was up to running affairs any longer. This same question lurked in a long letter from Savinkov's mother, Sofia Aleksandrovna.[21] Writing in "absolute confidence," she noted her son's faith in Reilly, "a knight without fear or reproach," and begged him to use his influence to persuade Boris to change his tactics. Continuing efforts to promote terrorism and insurrection in Russia were pointless, she argued. She felt he should commit himself wholly to propaganda. The ideal vehicle would be a newspaper, and one of its major themes should be the protection of Jewish rights in Russia and elsewhere. That, she believed, would secure the financial backing of "Jewish bankers" in Paris and New York. Because of his connections to those quarters, she thought, Sidney could be of special help. She alluded to a dangerous web forming around Boris, one into which he was bound to be drawn without his friend's intervention. Was this a reference to the Trust? Madame Savinkova's views were on the mark overall, but what she did not guess was that Reilly was one of the weavers of that web.

Elsewhere, new developments were underway. In Moscow, Lenin suffered a second stroke that left him half paralyzed and unable to guide the destiny of his Party or its state. To fill the vacuum, in early 1923 there appeared the so-called *troika* (triumvirate) consisting of two of Lenin's old comrades, Comintern boss Zinoviev and Lev Kamenev, plus the ambitious

Georgian, Yosif Stalin. The only thing uniting this trio was their common hatred of Trotsky, the man many saw as Lenin's most likely successor. Here was a conflict ripe for the System.

Meanwhile, in New York Wiseman formally joined Kuhn & Loeb, reward for a job well done in Central Europe. Wall Street also noted the 11 January return of Max May, the former vice president of Guaranty Trust who had bankrolled Martens' Soviet Bureau. May came straight from Moscow where he had enlisted as a director of a new Russian Commercial Bank, a nominally "private" institution that he intended to represent in America. "The interests behind the bank," he claimed, "included capitalists in [America], Sweden and England," but he declined to name names.[22] Reilly, no doubt, would have put Morgan at the top of the list.

No wonder, therefore, that at the onset of the new year Reilly's main attention was devoted to "American negotiations." At the center of it all was the proposal/ultimatum he recently sent to Vauclain via Dukes. After a spate of ineffectual maneuvering by both sides in late 1921, Reilly's suit lapsed again into legal limbo. His current offer probably proposed an out-of-court deal, but as incentive it would have included a threat if Baldwin rejected it. On 5 January, Sidney wrote Savinkov that he anxiously awaited a cable from New York. If the response was "9," a code he often used to signal success, then all their money problems would be solved.[23] Four days later, however, he wrote Pepita in Berlin to say that "the negotiations in America have fallen through completely," and noted that "here they are dragging terribly and it is quite impossible for me to predict the result."[24] He added rather cryptically that "I have ten days left [to 19 January], so you can imagine how I feel, and with what feverish energy I am working." "Everything seems to go against me," he concluded, "but I shall not give in to the very last." Ten days left until what?

On 20 January the *New York Times* ran a letter purporting to be from Samuel Vauclain.[25] The original was on Baldwin letterhead (courtesy of Vonsiatskii, perhaps?) and bore a convincing facsimile of Vauclain's signature. It warned that Baldwin's financial position was precarious because of worthless Polish and Rumanian bonds the firm had accepted as collateral for recent sales. In reality, the bonds were perfectly sound and the author was not Vauclain. Fortunately for him, someone at the *Times* decided to double-check and he was able to insert a disclaimer in the same edition. The certain intent of the scheme was to start a ruinous selloff of Baldwin stock. Given current "negotiations," Vauclain could have had no doubt as to who was behind it.

Reilly, naturally, had other irons in the fire. On 18 January reports circulated in London that Putilov and Krasin had reached a tentative agreement regarding the RAB and the Chinese Eastern.[26] Under this, the Russo-Asiatic would receive a 99-year lease on its former holdings in Russia and in return would recognize the legal authority of the Soviet government over the Bank and the CER. However, the deal would take months to work out and chances are these were negotiations that were "dragging terribly."

At the same time, Sidney was in touch with moves taking place in Berlin. During January a Soviet military delegation arrived in the German capital led by Reilly's old acquaintance, Gen. Mikhail Bonch-Bruevich. He wanted to engage German officers to help upgrade the Red Army's training and transport. The talks continued through mid-February, but were to be resumed in Moscow.[27] SIS kept abreast of this through an agent close to the negotiations (D/57). So did Reilly through "K" (Kol'berg? Klyshko?). In February, he learned that an unnamed agent had arrived in Berlin from Moscow with important information.[28] He soon made plans to check on the matter himself. Or did someone in SIS ask him to go?

There certainly was ongoing contact with SIS personnel. In January, he received a brief visit from Boyce, still "C"'s man in Helsinki.[29] This, too, must have had some bearing on Russian developments. The following month, Reilly offered to intervene with "my comrade" (*tovarishch*) chief of "British passport control" concerning a visa for one Yazbitskii. The former was Col. Herbert Spencer, another of Cumming's lieutenants. Most interesting is the 8 March description of Alley's intercession that secured Reilly a meeting with Col. Adrian H.F.S. Simpson, deputy managing director of the Marconi Wireless Telegraph Co.[30] Through him, he connected with the firm's chief, Godfrey Isaacs. This concerned Marconi's long quest for a Russian concession, a deal in which Krasin and Zaharoff were much involved. There may have been something more to the Marconi business than, well, just business. During the early '20s the firm played an important role in supplying training and equipment to Scotland Yard's wireless interception or "Y" Service.[31] That Service, in turn, cooperated closely with SIS and MI5. Getting Marconi personnel into Russia, therefore, could have played a valuable role in the development of an espionage network.

During the first weeks of 1923, Sidney also had meetings with Churchill, one of the few people in London willing to receive him openly.[32] These mostly concerned recent developments in Russia. On 11 February, he relayed a recent talk with Krasin who was about to return to Moscow.[33] Krasin allegedly was very pessimistic about conditions in Russia, all the more so because of Lenin's failing grip. During quick jaunts to Paris, Sidney conferred with Zhivotovskii and Jaroszynski, doubtless regarding the recent RAB-Soviet agreement.

From somewhere, he continued to supply Savinkov with driblets of cash. At the same time, he insisted again and again that his resources were scraping bottom. As a symptom of his reduced circumstances, Sidney moved out of the Albany at the end of February and relocated to somewhat less elegant digs at 5 Adelphi Terrace, near The Strand. On 16 March, he warned Boris that he faced the complete ruin (*krakh*) of his "material situation" unless things turned around.[34] To add to his miseries, creditors were hounding him. Lo and behold, four days later, he announced that all was saved, for the moment at least, by the deal he had put together for the German medical patents. That, however, necessitated another trip to Berlin. In the meantime he urged Savinkov to go to Rome and put his case before Mussolini.

Reilly remained in Berlin through the better part of April. On the way he stopped in Brussels and paid a visit on Margaret, his first in some time. She was still with the Wary family, ostensibly as their governess, a stern and plain middle-aged woman, with a small suitcase of belongings and a glass eye. With marriage to Pepita in the offing, he wanted to make sure that there would be no problems from Daisy. Besides actual or implied threats, he doubtless offered her money to keep her silence and her distance.

Besides finalizing the details of the patents agreement, Reilly's came to be at Pepita's side. She had been hospitalized by an attack of appendicitis and was only just getting back on her feet. The patent business concluded on 18 April, making Reilly the proud owner of all rights to two elixirs, *Rejuven* and *Humagsolan*, along with other pharmaceutical preparations extant or to be developed.[35] The key figure on the other end was a Russian chemist/physician, Dr. Joseph Laboshin, who received a personal contract as a technical consultant. One can only wonder if Laboshin knew something about the preparation and refining of opiates.

Reilly was back at Adelphi Terrace by the close of the month, fiancée and contracts in hand. The next step was to incorporate "Modern Medicine Ltd." on 4 May.[36] In the papers he identified himself as British and director of the Radium Co. of Czechoslovakia. He assumed the post of managing director of the new firm and sold back to it the rights he had acquired at a nice profit. It was the same technique he had employed in New York seven years earlier. Interestingly, one of his partners in Modern Medicine was an old crony of Aleksandr Weinstein. Rounding out the managerial triumvirate was Herbert Hugh Coward, former vice manager of the Russo-Asiatic Bank's London branch.[37] Coward also was British representative of the

New York-based Irving National Bank, the significance of which we will address directly. Yet another name from the past, ex-(?) MI1c man William Calder joined the board on the 17th, taking over Weinstein's slot when he returned to America.[38] With an office on Fenchurch Street, near the Lloyd's building, the company proclaimed itself to be in the general business of "chemists, druggists [and] chemical manufacturers" and to engage in the buying, selling, import and export of drugs and medicines, plus "electrical, chemical, surgical and scientific apparatuses" and just about anything else. Reilly's next step was to go the U.S. as the company's representative where he would sell the patents all over again.

First, of course, there was the matter of making Pepita an honest woman. As was his style, on 18 May bride and groom convened at the St. Martin's Registry Office and became man and wife in a brief civil ceremony. Bearing witness were the bride's sister, Alice "Cita" Menzies, and two of Sidney's old "spook" friends, Stephen Alley and George Hill.[39] Beyond bringing the shadow of the intelligence services to the nuptials, both men knowingly bore witness to bigamy, in fact, trigamy, since there was no legal dissolution of his marriage with Nadine, not to mention Anne Luke. But what was another little lie among friends in the Secret World?

During early June, there were meetings with Harold Williams, Arch Sinclair (i.e., Churchill) and Urquhart who reported that he was getting new feelers from Moscow about a concession. Meanwhile, on 8 May, Lord Curzon had issued another ultimatum to the Kremlin. He demanded that the Soviet Government cease and desist its foul subversion of the Near East and India which sent Anglo-Russian relations into another spate of acute tension. That same month, Lenin had a third stroke, completely incapacitating him. He would linger in this living death for months while Trotsky, Zinoviev, Stalin, Dzerzhinskii—and Yagoda—considered their options.

Of more immediate significance, however, on 10 May the Soviet emissary to Italy, Vatslav Vorovskii, was shot to death in Lausanne, Switzerland. The killer was a young White émigré, Moritz Konradi, who justified the killing as an act of protest against the Red regime and its crimes.[40] However, the real cause of the attack probably was the fact that Vorovskii was due to replace Krasin as representative in London, something Reilly and others found most inconvenient. Vorovskii's death kept Comrade Krasin in England though in July when Moscow finally announced Khristian Rakovskii would take his place. So far as can be determined, Reilly was in London when the killing occurred, but he had many links to those involved. Konradi was no lone gunman. His accomplice was Arkadii Poliunin, an intimate of Guchkov for whom he carried out certain "intelligence duties."[41] The Swiss attorney hired by Guchkov to defend Konradi and Poliunin, Theodore Aubert, was a past and future collaborator of Sidney's in the anti-Bolshevik cause.[42] Subsequent investigation by SIS' Oswald Rayner revealed that Konradi was linked to a secret cabal of Russian officers in London who had provided the financing for the attack in Vorovskii and who were planning a like move against Rakovskii.[43] Reilly's name was not mentioned, but it was a good bet that he had more than a passing acquaintance with the London conspirators.

Speaking of SIS, on 14 June Mansfield Cumming died. The passing of this curious man, so long secluded in his offices at 2 Whitehall, went unnoticed by most people, but Sidney must have taken note. Not long before his death, "C" initiated another attempt to dig up Reilly's past.[44] Why he would have bothered at this late date and what he hoped to find are more minor mysteries, but it shows that Reilly was still of some interest or significance. The operative he assigned to the task was George Hill and the place he sent him to search was Odessa, a city firmly under Bolshevik rule for three years. How Hill managed that feat also is unexplained, and in the end the only comment was that he "had not got much."

Regardless of his actual feelings about Reilly, "C"'s passing, like that of Melville and Nathan, meant that London's intelligence community was more and more populated by persons with little or no acquaintance with the Ace-of-Spies. Cumming's replacement at the helm of SIS, Admiral Hugh "Quex" Sinclair, was another short, avuncular Navy man, but there the resemblance mostly ended. Sinclair, it may be recalled, had earlier succeeded Hall as chief of Naval Intelligence, and was in charge when the flap arose about Reilly's impersonation of an RN officer in 1920. That surely did not predispose him to take a positive view of Mr. Reilly.

Yet another complication to arise was American oil tycoon Harry Sinclair who arrived in London in hot pursuit of a Russian deal. One of the most aggressive and unscrupulous of his breed, Sinclair would soon find himself embroiled in the notorious Teapot Dome Scandal at home. For the moment, however, he had his eye on oil concessions and the man he wanted to see was Leonid Krasin. Sinclair thumbed his nose at Deterding's "United Front" and was determined to pull a coup on his big-league rivals by snagging a deal to run the whole Soviet oil industry. At the same time, the Persian parliament revoked a recent concession compact with Standard and offered to negotiate a new one with Sinclair. More ominous, Sinclair was intimate with President Harding's former Secretary of the Interior, Albert B. Fall, and Fall was due to visit Moscow. The rumor was that Sinclair would use the promise of American recognition to gain the concession. Krasin tried to hold him off by insisting the American take his offer directly to the Kremlin. In short order, Sinclair dispatched one of his men, Mason Day, to do just that.

Sinclair's initiative not only posed a threat to Standard interests, in which Reilly had a stake, but also those of Shell and Anglo-Persian. This may have had something to do with Robert Waley Cohen's contemporaneous offer to Churchill to negotiate a merger of the two firms.[45] At the same time, Cohen may have looked to Reilly to handle more delicate matters.

As June came to a close, Sidney made plans for his trip to New York but, first, "company business" again called him to Berlin. On the way, he stopped in Paris to see Savinkov who had interesting news. He had been visited by a man calling himself Aleksander Petrovich Fedorov who claimed to represent an underground party of Liberal Democrats in Russia. They wanted his cooperation in toppling the Bolos.[46] If this sounds like the Trust, it was, or rather, a parallel aspect aimed at non-monarchists. Fedorov, or to give his real name, Mukhin, was, of course, an OGPU agent. Boris had his doubts about the visitor, but was also intrigued. Sidney promised to check on the matter in Berlin but again said nothing about what he knew already.

Returning to London, he had further last-minute details to attend to before heading across the Atlantic. Around 12 July, he dropped in on old chum Field-Robinson in an "agitated frame of mind."[47] "Robbie," he supposedly said, "I am broke—my credit in London is finished—I *must* get to New York to fight my case . . . will you help?" Robinson was more than happy to aid his "very great friend" who had booked tickets for himself and Pepita but had no means to pay for them. He and "Robbie" went to the bank where the latter drew £200. An hour later Reilly sent an IOU explaining that he was tied up in a "big board meeting" that could go on all night. As Robinson recollected the incident more than a decade later, he never got his money back, but he had no regrets; after all, "[Reilly] helped me get jobs." In fact, he added, "I might almost say that [Sidney] indirectly put me in the way of getting the job I have now—through Alley." It never occurred to Robinson to ask why his friend had to borrow money when his well-heeled wife could easily afford the tickets. No doubt Sidney would have insisted that he was too proud to use Pepita's money. That would have been a first, and what were they going to live on once they reached America? Reilly picked Robinson because he knew he would not ask questions and could be counted on to repeat the tale of destitution as needed.

Next it was Thwaites' turn to do a favor. On the 13th, he addressed a letter to Assistant Secretary Leland Harrison of the U.S. State Department.[48] Thwaites introduced "Capt. [sic] Sidney Reilly, M.C., late Royal Air Force,

and one of my colleagues in Intelligence work during and since the war."
Reilly was coming to New York on business, he continued, but "will probably be in Washington and I would like you and he to have a talk." He was
"amazingly well-informed on European matters and more especially on
Russian affairs."

Sidney paid one of his last visits on Spears, who responded with two letters, one to his Chicago-based father-in-law, John Borden, and the other to
Borden's partner, John Hertz. They were the dominant figures in the Yellow
Cab Co. and soon would be major players in the new General Motors
Corp. Both could be of real help in Reilly's coming endeavors, though not
necessarily with Modern Medicine. Spears explained that the bearer was
coming to America where he had "various business interests . . . in connection with what appears to be a very interesting scheme." "I have known Mr.
Reilly for a long time," he added, "He knows central Europe extremely well
and he has carried out very interesting business there, some of which I have
participated in to my advantage." Spears suggested that recipients might be
interested in Reilly's proposition, or know others who were.

In London, he also paid a visit on Boris Bakhmet'ev who had been
forced to abandon his position in Washington in mid-1922 because of
unwelcome scrutiny from American politicians concerning his financial
transactions. Bakhmet'ev's nemesis was a prominent Senator from Idaho,
William E. Borah, an outspoken proponent of normalized relations with the
Soviets. Reilly wanted to find all he could on that angle and whatever other
insights the former Ambassador could offer on the American scene. On the
same track, Sidney zipped across the channel for a quick meeting with an
"American banker" in Paris.[49] That was Lewis Pierson, a Wall Street bigwig
and staunch adversary of Borah and his ilk. He also happened to be the
head of Irving Trust and employer of Reilly's partner Herbert Coward.

SIS also took notice of Reilly's impending trip. On 24 July, Humphrey
Plowden, Reilly's "good friend," cabled the SIS station chief in Manhattan.
The latter had taken over the U.S. branch in late 1921 and knew little or
nothing of our man, so it fell to Plowden to fill him in. He noted that Reilly
had either already sailed on the *Adriatic* on the 23rd or would catch the
Majestic three days later. Soon after, he reported that they actually were on
the French liner *La Touraine*, though, in fact, that vessel was no longer in
service. In any case, Plowden briefed New York that "S.G. Reilly worked
for us during and after the war in Russia and knows a certain amount about
our organization as it was then constituted." "He apparently is familiar
with your name and asked for a letter of introduction to you personally in
case he had any difficulty with his passports," he continued. "We avoided

giving him any letter as although he probably thinks the Passport Control is a cover for this department, it is just as well that he not be certain," he added. "If he puts any question," Plowden went on, "it will be as well for you to say that your work is entirely passport control and you know nothing of any other work as the organization is now completely altered." In other words, lie. In conclusion, Plowden doubted that the traveler would be any trouble, but felt New York needed to know, if anyone should inquire, "that he has now nothing to do with us." SIS knew about Reilly's trip and had some contact with him prior to departure, further evidence that he was not completely cut off from the agency. What did they know or suspect? What were they worried about?

As a precaution, in the end Sidney and Pepita actually took passage on the *Lafayette* bound for Canada, so that any unwelcome eyes looking for them on the New York docks would be disappointed. The couple came to rest at the Gotham Hotel about 3 August. It was a place Reilly knew well from the war years. Whether he made any subsequent effort to touch bases with local British intelligence is uncertain; the SIS file again falls silent.

Further avoiding the Manhattan limelight, Sidney left at once for Chicago to present his introductions to Mssrs. Borden and Hertz. The last was plotting an "invasion" of Europe by Yellow Cab, including Warsaw and Prague, where Reilly's contacts and expertise could come in very handy. Some weeks later, Hertz made his first successful sales trip to the Continent and returned to New York just as Reilly prepared to leave.[50]

But Reilly may have had business in the Windy City of a more clandestine sort. As noted earlier, after his release from Red captivity in mid-1921, Kalamatiano returned to the U.S. After first pursuing and then, oddly, turning down a diplomatic post in Eastern Europe, he took a modest job as language instructor at Culver Academy, not far from Chicago. While at Culver, Kalamatiano is supposed to have spoken and even written about his experiences in Russia and branded Reilly in no uncertain terms a Soviet provocateur.[51] So long as Kalamatiano rusticated in small-town academic life, his opinions were no bother, but in the forepart of 1923, he contacted MID with an offer to resume intelligence work regarding Russia.[52] That was a problem for Sidney since America was going to be a vital base of operations.

In the winter of 1922–23, Kalamatiano suffered frostbite to one of his feet during a hunting trip, and in March he had to have three toes amputated. He had no further difficulties in the months following. Nevertheless, this incident often is assumed to have been the source of his later health problems, but medically there was no connection.[53] In August, however, soon after Reilly's visit to Chicago, Kalamatiano began to suffer from vague aches and pains. The symptoms came and went but steadily worsened over time, and in October he entered the hospital. There he seemed to rally, but then suddenly took a turn for the worse and died on 9 November, age 41. The formal cause of death was endocarditis—inflammation of the heart— coupled with anemia. These unrelated and non-specific ailments do not point to any clear cause, but the suspicious up-and-down pattern in his decline suggests a series of toxic doses administered over time with cumulative, fatal effect. Did Reilly have Kalamatiano killed to get him out of the way once and for all? He was, after all, was a chemist and who knows what other concoctions he picked up from Dr. Laboshin. In any case, from Reilly's standpoint, it was a most timely and happy demise.

There were other things going on near Chicago to merit his input or interest. During August, Soviet envoy Isaiah Khurgin (Hoorgin) arrived in the U.S., ostensibly as a representative for the Soviet-German shipping firm Derutra. Khurgin's true purpose was to set up a trade mission à la ARCOS and arrange deals with American interests in anticipation of recognition. After being hosted by W. Averell Harriman in New York, he pushed on to the Windy City where he concluded a draft agreement with the Gary Steel Works (a subsidiary of giant U.S. Steel). It bore a distinct resemblance to Sidney's past proposals: the Americans and Moscow would each put up $5 million to back a general trade syndicate. The real moving force behind the scheme was Krasin, and Reilly may have been on hand in his usual middleman role or as Krasin's stand-in. However, like the Urquhart deal, the agreement died in Moscow.[54]

Reilly was back at the Gotham on 27 August where he penned a letter to Leland Harrison in Washington.[55] Forwarding the note from "our mutual friend Col. Norman Thwaites," he offered that he had wanted to come down to Washington for some time but had been "absolutely nailed down" by business. Nevertheless, he did plan on making the trip soon and was "anxious to see you and to discuss with you certain matters concerning Russia which, I believe, would be of interest to the State Department." Alternately, he offered to meet Harrison in New York should the latter have occasion to visit.

Given the Kalamatiano and past incidents, Sidney had good reason to approach the State Department with caution. Harrison waited almost a month before replying to his letter, noting that he had been on vacation. He doubted that he would be making any trips to New York in the near future, but, if so, "I shall try to get in touch with you."[56] In fact, Harrison received the letter almost at once and immediately queried State's intelligence section

(U-2) about the sender. The short response was that the subject, "a former British secret service agent," was "nationally O.K., but morally and financially a rotter." [57] Reilly, it went on to note, "had Russian experience, numerous wives at the same time, [and] connections in this country." The compiler of this profile was Evan Young, late chief of the American Legation Riga where he had been Riis' boss. He also was the man who forced Riis' dismissal for disloyalty.

What Sidney most wanted to show Harrison was a document he recently acquired from Orlov in Berlin. Not to be deterred, he found a better-placed person to deliver it, Boris Brasol. The latter arrived in Washington at the end of August and promptly delivered the item to his friends at the Bureau of Investigation. On the 30th, BI Director William Burns (himself a former private detective) informed State "I am in receipt of a very confidential and reliable report setting forth the most recent instructions received by the Workers' Party of America." [58] This was a supposed letter from Grigorii Zinoviev, head of the Comintern, in which he exhorted American Communists to prepare to hoist the Red Flag over the White House by forming cells in the military, factories and other areas. As Burns later elaborated, "the original instructions were written in the Russian language, and while the Bureau has not been able to obtain a true copy of the same, they were viewed by a party in whom the Bureau had complete confidence [undoubtedly Brasol]. This individual made a copy of the original . . . signed by Zinoviev, his name being written in English letters." [59] Any doubts about this odd provenance vanished when an identical or similar document, also a "copy," handily appeared at the Riga Legation, a city where Orlov's operatives maintained an active presence.

These "Zinoviev Instructions," as we will see, were a trial run of a more infamous ploy used in Britain the following year. In both cases, they were designed to sway political opinion and policies towards Russia at a critical time. From Reilly's perspective, the Harding Administration presented a real threat of American recognition of the Soviets. That momentum, temporarily checked by the 1920 Wall Street Explosion, had gradually been rebuilt thanks to the pressure of business interests and the dogged efforts of politicians like Senator Borah, head of the influential Senate Foreign Relations Committee. Active behind the scenes was Reilly's old antagonist Morgan & Co. For instance, in October, Morgan partner Dwight Morrow and General Electric chairman Owen Young met with Borah to voice their support for recognition.[60] The situation was further complicated by the 2 August death of President Harding in San Francisco. His death is still a matter of some mystery, though we may safely say that Reilly, in this case, was blameless. Harding's passing transferred power to Vice President Calvin Coolidge, an unknown quantity in foreign affairs, and this only increased speculation that the new Chief Executive soon would extend full diplomatic privileges to Moscow.

Meantime Krasin's man Khurgin formed the Products Exchange Corp. (Prodexco), a front connected to ARCOS. He also received word from Moscow to prepare to assume an open role as the USSR's representative. Khurgin fully expected that he would become the first Soviet ambassador in Washington. He was not the only one. In Washington sat Boris E. Skvirskii who had come to the U.S. in late 1921 as emissary of the so-called Far Eastern Republic, a semi-autonomous "buffer state" in eastern Siberia. By 1923, the FER had outlived its usefulness and disappeared into the new USSR, but Skvirskii stayed in D.C. With close links to Sen. Borah and other American officials, Skvirskii naturally thought *he* would be the Kremlin's ideal ambassador. Then there was Skvirskii's quasi-assistant, the Russo-American Alexander Gumberg, who had worked on Lenin's behalf since attaching himself to the American Red Cross in Russia in 1918.[61] Gumberg, too, was very close to Borah.

Skvirskii was good friends with a U.S. Army officer, Col. Philip R. Faymonville. Later dubbed the "Red General," Reilly found Faymonville an object of some interest.[62] In the 1930s, Faymonville would become America's first military attaché to Moscow. By the end of the decade, he also would become a Soviet agent.[63] But that role began years earlier, something Reilly probably knew. In 1918, Faymonville was in Vladivostok where he held a seat on the Inter-Allied Materials Commission. That body oversaw the mountain of war supplies clogging the port and nearby depots. As a member of the Commission, Faymonville reportedly did his best to obstruct transfer of these stores to Kolchak.[64] It was in Siberia that he met Skvirskii. In early 1922, Faymonville went back to Siberia as U.S. military observer in Chita, capital of the Far Eastern Republic. The following year he shifted to Tokyo where he became assistant U.S. military attaché, rising to full attaché by 1924. From the Far East, he stayed in regular contact with Skvirskii as well as Soviet officials in China and Manchuria. As so many others, Faymonville took a particular interest in the status of the Chinese Eastern Railway.

The real danger, however, came from yet another Bolshevik official, Viktor Pavlovich Nogin, who arrived in the U.S. as representative of the recently-formed All-Russian Textile Syndicate (ARTS) in late November.[65] His aim was to buy up American cotton for Russian mills. The mission aroused Krasin's hostility because he regarded it as competition with his own efforts. And that meant it touched on Reilly's interests as well. That did not mean he would not try to make a little profit if he could. Just about this time, he claimed to have taken up cotton brokering under the name of Sidney Berens (Berns).[66] If so, there is no record of anyone doing business under that name in New York, but it will turn up again in a very different light some years hence.

Nogin was greeted by Borah and Gumberg. The Senator prepared a resolution supporting recognition to be introduced on 20 December.[67] Secretary of State Charles Evans Hughes, however, was not a champion of recognition, and he had a copy of the above Zinoviev Instructions. On the 19th, he released them to the press as object proof of why the United States could not enter into normalized relations with Moscow. Borah's resolution and Nogin's ambitions sank together. Sidney must have taken real satisfaction. In September he had characterized U.S.–Russian relations as rather like Trotsky's stance at the old Brest-Litovsk negotiations, "No War, No Peace," but with the possibility of going either way.[68] By October, he assured Savinkov and others that America would be the "last" of the Western Powers to recognize the Bolos, a prediction that proved quite correct.[69]

It was not until late August that Reilly got around to writing Boris. His letter sounded a typically despondent note.[70] "Not one of the people who through me made millions of dollars in the . . . war will give me a cent," he complained. Many, knowing his "situation," flatly refused to see him. The only bright spot seemed to be that his case against Baldwin was going well, though there was no settlement in sight. That was hardly a truthful representation of the situation. The only movement in Reilly's case since June of the previous year was a 28 May 1923 Notice of Trial, the third such notice since the case began. As usual, it was his attorneys who argued that a trial could not go forward because he was not in the country. But now that he was back on American shores, why did Vauclain's attorneys not pounce?

The answer is that Vauclain believed he now had an ace-in-the-hole if Reilly dared bring the matter into court. That "ace" was perennial wild card Tony Jechalski. By the beginning of 1923, Jechalski had returned to Poland as an employee of the Standard-Nobel Oil Co., a job probably acquired with Reilly's help. Never one for gratitude, the Pole was always on the lookout for a bigger and better deal, and Sidney's dispute with Vauclain offered just such an opportunity. He contacted Baldwin offering to tell all he knew about Reilly's activities during the war and since. Moving cautiously, in April Vauclain's agents made inquiries to the U.S. Embassy in Warsaw, and the probe finally worked its way back to the MID in

Washington.[71] However, Military Intelligence showed the same reluctance to divulge information from its files as it had with the earlier Polish inquiry. Nevertheless, Vauclain seems to have gotten what he wanted one way or another. Towards the end of May, word reached the U.S. Embassy in Warsaw that Jechalski was planning a visit to America. Despite his reputation as a spy, Tony received a visa and arrived in New York just ahead of Reilly.[72]

As if on cue, Riis appeared on the scene. His gig at the Estonian Embassy in London finally ended in April amid questions about his expenses and his status as an Estonian citizen.[73] The simple fact was that many in Tallinn found him too pro-British. Returning to Gotham in July, he resumed to his old trade of private detective, resurrecting his Confidential Bureau in a posh office on Park Row. Where he got the money for this endeavor (Riis had no obvious income beyond his small Estonian salary) is an open question. A good bet would be that friend Reilly again lent a helping hand. In an amazingly short time, Riis' agency established branch offices in fifteen cities, including San Francisco, London, Riga, even Shanghai and Harbin. Evidence that Riis was up to much more than spying on wayward husbands is his September 1923 overture to the Estonian War Ministry. He still had friends there, notably the Estonia Army's chief-of-staff, Gen. Juhan Torvand. Riis asked the General's permission to set up an "observation center" in Estonia for the express purpose of collecting intelligence on Soviet Russia.[74] Riis' outfit, no doubt, was one of the things that gave Reilly the means of "finding out information all over the world."

Anticipating a prolonged stay, in September Reilly and wife moved into an apartment at 38 West 59th Street. In letters to Savinkov, Sidney described himself as mentally and physically exhausted. "I am very tired," he wrote, "if it weren't for you and the *svoloch* [Bolsheviks], I would have left this vale of tears and suffering with pleasure. But it would be a shame to give up and die like a son of a bitch without having done anything."[75] He characterized the weeks that followed as a constant and mostly unrewarding effort to "brew-up affairs." He expressed a growing contempt, even hatred, of America and Americans. It was a "monstrous country," he assured Boris, dominated by the meanest of intellects and a money-grubbing, short-sighted business class. He could imagine of no worse indignity that to die there.[76] His complaints had a particular anti-Semitic ring. Jews, he averred, dominated banking and commerce, especially in New York. Beyond that, he was certain that many of the Russo-Jewish immigrants harbored pro-Bolshevik sentiments.[77] He blasted American immigration laws that, in his jaundiced opinion, had flooded the U.S. with the worst type of Jews and most other groups. Whether he counted the likes of Schiff and Rothstein in this category would be interesting to know. As ever, the question is whether the above truly reflected his opinion or was it another case of feeding back to Savinkov his own prejudices.

Starved of real news about Russia and with business at a standstill, he kept his mind occupied with books. These provide an interesting glimpse into his wide-ranging interests. In October, he told Boris that he was simultaneously re-reading Dostoevskii's *Brothers Karamazov* and Petr Uspenskii's *Tertium Organum*, a tale about the 4th dimension. Perhaps there, he mused, money was no longer a necessity. He noted interest in Einstein's latest theories and thought Savinkov might write a story based on these.

The settlement of his lawsuit, like the pot of gold at the end of a rainbow, was always just beyond reach. He thought things might come together by November, then January, then further delays pushed the day of reckoning to March. Or so he told Savinkov. In reality, there was no official movement in the matter during the latter part of 1923. His commercial hopes also seemed always to hang in the realm of possibility. "I have a few things going on here," he wrote in mid-October, "the realization of which completely depends on one person, in whom I cannot confide my present situation under any circumstances." [78] There were other vague mentions of an American-based syndicate or "combination" that might engage him to return to Europe in the New Year. Most likely it was an allusion to Hertz's Yellow Cab scheme. In any case, soon after, Sidney noted that another friend, one who knew all about his situation, offered him an "opportunity" that he jumped on without hesitation. At least it would pay the rent and keep food in his and Pepita's mouths. The "opportunity" interestingly coincided with the appearance of Aleksandr Weinstein at the close of October. He came from Berlin. Who there would have had a job for Sidney?

About the same time, Sidney greeted Dukes who left for Europe at the beginning of November. While they were together, Reilly persuaded him to take on the translation of Savinkov's novel—for free—and also extracted a promise to return to the states as soon as possible.

Another vexing matter in his exchange with Savinkov was the latter's ongoing contact with "R," Mussolini. Reilly described this as the "one ray of sunshine in our nightmarish existence." The flip side was that "if our affair with [Mussolini] fails, we are finished." [79] As the weeks passed, however, nothing tangible emerged from Rome, especially money. Still, Reilly voiced hope, but the real purpose was to keep Savinkov hoping and hanging on that idea until it was time to direct him somewhere else.

November brought more bad news on the business front. Word reached New York of an agreement between Sinclair's Mason Day and the Soviets for a concession on the entire Baku and Grozny oil fields. In return, Sinclair promised to back a big loan for the Reds on Wall Street.[80] As might be expected, this aroused intense resentment at Standard and among other competitors. However, in October the U.S. Senate initiated a full inquiry into the aforementioned Teapot Dome affair. By year's end, Sinclair was under mounting scrutiny and attack, and one casualty, and not an incidental one, was the Russian deal. We can only wonder: did Reilly, with help from Riis, Said and others, help bring Sinclair to that unhappy state?

Another who might have assisted such a scheme was Brasol, who maintained his links to the U.S. Justice Department and other official channels. He was a frequent witness in the ongoing suits over Russian wartime contracts. That certainly had interest to Reilly, not the least because of his battle with Vauclain. For example, during 1923, Brasol testified in at least two cases in which our man had some interest, financial or otherwise. A prime example was an action by Claude Nankivel (Kalamatiano's former employer) and John MacGregor Grant to recover the cost of automobiles supplied to the defunct Kolchak regime.[81] Most importantly, through Brasol, Reilly made contact with Ford's people.[82] Brasol also was the key to American financier, Lewis Pierson, head of Irving National Bank and Trust Co. Pierson, recall, hated Borah and opposed all efforts to aid or recognize Bolsheviks.[83]

Brasol also was the personal representative of the Grand Duke Kyril (Cyrill) Romanov in America. Kyril had proclaimed himself Tsar-in-exile, a move that deeply divided the monarchist movement and his own family. Sidney also noted dealings with two of Brasol's close associates, Gen. K.V. Sakharov, a former Kolchak commander with strong ties to émigrés in Manchuria, and Father Varsonofei, agent of the Russian Church and, supposedly, of the Patriarch held virtual prisoner in Moscow. The Father warned that the Bolsheviks were seeking to infiltrate the Church abroad, and at this very moment a Soviet appointee was challenging the legitimacy of the Orthodox Metropolitan in American, Platon.[84]

Two other Russians of significance to drop anchor in New York in this period were Emil Nobel and Prince Yusupov. The first came as a representative of Standard-Nobel Petroleum and the *Torgprom*. Yusupov was a rarity among the exiles, one who managed to get away with a stash of gems and artworks that he sold or "pawned" to keep him in some semblance of the style to which his class was accustomed. On 27 November, Sidney wrote Savinkov of Yusupov's arrival in New York, noting with obvious sarcasm his claim to be the "Saviour of Russia" by slaying Rasputin. Reilly, remember, likely knew who really was responsible for that. Nevertheless, Sidney approached Yusupov, probably with money on his mind. The Prince cut him dead, a slight for which Reilly may have extracted revenge in the not-too-distant future.

A passing reference to Savinkov about a Canadian timber deal is oddly revealing. The roots of this go back to 1920–21 when Jonas Lied, on Krasin's behalf, persuaded Canadian entrepreneurs to purchase Russian logs shipped via Archangel and the Baltic.[85] Why would Canadians purchase Russian logs when they had plenty right in their own backyard? The simple answer was price and the opportunities for other trade. To secure a foothold in a market, the Soviets offered timber dirt-cheap. They kept costs down by using prison labor in the expanding network of northern labor camps—the beginnings of the infamous *Gulag*. The man who kept a close eye on the operation establishments was Genrikh Yagoda who worked closely with Krasin's foreign trade nexus. The logs went to pulp mills in Nova Scotia; pulping the timber eliminated any trace of its origins and pesky questions about the trafficking in "stolen" goods. On the return, the ships were loaded up with machinery, cotton and other goods needed in the Proletarian Utopia. During 1923 another veteran of Reilly's New York "rat pack," ex-naval officer Tikhon Agapaev, took over management of a large pulp mill near Halifax.[86] Just before Christmas he came to Manhattan on some business, perhaps to touch base with Sidney prior to his departure.

Although seemingly deeply disenchanted by his American ventures, Reilly was uncertain just how long he would have to remain there. He initially spoke of staying until March or April, but in December he suddenly saw his way out or the need to get out. Curiously, this change in plans followed right after Claude Dansey's arrival in New York on the 2nd. Did Dansey bring him some needed information, or did Reilly smell trouble in the presence of a man closely connected to Sinclair's SIS and, possibly, Margaret?

Or was Dukes' fresh arrival the deciding factor? As before, he needed Paul as an observer and stand-in while he attended to business in Europe. Dukes finally disembarked Stateside on Christmas Day. Three days later, Reilly and Pepita were on their way back across the stormy winter Atlantic.

NOTES
1. PRO, FO 371/7513, 14789. The actual file on this incident is missing; only a summary reference remains.
2. USDS, 861.516/152, Wheeler to State, 19 Jan. 1923.

3. Boris Prianishnikov, *Nezrimaia pautina* (Silver Springs, MD, 1979), 69–70.
4. *NYT* (8 Oct. 1922), 3:2.
5. Vladislav Minaev, *Podryvnaia deiatel'nost' inostrannykh razvedok s SSSR* (Moscow, 1949), 85.
6. *NYT* (3 Oct. 1922), 20:7.
7. HIA, Lockhart, 6, Reilly to Dukes, 23 Oct. 1922.
8. PRO, WO 339/19912, Stevens & Brown to WO, 14 Sept. 1921.
9. CAC, SPRS 1/326, Thwaites to Spears, 29 Sept. 1921.
10. Zhivotovskii's firm was the *Société Nouvelle d'Études pour l'Industrie en Russie*.
11. MI5, Reilly, CX Prod., 15 Dec. 1922.
12. Ibid., Alexander to Morton, 10 Jan. 1923.
13. GARF, 5831, 25 Oct. 1922.
14. Gill Bennett, '*A Most Extraordinary and Mysterious Business*': *The Zinoviev Letter of 1924* (London, 1999), 31, quoting Morton to Ball, July 1924. Numerous SIS reports based on information supplied by real or alleged agents in the Soviet establishment can be found in PRO, FO 371/ 8718, 8719, 9337. The last contains a report on the organization and structure of the GPU/OGPU as of 1923.
15. Bortnevskii, "General P.N. Vrangel' I bor'ba za rukovodstvo prsskoi emigratsiei v 1920-x gg.: Zagadka smerti belogo vozhdia," [unpub., 1997.], 7–10.
16. *NYT* (14 Sept. 1926), 18:5.
17. Chambers died intestate which left his entire estate to Pepita.
18. MI5, Reilly, Re: Isabel Burton, 1 Dec. 1919 and Pepita to Maj. Reeves and reply, 14 Feb. 1917.
19. CSA 215, Sharpe to Bannerman, 13 Dec. 1924, attachment.
20. Serge Savinkov to author, 15 May 1999.
21. University of Indiana, Lilly Library, Lockhart Coll., Reilly material, Savinkova to Reilly, 19 Dec. 1922.
22. *NYT* (12 Jan. 1923), 28:4.
23. GARF, 5831, 5 Jan. 1923.
24. HIA, Lockhart, 6, Reilly to Pepita, 9 Jan. 1923.
25. *NYT* (20 Jan. 1923), 14:1.
26. USDS, 861.516/152, and Carley, 744–745.
27. PRO, FO 371/9357, 2360, [March 1923].
28. GARF, 5831, 11 Feb. 1923.
29. Ibid., 11 Jan. 1923.
30. Ibid., 8 March 1923.
31. PRO, HW3/81, "A Brief History of the Events Relating to the Growth of the 'Y' Service."
32. Ibid., 31 Jan. 1923
33. Ibid., 11 Feb. 1923.
34. GARF, 5831, 16 March 1923.
35. PRO, BT 31/27894/189767, Agreements of 14 and 18 May between Drs. Laboschin [sic] and Pariser and attachments.
36. Ibid.
37. *LT* (26 Sept. 1923), 17f.
38. Weinstein's departure probably stemmed from a need or desire to make the firm a wholly "British" affair.
39. Marriage Certificate, St. Martin's Registry Office, London, #29, 18 May 1923.
40. Alfred Erich Senn, *Assassination in Switzerland: The Murder of Vatslav Vorovsky* (London, 1981).
41. Bortnevskii to author, 9 June 1995.
42. Reilly seems to have first met Aubert in early 1918 when he was in Switzerland looking into Bolshevik bank transactions. Aubert was then close to K.M. Onu, the Russian consul in Berne.

43. PRO, FO 371/9371, 5351, 9 Aug. 1923.
44. SIS, Most Secret, 27 July 1939.
45. Yergin, 192–194.
46. Fedor Gladkov and Nikolai Zaitsev, *I Ia emu ne mogu verit'*. . . (Moscow, 1983), 113.
47. HIA, Lockhart, 6, Field-Robinson to Hill, 9 Sept. 1935.
48. Library of Congress, MSS Div., Leland Harrison Papers, RE folder, box 9, 13 July 1923.
49. GARF, 5831, 15 July 1923.
50. *NYT* (22 Dec. 1923), 20:2.
51. Allen and Rachel Douglas, "The First Chapter of the Trust: The Lockhart Plot," *Executive Intelligence Review*, (Nov. 1988), 10 and John Loehrs and Vicki Pare, Culver Academy, 12 and 15 Oct. 1997.
52. MID, 10039-2346.
53. Dr. Sally Fitterer to author, 30 Dec. 1995.
54. PRO, KV 2/574, VSO report, 17 Nov. 1933.
55. Library of Congress (LOC), Leland Harrison Papers, box 5, RE folder, Reilly to Harrison, 27 Aug. 1923.
56. Ibid., Harrison to Reilly, 25 Sept. 1923.
57. USDS, 862,.2-412, U-2, Young to Harrison, 28 Aug. 1923.
58. Ibid., 811.00B/212, Burns to Armour, 30 Aug. 1923.
59. Ibid., 811.00B/213, Burns to Armour, 20 Dec. 1923.
60. *NYT* (7 Oct. 1923), 8:2.
61. See: James K. Libbey, *Alexander Gumberg & Soviet-American Relations, 1917–1933* (Louisville, KY, 1977).
62. John Daniel Langer, "The 'Red General': Philip R. Faymonville and the Soviet Union, 1917–52, *Prologue* (Winter 1976), 208–221.
63. HIA, Ivan Yeaton Coll., "Faymonville" file.
64. Crowley and Corson, 463.
65. Phillip S. Gillette, "Conditions of American-Soviet Commerce: The Beginning of Direct Cotton Trade, 1923–1924," *Soviet Union*, vol. 1, #1 (1974), 74–93.
66. TsAFSB, 303330, Protokol, 9 Oct. 1925.
67. Congressional Record, U.S. Senate, 68th Congress, 1st Session, LXV, Pt. 1, Senate Resolution 50, 20 Dec. 1923.
68. GARF, 5831, 17 Sept. 1923.
69. Ibid., 26 Oct. 1923.
70. Ibid., 28 Aug. 1923.
71. MID, 9140-1496/356, 18 April 1923.
72. Ibid., 1496/360, 28 May 1923.
73. Estonia, Eetsi Riiigiarhiiv (ERA), fond 4002, Military Attaché, Medijainen to author, 30 Nov. and 22 Dec. 1999, and PRO, FO 371/9269, Leslie to Curzon, 23 Jan. 1923.
74. ERA, Ministry of Defence, Personal file 495/7.
75. GARF, 5831, 18 Oct. 1923.
76. Ibid., 17 Sept. 1923.
77. Ibid.
78. Ibid., 15 Oct. 1923.
79. Ibid., 18 Oct. 1923.
80. *NYT* (22 July 1923), VII, 15:5 and (25 July), 28:2.
81. HIA, Russia, Posol'stvo, 141/1-3.
82. HIA, Vrangel, box 149, f. 39, Brasol, "Ocherk deiatel'nosti russkikh monakhicheskikh organizatsiia v S-ASSh," Sept. 1922 on his links to Ford.
83. USDS, 861.50 Am 3/38, Bertron to Hughes, 7 June 1923.
84. *NYT* (14 Oct. 1923), II, 1:4 , (8 Nov. 1923), 21:3 and (31 Dec. 1923), 5:3.
85. HIA, Vrangel, Report, 19.
86. *NYT* (5 Dec. 1931), 17:5.

Chapter Fifteen

THE RED LETTERS

Back in London, a stunning electoral upset brought a new government to power, one headed by the socialist Labour Party under J. Ramsay MacDonald. The Labourites lacked a majority and held power through a tenuous alliance with the third-place Liberals. That made MacDonald and his comrades all the more determined to press their agenda while they could. On 1 February, MacDonald extended formal recognition to the Soviet Government. The timing, if not the move itself, may have taken Reilly by surprise; a few weeks before he had assured Savinkov that the French would be the first to recognize the Bolos.

Reilly kept a low profile and avoided many of his London haunts. If nothing else, it helped him dodge increasingly aggressive creditors. Interestingly, in her later version of events, Pepita eliminates all mention of their return to Europe in the forepart of 1924. According to her, they remained in America straight through the first half of 1924. Given that this was a sizable span of time to simply forget, we have to wonder why she, or someone, swept it under the rug a few years later. The truth was that she and her husband first appeared in Paris where Savinkov failed to meet them as arranged. By 10 January, they surfaced at London's Hotel Washington where Sidney wrote Boris a letter laying out the present state of affairs.[1] Most of his energies, he claimed, were taken up trying to keep the wolves at bay and putting together new deals in the hope of restoring his (and Savinkov's) finances. That, he expected, would keep him in London for a month or so.

A few days later, the Reillys shifted abodes to 7 Park Place in St. James, an address previously used by Dukes. Soon after, Sidney signed a new contract with Rosen for tobacco sales in Eastern Europe. He also recorded fresh encounters with Sinclair and Zaharoff ("Z") and the pseudonymous "Plantagenet," possibly a nickname for Balfour or Admiral Hall. In any case, he was conservative with connections to Parliament and Churchill.[2]

Most of the talk concerned the coming recognition debate in Parliament and the likelihood of new credits or loans flowing to Moscow.

Reilly was anxious to come over to Paris and discuss related matters with Boris, especially reports recently received from his agents in Russia. Some months earlier, Savinkov had persuaded one of his best guerrilla commanders, Col. S.E. Pavlovskii, to undertake a lone mission to Moscow. His task was to check on the claims made by Trust representatives. Pavlovskii reached the Red capital in August where he was immediately grabbed by the OGPU. Reilly was among the privileged few who knew about the mission. That, of course, also gave him the ability to betray, though he was not the only one. In any case, the Chekists soon persuaded Pavlovskii to send favorable reports back to Paris. His messages were full of more or less authentic military data that was meant to show the reach and power of the shadow government, the Trust. He argued that things were already so far gone for the Bolos that all that was needed was a man capable of leading the opposition in a quick seizure of power. That, naturally, had to be Savinkov himself. Even in his present state, common sense and long experience told Boris that the Trust, the Liberal Democrats, or whatever they called themselves were just a little too good to be true. Reilly still remained mum about what he knew.

New winds certainly were stirring in Russia. On 21 January, Lenin's frail, stricken body finally gave up the ghost. Whether his was an altogether natural death is open to serious question. Just two days before, his comrades in the Politburo had received an optimistic report from doctors stating that the Leader of the Proletariat was improving and would be able to return to work. Of course, not everyone found that a welcome possibility, least of all the ambitious Stalin. The latter had broached the subject of freeing Vladimir Ilich from his mortal coil, and Trotsky and others later became convinced that Stalin had poisoned their Lenin for his own nefarious ends.[3] For our purposes, the most important thing is Yagoda's alleged role as Stalin's accomplice.[4]

Lenin's death occurred in the midst of the XIII Party Congress where Stalin and his new allies Kamenev and Zinoviev launched a blistering attack on Trotsky. Whatever his other gifts, Trotsky had neither talent nor stomach for down-and-dirty politics and it was apparent to most that he could never fill Lenin's shoes. Mastery of the Party and the Kremlin was now up for grabs. This signaled to Reilly that the cracks always present among the Bolshevik elite were widening, offering fresh opportunities for exploitation. For instance, from Krasin or Klyshko Sidney picked up the rumor that Trotskii was plotting to seize power through a *coup d'état*.[5] This probably was disinformation spread by his enemies, but considering that he still held sway over the Red Army, it was not a possibility to be dismissed out of hand. Dzerzhinskii's star, on the other hand, was ascending. On 2 February, along with his control of the OGPU, he assumed chairmanship of the Supreme Council of the National Economy (VSNKh-*Vesenkha*), a role that gave him new clout in trade and related matters. His deputy, once again, was Genrikh Yagoda.

Yagoda was emerging as the key man in Reilly's evolving plan. Inside the OGPU, Dzerzhinskii's #2, or first deputy director, was a fellow Pole, Viacheslav Menzhinskii. A sickly man who prided himself on his aesthetic sensibilities and courtly manners, Menzhinskii left much of the hands-on work to the second deputy director, Yagoda.[6] The latter also still held his seat on the OGPU's executive board and direct control of the Special Section that oversaw a network of spies and informants in the armed forces. As Menzhinskii's factotum, he exercised strong influence over the Secret Operational Administration (*Sekretno-operatinvoe upravlenie*—SOU). That body handled the ticklish area of "political opposition," including dissent within the Party, and oversaw the activities of other OGPU departments.[7] This brought Yagoda into collaboration with stocky, goateed Chekist Artur Artuzov who, as noted, oversaw the Trust. Artuzov's main job was chief of the CounterIntelligence Department or KRO (*Kontr-Razvediavatel'nyi Otdel'*) which combated espionage and subversion directed *against* the Soviet Republic.[8] One of Artuzov's assistants, in turn, was a moon-faced young Latvian/Estonian officer, Vladimir Andreevich Styrne. Each of these *chekisty* is destined to play important roles in our story.

Artuzov's KRO was locked in a turf war with the Foreign Intelligence Department, INO (*Inostrannyi Otdel'*), run by Mikhail Abramovich Trilesser. The latter believed that all operations outside the Socialist Motherland should be under INO control and felt the Trust was an unwarranted intrusion on his territory. Thus, Trilesser decided to initiate his own efforts to penetrate émigré groups and simultaneously spy on the activities of his rivals.[9]

Outwardly, Reilly declared he was too depleted of money and energy to pursue political intrigues. His health, he claimed, was near the breaking point, and he had to escape the pressures of London if he was to preserve his sanity and even his life. To Savinkov, he compared himself to Voltaire's hero Candide, whose naïve optimism was inexorably ground down to a stoic realism. So, too, he compared Russia to Candide's elusive object of desire, the once-beautiful Cunegonde, whom time and travail reduced to a dilapidated hag. Towards the end of January, Sidney and Pepita headed to the Riviera. On a brief stop in Paris, the new Mrs. Reilly got her first glimpse of the legendary Savinkov. She was not impressed: "a portly little man . . . with the most amusing air of self-assurance" given to striking "Napoleonic poses" and "theatrical gestures."[10] By the time news from London proclaimed recognition of the Soviet Government, she and her husband were ensconced in the comfort and relative isolation of the Hotel de la Terasse in Theoule, a small seaside town a few miles from Cannes. Reilly called it "the most beautiful spot on the whole Riviera."

Despite his claims to the contrary, Sidney was still very much involved with "Russian Affairs." The difference now was that he felt the need to pursue this away from his usual haunts. On 7 February, he told Savinkov that through a "small bureau" in Riga, "the center of anti-Bolshevik intrigue," he received various reports and documents concerning Russia.[11] Most likely this was a reference to Orlov's network, but it may also have been Riis' agency that also had a Riga branch. Nor was this Reilly's only source of information. Supposedly through sources at *The Times*, he sent Boris a paper on opposition forces within the Soviet Communist Party. Besides Trotsky's loyalists there was an "economist" clique led by Krasin. The latter was opposed to the Comintern and the hardcore ideologues and sought a common front with the SR committee in Prague. Dzerzhinskii and Zinoviev considered Krasin's group dangerous and were determined to root it out. In doing so, Iron Feliks faced a problem because among its adherents were members of his own OGPU. Was Yagoda one? In early March, he got more information from a "former comrade" in London ("comrade" being Reilly's usual term for British intelligence associates). This was a report compiled by a British operative in Moscow connected to the Marconi negotiations.[12] According to this, despite the modest improvement wrought by the NEP, the overall economic situation remained wretched. Far from relaxing their control, Dzerzhinskii and the Party hardliners were determined to hold on to power through an intensified Red Terror.

Reilly mentioned a meeting with El'vengren, who was still plotting attacks on Bolshevik diplomats. Did he come to Sidney for money, information or both? Guchkov stopped by for a visit as well. What information did they have to convey—or receive? Something that Sidney did not mention to Savinkov was his trip to Geneva at the start of March. There he took part in the founding of the International Entente against the Third International, AKA the International Anti-Bolshevik League.[13] At its head stood Theodore Aubert, the Swiss lawyer who defended White assassins Konradi and Poliunin. To combat the Bolshevik scourge, the Entente aimed to organize like-minded groups in America, Asia and every corner of the

globe. In short order, it had filials in more than twenty countries, including
Britain, the U.S., even Australia and Argentina.[14] Aubert forged a close
alliance with Orlov's network in Berlin that, in effect, became the League's
intelligence service.[15]

Among the British groups linked to Aubert's net was the Economic
League. It represented an array of right-wing industrialists and financiers
dedicated to a "crusade for capitalism" and battle against socialism in all its
forms. It also was aligned closely with the Conservative Party and shared
goals and many members with organizations like the British Empire Union,
the Anti-Socialist League and even the British Fascisti.[16] Among the members
of the EL and its kindred societies were various "military intelligence
experts," notably Reilly stalwarts Basil Thomson, Sir Alfred Knox, and
Norman Thwaites.[17] By far the most important, however, was the founder
of the Economic League, ex-Director of Naval Intelligence, Admiral
"Blinker" Hall. He was spiritual leader of the arch-conservative "Diehard"
wing of the Tories and assumed the powerful post of Conservative Party
Principal Agent in 1923. He remained, however, much more a spy than a
politician. According to one biographer, Hall was fixated on "the world of
spies, agents, deception, bribery, disinformation, destabilization, and all that
side of intelligence now stigmatized as the 'Dirty Tricks' department."[18] In
that realm he could find any number of uses for the Ace-of-Spies.

Close to the above sphere, if less obviously so, was Churchill, and how
convenient that Winston planned a visit to Cannes while Reilly was nearby.
Sidney told Savinkov of an anticipated visit in February. A little further up
the coast was Monaco where Zaharoff had taken an interest in the famous
Monte Carlo Casino. After the costly fiasco of the Greco-Turkish War, the
75-year-old Greek had slowed down a bit, physically and financially, but he
still had an ample appetite for deal-making and attendant intrigues.
Vickers, and Sir Basil personally, had huge investments in Russia before the
Revolution, and they were as anxious as any to recoup those losses one way
or another. In February 1924, just after Reilly set up camp in Theoule, one
Efim Grigorevich Shaikevich arrived in Monte Carlo to offer Zaharoff just
such a deal through which Vickers could regain control of the giant
Tsaritsyn arms works.[19] A past and present director of the International
Commercial Bank in Petrograd, Shaikevich was well known to Reilly.[20] The
Greek was interested, but Vickers' men in London were more skeptical.
How did one know if this Russian possessed the influence and resources
claimed? The only way to be sure was to send someone to Russia to find
out. Who was available and better suited to undertake that kind of fact-
finding than Sidney Reilly?

On 15 March, Reilly wrote Boris that his suit in New York was coming to a head (it was not) and he had to return to America. First he had some pressing matters to attend to in Paris and London. Sidney and Pepita breezed through the French capital on the 19th where he and Savinkov had a brief but very important meeting, of which more below. Afterwards, Reilly dropped from sight. He would not arrive in New York until the middle of May, so where did he go and what did he do for the next several weeks? A key to this puzzle is contained in a 1927 statement given to Scotland Yard. The informant was a Russian attached to the Soviet Mission in London, and circumstantial evidence points strongly at Nikolai Klyshko. While the statement contains some dubious and erroneous secondhand information, the informant personally attested that he knew Reilly well and met him outside the Opera House in Moscow in 1924.[21] French investigative writer Hauteclocque also puts Reilly in Russia during the year, and Alekseev's inquiries produced the same result.[22] The "blank page" from late March through early May was the only time the trip could have been made.

Getting into Russia was not a great problem. The long Soviet frontiers were quite porous; partisan raiders and a small army of smugglers crisscrossed them on a routine basis. Remaining in the country for any length of time posed greater difficulties, but not insuperable ones, especially for someone with Sidney's experience. The Soviet Republic, after all, was no longer shut off from the outside world. Britain, Germany, Italy and a bevy of smaller states now had formal diplomatic missions there that gave their nationals the ability to travel openly and in relative safely. A suitable identity was simple enough to arrange. Reilly could pass himself off as a German, Frenchman, Belgian, Italian, even an American, or as one of the multitude of returning émigrés. Despite fears that foreign powers, especially Britain, would exploit this reverse exodus to infiltrate agents, it was impossible to inspect and watch them all.[23] Indeed, Sidney may have been as interested in concealing himself from London's gaze as the Kremlin's. There was now a British mission in Moscow, the opposite of Krasin's, and SIS had its eyes and ears therein.

The most important question, however, is why Reilly took the risk at all, considering that he had a death sentence hanging over his head. The Shaikevich matter was no more than a blind for a more personal and sensitive purpose. This is where we go back to his quick meeting with Savinkov in March. Boris confided was that he was willing to take up the Trust on their offer of return. It was a desperate move, but he was a desperate man. As usual, neither Savinkov nor Reilly were entirely open and honest with the other. Savinkov did not mention his strong suspicion that behind the Trust's overture was the hand of the OGPU. And Reilly kept quiet about what he knew on the same count.

Nor, of course, did Sidney let on he was about to visit Russia himself. Savinkov's decision was exactly what he had planned for, and his main mission in Moscow was to deliver that news to certain quarters with a promise to deliver Savinkov himself when the time was right. The basic plan went back at least as far as Boris' meeting with Krasin in late 1921, a meeting that Reilly had so doggedly arranged and stage-managed. The critical thing, however, was that the stubborn and mercurial Boris come to the decision himself. A subsequent OGPU report on the Trust admitted that the neutralization of Savinkov was an unexpected bit of "good fortune" as opposed to real design.[24] Whatever his limitations, Savinkov was a symbol of resistance and his surrender would demoralize the emigration, even those who hated him.

The man Reilly needed to see in Moscow was Yagoda. That he was willing to do this on the latter's ground was a sign that the OGPU deputy was a man he could trust or, more accurately, one on whose mutual interests he could rely. Their partnership was not based on friendship or shared ideology but on simple, common desire for money and power. So long as he was a greater value to Yagoda alive than dead, Reilly knew he was safe. Should that change, he also knew the relationship would terminate at once, and probably with extreme prejudice.

Getting Savinkov into the bag was only the first step in a bigger deal, one that would involve millions of dollars and, eventually, another trip to Russia for Sidney. What Reilly could put on the table was money, or its promise, and that network of contacts all over the world. With these at his disposal, Yagoda could further enhance his power within the OGPU. Soon after the meeting, Yagoda established a secret personal account in Switzerland, a detail probably arranged with Reilly's help.[25] Did Yagoda realize that Savinkov was but the head of the Trojan Horse pushing open the gate? He, however, may have had his own ace up the sleeve—Anne and the children. That latter were now young adults, the boy almost twenty, but if they were in Russia, Yagoda had or could soon put his finger on them. Their safety and, as we will see, the prospect of their ultimate release, was a very useful bit of leverage in dealing with the notoriously slippery Mr. Reilly.

Yagoda's great importance lay in his position at Dzerzhinskii's elbow, for Iron Feliks needed careful watching. Dzerzhinskii saw security threats everywhere, especially from the crafty and treacherous English. For that reason, he had instructed the Trust to steer clear of the British.[26] The whole operation worried him. Too many of the key operatives, men like Opperput and Yakushev, were not true *chekisty* but opportunists and turncoats whose loyalties were far from certain. Might the Trust become a Frankenstein monster and turn on its creators? Such concerns were not baseless. During 1924 OGPU agents did briefly lose control of the MOTsR branch in Petrograd. The authentic monarchists gained control and murdered Artuzov's man, prompting a hasty crackdown before things got further out of control.[27] Dzerzhinskii also balked at the Savinkov deal, insisting the old plotter was too dangerous to do anything with but shoot.

During March and April, Feliks' paranoia and uncertainty about who was in charge goaded the OGPU into an "orgy of arrests and death sentences."[28] Moscow was the epicenter of this crackdown with businessmen and former officers among its main victims. Under the circumstances even Yagoda could not guarantee absolute security. It was at this time that Scotland Yard's informant recalled meeting Reilly outside Moscow's Opera House. He warned Sidney to "clear out" of the Capital at once because his name (presumably his alias) was "on our list."[29]

The Ace-of-Spies got out of Russia via Riga and briefly surfaced in Berlin at the beginning of May. Through Orlov he arranged a meeting with Col. Max Hoffmann. It probably was not their first. During the latter part of WWI, Hoffmann more or less ran Germany's Eastern Front and orchestrated the Brest-Litovsk negotiations opposite Trotsky. The experience left him with an abiding hatred of Bolshevism and an obsession with unfinished business, or, as he termed it, "lost opportunities," in the East.[30] Since early 1919, Hoffmann had advocated an anti-Bolshevik crusade by the Western Powers and had tried to rally British and French, not to mention German, support for the idea. Thwaites talked with him in Berlin in 1920.[31] In early 1924, Hoffmann was mixed up in a strange amalgam of Russian monarchists (led by Brasol's crony, Gen. Vasilii Biskupskii), Georgian nationalists and German mercenaries in a scheme to foment an anti-Moscow rebellion in the Caucasus. That meant oil, and to no surprise the bankroll behind the venture was Deterding.[32] In the end, nothing came of it, but Reilly's friends at Standard, among others, would have been very curious about what their Dutch rival was up to.

From Berlin, he rushed to Paris to peek in on Savinkov and make sure the game was still on. With Pepita in tow, it was on to Boulogne and the *Nieuw Amsterdam* that had them back in New York by the 17th. Their new base of operations was the Netherlands Hotel. During the war it earned dubious notoriety as a center of German intrigue, and a reputation for shady dealings and clientele still hung over the place.[33] Interestingly, Claude Dansey had stayed there on his recent visit. Sidney was bound to feel quite at home for there were familiar faces to keep him company. The manager was H.C. Manger, the same man who headed up Reilly and Helm's China and Japan Trading Co. Another regular was a Baltic German, Carl von Hoffman, seemingly no relation to the Colonel. A photographer by trade, during 1919–20 Hoffman worked for the Kolchak regime making propaganda films. For reasons never fully elucidated, American military authorities expelled him from Siberia as a security threat.[34] Among other things, they suspected him of being a German agent. Thereafter, he kicked around China and Manchuria, that area of such interest to the Ace-of-Spies, and ended up working for China & Japan Trading. In New York, he at once established a close association with Reilly.[35]

As usual, there were assorted problems to be dealt with. Back across the Atlantic, Modern Medicine, saddled with his worthless patents, was under attack by angry shareholders. To avoid all further responsibility, on the 20th Reilly resigned as managing director, a move that further cemented his reputation as a bankrupt cad in British circles. Interestingly, he gave his address c/o Alexander Weinstein in New York, an indication that he was back in league with that old partner in one way or another. Next, a process server was waiting to hand him a summons for the Baldwin case. In a letter to Savinkov, Sidney complained that his opponents were doing their best to wear him down and had offered a paltry $25,000 settlement.[36] No matter how desperate his straits, he would take nothing less than the whole $750,000. Armed with the dirt supplied by Jechalski, Vauclain's lawyers tried to force a judgment, but on 2 June Reilly's team filed an opposing motion that again brought things to a halt. With his supposedly nonexistent assets, Sidney had hired a new legal-eagle, David L. Podell.[37] A former federal prosecutor, Podell had plenty of experience fighting corporations, and an almost unbroken record of victories. He also had personal connections to U.S. Supreme Court Justice Louis Brandeis who, it happened, was a friend of Wiseman's.[38] Podell at once launched a legal counterattack that stymied Vauclain and delayed the day of reckoning until the fall session.

Brasol, as ever, was a valuable source of information and contacts. Reilly also came as the accredited representative of Aubert's Entente and helped Brasol set up an American branch of the International Anti-Bolshevik League. Sidney, in turn, served as that group's representative to the European headquarters. As nominal head of the New York organization, Sidney and Brasol installed the colorful Count Arthur Cherep-Spiridovich, a former Tsarist spy and almost psychotic anti-Semite.[39] Brasol had more influential and well-heeled recruits. Among these were "geographer-explorer" Alexander Hamilton Rice (married to a very rich Philadelphia widow) and investment banker Francis Kinnicutt.[40] These were just the sort Sidney wanted to meet. Also among Brasol's intimates was Philadelphia bond broker Francis Ralston Welsh. They had worked together investigating "subversives" for the Justice Department.[41] Welsh was a ferocious anti-Communist and another mortal enemy of Borah and his ilk. That, along with Reilly, connected him to the aforementioned Lewis Pierson.

Dukes was in town having just completed another speaking tour berating the Bolsheviks. He had been working on the translation of Savinkov's novel, and Sidney now helped him complete it. In the process, Reilly dropped a very important bit of information. "Savinkov is going back to Russia to give himself up," he confided, "[and] I too will return, but to fight." [42] It demonstrates that Reilly knew exactly what Savinkov intended to do, possibly even before Boris did.

Another matter to compel Reilly's attention Stateside was the inauguration of the American-Soviet trading firm Amtorg in May. At its head was Krasin's man Khurgin, who also had a seat on Nogin's ARTS textile board. His position was further strengthened by Nogin's untimely death in Moscow in May.[43] The significance of Amtorg is that it would channel most Russian-American commerce through a single front and through the hands of whoever could control it. From that standpoint, it was of greater value to Yagoda than Krasin.

Events of note were happening in other corners of the world. During the first half of the year, negotiations continued in London between Soviet representatives and Putilov over the fate of the RAB. The deal was clinched in July when a Soviet-designated director, Mikhail Nentskii, took a seat on the Bank's board. Intelligence reaching the U.S. State Department claimed that Putilov and Batolin had first bought up every RAB share they could find and then sold them to Moscow at a handsome profit. More interesting, in doing so Putilov and Batolin "acted in the name of an Englishman and Ukrainian resident in London." [44] Was the former Reilly?

The same information held that the real object of the purchase was to "give the Soviet Government complete power to dispose of the Chinese Eastern Railway." In fact, Moscow had just reached agreement with Wu Peifu's government on the status of the Chinese Eastern. Beijing recognized the Bolshevik regime and its administrative control of the line. Also about this time, Sergius Riis left his agency in New York and traveled to China. He was supposed to be on a job for Texaco Oil and ended up at the CER hub of Harbin. There, he certainly kept his eyes open for Reilly. State Department agent R.S. Sharp could not figure out just what was going on but was certain he had discovered Reilly involved in "peculiar Far Eastern Relations with Bolshevik elements."[45]

In Paris, during the early part of June, American Consul Charles Westcott received a handwritten copy of what purported to be the minutes of a 2 March 1924 meeting of the Comintern Executive Committee. The document outlined subversive plans for Britain, America and other countries and the money allocated to support them.[46] This followed in the footsteps of the previous Zinoviev Instructions, right down to the fact that it was a reproduction, not an original document. Westcott identified the purveyor as "an accredited agent of the Anti-Bolshevik Secret Service with headquarters in Paris," known as "AB-1."[47] This was the Aubert-Orlov outfit. AB-1, based in Berlin, may have been Orlov himself. Could this item have been something recently dropped off in Berlin by Reilly? It would bear a definite link to a similar document to emerge in just a few months.

For the moment, the issue is why Orlov chose this time, place and recipient. The answer lies in the fact that Westcott was good friends with a Philadelphia lawyer, Dillworth P. Hibberd, and Hibberd a friend of the above Francis Welsh. As Reilly was preparing to sail back to Europe in July, Hibberd was readying a trip to London and Paris. Sidney tipped off Orlov, who made sure Westcott had a copy on hand when Hibberd appeared in August. Hibberd, in turn, dutifully brought it home to Welsh. The purpose of all this was to render any tracing of the document's origin and authenticity all but impossible.

In the early days of July, Savinkov wired Reilly and urged his friend to return to Paris at once. Boris had just had another meeting with the "friends from Moscow" who brought a note bearing Kamenev's and Trotsky's signatures. This promised that if Boris surrendered, publicly confessed his errors and acknowledged Soviet authority, he would receive a prison sentence with possibility of early release.[48] Whether those two bitter rivals would have cooperated in such a proposal is questionable, but Savinkov was convinced and was champing at the bit to leave for Russia. Things seem to have moved a little faster than Reilly expected. To stall for time, he urged Boris go to Rome and make one last appeal to Mussolini. The agitated drug addict had to be kept hanging on futile hope just a bit longer.

Before leaving America, Sidney probably met with two other Russians recently arrived. The first was Emil Nobel, exiled oil magnate and *Torgprom* stalwart, who was in New York to negotiate some hush-hush deal with Standard. Perhaps that also had some bearing on the Manchurian maneuver. The other was Yakov Maller who arrived from Paris at the end of June. He now billed himself as the head of the Russian-American Commercial Agency that immediately sought contracts with Amtorg on behalf of U.S. concerns. Right after Reilly's departure, Wilhelm Lucas sailed into Gotham from Finland and went straight to the Netherlands Hotel. A day later, Tikhon Agapaev showed up too. He, recall, was the former Russian naval officer who oversaw the operation of a Soviet-supplied lumber mill in Halifax. Was this all coincidence, or were these veteran Reilly operatives gathering for some common purpose?

The Reillys sailed on the SS *Paris* on 12 July and reached Paris around the 20th. A disappointed Savinkov came back from his visit to the Duce that yielded nothing of substance. Boris was prepared to head East and submit his fate to his longtime enemies. The Ace-of-Spies later claimed he tried to talk his friend out of going to Russia.[49] Burtsev, for one, doubted that but knew Reilly was deeply involved in Savinkov's return and that the whole affair was "complex."[50] In the weeks following, Sidney carefully orchestrated his public reaction to Savinkov's stunning "betrayal." The first stage was protests of disbelief and insistence that Boris had been killed and an impostor tried in his place. Gradually this gave way to acceptance, complete with anger and disgust, that his comrade had gone over to the other side.

On 8 August, from the Hotel Montplesier, Reilly wrote Savinkov kinsman Aleksandr Miagkov in Prague.[51] He expressed reservations about Boris' venture but also cautious hope. Two days later, Savinkov, accompanied by the Derentals and Mukhin, departed Paris bound for Berlin, Warsaw and the "window" through the Soviet border. By the 20th, he was in Minsk and in the hands of the OGPU. Reilly told Miagkov that he planned to stay close to Paris waiting for news, but he probably shadowed Savinkov as far as Warsaw and, perhaps, all the way to the frontier to make sure that there was no last-minute change of heart. In any case, his almost daily flow of letters ceased until the 20th when, from the Montplesier, he wrote Miagkov with concern about the lack of news. Again, this was the very same day of Savinkov's arrest. It was nine more days before news of the arrest, trial and recantation appeared in the Soviet press and swept like wildfire through the émigré community. Reilly at once raised the impostor theory with Burtsev and Miagkov, telling the latter that Soviet reports were "incredible."[52]

Savinkov's public trial ran from the 27th to the 29th and featured a long and detailed questioning from the prosecutor and panel of judges. Boris expounded on all his past dealings with enemies of the people, foreign and domestic.[53] Most of what he had to say was quite true. Churchill's name came up several times, and many others. However, one name was completely absent—Reilly's. It is not simply that the accused failed to mention his conspiratorial mainstay for the past few years; the prosecution never asked about him either. It cannot have been accidental, but what purpose could there have been in keeping his name out of the proceedings? Among other things, Sidney had no need of publicity. If Boris had revealed even half of what he knew about his comrade's connections, it could have stimulated all sorts of inconvenient and embarrassing questions, and not for Reilly alone. Another reason may have been that the conspicuous silence was a signal to Sidney that all was going as planned and Yagoda was keeping his end of the bargain. For his long list of crimes, Boris Savinkov received a sentence of death. However, because of his "honesty" and in the interest of proletarian justice, the court commuted the sentence to ten years' imprisonment with the recommendation that he be eligible for release in three, possibly sooner.

On 3 September, Reilly dispatched a long letter to the *Morning Post*, with a copy to Churchill, in reply to the paper's editorial, "Savinkoff's Nominal Sentence."[54] He vociferously denied that Savinkov's surrender was a "stunt" cooked up with Soviet agents. Avowing himself one of Boris' "most intimate friends and devoted followers," he claimed the right to vindicate his friend's honor. He branded the trial and its revelations a "colossal libel" and the "vilest of Bolshevist *canards*." The whole affair was a fraud and Boris' supposed confession cooked up from "old political tittle-tattle" that had floated around for years. All evidence and common sense, Reilly argued, led to the conclusion that "Savinkoff *was killed when attempting to cross the Russian frontier* [italics added], and a mock trial, with one of their own agents as chief actor, was staged by the Tcheka . . ." This had nothing to do with Savinkov, but, interestingly, Reilly described a scenario eerily similar to his supposed fate just a year later. Was this precognition, or had the Ace-of-Spies let slip what was already on his mind, perhaps already planned?

In due course, he changed his tune. On 15 September another letter ran in the *Morning Post* in which he admitted that "the testimony of reliable and impartial eyewitnesses" (unnamed) had finally convinced him of his past comrade's "moral suicide" and "treachery beyond all reasonable doubt."[55] To Miagkov, he summed up the whole episode as a "unending nightmare."[56]

Sidney's statements generated some official interest. On 16 September, Capt. Guy Liddell of Scotland Yard sent Plowden a recent extract from the

Russian Information Review (a pro-Soviet publication) that chided Reilly's latest as "the usual tirade of threadbare abuse of the Soviet Government." [57] The writer poured particular scorn on the allegation that Savinkov had been shot at the border and a ringer tried in his place. The piece warned, even threatened, Reilly that he would do well to heed his friend's example and "meditate a little while upon the consequences" of the policies he had so long pursued and abetted. There even was a reference to his role in the 1918 plot. What so interested Liddell is not evident, but from this point on, he took a special interest in Reilly and compiled a growing dossier on him.

There were other interested parties in London and in the U.S. During the summer of 1924, men identifying themselves as British secret service operatives contacted the U.S. State Department's special agent in New York, R.S. Sharp. They claimed to represent a "reform faction" that had come into being in "British intelligence" after the fall of Lloyd George's government nearly two years earlier. The SIS file suggests no connection to their efforts, so we may guess MI5. Then again, perhaps they were not British at all. In any case, their investigation was of questionable persons and activities going all the way back to the war. They seem to have been interested in Reilly because of his connection to Wiseman who, according to Sharp, was under investigation for "treachery and treason." [58] Among other things, they suspected Sir William of conniving with Indian nationalists to the benefit of his new employers, Kuhn & Loeb. In the process, their investigation had "uncovered the real life and history of Sidney G. Reilly," though his mysterious British friends seem to have imparted only bits of it to him.[59]

Perhaps at their instigation, Sharp began to dig on his own and quickly discovered all manner of suspicious characters, including Helm, von Hoffman, Weinstein, Jechalski, Zhivotovskii, Jerome Landfield, William McAdoo, Benny Sverdlov and many others. He was never able to piece together this puzzle but became convinced that Reilly and Wiseman had been "planted" on His Majesty's Government by the "same secret influences." His big picture took on a marked anti-Semitic tone, complete with reference to the *Protocols of the Elders of Zion*, but the many details he churned up were mostly authentic.

America was much on Reilly's mind; he was awaiting word from New York about the pending showdown with Vauclain. On 27 September, though, he told Miagkov that departure for America was postponed for two more weeks.[60] Something had come up. It was what would be known as the Zinoviev Letter Affair. This "most extraordinary and mysterious business" remains one of the outstanding political riddles of modern British history and one unlikely to ever be solved. Even with access to SIS and Russian archives, a recent effort by the Chief Historian of the Foreign and Commonwealth Office to clear up the mysteries left many unsolved and created some new ones.[61]

In brief, the origin of the scandal goes back to the establishment of the Labour Government at the beginning of the year. Despite the fears of the Right, MacDonald's regime actually steered a moderate course, effectively banning Communists from its ranks.[62] The only area where MacDonald & Co. might be accused of pushing a Red agenda was in foreign policy. Beginning with the recognition of the Soviets, there were continuing efforts to secure a large loan and credits package for Moscow. As the treaty worked its way through Parliament in the summer, the Conservatives accelerated their attack. The Tories also harped on the Government's laxness in the face of ongoing Red propaganda and subversion. The result of all this was that on 8 October MacDonald lost critical Liberal support in Parliament and was forced to call new elections. To some, the fate of Britain hung in the balance. Certainly, its Russian policies did.

On 26 October, in the midst of the heated electoral campaign, the *Daily Mail*, a paper closely linked to the Conservative Party, printed the text of an alleged letter from Comintern head Grigorii Zinoviev to the British Communists. He exhorted his comrades to arouse the British proletariat in support of the pending treaty and to redouble efforts to form Red cells in the Army and Navy. Zinoviev promised help in the form of money and propaganda materials.[63] There was really nothing new or shocking in any of this; Zinoviev certainly had uttered much the same in the past. The volatile issue was the accusation that MacDonald had attempted to suppress or delay publication of the letter until after the election. While Labour actually increased its vote at the polls, it lost the government and the Tories returned to power with a vengeance. Ever since, the British left has decried the Zinoviev Letter as a forgery and a damned dirty trick by the opposition. On the right, belief in the Letter's basic validity remained almost as strong.

From our standpoint, whether the Letter was real or fake is not the issue, but, rather, what part Reilly played in the affair. Writers such as Michael Kettle and Robin Lockhart have long maintained that Sidney was largely responsible for the Letter; Kettle insists he actually *wrote* it.[64] Lockhart states that Reilly later admitted his responsibility to Alley and "how pleased he was with this coup."[65] Certainly the tale spread from Sidney's lips or someone's. Little over a year later, the London *Sunday News* ran an otherwise none-too-accurate article by "one of his friends" that declared "[Reilly] was the man who was responsible for the British

Government getting hold of the now notorious Zinoviev Letter." [66]

Kettle again cites handwriting analysis to prove the Ace-of-Spies' authorship. However, Kettle compared a single example of Reilly's flowing *Latin* cursive to the rather careful *Cyrillic* printing of the Zinoviev Letter. When compared to an array of our man's Russian writing, there are similarities, but not conclusive ones. Simply put, Reilly could have written the Letter, but so could any number of other people. The author of the recent FCO study, Gill Bennett, concluded that while it is "impossible to prove that Reilly had no connection with the Zinoviev Letter," there simply is no tangible evidence to argue he did. [67]

Well, not quite; the truth seems to lie somewhere between Bennett and Kettle. To understand this, we need to look more closely at the character and provenance of the Letter. The first thing to understand, and frequently overlooked in discussions, is that no one involved ever claimed to had seen or possessed an *original* letter. According to SIS, the original never left Moscow. It was hand-copied by a agent working in the Comintern offices, one who had supplied valuable information in the past. Opponents argued, and still do, that there never was a Kremlin agent and no original letter, just a "forgery" concocted by SIS or some other entity. Of course, it is fruitless to argue about the ZL being forgery if all that ever existed was the alleged copy of an alleged document by an alleged agent. It all came down to whether one placed faith in the source, as SIS insisted they did. After all they had been receiving high-grade ("A-1") reports from agents in Moscow since at least 1921, and if not all of these had proved entirely reliable, many had. On the other hand, when pressed, Desmond Morton admitted that SIS did not know the true identity of the Kremlin source and had doubts about some of the intermediaries involved. [68] Was one of them Reilly?

The basic nature of the ZL, a "copy" attested by supposedly impeccable sources, is, of course, identical with the earlier cases of the American Zinoviev Instructions and Consul Westcott's Comintern Note. Furthermore, there is no doubt that the handwriting of the March Comintern document and the Zinoviev Letter is identical, proving that both items one way or another emanated from a common source. The role of Orlov's organization also is evident. On 24 October, right after it reached the office of the *Daily Mail* in London, Westcott in Paris was handed an *identical* copy by the same agent, AB-1. [69] Yet another link in the chain was a document that came into the hands of the U.S. Legation in Riga on 16 August, a so-called "Comintern Letter on Balkan Affairs." [70] Dated 7 August 1924, it detailed subversive plans for Bulgaria, Yugoslavia and neighboring states. Once again, it was a "copy" of an original document, and style and subject matter argues that it was the handiwork of the same source(s).[71] The most important clue, perhaps, was its appearance in Riga.

Soviet inquiries lay these "forgeries" at the feet of a former Russian naval officer, Lt. Ivan Dmitrievich Pokrovskii, stationed in Riga. Despite later claims that the Letter was created in Berlin (and, perhaps, another letter was), the path of the "genuine" ZL clearly begins in Riga. Pokrovskii ran an "information center" closely affiliated with Orlov's Berlin outfit. He probably was Riga-based operative "AB-3" mentioned by Westcott in connection with the ZL and like documents. The Soviet report, from an informer inside the Orlov circle, alleged that Pokrovskii cooked up the ZL on the express orders of an SIS officer, "Capt. Black." [72] However, no SIS man with that name can be found in the Baltic or anywhere else. Could it have been another Reilly alias? Possibly; recall his "disappearance" in mid-August. If he traveled as far as Warsaw, a quick visit to Riga would have fit nicely. Pokrovskii had a clandestine career that went all the way back to Petrograd in 1918 where, just like Reilly and Orlov, he was connected to the local Cheka. He later became affiliated with Dukes' operation, but somehow avoided the ruin that befell most of its members.[73] All of this suggests past acquaintance with the Ace-of-Spies.

On 2 October, SIS Riga station chief and Reilly associate Ronald Meiklejohn forwarded an English translation to London noting that its "authenticity is undoubted." [74] This, he later explained, was a translation of the Russian copy received from the agent in Moscow. It arrived in London about the 8th, the same day MacDonald's Government fell, and the same day one Conrad Donald im Thurn received a visit from an old acquaintance. This individual, called "X" in im Thurn's diary, was an "old enemy of Apfelbaum" (Zinoviev's true name) and well-connected to Russian circles in London. He also had sources of information in the press and intelligence circles. "X" claimed to be in communication with Moscow, for he pointedly mentioned a story circulating there that Zinoviev had sent instructions to the British Communists.[75] His host was intrigued and begged his visitor to dig up more details. He also started making inquiries on his own which helped spread word of the Letter.

Donald im Thurn was a former MI5 officer turned investment banker with an eye to import-export. He currently worked with the London Steamship Co. which brought him into contact with a wide array of local Russians from monarchists to employees of ARCOS. Politically, he was an ardent anti-Bolshevik and arch-Conservative. He and Sidney definitely moved in the same circles. While im Thurn seems to have used "X" to designate more than one person in his diaries, in this case all things point to

Reilly as the mystery figure.[76] Sidney was in London during 8–14 October when the meetings transpired, and, just like "X," vanished immediately thereafter. On the 15th, he and Pepita caught the *Olympic* for New York, once more getting out of town before the storm broke.

By getting im Thurn to start asking questions and rattling cages, Reilly made sure the Letter got plenty of "buzz" in the right circles. On the other hand, the whole im Thurn gambit may have been a diversion to disguise a more direct transmission from Sidney or others connected with the intelligence services (though not SIS *per se*) to the Conservative Party. Key there was retired spy master and Principal Agent Admiral Hall. The best bet is that Hall and friends deliberately used the ZL to sabotage Labour's electoral chances and stop the Anglo-Soviet Treaty dead in its tracks. Through Baldwin Raper, "Plantagenet," and, of course, Churchill, Sidney had long and solid ties to the "anti-socialist" camp. Im Thurn ultimately coaxed £10,000 out of the Tory Central Committee to compensate "X" for his efforts.[77] Reilly was never above squeezing money out of a deal even in the best of causes. According to im Thurn, Mr. "X" conveniently slipped off to Buenos Aires. That, interestingly enough, is precisely where Pokrovskii retired in the aftermath of the affair along with his supposed co-conspirator, "Capt. Black." All of this probably was designed to lead any hounds well away from the fox.

Another possible mask worn by Reilly was that of a mysterious "Mr. Singleton" cited by Soviet Charge d'Affaires Rakovskii and a Communist-inspired work, *Anti-Soviet Forgeries*, as a purveyor of forged and dubious documents.[78] "Singleton" also vanished after the ZL scandal. As the story went, he had many aliases, was "an unscrupulous scoundrel" and well-known to British intelligence and Scotland Yard.[79] That does sound like someone we know. Furthermore, "Singleton" was close to Orlov's operation and a "White Russian organization in Paris," certainly Aubert's Entente or *Torgprom*.[80] If nothing else, Sidney knew about the Zinoviev Letter before it was public knowledge and almost certainly had a hand in authenticating and disseminating it in a properly obtuse manner. His boasting to Alley, therefore, was not all hot air.

Hauteclocque later alleged a very cozy, unofficial relationship between Reilly and the Baldwin Cabinet. He certainly had some friends there. Churchill, turned Tory, became Baldwin's Chancellor of the Exchequer, a post that put him right in the middle of the financial and economic affairs so dear to Reilly's heart. According to Hauteclocque, the new administration was determined to purge the Foreign Office and other departments of Red sympathizers and commissioned Reilly to draw up a list. In so doing, he had a wonderful opportunity to avenge himself on some who had long persecuted him. Allegedly, one of the names on that list was former British vice consul in Baku, A. Ranald MacDonnell, who had gone over "body and soul" to the Bolsheviks and served their interests.[81] How much truth lies in this story is difficult to determine. There is nothing else to connect Reilly with McDonnell, but the latter was involved in activities that would have drawn his interest. For instance, from later 1917 through 1919, MacDonnell was a special representative in Tiflis (Tblisi), deep in the oil-soaked Caucasus. In late 1922, he was slated to lead a special economic mission back to the same region. What became of him during 1924–25 is unclear and it is not at all certain he was even connected to the government. However, when Labour returned to power in 1929, MacDonnell popped up to request a diplomatic post in the USSR.

According to Hauteclocque, Reilly also served the cause of anti-Bolshevism across the Channel. In Paris, the government of Eduard Herriot was plagued by Communist-inspired unrest. Baldwin paid a visit in early December and supposedly provided his French counterpart with a dossier detailing Red subversion, once again, the handiwork of Sidney Reilly.[82] A general crackdown on Communists ensued. This flap, by the way, neatly coincided with Krasin's arrival in Paris as the new Soviet ambassador. That was a move Sidney (and Krasin) opposed and would have been glad to disrupt. Krasin's tenure in France would prove to be very brief. Donald McCormick alludes to the same incident, but gives a different twist to Reilly's motives. McCormick insists that he deliberately directed attention away from the most dangerous Red agents, as part of his service to Moscow.[83] As ever, there was nothing to prevent him from doing both so long as it furthered his own byzantine interests.

There is an interesting epilogue to the Zinoviev business. In 1968, an odd item turned up in the vaults of Harvard Law Library.[84] It was a set of three roughly 10x12-inch glass photographic plates bearing the negative image of the handwritten ZL. The text is identical to the London and Paris copies and the plates, presumably, were used to produce one or both. How they got to Harvard no one could determine. One guess was that the plates were acquired in the late 1920s by Walter Batsell, a bibliophile who sometimes acquired Russian materials. On the other hand, Reilly may have had the plates on him when he left Southampton for New York. He would not have overlooked their potential for future extortion and possession of the plates may have been the source of his claim that the Letter was "his." The fact that he had no connection to Harvard Law made its library an ideal hiding place. However, some of his associates, notably lawyer David Podell, did have contacts there.

One man who had his own questions about the Zinoviev Letter was the head of SIS, Admiral Sinclair. During the early '20s, SIS received information from at least three groups of agents in Russia, some, like the purported source of the ZL, in very sensitive positions.[85] If the Letter was a fake, it raised very serious questions about the validity and reliability of these Russian sources. Was SIS itself being deceived? If so, by whom? The Admiral would not have overlooked Sidney's recent presence in London. What, he must have wondered, did Reilly know about the ZL and, more importantly, what might he do with such information? Did he have means to embarrass the Service, the Government or worse?

Such concerns doubtless explain SIS' sudden interest in the Ace-of-Spies. On 18 November, Plowden wired the New York station to request that any press reports regarding Reilly be forwarded to London at once. "We are particularly anxious to have anything, "he added, "that may appear in connection with Reilly's nationality." Plowden also expressed special interest in the Baldwin case. Was there fear that Vauclain's lawyers could make a connection between Reilly and SIS, one they might air in public? Ten days later, New York sent a special "Report on Sidney G. Reilly." It mostly recycled information from the war years noting the subject's association with Germans, Japanese and assorted dubious types.[86] Interestingly, notations also revealed that Reilly's cronies Zhivotovskii, Ginsburg and Skidelskii had either been the objects of SIS investigation or informants in their own right.[87] The same was true for Benny Sverdlov who had been the target of an MI5 probe on 1921. Current information indicated that the subject and wife were at the Netherlands Hotel, a past and *current* "centre of German espionage." As far as Reilly's nationality was concerned, everything pointed to him being a "Russian Jew." New York promised to keep him under observation.

The Americans were watching too, especially Sharp. He noted continued meetings with von Hoffman and Franklin Helm, who were cooking something up with Sidney. Sharp suspected the gang was plotting some mischief in Latin America, but the reality of their scheming probably exceeded his darkest imaginings. A brief note in Reilly's MI5 dossier reveals that during 1924 he, Wiseman, Helm and Slevin were in league with the Flint Arms Co. in putting together a clandestine contract for 2 million rifles for the *Soviet* military.[88] This must have been a part of Krasin's arms pipeline destined for transit via the Chinese Eastern. Then again, there may have been something to the Latin American angle. Was Sidney laundering the ZL payoffs through New York, or was the money actually coming to *him* via South American channels? Then as now, South America also was the source of cocaine, a commodity much in demand by Rothstein's syndicate. The "mules" used to carry raw coca to European labs were Russians, mostly former officers.[89] Were Sidney and his partners mixed up in this as well?

Sharp sensed something even more insidious at work. Behind Reilly and the "intrigues and revolutionary activities" were "certain international banking elements in New York City" who used him and his associates as agents.[90] In Sharp's mind, a key element in this conspiracy was Kuhn & Loeb. That, naturally, made him very curious about the relationship between Wiseman and the Ace-of-Spies. Around 10 December, he had a woman in his office phone up Wiseman pretending to be the sister of a man who had served with the Royal Flying Corps. She was anxious, she claimed, to locate her brother's old friend from Toronto, Lt. Sidney Reilly. Did Sir William know where he was? Wiseman, "with great pleasure," informed the young lady that Reilly was at that moment in New York and staying at the Netherlands.[91] Wiseman, Sharp noted, seemed to be in close contact.

In the meantime, the Baldwin suit finally came to trial. In September, Podell journeyed all the way to Paris to tell Sidney that delaying tactics were exhausted. The case went before a jury in early November. Beforehand, Vauclain's lawyers did their best to paint Reilly in the most unsavory colors.[92] They argued that while a commission contract with Vauclain did exist, it had been obtained under duress by a notorious crook and the defendant was on firm moral ground in dishonoring it. The jury concurred, and on 28 November handed down a verdict in Baldwin's favor. To add insult to injury, the judge saddled Reilly with court costs and flatly rejected an application for a new trial. According to Dukes, who was present at the decision, the ruin of his long-nurtured hopes plunged Sidney into an uncharacteristic outburst of public anger. He had oft described the suit as his last chance, and by that logic he should now have been completely and irretrievably ruined. Or was he?

On 23 December, barely two weeks after the judge turned down his final motion in the Baldwin case, Reilly incorporated a new company under the laws of the State of New York. This was Trading Ventures Inc., the declared intent of which was to "export, import, buy, hold, own, manufacture, produce, lease, mortgage, sell, or otherwise dispose of" everything under the sun. It was an all-purpose shell company for overseas commerce. It is an interesting coincidence that on the very same day who should again pop up in New York but Tikhon Agapaev, fresh from pulping Russian logs in Nova Scotia. Was Trading Ventures somehow linked to this operation?

As headquarters for his new enterprise, the supposedly bankrupt Reilly first took offices at 115 Broadway, near his old base of operations. He also issued 1100 shares of stock, including $10,000 in preferred shares. A regulatory inspection of Reilly's assets showed that he possessed, in his personal accounts, "adequate cash balances" to support his new company and its stock.[93] For a man who a year earlier bemoaned his inability to raise a penny in Gotham and had just lost a major lawsuit, this was a sudden change in fortune, indeed. His partners in Trading Ventures were unlikely to have been much help in the money department. Sidney, naturally, was managing director. Under him was loyal standby, Upton Thomas, and rounding out the board were Vincent E. Howard, Suzanne Johnston and Edward S. Silver. Howard was a small-time stockbroker, and Silver a young attorney linked to Podell and Brandeis. Johnston was a humble court stenographer, in fact, *the* stenographer who had taken the transcript of the Baldwin trial. Under the rules of the day, that document remained her property, and we may be sure that her recruitment in Sidney's new venture involved the surrender of the transcript to his hands.[94]

Reilly, of course, was not and never had been broke. The sums propping up Trading Ventures were only the tip of the iceberg. Over the next several months the only substantive activity in which TV engaged was the transfer of money from banks in New York and Philadelphia to accounts in Switzerland and Germany, notably the Banca di Roma Suizza (BRS) based in Lugano. Ostensibly the money was to finance buying in Europe, except that TV never seems to have bought or imported anything. Furthermore, Reilly appears to have set up this money pipeline *before* the formation of Trading Ventures. On 13 December, the day following the loss of his case, he received a coded telegram from Berlin. In Russian, it asked "Please advise method and date of transfer."[95] Immediately after Christmas, he wired back indicating that "40MM" would be deposited in the BRS as of 1 April. This presumably indicated 40 *"Millionen Mark"* [German *Reichsmarks*] which in current exchange represented just under $10 million. The laundering of the money into marks was a standard step to disguise its origins. Notably, while dollars could not be imported into Russia, marks could.

It is by no means impossible that Reilly had accumulated this sum over the years. However, the above transfer was not the only one. Most likely, however, Sidney was tapping resources other than his own. Pure salesmanship aside, he possessed an effective, time-tested means to discreetly extract large amounts of cash—extortion. Remember that during the war he had links to at least two incidents of alleged sabotage with strong suggestions of insurance fraud, the destruction of Russian munitions at Black Tom and Kingsland. In the years following, these blasts gave rise to a tangled web of suits and claims that still clogged U.S. courts. The American Government tried to prove that German agents had been responsible for the destruction, while the Germans denied any official responsibility. In an effort to resolve the thorny issue, Washington and Berlin created a Mixed Claims Commission (MCC) to assess the evidence. Though the Americans finally prevailed in the late '30s by default, German responsibility remained unproved.[96]

The simple fact was the Germans were not responsible, but if they could be saddled with the claims, everyone else was off the hook. Such was the position of the Lehigh Valley Rail Road (LVRR), operator of the Black Tom terminal. Back in 1918, Kerenskii's ambassador Bakhmet'ev had filed a $1,700,000 suit against LVRR (one of many) to collect on Russia's lost munitions. The case simmered for years with little result.[97] In early 1925, however, things suddenly heated up. The legal expert for the "State of Russia" was none other than Boris Brasol. At the same time, five American claimants filed their own actions against Lehigh, a timely coincidence to say the least.[98] Reilly could do more than instigate lawsuits. Through such actions, he could threaten to introduce evidence, genuine or concocted, to prove that the disasters at Black Tom and Kingsland were not sabotage but fraud. Indeed, mere suspicion about what he knew and what he might do with such knowledge could have been sufficient to encourage an investment in his silence.

As strange as it may seem, some of his dollars may have been Baldwin's. It is possible that he finally did reach some accommodation with Vauclain. For instance, Sidney could have appealed the verdict, a logical step if he really was as desperate as claimed. He made absolutely no move to do so. While Vauclain's men had dug enough dirt to scuttle Reilly's chances before a jury, he had the means to come up with or concoct some of his own. The deal may have been this: Reilly agreed to publicly lose the case and even make a big show of his disappointment. Vauclain agreed to a payoff under the table. This arrangement had the advantage of enhancing Reilly's portrayal of a desperate man at the end of his rope, the type who might be driven into taking a suicidal gamble like returning to Russia. A gamble it would be, but Reilly was going to do everything he could to stack the odds in his favor.

NOTES
1. GARF, 5831, 10 Jan. 1924.
2. Ibid., 18 Jan.
3. Brackman, 176.

4. Ibid.
5. GARF, 5831, 18 Jan. 1924.
6. Leggett, especially 231–232, 292–300, and 461.
7. Teodor Gladkov, *Nagrada za vernost'-kazn'* (Moscow, 2000), 270–271.
8. Artuzov's true surname was Fraucci; his family was of Italian-Swiss origin.
9. Leggett, 232, 298.
10. Reilly, 115.
11. GARF, 5831, 7 Feb. 1924.
12. Ibid., 5 March.
13. *L'Entente Internationale contre le III Internationale*. R. Mennevee, "L'Entente Internationale contre le Communisme," *DPDF*, July, Aug. 1925.
14. Henri, 296–298.
15. Arthur McIvor, "A Crusade for Capitalism: The Economic League, 1919–39," *Journal of Contemporary History*, vol. 25 (1988), 642.
16. Ibid., 634 and John Hope, "British Fascism and the State, 1917–1927: A Re-examination of the Documentary Evidence," *Labour History Review*, vol. 57, #3 (Winter 1992), 72–83.
17. CAC, SPRS 1/326, Thwaites to Spears, 25 Sept. 1923. Thwaites was promoting a right-wing publication called *The Watchman*.
18. Patrick Beesley, *Room 40—British Naval Intelligence*, xxxx.
19. Allfrey, 230–231.
20. Bokhanov, 250. In addition, Shaikevich was a board member of the Mantashev Oil Co.
21. SIS, Memo from Special Branch, 9 March 1927.
22. Hauteclocque, RSSS, 348.
23. Russia, *Rossiiskii tsentr khraneniia I Izucheniia dokumentov noveishei istorii* (RTsKhIDKI), fond 76, opis 1, delo 306, I. "O deiatel'nosti, K.R.O.OG.P.U. za 23/24 oper. god."
24. Ibid.
25. Yagoda family member to author, 11, 12 May 1998.
26. RTsKhIDKI, f. 76, op. 1, d, 356, Styrne, "Osnovye momenty v razrobotke Yaroslavets/Trest."
27. CIA, "Trust," 34–35, 50. The chief of the Petrograd monarchist cell was Alexander Sergeevich Putilov, a former Tsarist counselor but no apparent relation to A.I. Putilov.
28. *NYT* (16 April 1924), 14:1.
29. SIS, Memo from Special Branch.
30. For Hoffmann's views see *An allen Enden Moskau: Der Problem des Bolschevismus in seinen jungsten Auswirkungen* (Berlin, 1925).
31. Thwaites, 242.
32. Roberts, 263–264, 300–309, 402–409; Pool, 60–61, 321–322.
33. CSA 215, Sharpe to Kinsey, 25 Aug. 1925.
34. MID, 10080-906/63, Memorandum of Conversation between Major Hicks and Carl von Hoffman, 8 Sept. 1920.
35. CSA 215, and Sharpe to Bannerman, 13 Dec. 1924, 3–4.
36. GARF, 5831, 9 June 1924.
37. *NYT* (2 Feb. 1947), 57:3. See also (2 Oct. 1918), 10:1.
38. *NYT* (2 Nov. 1921), 21:2. Susan Brandeis, sister of the Justice, worked as an assistant in Podell's office.
39. Cherep-Spiridovich was author of *The Secret World Government or The Hidden Hand* (New York, 1926), a rambling exposé of the "Jewish conspiracy" that relied heavily on the *Protocols*.
40. Anti-Defamation League, Report on Boris Brasol, c. 1940. The "explorer" angle may also have linked Rice to Hoffman.
41. USDS, 811.00B/434 and /678, Welsh to State, 4 March 1924 and 4 Feb. 1927.

42. R. Lockhart, *Ace*, 138, and Van Der Rhoer, 166.
43. Nogin expired during a routine ulcer operation. Rumors that this was no accident arose at once.
44. USDS, 861.516/214, Coleman (Riga) to State, 14 Aug. 1924.
45. CSA 215, Sharpe to Bannerman, 24 Aug. 1925.
46. USDS, 861.00B/259, Westcott to State, Foreign Service Report #45, 25 Nov. 1924.
47. Ibid.
48. Spence, *Savinkov*, 349.
49. Reilly, 145.
50. Burtsev, "Pechal'nyi konets B.V. Savinkova," *Byloe*, #1–2 (1933), 48–49.
51. GARF, f. 6756, d. 18, 8 Aug. 1924.
52. Ibid., 20, 29 Aug. and 2 Sept. 1924.
53. BSPVKVS, 139–145.
54. *Morning Post*, Letters, 8 Sept. 1924. Reproduced in Reilly, 149–152.
55. Reilly, 154–155 and GARF, 6756, 13 Sept. 1924.
56. GARF, 6756, 21 Sept. 1924.
57. SIS, Liddell to Plowden, 16 Sept. 1924, enclosing item dated 13 Sept.
58. CSA 215, Sharp to Bannerman, 13 Dec. 1924, 4.
59. Ibid., 6–7.
60. GARF, 6756, 27 Sept. 1924.
61. The most recent and comprehensive study is Bennett, *"A Most Extraordinary and Mysterious Business": The Zinoviev Letter of 1924*. For an earlier but still useful study, see Lewis Chester, Stephen Fay and Hugo Young, *The Zinoviev Letter: A Political Intrigue* (London, 1967). Useful insights are provided by Natalie Grant, "The Zinoviev Letter Case," *Soviet Studies*, vol. 19 (1967–68), 264–277 and items in HIA, Alexandre Tarsaidze Coll., box 7, "Zinoviev Letter."
62. Bennett, 6.
63. Ibid., 93–95, English text of ZL.
64. Kettle, 121.
65. R. Lockhart, *Ace*, 153.
66. SIS, *Sunday News* clipping, "Man Who Exploded Plot by Bolshevists" (20 Dec. 1925).
67. Bennett, 30 n. 67.
68. Ibid., 86–87.
69. USDS, 861.00B/259.
70. Ibid., /225, Coleman to State, 21 Aug. 1924.
71. William Butler, "The Harvard Test of the Zinov'ev Letter," *Harvard Library Bulletin*, vol. 18, #1 (Jan. 1970), 60–62.
72. Bennett, 89–91 and Nigel West and Oleg Tsarev, *The Crown Jewels: The British Secrets at the Heart of the KGB Archives* (London, 1998), 40–43.
73. Berezhkov, 59.
74. Bennett, 34–35. The story varies, but he actually seems to have sent two copies, one to SIS central and the other addressed to the British Communist Party. The text of the "original" from Moscow would later be introduced to demonstrate the authenticity of the English version.
75. Bennett, 40–41.
76. Kettle, 122–123, also arrived at this conclusion, if for somewhat different reasons.
77. Chester et al., 186–188.
78. Bennett, 76–77. *Anti-Soviet Forgeries* appeared in London in 1927.
79. Ibid., 77.
80. Ibid., 79.
81. Hauteclocque, "Sidney Reilly."
82. Ibid., and *NYT* (7 Dec. 1924), 1:8.
83. Deacon, *British Connection*, 37.

84. Butler, 43–62.
85. Various reports from these networks may be found in FO 371/8718, 8719 and 9337. The last includes a organizational structure for the OGPU from 1923.
86. SIS, YN356, 28 Nov. 1924.
87. Ibid., referencing CX 7697 ("Jivatovsky") and CX 12650/1329 (Ginsburg, Skidelski).
88. MI5, Reilly, SZ/835, note dated 15 Sept. 1927.
89. NYT (14 Sept. 1926), 18:5.
90. CSA 215, Sharp to Bannerman, 13 Dec. 1924, 1.
91. Ibid., 3.
92. Jechalski did not go without reward. He later took a job in Poland with the Warsaw-based First Locomotive Co., a Baldwin affiliate.
93. CSA 215, Sharpe to Kinsey, 25 Aug. 1925, attachments.
94. As was the norm, court records did not retain a copy of the transcript. One copy survived in the files of Vauclain's attorneys, White & Case, until the 1980s but subsequently was lost or destroyed in a purge of old documents.
95. Thanks to G.L. Owen for this information and his valuable insights.
96. MID, 2778-B-1, G-2 to CoS, 6 March 1925; Russell van Wyk, "Enduring Myths: Accusations of Unrestrained German Sabotage in the United States," paper presented at the Moscow Conference on the First World War, May 1994, and NYT (1 Feb. 1930), 35.
97. NYT (3 July 1925), 6:4.
98. NYT (11 Dec. 1924), 11:3.

Chapter Sixteen

THE SPY WHO WENT INTO THE COLD

Feliks Dzerzhinskii felt very pleased with himself. Despite initial misgivings, he had come to view the "capture" of Savinkov as a great psychological triumph for the Soviet regime. After Boris' arrival in Moscow, Iron Feliks had a series of long conversations/debriefings with the ex-terrorist and came away convinced of his change in heart.[1] Perhaps Boris himself even believed what he was saying. Dzerzhinskii added his voice to those insisting that Savinkov's life be spared. What the long-term fate of the broken-down drug addict would be remained to be seen, but the possibility of parole was not out of the question. Reilly had carefully molded his friend's psychological state and guided him into Dzerzhinskii's hands with just this purpose in mind. With Feliks' acceptance of Savinkov, the Trojan Horse edged further through the gate.

Dzerzhinskii was so taken with the success against Savinkov that he almost immediately sanctioned a like operation to entrap another, even more dangerous, enemy, Sidney Reilly. As a sign of good faith, perhaps Savinkov offered his assistance. More importantly, perhaps, *Yagoda* informed his boss that a captive Reilly could provide vital information on British and other spy networks inside Russia, perennial objects of Dzerzhinskii's concern. On 31 August, Iron Feliks summoned KRO chief Artuzov and charged him with mounting a special operation to lure Reilly onto Soviet territory and take him alive. He assigned *Yagoda* to oversee the operation.[2]

According to the later Chekist defector Aleksandr Orlov (no relation to Vladimir), the agent specifically designated to "get Reilly" was Fedorov, the same Fedorov/Mukhin involved in the Savinkov case.[3] However, as we will see directly, Sidney knew all about Fedorov's association with the OGPU well in advance of his return. There is no way Reilly could have been taken in by him unless he wanted to be. More problematic is that Fedorov/

Mukhin's name is completely absent in all Soviet documentation of the case. As we will see, Orlov's recollections, based almost entirely on hearsay, are far from a reliable guide, though not without their kernels of truth.

Savinkov's capture made Artuzov's KRO outfit the fair-haired boys of the OGPU and even gave the lackluster Trust operation a new lease on life. None of this went down well with Trilisser at the rival INO who viewed the Reilly gambit as another invasion of his domain. Trilisser long had taken a keen interest in the activities of the Ace-of-Spies and had compiled an extensive dossier on his association with Dukes, Orlov, Aubert and a host of other émigré and foreign enemies. The INO chief was convinced Reilly was a central figure in an international conspiracy against the Soviet regime, and monitoring him could reveal the dimensions and intentions of this plot. From that standpoint, he argued that the KRO's plan would disrupt an important source of information. Thus, he balked when Artuzov asked for the Reilly materials in his files. Yagoda appealed to Menzhinskii, perhaps to Feliks himself, and on 17 September, Artuzov informed his deputy Vladimir Styrne that INO was to turn over all materials relevant to Reilly, Dukes and related matters going back to 1918.[4] KRO had won this round, but Trilisser was not about to give up the fight. He ordered his own agents to redouble efforts to gather information on Sidney and his associates. Did he suspect that there was more to Artuzov's and Yagoda's plan than they told Dzerzhinskii?

In early October, Savinkov revealed his new state of mind in a series of letters to his family and close friends, including Sidney. Reilly was the recipient of a particularly long one that extolled a vibrant Moscow replete with "shops, theatres, cinemas, motorists . . . electric lights."[5] He lauded the humane prison system in which no one served "more than three years." Ensconced in the relative comfort of the Lubianka's Inner Prison (including conjugal visits from Mrs. Derental) his perspective was decidedly warped. It was a brave new world that he described, and himself as a man reborn in it. He reserved special praise for the OGPU wherein he had met men "spiritually closer to me than" any in the emigration. The latter, in all its forms, he declared politically and morally dead and proclaimed with absolute assurance that the Russian people are "with the Soviet Government."

Boris admitted that as early as 1923 he had privately come to the conclusion that it was "impossible and perhaps unnecessary" to fight the Bolsheviks but had *not* admitted such to Reilly. The appearance of the "friends from Moscow," i.e. the Trust, actually delayed his decision by raising hope that some opposition might exist. He had never taken that possibility too seriously and now admitted that there "was not any ghost of an organization"; Fedorov/Mukhin, Yakushev and the others were all tools of the Bolsheviks. He acknowledged that Reilly had been present at meetings with these men. He urged Sidney to follow his example and warned that "some day, very soon, you will convince yourself that not you are right but I am." These comments again show that Sidney was familiar with the Trust and fully appraised of its true nature long before his return. Note also that the Chekists who reviewed Savinkov's outgoing mail made absolutely no effort to conceal these facts. This was a very strange oversight if they really planned to use the same means to ensnare Reilly, and stranger still if they sent one of these blown agents to do it. But that all depends on whom they really sought to deceive.

Reilly received Savinkov's letter before he left for New York but said nothing about it for months. In March, however, he sent a translated and edited copy to Churchill, Arch Sinclair and Spears. To the last he described the letter as reeking of "hypocrisy, cynicism and callousness" and declared Savinkov "dead as a doornail inside and outside of Russia."[6] He also expressed confidence that the letter "was written under supervision and censorship," and noted that it failed to make mention of "a number of purely personal matters which held considerable interest for both of us." Privately, of course, he was very satisfied with the letter because it was proof that Dzerzhinskii had taken the bait.

Boris, though, became more and more restless in his genteel confinement. Furloughs to visit cabarets and race tracks, under guard of course, were not what he had bargained for, nor was writing letters extolling the virtues of the Soviet system his idea of meaningful work. He pestered Dzerzhinskii to set him free and give him real work. According to defector Grigorii Bessedovskii, in early 1925, Feliks was willing to see the old wolf set free and given some safe job in the economic planning department.[7] Interestingly, such work would have placed him right in Yagoda's bailiwick. Stalin, however, voiced strong opposition, insisting that if the repentant enemy wanted his freedom he could come beg for it in person.

Vladimir Burtsev later picked up a story from other defectors that after his arrest Savinkov was approached by certain men in the OGPU, the very ones who saved him from execution, about assisting them in a secret struggle against Trotsky and Zinoviev.[8] And what better way to use a terrorist than as a terrorist. What would have been the result of a liberated Savinkov gunning down or blowing up a prominent Bolshevik or two? It was not even necessary for him to actually carry out the deed; Yagoda had steadier hands to arrange that. Boris would provide the perfect scapegoat. Who would take the heat for this gross error in judgment? Not Stalin, who had gone on record time and time again opposing any release. Dzerzhinskii would have taken a hit, but perhaps the most compromised would have been Trotsky and Kamenev whose signatures, recall, were on a document inviting Boris back home. Just as they tried in 1918, Reilly and his collaborators could have shifted the balance of power in the Bolshevik hierarchy and opened up new avenues for their own influence and advancement.

Meanwhile, Sidney had plenty to keep him occupied in New York. In January, he moved into bigger offices at 25 Broadway. This was the Cunard Building and it lay just across the street from Standard Oil's headquarters at #26. Boris Said also had an office at #25 as did a very intriguing character named Sergei Romanovskii. On Christmas Day 1924, Romanovskii, who claimed to be "Duke of Leuchtenburg" and a distant cousin to the late Tsar, arrived from Italy.[9] He was a bosom friend of the art dealer and collector Joseph Duveen, and an artist and musician in his own right. It was, therefore, rather out of character for him to take an interest in the import-export business. Nevertheless, he soon formed the Russian-American Transatlantic Co. (RATC) for the declared purpose of trading with the Bolos. Not only did he do business in the same building as Reilly, but the two firms had the same post office box address. There is some question whether Romanovskii's outfit ever really existed at all. There is no record of it having been incorporated in New York or having engaged in any business. The conclusion is that the Duke was another front manipulated by Reilly, but to what end?

The answer lies in ongoing efforts to find Tsarist and Russian assets. As noted in earlier chapters, millions of dollars in Russian gold and personal effects of the Imperial family had gone missing since 1917. Some of it probably lay forgotten or hidden in American banks. During late 1924 and early 1925, New York was a sudden focus of attention for various Romanovs or Romanov agents in search of such treasure. Also in December, the self-proclaimed Tsar-in-exile, Kyril, sent his wife, the Grand Duchess Victoria Fedorovna, to the U.S. to hobnob with rich Americans and lay claim to any family money she might find. Kyril naturally felt that anything that had been Nicky's was now his. A month later, Kyril's younger brother Boris came to town. The Russian rumor mill had it that he hoped to locate assets and coax cash out of Henry Ford. Brasol was still Kyril's personal representative in the U.S. and the liaison with Ford, so Sidney had an inside source. He would have wanted to know about anything the monarchists turned up but had no desire to see them get their hands on it. He had his own plans for such loot. He may have introduced the Duke into the picture as his cat's paw and to obstruct other claims. Romanovskii eventually sought a court order granting him right of administration over any assets of the late Tsar.[10]

Romanovskii was linked to another strange episode centering on Prince Yusupov, the supposed killer of Rasputin. In 1923 in Paris, Sidney and Savinkov had spent some effort trying to locate Yusupov's personal secretary, Georges de Mazirov. Exactly what they wanted from him is unclear, but it certainly was not to chat about old times. Recall that the Prince had evacuated a sizable fortune from Russia. More interesting, perhaps, were stories that he left riches behind, safely hidden but inaccessible. In the spring of 1925, Yusupov was in New York pursuing legal action against Joseph Widener, a(nother) rich Philadelphian. The Prince had previously "loaned" two Rembrandts to Widener and now wanted them back.[11] Romanovskii testified as did Duveen and Calouste Gulbenkian, Zaharoff's shadow. From this, Reilly may have collected enough clues to figure out the whereabouts of Yusupov's hidden treasure. During June, Yagoda sent agents to search Yusupov's residence in Leningrad (the former St. Petersburg/Petrograd) and happily discovered a secret safe containing $3 million in gold and gems.[12] Was this just good luck or further demonstration of the Ace-of-Spies' good faith and utility?

In early March, Trading Ventures went through a major reorganization. Howard, Johnston and Silver dropped from the board, while Yakov Maller joined as vice president and Thomas became secretary-treasurer. Soon another new face was added, Paul M. Herzog, a lawyer pal of Podell and an "authority" on Manhattan real estate.[13] Herzog had plenty of connections on Wall Street, especially to its more speculative quarters.

It was during the first months of 1925 that Reilly became involved in two ongoing and revealing exchanges of correspondence. The first, with Spears, Sidney seems to have initiated with a letter dated 22 January on Trading Ventures stationery.[14] Spears, in fact, was in New York, having come over at the close of 1924. "As you will see," Reilly began, "I am now permanently established in New York [and] president of the above company which I have formed and in which I own a large interest." He went on to ask "whether you are still in any way interested in business, and . . . if this is the case, could not we do something together here?" Reilly described his main interest as "bond issues for foreign municipalities and foreign industries" and boasted "excellent connections" to Kuhn & Loeb (via Wiseman, presumably), Metropolitan Trust (Lewis Pierson territory) and his old friends at National City. He expressed a keen interest in Anglo-American trade and "the placing and financing of British inventions and processes" in the U.S. Thanks to the recent loss of his suit, he lamented, his finances had been "rather precarious" which necessitated a withdrawal from "active participation in Russian politics." He declared himself ready to "jump in again as soon as my financial circumstances are somewhat improved and there is something doing."

Reilly only briefly mentioned their past partner in the tobacco business, Leon Rozen. He cautioned Spears that should Rozen bother him about an "outstanding account" to just ignore it. It was a matter, he declared, he would settle "in due time." Soon enough, Spears did hear from Rozen who demanded £75 due him in commissions. Spears argued that Rozen's claim arose from a separate pact with Reilly which neither he nor Brunstrom knew about and from which they reaped no profit.[15] He thought it only fair that Sidney settle the matter at once, something he seemed quite able to manage.

To Spears' annoyance he just ignored it and continued to solicit help. On 17 March, he wrote, "I am in frequent correspondence . . . with Brunstrom with regard to some Central European bond issues."[16] "I should be very pleased . . . if you could either directly or indirectly through your city connections find suitable British, Colonial or even Central European objects for American bond issues," he continued, "I have excellent connections here in this line of business . . . ." Sidney noted ongoing interest in radium, and his interest in politics had revived. "I am keeping myself extremely well-informed on Russia affairs and am more optimistic as regards impending doom of the Bolshevik regime than I ever was," and added, "I hope no one in England is taken in by their recent widely advertised moves to the right. All this is nothing more than eye-wash . . . the real significance behind these moves is that the position of the Bolshevik Government as far as the peasants are concerned is becoming more untenable." "There is a lot of rumour floating about as regards the possibility of the U.S. administration recognizing the Soviet Government in the near future," he concluded, "I am following this very closely and I feel certain that there is not a ghost of a chance for it under the Coolidge administration." Interestingly, on 15 February, the *NYT* noted a new "Comintern Letter to America," bearing the all the usual hallmarks. It helped stymie a fresh push by Borah to bring up the recognition issue.[17] Perhaps Reilly knew that the Senator was in contact with at least two Trust agents.[18]

In April, Spears found himself sued by Rozen for the still-unpaid commission. The "sickening" part to Spears was that Reilly simply refused to be bothered. In desperation, he turned to Brunstrom; "I rely on you to bring strong pressure on him." That had no effect, and on 5 May Spears wrote Reilly for the last time, insisting that "I shall expect you to reimburse me for any expenses to which I am put in this matter, concerning which I am exceedingly annoyed. I think the least you can do is immediately . . . send Rozen's cheque, and I should be glad if you would notify me by cable that you have done so." [19] He also threatened to call in the £500 loan he and Brunstrom had made to Lockhart at Sidney's behest some years before. Why did he think that would matter?

Reilly's behavior is puzzling. His cavalier indifference to this niggling debt seemed calculated to alienate Spears, a man whose cooperation he at the same instant sought. Perhaps it was delayed payback for Spears' abrupt severing of their business link in 1922 or for some other real or perceived slight. For Reilly, revenge was always a dish best served cold. In any case, Spears simply did not matter. All the talk about bond deals and the like was just talk, just like Trading Ventures was a firm trading nothing. It was all part of an ongoing act disguising his true intentions.

Those plans peek through in other correspondence with SIS colleague Ernest Boyce and one of his Russian agents, Nikolai Nikolaevich Bunakov. To put this in perspective, we must backtrack a bit. Bunakov was an adherent of Savinkov's Union in 1918 and worked with Dukes during 1919–20. By 1923 he headed up Savinkov's organization in Finland and simultaneously was an agent for Finnish military intelligence and Boyce's Helsinki station. In June of that year, the same time Savinkov had his first visit from the Trust in Paris, Bunakov was visited by Yakushev who spun his tale. Bunakov informed Boris, who ordered him to test Yakushev. Yakushev agreed to arrange a rendezvous with Bunakov's brother, still in Russia and an active member of the Trust. Of course, Bunakov also appraised Boyce of the situation, who sought his own Trust connection. Artuzov's men, however, at first kept their distance. A February 1925 report on the Trust noted British overtures via Bunakov were treated with great circumspection because of standing policies about dealing with the perfidious English. [20] The not unrealistic fear was that they would seek to turn the Trust to their own ends, or even betray the operation, especially if they sensed it was an OGPU front.

Another man with interest in the Trust was Gen. Aleksandr Pavlovich Kutepov who headed the main White Russian military forces in exile under the banner of the Russian General Military Union (*Russkii Obshche-voenskii Soiuz*) or ROVS. The astute and cautious Kutepov listened closely to his advisor, Col. Nikolai Chebyshev, who thoroughly mistrusted Yakushev and his supposed organization. [21] Nevertheless, in the fall of 1924 Kutepov chanced the lives of five agents by sending them into Russia under the wing of Opperput. Two of the five were husband and wife, Georgii (Yurii)

Radkevich and Maria Zakharchenko-Radkevich. Georgii was a boyish figure dominated by his small, intense spouse. Aleksandr Orlov described Maria as a "beautiful blonde" codenamed the "Sorceress" by the OGPU.[22] Again, he is way off the mark. In fact, she was a thin, dark-haired, very plain woman animated by nervous energy. Reilly described her as an "American schoolmarm type."[23] Born Maria Vladislavovna Lysova, she had outlived two husbands and fought in the civil war before marrying Radkevich.[24] She also happened to be Kutepov's niece and a trusted member of his elite Combat Organization. What the General did not know was that Opperput had recruited both Radkeviches into the OGPU's service, though whether they realized that is another question.

Opperput, as ever, was an enigmatic figure. He now operated as Eduard Ottovich von Staunitz, a Baltic German, though he also used the names Levine, Ring—even Fedorov—as occasion demanded. Despite his work for the men in the Lubianka, he remained a hireling, not a true Chekist—"among us, but not one of us"—and not entirely trusted.[25] His "outsider" status made him suitable for certain specialized work. According to his version of events, during 1922–23, Artuzov tapped him to form a secret "special operations" unit for the KRO. This was composed of persons, like Opperput, outside the OGPU proper. Their job was to spy on regular *chekisty* and liquidate those who strayed out of line, or anyone else who proved an obstacle but too sensitive to eliminate through usual channels. Opperput's group was an "OGPU within the OGPU," an internal security cell-*cum*-hit squad whose existence was known only to Artuzov and a few others, most notably Yagoda. It is impossible to confirm Opperput's story, but it seems plausible enough. Such a unit would have been very useful to the Yagoda—and others. But there also remains the possibility, later picked up by Chebyshev, that Opperput was a *British* double agent.[26] Or was he, simply, Reilly's agent?

In January 1925, the Radkeviches, who now called themselves Shults (Schultze), reappeared in Helsinki claiming to be representatives of a secret underground government in Russia. Their special goal was to establish contact with the famed anti-Bolshevik crusader Sidney Reilly. They connected with Bunakov who introduced them to Boyce. They, certainly, were Artuzov's response to Dzerzhinskii's directive to get Sidney. He knew Boyce was the right man to carry the message. What he may not have known is to whom else Boyce delivered it.

On 26 January, Boyce sent Sidney a letter from Tallinn. He enclosed *another* letter also written in Tallinn and dated the 24th.[27] The writer of the latter assumed that Sidney was in Paris or soon would be. He told him to expect a visit from the "Krasnoshtanovs" (Radkeviches) who were representatives of a "big concern" (the Trust). They brought some interesting news from "California" (Russia). In true cloak-and-dagger form, they would offer a quote from Omar Khayyam to which Reilly would respond. The supplicants sought Reilly's help in establishing links between their concern and "European and American Markets" (political sympathizers and financial backers). At the present time they faced opposition from a powerful "International Group" (the dominant Kremlin clique), but had offers of help from "German" and "French" interests. Fearing potential domination by the "Germans," they wanted Sidney's help in opening negotiations with an "English" group. The writer could not reveal "the name of the man at the back of the enterprise," but "some of the persons involved are members of the opposition groups" (members of the Communist Party and Soviet Government). He thought this might interest Reilly as compensation for the collapse of his last "big scheme" (Savinkov). He added that as "a government official," presumably a British one, he had to keep his involvement "from the knowledge of my department" and asked Sidney to look after "my interest."

Subsequent references to the 24 January letter, including Pepita's, have declared it Boyce's. It was not. Reilly's 10 February reply only referred to Boyce's letter of the 26th but thanked him for the "extremely interesting enclosure."[28] Extant copies of the 24 January letter are typed but variously bear the signature "E" or "ST2," the last Boyce's SIS code name. But inspection of the copies reveals that "E" was pasted over "ST2" and that, too, could have been added easily at a later date. That is not the only oddity. In fact, Boyce's designation as station chief was ST0, not ST2. That change occurred in early 1921.[29] Reilly knew this and had referred to Boyce as ST0 in SIS correspondence.[30] Whoever forged "ST2" was not aware of that little detail.

The true author of the letter of the 24th was George Hill. Much later, in an effort to disguise his authorship, he mistakenly used Boyce's old code name. Why the subterfuge? The "Explanatory Note" added to Reilly's case file by Styrne provides the answer: Hill was a "collaborator of the OGPU."[31] Captain George, remember, was born and raised in Russia, and his British service hardly earned him the rewards he thought he deserved. No doubt he and Reilly had discussed their mutual dissatisfaction in that regard. His "collaboration" went right back to 1918. In helping set up the Cheka's counterintelligence section, he had worked closely with Dzerzhinskii. Jolly George, not the amateurish Buikis or the lovesick Lockhart, was the real "Dzerzhinskii agent" inside Reilly's Latvian Plot.

Sidney, remember, had "explained to [Hill] all that had been done," briefing him on every meeting with Berzin.[32] But if that was so, why did he later help Reilly escape? Betraying him is the one thing Hill could not do without tipping his hand. Keeping Reilly at large diverted suspicion, quite successfully as it turned out. Hill's loyalties did raise questions. One of his later colleagues accused him of being a "triple-agent" who supplied information to the Soviets, British and Germans.[33] A more recent Russian source says exactly the same, and also ties him to the Trotskyites.[34] So, exactly whom was he serving in 1925?

The key question is how much Reilly knew about all this. He may have suspected Hill's duplicity as far back as 1918. Recall that George said he saw Sidney off on 8 September, while Reilly put his final exit three days later. It would have been simple enough for him to slip off the train at the station or double back giving him a few days free of Hill's observation. In any case, it seems extremely unlikely that an experienced intriguer like Sidney would have failed to put two and two together in the years that followed. Here is no evidence that he extended Hill any special trust. At the same time, he would have looked for a way to use Hill's duplicity to his advantage even through the simple expedient of blackmail. What must not be overlooked is the possibility that he and Reilly actually were working together in 1925 in the common purpose of getting Sidney back into Russia.

However, Styrne's report contains another surprise: Ernest Boyce also was an "agent" of the OGPU. As a serving SIS officer, a station chief no less, his treachery was a much more serious matter from both the Russian and British perspectives. When and how Boyce became a Soviet collaborator is more difficult to determine. Though he did not reveal it until the early 1970s, Aleksandr Orlov assured the U.S. FBI that Boyce was "the principal who ultimately sent Reilly to his death." [35] Orlov claims the motivation was money, but a survey of his personal finances reveals no obvious difficulty.[36] Also, Orlov elsewhere described the man as a "young Englishman," something that Boyce in his late 30s with a head of prematurely gray hair did not fit at all. But that is not the only question. As important as he was, it was most irregular for the OGPU to risk exposing him by involving him in Reilly's capture. Perhaps that is why Hill was brought in, yet Boyce still ended up entangled in the plan. Moreover, involving two operatives in the same gambit, even if they were ignorant of their mutual affiliation, risked exposing both if something went wrong. Was Boyce, perhaps, connected to Artuzov's organization while Hill worked for Trilesser's INO?

There may have been another level of deception. As mentioned with regard to Hill, was Boyce's collaboration really also part of a plan *with*

Sidney to allay Iron Feliks' suspicions and further embellish the prestige of
the Yagoda-Artuzov clique? If so, who else in London knew about the
scheme? The letter of 24 January bears an interesting notation. In the lower
left corner of the last page, in Boyce's hand, is written "copy to London
address." Whose was it? There existed a gray area of communication
dubbed the "Demi-official," or DO Letter. This was the use of ostensibly
private correspondence to convey "official" information. If this was the
case here, to whom was Boyce reporting? In years to come, the constant
refrain from SIS was that any dealings Boyce had with Reilly were entirely
on his own and contrary to instructions, but that does not mean everyone
there took the same view. And Sidney, remember, had other friends in
London.

In his reply to the above, Sidney regretted missing the "Californian
couple," but noted that from New York he was in "constant correspondence with the different manufacturing groups [émigré factions] in the various countries." He thought the proposal had possibilities, "especially since
the recent fight for share control which has been going on in the Board of
Directors," i.e. the Kremlin leadership. "I have finally convinced myself,"
he continued, "that the initiative must come direct from among the present
minority interests," and that the latter must "make up their minds to sacrifice a good portion of their original ideas . . . in a manner which will be
acceptable both to the internal and international market." "Minority interests" were pragmatic elements among the Bolsheviks, men like Krasin and
Yagoda. Basically, this was the same idea he had been promoting since
1918. He was willing to talk to the "Californians" but was quick to remind
Boyce that any approach to the émigrés was "a waste of their time."
Guchkov alone was worth talking to because of his connections to certain
"minority interests" among the Reds. As for money, it could be made available but only to the right sort of organization led by practical people. He
spoke of negotiations with "the largest automobile manufacturer," certainly Ford, who would come up with the cash provided he was convinced
that the "patents [plan] will work." It would be Reilly's part to give that
assurance. He also thought "Marlborough" [Churchill] would be amenable
on the British end.

Reilly played it cool. He showed some interest but offered no commitment, least of all of himself. Nevertheless, on 20 February, Bunakov
reported to Moscow that Reilly was hot for the deal and had "important
personal political and economic connections in England as well as
America." [37] Styrne took this one step further and informed higher-ups that
Sidney actually expressed a desire to come to Russia. [38] The person being

THE SPY WHO WENT INTO THE COLD 423

deceived here was Dzerzhinskii who was encouraged that everything was going according to plan.

Over the next several weeks, Reilly exchanged several letters with Boyce, Bunakov and, possibly, Hill. On 9 March, Boyce advised the Ace-of-Spies to conduct all further negotiations through Bunakov, though he definitely wanted to stay in the loop. What Sidney actually said to Bunakov was unimportant, assured Boyce, so long as it "showed that you are in a position to help them" and Bunakov could prove that he was "working on the matter." Again, just who was trying to con whom?[39] In further letters dated 25 and 30 March, Reilly again voiced interest in the "syndicate" proposed by the Trust representatives but also noted strong reservations. He characterized their ideas as "too vague" to attract outside support. Like the Boy Who Cried Wolf, hopes of Bolshevism's collapse had risen and fallen so many times that no one in America or anywhere else was interested in pouring money down another Russian rat hole. In direct contradiction of what he recently told Spears, Reilly saw no chance that the present order in Russia would change on its own; Bolshevism wasn't going to be talked to death. "Only *action*," he insisted, could arouse real interest and support. As a first step, the Syndicate should make its existence known to the world. If it really had the influence claimed, it ought to be able to withstand the attack of the opposition; if, not, what good was it? In effect, he was asking the Trust to acknowledge itself a Soviet organization. Although his affairs were "in a hellish state" . . ."if I see the right people and prospects of real action, [I am] prepared to chuck everything and devote myself entirely to the Syndicate's interests." "I was fifty-one yesterday, and I want to do something worthwhile whilst I can," he concluded.

A few days later, Reilly reiterated that he was "sick and tired of continuous theorizing" and was sending some specific proposals for the "Board's" [Trust leadership's] consideration. If they declined them, they would do without his help. He again attacked the organization's overtures to the émigrés, especially the monarchists like Kutepov. Sidney had nothing against Kutepov or monarchism in the right circumstances, he added, but in the present ones a whiff of reaction would be "absolutely fatal" to foreign support. On 27 March, Reilly sent a letter to Bunakov that took a distinctly militant tone. He identified three keys to combating Bolshevik power—organization, propaganda and terrorism. The last, he argued, was of special importance, for terror alone could demolish the aura of invincibility surrounding the Bolos. One "major terroristic act" would generate more consternation among the Bolos and attract more outside attention that any amount of empty scheming and endless proposals.[40] It was time for the opposition to quit talking and do something. On 4 April, Sidney noted that the "Board" had rejected some of his proposals and he had strong disagreements with the "Directors." Nevertheless, he accepted their recommendation that the best thing was for him to "come out and inspect the factory personally." That, however, would have to await the arrangement of his affairs in New York.

Thus, after much dickering and posturing, Reilly finally gave Dzerzhinskii what he wanted, a promise to return to Russia. Feliks then gave Yagoda the go-ahead to reel him in. It was Dzerzhinskii, however, who was being deceived. Sidney, as we know, began planning his return months before. What was being played out now was a dog-and-pony show for Dzerzhinskii's consumption. His decision to return had to look convincing, and that meant it could not come too easily or quickly. By playing hard to get, Reilly made his "capture" seem all the more desirable and important. The Horse was now all but inside the gates.

Boyce now sought to set up a new meeting. The Radkeviches and Yakushev were planning a conference with Gen. Kutepov in early July and he thought it would be ideal if Sidney could be there. On 19 April, Boyce wrote to say that another of Reilly's SIS chums, Arthur McPherson, was cooperating and more assistance could be expected from persons connected to the American Relief Administration.[41] One can only wonder if some of this was coded reference for something else. More letters followed on 28 April, 9 May and 5 June, the last informing Sidney of the Paris meeting and thoughtfully providing Kutepov's address.

Reilly did not rush to reply to any of these communications for the simple fact that for most of the time he was not in New York. In late April, he quietly returned to Europe. This conveniently coincided with the closing of the Netherlands Hotel, and the Reillys' relocation to the Times Square Hotel. In fact, he *did* go to Paris but not to see the Trust. His main task was to check on and finalize his financial arrangements, something that demanded great caution. To help, he may have enlisted the help of old friends Sasha Grammatikov and Abram Zhivotovskii, both on hand in Paris. He also looked up Aubert and Orlov who were busy organizing the second congress of the International Entente against the III Internationale.

Reilly's European sojourn coincides with a marked downturn in the fortunes of Armand Hammer. The Ace-of-Spies had kept a watchful eye on Hammer's activities, and current plans made it all the more important to curb the American's activities. It is possible, if no more, that our man was behind the 1924 report to J. Edgar Hoover from "a source apparently well-located in the Comintern hierarchy" (shades of the Zinoviev Letter).[42] The source alleged that Moscow had supplied Hammer with $75,000 to finance Comintern activity in the U.S. American surveillance of Hammer became much tighter. Another factor working in Reilly's favor was that Hammer's activities came under the direct scrutiny of Yagoda.[43] In May 1925, Hammer's primary financial prop, the Estonian Harju Bank, suddenly went belly-up. One of the bank's hidden functions was to launder money going to and from Russia. Bad management was the basic problem, but Yagoda insured the Bank's failure when he refused to provide money to cover the losses.

Sidney's next stop was Vienna. Orlov had directed him to Col. Ivan Borodin who led a local group of White officers. Reilly promised all the money they would need if Borodin would assassinate Moscow's representative in Vienna, Yan Berzin, a former comrade of Krasin's in London.[44] He pledged like support for attempts on Soviet officials in Warsaw and Prague. The attacks were to commence on a specific signal. In March, the Foreign Office picked up reliable reports of a meeting in Paris in which unnamed French, Polish and Romanian elements pledged money to finance armed action and insurrection against the Soviet regime. Even British capital was said to be involved. Interestingly the man handling that was Donald im Thurn, late of the Zinoviev Letter scandal.[45] Trilesser's agents picked up reports of the same thing, and he was convinced Reilly was somehow involved. That, certainly, is exactly what Sidney wanted to accomplish. By increasing his real or potential threat to the Red regime, he made his capture all the more important and desirable.

Another man Sidney saw in Vienna was Capt. Vladimir Stepanovich Nesterovich, a former Tsarist officer. Joining the Bolsheviks, under the name Yaroslavskii he rose to command a division in the Red Army. By 1924, he was resident agent of Soviet military intelligence (*Razvedupr*, later GRU) in Austria and worked closely with Comintern and OGPU agents like the redoubtable Dr. Efraim Goldenstein.[46] He had been up to his neck in planning various schemes to advance Communist power in the Balkans. Yaroslavskii may have had a hand in providing information for the Comintern "Balkan Letter" that surfaced in Riga the preceding summer. He supplied other information to Orlov and, as Trilesser discovered, "had secret connections with Reilly for a long time."[47] Sidney had a new mission for him, one that would compel him to break with the Soviets.

Next, it was south to Rome where a Soviet delegation was negotiating a trade pact with Mussolini's regime. Krasin was on hand as was another familiar face, Nikolai Klyshko. Again, it may have been Klyshko who told Scotland Yard he ran into Reilly in the Italian capital in the spring of 1925.

Was he there to confer with Krasin out of the Parisian spotlight or was it Mussolini he came to see? Then again, the headquarters of the Banca di Roma may have been the main attraction.

Reilly was back in New York by the first week in June. At the beginning of that month Isaiah Khurgin, the head of Amtorg, also returned from a seven-month visit to Russia. Perhaps this was what Reilly had wanted to discuss with Krasin. During Khurgin's absence, Amtorg's leadership was in limbo, presenting an ideal opportunity for others, such as Sidney and Yagoda, to expand their influence. From their perspective, Khurgin's return was a real inconvenience, especially with Reilly preparing his own departure.

In June, Yaroslavskii fled Vienna for Paris, taking with him a large cache of money and documents. Trilesser was convinced that there was more to this than a routine defection and theft. He learned that in Paris, Yaroslavskii had met with an agent of Reilly's, an Englishman who had just come from America.[48] This was either Dukes or Wiseman. Other information suggested that the fugitive had supplied Reilly with details about "valuables" hidden in Leningrad.[49] The INO chief was convinced that Yaroslavskii, who previously served in Berlin, had long funneled information to the British and Americans "through Reilly's agency" and that the latter could provide invaluable information on other traitors in Red service. The INO chief decided that the efforts of his KRO comrades might prove useful after all. At the same time, he decided to take a closer look at just what they were doing.

Others taking a renewed interest in Reilly were Admiral Sinclair and SIS. Since the previous, SIS and Scotland Yard had obtained a number of new "Zinoviev Letters," apparently genuine but of the usual vague provenance. SY Inspector J.F.C. Carter, who had past contact with Sidney, would only admit that they came from a source "who had proved reliable in many respects."[50] What made this all the more worrisome was that Labour MPs were pushing for Parliamentary investigation into the "whole circumstances " of the ZL.[51] What Reilly knew and what he might do with that information was one of several imponderables. On 16 July, Sinclair ordered the New York station to "ascertain as soon as possible the present whereabouts of Sidney G. Reilly," and a week later he received a report from operatives there.[52] Inquiries showed the subject presented himself as a British subject and claimed to have "served in the British Army in France during . . . the war." He appeared to have last returned to the U.S. in November 1924, which shows his most recent European foray had escaped detection. The report noted his presence at the Cunard Building and his operation of Trading Ventures in close association with Thomas, Maller and Herzog. An agent who visited Reilly's offices found the premises "well-furnished" and the subject "in a prosperous condition." The place seemed very busy and employed a number of stenographers and other help, all of whom "seem to be of German and Jewish origin." "The whole atmosphere of the office," the observer concluded, "is foreign." The agent managed a brief interview with Sidney during which he claimed to have been attached to the wartime British and Canadian Recruiting Mission in Manhattan. However, the agent's doubts were raised when Reilly could not identify the former commanding officer of that body or many of the other officers so attached. The report added that American authorities regarded Reilly "as a suspicious character and former German spy" and "also in the employ of the Japanese." Also noted was the past and present connection to Helm, "whose notorious connections have been the subject of many comments in reports from this office" and the strange business of exporting aircraft and other military materials to China. The subject not only was evasive about his past, but presently involved in an undertaking the nature of which was closely guarded.

In the interim, Moscow reported on 7 May that Boris Savinkov had killed himself by jumping from a prison window. The desperate act seemed in response to Dzerzhinskii's continued refusal to release him from custody. Indeed, a few days before Boris had written another appeal insisting that Iron Feliks "either shoot me, or give me a chance to work." [53] One way or another, Boris probably did bring about his demise, though whether the situation was as simple as official reports described is questionable. His sister and ex-wife, for instance, insisted he was murdered. Earlier the same day, Boris had been out on a visit to the countryside. After his fatal plunge, the body lay for a long time in the courtyard. One scenario, which falls somewhere between suicide and murder, is that he made an escape attempt during the outing and was shot or seriously injured by his guards. Not knowing what else to do, they brought the dying prisoner back to the Lubianka and finished the job as a "suicide." [54] Other rumors circulated that the old terrorist was not dead at all, but living somewhere under a new identity. [55]

Our question is how Savinkov's demise affected Reilly's plans, and the simple answer is that it fit quite nicely. Sidney knew all about Boris' intention to return to Russia, but whether the latter knew about Reilly's is doubtful. Reilly knew Savinkov was too unreliable to be a partner in any serious conspiratorial undertaking. Having paved the way for Sidney's return, his job was complete and his elimination a virtual necessity.

As noted, the original idea may have been to sacrifice Savinkov in a "terrorist" act against one of the Red leaders, but changes in that arena rendered the plan unnecessary. At the beginning of 1925, Kamenev and Zinoviev led an attack on Trotsky that stripped him of his most important post as War Commissar. Trotsky's political fate was sealed. Having let his partners do the dirty work, at the March Party gathering Stalin repudiated Kamenev and Zinoviev and made a new alliance with the Party's right wing, a right wing that included Yagoda. Having Boris kill Zinoviev in the name of Trotsky or vice versa no longer had much utility.

There are good reasons why Reilly would have welcomed Stalin's rise. The Georgian seemed more pragmatic than his rivals, something Sidney always regarded as a positive indicator. He appeared a manifestation of that resurgent nationalism Sidney had long predicted, right down to the exploitation of anti-Semitism in the struggle against his Jewish opponents. Beyond this, Reilly certainly knew of Stalin's past work for the Okhrana. As with Peters, Krasin and others, this offered a means to exert influence as the need arose.

Soon after his return to 25 Broadway, Sidney received a new letter from Boyce that outlined plans for a meeting in Paris in early July. The Radkeviches and the Trust's "foreign minister" Yakushev were coming to confer with General Kutepov. It would be splendid, thought the Commander, if Reilly could attend as well.[56] On 6 July (the day of the gathering), he wired Kutepov and Boyce to explain that business had him tied up in New York and he saw no way out before mid-August. Dzerzhinskii had to be kept waiting just a while longer.

This delay may have been because Sidney was waiting for another bit of business to complete, a most secret and personal one. In mid-June 1925, a woman and her daughter presented themselves at the British Consulate in Leningrad. She identified herself as "Mrs. Z.Z. Zaharoff," a British subject, and formally requested repatriation.[57] The file on this case long ago disappeared, but the result was that London approved the application and the women departed Russia in the summer or fall of the year. As noted earlier, part of Reilly's arrangement with Yagoda may have included the "release" of Anne and the offspring. That would have to be settled before he came over. The suggestion has been made that the mysterious Mrs. Zaharoff, not your usual British name, had some connection to Sir Basil, also known as "ZZ."[58] There is, however, absolutely nothing to suggest that Basil Zaharoff had a stray wife and daughter in Russia. He might, however, have been willing to lend his name and influence to assist an old friend. Was this something the two worked out in their meeting the previous spring? Anne hardly could have applied for repatriation under the name of Mrs. Sidney Reilly without raising all sorts of inconvenient questions, both in London and Moscow.

Meanwhile, Reilly had other loose ends to tie up and a few more to leave hanging. In American courts, Brasol had managed to secure a positive outcome to the lawsuit against Lehigh Valley RR. In July, a federal court awarded the "State of Russia" more that $850,000 in compensation for goods lost at Black Tom. The question was: who got the money? The immediate answer was former Tsarist financial agent, Sergei Uget, who would hold the funds in trust until such time as a "legal" Russian government existed. This opened the door to eventual Soviet possession via formal recognition or another court ruling the Bolshevik regime to be the de facto State of Russia. Thus, it was one more potential offering to Yagoda, or did Reilly figure out a way to divert this loot into his own coffers? About this same time, Brasol gave testimony in another case involving Russian assets in Washington, D.C. In this instance "his testimony was favorable to the Soviet" which earned him "good Soviet contacts."[59] Indeed, for the next several years, while never repudiating his outward stand as a virulent anti-Bolshevik, Brasol quietly functioned as "an agent of Amtorg and the G.P.U. [OGPU]."[60] More to the point, perhaps, he functioned as Reilly's and Yagoda's agent.

Another useful figure to return to Gotham was the roaming Sergius Riis, back from Manchuria. He resumed management of his Confidential Bureau on Park Row and was at Sidney's disposal. Riis probably brought Sidney information about U.S. military attaché Faymonville. In any case, Reilly somehow learned that Faymonville maintained secret contact with Moscow via a "young English agent," someone connected to British concerns in China, perhaps even SIS.[61]

Pepita later recounted that just prior to their final departure, her husband "accepted a position as director of a large firm in Europe."[62] This was a vague reference to General Motors that was busy buying up European subsidiaries, including Vauxhall Motors in Britain.[63] Sidney secured a berth through Hertz as payoff for previous good work for Yellow Cab. His likely job was to scout and broker new acquisitions in Central and Eastern Europe not excluding, perhaps, Russia. If nothing else, the slot was convenient cover for his coming travels and, should other plans change, a fallback position. Remember the System's rule: always hedge your bets. Meantime, Sidney reassured parties in New York that he would be returning Stateside before year's end.[64]

In Moscow, Dzerzhinskii and others were impatient as Reilly "delayed and delayed" his return.[65] Finally, on 20 August he wired Helsinki that he would depart New York on the 26th bound for Havre. Artuzov got wind of this at once and passed word up the chain.

There may have been one final thing to take care of before departing. On 25 August, Khurgin welcomed a new face of Bolshevik officialdom, Efraim M. Sklianskii, to Manhattan. Sklianskii came as representative of the Moscow Textile Trust but until recently he had been Trotsky's "right-hand man in the creation and management of the Red Army." [66] Sklianskii remained a "close friend" and devoted partisan of Trotsky and the posting to America may have been a plan to separate them. [67] On the other hand, Sklianskii was positioned to act as Trotsky's representative in America, and rumors buzzed in Moscow that Comrade T would become a special Soviet emissary to the United States. [68] Who knew how it might impact Amtorg and other carefully laid plans? On the same day Sidney and Pepita sailed, Khurgin, Sklianskii and three other Amtorg staffers adjourned to the Sagamore Hotel on Long Lake in the picturesque Adirondacks for a brief vacation. The following afternoon, the group went boating on the lake. For reasons never made clear, Khurgin and Sklianskii ended up in a canoe out of sight and "several hundred yards" from the rest of the party. [69] The later assumption was that a freak gust of high wind capsized Khurgin's and Sklianskii's canoe, drowning both, though Sklianskii reputedly was a strong swimmer. While conditions on the lake were breezy, there were no other reports of capsizing or troubles due to wind. There also was confusion about the number of the dead men's companions; were there three or *five*?

Back in New York, rumors floated around Amtorg that the two men had been murdered. The NYPD tried to investigate but could find no one willing to substantiate the charge or any other solid evidence to go on. The deaths not only eliminated one of Trotsky's loyalists, but left Amtorg even more susceptible to control by the OGPU. Arranging the demise of Khurgin and Sklianskii would have been a simple task for a man with Reilly's connections and another demonstration of good faith to certain people in Moscow. Interestingly, not far removed from the fatal scene, on nearby Placid Lake, was the secluded summer home of Boris Brasol.

The Atlantic breezes must have been a welcome relief from the heat wave gripping New York. As always, the leisurely pace of transoceanic travel gave Reilly time to reflect and plan. It was more important than ever now, for he was about to embark on a course from which it would be very difficult to turn back if something went wrong. How far could he really trust Yagoda? Was Boyce working for or against him, and what about Hill? For that matter, what of Pepita; was she really the guileless innocent she seemed? Something to keep in mind is that Reilly was not one to take foolish or unnecessary risks. He was a methodical planner and had absolutely no illusions about the nature of the Trust or the people he was dealing with.

If simply getting into Russia was his goal, that could be accomplished in a much less obvious fashion. What was about to unfold was a deliberate, orchestrated performance, the role of a lifetime.

The Reillys reached Paris late on 3 September and were met by Boyce, or so recollected Pepita. Early the next morning, Sidney shunted Pepita off to Belgium to visit her mother and sister while he got down to business. On the 3rd, Gen. Kutepov wired his people in Helsinki informing them that Sidney soon would arrive in Finland. He advised that the Englishman be treated with the "greatest caution," which suggests the General was not altogether certain what the Ace-of-Spies was up to.[70] Over the next few days, Reilly held a series of meetings involving Boyce, Kutepov, Grammatikov and Vladimir Burtsev. No one from the Trust was present. Guchkov was supposed to have attended but was held up by illness. They were, for the most part, old and trusted (so far as he trusted anyone) associates. How much Sidney revealed of his plan, and whether he told the same to everyone, is unknown. The gist of this conference, as relayed to Pepita, was that all present "agreed to lay all cards on the table" and there was "complete agreement as to the theoretical appreciation of the entire situation" whatever that may mean.[71]

Following this, Sidney disappeared from Paris for the better part of a week. He made a quick visit to London, but whom he saw there and why are a matter of enduring confusion. In his later statements, or alleged statements, to the OGPU, he claimed to have consulted with an interesting trio just prior to his return: Churchill, Spears and Guy Gaunt. The first makes sense; if anyone would have been willing to meet with him it would have been Winston. As Chancellor of the Exchequer, his opinion and influence would play an important part in Sidney's plans. As later reported to Dzerzhinskii, Reilly told Churchill of his plans to meet with the Trust and sought his support. Winston declined to promise anything until he had "concrete evidence" of a viable "counter-revolutionary *movement*" [italics added] inside the Soviet state as opposed to some or various counter-revolutionary organizations.[72]

Given Spears' recent difficulties with Reilly, it is hard to see what they would have had to talk about, but perhaps he participated at Churchill's request. Gaunt's, however, is a frankly bizarre name to pull out of thin air. Reilly had had no discernible contact with him since 1917, and that, recall, was not exactly chummy. Or was that just the way Gaunt later portrayed it? Was his denunciation of Sidney as a German agent itself an act to make sure the Americans did not mistake him for a British one? Then again, perceptions can change in seven years. But stranger still, in his

OGPU statements Reilly identified Gaunt as "chief of the Secret Intelligence Service."[73] The Chekists appear to have taken the story as fact and repeated it for years after.[74] Of course, Sidney knew very well that Admiral Sinclair was SIS chief.

So why the lie? It was not just to keep "C"'s identity secret. Chances are, Sidney really met with Gaunt, not as head of SIS, but as a representative of Admiral Hall and his "private secret service." The two retired Navy men were close, personally and politically. Like "Blinker," Sir Guy was aligned firmly with the Tory "Diehards." His past intelligence duties made him an ideal assistant to take care of clandestine matters.

So what did Sidney want from these men? He later told Styrne that he did not contact them for instructions or sanction but only to offer an "appraisal" of his gambit.[75] All, supposedly, voiced "disapproval." He must have offered some assurance that however things might seem, he would continue to serve Britain's best interests. He also may have cautioned them not to raise any fuss or inquiry over his disappearance. In his pending venture, he knew he could expect no official help from His Majesty's Government. Indeed, many therein would be more than glad to see him vanish off the face of the Earth. Hall's apparatus, and Churchill, provided means for private communication with higher quarters in state and business. If necessary, he could have leveraged such cooperation by pointing out that even if he was in Russia, friends in the West had access to information, about the Zinoviev Letter and many other things, that could prove very embarrassing.

Many years later a story circulated among Russian émigrés that another man Sidney saw in England prior to his departure East was Franz Rintelen.[76] Rintelen may be recalled as a short-lived but effective German agent who was nabbed by Hall, probably with Reilly's assistance, on his way back to Berlin in 1915. He and Hall later became great friends. Following an unrewarding homecoming in Germany in the '20s, Rintelen drifted back to England where he found support from Hall. As the story goes, Reilly entrusted the German with various papers, some of which pertained to his recent transatlantic financial transactions, including account numbers. Why would he have entrusted such to Rintelen? Unlike Thomas, Weinstein, Brasol, Spears or Churchill, Rintelen was the perfect choice because he had no visible connection to Reilly; anyone trying to ferret out such information would not likely look to him. Sidney knew the German was a man who could keep his mouth shut, and who knows what other secrets he had to insure that silence? While the Rintelen story cannot be taken as fact, it does make sense by the standards of the Secret World.

Finally, if it really was Anne who emerged from Russia earlier that summer, her long-estranged husband would have made some effort to check on her and his daughter's welfare and to make necessary arrangements for their needs. Perhaps Rintelen fit in here, too. Again, with no obvious links to the Ace-of-Spies, he would have been a good choice to look after the women's affairs.

Reilly was back at the Hotel Terminus in Paris by the 11th where he rendezvoused with Pepita, Boyce and Kutepov, and even crammed in a belated meeting with Guchkov. That same day, a message reached Moscow from Tallinn, probably from Hill, stating that Reilly would arrive in Helsinki on the 23rd. This supports the notion that Boyce and Hill were in contact. According to Pepita, her husband swore that he was "convinced of the sincerity and potentiality" of the mysterious anti-Bolo organization and would leave at once to meet its principals in Finland.[77] He would not, he assured her, venture into Russia itself and would be back in her arms by the end of the month. If these were his words, he was lying to her at every step.

Departure from Paris was on the 15th. As a security precaution, Sidney waited until the last minute to buy tickets to Berlin. Pepita recounted some unsettling incidents as the trip got underway. On the way to the station, a stranger snapped their picture and dashed off in a cab. On being appraised of this, Boyce "became very alarmed and asked all sorts of questions."[78] On the train, they ended up sharing a compartment with a genial young stranger who addressed her husband in Russian, a strange assumption to make in Paris, she thought.

At Köln, on the Rhine, Sidney and Pepita parted company. She proceeded to Hamburg to visit friends and await his return. He was supposed to continue on to Berlin, but first he took a detour to the nearby town of Mainz. The person he originally intended to see there was Vladimir Yaroslavskii, the Soviet military intelligence officer who had defected from Vienna. After meeting with Reilly's man in Paris, Yaroslavskii had offered his services to the French who assigned him to the *Deuxième Bureau's* outpost in Mainz. There he worked under Capt. Pierre Laurent, Reilly's old collaborator from Russia during 1917–18. Yaroslavskii's job was to point out Red agents. Unfortunately, he failed to recognize one of Trilesser's men who poisoned him in late August.[79] What Sidney was after was information Yaroslavskii had left for him concerning "valuables" hidden in Leningrad. It was from Mainz, on the 16th, that Reilly cabled Bunakov to confirm that he would arrive in Helsinki no later than the 23rd. He gave precise instructions concerning the preparation of a new passport.[80] This specified the name, Nikolai Nikolaievich Steinberg, profession (merchant) and details of height, weight, etc. This is the passport that he would use in Russia and further evidence that the decision to return was a fait accompli.

Reilly stole into Berlin late on the 17th where he lingered for the next three days. He wired Pepita that he was waiting for "O." That, most likely, was Orlov, but it may have referred to another "O," *Opperput*. According to German investigative journalist Berndorff, several persons remembered Sidney dining in a well-known Russian restaurant in the Charlottenburg district with a trio identified as Trust-niks Opperput, Yakushev and Fedorov/Mukhin.[81] The story continues that at this meeting Sidney first learned of the Trust and hatched the idea to enter Russia. Definitely untrue, but it may have been a tale Opperput laid on Kroshko, Trilesser's man in Orlov's camp. If so, it was to cover up a meeting for some very different purpose.

After a "rotten trip" across the storm-tossed Baltic, Sidney reached Helsinki on the evening of the 22nd. Boyce was nowhere to be seen; the Commander made himself conspicuously scarce for the next several days, "on holiday" as he later explained. One might think that would raise Reilly's suspicions unless, of course, it was precisely what he expected. In Boyce's place was his young, "keen as mustard" assistant, Harry Carr. Was he the Soviet agent; did A. Orlov later get him confused with Boyce? In any case, Carr introduced our Ace to Bunakov and the "Schultzes," i.e. the Radkeviches. Georgii struck him as a "nincompoop" and Maria, as mentioned, a hyperactive plain Jane who "did most of the talking." [82] Other people were coming over from Russia, but something had caused them delay. Reilly wired Pepita that he would have to remain in Finland longer than planned, at least until the 26th. He also had to travel to Vyborg (Viipurii), close to the Soviet border. Everything, he promised, would be perfectly fine.

What happens next is a matter of much confusion and disinformation. From this point on we enter a realm where it is impossible to be absolutely certain of almost anything. Still, with patience, skepticism and some speculative insight, it is possible to recreate a picture of what transpired. According to the KRO's after-action reports, Reilly reached Vyborg on 24 September. He was met by *seksot* (secret collaborator) "A," (Yakushev), one of those he is supposed to have met just a few days before in Berlin. Yakushev later wrote that his "first impression" of Reilly was a rather unpleasant one.[83] Of course, that was not their first meeting. There was something "hard and thorny" in the gaze of his protruding, dark eyes, Yakushev recalled, and a disagreeable pout to his full lower lip. Overall, he gave an impression of arrogance and contempt. He was immaculately dressed in a light gray overcoat and "flawless" gray check suit. Everything about him seemed too fastidious and calculated, from his shiny black hair and manicured hands to his well-polished yellow shoes and perfectly creased trousers.

Yakushev showed Sidney a letter from a "British intelligence officer" whose handwriting he recognized. This vouched for the existence of "bona fide anti-Kremlin groups" whose overtures "should be taken seriously." [84] This had to have been from Hill. But once more, this was not telling Reilly anything he did not know or would take seriously. Yakushev next escorted Reilly to the house of another collaborator, one Karpinen, who lived right on the frontier. There they finally met the expected emissary from the other side, a Soviet official of some note and the representative of an even higher-placed personage. According to Stalin-era defector Aleksandr Orlov (no relation to Vladimir O.), the man was Chekist Terentii Dmitrievich Deribas. As elsewhere, Orlov's recollection must be taken with a hefty dose of salt. He had no direct knowledge of anything concerning the Reilly case but recycled Lubianka gossip larded with his own imaginative details. Like Fedorov, Deribas' name is lacking from any documents or other accounts. Still, he was chief of the OGPU's Secret Operational Administration that made Yagoda his superior. As head of the department charged with keeping tabs on the "opposition," Deribas was uniquely qualified to represent it. He allegedly handed Sidney a letter from the prince of opposition, Trotsky. In it he proposed that in return for helping him wrest power from Stalin, he was prepared to grant broad concessions to the citizens of helpful governments and to offer a sweeping amnesty for the émigrés. Trotsky almost certainly did not write the note. As the similar offer to Savinkov, it was a handy incriminating item to generate, one that could be used to generate all manner of subsequent mischief. Stalin would have found it very useful.

Opperput later offered a different version of events. According to this, Reilly came to Finland as a journalist with the aim of collecting material on current Russian conditions. There is no mention of Deribas. He notes only that Yakushev "was sent from Russia to meet [Reilly]" as emissary of the Trust. Before going to the meeting, Yakushev "obtained a promise from members of the collegia of the [OGPU]" that Sidney would not be arrested.[85] That body was headed by Dzerzhinskii and included Yagoda, Artuzov, Styrne and Trilesser. The whole point was that the Englishman would be treated to an elaborate dog-and-pony show to convince him of the Trust's power and then set free to carry that word abroad. Just who was being deceived here is far from clear.

Despite the entreaties of Hill, Deribas, Yakushev or whomever, Reilly balked at proceeding further. He had booked return passage to New York on the 30th, he claimed, so there simply was not enough time for a trip across the border. He might be able to do it in two or three months. For a moment, reported Styrne, the quarry seemed about to slip from their grasp. That, no doubt, was exactly the impression intended. In the end, Styrne gave credit to an unnamed "collaborator" who "worked so cleverly" to change Reilly's mind. A. Orlov assigns that role to Maria Radkevich, but elsewhere says Deribas claimed to have lured Reilly into the trap by making his "eyes glitter" with assurances of the vast profits to be made under the new order.[86] Other versions have Yakushev doing the last minute persuading.[87] Perhaps there is such confusion on the point because it never happened at all. Who had to be persuaded that Reilly was persuaded?

There was a performance going on, and Reilly was the star and director of the show, not its audience. How many others fully understood the roles they were playing is hard to say, but it really mattered little one way or another. Sidney was not undupable, but it seems impossible that a man of his experience and caution would have been taken in by any of this even if he did not already know exactly what the Trust was and was not. In the System you never bet your life, at least not without good odds.

That Reilly would never have walked into such an obvious setup struck Natalie Grant, a researcher who spent decades studying the Trust and its like. Among other things, she guessed Boyce's deal with the OGPU.[88] Regarding Reilly, she concluded that in Vyborg or somewhere near the frontier he was drugged and carried into Russia.[89] Soviet agents were not loath to use kidnapping as means to an end. Grant also feels that Moscow was closed-mouthed and deceptive about Reilly's case because it did not want this means revealed. Reilly, of course, went back willingly and knowingly, but Grant noted another very important detail that we will come to shortly.

The next day, the 25th, Pepita received a wire from her husband confirming that he would depart Helsinki on the 30th and rejoin her in Hamburg two days after. What she did not yet know was that later that day Reilly wrote her a letter explaining that he was making a quick visit to Leningrad and Moscow but would still catch the boat out on the 30th. Why did he not wire this information as before, especially as it was such an important decision? Obviously, Pepita was not to receive this news until well after he set foot in Russia. "I would not have undertaken this trip unless it was absolutely essential," he explained, "and if I was not convinced that there is practically no risk attached to it." [90] However, he warned that in the off chance something should go amiss, "you must not take any steps." Asking questions might compromise his new identity. "Every noise, etc.," he cautioned, "may give me away to the Bolshies." It was much the same advice Reilly had handed out to his women many times before: keep quiet, sit tight and wait.

That evening, Reilly dined with Bunakov, Yakushev and the Radkeviches. Afterwards, since his fancy American clothes would attract attention, he took Georgii's coat, cap and long Finnish boots. Bidding farewell to the others, he, Georgii Radkevich and a Finnish border guard officer, Capt. Ruzenstrem, headed out for the frontier station of Kuokkala. Arriving there about 10 p.m., they went on foot to Karpinen's house. From there, about midnight, they joined a group of Finnish guards and smugglers to make their way through the dark, swampy forest and across the Sestro River to the Soviet side. The going was painfully slow and Reilly's new boots creaked noisily. To prevent that, his companions forced him to soak them in the cold water. Further delay was caused by his need to unwrap and re-wrap elastic bandages around his legs. The purpose of the bandages, he explained, was to relieve the varicose veins in his lower limbs. It is a curious detail, for nowhere else is there any indication of Reilly suffering from this condition. He endured much discomfort as the journey continued by foot and cart, albeit, the report noted, with a measure of stoicism.

Waiting in the gloom across the river were two more Trust operatives: the Soviet border guard Toivo Viakhia (true name I.M. Petrov) and one Shchukin. Both were OGPU as well. Shchukin handed Sidney the new passport in the name of Steinberg. It is here that Grant notes a very odd occurrence. Once across the river, Reilly turned back and ostentatiously shouted good-bye to the Finns in *English*. Not only was this a strange and seemingly dangerous thing to do under the circumstances, but it is even stranger that he would have bid farewell in English to a group of Finns and Russians. He would if the whole point was to reinforce the notion that an Englishman was there. It was another performance, but for whom? Based on her kidnapping thesis, Grant argues that the man who bid farewell was not the real Ace-of-Spies but an "actor" used by the OGPU to cover the abduction.[91] Was the man with the varicose veins an impostor? Certainly, the midnight journey through mud and water was completely unnecessary. The Trust (OGPU) could have arranged a quick, comfortable train ride to Leningrad. Did Reilly take another route, while an unfortunate stand-in waded across the Sestro? It is only the first of many questions.

NOTES

1. Spence, *Savinkov*, 356–357.
2. Savchenko, 301.
3. Edward Gazur, *Secret Assignment: The FBI's KGB General* (London, 2001), 506–507.
4. TsAFSB, 302330.
5. HIA, Lockhart, 6, Savinkov to Reilly, 7 Oct. 1924.
6. Ibid., Reilly to Spears, 17 and 20 March 1925.
7. G.Z. Besedovskii, *Na putiakh k' termidoru* (Paris, 1931), 8–9.
8. HIA, Nicholas de Basily Coll. Burtsev, untitled document beginning "En 1924 . . ."
9. *NYT* (26 Dec. 1924), 7:1.
10. *NYT* (7 Oct. 1925), 55:3.
11. *NYT* (14 Apr. 1925), 4:3 and subsequent days.
12. *NYT* (28 June 1925), 1:2.
13. *NYT* (13 Nov. 1925), 19:5.
14. HIA, Lockhart, 6, Reilly to Spears, 22 Jan. 1925.
15. CAC, SPRS 1/299, Spears to Abrahams, 4 May 1925.
16. HIA Lockhart, 6, Reilly to Spears, 17 March 1925.
17. *NYT* (15 Feb. 1925), 6:2.
18. RTsKhIDNI, f. 76, d. 356, Artuzov, "Osnovnye momenty v razrabotke Yaroslavets," [Feb. 1925], 5.
19. CAC, CHAR, SPRS 1/299, 5 May.
20. RTsKhIDNI, Ibid.
21. CIA, "Trust," 12.
22. Gazur, 518, and Smith, "Who Murdered . . . ."
23. Reilly, 190.
24. N. Tsurikov, "Za Rossiu-Mariia Zakharchenko-Shults (1893–1927), Biografichekie dannye . . . ," *Rossiia*, #12 (12 Nov 1927) and HIA, Prianishnikov, #5, "Materialy Opperputa."
25. Chebyshev, "Iz proshlogo: O tak nazyvaemom Treste," *Pereklichka*, #136–137 (March-April 1963), 10–13 and Gladkov, 101–102, 254–256.
26. Chebyshev, 10–11.
27. HIA, Lockhart, 6, "E" to Reilly, 24 Jan. 1925; see also Reilly, 172–174.
28. Reilly, 175.
29. Thanks to Phil Tomaselli for this detail.
30. SIS, to ST0, Helsingfors, 22 Jan. 1922.
31. PZZ #73, 7.
32. PRO, Hill Report, 17/36.
33. Gladkov, 203.
34. L.H. Manderstam, *From Red Army to SOE* (London, 1985), 146–149).
35. Gazur, 519. See also Nigel West quoted by Michael Smith, "Who Murdered the Ace of Spies," *Daily Telegraph* (3 Oct. 1998).
36. Thanks to Phil Tomaselli.
37. Igor Prelin, "Zhizn' I smert' Sidnei Reilli," (Moscow, c. 1991), 4. In edited form this appeared under the name of Iurii Miliutin as "Konets shpiona Reilly," *Sovershenno sekretno*, #12 (1990), 21–23.
38. TsAFSB, 302330, Styrne, "O priezde R."
39. Reilly, 9 March.
40. Prelin, 4–5.
41. 19 April 1925.
42. Epstein, 73.
43. Ibid., 106.
44. Jan Berzin was no known relation to Col. Eduard Berzin, though both were Latvians.

45. PRO, FO 371/11010, 75138, Bentinck to FO, 3 March 1925.
46. Orlov, *Dvoinoi*, 348.
47. SIS, translation of 1 Oct. 1925 Trilesser memo.
48. SIS, Trilesser memo and HIA, Nicolaevskii.
49. SIS, Trilesser memo.
50. PRO, FO 371/11011, Note of J.W. Olive, 20 Aug. 1925.
51. Ibid., 5431 and *Daily Express* (24 Sept. 925).
52. SIS, CSS, CXG 817, 16 July 1925 and YN 1215, "Sidney G. Reilly," 24 July 1925.
53. Spence, *Savinkov*, 369 and *Parizhskii vestnik*, #11 (16 May 1924), 1.
54. Ibid., 370.
55. Ibid., 371–372 and Walter Duranty, *The Curious Lottery* (New York, 1929), 132.
56. HIA, Lockhart, box 6, E to Reilly, 5 June 1925.
57. PRO, K8230/8230/238.
58. Allfrey, 230.
59. ADL Report.
60. Ibid.
61. TsAFSB, Diary, 4 Nov. 1925.
62. Reilly, 183.
63. *NYT* (29 Aug. 1925), 16:1, and (31 Oct. 1925), 6:2.
64. Alekseev, "OGPU . . . ," 3–4.
65. TsAFSB, "O priezde R."
66. *Tupper Lake Herald* [TLH] (4 Sept. 1925), 1 and *NYT* (30 Aug. 1925), 12:1.
67. *NYT* (30 Aug. 1925), 12:1.
68. *NYT* (27 Feb. 1925), 4:5.
69. *NYT* (30 Aug. 1925), 12:1, and *Glen Falls Post-Star* (28 Aug. 1925), 1.
70. TsAFSB, "O priezde R."
71. Reilly, 184.
72. TsAFSB, "O priezde R."
73. Kichkassov, 30.
74. Ibid. and Minaev, 87.
75. TsAFSB, 302330, Styrne, 31 Oct. 1925.
76. Thanks to G.L. Owen.
77. Reilly, 185.
78. Ibid., 186.
79. Orlov, *Morder*, 160.
80. TsAFSB, "O priezde R."
81. Berndorff, 43–47.
82. Reilly, 190.
83. Prelin, 7.
84. Brook-Shepherd, 290.
85. SIS, "The Shooting of the English Officer Sidney Reilly," 1, and HIA, Nicolaevsky, 300-1, "Rasstrel' angliiskago ofitsera Sidnei Reili" (Russian original).
86. Brooke-Shepherd, 290–291.
87. Prelin, 7–8.
88. Grant interview with Andrea Lynn, 14 Nov. 1998.
89. Ibid.
90. Reilly, 199–203.
91. Grant interview.

Chapter Seventeen

WANTED DEAD OR ALIVE

A ccompanied by Shchukin and Viakhia, Reilly arrived at Leningrad's Finland Station about 7 a.m. Yakushev was there to greet him, having taken the train from Vyborg the night before. They all bundled into a car and headed for their "conspiratorial quarters," Shchukin's flat. Later Styrne arrived to join the crowd. If the goal was to lure the Ace-of-Spies into a trap then surely he was in it. Why was he not arrested? For that matter, why was he not grabbed as soon as he crossed the Sestro? Obviously, this was not a simple bait-and-capture operation, but when did the orders change, and on whose authority? Opperput later claimed there was a split in Moscow's higher quarters as to what to do with Reilly. Artuzov argued that by letting him come and go unmolested, the Trust would receive a big boost whereas his arrest could only do harm. Dzerzhinskii had seemed to accept this but now changed his mind. Nor were these the only persons concerned.

For a man who supposedly had been up all night trudging through swamps and streams in great discomfort, Reilly was amazingly energetic. In the company of his new "friends," he strolled around town, taking in the familiar sites and dining at two of the better restaurants that had recently reopened. He stopped into church for vespers, not something he usually took much interest in. If old Petersburg was not quite what it once was, it definitely was an improvement over the dismal days of 1918–20. The cars of new millionaires, the so-called "Nepmen," rolled up and down the Nevskii Prospect and the gray city had regained a measure of its energy and cosmopolitan color. It was not New York or Paris but was it a place the Ace-of-Spies could again call home?

One landmark Sidney strolled past was the old British Embassy. Interestingly, at the same time Reilly landed in Helsinki another British agent arrived in Leningrad from Moscow. He was Oswald Rayner, an officer with long experience in Russia including wartime work for MI1c, including a stint under Reilly's ST boss, Scale. More recently we encountered him poking into White Russian intrigues in London and Switzerland. Rayner had returned to Russia as a member of the British Mission under Sir Robert Hodgson but retained connection to SIS. His apparent task in Leningrad was to look over the old Embassy archive that had been handed over by the Soviets.[1] The arrangements for this assignment commenced back in July, the same time Reilly finalized his travel plans. There is every chance that Rayner's presence in the city was just a coincidence, but the timely presence of a man with SIS links must raise a question. His unofficial task could have been to monitor Reilly's arrival and activity. If so, that means someone in London was interested—and knowledgeable.

That evening, Styrne departed for Moscow to make arrangements for the following day. Or so he claimed. Opperput insists Styrne arrived in Moscow the next morning on the same train as he and Sidney.[2] Did Styrne fake the earlier boarding so he could keep a surreptitious eye on the others? If so, who was it he did not trust? In any event, later that night, Reilly, Yakushev and another Trust operative, one Mukalov-Mikhailov (supposedly a "true" monarchist), caught the Moscow sleeper. The Englishman and his companions took berths in the "international car" earmarked for foreign travelers.[3] It was just the way he left Moscow back in 1918.

Our traveler still seemed surprisingly energetic, sitting up to chat with his companions. In Vyborg, he had first brought up the all-important subject of money. He knew that the Moscow organization expected him to provide lots of it. That, he proclaimed, was "impossible" for the time being.[4] No one was going to help the Trust until they helped themselves. He insisted the organization get its hands on artworks and similar valuables. These, he assured, could be smuggled abroad to fetch huge prices on the black market.[5] He noted the Bolsheviks had fenced jewels and art in the West for years; it only made sense for the opposition to compete. He also suggested a ready means of getting money through collaboration with "English counterintelligence." The British would pay for information, he assured, if it was the right stuff. He asserted that he had worked for the British for years and had achieved "impressive results." However, his "official" connection had ended in 1922 over questions about methods and certain operations that "ended badly."[6] Was that a reference to Savinkov's abortive assassination effort? Nevertheless, through his "long and close" relationship with Churchill and other personages he continued to supply information to London on an informal basis.[7] For instance, he had supplied reports on the intelligence and counterintelligence services of various countries, including the U.S. and Germany, with details of personnel, structure and operations. Now he was after "special" information that might restore him to official favor. Most of all, he wanted material on the Comintern, that "annoying pest" of Western governments.[8] He wanted Trust agents to infiltrate and gain control of the Comintern and use it against the Kremlin clique. When Styrne challenged that this would be hard to do, Reilly retorted that there were British agents already in the Communist Party, even among its most "rock hard" adherents.[9]

He also offered opinions on everything from politics to religion. He insisted that a post-Bolshevik Russian regime would have to be a dictatorship to preserve order, but later the people might be able to choose another. He thought most social elements were disaffected from the Bolshevik regime, especially the peasants and the Red Army, an institution in which he had a number of friends and placed much confidence.[10] The Orthodox Church would be restored but kept under firm political control. Religion brought up the Jewish Question on which Sidney made familiar-sounding comments. As before, he expected the fall of the Red regime would unleash a wave of pogroms, an inescapable expression of "popular feeling." A new government had to avoid any overt connection to these pogroms or risk losing critical financial assistance from the West. The simple fact, he declared, was that British and French capital was "completely in the hands of Jews" and in America they controlled "a third, if not more."[11] A liberal Jewish policy was an absolute necessity. In foreign affairs, he warned of a rapprochement between London and Berlin that would be used to bring pressure on France. Once the French came on board, there would be a common anti-Soviet front that would spell the end of Bolshevik power. Britain was the dominant force in Europe and it was absolutely necessary for the new Russia to be on good terms with it.

Sidney even offered his views on certain prominent Bolsheviks.[12] As the most "disgusting" example, he chose Nikolai V. Krylenko, a one-time German spy become state prosecutor, whom he branded a "degenerate and sadist." Zinoviev he dismissed as a mediocrity who had run the Comintern into the ground and whose political career was finished. Dzerzhinskii was a "very cunning" fellow although Sidney branded the OGPU itself an illegitimate and "horrid" institution.[13] He offered kind words for his old collaborator Gen. Bonch-Bruevich who, he suggested, had taught Trotsky everything he knew about military affairs. He also expressed an interest in the whereabouts of Col. Berzin, his coconspirator in the Lockhart Plot. Yakushev carefully noted everything his companion said and delivered it to Styrne the next day. In his subsequent talks with the Ace-of-Spies, Styrne was impressed by the breadth and depth of his knowledge of Russia and the Soviet regime. He knew official Party policies on all issues and familiar with the membership of its Central Committee, Politburo and other key institutions. He had read, it seemed, every issue of *Izvestiia* and could converse on almost any issue.[14]

On the morning of the 27th, Sidney and his party were met by Styrne and two more Trust agents. These were F.S. Shatkovskii and Dmitrii Kokushin, also known as Dorozhinskii. The latter was Styrne's brother-in-law and owner of a *dacha* (country house) where the main meeting was to be held. A former Gendarme officer, it is possible Reilly knew him from past encounters. These two escorted Sidney into an auto and drove him to the *dacha* in Malakhovka, a small town of summer residences about twenty miles southwest of the Kremlin. This was a change in plans. Reilly was supposed to have gone with Opperput, who had arrived on the scene, Yakushev and Gen. Nikolai Mikhailovich Potapov, a former Tsarist intelligence officer who acted as the Trust's titular military chief. Styrne ordered the trio to go to Opperput's nearby apartment on Maroseika Street and wait while he checked in with his bosses at the nearby Lubianka. After Styrne was gone for more than an hour, Opperput wondered out loud if there had been a more serious change in plans. There must be, he argued, some disagreement in the OGPU about Reilly. Yakushev seemed assured there was nothing to worry about.

Styrne finally showed up in a car and they set out for Malakhovka. On the way, Yakushev brought up Opperput's suspicions, but Styrne "firmly and categorically denied them." [15] Halfway there, they ran into Shatkovskii coming back. In front of the others, Styrne gave him money to buy return tickets to Leningrad for himself and Reilly. Opperput was momentarily reassured, but his doubts returned as soon as they reached the *dacha*. The place was swarming with "some of the best of the [OGPU] agents" disguised, none too convincingly, as summer residents out for a stroll. Opperput again voiced his misgivings and Styrne explained that the additional agents were on hand to cover escape in case of "trouble with the militia," i.e., the regular police. That did not convince Opperput, but at the same time it made no sense to have a legion of agents on hand to capture one man who had been in their grasp for more than twenty-four hours. Were the extra operatives really there to guard against Trilesser's INO and to seal off the proceedings from all unwelcome eyes?

Inside the house, Sidney dined with the executive committee of the Trust, the supposed shadow government of Russia. After a sumptuous meal, everyone adjourned outside and seated in a circle beneath the trees to hear the honored guest's address. With cigarette in hand, Reilly repeated almost word for word what he had already shared with Yakushev and Styrne. It was as if he was reciting a script, and perhaps it was. Was the man addressing the congregation the real Sidney Reilly or an actor reciting his lines? Opperput recollected that at one point Styrne asked him if he recognized Reilly, a question he found a bit odd. Opperput knew what the Ace-of-Spies looked like; was Styrne seeking assurance that the impostor could pass muster?

The speaker, whoever he was, reiterated that no European government could spare money to invest in the Trust, least of all Britain, which faced serious unrest in its laboring population and in its farflung dominions. On the other hand, because Bolshevik subversion was to blame for much of this unrest, London had a powerful interest in seeing the end of the current Kremlin administration. Churchill and he shared the conviction of the inevitable collapse of the Red monstrosity. They were willing to assist such efforts as they could, but the main energy and resources had to come from within Russia. Sidney pushed his idea of selling artworks as the best way to raise cash and again proposed active collaboration with British intelligence. Those who found this unpalatable, he added, were letting "useless sentimentality" stand in the way of saving Russia.[16]

This was not what the assembled expected or wanted to hear. Most of them were genuine opponents of the Bolos and considered themselves Russian patriots above all else. Acting as thieves, smugglers and spies did not sit well with that image. Far from galvanizing and energizing the Trust leadership, Reilly's speech provoked disappointment and consternation, even anger. Was that what it was designed to do? Had Reilly come to help the Trust or destroy it?

All afternoon, Opperput watched Styrne become more and more nervous. The meeting broke up as evening fell, but the car that was supposed to take the visitor back to the October Station was late. Styrne seemed to be waiting for it to grow dark. Wandering into the garden, Opperput noticed that the OGPU men who had been posted to the periphery of the grounds had closed in and the *dacha* was completely surrounded. He rushed back to the house to confront Styrne. The latter pulled him aside and admitted that his earlier guess was right—Reilly was to be arrested, though for some reason not at the *dacha*. Yakushev soon got into the act, and he and Opperput did their best to dissuade Styrne; everything they had worked for would be ruined. Yakushev went so far as threatening to shoot himself on the spot. In his defense, Styrne declared that "I was against the arrest and so was Pilyar, and we argued for two hours." Their effort was in vain, however, "as instructions in this matter have already been issued by the [Politburo], and no one has the power to change them." Stalin had stuck his nose in, he added, and was demanding updates "every half hour."[17]

Two cars soon pulled up, one Dzerzhinskii's personal machine. At the wheel was S.V. Puzitskii, another deputy-chief of the KRO. With him was another agent, a young athlete known as the "Procurer" who had a reputation for physical strength and strong-arm methods. If that was not enough, also along for the ride was one Ibragim, reputedly the "best shot in the [OGPU]."[18] Why such muscle was needed to apprehend a single, slight, fiftyish subject is nowhere explained. According to Opperput, he made one more appeal to Styrne and got him to agree to go to the Lubianka and try to get the order rescinded. In the meantime, Opperput offered to keep Reilly at his apartment. Styrne agreed, but ordered Puzitskii and the Procurer to stay with them.

Styrne, to no surprise, gave a different account of this episode, mentioning nothing of Opperput's suspicions and entreaties, but noting that Reilly headed back to Moscow with Puzitskii and two other OGPU men while Yakushev and Potapov followed in the second car. The original idea was to take him straight to the Lubianka, but on the way Sidney suddenly expressed the desire to post a letter in Moscow as later evidence of his trip. This struck the Chekists as a wonderful idea and they postponed his arrest. However, rather than simply driving him to the post office, they took him to Opperput's apartment. Styrne then left for the Lubianka to meet Pilyar and, most importantly, Yagoda to "coordinate" the next step. In the meantime, back at Opperput's, Reilly relaxed and wrote out a postcard to Pepita. When Styrne returned, he took Puzitskii aside and instructed him to get Sidney back into the car as if taking him to the station. Once underway, he was to arrest the Englishman and take him directly to Pilyar's office in the Lubianka. Again, there is no explanation as to why, in a room full of Chekists, he was not grabbed on the spot. Were they afraid that Opperput and Yakushev would make a scene, and why would that have mattered?

Overall, Opperput's account makes more sense if still incomplete. He makes no mention of any letter. Instead, the party arrived at his place to find Shatkovskii waiting, somewhat perturbed, with the train tickets. He handed one to Reilly and left. Some fifteen minutes later, the phone rang; it was Pilyar from the Lubianka who ordered Puzitskii to "carry out his instructions." Again, instead of arresting Sidney on the spot, they piled everyone, including Opperput, into the car. Finally, as they turned onto Zlatoustinskii Lane, Puzitskii turned to Reilly and whispered "not a word; you are arrested." One of the assistants handcuffed him and the car sped to the gates of the Lubianka that were "under a specially strong guard." Reilly was hustled inside and Opperput driven back to his place. Had he been brought along as a witness for the express purpose of later attesting these events?

An hour or so later, Opperput was rejoined at his flat by Styrne, Pilyar, Artuzov, plus Yakushev, Potapov and other Trust bigwigs. The latter group insisted that Reilly's apprehension would ruin their organization. Artuzov and his deputies countered that they had taken unspecified measures to protect it. As they spoke, he explained, Puzitskii and a team of agents were on their way to Leningrad. They would proceed to the frontier to act out a repeat of the midnight crossing. This time, however, they would be intercepted by a Soviet border patrol. In the ensuing gun battle Reilly or, rather, *a man made to look like Reilly*, would be killed. His death would be a tragic accident and the Trust's reputation would remain intact.

Opperput later made it a point to learn all he could about this gambit that, he discovered, did not go quite according to plan. On the night of 28 September, four men set out through the woods and mists for the Sestro River. The leader was Viakhia, the border guard who had met Sidney a few nights before. His three companions were Shchukin, another OGPU-Trust operative, Bakonin, and a third, unnamed "member of the Leningrad KRO" who was "made up to represent Reilly."[19] Waiting for them on the other side were Karpinen, Georgii Radkevich and the Finn Ruzenstrem. As Viakhia and the others approached the crossing point, they ran into, as planned, a group of guards led by Puzitskii. The latter opened fire, shooting over the heads of their comrades, or at least they were supposed to. For some reason, Shchukin panicked and fired back, narrowly missing one of Puzitskii's men, and the whole thing halted at once. Did he fear that he and the others might be liquidated for real? Shchukin, Bakonin, and their nameless comrade were daubed with red paint and carried back to Leningrad "as dead men." Shchukin's and Bakonin's "corpses" later arrived at a Moscow mortuary. What became of the third body, *"Reilly's" body*, no one mentions. Other versions held that Viakhia was killed also, while still others said "Reilly" had been wounded and captured. Opperput finally determined that Viakhia, Shchukin and Bakonin were very much alive under new names. That leaves the interesting question of whose bodies went to the Moscow morgue. The mysterious Leningrad KRO man, the "fake Reilly," simply vanished.

The above incident was supposed to have been reported in the Soviet press, including *Izvestiia*, but no copy of the notice can be found.[20] The Finns, for their part, took little notice; gunfire on the Russian border was not that unusual. Nevertheless, it seems safe to assume that the episode occurred more or less as described. It also shows that there were, at one point, two Reillys, one real, one phony. But when did this doubling occur? Was the phony introduced as early as the initial crossing as Grant suggests? Was the man who ostentatiously bid goodbye in English the same one "killed" going back? Did this actor also perform Reilly's speech at the *dacha*? It is possible that a switch was made when Styrne first sent Reilly ahead to Malakhovka; on the way, the genuine Sidney was diverted elsewhere and the double took his place.

Dzerzhinskii, recall, initially ordered the simple entrapment and liquidation of an enemy of the regime. Stalin, apparently, was of like mind. Trilesser wanted to get his hands on Sidney to interrogate him. Yagoda, however, was after something else, the acquisition of Reilly—and his money—for his organization. Yagoda's fundamental problem was how to get Reilly back to Russia without losing control of him in the process. Substituting a ringer was one way to do that. Of course, having served his purpose, the double would have to be eliminated lest his impersonation be discovered. The best bet is that the fake Sidney was killed at the border and his body kept on ice for one last performance.

Meanwhile, the genuine article, presumably, was in the Lubianka, seated in Pilyar's office. There, on the evening of the 27th, he underwent an initial questioning by Yagoda and his deputies Styrne and Stanislav Adamovich Messing. Trilesser was on hand, doubtless to bear witness that the dangerous enemy of the people was safely in OGPU hands. Reilly's acting job was just beginning. If his capture had been made drawn out and complicated, his final surrender and interrogation would prove likewise. He admitted his identity and that he had entered Soviet territory for the purpose of conferring with a counter-revolutionary organization, but refused to say more. All the while, he exhibited an imperturbable self-control.[21] After a hour of fruitless questions, mostly from Trilesser, the prisoner went to the overnight cell of the Lubianka's Inner Prison.

In Hamburg Pepita grew anxious, or so she later claimed. The last message she had from Sidney said he would be back in Finland by the 28th. However, as of the 30th he had not arrived at the hotel in Vyborg. She fired off an urgent wire to Boyce who, on 1 October, replied that he had "heard from no one regarding Sidney's condition."[22] He declared himself "rather surprised" that Reilly had "undergone the operation after all," i.e. gone into Russia. This would be his standard refrain, officially at least: he was completely unaware of Reilly's decision to cross the border and had advised him against any such move. He was certainly lying, but why?

Pepita's motives and whereabouts are not without question. She insisted that she remained in Hamburg obedient to her husband's wishes until about 7 October when she headed back to Paris. Bunakov, however, later reported that she had followed Reilly to Finland and was there at the time he crossed over. He also voiced doubts about the exact nature of her relationship with the Radkeviches who he was certain were Red agents of one kind or another.[23] Could Pepita have been Orlov's "Sorceress," and did she play some part in "luring" her husband into Russia? Her actions likely have another explanation, but she certainly knew more about his disappearance than she later admitted. What she was not certain of and needed to know was whether he was dead or alive.

The same day Boyce mailed the above letter, he sent Pepita a wire saying he had just received Sidney's card from Moscow, presumably the one written at Opperput's. Boyce took this as a sign that there was "nothing to worry about yet."[24] A few days later, he wrote to say that he had nothing new but urged her to sit tight and not make any further inquiries to the "doctors" (Trust representatives) in Finland as it "only harasses them." To further mollify her, he offered to forward a letter Reilly had written before his departure to be delivered in the event anything "went wrong." On the 11th, however, a fresh letter from Boyce sounded a more ominous note. Everything had gone fine, he wrote, until an "unfortunate coincidence" in which her husband and comrades "fell across an influence which was work-ing on different lines" and that "entering into the case, completely upset all the plans and left the parties concerned in a most parlous condition."[25] This seems to coincide with Opperput's story. Could the "opposing influences" that caused so much trouble have been Trilesser who brought the KRO's operation to the attention of Stalin, thus provoking the change in plans? Soon after Reilly's arrest, on 1 October, Trilesser sent an urgent message to the Soviet mission in Vienna demanding more information on the links between Reilly and Yaroslavskii. He was most interested in the story that Yaroslavskii had asked Sidney to retrieve certain "valuables" hidden there and noted that he actually had some of these on him when he was arrested.[26] If so, that raises more questions. Why would Reilly, who sup-posedly was never out of the company of OGPU agents, have picked up these valuables going into Russia as opposed to the way out? Was that because he was supposed to hand them over to the Trust—or Yagoda? Absolutely no mention of these valuables appears in any KRO reports and Sidney, of course, told the Trust he had no money for them at all.

Meanwhile, Boyce was telling a rather different tale to SIS. On 13 October, he reported that Reilly, working through Bunakov, had made contact with the "Monarchist Centre" in Moscow and "against my advice unexpectedly went illegally into Russia under an assumed name." [27] On the way back, he continued, Reilly's party was ambushed near the border and "all reported killed." However, his true identity was not discovered by the Reds who mistook the dead men for Finnish agents. "It is in everyone's interest, excepting [his] wife," he added, "to hush up matter." Soon after sending the message, Boyce headed for London to report in person. Clearly there were people in London interested in Reilly's actions and fate. Officially, however, not a word was spoken nor a question asked. Later rumors tied Reilly's disappearance to efforts to stymie Parliamentary investigation of the Zinoviev Letter. Another maintained that he was "eliminated" to forestall a broader inquiry into past British operations in Russia, including a supposed plan to gain control of the Baku oil fields.[28] Whether or not Sidney held the secrets to these matters, he undoubtedly held others and his reported death must have come as welcome reassurance in some quarters. At the same time, others within SIS and elsewhere suspected, or feared, that his reported demise was simply a disguised defection.

From Stockholm on the 19th, Boyce informed Pepita that "situation was worse than I had hoped." He repeated the border-shooting tale he had just sent London with one critical difference.[29] In this version, Reilly's party was waylaid by "brigands" who left two dead, Reilly "seriously wounded" and the fourth captured. Boyce suggested the incident was pure bad luck but had no further details about her husband's present location or condition. He wrote her again on the 23rd to say that urgent business was calling him abroad and that he would have "no permanent address for some time." [30] However, in a parting gesture of quasi-helpfulness, he noted that Bunakov would soon be in Paris bearing Sidney's last letter. Bunakov did show up with the letter, but it did nothing to solve the puzzle. In it, Sidney merely noted that he was going to Leningrad and Moscow for three days. In the very remote chance that something might go wrong, he again instructed "you must not take any steps." [31] So long as the Bolos did not know who he really was, he emphasized, he would be safe, so "keep your head."

Perhaps tipped off by some helpful party, in late October Pepita arrived in London where she found Boyce still very much at ease. Her appearance "obviously disconcerted" him, but he offered an excuse for his deception: he was acting on the strict orders of SIS to avoid having "the Service" drawn into the affair.[32] That may have been true. Beyond that, he insisted, he could add nothing. Reilly had been badly hurt and his present condition was unknown. There was nothing to do but follow Sidney's advice and wait.

The uncertainty left Pepita agitated and dissatisfied, but not really out of loving concern for her missing hubby. At least as far back as her marriage to Chambers, she had been a dedicated gold-digger, and the same thing was behind her whirlwind courtship of Reilly. She was smart enough to smell his money, real and potential. Despite his obfuscation, her proximity over the past few years must have allowed her to gather some notion of his holdings. Sometime in 1924, she later wrote, Sidney had made "elaborate arrangements for my future in the event of his meeting with some mysterious accident."[33] But that was not all; so far as she knew he had no other wives or other dependents, so everything he had would go to her. Perhaps he even showed her a will to that effect. What she now was after so desperately was his money. However, to get her hands on it she also needed him *dead*. Is that why she had been willing to assist the Radkeviches?

With Moscow stubbornly silent on Reilly's fate, Pepita hoped for some British statement on his death to make her a widow. She visited Harold Williams of *The Times* and begged him to publish the story "in some form that might reflect upon the British" and force persons in authority to divulge what they knew. Williams was reluctant to involve himself that far, but he did agree to publish a death notice if and when she asked him to.[34] On 27 October, she looked up Norman Thwaites. As he reported it to SIS two days later, she declared Sidney had been "killed by Bolshevist agents in Russia as he was attempting to cross the Finnish border."[35] She admitted to having been in Helsinki waiting for his return when this occurred. He had gone to Moscow, she insisted, on "some secret mission" for British intelligence. She further claimed he was persuaded to do so by a British agent (Boyce?) "to engage in getting certain information and establishing a service between London and Moscow." What she wanted was more information on the precise nature of that mission (just what Trilesser wanted) and a "statement from authorities here clearing him of the suspicion obtaining in certain quarters that Reilly had gone over to the Bolsheviks just as did his friend Savinkov." If she could get an admission that Reilly had been working on Britain's behalf, it would be worth a pension at least. Thwaites insisted he could do little but did admit her husband's past service and that he "did very well" in that role. Thwaites concluded that Mrs. Reilly "has not got the whole truth or is misleading me." He suggested to SIS that it seemed a good idea for someone to get to the bottom of the matter, whether or not they informed Pepita. It might be possible, he thought, to get something through "German channels," probably a reference to Orlov.

In reply to Thwaites, SIS branded Pepita's story as "absolutely and categorically untrue from start to finish," and added that Reilly had "no connection whatsoever with us" for some years.[36] Berlin, however, hosted too many forgers and other dubious types there to trust anything from there. Sinclair made the official stance even clearer in a subsequent message to Boyce: "This matter has nothing to do with us and we are not to have anything to do with *it*."[37]

Undaunted, Pepita headed back to Finland where she hoped to dig up information with the aid of the Radkevich duo, or was it to report to them? Perhaps at Thwaites' suggestion, she wrote Orlov in Berlin asking him to make inquiries into the fate of "H. Sternberg" (actually, N. Steinberg). Bunakov also reported to Boyce that Mrs. Reilly boasted of having left a "complete history of affairs" with her solicitor and a note with *The Times* to be published in the event she did not return in a specified time.[38] Boyce dutifully relayed that bit of information to London. Openly mistrustful of Bunakov, Pepita connived with the Radkeviches to publish an announcement of Reilly's death. That, she hoped, would force a statement out of the Soviets or the British. She intended to make "definite accusations" against SIS and Boyce specifically and would "quote the Paris meeting in support," an apparent reference to Reilly's conference after his arrival in September. Boyce's impression was that the Radkevich pair were "planning the whole thing" with the obvious intent of incriminating SIS.[39] The Commander, of course, had his own interests to protect.

In November, Pepita approached one of Sidney's Diehard allies, Oliver Locker-Lampson, and asked him to raise a question in Parliament about her husband's fate. He finally agreed to query how many Britons were being held in Soviet custody and how many on "political" charges.[40] The official response was "none." Finally, she again asked William's help. On 15 December, *The Times* ran this among the front page death notices: "REILLY.—On the 28th Sept., killed near the village of Allekul, Russia, by G.P.U. troops, Captain Sidney George Reilly, M.C., late R.A.F., beloved husband of Pepita N. Reilly." The *Times* offered no further comment, but over the next few days other papers picked up the story in Britain, France and the U.S. with most adding some color and details. The London *Daily Express* gave the story a full column and asserted that "a thrilling story of drama and romance" lay behind the announcement of Capt. Reilly's "mysterious death."[41] The writer acknowledged the deceased as a "British secret service agent" who had won great renown for his actions in Russia after the Revolution, an assignment in which he posed as "Comrade R," a "fanatical adherent" of the Bolsheviks. This and a similar, shorter piece in the *New York Times*, identified Reilly as the son of an Irish seafaring father and Russian mother.[42] Interestingly, the London *Daily News* proclaimed that the story of the Captain's demise "is at present the subject of an official investigation."[43] The *Express* followed up by sending reporters to the Foreign Office and the Air Ministry for statements. The FO responded that Reilly was known to them, but they could not make any official statement without more information. Nor would they confirm or deny that he was involved in FO work at the time of his death.[44] The Air Ministry would say only that he was in no way connected to their department.

Probably the strangest response to Reilly's passing came from the London *Sunday News*.[45] If nothing else, it shows the almost immediate appearance of the Reilly Legend. In addition to declaring him the man behind the Zinoviev Letter, the article transformed him into a "typical Irish adventurer" nicknamed "Red Reilly," an all-around "general good fellow." Early in the war, his swashbuckling nature found the poor bloody infantry too tame, and he went into the RAF. He was more than once dropped behind enemy lines to perform feats of derring-do, including bringing back the secrets of the 1918 German offensives. According to this, he did not set foot in Russia until after the Armistice, but in short order managed to make himself an "important figure" in the Soviet Government, and performed all manner of useful work for King and country. Did they think up these bogus details on their own, or were they supplied by someone else? If so, to what purpose?

On the 17th, SIS in New York informed London that Mrs. Reilly had cabled the superintendent of the Cunard Building with news of her husband's demise.[46] She also contacted Upton Thomas to order he take charge and clear up the offices. She was clearly staking claim to Reilly's assets, if only she could pin them down. Thomas eventually shut down the office, but transferred nothing to her name. He kept Trading Ventures running, on paper at least, until 1930 though it never appeared to transact any business. Wherever she turned, East or West, all that issued was a deafening silence.

Back in the Lubianka, our man was trying to work the biggest con of his career. From his standpoint it also was useful that Sidney Reilly be thought dead. As he had done before, he would assume a new identity and continue collaboration with Yagoda free of all the baggage that burdened the Reilly identity. It was a simple as a serpent shedding its skin. The initial idea may have been that Yagoda, one way or another, would convince Dzerzhinskii to accept Reilly's collaboration, much as he had turned around on the Savinkov issue. The interference by Trilesser and Stalin complicated matters, but not beyond repair. Sidney's immediate job was to keep himself alive.

According to Opperput, the OGPU at first dealt "very gently" with their captive. They put him up in the same rooms formerly occupied by

Savinkov and, just like Boris, provided him amenities such as whisky and chaperoned outings to the countryside. On 7 October, some ten days after his capture, the Ace-of-Spies made his first significant statement in the form of a brief autobiography. Just like SIS, the OGPU had very little information of its own to go on. For instance, was their prisoner a genuine Britisher or a Russian? Sidney festooned his statement with the usual lies. "Captain Reilly" again proclaimed himself a native of Clonmel, Ireland and the son of a Navy captain.[47] He further declared himself a graduate of Heidelberg University and the Royal School of Mines, but added a dose of truth by noting specialization in chemistry. Politically, he affirmed himself a staunch Conservative. He freely admitted that he had been sentenced to death in absentia by a Soviet court. The report, however, focused on his activities since 1917. He gave a spare, but reasonably accurate, rendition of his role in the 1918 plots, but mentioned only Lockhart and Berzin. He described his escape from Red territory in some detail, perhaps to answer Dzerzhinskii's lingering questions about just how he managed to slip through the Cheka's fingers. He mentioned his 1919 mission in the South and close work with Savinkov. Also noted were his connections to émigré groups and foreign business and political figures. He admitted having "discussions" with Krasin on economic projects, but dismissed them as unfruitful. Personal and financial problems, he explained, had led him to sever ties with British intelligence and concentrate on his own affairs. The Trust came along to reawaken his interest in Russia.

Two days later, he gave a second deposition adding details about his prewar career in Russia. Interestingly, he dated that starting only in 1909. He mentioned his friendship with Guchkov and Guchkov's clandestine dealings with Savinkov.[48] Regarding his present situation, Sidney insisted he had come to Russia on his own initiative and "had no connection whatsoever to the secret service." He came as a journalist to "get acquainted with conditions in Russia." His intention, he insisted, was to write articles under the title of "The Great Bluff" in which he would show "the true face of the Soviet Government."[49]

In terms of hard information, Reilly gave his captors a few tantalizing bites but no meal. Dzerzhinskii and others wanted much more: names and dates and every other detail he could supply on his political and business connections. About 12 October, Styrne brought an ultimatum from his superiors, probably from Feliks himself. Given the 1918 verdict, he could be shot at without further ado. He was, in fact, already "dead" courtesy of the incident on the border, but no formal announcement had been made. Sidney was as yet neither alive nor dead, and which he remained depended on his level of cooperation. He had value as a collaborator of the Soviet State, value that could buy him a return ticket to the land of the living. He might even be allowed to leave Russia on the following conditions. First, he would have to provide the OGPU with precise and accurate details about his past activities and everyone he knew, especially persons in high positions in England and America. This included any useful "dirt" he had on them. Next, once free he would continue to supply information on an regular basis. He would desist from advocating or abetting any anti-Soviet activity and would instantly inform on any plans he came across. Finally, he would never say a word about what happened in Moscow and would do nothing to compromise the Trust. Rather, he would assist it in every way possible.[50]

That was very much the response he wanted, but, again, he could not look too eager. So, on the 13th, he laid out a counter-proposal to Styrne. He protested "with all the sincerity of which I am capable," that he could not agree to the terms presented. He realized that his freedom and life hung in the balance, but he could not see it differently. He had no problem with protecting of the Trust and assisting its efforts abroad. He was willing, even anxious, to do that. No, the objection was to handing over his personal trove of secrets and connections. With him on their side, the masters of the Lubianka did not need that information themselves, nor would they know what to do with it. Clumsy effort at infiltration or blackmail would only destroy his credibility with the very people they needed to him to cultivate. He hastened to add that an accommodation between himself and 'Soviet organs" was possible. In exchange for his freedom, he offered his "profound and sincere assurance" that he would render every assistance to Soviet agents abroad. In Britain and America he would use his special channels to "persuade the appropriate spheres" of the solidity of the Moscow regime and the benefits from closer Soviet ties. He offered to use his influence among the émigrés to discourage them from hostile words and actions. Even further, he declared it unthinkable that he would engage in anti-Soviet intrigues for the simple reason that they would not reap him any material reward. This arrangement likely was a description of the deal earlier made between him and Yagoda.

On 17 October, Sidney addressed a second, much longer letter to Styrne. It was obvious that higher-ups had not given his counter-proposal a positive reception. Their demand remained that Reilly would have to give a full and accurate accounting of his associates and activities. Obviously, he had not convinced them of his sincerity. Thus, he tried again to make his feelings and position absolutely clear. Soviet authorities, he noted, had not expended so much effort on his capture just to shoot him. If so, he would be dead already. They wanted to use him, and he was willing to be used. But he could not render the "complete, accurate and detailed information" they wanted without compromising himself and others. He felt Dzerzhinskii should understand his refusal; after all, would he expect any less of his own agents in a like situation? Was this not evidence that the OGPU could put their confidence in him as well?

The basis for agreement was the manifest desire of the Soviets to employ him as a secret collaborator and agent of influence abroad. He was prepared to execute that role "loyally and completely" if the OGPU promised to refrain from punitive or provocative measures against persons he knew or with whom he came in contact. The foreign policy of the Soviet Union, overt and covert, he argued, had achieved little success. Moscow had gained recognition in London, Paris and Rome but it had not been able to secure loans, credits or technology to revitalize the Russian economy. Relations with the economically most powerful of the Western Powers, America, remained in limbo. On the other hand, Sidney attested that there was great interest in Russia in London and New York and the general belief that normalized relations were "necessary and inevitable." He offered himself as an "unofficial middleman" in setting up deals between the Soviet Government and interested parties in Britain, America and elsewhere. Reilly compared his situation to an officer captured in war. In return for his release, he gave his word of honor that he would not again take up arms against his captors. That was the best guarantee he could offer, he claimed, of loyal adherence. He did not regard the abandonment of political struggle as a great price to pay for liberty. He was glad to exit himself from a realm that had brought him nothing but disappointments and difficulty for several years. However, he did not portray himself as a newborn Bolshevik. He proclaimed unwavering conviction that Communism was doomed to fail in the long run. For the foreseeable future, however, it held sway in Moscow, and he recognized forceful efforts to unseat it as unworkable and counterproductive. Sidney made the frank admission that in opening up Russia to the West, he simply would be combating Bolshevism in a different way. Western ideas and methods must, he was certain, eventually undermine and replace Lenin's experiment. It was a bold and sensible proposal, Reilly playing his best "ingenious diplomat." But would Iron Feliks go for it? And how serious was Sidney? After all, he had built his whole career by betraying secrets.

His new proposal must have caused debate within the OGPU and, perhaps, beyond. In the end, however, the answer was still no: the prisoner must confess all. According to Opperput, the Lubianka regime tightened and threats increased. Guards kept a constant watch on the captive and he was treated to graphic descriptions of the "whole arsenal of means and methods with which the [OGPU] broke anybody's will." [51] Styrne later boasted that Reilly was broken by being forced to watch a grisly execution in the Lubianka cellar. It was the sort of thing "civilized Europeans cannot stomach," Styrne claimed, "this spectacle kills every illusion of an honorable death and . . . produces an uncontrollable desire to escape [such a fate] at any price." [52]

There are two documents that suggest a different picture. The first is a short letter from Sidney to Dzerzhinskii dated 30 October 1925. Reilly agrees to tell all he knows concerning British and U.S. intelligence and the Russian emigration. [53] The handwriting gives every indication of being his. The other is a diary kept by Reilly in the last days of his imprisonment, also commencing on 30 October. [54] It purports to be a secret account, recorded on three small pieces of paper in a cramped but very recognizable hand. Later discovered in his cell, or so claimed the OGPU, they appended it to his file. It is in English, though with occasional words or names in Russian script. There seems no serious reason to doubt that Reilly wrote both; the question is why. The Diary poses the biggest problem. Sidney certainly knew it would be found and produced later as evidence of his presence and a record of what he said and *did not* say.

Something definitely happened on the 30th. Reilly began the diary noting an "additional interrogation" late that afternoon. Guards forced him to change into "work clothes" and removed his possessions. Later rousted from sleep, they led him to "a room downstairs near [the] bath." He noted having had an odd premonition about the place. Inside, however, was no bloody scene but Styrne, "his colleague" (probably Yagoda) and a handful of other Lubianka functionaries including the "executioner," Karl Yanovich Dukis, another Latvian and the chief warder. [55] Styrne's colleague, the only one seated, was in charge. He announced that the OGPU *kollegiia* had "reconsidered" his 1918 sentence, and that unless he agreed to tell all he knew, his execution would be carried out immediately. The prisoner expressed no surprise but again refused and pronounced "I am willing to die." Styrne offered him an hour to reflect and he returned to his cell. As he recorded it, he made a small parcel of his things, smoked a couple of cigarettes and "prayed inwardly" for Pepita.

After a long hour, he came back in the basement room where now there were only Styrne and a single young assistant. From the adjoining room, he could see the executioner and a deputy all "heavily armed." Questioned by Styrne, Reilly again voiced his refusal and demanded to make a written statement. He noted "I am glad that I can show them how an English Christian understands his duty." The request was denied. He asked to have his belongings sent to Pepita; also refused. Styrne taunted that his "death will never be known," but tried another "long, rambling persuasion—same as usual." In the course of this, "M's case was mentioned." There is no other indication who this might have been, but it may have been a reference to Moura Benckendorf/Budberg, Lockhart's old (and continuing) paramour who was pursuing a highly successful career as a Soviet agent of influence. Did this mean she had originally turned informer to save her own skin? Reilly retorted that Styrne and his friends were fools; killing him would be "blasting the water supply" (i.e., "killing the goose that laid golden eggs"). After about forty-five minutes, an exasperated Styrne called in Dukis and his men. They handcuffed Reilly and left him in the room while "the distinct loading of arms" came from beyond the door. A few minutes later, they took him out to a waiting car. After a short drive to a garage where the driver tinkered with the engine in the freezing drizzle, the party drove out of the Lubianka. Reilly assumed he would be taken someplace out of town and shot. Instead, after a short drive, the car returned to the Lubianka through a different entrance, i.e., the eyes that saw them leave did not see them return. Waiting there was Styrne who informed him that his execution was postponed for at least another day. Sidney returned to his cell where he wrote down "Terrible night, Nightmares." Nowhere is there any mention of a letter to Dzerzhinskii. Interestingly, in his diary Sidney described events very similar to those allegedly befalling a few days hence.

Then again, perhaps Reilly did write Dzerzhinskii. Certainly he recounts a much friendlier scene the next day. That morning about 11 a solicitous Styrne arrived and introduced Dr. Sergei Ivanovich Kushner, a physician. He examined Reilly for much of the day in Room 176, a special accommodation of some sort. His report "much impressed" Styrne and ordered "increased attention" to the prisoner. The implication is that Reilly's health was somehow precarious, though from what is never elaborated. Kushner provided him with Veronal, a powerful sedative, to aid with sleep. That evening, Reilly went for another drive and a pleasant walk in the country. The most interesting detail, though, is that he did so "dressed in GPU [OGPU] uniform." He was being passed off as a Chekist—but why? Was his presence being concealed and, if so, from whom? Surely this was not standard dress for condemned prisoners. Back in town, he went to a "nice apartment" (Opperput's?) where he met Styrne and Ibragim and all partook of tea and a good meal. Later alone with Styrne, the subject turned to "that protocole [sic, *protokol*, 'interrogation minutes'] expressing my agreement." Styrne left to deliver the *protokol* to Dzerzhinskii. So Sidney does seem to have capitulated, but a day after his supposed letter. Returning a half-hour later, Styrne informed Reilly that the death sentence had been "stopped" and offered agreement "in principle with my plan," presumably the one outlined in the letters of 13 and 17 October. Just who had surrendered to whom, and what was the basis of this sudden change of heart all around?

After some sleep thanks to Veronal, Styrne called again the next morning and the two "devised [a] program" about the topics to be covered in future reports. Once more, Sidney donned an OGPU uniform as part of "precautions that I not be seen." The result of their effort was the following list:

1. 1918 [Latvian Plot, Kalamatiano, etc.]
2. SIS, and 2a) Savinkov
3. Political spheres in England
4. American S.S. [Secret Service]
5. Politicians & banks in the U.S.A.
6. Russian émigrés

Reilly completed most of 1–3 before parting with Styrne late in the afternoon. After dinner and rest in Room 176, he dictated #4 and #5 to a secretary, Ilkina. Then it was back to his cell for a sleepless night. Regarding the 1918 report, the Diary notes that the "main object," presumably of Reilly's initial operation, was "German identification," and that this had been carried out with the help of "B-B" [certainly Gen. Bonch-Bruevich] and with the "knowledge of Tr[otsky]." Another key issue was the matter of blowing up bridges and rail lines to isolate Petrograd and Moscow. Reilly denied any Allied plan to "cut off supplies" and alleged provocation. A reference to the "scene at Am[erican] Cons[ulate]" must have involved the fateful meeting in late August. Even Manasevich-Manuilov (shot by the Cheka in early 1918) somehow figured into the picture. Later, Reilly was quizzed about "my intentions if Sav[inkov] returned," the ill-fated Balakhovich campaign and the "story of Opperput [and] Yakushev." Another topic was the "object of my trip." Contrary to earlier statements, he Ace-of-Spies revealed he had discussed it with "W.C." [Churchill], "Sp[ears]" and "G[aun]t.," also noting their disapproval and "my unexpected decision in Vyborg."

Among his somewhat confused notes for 1 November, Reilly recollected that during the interrogation late on the 30th, his questioners had laid "tremendous stress" on whether the current British charge d'affaires in Moscow, Sir Robert Hodgson, had agents inside the Comintern or elsewhere in the Soviet administration. Agents, that is, like Oswald Rayner. Sidney made no mention of him but indicated "Burberry," the Mission's 3rd Secretary Arthur V. Burbury, as the one handling intelligence.[56] Other questions concerned Dukes, Kiurtz and Peshkov, surely Zinovii Peshkov. The notes also reference another "scene" or interrogation on 29 October that included "lots of talk" about Pepita and "offers [of] any money or position," though whether for him or her is not clear. Much of the day he spent "correcting the Amer[ican] report," but there was time for a drive in the afternoon.

The following day, he and Styrne worked more on the SIS report. This included repeated questions about Burbury, L.A. Hudson, SIS station chief in Denmark, now in Prague, Yaroslavskii and "the Norwegian Ebsen." The last was Lt. David Ebbesen, the recent Norwegian military attaché in Moscow, and friend of another Norwegian diplomat, Vidkun Quisling. Where the Norwegian Connection fits into the picture, we will see later.

Reilly fielded repeated questions about British agents in Russia, a matter about which the OGPU was very interested, and they seemed convinced he could tell them something. Sidney steadfastly insisted that there had been no significant network in since Dukes' departure in 1919, and that maintaining agents in Russia was all but "impossible." Of course, as he and we know, that was quite untrue and conveniently denied the existence of operatives like D 57 and Rayner. The fact that he came personally to check out the Trust suggested that London had no onsite agents to do so. Was one of the aims of his return to Russia to convince the OGPU, or at least Dzerzhinskii, that no British espionage network existed there? But that would argue he was working hand-in-glove with SIS or someone therein, the very thing they so vociferously denied.

A closer look at Reilly's SIS report raises other questions. In 1927, parts of it were read into the transcript of a trial of White Guard terrorists in an effort to link their activity to the influence of the nefarious Capt. Reilly and his British employers.[57] In it, Reilly described the Secret Intelligence Service as a "completely autonomous establishment" which served the interests of other ministries and departments but was under the control of none. It worked closely with Admiralty, Home Office, War Office intelligence and the like, and maintained close links to the military staffs and intelligence services of "friendly" nations such as the Baltic States and Poland. The work of Polish, Finnish or Estonian agents in Russia largely served London's interests. The SIS carried out all its activities under the mantle of great secrecy and officially did not exist. Only the prime minister and a few select officials knew the identity of the Service's chief, "C," and his key lieutenants. In most cases, the families of officers had no idea as to the true nature of their work. That much was broadly true and probably told the Soviets nothing they did not already know. When it came to specifics, however, Sidney was less than reliable. As noted, he falsely identified "C" as Sir Guy Gaunt and named head of the "Russian section" as a Col. Warburton. He had to gamble that Dzerzhinskii did not know such details, but did he?

Later that day, the topic switched back to 1918, and Sidney recounted his encounter with Admiral Kemp and the "misunderstanding with Lockhart." Other names popping up were SIS operatives Frank Foley (Berlin), Boyce's assistant Harry Carr, and Leslie Humphreys who operated in Central and Eastern Europe. That same day, the diary noted a visit from Artuzov, the only interrogator mentioned by name besides Styrne. He put questions about the New York émigré activist (and Brasol intimate) K.A. Kovalskii and asked about "Zinovieff's Letter." Styrne wanted to have all reports done by the 4th, but the pace seemed to be taking a toll on the prisoner. Dr. Kushner expressed concern over his "state," and Reilly recorded little sleep despite the drugs. He felt himself "getting very weak."

The 3rd he spent mostly on his own polishing the reports. He was "hungry all day," and also made note of "Frunze's funeral," a reference to Gen. Mikhail V. Frunze, Trotsky's successor as War Commissar and another casualty of a medical "error." Rumors circulated, even in the Lubianka, that this was no accident.[58] At the least, the reference shows that Sidney was not unaware of other developments in Moscow. That evening, Styrne sent Reilly a letter via his assistant Ivan Feduleev. This included a fresh batch of questions concerning MI5's Vernon Kell and Hugh Miller, Anglo-German collaboration, "Dukes' agents" and "China." One name mentioned in response was Walter Bartels, Orlov's German connection. After a friendly chat with Feduleev and writing down his responses, Sidney took Veronal and "slept well."

The 4 November entry opened with "very weak." Again, there is no hint as to what was at the root of this debility, though it simply may have been the aftereffects of Veronal, a powerful barbiturate. Styrne showed up late morning in a very friendly mood, and they worked together through the afternoon. The discussions covered a huge range of topics, from Basil Thomson and Scotland Yard to Reilly's thoughts on Amtorg, ARCOS and the Urquhart Concession. Other issues were "petroleum," "financing debts in the U.S.A." and ideas "concerning an agreement with England." Reilly cited Churchill, Balfour and Baldwin as key figures in that regard. Others were Krasin, Boris Said, "questions about Persia" and the American military attaché in Japan, Faymonville.

After dinner came a visit from another Chekist, V.A. Ukolov. The latter had just returned from Paris or was about to go there and they engaged in a "long conversation about his trip." The suggestion is that his task was to contact some of Sidney's intimates there, perhaps Grammatikov and Zhivotovskii. Ukolov knew Yakov Peters and had worked with him in Central Asia. Moreover, Ukolov also had connection to OGPU operations in China and was due to take up an important post there soon. Afterwards, there was another evening drive in OGPU disguise. At the end of the busy day, Reilly went to bed about 2 a.m. and managed to sleep without Veronal. His last entries sounded a note of mortality and hope: "Feel at ease about my death . . . I see great things ahead." He certainly was not talking about any immediate demise; so far as he knew he had made a deal that spared him the firing squad. Rather, it was another expression of his concern about "achieving something" before he died. He had pulled off something big and he had every intention of sticking around to reap the rewards.

Sidney Reilly, in one form or another, had less than twenty-four hours to live. In his analysis of the Reilly case, former KGB officer Igor Prelin offers three reasons why the OGPU, including Iron Feliks, reneged on their agreement and carried out the 1918 sentence.[59] First, they suspected their captive was dragging out his depositions, stalling for time by claiming ill health. That, they concluded, was because he hoped the British eventually would demand his release. However, the diary suggests he kept pace with Styrne's timetable. Besides, the British Embassy in Moscow had not made the slightest peep about him and they would not do so. The next issue was that the Chekists were dissatisfied with his information. Prelin insists they already had excellent sources of information about White émigrés and foreign intelligence services and Sidney's statements added little or nothing. But if that was the case, why were they so broad and insistent in their questioning, and why did they not challenge his falsehoods if they could detect them? But what of his value as an agent of influence, the central point in the agreement? Prelin's third point was that Dzerzhinskii and friends decided the Ace-of-Spies could not be trusted. If set free, there was nothing to stop him revealing what he knew about the Trust, endangering the whole operation and the operatives connected to it. Yet these same men had been more than willing to endanger the Trust's security in other ways.

On 6 November, Feduleev sent the following report to Styrne. In obedience to the latter's instructions, about 8 p.m. on the evening of the 5th, Feduleev, Dukis, Ibragim, a fourth Chekist, Grigorii Syroezhkin, and a driver took "Prisoner #73" out of the Lubianka by car and drove north in the direction of Bogorodsk. That was entirely routine. "Prisoner #73" *pre-sumably* was Reilly, but nowhere in this or subsequent documents is his name used, an odd precaution in internal communications in which every-one knew who they were talking about—or did they? An essential point is that #73 designated not an individual but the cell in which the prisoner was held.[60] Thus, there were many "#73s," though usually only one at a time. Change a man's cell and you had, administratively, changed his identity.

The prisoner chatted with his companions as they drove. Sometime after 8:30 they reached Sokolniki, a sprawling park on the northern out-skirts of the city. As they entered, the car started to have problems, and the driver pulled over. Note how this echoes the earlier episode described in the diary. Feduleev asked how long the fix would take, and the driver said five to ten minutes. In the interim, he suggested to the prisoner that they get out and stretch their legs. As they walked away from the vehicle, Feduleev was to #73's right, Syroezhkin behind him while Ibragim on the left. About thirty yards on, Ibragim, who had fallen back, pulled a Mauser pistol and fired a single shot into the prisoner's back. The latter uttered a "deep gasp" and fell to the ground. Feduleev found a pulse and Syroezhkin fired another bullet into the chest. After ten to fifteen minutes, another check found no pulse, so they loaded the body into the car had headed back to the Lubianka. They delivered the corpse to the infirmary where the same Dr. Kushner was waiting with a photographer. None of this was standard pro-cedure in executions, particularly taking the condemned on a drive before shooting him. Why not a simple bullet in the back of the head in the base-ment? Opperput questioned this and was told by Styrne that Reilly was killed "unawares" as a kind of "special grace," something else the OGPU was not known to dispense freely.[61] The whole business continued the elab-orate ruses and intense secrecy that attended him from the moment he arrived in Russia. Yet another strange feature was that the deceased arrived with his head covered in a sack. Feduleev explained to the infirmary staff that the man had been run over by a tram. There was no injury to #73's head; the real purpose of this was to conceal his features. Why? So that none but the chosen few could view and identify the victim? Was this the earlier "double's" body, now playing his final role? In more secure sur-roundings, the body, unmasked, was photographed, or was it another body? The OGPU file includes a photo of a man resembling Reilly laid out, fully clothed, on a morgue table. He seems oddly composed and well-kept for a bundled-about corpse. Feduleev recorded the whole operation com-pleted by 11 p.m.

There were two follow-up reports. On 10 November, Feduleev informed Styrne that, as instructed, the previous afternoon Comrade Dukis had removed #73's corpse from the infirmary morgue. With the help of three other personnel, he transported the remains to a pit prepared in the inner prison. Why it took almost five days to do this is not explained. The body, furthermore, was concealed in a sack so none of the workers saw the contents. What possible difference could that make? The same day, Styrne compiled the "Explanatory Note" to the file of Prisoner #73. Explanation for whom and for what purpose now that the subject was dead? The intended audience must have been Dzerzhinskii and, perhaps, Stalin and the Politburo. This report, as we have noted, contained a wealth of biographical material on Reilly, some of it accurate, but some very misleading, especially where his true identity was concerned. This is the same document that identifies Boyce and Hill as OGPU collaborators. It is probable that much or most of the information originated with George Hill because it largely duplicates the story he gave the younger Lockhart many years later.

So had the Ace-of-Spies gone one bet too far and lost the biggest gamble of his life? That would seem the simplest explanation, but there are so many questions and peculiarities about the Soviet version, or versions as we will see, that it cannot be taken at face value. Moreover, there is much circumstantial evidence to suggest other answers, albeit none of them conclusive. Having killed Reilly, the OGPU kept strangely quiet about their great coup. They showed no such concern in other cases involving foreign subjects. Moscow would not issue a statement until in 1927 and that merely stated that he had been wounded and captured in late 1925, not executed.[62] To add further confusion, another version held he was taken into custody until 1927.[63] Or did this mean taken into custody *again*? A article in the 1930 edition of the *Malaia Sovetskaia Entsiklopediia* stated that the subject "perished while crossing the Soviet border" in 1924. More recently, the presumably authoritative *Ocherki Istorii Rossiiskoi Vneshnei Razvedka* ("Essays on the History of Russian Foreign Intelligence"), vol. II, puts his death on 3 November 1925.[64] This is an astounding degree of confusion from the same general source over what should be a simple fact to establish. A man can die only once. Moreover, the OGPU dossier, in its current, edited form, contains a photo of a living Reilly allegedly taken in 1925. It is a picture of Sidney, all right, but one obviously taken years earlier, probably during WWI. Men do not grow younger, either. In their mutual contradictions, Soviet accounts are not complete or wholly believable.

Yagoda had a very strong reason to keep Reilly alive. Sidney would have insured that only he, personally, could access the money stashed in

Swiss and German banks. Despite his interest in the case, Dzerzhinskii took no direct part in Reilly's interrogation and left the matter firmly in Yagoda's and Styrne's hands. Both of them, along with comrades Messing and Viakhia, won "Red Banner" awards for their work.[65] If Yagoda had tried to cover up Reilly once by faking his death, why not do it again?

One man clearly frustrated by Reilly's abrupt demise was Trilesser. On 3 January 1926, he submitted a special report to Dzerzhinskii, with copies to Yagoda, Messing, Artuzov and others.[66] He noted that in mid-December, right after Pepita's announcement of Reilly's death, sources indicated the Foreign Office had sent a confidential circular to all British missions. This instructed them to closely monitor émigré and foreign economic publications for news of any developments concerning Russian ventures or concessions. He also reported that SIS made special inquiries in Paris and Prague. There was a particular interest in anything touching upon Manchuria and the Chinese Eastern Railway. This convinced Trilesser that London was very interested in Reilly and believed him still alive. Was that because the British feared Sidney had defected, Trilesser wondered, or because he had entered Russia as their agent?

Though there were no official pronouncements about Reilly, East or West, many rumors circulated among the Russian emigrants. Opperput noted that two very different stories seemed to originate in Moscow. One still insisted the Ace-of-Spies had died in a frontier shootout, while another argued he had joined Savinkov and "taken service with the Soviet Government."[67] Still others held he was alive but in prison, while another version insisted it was a British demand for his release that prompted his execution.

Pepita continued her crusade, to little effect. Maria Radkevich, Opperput and Yakushev yielded nothing but contradictory stories as the above. Most disappointing was that aside from a few convenience accounts she could not locate her husband's money. Like him, it seemed to have vanished into thin air. Settling in Paris, she posed as an anti-Bolshevik crusader but her supposed adventures in that realm seem more imaginary than real. One report to SIS linked her to a plot to assassinate Rakovskii at the end of 1926. The same item claimed she was very close to Abram Zhivotovskii, Reilly's old business partner. More interesting, the same unnamed source claimed Zhivotovskii was in the employ of the Soviets, and that he somehow aimed to "get her back to Russia."[68] Some years later, a like anonymous report asserted that Pepita had been under the constant surveillance of Red agents, among them one "Chernyi," actually Sasha Grammatikov.[69] Why would the OGPU have been so interested in her activities? Surely, her capture would have had no value. Instead of being spied upon by Soviet agents, was Pepita actually working with them? Or were old friends Abram and Sasha keeping tabs on Mrs. Reilly, not for the OGPU but for her late husband?

The death issued by Pepita also brought Margaret out of the woodwork and in search of money. At the end of 1925, she appeared in London and engaged a law firm, J. Bartlett & Sons, to hunt for her husband's will and assets. She was prepared to claim that as the missing man's only legal spouse, she was entitled to his entire estate. Her solicitor contacted the Foreign Office asking if they had any definite information regarding Mr. Reilly's reported death. This received a curt reply that no such information was at hand.[70] About the beginning of February, Margaret addressed a "pathetic letter" to Picton Bagge at the FO in the hope that he could help find out what had become of her husband. Reporting to his superior J.D. Gregory, Bagge said she claimed to have certain information independent from her husband's present case which "would be of great interest" to the Government.[71] Was there the whiff of extortion here? Was she referring to what she knew about Reilly's early work for British interests?

Bagge declared the matter "not my pigeon" and asked Gregory's advice. That was to ignore her. On 25 February, Margaret wrote another letter to the Chancery.[72] She described her missing spouse as a "prosperous ship-broker" in prewar St. Petersburg who later joined the British Army and became a "political officer" in Russia. He rose to become "one of the most active ring-leaders of the anti-Bolshevik movement." She implied some direct knowledge that he had returned to Russia "at the end of October last." Had Sidney informed her of his plans, or someone else? Before Christmas, she claimed, she saw press reports of his death there on 28 September. "Too stricken" to make a personal inquiry, she hired a solicitor to find out what he could, especially about his will. "All that I possessed," more than £12,000, she asserted, had been in her husband's hands, but he had spent every penny of it on his anti-Bolshevik activities. She was coming over to London soon to seek "official help" in the matter. In response to further inquiry, the FO told Daisy "we are making some enquiries of Picton Bagge who apparently has some special information before answering you officially."[73] In other words, they were referring it back to them who had told them he knew nothing about it. They would not give her a penny. There were questions no one wanted asked, and answers no one wanted found.

NOTES

1. Reports noting Rayner's activities in Russia may be found in PRO, FO 371/6905, 6906.
2. SIS, "Shooting . . . ," 1.
3. Prelin, 10.
4. TsAFSB, 302330, Styrne to Pilyar, 2 Oct. 1925.
5. Ibid., "O priezde R."
6. Prelin, 11.
7. TsAFSB, 302330, "O priezde R."
8. Ibid.
9. Ibid.
10. Ibid., Styrne to Pilyar, 2 Oct. 1925.
11. Ibid.
12. Ibid.
13. Ibid., "O priezde R." and Styrne to Pilyar, 2 Oct. 1925.
14. Ibid., "O priezde R."
15. Ibid.
16. Prelin, 10.
17. SIS, "Shooting . . . ," 2.
18. Ibid.
19. Ibid.
20. Prelin claims the notice appeared in the Leningrad *Krasnaia gazeta*, but that, too, cannot be located.
21. Prelin, 12.
22. Reilly, 192.
23. SIS, [ST]28 Reports, 17 Nov. 1925.
24. Reilly, 194.
25. Ibid., 196–197.
26. SIS, Translation of Trilesser Memo, 1 Oct. 1925 and HIA, Nicolaevsky, 217/6.
27. SIS, ST0 to CSS, 13 Oct. 1925.
28. John Coleman, *The Conspirator's Hierarchy: The Committee of 300* (Carson City, NV, 1992), 160.
29. Reilly, 197–198.
30. Ibid., 198.
31. Ibid., 202–203.
32. Ibid., 210.
33. Ibid., 117.
34. Ibid., 212–213.
35. SIS, "Capt. Sidney Reilly MC, late RAF," 29 Oct. 1925.
36. SIS, G.S. to Thwaites, 30 Oct. 1925.
37. SIS, CSS to Boyce, 24 Nov. 1925.
38. SIS, [ST]28 Reports.
39. Ibid.
40. PRO, FO 371/11029, 6544, 25 Nov. 1925.
41. *Daily Express* (16 Dec. 1925).
42. *NYT* (16 Dec. 1925) 6:2.
43. *Daily News* (17 Dec. 1925).
44. *Daily Express* (17 Dec. 1925).
45. SIS, press clipping, *Sunday News* (20 Dec. 1925).
46. SIS, YN0 to CSS, 17 Dec. 1925.
47. TsAFSB, 302330, Protokol, 7 Oct. 1925.
48. Ibid., 9 Oct. 1925. Extracts of both protocols can be found in *Izvestiia* (17 June 1927), 2.

49. SIS, "Shooting . . . ," 2.
50. TsAFSB, 302330, Reilly to Styrne, 13 Oct. 1925.
51. SIS, "Shooting . . . ," 2.
52. Ibid.
53. TsAFSB, 302330, and "Konets Sidnei Dzh. Reili," *Novoe Russkoe Slovo* (23 Aug. 1964).
54. Richard Spence (ed.), "Sidney Reilly's Lubianka 'Diary' 30 October–4 November 1925," [hereafter Diary] *Revolutionary Russia*, vol. 6, #2 (Dec. 1995), 179–194.
55. Ibid., 190, n. 49.
56. Ibid., 189, n. 42. Minaev, 89, accuses Burbury of gathering political intelligence on the Comintern and Communist intrigues in the Far East.
57. Kichkassov, 30–32, quoting Reilly's *pokaznaniia* ("confession") of 31 Oct. 1925 and *Izvestiia*, "Oglashenie pokaznanii Sidnei Reili" (23 Sept. 1927).
58. Brackman, 189.
59. Prelin, 28–29.
60. Ibid.
61. SIS, "Shooting . . . , " 2.
62. *Izvestiia* (9 June 1927), 2.
63. Minaev, 87–88.
64. OIRVR, II, 123.
65. Ibid.
66. RTsKhIDNI, f. 76, d.384.
67. Ibid.
68. SIS, Memo from Special Branch, 9 March 1927.
69. SIS, translated letter, 27 June 1931.
70. PRO, FO 371/3332, Bartlett to FO, 24 May 1928, referencing FO reply of 5 Jan. 1926.
71. PRO FO 371/11793, Bagge to Gregory, 9 Feb. 1926.
72. Ibid., Margaret Reilly, 25 Feb. 1926.
73. Ibid., FO to Chancery, 12 March 1926.

Chapter Eighteen
LEGENDS

"The greatest trick the devil ever pulled
was convincing the world he didn't exist."
Verbal Kint, *The Usual Suspects*

Moscow's silence on the Reilly case ended on 8 June 1927 when an official statement admitted the apprehension of a so-called merchant, one Steinberg, in the "summer of 1925." The details appeared in *Izvestiia* the following day.[1] Wounded by Soviet frontier guards, he was captured and subsequently admitted to being RAF Capt. Reilly, "one of the principal organizers of the Lockhart Conspiracy." He confessed to having come back to Russia to instigate "terrorist attacks, arson, insurrection" and other hostile acts. In doing so, he acted on the personal instructions of Churchill and other British officials. Reilly's full written statement was in the hands of the Soviet Government and his statements "had been confirmed fully by materials seized in later arrests." There was, however, absolutely no reference to his eventual fate.

Over the next few months, the Soviet press offered up more snippets of information in its coverage of ongoing trials of assorted terrorists and spies. On 17 June, *Izvestiia* quoted at length from Reilly's "confession" apparently compiled from his depositions of 7 and 9 October 1925 and letters to Bunakov. The central point was his advocacy of terror as a weapon against the Revolution.[2] "I am sure that terroristic acts on a large scale would make a great impression," he supposedly claimed.[3] This would "arouse hope on the early fall of Bolshevism and create a wide interest in Russian affairs." However, the *Izvestiia* article also quoted him as saying that he had come to Russia in 1925 "on my own initiative" to promote the "peaceful intervention" of British capital into the country through collaboration with a "serious and active anti-Soviet group." The article dismissed that as a crude blind for his true, destructive purpose.

News of Reilly's "confession" reached the American press. The *New York Times* made note that Soviet reports claimed he had spied "indirectly" for the U.S. because "the English Intelligence Service hands over to the American Intelligence Service information regarding Russia . . . ."[4] According to the *New York Times*, the Foreign Office admitted that "a man named Riley [sic], believed to be a British subject" was reported by Soviet authorities to have been shot on the Finnish border two years prior. Of course, the Soviets had reported no such thing, publicly anyway. London added that the present "circumstances of the affair were not known to the British Government."

Reilly's was not the only name to surface in Russian spy trials. In July, Moscow announced the smashing of a conspiratorial group led by an ex-naval officer Albert Hoyer (Goier).[5] He had past connections to Reilly and Dukes, but his most recent "control" was Commander Boyce. In the months to follow, Soviet prosecutors and press repeatedly invoked Boyce as the guiding hand behind plots and terrorism. If the Commander really was an important OGPU asset, this was an odd strategy, for in giving Boyce such notoriety, SIS was obliged to relieve him from his post. Was Boyce's exposure linked to Sidney's, and was the reason because someone in Moscow figured out that he was not on their side after all?

Reilly's name appeared with renewed prominence in the September trial of five "Kutepovite terrorists." He was featured as the "British chief directing terrorist acts in Soviet Russia" and "the resident of English counterintelligence," suggesting that he had direct contact with the defendants and had been active until fairly recently.[6] But that was impossible if he had been arrested and executed in 1925. Still, the reports made no mention of his death, only wounding and capture at the frontier. That question appeared to be answered by another *Izvestiia* item, dated 18 September, which reminded readers that Capt. Reilly was "mentioned in the list of twenty counter-revolutionaries and spies shot *this summer* [ital. added] . . . and was one of the most prominent figures among them." Interestingly, the execution in question took place on 9 June, the exact day as the initial *Izvestiia* story. The execution and the list of victims was noted widely in the foreign press, including *The Times*.[7] Curious persons in the Foreign Office noticed a strange discrepancy. Almost all the executed were ex-officers or noblemen connected to monarchist conspiracies and many had past links to British intelligence or the British Mission in Russia. For instance, one was M. Skalskii "who supplied a British spy in Finland named Bunakov" with military information.

The most familiar was Capt. Georgii El'vengren, "one of those who with Captain Riley [sic], an officer of the British Intelligence Service, took part in the organization of the attempt on the Soviet Delegation at the Genoa Conference." There was no mention, however, of Reilly's name among those shot. The only person on the list who did not fit the general profile was a Jewish journalist, Solomon Naumovich Gurevich, who allegedly had attempted to assassinate Stalin, Bukharin and Rykov in March. Could that have been a Reilly alias? Nothing else suggests so. Was this whole story a matter of gross confusion or of deliberate disinformation? And if the latter, to what purpose? Curious persons at the FO thought it unlikely *Izvestiia* could have been mistaken about such a simple matter and noted the paper was "basically controlled by the OGPU." Thus, what first seemed to be a solution to the Reilly mystery merely deepened it. It left the same question: was he dead or alive?

To put things in context, we must consider some recent events. In July 1926 came the sudden death of Feliks Dzerzhinskii. If Yagoda had conspired to keep Reilly alive against his boss' wishes, neither he nor Sidney could rest easy so long as Iron Feliks drew breath. On 20 July, Dzerzhinskii delivered a long, rambling speech "punctuated by hysterical outbursts" to assembled comrades. Before he finished, he collapsed and died. Natural causes could have been to blame, but rumors immediately spread that he had been poisoned. Author Roman Brackman offers an intriguing answer to by whom and why. Just a few days prior, Stalin's Okhrana file surfaced among a shipment of old police documents from Leningrad.[8] By some unknown hand within the OGPU, Brackman believes, the file landed on Feliks' desk. What so upset him the day of his death was the information contained between its covers. Stalin guessed—or was he tipped off—what Dzerzhinskii had stumbled upon, and poisoned the water Feliks drank at the podium. The timely appearance of this file and its presentation to Dzerzhinskii brings to mind the Sisson Documents and the Zinoviev Letter. Simply put, did Reilly and/or Yagoda use the incriminating dossier to goad Stalin into eliminating Dzerzhinskii and at the same time secure an important piece of leverage over the Georgian? Iron Felik's removal elevated Yagoda from #3 to #2 in the secret police hierarchy. Under the lax oversight of Menzhinskii, he was little less than de facto chief.

Another figure to depart the scene was Leonid Krasin who died of leukemia in November 1926. In the last months of his life, he returned to London as Moscow's ambassador. What links, if any, he may have had to a Reilly-Yagoda gambit are unclear, but he definitely took many a secret to his grave.

In the spring of 1927, Anglo-Soviet relations entered a perilous phase. In April, Chinese authorities, egged on by the British, conducted a series of raids against Soviet missions in Canton, Shanghai and Tientsin. This was part of Chiang Kai-shek's break with the Russians. One of the Red functionaries killed in these raids was V.A. Ukolov, the Chekist who had visited Reilly in his cell. Was it simple misfortune, or the elimination of another who knew too much? At the same time, French authorities arrested several Communists and Army officers on charges of passing military secrets to Moscow.[9] On 12 May, British police conducted a massive raid on the ARCOS offices in London. The ostensible reason was that the premises held a copy of a missing RAF plan book, never found. Around the world, Soviet missions came under intensified scrutiny and assault. Was this an imperialist conspiracy, as the Kremlin alleged, or were secrets compromised by someone inside the Red establishment? In the case of the ARCOS raid, some point a finger at oil tycoon Deterding, who was still waging a private war against Moscow.[10] Guy Liddell, the MI5 man who had taken such an interest in Reilly, played a guiding role. One casualty of the incident was a £10 million Russian loan proposed by Midland Bank. The larger impact was Britain's severance of diplomatic relations, a condition that would endure for two years. McCormick suggests that Sidney conspired to provoke the raid again in the hope of revealing British codebreaking. If he was alive, the incident surely affected him one way or another. Did it provoke the Soviet reports of his capture and/or execution? Was that because certain parties demanded assurance that he really was out of the picture, or was it intended as a signal of precisely the opposite?

It also was in April that Opperput, AKA Staunitz, and Maria Radkevich reappeared in Finland claiming to have once and for all split with the OGPU. The Trust was unraveling of its own accord and he may have sensed his utility to the OGPU coming to an end. In any event, he dealt the Trust a *coup de grâce* by trumpeting its true nature in articles for the Finnish and émigré press.[11] Whether this was an act of defiance or simply more OGPU spin control is another question that defies an easy answer. His long history as a serial turncoat did not recommend his honesty. The Finns, for instance, viewed him with strong suspicion while at the same time taking in all he had to offer.[12] As for the British, they had him interviewed by two "intelligence officers," Capt. Alexander Ross and R.L.J. Farina. The former felt that Opperput "knew too much by British Intelligence," but Farina, a former MI5 Red hunter, "discounted" most of the subject's claims.[13] Something noted in British reports was that Opperput and Maria R. were followed to Finland by a second, unnamed man who thereafter simply vanished.[14] Opperput's own reports claimed that the Kremlin had abandoned hope of spreading Communism in Europe and now placed its hopes on the East, above all China. He described plans to use Afghanistan as a base of operations against India. Oddly, his report on Reilly's fate would not come to light for months.

In the aftermath of the ARCOS raid, the OGPU station in China intercepted a message that revealed one of its own, Evgenii Kozhevnikov, was a double agent for the SIS man in Shanghai, Patrick Givens. Kozhevnikov, better known as Comrade Pick, had been a coworker of the deceased Ukolov. Kozhevnikov promptly vanished, but he is destined to play a very interesting role a bit further on. At the end of May, Opperput, Maria Radkevich and a young Kutepovite activist, Yurii Peters, suddenly returned to Russia to attack the OGPU in its lair, the Lubianka. The terrorist foray failed and Opperput and his accomplices fled back towards the Polish border. About 19 June, Opperput, somehow separated from the others, allegedly died in a shootout with militia. Some days later, Maria and Peters met a like fate in the woods of Belorussia. The man who spearheaded the destruction of these counter-revolutionary miscreants was Comrade Yagoda.[15] However, soon after, reports reached the West that Opperput was alive, and under a new name was on his way to *China*.[16]

This, then, was the chaotic atmosphere in which Reilly's name reappeared. What was the connection? On the British end, there had been almost no movement or comment on his case since Margaret's inquiries in early 1926. His SIS file does include one cryptic cross-reference dated 27 April of that year. It notes that a "large packet of private papers" regarding Reilly was passed to a Miss Henshawe from a Miss Cook. This and a few other items suggest someone in SIS retained an interest in their former agent. In May, they received a copy of Trilesser's INO memo from the previous October requesting information about Reilly and Yaroslavskii. Why was that of significance now? An accompanying note, dated 20 May, explained "a German friend of 26 III obtained it from a person in the Soviet Legation in Berlin."[17] In late November 1926, the Service received a letter from Sidney's friend Gwynne at the *Morning Post* saying he had recently been treated to a visit from a "desperate" Margaret who was still trying to find her husband, or at least his money.[18] She was absolutely convinced he remained alive.

In early March 1927 SIS received the previously discussed memo from Special Branch, which arrived bearing a Russian informant's recollections of Reilly in Moscow and Rome. This included the claim that when Sidney was shot in Russia, the "Bolshevik Department concerned with him did not

know he was Reilly," though "one or two of us did." The informant opined
that it was Abram Zhivotovskii "who gave poor Reilly away," though how
or why he did not elaborated. More significant, perhaps, was his opinion of
George Hill, especially in light of what we know. He was a "blackguardly
spy" of "poor moral character." Reilly's old chum Desmond Morton
thanked Scotland Yard's Hugh Miller for sending the report, but told him
that "As a matter of fact, we have no questions to ask, since we have no
official interest in Reilly who was not working for us or for the British
Government when he met his death." [19]

But if Morton and others had no questions, they may still have been in
search of answers. Opperput's description of Reilly's arrest and execution
came into SIS hands sometime in "mid-1927." An internal "analysis" of
Opperput's report, possibly by Boyce, mentioned receipt of an earlier report
from the Trust and a letter from Yakushev which promoted the border
shooting story. That was taken seriously until the Trust people, "who evidently had very good connections with the GPU [OGPU]," balked at providing further details. This suggests SIS was well aware of the Trust-OGPU
link. Nevertheless, the writer still thought it "quite feasible" that Maria
Radkevich had been "genuinely deceived." The only thing that seemed clear
was that Opperput's, Radkevich's and Yakushev's words could not be taken
for anything. Doubts deepened when Toivo Viakhia, supposedly killed in
the skirmish, was found to be alive and well and in a new post on the
Estonian frontier. Of course, he had a new name as well. All this gave some
plausibility to recurrent rumors that Reilly was alive. However, the analysis also noted that some of those rumors could be traced back to Orlov,
another very dubious quantity. Curiously, Orlov's only published statement
regarding Reilly, appearing in 1929, had him the victim of an OGPU trap
but left open the possibility that he had somehow escaped their clutches.[20]

In Parliament, Communist MP Shapurji Saklatvala cited the Russian
press stories to demand a statement from the FO regarding Capt. Reilly's
alleged work for Lockhart in 1918. Saklatvala also wanted to know if the
Government had any information of that individual's attempt to enter
Russia in 1925, if he did so with the Foreign Office approval, and if it had
knowledge of his present whereabouts.[21] In an response dated 21 June,
the FO's Neville Bland admitted that "It is perfectly true that we did at
one time make considerable use of Reilly. He was a man of great courage,
inspired by a violent hatred of the Bolsheviks, which, coupled with a
somewhat unscrupulous temperament, made him a somewhat double-
edged tool."[22] He added "this did not prevent people in high places,
including Mr. Lloyd George, from coquetting with him." One of Reilly's

more negative characteristics was a marked tendency to "exaggerate his own importance" and "go about boasting of his subterranean activities." This, Bland suggested, undoubtedly had something to do with his fate. As for his relation to Lockhart, Reilly had supplied information but "there is nothing to show that he was actually employed by him." "In all circumstances," he advised, "I think the less that is said in answer to this question the better." In the end, Parliamentary Secretary Gregory Locker-Lampson offered a laconic "affirmative" to whether the Government had taken notice of the recent Soviet statements on Reilly, and a blunt "negative" to all the other questions. He also quite inaccurately proclaimed that the British Government employed no spies in Russia at all.

The Communist press also chimed in. On 17 June, *Workers Life* ran "Sidney Reilly—British Spy: Further Exploits." This included excerpts from Rene Marchand's account of the meeting at the American Consulate where Sidney plotted the demolition of bridges with the aim of "starving the workers of Petrograd."[23] A few months later, the *Sunday Worker* ran "How British Spies Work," based on testimony from recent Soviet trials and repeating parts of Reilly's report on the "British secret service."[24] But the Red press was not the only media to run with the story. On 3 July, the *New York World* printed an article by special London correspondent John Balderston.[25] Balderston presented a bizarre biography that turned Reilly into an Oxford graduate (1907). Thwarted in his desire to marry "the beautiful daughter of one of the richest and noblest peers in England," he joined the "espionage service of the British Foreign Office" and became one of England's most redoubtable agents. He spent "several years training at a special spy school" before being sent to Russia as a resident agent. Thereafter, in no certain order, he "built the first aerodrome at Moscow, learned the Russian language . . . and gradually Russified himself." During the war, Reilly "was the first to report on Rasputin's influence over the Imperial Family." After the Revolution, he became one Relinsky, "a pretended Bolshevik leader" and supplied "Downing Street" with regular reports on Russian events. He traveled back and forth between Britain and Russia several times until finally caught in a trap in September 1925. Adding another twist, Balderston alleged that "he escaped in some miraculous way," but was apprehended and shot by the Bolos sometime in *December* of that year. Again, we find some more or less accurate details (e.g., "Relinsky") embedded in an otherwise fictional story.

Balderston seems to have copied most of his story from a recently published French "exposé" of the British intelligence service by Robert Boucard.[26] Boucard's book was banned in Britain and that may explain why the Foreign Office was disturbed by the Balderston piece.[27] There was, however, special sensitivity over the Reilly references. A. Gascoigne called Balderston's revelations "most indiscreet" but suggested taking no action because "the less we say about Riley [sic] the better!" Neville Bland dismissed the story as "fairy tales," but observed that "we can hardly chastise him without pointing out to him in what respects his version differs from the truth—a process that would be tedious and unprofitable."[28] Could Balderston's aim, or the aim of those behind him, have been to smoke out the truth? A salient point may be that Balderston was a good friend of Norman Thwaites and the latter still had solid links to the Diehard Right where persons maintained a lively interest in the departed Ace-of-Spies.

Along with the Balderston article, the British Library of Information in New York forwarded a copy of a recent exchange in the *New York Times* between a public relations man for the Rockefellers, Ivy Lee, and Reilly's past ally in anti-Bolshevism, Lewis Pierson.[29] At issue was Lee's suggestion that the U.S. Chamber of Commerce open a branch in Moscow to promote trade and access the "virtually untapped markets of Russia." Pierson, President of the USCC, vehemently opposed the idea and countered it would do nothing but harm American interests. Lee had just returned from Russia where he had helped Standard Oil of New York negotiate a new deal to purchase and distribute Soviet oil products. Perhaps it was nothing more than a coincidence that this and the Reilly story came linked together, or was it because of Sidney's past links to Standard and Pierson? Did someone, perhaps, suspect ongoing links? If Reilly was alive and doing business, Lee's deal was exactly the type of thing he would have had his finger in.

The autumn of 1927 saw several other comments emerge on Reilly's fate, none of them definitive. On 26 September, the Riga-based *Segodnaia* ran a piece by Vladimir Brunovskii who had just arrived in Latvia after a stint in the OGPU's prisons.[30] He had some familiar connections of his own. Before the Revolution, he worked beside Guchkov in the Red Cross. Later, as a *spets*, he held economic posts which brought him into contact with Krasin and, interestingly enough, the Norwegian Jonas Lied, and Lied's countrymen Frederik Prytz and Capt. Vidkun Quisling. Prytz and friends were connected to a big timber concession. In late 1923, the OGPU accused Brunovskii of using the Norwegians to pass information to the British. Brunovskii denied that, but he did recollect, almost offhand, that while in the Lubianka Inner Prison in early 1926, he heard stories of an "important British spy" held in the prison hospital. He tried to find out more, but only gathered a few snippets of information. He recorded those on scraps of cloth sewn into his overcoat. Only after his arrival in Riga did he discover them but no longer remembered exactly what they were about.

The message Brunovskii wrote to himself read "British officer Reilly. Persia. Father-in-Law."[31] The latter was the Russian word for a man's father-in-law, *Test*, which, of course, had a very different meaning in English. Brunovskii was certain that Capt. Sidney Reilly had been alive and in custody in early 1926. Of course, it also could have been just about anyone *claiming* to be our man.

Brunovskii's story provoked a testy counter-article from Vladimir Burtsev in *Segodnaia* on 11 October.[32] He cited Opperput's version of events as proof that Reilly was dead though he elsewhere admitted that Opperput was a less than reliable source. Why did it matter to Burtsev one way or another? The Brunovskii tale may not have been wholly imaginary. Persia hinted at oil, a common element in Reilly's career. The place was to feature in later stories as well.

Reports of Reilly's survival just kept coming. In late November, in far-off Tientsin, the Russian paper *Nash Put* published an article by a "White officer" claiming Reilly was alive in Orlovskii prison in 1926 but "insane."[33] Similar rumors arose from the émigré grapevine alleging the Captain was alive as of 1927, but invariably, mad or in a dying condition. Inspired by these tales, Pepita wrote Churchill in December and pleaded with him to use his influence to force an official inquiry into her husband's case. Through his secretary, Eddie Marsh, Winston politely declined. He again pointed out that Reilly had gone into Russia on his "own private affairs" so there was no basis for the Government to involve itself. Besides, he added, "latest reports" indicated that Sidney had met his death there not long after his arrest.[34]

Things remained quiet for several months, but in May 1928 Margaret's new solicitors tried to pry information out of the Foreign Office and received the closest thing yet to an official response, if a most uninformative one. On 8 June, G. Agar Robartes for the FO wrote Bartlett & Sons, Solicitors that "I am directed to inform you that this department has no confirmation of [Reilly's] death in Russia and no information as to his executor."[35]

Soon after, a new report surfaced attesting to Reilly's post-1925 survival, this from a Miss Lauder-Brunton, an honest and sober member of a Quaker mission in the USSR. According to her, Sidney was alive as late as the end of 1926 in a Moscow prison. Other information put him in the same place as recently as the summer of 1927.[36] Inspired by these stories, in October Sir Alfred Knox, ex-military attaché in Russia and stalwart of the Anti-Bolshevik League, mounted a new campaign for an official inquiry. He believed Reilly was most likely dead, but that "no stone should be left unturned." In reply to Knox, the FO's Gregory Locker-Lampson admitted "information is too scant to confirm anything."[37] However, he offered that an inquiry through the Norwegian Legation, which now handled British interests in Russia, might "produce something."

On 22 November, London asked its man in Oslo, Gascoigne, to approach the Norwegian foreign minister on using his legation in Moscow to try and determine the "true fate of Capt. Reilly."[38] During early 1929, Norwegian Ambassador Andreas Urbye submitted the question to L.I. Kogan of the Commissariat of Foreign Affairs. Most of the documents generated by this overture have disappeared from FO files, but a later reference shows that as of 2 April 1929, the Norwegians reported Kogan had informed that Reilly "perished under circumstances as formally stated."[39] But as noted by the FO, which "formal circumstances" were these—the 1925 shooting, Opperput's version, or the execution in 1927? Was Kogan being coy, or was the simple fact that he and his superiors did not know the answer either? The situation was no clearer than before.

Urbye's overture was handled by a special secretary in charge of British affairs, Vidkun Quisling. Best known as the man whose Nazi collaboration made his name a synonym for treason, Quisling's earlier career had many parallels with Reilly's, not the least of which was a certain relationship with British intelligence.[40] Another was a long interest and experience in Russia. The tall, austere Norwegian was there in May 1918 as Oslo's military attaché, and he was on hand as the Ace-of-Spies' plots blossomed and withered. As mentioned, Quisling knew Lied and was very close to Frederik Prytz, who before the war was a timber merchant and ship-broker, activities right in Reilly's sphere.[41] During 1919–21, Quisling was a Norwegian intelligence officer in Helsinki where he collaborated with Scale and Boyce. Whether he formally enlisted as a British asset is uncertain, but he did make a mysterious trip to London in the summer of 1920. Quisling was in and out of Soviet Russia repeatedly in the mid-'20s as a representative of the Nansen relief organization, a job that brought him into regular contact with Krasin. In early 1926, he came to Moscow to work for Prytz's timber concession, an arrangement that brought him into contact with the OGPU and Yagoda. The following year, however, Prytz's venture collapsed amid rumors of currency speculation and the smuggling of *valiuta* via "Turkish and Persian merchants."[42] Nevertheless, soon after persons in London thought him the ideal man to look after their interests from 1927–29. Where Reilly was concerned, was Quisling really in search of the truth, or party to the ongoing cover-up?

In the fall of 1930, five years after Sidney's disappearance, a new angle was added to the saga. This was the publication in Berlin of Berndorff's

Diplomatische Unterwelt. Its chapter on the "Death of Captain Reilly" was only part of an ambitious exposé of espionage and secret diplomacy. For the most part, he followed Opperput's scenario.[43] However, in Berndorff's version, Opperput, Yakushev and the OGPU's spy in Orlov's entourage, Nikolai Kroshko, became the key figures in luring the Ace-of-Spies into Russia. Styrne, Puzitskii and most of the other Chekists vanish. The minor Shatkovskii became the agent who arrested Sidney in the car in Moscow. It certainly was Kroshko himself who gave Berndorff this "sanitized" version, and he did so on orders from Moscow. But whose orders were they, and why? It is interesting that Hill, in early 1931, assured a wary Lockhart that Reilly's death "was more or less" as Berndorff described it. It also seemed evident, Hill added, that Sidney was "in the hands of the Cheka from the beginning."[44] Of course, he had special insight on that point.

The most sensational part of Berndorff's tale was the alleged appearance in the German capital, sometime in 1928 or 1929, of a British intelligence agent using the code name "Stenly" or "Stanley." He came to meet a Soviet defector, one "Andrei," who claimed to have information about Reilly's fate as well as the names of Russian agents inside Scotland Yard.[45] There was the implication that the two were somehow connected. The Englishman, however, recognized "Andrei" as Kroshko and dismissed his evidence as so much Soviet disinformation. "Stanley," of course, was an alias used by Desmond Morton. Did he go to Berlin in search of news about Reilly and, if so, on whose orders?

Meanwhile, news in London was that Pepita was preparing to publish her husband's "memoirs."[46] Determined to cash in on Sidney one way or another, she teamed up with a journalist, Stuart Atherley, to edit Sidney's account of his 1918 adventures and her own experiences into a salable volume. Getting wind of this, on Halloween 1930, Churchill wrote Morton wondering if the book might not contain "indiscreet stuff."[47] This was the first Morton had heard of the matter, but felt certain the Official Secrets Act could be imposed if necessary, though he suspected an "unscrupulous publisher" could "drive a coach and horses through that."[48] After doing some checking, Morton informed Winston that Pepita's publisher, London General Press, was a "hole and corner establishment" and "no one reputable" had ever heard of Atherley.[49] Even so, he felt they should get a look and the manuscript and worried that Atherley "may possess secret information." Secret information about what, one must wonder? Churchill, Hill, Lockhart and SIS successfully demanded deletions before publication. Lockhart felt the Reilly manuscript, which he referred to as "diaries," contained "some very inaccurate statements about me."[50] He was in the midst of preparing his own memoir, *British Agent*, as was Hill, and neither wanted to be contradicted or embarrassed by Reilly. Interestingly, after reading Pepita's materials he felt quite convinced that Reilly was "trapped back into Russia by the Cheka."[51] "Apparently," he added, "they got hold of Boyce first." Had he had guessed the Commander's collaboration?

Lockhart still had questions about Sidney's fate. In early 1932, he put the question to Moura Budberg who had all manner of contacts inside Russia. In a letter from Estonia dated 13 March, she concluded with "R. is *not* dead, as our friend said."[52] Who the friend was we can only guess, but Lockhart later assured his son that "R" meant Reilly. Of course, Moura was herself a Soviet agent with a very flexible approach to the truth. Still, why would she deceive her beloved Bruce on this point at this time, and why did *he* make no public mention of her revelation? Later that year, Lockhart questioned Hodgson who had headed the British Mission in Moscow in 1925. Hodgson claimed to have no direct knowledge of the Reilly cases at all but felt "confident" that had been killed.[53]

"The Secret Documents of Sidney Reilly" appeared in serialized form in the *Evening Standard* beginning 11 May 1931 and ran almost simultaneously in *Paris Soir* and later in Russian papers.[54] A book version, *The Adventures of Sidney Reilly*, came out later that year. In addition to presenting her husband and herself in the most heroic of light, Pepita made it absolutely clear that she still believed him alive and probably a prisoner. Dead or captive, she would still be heir to his estate, if only she could find it.

Of course, she was not the only one with such ambitions. One person to sit up and take notice when the serial hit the French press was Margaret, then eking out a living as a nanny for an English family in Brussels. Daisy took serious issue with Pepita's claim to be "Mrs. Sidney Reilly," and was determined to prove otherwise. She engaged her own lawyer and sued Pepita and the *Evening Standard*. She also vented her feelings to British officialdom. On 29 May, she appeared at the Embassy in Brussels with a letter from her solicitor, attesting her lawful marriage to one Sigmund Rosenblum, later known as Sidney Reilly. The report from Brussels to London rendered his original name "Rosenbaum or Rosenblaum." That, in turn, provoked an inquiry from the FO to SIS asking if Reilly had ever been known as "Rosenbaum." In reply, "C" could find nothing of the sort, but he could find no mention of Margaret either, odd since she had corresponded with SIS more than once before.[55] Margaret, moreover, specifically asked that a special message be delivered to "Capt. Spencer" at the War Office. That, recall, had been Cumming's old alias. The Embassy advised that Daisy seemed "unstable" and liable to commit some "desperate act" if not treated carefully.[56] Up to now, she claimed, she had kept quiet about her husband's "true origins" because she believed he was working against the Bolsheviks. However, in light of "recent events," she had doubts that his efforts were genuine and thought "he may be alive and safe in Russia." She did not elaborate, but went on to say that she knew things about many of the people mentioned in Pepita's book and, as a loyal British subject, was willing to furnish "further particulars." Was there a genteel threat of extortion here? How much did she really know?

Margaret ultimately decided to follow Pepita's example and write a book. She got as far as a short synopsis that made the rounds of London papers and publishing houses in late 1931. The *Evening Standard* itself received a copy. So did SIS. How much it had to say about Reilly is hard to determine. After looking it over, Stewart Menzies concluded that it was mostly "the true story of her life" and found nothing objectionable from SIS's standpoint.[57] If Daisy had hoped to be paid to keep her mouth shut, the scheme fell flat, nor did anyone bite on the publishing end.

Pepita's book produced several informants who claimed to have information about her husband, though none, apparently, of real significance. There was at least one such letter, however, that she never saw. On 7 August, the War Office dispatched a "secret memo" to Maj. Valentine Vivian of SIS informing him that a few days prior the Admiralty had obtained a letter addressed to "Mrs. Sidney Georgievich Reilly." The undelivered letter had been opened and duplicated and a copy attached, and the question now what to do with the original.[58] Dated 27 June 1931 and signed "a Friend," the letter detailed the shadowing of Pepita by Grammatikov and other "Soviet" agents in Paris.[59] The writer vouched that Reilly was alive because "I personally heard this from the chief of the Soviet espionage in November or December 1925 and in the autumn of 1926 from his substitute." Both men, he assured, were "prewar friends of mine." The writer suggested that if Mrs. Reilly desired further communication, she should put an ad in the Paris Russian paper, *Poslednie Novosti*. Admiral Sinclair's curt answer was "no action." On 11 August, Vivian wrote MI5 insisting the letter not be forwarded, but suggested placing an ad in *Poslednie Novosti* "to see what happens."[60] On the other hand, he cautioned, the whole thing smacked of "provocation" and "we think it better to leave it alone." The most interesting thing about this incident is that it appeared to involve almost every branch of British intelligence. Clearly, there was still some interest where Reilly's name was concerned.

Things stirred in Parliament. In May, Tory MP Geoffrey Shakespeare raised new questions about Reilly's fate. In light of recent reports, he demanded to know if the Secretary of State intended to make inquiries to the Soviet Government as to whether or not "Capt. George [sic] Reilly is imprisoned" there.[61] In response, FO Undersecretary Hugh Dalton replied that he had looked at all available material that "might throw some light on" the issue, including Brunovskii's book, but without result. He consulted Vivian on the matter who noted the striking inconsistencies in the Soviet accounts, all of which he deemed "unacceptable." Vivian could not find, for instance, any trace of a Soviet account of Sidney's death or capture in Russia in 1925, and pointed out that the 1927 reports stated that the Captain had been wounded and taken prisoner, not killed. Taken as a whole, Vivian felt this lent credence to the stories of Brunovskii and others without, of course, providing any real solution.[62] Nevertheless, Dalton assured Shakespeare that there "remains no reasonable doubt that Reilly died, probably after undergoing much suffering and finally losing his reason, several years ago."[63]

This was not the end of the matter. In July, Pepita's man Atherley made a personal appeal to Philip Kerr (now Lord Lothian), Lloyd George's former secretary. On behalf of Mrs. Reilly, who was "under great strain," he pleaded with Kerr to use his influence to provoke a fresh inquiry to Moscow concerning Reilly's fate.[64] He sent identical appeals to Lady Astor and George Bernard Shaw. Kerr agreed to forward letters from Pepita to Sir Esmond Ovey, the new British charge d'affaires in Moscow. In a cover letter, dated 19 October, Kerr noted Atherley's question as to why the British Embassy, which functioned in the Red capital throughout 1925–26, made absolutely no effort to inquire into Reilly's case.[65] Ovey ignored that question, but sent along a copy of the Norwegian report from 1929. In light of that, he opined, it made "little sense" to pursue new inquiries.[66] Kerr got a more formal response from the FO's Anthony Eden in December. He acknowledged all Soviet versions were full of holes and unreliable, but he, too, saw no reason to suspect that putting the same questions to the same sources would result in anything but the same answers.[67] That, so far as the Foreign Office was concerned, was the last word on Sidney Reilly.

Margaret and Pepita kept up sporadic, parallel efforts to coax help and money out of His Majesty's Government. In November 1931, Daisy was in London and met with SIS via Capt. Issacs. She asked him if "a little financial aid for personal needs could not be afforded by your department." She claimed that the publication of her husband's memoirs had lost her a good position in Brussels and she was back to relying on the "kindness of Belgian friends."[68] Actually she voluntarily quit her post with the British family soon after the articles appeared and was back with the Warys, the same

Belgians with whom she had been connected since at least 1917. She came to England, she explained, to halt proceedings against Pepita, et al. because the court had ordered her to put up a surety bond she could not afford. She wanted SIS to ring up the *Evening Standard* and get them to back off. The hint of blackmail appeared again in her assertion that a quiet resolution of the case would prevent a "great amount of sensational scandal." Her marriage to Rosenblum, she complained, had brought her nothing but a "great amount of trouble." Isaacs reported to "the Colonel" (Morton?) "she is undoubtedly unbalanced, moving and speaking like a woman who had suffered . . . mentally." Reilly, whoever he was, "has left a twisted bit of humanity to float around the world."[69]

Two days later, Margaret came to him again.[70] Her lawyer wanted to go ahead, but she did not relish going into court and "have it all thrashed out." Isaacs told her that SIS could do nothing without verifying her story; they had no proof that she was Reilly's wife. This must have been what prompted her to provide him a copy of her "synopsis." He described her as a "poor, broken, lonely, twisted woman whose very soul seems crushed by her 'punishment for having done wrong'." She clung to the idea that Reilly was alive in Russia, but "how far Rosenblum is Reilly," he confessed, "I don't know." In a follow-up letter dated 17 November, she told Isaacs that her husband's case was being looked into by "persons qualified to deal with the matter," without saying who they might have been.[71] She also disavowed earlier doubts, proclaiming her "absolute conviction that Reilly has been perfectly honest and loyal in his relations with England." As evidence, she related a story that once in Paris her husband had been offered £50,000 by an "important Jewish gentleman" for a copy of a report Sidney was preparing for persons in London. Reilly turned down the money. Was that an episode in her book? Not only was he alive, she insisted, but was still "working for England against Bolshevism." Why this change of heart? She now wanted to halt her action to avoid dragging certain matters into open court but seemingly hoped the Government would "compensate" her somehow. Isaacs simply informed her that the War Office wanted nothing more to do with her or her case.

Back in Brussels, Daisy sent a letter to SIS complaining that Isaacs was the wrong person to deal with her.[72] He knew nothing about Russian affairs, she argued, so she had not told him certain facts that pertained to that part of the world, relevant to her husband's fate. She went on with a rambling story of how Jews, bent on revenge for past abuse, had seized control of Russia under the guise of revolution and Bolshevism. Strangely, she presented Lenin, "a perfectly sincere man—an illumine," as an unwitting tool of these unscrupulous men. Whether she had derived this information from Sidney or someone else she did not reveal. Parts of her scenario, however, are remarkably similar to passages of Count Cherep-Spiridovich's anti-Semitic "exposé." Was Reilly the common source? Her husband, she claimed, had fought against this conspiracy almost single-handed. The only official response was an internal note that stated "this information, even if it is correct, is of no value to us." It was the last word from Daisy. On 31 March 1933, she died in Brussels, age 59. She left £200 of effects in England, and little else to mark her passage through the world.

Pepita did not go away so quickly. Throughout the '30s she remained close to Atherley and in contact with Hill and Boyce. Much to Lockhart's surprise, she sued him in 1932 because in his book he acknowledged Margaret, not her, as Mrs. Reilly. He considered her "dangerously hysterical."[73] In March 1939, Maj. Hore-Belisha of the Air Ministry received a letter from Atherley on a "highly confidential matter."[74] This was a pension for "Mrs. Haddon Chambers," the widow of RAF Captain Reilly who had "disappeared in Russia in 1925." Reilly rendered "sterling service" to the British Government for many years, claimed Atherley, and in 1925 he had gone into Russia "at the suggestion of a British official, Commander Ernest Boyce." At the time, "a pension was mooted for his widow," but she "rejected it with anger." Now of a "different frame of mind" and in distressed finances, she desperately needed it. Atherley suggested Mr. Churchill and Archibald Sinclair would testify to the value of Reilly's past services.

The Air Ministry forwarded the letter to SIS where it landed on the desk of the new "C," Menzies. Citing his predecessor's letters dated 5 November 1925 and 1 July 1927, Menzies insisted Reilly's activities after 1921 were his own affair and had "no connection whatsoever in any shape or form with this organization."[75] Moreover, that Sidney had entered Russia at the suggestion of Boyce had been "categorically denied by the latter." "In light of the deceased's somewhat complicated matrimonial tangles, which have never been satisfactorily elucidated, I think it would be inexpedient to make any compassionate grant to Mrs. Haddon Chambers," he concluded. How many other Mrs. Reillys might come out of the woodwork to claim the same?

Menzies instructed that all further communications from Atherley be ignored, but the latter claimed he could prove that Boyce had encouraged Reilly's final trip. In July, Atherley was approached by C.E.S. Williams, who claimed to represent the Foreign Office's Sir Alexander Cadogan. Williams wanted to convey verbally the decision not to make any "compassionate grant" to Mrs. Reilly and to stress that Cadogan was "emphatic that under no circumstances could the matter be reconsidered."[76] He reiterated that

Reilly had no formal association with the Government after 1921 and that high quarters, in fact, had done their best to discourage his "embarrassing" activities. Williams was really Col. Sykes Wright acting for SIS to find out what Atherley knew and, more importantly, what he could prove. "Williams" denied Boyce's role and stressed the Commander "had categorical instructions to tell Reilly to stop." Atherley insisted he had a letter showing "Boyce did work with Reilly" in the matter. If so, replied his visitor, he did so "against instructions." There was further banter about the Ace-of-Spies' origins and the role of Margaret, but nothing really new or conclusive. One way or another, Atherley was persuaded to drop the matter.

Pepita made one last appearance in the fall of 1940. Europe was again at war, and she wrote to Menzies asking for a job as a spy. Curious, perhaps, he sent a man to talk with her. Described her as "voluble and very excitable" and "evidently very hard up." She appeared to drink a bit and definitely was not agent material. Her whole room was "plastered with pictures of Sydney George [Reilly]." She claimed to be on very good terms with French General Maxime Weygand, presently collaborating with the Germans, via her past "anti-Bolshevik work." With the right incentive, she thought she could convince him to break with the Vichy regime. She also mentioned her connection to Boyce and Hill. Interestingly, both those worthies had returned to the intelligence fold. Hill, in fact, was to return to Moscow as official liaison to Stalin's NKVD, the renamed OGPU.[77] She added an "amusing" story of telling "Mr. Mansfield" (Cumming? Sinclair?) about a man named "Dansey" (certainly Claude Dansey) who might have saved her from a bigamous marriage if only he had told her what he knew about Reilly's "first wife." She also advised that Boyce's organization in Finland had been "riddled with Bolshevik agents" and it was "through [Sidney's] dealing with Boyce that they eventually caught him." One can only wonder how much she really knew about that episode and other things.

MI5 kept tabs on her throughout WWII with interesting results. In late 1941, she wrote to Sidney's old crony Aleksandr Weinstein, then in London, asking for money to start a small business. She made the overture despite, she claimed, having been "threatened with all sorts of things if I communicate with you."[78] Who made the threats, she did not say. Weinstein had some contact with the Soviet Embassy, and she wondered if, in light of Britain's and Russia's new alliance, Moscow might "release Sidney (if still alive)" or at least pay her some compensation. In late 1944, she sent a letter to SIS addressed to "Mansfield."[79] In it she asked if a man named "Simonovitch," possibly Aron Simanovich, had been seen in

London and declared him an agent of a "Nazi-Fascist murder organization." She offered to produce further details on this character and other
dangerous agents, but SIS simply forwarded the letter to MI5 for them to
deal with or not. An unnamed SIS captain noted in passing that the subject's
late husband had "disappeared *on service* [ital. added] in Russia."[80] Was he
just misinformed, or were all those past assertions about Reilly's fateful trip
having no official sanction less than truthful? Pepita lived three more
decades in impoverished alcoholic obscurity before dying in London in
1974. She remained close to, some would say dependent on, Hill until his
death in 1970.

Jolly George had a powerful influence on the evolution of the Reilly
myth. During the '20s and '30s, he gained a reputation as a raconteur and
a drunk. In 1935, he told Field-Robinson that he was planning to write a
book on Reilly, but nothing came of it. He used it as pretext to collect various documents on the Ace-of-Spies, including examples of his handwriting.
Could he have had some ulterior motive? Hill's wartime work with the
NKVD, while receiving all official approval, left dark suspicions in the
minds of some of his British colleagues.[81] Ultimately, he became Robin
Lockhart's primary source for the 1966 *Ace of Spies*. By spinning Reilly as
an untarnished British hero, Hill indirectly polished his own reputation.
Shortly before his death, however, Hill confessed he had not told the whole
truth. During his WWII days in Moscow, he claimed, Russian officer friends
confided that Reilly was still alive and still in Russia.[82] Indeed, Sidney had
defected and had been working with the Soviets ever since. Interestingly,
Donald McCormick [Richard Deacon], who helped debrief Hill after his
return from Russia, held precisely the same conclusion about Reilly. Did he
get that from Jolly George or someone else? Stimulated by Hill's "confession," Lockhart penned his 1987 sequel, *Reilly: The First Man*, which portrayed him as the architect of Soviet penetration of British institutions,
including the infamous Cambridge Spy Ring.

It was in 1940 that the Soviets issued what purported to be the most
complete and authoritative statement yet on Reilly's demise. The source
was Vladislav Minaev's *Podryvnaia deiatel'nost' inostrannykh razvedok v
SSSR* ("The Hostile Activities of Foreign Intelligence in the USSR"). This
was the period of the Hitler-Stalin Pact, so Minaev's attention focused
almost entirely on the nefarious actions of Western agents, especially
British. As the "court historian" of the NKVD, Minaev presumably had
access to official sources. In the summer of 1925, he wrote, the well-known
English operative Sidney Reilly illegally crossed the Soviet border using the
name of Steinberg. "Arrested by the OGPU in *1927* [ital. added], Reilly

confessed that he came to the USSR in 1925 [ital. added] with the aim of organizing terrorist assassinations, arson, uprisings, etc." [83] Within the Soviet Motherland, Minaev continued, he carried out his vile work as "Comrade Rellinskii" attached to the Leningrad criminal investigation department. He even managed to become a candidate member of the Communist Party. Under this cover he conspired with monarchists and other miscreants to carry out terrorist actions before finally being struck down by the avenging hand of the OGPU. [84] In other words, Sidney had been alive, free and working in the Soviet administration for almost two years before he was "discovered." There is no mention of wounding and capture at the border. Would Reilly have reverted to the same alias he had used in 1918, one definitely known to the OGPU in 1925? Would that matter if he had been working for them all along? Or was Minaev deliberately misinformed? It is worth noting that Minaev's book portrayed Yagoda as a "Right Deviationist" and conniver with enemy agents from the early '20s, and protector of terrorists and spies. [85]

Yagoda ascended to the top position in the OGPU, soon the NKVD, with Menzhinskii's death in 1934. His triumph was short-lived. A pragmatic ally but never a confidant of Stalin, they maneuvered against each other in the early '30s. Yagoda's fall came in late 1936 when Stalin sacked him. The following spring, his successor, Stalin's dog-like henchman Nikolai Yezhov, denounced Yagoda as a former Okhrana agent, embezzler and tool of terrorists. Arrested in April 1937, Yagoda was subjected to a long interrogation before being tried and shot with the rest of the "Rightists" the following year. In compiling his indictment of Yagoda, Yezhov requested all records pertaining to Reilly. Obviously, he discerned some connection, but how much? When finished, on 25 March 1937, he ordered Reilly's investigative KRO-OGPU file, #249856, remanded to the care of the "most secret" collections of the Osobyi ("Special") Arkhiv, apparently a secure repository within the NKVD. [86] No one was to see the file, or obtain any information from it, without written authorization. In 1939, Yezhov himself went to the execution and what secrets died with him can only be guessed. Was Reilly's one of them?

In June 1933, OGPU agents in Vologda descended on the house of local resident N.M. Druzhinin. The latter had lived there since 1918 when the house served as the temporary British Consulate. The agents interrogated Druzhinin about the English officials he met at that time, especially Gillespie and Reilly. Druzhinin denied dealing with Reili, but his description of Gillespie convinced them that the two men were one and the same. [87] That detail was noted by Styrne in 1925. Why were they unaware of it? Or were they investigating the veracity of that report? Most importantly, why did it matter now? What difference could it make if Reilly had used Gillespie's identity fifteen years earlier? By identifying Sidney with Gillespie, could someone else be linked—and thereby incriminated—with the latter? It is possible the inquiry was fallout from the recent Metro-Vickers Affair, a January 1933 trial of British engineers and their Russian assistants charged with sabotage and spying.[88] Reilly, of course, had old links to Metro-Vickers. Moreover, among the defendants were at least two former (and present?) MI1c contacts, Allan Monkhouse and C.S. Richards, who had been active in North Russia along with Gillespie/Reilly.

A curiosity of the first water was the mysterious return of Reilly's Military Cross to the Air Ministry in the spring of 1936.[89] There is no indication of how or from whom it was received. Perhaps Pepita sent it back as a protest, though there is no indication she ever had it. But if not, who did? Was someone sending a message? The brief file indicates that on 26 March 1936 "MI/5" took an interest in the matter. What were they looking for?

Even the Gestapo added to the mystery. In anticipation of the invasion of England, in 1940 the Germans drew up a *Sonderfandungsliste* ("Special Arrest List") to be rounded up once in control. The names included many past or present British intelligence agents, and among them was:

"*Reilly, Sidney Georg, 24.3.74, Dublin, brit. Kapitan u. N.-Offizer, vermutl. England, RSHA IV E 4*"[90]

The entry shows that they still counted him a British intelligence officer and suspected he might be in England. The *Sonderfandungsliste* was far from perfect and contained all sorts of inaccurate information. On the other hand, Reilly's presumed death had been known for years in Germany (e.g. Berndorff), so would his name have appeared on the list without some information to the contrary? The reporting section, IV E 4, was run by SS Col. Walter Schellenberg. One of his key informants was Kurt Jahnke.

Reilly's fate was a question that almost no one, East or West, wanted to examine very closely. Most wanted to ignore it completely, and if Sidney was alive, that is what he would have wanted as well. Prior to WWII, only one man attempted a real investigation of the mystery, and he did not get far. This was Nikolai Alekseev, the Russian émigré journalist mentioned several times in the preceding chapters. Alekseev, recall, first met Reilly in London in 1919 and his interest was piqued. To no surprise, he had a rather colorful and dubious past of his own. He served with Vrangel's forces in the Crimea and accidentally, so he claimed, delivered a boatload of White officers to the Reds. Afterwards, he entered Soviet service, acting as a *spets* first in Moscow, then Germany and Yugoslavia. By 1923 he was working for

Krasin's foreign trade apparatus, a sphere that may have brought him into further contact with Reilly. Alekseev subsequently parted with the Bolos, but he retained a dubious reputation in White circles, some regarding him a Soviet agent.[91]

However, he retained the confidence of Guchkov who got him a job at *Vozrozhdenie* ("Resurrection"), one of the main Russian newspapers in Paris. Possibly at Guchkov's instigation, Alekseev began digging into the Reilly case in 1929. Right away, he ran into the basic questions: was Reilly English, or Russian, or Jewish? Was he an enemy of the Bolsheviks, or a secret collaborator? Alekseev's personal experience, no doubt, had taught him a thing or two about duplicity. He interviewed ex-officers and businessmen, including the French police/intelligence officer Faux-Pas-Bidet, a mysterious female associate of the Ace-of-Spies (Natta Azef or, possibly, Nadine), and Aleksandr Matzebovich who provided details about Reilly's early career. It was Matzebovich who told Alekseev that he had worked with Reilly in the "Bolshevik underground during Lenin's time," presumably the early '20s but, perhaps, earlier. Matzebovich seems to have had quite an interest in the subject, for in September 1932, he offered the British Embassy in Paris information about the "alleged Bolshevik activities and death" of Sidney Reilly.[92] Through contacts in Russia, Matzebovich assured Alekseev that Sidney's exact fate was unknown but there was no proof he had been executed. Alekseev learned that Reilly recently had reappeared abroad and had been traveling "between London and Moscow" on some unknown business.[93]

Alekseev located other former associates who swore that Reilly was alive and operating under a new identity. Some vouched to have seen him in Paris, and recently. One informant insisted he had seen Reilly in Ciro's, a posh Parisian restaurant, toward the end of 1929.[94] There had been others present to bear witness. Sidney supposedly had been in the company of "S" who was involved in oil matters; Boris Said, perhaps? Alekseev looked up "S" who admitted knowing Reilly but denied the incident and claimed he had not seen Sidney since '25. Alekseev was not convinced. Another man who had known Reilly in old Petersburg was shocked to run into him on a Parisian street, also during 1929. When he tried to speak to his old friend, Reilly ducked into a doorway and disappeared.[95] Alekseev discovered Reilly had placed an order of personal linen with a Parisian shop just before leaving for Finland, to be ready when he returned. The linen sat in the shop until mid-1927 when an unknown man paid for it and took it away.

As a result of his sleuthing, Alekseev became convinced that Reilly was alive and that he was now, and probably had been, a secret agent of the

Soviets. With signs pointing to his presence in Paris in the latter part of 1929, Alekseev suspected that Sidney had played a part in the January 1930 abduction of Gen. Kutepov. Snatched by OGPU agents right off a Paris avenue, Kutepov was smuggled back to Moscow, interrogated and later shot.[96] The loss of his charismatic leadership was a major blow to ROVS and demoralizing to the emigration as a whole. Faux-Pas-Bidet, who was involved in the French investigation into the General's disappearance, fed Alekseev his suspicions about Reilly's possible involvement.[97] Reilly might have been able to gain the General's confidence in 1930, especially if he came offering vital news from inside Russia. Another intriguing detail is that one of the OGPU agents who snatched Kutepov was S.V. Puzitskii, the very same operative who supposedly arrested Sidney in Moscow four years before.[98] Or was Alekseev just another Soviet disinformation agent, spawning rumors and red herrings?

Alekseev used Guchkov to get to Pepita. In early 1930, he appeared at her door in Paris and boldly asked to see her husband. Alekseev thought he might still be in town or that Pepita knew where he was. Taken aback, she assured her caller that Reilly was alive but in a Bolshevik prison. Alekseev agreed with her first point, but insisted her spouse had recently been right in Paris. He swore that if she told him what she knew he would treat the information with confidence. She countered that she had communicated with Sidney in Moscow, and that he had been badly wounded, but had recovered.[99] Alekseev did not end up publishing his findings until early 1933, and then in summary form. He was discouraged from pursuing Reilly's case further, he claimed, by Guchkov and others. Had the journalist, perhaps, come a little too close to something?

The appearance of Alekseev's article, which focused on Kutepov's disappearance, generated an angry letter from Pepita to *Vozrozhdenie*.[100] She categorically denied his allegation that Sidney had any part in betraying Kutepov and denied meeting with him. She took umbrage at his description of her as a "cabaret artiste." In response, Alekseev agreed to call her an "artiste" but stuck by his story of their meeting and that Reilly was very much alive.

Donald McCormick later insisted on supposedly compelling, if unidentified, evidence that Reilly spent the late '20s abetting various anti-British schemes hatched in the Kremlin. One of these involved the raising of a Royal Navy sub, the L 55, lost in the Baltic in 1919.[101] In 1927, the Soviets located and raised the vessel and ultimately used it as the template for new designs of their own. Submarines definitely were familiar territory to the Ace-of-Spies, but whether he had any connection to this episode is doubtful. Perhaps the most interesting thing is that someone *thought* he might have.

So where does this leave us? Did Reilly perish in 1925, 1927 or, as Alekseev claims, was he alive in 1930 or, according to Hill, 1944? Was he working with the Soviets or against them or for whom? If he was alive, there is no reason to believe he was doing anything but what he had always done: play both sides against the middle to the System's tune. If anyone could have pulled it off it was he. He had done it before. The period is replete with agents who "died" only to reappear under new identities. Besides those noted in the Trust, there was Boris Bazhanov, Stalin's former secretary who escaped to Paris in the late '20s. Reportedly liquidated by Yakov Bliumkin in 1929, he actually lived until the 1980s.[102] But if he ceased to be Reilly, who did Rosenblum become?

There are other sources, emerging as recently as the 1990s, which may offer clues to what really became of *Sidney Reilly*. They are, it must be said, recollections of dubious provenance and dubious persons, or simply anonymous. The primary reason for not dismissing them out of hand is that, despite disparate origins, they contain some oddly consistent and accurate information.

The first is a series of statements or stories recounted to researcher G.L. Owen in San Francisco in the early 1960s.[103] The informant was an elderly man of apparent White Russian background. He gradually spun out a tale of his own past association with Reilly and the latter's survival in and out of Russia through at least through the late 1930s. The gist was that Sidney made a deal with elements in the OGPU in 1925. For the next decade or so he acted as their secret economic agent in Western Europe, America and the East. However, from the beginning, his true purpose was to act as a "mole" or the "Trojan Horse" as described. As such, he continuously funneled information to the West, apparently to his longtime secret collaborators in Britain. He employed his usual multiple identities, one of them "George Rose." Sometime after 1935, as Yagoda fell, he left European Russia for the last time and headed East. He next surfaced in Manchuria and, later, possibly, Shanghai. There the trail runs cold, but there were suggestions that he survived the war and remained active into the 1950s.

The next item first appeared in London in 1992 in response to press accounts of new Soviet information about Reilly, specifically, his execution in November 1925.[104] The unsigned author claimed to be the son (or daughter) of a "brother officer," presumably British, who last saw Reilly about 1924. He described Reilly's 1925 "death" as a carefully orchestrated defection and that Sidney worked for the Soviets through the 1930s helping them recruit

British agents. In that, it conforms to the McCormick-Lockhart view. According to the writer, it was the rise of anti-Semitism, especially Nazism, that "gave Reilly the chance to mastermind the penetration of the British Establishment," the same crowd who had "abandoned him to his fate in the Lubianka." In this case, he made his deal directly with Dzerzhinskii. Reilly's biggest coup was his ability to persuade "a member of one of Britain's most powerful financial families" that the USSR was the only sure bulwark against Nazism. That individual was Jewish and closely connected to the affairs of British Petroleum and Shell-Mex Oil. Such clues suggest Sir Robert Waley Cohen. Through such means, Reilly was able to "set in motion a train of events that made Russia into a nuclear superpower." This hints that our man had some hand in the evolution of Soviet atomic espionage. The author's most intriguing comments, however, concern Reilly's whereabouts from the late 1930s, and here the story begins to converge with Owen's informants. In 1938, it is claimed, Sidney fled the USSR to Manchuria one step ahead of the NKVD that had liquidated his collaborators. Indeed. Along with Yagoda, almost everyone connected to Reilly's 1925 arrest perished during 1937–39: Styrne, Artuzov, Puzitskii, Deribas, Messing, Trilesser, Yakushev and Syrozhekin all vanished into the "whirlwind" of the purges. So did Peters, Berzin and Karakhan. Berzin may have sheltered him in Eastern Siberia through 1937. The following year he appeared in Harbin but soon left for Shanghai where he "took cover in the White Russian community." Accompanying him were a wife and daughter, whom he either brought from Russia or picked up in Manchuria. Could they have been the "Mrs. Z.Z. Zaharoff and daughter" who left Russia years before? If so, Harbin or Port Arthur would have been a safe, familiar and accessible place to keep them.

In addition to Stalin's men, Reilly was anxious to avoid the Japanese who were rampaging through China and tightening their grip on Shanghai's International Settlement. Through careful planning, he married his daughter to an "English official in the Hong Kong administration," and by that means reached Hong Kong. Just before the Japanese attack of December 1941, however, he followed daughter and son-in-law to Australia and later to Palestine. At some point in this process he took the name of George Rosenblum, curiously similar to George Rose. As Rosenblum, he lived and eventually died in Israel. The author's most astounding assertion was that Reilly/Rosenblum was still in 1968 at the ripe old age of 94, "active both physically and mentally." His daughter and grandson had no knowledge of his true identity, an ignorance that kept them "safe" from some lingering menace.

The most that can be said is that some of Sidney's Rosenblum relations did live into their nineties, and however much it may strain credulity, like the rest of the story, it is not impossible. If Reilly was alive until the late '60s, is it possible that through the likes of Hill he helped shape Lockhart's book? After all, the book portrayed him in a very heroic light, just as he would have wanted it. Unfortunately, key details in the "London Letter," the daughter's marriage, the exodus from Hong Kong and George Rosenblum's death, defy confirmation—or definite refutation. Prewar civil records and evacuation rosters from Hong Kong are incomplete, and the Shanghai Municipal Police files provide no obvious clues. Private and public inquiries in Israel produced no leads on George Rosenblum or his descendents, at least none that fit the criteria given.[105] Oddly, a query to the British Consulate in Tel Aviv (Rosenblum's daughter and grandson were supposed to be dual-nationals), elicited a reply that Consulate records had nothing on George Rosenblum or Sidney Reilly. No mention of the latter appeared in the query. Had someone alleged a connection before? The late Michael Kettle was convinced that all evidence of Reilly's presence in Israel was concealed because of his subsequent work for Israeli intelligence, Mossad. Like so much else, it is not beyond the realm of possibility, but certainly beyond the realm of objective proof.

During my research on Savinkov, I made contacts among the Russian community in San Francisco. Many of the older "White" émigrés hailed from the extinct colonies in Shanghai and Manchuria. Few could or wished to offer information where Reilly was concerned. In 1999, apparently in response to my participation in a *History Channel* program dealing with the *Ace of Spies* television series, an anonymous individual offered another twist on the legend of Reilly's survival. He was a Russian who had grown up in Shanghai during WWII. The primary source for his information was an older, deceased acquaintance called "Hoovans" or "Morskii." Their exchange seems to have taken place around 1960, provoked by a press article that mentioned Reilly's 1925 execution. "Hoovans" insisted that was not the case at all, for he had met the subject in China in the late 1920s and again in Shanghai in 1938.

"Hoovans" or "Hovans" and "Morskii" were aliases of the aforementioned Evgenii Kozhevnikov, the British double agent who deserted the OGPU in China in 1927.[106] Born in Riga about 1899, his many names included Eugene Pick and Dr. Eugene Clige.[107] He is, to say the least, a problematic source. From the late '20s through WWII, he was a denizen of Shanghai's underworld as well as being an actor and sometimes journalist. Like many others in our story, he was a freelance broker of information. In 1929 his name cropped up in a plot to sell British intelligence documents, forged or genuine, to an American journalist. Interestingly, in Europe,

Vladimir Orlov was embroiled in exactly the same sort of scandal. Soon after, he was involved in a scheme to pass phony Russo-Asiatic Bank checks.[108] Both hint at the possibility of some connection to Reilly's machinations. On the other hand, there is no doubt that Kozhevnikov was a "lying opportunist of the first magnitude."[109] But what did he have to gain in this instance?

As his story goes, in 1937–38 he assisted the Russian Emigrants' Committee in Shanghai by using his knowledge of Soviet agents to vet dossiers of new refugees, especially those coming from the USSR. It was among these that he spotted Reilly. Perhaps out of curiosity, or sensing an opportunity for extortion, he confronted him. The former Ace-of-Spies readily confessed his identity and asked for help. He, plus his *wife and daughter*, were on the run from Stalin's henchmen and the Japanese who, for some reason, wanted him. He had plenty of money and used Kozhevnikov's underworld channels to acquire papers identifying him and his companions as Jewish refugees. Were these the Rosenbergs from Breslau? The difference in age would have been a minor matter. So far as Kozhevnikov knew, Reilly revealed his identity to at least one other, the chief of the Emigrants' Committee, Karl Metzler, a former Tsarist diplomat. After Metzler's murder by Japanese agents in August 1940, Reilly felt unsafe.[110] Kozhevnikov was not sure how he effected his exit from Shanghai (no mention of the daughter's marriage) but thought it was with the help of certain British or Americans, notably the American insurance man *cum* intelligence agent, Cornelius Vander Starr.

The consistent point in all these stories is that Reilly surfaced in the Far East, most clearly in Shanghai, in or about 1938. Assuming that much is accurate, what had Sidney been doing for the past dozen-plus years? Looking at events around the globe and the actions of some of his known collaborators, the following scenario can be constructed. It is, of course, wholly speculative. But, if he did stay alive. . . .

According to Kozhevnikov, Reilly's first duty stations for the OGPU, around 1926, were Afghanistan and Persia.[111] Though Central Asia may seem an unlikely spot to employ his talents, it makes sense. An immediate return to Europe was out of the question. The "Reilly" trail had to cool and fade in and out of Russia. The turbulent Afghan kingdom lay on the border of British India and was an ideal base for mischief aimed against the Raj. In August 1926 Moscow's representatives signed a mutual neutrality and non-aggression treaty with the Kabul regime and established a large mission there.[112] Persia, of course, was the focus of long-standing intrigues over oil, something Sidney had always had an interest in. Recall that his Lubianka reports included details on Persia, "petroleum groups," and oil broker Boris Said. And Persia, too, appeared in the message Brunovskii found in his coat.

In 1927, Sergius Riis came to Poland as agent of Standard Oil of New Jersey. He actually worked for the local subsidiary, Standard-Nobel, the same firm Reilly had represented, and remained in Warsaw until 1934. But Riis was doing more than oil business. He later claimed his job in Poland was cover for work with a secret "Polish-British-American network" operating *in* Russia.[113] In 1931, the U.S. military attaché in Warsaw reported that Riis had "considerable information on affairs in Russia," and some of it was "at variance with all other information . . . bits of it are startling." [114] Was Riis still acting as Sidney's collaborator, perhaps a conduit to the "outside world"? Another "old friend" active in the same place was Tony Jechalski, working for the Warsaw First Locomotive Co. In 1935, he returned to the U.S. as part of a Polish mission interested in purchasing American arms, especially tanks.[115] Could he have been back in business with Sidney?

By 1928, Reilly must have been in China, probably in Manchuria where the Soviets had taken over management of the Chinese Eastern Railway. This neatly corresponds to Opperput's reported resurfacing in the Far East. That worthy, however, was never positively identified there. As he had done so many times before, did Reilly "appropriate" Opperput's identity briefly before morphing into someone else?

One matter Sidney was perfectly suited to handle in the Far East was the narcotics pipeline. In 1926 the cartel suffered a serious blow thanks to a bust of Rothstein's men in New York who were caught with $600,000 in heroin and cocaine.[116] In an odd coincidence, the federal prosecutor handling the case was Reilly's former partner in Trading Ventures, Edward Silver. The Gotham arrests followed like raids in Berlin, Geneva, Riga, Harbin and Shanghai. Dozens of persons were arrested, most "White Russians." In the end, though, most of the accused went free. In Berlin all evidence mysteriously vanished from police custody.[117] Nevertheless, there would have to be changes made. A bigger crisis must have occurred when Rothstein died in a card game shooting in November 1928.

The Orient also afforded to put Sidney close to another veteran accomplice, Kurt Jahnke. The latter was on excellent terms with officials of the Nationalist regime. In Germany, he ran yet another private intelligence service, the *Jahnkeburo*, a mysterious enterprise involved in "diverse operations involving contacts in various parts of the world." [118] That certainly has a familiar ring to it. Although disdainful of the Nazis, Jahnke somehow made himself indispensable to Hitler's key lieutenant, Rudolf Hess. Despite overwhelming evidence that he was a British double agent, Jahnke was protected by the *Abwehr's* Admiral Canaris and later by Schellenberg.[119]

If Alekseev is correct, Reilly reappeared in Paris in 1929. His evident interest in oil and collusion with Said suggests a next stop, New York. During 1929–30, Said formed a syndicate to handle the exchange of Soviet oil for American goods and machinery. Again according to McCormick, the late '30s OGPU defector Walter Krivitsky claimed that a Soviet agent called "Sidney Berns" "first penetrated the American Secret Service" and that a "substitute" used the alias up to 1936.[120] Reilly's use of the name "Sidney Berens" is mentioned in his Soviet depositions. If Krivitsky was right, was our Sidney the original or substitute?

There are two incidents that just might have some connection to his reappearance on American shores. On 17 November 1929, old rival Henry Kuntz, friend and partner of Armand Hammer, was found dead in his office at 180 Broadway. Authorities guessed suicide, but the cause of death, seemingly an "unknown poison," was a mystery.[121] Was Kuntz eliminated because he could or did identify Reilly? A man who posed a similar problem was Upton Thomas. Like many in the Depression, Thomas had fallen on hard times. He was a needy loose end that might compromise a new identity and mission. Perhaps he tried to shake down his old boss. Whatever the case, on 5 October 1930, Thomas jumped—or was pushed—off the roof of his Bronx apartment building.[122]

One man Reilly would have contacted in New York was Brasol. While dallying with Amtorg agents, Brasol maintained his stance as an inveterate enemy of Bolshevism. He had amassed important contacts and real influence in right-wing American circles, including Charles Lindbergh and Father Charles Coughlin.[123] In June 1930, Brasol took credit for the defection of five cipher clerks from the Amtorg office. What might Sidney have had to do with that?

Reilly has been alleged the "schemer" behind a Soviet-inspired counterfeiting scheme in the U.S. that came to light in 1934, though none of his recognizable names are connected to the case.[124] The apparent man in charge was Soviet agent Nicholas Dozenberg, but Sidney could have offered some advice. After all, one of his earliest conspiratorial ventures was the counterfeiting operation in London back in 1899, and he had ample experience with fakes and forgeries of all kinds.

If Owen's informant recalled correctly, the wandering Ace-of-Spies was back in Moscow, and in NKVD uniform, in 1935. Sensing the changing winds, he soon headed East, either to the huge OGPU/NKVD penal kingdom in Eastern Siberia ruled by his co-conspirator from 1918, Eduard

Berzin. This, for a time, insulated him from the purges that cut down Yagoda and his other allies. He could expect Yagoda would betray him if he could, but did Reilly, perhaps, have a hand in bringing down his old partner? Was he again hiding his trail by eliminating those who could point it out? Back in the Far East, did he do something to arouse the Japanese; is that why they were on his track? Or were they, too, just curious? In November 1937, Berzin received orders to return to Moscow and was arrested en route. Perhaps he gave away Peters, nabbed in Moscow a month later. In May 1938, Stalin's killers finally appeared in the Soviet Far East. Their reach extended to the Russian colony in Harbin, so Shanghai was one of the few places he and his could have found a modicum of safety, lost among an army of the displaced, dispossessed and the desperate.

In one respect, Reilly's end, whatever it was, was just how he would have wanted it. His entrance and exit from the world are equally shrouded in mystery. In life itself, he often seemed more phantom than flesh and blood. It is tempting to believe that he ended his days not in a chilly Moscow wood, but on some sun-drenched shore surrounded by his family and his secrets. Let us end with a final twist. Perhaps the most intriguing theory about Reilly's fate is that he never went back to Russia at all in 1925. Pointing in one direction, he was, in fact, headed in another. The man or men captured and shot were impostors pure and simple. If the OGPU would never admit they had been duped, and if everyone was searching for him in Russia, no one would look anywhere else. In a final, gigantic swindle, he took the money from the Swiss accounts and ran off to South America, just as he was supposed to have done thirty years before. Was this plan what Agent Sharp had stumbled upon in his investigation, without realizing it of course? What became of the millions he stashed via Trading Ventures? Pepita and Margaret never found it and neither, so far as can be told, anyone else. Improbable? Implausible? Impossible? What do such words mean when applied to the remarkable, inscrutable Man Who Was Sidney Reilly?

NOTES
1. *Izvestiia* (9 June 1927), PRO FO 371/12605, 3088.
2. Ibid., (17 June 1927) and PRO, ibid.
3. *NYT* (18 June 1927), 7:5.
4. Ibid.
5. PRO, FO 371/12593, 3578, 28 July 1927, 4279, 9 Sept. 1927 and *Izvestiia* (31 Aug. 1927).
6. PRO, Ibid., 4643, 3 Oct. 1927 and *Pravda* (25 Sept. 1927).
7. *LT* (10 June 1927), 14b.

8. Brackman, 191–193.

9. *NYT* (11 Apr. 1927), 4:2.

10. See: Francis Delaisi, "Oil and the Arcos Raid," *Foreign Affairs* [Brit.] (Oct. 1927), 106–108, and (Nov. 1927), 137–138.

11. PRO, FO 371/12602, "Activities of Opperput-Upelinz," 27 April 1927, quoting Opperput article in 25 April *Hufvudstadsblatet*, Helsinki.

12. Finland, Foreign Ministry Archive (Ulkoasiainministerio), Etsiva Kekuspoliisi, 1/355, 1927 and 124/1365, 1928.

13. MID, 9944-A-183, AA2-6015, Swett to G2, 7 Sept. 1927.

14. PRO, FO 371/12546, Rennie to Gregory, 15 July 1927.

15. *Izvestiia* (8 July 1927) and MID, 9944-A-183/1 (translation).

16. PRO, FO 371/13213, Mounsey to Lampson, 13 Jan. 1928., and MID, 9944-G-183/5, "Russian Communist, E. Opperput-Staunitz," 5 April 1928. See also *Morning Post* (27 July 1927), which claims Opperput received an Order of the Red Banner for his recent feats.

17. SIS, attached note of 20 May 1926.

18. Ibid., Gwynne letter, 24 Nov. 1926.

19. SIS, Morton to Miller, 14 March 1927.

20. Orlov, *Morder*, 222–223.

21. PRO, FO 371/12605, 4149, attached Parliamentary Question, 22 June 1927.

22. Ibid., Bland note.

23. Ibid., attached clipping.

24. SIS, attached clipping dated 2 Oct. 1927.

25. PRO, FO 371/12605, 4149, attached.

26. Robert Boucard, *Les dessous de l'espionage anglais—Des documents, des faits* (Paris, 1927), 148–51. Boucard emphasized the anti-French activities of *les espions anglais*. Much the same material was repeated by a German writer, Winfried Luedecke in *The Secrets of Espionage: Tales from the Secret Services* (Philadelphia, 1929).

27. PRO, FO 371/12606, 4149.

28. Ibid., Bland note, 12 Sept. 1927.

29. *NYT* (26 July 1927), 3:3.

30. PRO, FO 371/9373, 8133, "Espionage Trial of Brunovsky in Russia," 4 Oct. and 3 Dec. 1923.

31. Reprinted in Reilly, 282–283. Brunovskii's memoirs appeared in English as *Methods of the OGPU* (London, 1928).

32. PRO, FO 371/12602, 1874, to Liddell, translation of Burtsev article.

33. PRO, FO 371/15621, Dalton to Shakespeare, 12 June 1931.

34. Reilly, 244.

35. PRO, FO 371/13332, 2940, Bartlett to FO, 24 May 1928, Agar-Robartes to Bartlett, 8 June 1927.

36. Ibid., 2940, re report of Lauder-Brunton, 1 Nov. 1928.

37. Ibid., Knox to Locker-Lampson, 30 Oct. 1928, Locker-Lampson to Knox, 10 Nov.

38. Ibid., Villiers to Gascoigne, 22 Nov. 1928.

39. PRO, FO 371/14048, 2005 (missing) and 371/15621, Norwegian note, 2 April 1929.

40. Perhaps the most complete biography of Quisling is Hans Frederik Dahl, *Quisling: A Study in Treachery* (London, 1999). On his Russian experiences see pp. 27–69. Rumors later circulated in Oslo that he had been a British agent (66).

41. Dahl, 30.

42. Ibid., 63–64.

43. Berndorff, 32–58.

44. HLRO, Diary #14, 5 Feb. 1931.

45. Ibid., 59–68.

46. Boris Orechkin, "Za kulisami Trest'," *Segodnaia* (20 Nov. 1930).

47. CAC, CHAR, 2/169, Churchill to Morton, 31 Oct. 1930.
48. Ibid., 3 Nov. 1930.
49. Ibid., 4 Nov. 1930.
50. HLRO, Diary #15, 10–11 Feb. 1931.
51. Ibid., Diary #14, 11 Feb. 1931.
52. HIA, Lockhart, box 6. See also R. Lockhart, *First*, 59.
53. HRLO, Diary #16, 11 Oct. 1932.
54. The ES serialization ran 11–23 May 1931.
55. SIS, Sinclair to Norton, FO, 18 June 1931.
56. PRO, FO 372/2756, Note of G.S. Martin, 14 July 1931.
57. SIS, Isaacs, 17 Nov. 1931.
58. SIS., WO to Vivian, 7 Aug. 1931.
59. Ibid., attachment.
60. Ibid, Vivian to Harker, 11 Aug. 1931.
61. PRO, FO 371/15621, 3546, Shakespeare question and Norton note.
62. Ibid., Vivian to Seymour, 11 June 1931.
63. Ibid., Dalton to Shakespeare, 12 June 1931.
64. Ibid., Atherley to Lothian, 31 July and 23 Sept. 1931.
65. Ibid., Lothian to Ovey, 19 Oct. 1931.
66. Ibid., Ovey to Seymour, 23 Nov. 1931.
67. Ibid., Eden to Lothian, 3 December 1931.
68. SIS, Margaret to Isaacs, 11 Nov. 1931
69. Ibid., Isaacs to Colonel, 11 Nov. 1931.
70. Ibid., Isaacs to Col., 13 Nov. 1931.
71. Ibid., Margaret to Isaacs, 17 Nov. 1931.
72. Ibid., Margaret, 28 Dec. 1931.
73. HLRO, Diary #16, 9 Nov. 1932.
74. SIS, Atherley to Air Ministry (forwarded to Jebb), 15 March 1939.
75. Ibid., Menzies to Jebb, 14 April 1939.
76. Ibid., "Most Secret" 27 July 1939.
77. HIA, 96/800-10.V., George Hill, "Reminiscences of Four Years with the NKVD."
78. MI5, Reilly, three letters from Pepita to Weinstein, first dated 1 Sept. 1941.
79. Ibid., SIS to MI5, 28 Nov. 1944 and attachments.
80. Ibid.
81. Manderstam, 159.
82. Lockhart, *First*, 64–65.
83. Minaev, 87.
84. Ibid., 88.
85. Ibid., 157, 199, 201, 209.
86. In any case, it was not the so-called *Osobyi Arkhiv* created after WWII to house captured war booty and such rarities as pieces of Hitler's cell.
87. Bykov, quoting OA UFSB BO [Vologda regional security archive], delo 19, "Pokaznanii N.M. Druzhinina," 3 July 1933.
88. PRO, FO 371/17270, Metro-Vickers Case, and G.L. Owen, "The Metro-Vickers Crisis: Anglo-Soviet Relations between Trade Agreements, 1932–1934," *Slavonic and East European Review*, #114 (Apr. 1971), 92–112.
89. PRO, WO, 329/2302.
90. *The Black Book (Sonderfandungsliste G.B.)*, Imperial War Museum reprint (London, 1989), 172. Boyce and Moura Budberg also made the list.
91. Bortnevskii to author, 11 Feb. 1996.

92. SIS, Transfer Sheet, Consul General Paris, 8616/148, 24 Sept. 1932. The report itself, if any, is not in the SIS file.

93. Alekseev, "OGPU . . . ," 3–4.
94. Ibid.
95. Ibid.
96. Brackman, 213–214.
97. Interestingly, Alekseev mentions Bidet but says nothing of Reilly in work, co-authored with Boris Bazanov, *L'Enlevement du General Koutepov* (Paris, c. 1933).
98. Brackman, 214.
99. Alekseev, "OGPU . . . ," 4.
100. *Vozrozhdenie* (28 Feb. 1933).
101. Deacon, *Greatest Treason*, 62.
102. Boris Bazhanov, *Vospominaniia byvshego sekretaria Stalina* (Paris, 1980) also printed as *Boris Bazhanov and the Damnation of Stalin*.
103. My sincere thanks to G.L. Owen for this information and his invaluable work in decoding and evaluation.
104. Thanks to the late Michael Kettle for bringing this item to my attention and for his thoughts on same.
105. Special thanks to Eric Lee for assistance with this matter.
106. Roger Faligot and Remi Kauffer, *The Chinese Secret Service* (New York, 1987), 43.
107. Bernard Wasserstein, *The Secret War in Shanghai: Espionage, Intrigue and Treason in World War II* (New York, 1999), 44–47.
108. Faligot and Kauffer, 43.
109. Wasserstein, 286, quoting a 1950 U.S. Counterintelligence Corps report. According to these reports, Kozhevnikov/Pick was last identified in Taiwan, in jail, in 1950. He certainly had some friends in the American intelligence sphere, so his later arrival in the U.S. is entirely possible.
110. Metzler was assassinated at this time.
111. Kozhevnikov himself claimed to have served in the Soviet mission in Kabul, though apparently pre-1925. A possible source for this information was Ukolov.
112. *NYT* (10 Oct. 1926), IX, 13:1, and (12 Nov.), 1:4.
113. Guy Richards, *The Rescue of the Romanovs* (Greenwich, CT 1975), 161, quoting Riis' "autobiography."
114. MID, PF 60340, Yaeger to Foy, 16 Apr. 1931.
115. MID, 304-W-27, Polish Legation, 10 Dec. 1935.
116. *NYT* (13 July 1926), 18:2 and (24 Feb. 1927), 14:5.
117. *NYT* (8 March 1927) 17:3.
118. Doerries, "Jahnke," 38.
119. Schellenberg, *Memoirs* (London, 1956), 299–305.
120. Deacon, *British Connection*, 39.
121. *NYT* (17 Nov. 1929), 26:1.
122. *NYT* (6 Oct. 1930), 32:8.
123. ADL Report.
124. R. Lockhart, *First*, 166. McCormick made the same accusation but, again, without specific evidence.

Note on Transliteration

In general, Russian names and terms are rendered into Latin script using a modified version of the Library of Congress system. Unlike the LC style, initial "Ia," "Io," and "Iu" are rendered as "Ya," "Yo," and "Yu," e.g., Yagoda rather than Iagoda. Certain names follow common English usage, e.g., Trotsky rather than Trotskii.

Note on Basic Sources

Unless otherwise noted, general biographical data derives from *Who Was Who* (British and U.S.), *Dictionary of National Biography* (Britain), *Cyclopedia of American National Biography*, the *Great Soviet Encyclopedia*, *Who Was Who in the USSR*, A. Markov, *Entsiklopedia belago dvizheniia*, and *Foreign Office, War Office, Army* and *Navy Lists* (Britain).

Information on ship movements and dates of arrival, especially between Europe and New York, are drawn from U.S. Immigration records, principally the Port of New York records accessible at www.ellisislandrecords.org.

BIBLIOGRAPHY

Detailed source notes are provided at the end of each chapter. The following, consisting mostly of available works in English dealing with Reilly, espionage or related topics, is offered as a suggestion for further reading.

Agabekov, G., *OGPU: The Russian Secret Terror* (New York, 1931).

Allfrey, Anthony, *Man of Arms: The Life and Legend of Sir Basil Zaharoff* (London, 1989).

Andrew, Christopher, *Her Majesty's Secret Service: The Making of the British Intelligence Community* (New York, 1986).

Bailey, Geoffrey, *The Conspirators* (New York, 1960).

Bazhanov, Boris, *Boris Bazhanov and the Damnation of Stalin* (Athens, OH, 1990)

Bennett, Gill, *"A Most Extraordinary and Mysterious Business": The Zinoviev Letter of 1924* (London, 1999).

Brackman, Roman, *The Secret File of Joseph Stalin: A Hidden Life* (London, 2001).

Brook-Shepherd, Gordon, *The Iron Maze: The Western Secret Services and the Bolsheviks* (London, 1998).

Chester, Lewis, Fay, Stephen and Young, Hugo, *The Zinoviev Letter: A Political Intrigue* (London, 1967).

Churchill, Winston S., *The World Crisis*, vol. V (London, 1931).

Deacon, Richard, [Donald McCormick], *The British Connection: Russia's Manipulation of British Individuals and Institutions* (London, 1979).

_____, *The Greatest Treason: The Bizarre Story of Hollis, Liddell and Mountbatten* (London, 1990).

_____, *A History of the Japanese Secret Service* (London, 1982).

_____, *A History of the Russian Secret Service* (New York, 1972).

_____, *Murder by Perfection: Maundy Gregory, the Man behind*

Two Unsolved Mysteries? (London, 1970).

_____, *Super Spy: The Man Who Infiltrated the Kremlin and the Gestapo* (London, 1989).

Dobson, Christopher and Miller, John, *The Day They Almost Bombed Moscow: The Allied Intervention in Russia, 1918–1920* (New York,1986).

Dukes, Sir Paul, *The Story of "ST 25": Adventure and Romance in the Secret Intelligence Service in Red Russia* (London, 1938).

Dziak, John, *Chekisty: A History of the KGB* (New York, 1988).

Foglesong, David, *America's Secret War Against Bolshevism: United States Intervention in the Russian Civil War, 1917–1920* (Chapel Hill, NC, 1995).

Fowler, W.B., *British-American Relations, 1917–1918: The Role of Sir William Wiseman* (Princeton, 1969).

Gaunt, Sir Guy, *The Yield of the Years* (London, 1940).

Gazur, Edward, *Secret Assignment: The FBI's KGB General* (London, 2001).

Hanighen, Frank C., *The Secret War* (Westport, CT, 1934).

Hill, George A., *Go Spy the Land* (London, 1932).

_____, *Dreaded Hour* (London, 1936).

James, Admiral Sir William, *The Eyes of the Navy: A Biographical Study of Admiral Sir Reginald Hall* (London, 1955).

Jeffreys-Jones, Rhodri, *American Espionage: From Secret Service to CIA* (New York, 1977).

Judd, Alan, *The Quest for C: Sir Mansfield Cumming and the Foundation of the Secret Service* (London, 1999).

Kettle, Michael, *Sidney Reilly: The True Story of the World's Greatest Spy* (London, 1983).

Leggett, George, *The Cheka: Lenin's Political Police* (Oxford, 1981).

Lewinsohn, Richard, *The Career of Sir Basil Zaharoff* (London, 1929).

Lockhart, R.H. Bruce, *Memoirs of a British Agent* (London, 1932).

_____, *Retreat from Glory* (London, 1934).

Lockhart, Robin, *Ace of Spies* (London, 1967), reprinted (New York, 1984) as *Reilly: Ace of Spies.*

_____, *Reilly: The First Man* (London, 1987).

Mossolov, A.A., *At the Court of the Last Tsar* (London, 1935).

McNeal, Shay, *The Plots to Rescue the Czar* (London, 2001).

Nikitine, B.V., *The Fatal Years: Fresh Revelations on a Chapter of Underground History* (London, 1938).

Occleshaw, Michael, *Armour against Fate* (London, 1989).

Orlov, Vladimir, *The Secret Dossier: My Memoirs of Russia's Political Underworld* (London, 1932).

Reilly, Pepita and Sidney, *The Adventures of Sidney Reilly* (London, 1931), U.S. editions *Britain's Master Spy: The Adventures of Sidney Reilly* (1933, 1986).

Romanov, B.A., *Russia in Manchuria, 1892–1906* (Ann Arbor, MI, 1952).

Ruud, Charles and Stepanov, Sergei, *Fontanka 16: The Tsar's Secret Police* (Montreal, 1999).

Smith, Michael, *Old Cloak, New Dagger: How Britain's Spies Came in from the Cold* (London, 1997).

Spence, Richard, *Boris Savinkov: Renegade on the Left* (Boulder, CO, 1991).

Stafford, David, *Churchill and the Secret Service* (New York, 1996).

Sutton, Antony C., *Wall Street and the Bolshevik Revolution* (New York, 1974).

Thwaites, Norman, *Velvet and Vinegar* (London, 1932).

Van Der Rhoer, Edward, *Master Spy: A True Story of Allied Espionage in Bolshevik Russia* (New York, 1981).

Volkov, Fedor, *Secrets from Whitehall and Downing Street* (Moscow, 1986).

Voska, Emanuel and Irwin, Will, *Spy and Counter-Spy* (London, 1941).

West, Nigel and Tsarev, Oleg, *The Crown Jewels: The British Secrets at the Heart of the KGB Archives* (London, 1998).

Yergin, Daniel, *The Prize: The Epic Quest for Oil, Money and Power* (New York, 1991).

INDEX

A

Abbot, Lt. Col. Frederick 145, 153, 174

ABF-Economizer Co. 214, 367

Abrahamson, Sir Martin 302

Abramovich, Lt. 207, 244

Abwehr 495

Agapaev, Tikhon 289, 306, 383, 397, 406

Agar-Robartes, A. 497

Aggeev, K.M. 217, 253

Akashi, Col. Motojiro 46, 52, 53, 61, 63, 72

Alekseev, Gen. M.V. 171, 174, 175, 194, 208, 212, 217, 221, 225, 247

Alekseev, Nikolai 15, 20, 52, 53, 70, 75, 76, 77, 91, 273, 294, 322, 391, 439, 487, 488, 489, 490, 495, 499

Aleksinskii, Grigorii 271, 277

Alexander, Maj. W.A. 364

Alley, Stephen 2, 157, 189, 190, 198, 205, 270, 333, 344, 356, 369, 371, 373, 400, 403

Allied American Corp. (Alamerico) 352

Allied Machinery Co. 134, 135, 142, 143, 147, 159

All-Russian Textile Syndicate 378

Altendorf, Paul 305

American Art Galleries 36, 134, 316, 327, 336

American International Corp. (AIC) 134, 264

American Relief Administration (ARA) 325, 424

American-Russian Industrial Syndicate 276

Amsinck & Co. 117, 135

Amtorg 395, 397, 426, 429, 430, 460, 495

Andersen, Capt. Hans Nils 43, 44, 73, 143, 282, 302

Andrews, Dr. 30, 37

Anglo-Magyar Bank 333

Anglo-Persian Oil 57

Anglo Russian Sub Committee 138

Anglo-Russian Supply Committee 251, 299

Anti-Socialist League 390

Anusilam Samiti 85, 98

Archbold, John 58, 59, 75

ARCOS 352, 376, 378, 402, 460, 471, 472, 497

Armitstead, Henry 188, 203

Armour Co. 264, 276, 385, 503

Aron, Jules 79

Artamonov, Yurii 337, 338

Artuzov, Artur *101*, 388, 393, 409, 412, 413, 418, 421, 422, 429, 435, 438, 440, 446, 460, 464, 491

Aschberg, Olaf 124, 155, 176, 183

Ascherson, Charles 184, 186, 198

Astor, Lady 481

Peshkov, Zinovii 153, 168, 175, 176, 459

Peters, Yakov *102*, 131, 132, 205–7, 213, 214, 220, 222–25, 227–29, 231–35, 237, 244, 255, 280, 287, 308, 310, 338, 428, 461

Peters, Yurii 472, 491, 496

Petlura, S.V. 247, 252, 254, 298, 310, 312

Pierson, Lewis 375, 382, 395, 416, 475

Pilenas (Palmer-Pilenas), Casimir 26, 162, 164, 165, 205, 315

Pilsudski, Marshall Josef 282, 283, 298, 307, 309, 312, 332, 335, 341, 355

Pimenov, Revolt 197, 200, 229, 230

Platon, Metropolitan 125, 139, 282

Plowden, Capt, Humphrey 260, 288, 313, 356, 374, 375, 398, 405, 410

Podell, David L. 394, 404, 406, 407, 409, 416

Pokrovskii, Lt. Ivan 402, 403

Poliakov, R.V. 133, 136, 166, 289

Poliunin, Arkadii 371, 372, 388

Poole Engineering Co. 135, 154

Poole, De Witt C. 210, 224, 226, 235–38, 241, 288

Poole, Gen. F.C. 188, 198, 201, 202, 203, 220, 226, 229, 248, 249, 265

Popov, D.I. 220

Potapov, Gen. M.N. 443, 445, 446

Pougher, H.F. 347, 348, 358

Prelin, Igor viii, 36, 438, 439, 461, 466, 467

Prodexco 378

Proskey, Winfield 121, 165

Protocols of the Learned Elders of Zion 13, 18, 65, 399, 409

Pryor, Samuel 121, 122, 261

Prytz, Frederik 475, 477

Pulitzer, George 149

Putilov Works 69, 73, 85, 95, 96, 97, 100, 111, 112, 135, 137, 141, 206, 239, 275, 360, 276, 277, 291, 296,

299, 303, 307, 316, 333, 346, 352, 360, 368, 395, 409

Putilov, Aleksei 69, 96, 111, 112, 127, 132, 155

Puzitskii, S.V. 445, 446, 478, 489, 491

Q

Quisling, Vidkun 459, 475, 477, 499

R

Rachkovskii, P.I. 13, 14, 22, 23, 25, 35, 36, 40, 48, 59–62, 82

Radium Corp. of Czechoslovakia 331, 370

Radkevich, Maria (AKA Shults, Zakharchenko, etc.) 451, 464, 470, 472, 473

Radkevich, Yurii (Shults) 418, 419, 437, 446, 451

Raevskii, Nikolai 87, 89, 95, 99

Rafalovich, Artur 59, 79

Rakovskii, Khristian 350, 371, 372, 403, 464

Raper, A. Baldwin 277, 296, 354, 403

Rasputin, Grigorii 48, 79, 82, 83, 98, 100, 112, 137, 141, 143, 146, 157, 169, 189, 250, 383, 416, 474,

Ratkov-Rozhnov, A.V. 89

Rayner, Oswald 157, 372, 440 ,441, 459, 466

Reddan, J.H. 32, 33, 37

Redkozubov (ST89) 330, 347

Redwood, Sir Thomas Boverton 24, 26, 28

Reem, Marion 345, 346

Regnart, Capt. "Roy" 69

Reile, Anna (wife?) 142

Reilinskii (Rellinskii), Sidnei (alias) 200, 201, 229

Reilly, George (claimed father) 125

Reilly, Nadine (Nadezhda Petrovna) 95, 97, 110, 115, 124, 125, 126,

Standard-Nobel Oil Co. 344, 379, 382, 494

Starzhevskaia, Olga 207, 230, 234, 235, 236

Steed, Henry Wickham 259

Steinberg, Nikolai (alias) 433, 437, 451, 468, 485

Stepniak (Kravchinskii), Sergei

Stern, Sigmund (alias) 22, 23, 35

Stettinius, Edward 123, 168

Stevens, John F. 99, 291, 384

Stolypin, P.A. 80

Strubell, Maj. T.F.G. 173, 182, 247, 347

Stump, Charlie 58, 59

Styrne, Vladimir *104*, 231, 326, 388, 409, 413, 420–22, 432, 435, 436, 438–47, 453, 454, 456–64, 466, 467, 478, 486, 491

Summers, Maddin 178, 210

Supreme Monarchist Council (VMS) 289, 337

Suvorin, A.S. 81

Suvorin, Boris 74, 81, 82, 86, 87, 89, 90, 92, 93, 95, 98, 132, 146, 192, 193, 248, 271

Sverdlov, Veniamin "Benny" 85, 131, 144, 153, 206, 207, 399, 405,

Sverdlov, Yakov 85, 131, 153, 206

Svirskaia, Tamara 126

Syroezhkin, Grigorii 461, 462

System, The 25, 31, 47, 48, 52, 59, 65, 71, 72, 87, 110, 114, 115, 118, 122, 133, 134, 137, 147, 164, 173, 189, 191, 217, 268, 271, 277, 278, 281, 285, 303, 305, 332, 344, 354, 361, 363, 368, 429, 436, 490

Syvorotka, Aleksei 292

Szek, Alexander 130

T

"Tacticion" (Japanese agent) 72

Takata & Co. 48, 53

Talbot, Capt. D.S.

Teapot Dome 245

Texaco Oil Co. 395

Thomas, Margaret Callahan (wife) 28, 30, 365

Thomas, Olive 125

Thomas, Rev. Hugh 28–30, 37, 50, 365, 366

Thomas, Upton Dale 124, 129, 137, 140, 267, 289, 407, 416, 432, 452, 495

Thompson, William Boyce 135

Thomson, Sir Basil 268–73, 280, 285, 290, 295, 300, 301, 305, 313, 318, 322, 326, 342, 354, 356, 363, 390, 460

Thornhill, Maj. C.J.M. 201, 202, 229

Thorpe, Michael 26, 36, 162

Thurston, Sir George Owens 65, 76, 182, 198

Thwaites, Norman G. 149–54, 158, 162, 166, 168, 172, 173, 180, 185–87, 197, 198, 231, 259, 262, 276, 286, 290, 296, 305, 316, 363, 366, 373, 376, 384, 390, 393, 409, 450, 451, 468, 475, 503

Tikhon, Patriarch 218, 221, 289, 383, 397, 406

Tikston, Pavel 346

Torgprom 277, 290, 291, 316, 346, 347, 350, 353, 355, 382, 396, 403

Torvand, Gen. Juhand 380

Toye, Edward 270

Toye, Eleanor 270, 271, 350, 355

Toye, Francis 270

Trading Ventures Inc. 406, 407, 416, 418, 426, 452, 494, 496

Transatlantic Co. 302, 354, 355, 415

Trebitsch-Lincoln, I.T. 126, 272, 286

Tremaine, Beatrice 136, 144, 158, 166, 173, 216, 270

Trester, Maksim 177, 207, 230, 236

Trilesser, Mikhail 388, 413, 425, 426, 433, 434, 435, 439, 443, 447, 448, 450, 452, 464, 466, 472, 491

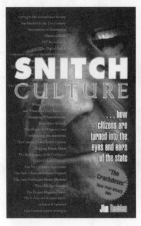
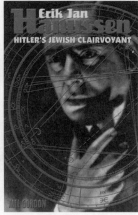